The Leigh Family
From New York Westward

Family Genealogies of the following families:

Nathan S. Leigh settling in Deposit, New York

Henry B. Webb from Delaware County, New York

Humphrey Turner from Kent, England

by Karen Emery Dwyer

Author's Notes

1. There are no living people mentioned in this book except for my immediate family from who I have permission.

2. Very often, a name, especially in the census records, would be misspelled. It was spelled as it was pronounced.   You will see in this book various spellings of the same name as I spelled the name the way I found it in the research record.

3. Siblings and descendants often spelled their last names differently than their parents for many different reasons. In most cases, this was done to Americanize their name.

ISBN - 13: 978-1725809659

EAN-10:1725809656

Printed in the United States of America by CreateSpace, a DBA of On-Demand Publishing LLC, part of the Amazon group of companies.

Dedication

A special thanks to Rev. Laverne E. Leigh, who wrote the Leigh Family Genealogy in 1975. I stumbled upon that genealogy in 2017, contacted Rev. Leigh and proceeded to put this book together. He supplied all the family stories that I would not have known and many of the family photos. Rev. Leigh was a true inspiration for me to compile this book.

Photo of Rev. Laverne E. Leigh and his wife Betty. This photo was given to me by Rev. Leigh and used with permission.

Letter from George H. Leigh to his niece, Minnie Augusta Leigh dated April 5, 1896

Dear Niece:

I trust I may call you so as your letter found me yesterday and found the right party this time as I am the youngest son of William Todd Leigh. Although I had not seen him since I was five years old. And never saw any of my brothers after I was eight until I was twenty one years old. So you see that I was not very well known to my folks for a long time and I did not know that I had a niece until your letter found me yesterday and I was glad to hear from you. Of course I never knew your father or my own for that matter either. I am sorry that you have lost both of your parents as they were your best friends. I buried my youngest girl three weeks ago today. I have two girls and one boy left. My last one would have been 5 years old in August. I shall write to Brother William as soon as I hear from you again. My Bro John, your Uncle, is very much alive and the daddy of two children. One boy and one of the feminine gender. I saw him last fall. He lives in Gilbertsville, Otsego County, NY. Uncle Tom Webb of Blue Earth City told me of Fathers death and that William S. Leigh claimed that he was the only heir to property that he left. Did he leave any property or not. Uncle Tom Webb claims that he (word omitted) some land and money in Kansas when he died. Uncle Tom Webb was my mother's Brother. Well Minnie, I wish I could see you and shake hands with you and as I cannot think of anything more at present. I will close this by saying write soon to your Uncle George H. Leigh, Oneida, Madison Co., NY 13 Bennett Street. P.S. Send me your photograph.

G.H.L.

Letter, May 17, 1896

In my father's family, there was eight of us Lewis, Luman, Lydia, Nathan, John, Anna, Agnes and yours truly, George. Now there are only John and myself.

These letters written by George H. Leigh to Minnie Augusta Leigh are the only information known to the compiler concerning this branch of the family and indicates that eventually they did know one another existed.

A Word about the
Genealogical Number System

The numbering system used in this book is the Simple Register Report format, the format accepted by the New England Historic Genealogical Society, one of the oldest genealogical societies in the country. The format dates back to 1870 and is used to establish "pedigrees".

This book consists of three chapters of Genealogical Summaries. Numbers are assigned to the people covered in the genealogy.

The progenitor is given the number 1. Each child is then numbered in order with lower-case Roman numerals (i, ii, iii, iv, v, etc.) and those whose lines are carried on are also given an Arabic number. For instance, No. 1 may have had seven children (i through vii), but only one of these had descendants, say iv. Number iv is then also given the Arabic number 2 and his children, in turn, are numbered from i on, with, perhaps, numbers. i, iv and vi given the additional identification of 3, 4 and 5.
For example, in Chapter One:

4. Mary Abigale Leigh[3] (Elijah Leigh[2], Nathan S.[1]) was born on 24 Jan 1836 in New York State and died on 31 Jan 1904 in Money Creek, Minnesota.

Cyrus Gilbert Berry and Mary Abigale Leigh had the following children:

      i.   Mary Etta Berry was born in 1860 and died on 20 Jun 1891 in Money Creek, Minnesota.

11.   ii.   Cyrus Nathan Berry was born on 06 Dec 1862 in Money Creek, Minnesota and died on 27 Jun 1942 in Alma Center, Wisconsin.

The bold numbers are Mary Abigale Leigh and Cyrus Nathan Berry's unique Arabic numbers in the system. The number **11** for Cyrus Nathan Berry indicates he had children. Whereas Mary Etta Berry did not have children.

Table of Contents

<u>**The Leigh Family first settled in Deposit, New York in Delaware County.**</u>

Deposit is situated in the valley of the Delaware, sixty miles from its source, nestled among mountains which surround it on all sides, with their summits nearly a thousand feet above the bed of the river. (Illustrated History of Delaware County 1880).

The name Deposit was logical because in early times vast quantities of pine lumber were drawn in winter on sleighs, from as far away as the Susquehanna, and deposited on the banks of the river here to await the Spring high waters when the logs were fashioned into rafts sometimes as large as 200 feet in length, and taken to Philadelphia's market. This was in most cases the only cash income for these early settlers, who did business the rest of the year by bartering and the giving of notes of promise to pay.

Before the coming of white settlers, this part of the Delaware River Valley was inhabited by Indians from several different tribes. The Lenni Lenapes, or Delawares, were most numerous, but the Mohawks held the upper hand. There were also some Oneidas and Tuscaroras. Their council ground, where they held public meetings and performed ceremonial dances, was on a level piece of ground about 8 rods square, situated a few feet south of the present location of the Revolutionary Cemetery. On the flats below the railroad they had cleared 30-40 acres of land where they raised corn and apple trees.

To the Indians this area was known as Koo Koose (Cookose, Cookhouse) the place of owls. The local chapter of D.A.R. has adopted the name Koo Koose.

The first permanent settler was John Hulce who came from Orange County in the Spring of 1789 and settled on the west side of the river at the northerly side of the village. Next was Phillip Pine who came from Fishkill on the Hudson in 1791.

In 1790 Captain Nathan Dean a native of Taunton, Massachusetts, removed to Kortright, Delaware County, where he remained until June 1791. Then, as there were no roads, he lashed two canoes together and loaded his family and goods thereon and floated down the river to Cook-house, where he found an empty log house and lived there until he could provide one for his family on his farm consisting of two lots of two hundred acres each covering that part of what is now Deposit, in Broome County, of which he was the first settler. Later streets were laid out and the area became known as Deansville. In 1811 the village, containing twelve dwellings, on the westerly side of the river, on land consisting of Lot No. 43 of the Evans patent, containing 156 acres extending only to "the property line" was incorporated. In 1851 the charter was amended to include 400 acres in the Town of Sanford, Broome County. A provision was inserted that the village, except for elections and schools, should be regarded as belonging to either or both counties. The next and present charter, made in 1871, was a very special act of the State Legislature because of the unique location of Deposit in two counties. We even have a special date for village elections. But our dual "nationality" has created some problems over time. Logging was at first the main industry as settlers cleared the land for residential purposes. Then this part of New York State became agricultural with some very large farms in existence. But the rebuilding of highways and changing economy has reduced farming to a minimum.[1]

Photo of Deposit, New York taken at the turn of the century from the authors collection.

---

[1] http://www.villageofdeposit.org/histandstats.html

<u>**The Leigh Family moved to Fairmont, Minnesota about 1865.**</u>

Fairmont Minnesota history can be traced back to the days before Minnesota became a state. In 1826, a fort was established which served as an army post and trade center on the site now covered by the Martin County Courthouse. The first permanent settlers were E. Banks Hall and William H. Budd. In June 1857, these men built their homes on lakes that still bear their names. Mr. Budd recorded that in January of that year, twenty men, nine women and twenty-three children lived in the Fairmont area.

Fairmont was platted in October 1857, by the Des Moines and Watonwan Land Company, by whom the name was applied. The City was named for the rolling hills which surrounded the adjacent lakes. The original name was Fair Mount, but this was later changed to Fairmont. Fairmont had the first post office in Martin County, dedicated on October 9, 1858, with William Budd as the first postmaster.

Fort Fairmont was established in 1862, shortly after the Sioux Indian Uprising which terrified settlers throughout southern Minnesota. With the end of the Civil War and subsiding of Indian troubles, Fort Fairmont was abandoned. Closely following the hard times after the Civil War, the "Grasshopper Plague" of 1873-1877 descended on the impoverished farmers, and many were forced to abandon their holdings and leave Martin County. This gloomy picture was brightened by the arrival of English colonists during the same period. They came to develop new methods of growing beans, spent their money lavishly, built a number of beautiful homes and brightened the hillsides with their scarlet foxhunting expeditions.

The Southern Minnesota Railroad was completed to Fairmont in 1878, and marked the beginning of a new period of development for the area. In 1896, the first switchboard and telephones were installed in Fairmont providing services for 35 subscribers. Electricity became available in 1890 from a privately owned plant which provided service from sun up to 10:00 p.m. The City purchased the generating plant in 1902. City water became available in 1897 from Budd Lake, but it was unfiltered. The initial filtration plant was built in 1924.

Industrial development of note began in 1909 when Fairmont Railway Motors was established to make small farm engines. These engines became useful on railway hand cars. Agriculture related industries, such as the Fairmont Canning Company and Stokely-Van Camp added to Fairmont's industrial growth.

From the mixed agriculture-industrial-based economy, Fairmont has grown and prospered into one of the state's leading rural communities. Adding to the steady growth and stability of the Fairmont economy are several leading industries which have settled in the community.

Fairmont has also situated itself to be a leading regional health care center with the continued growth and expansion of the Fairmont Medical Center – Mayo Health System, Center for Specialty Care, Dulcimer, REM, Goldfinch Estates, United Health District, MRCI and Lakeview Methodist Health Care Facility.

Fairmont is restructuring its claim as a retail trade center as well. Many national name retailers have moved to the community and more than 880 different businesses are active in the corporate limits of Fairmont today[2].

Photo found on the Fairmont, Minnesota Chamber of Commerce web site.

x

<u>Town of Sciatuate, Massachusetts is where the Turner family from Kent, England settled.</u>

In this text we propose to set forth not a complete history of the Town of Scituate. This is a very abbreviated account giving the fundamentals of such history, and which might be of interest to our newer citizens and to those who may at some time wish to become residents.

The name Scituate is derived from an Indian word which the early settlers understood as Satuit, which means "Cold Brook", and referred to the small stream flowing into the harbor; this they spelled in various ways as Sityate, Cituate, Seteat, etc., and it was not until about 1640 that the name came to be universally spelled in its present form. No one knows why the silent "c" was added, but around that time it was quite common to add this "c" to such words as site, situation, etc.

Scituate more than any other location along the shore of Cape Cod Bay presented to the explorer a distinctive front toward the sea which very soon after the settlement at Plymouth attracted venturesome colonists to our shores looking for fertile lands to cultivate and perhaps to find a suitable place to live and establish their homes. The sea front marked as it was by four water washed gravel cliffs suggested good planting lands in the interior, and it was on one of these cliffs that the first use of the land was made for this purpose, this was previous to 1628, we do not know for sure the exact year the first plantings were made here.

In some part of the years 1627 or 1628 a group from Plymouth augmented by new arrivals from the County of Kent in England came here and formed the first permanent settlement. They laid out their village a mile or so back from the coast behind one of the cliffs, established a public way or street, which they named Kent Street, which name it still bears, and allotted space on this street to the various householders forming the Company. They were of course under the jurisdiction of the General Court at Plymouth, and it was not until 1636 when the population had increased that permission was given to elect certain officers and to some extent carry on their own affairs, an act which we refer to as the incorporation of the Town, and its boundaries were established. Other grants were later, viz. the so called Two Mile in Marshfield and the Hatherly Grant of three miles square on the westerly side of the above boundaries which is now contained in the Town of Rockland, then a part of Abington.

In establishing the bounds of Scituate the General Court at Plymouth took the somewhat strange action of reserving a section in the northerly part of the Town for the exclusive benefit of certain individuals, viz. Messrs. Hatherly, Beauchamp and Shirley. This grant included the entire part of the Town northerly from Satuit Brook and extending to the Conihasset marshes; as the bounds were not definite and some settlers had previously occupied parts of this land. Controversies arose which were not adjusted for several years. In the meantime Mr. Hatherly purchased the entire tract from the other grantees and in 1646 divided it into thirty shares, reserving one fourth of them for himself and sold the remaining for 180 pounds to a company which became known as the Conihasset Partners, which Company functioned as a Government, carrying on its own affairs, building its own roads, keeping its own records etc. in disregard of the fact that they were legally and technically a part of the Town of Scituate with no objections on the part of the Town, which was due probably to the fact that the proprietors of the Conihasset Grant were also men interested in the government of the Town itself. The last meeting of the Partners was held in 1767, after which their affairs reverted to the town.

As time when on and the population in the westerly part of the Town increased the people there becoming desirous of self government. A portion of the original grant was separated and incorporated as the town of Hanover in 1717. This seems to have been accomplished without any serious opposition by the parent town, and in 1849 a further reduction in the territory of the town was made by the separation of another westerly section which became the town of South Scituate, which name was later changed to Norwell, in honor of a prominent citizen and benefactor of that town. The section referred to above as the Two Mile, really a part of Marshfield was cede back to that town in 1788, again without any serious opposition on the part of the people of Scituate. Thus the town became as it is now, containing about 10,000 acres and in possession of its greatest asset, the several miles of shore line and beaches, which was formerly considered a useless liability, but is now the most valuable property in town.

Scituate in common with other country towns was a slow growth in population during the first two centuries of its existence; the lack of good roads and the difficulties of transportation did not encourage people to settle here so the greatest increase was in or near large cities.

The coming of the railroad in 1871 helped to some extent, but it was not until the advent of the automobile and the building of better roads that any marked increase was noted. As late as 1900 the population hardly exceeded 2,000. From then on the increase was rapid and in the last ten years a great increase in population has occurred so that the census of 1960 gives it as between eleven and twelve thousand[3].

xii

---

[3] https://www.scituatema.gov/about/pages/a-historical-overview

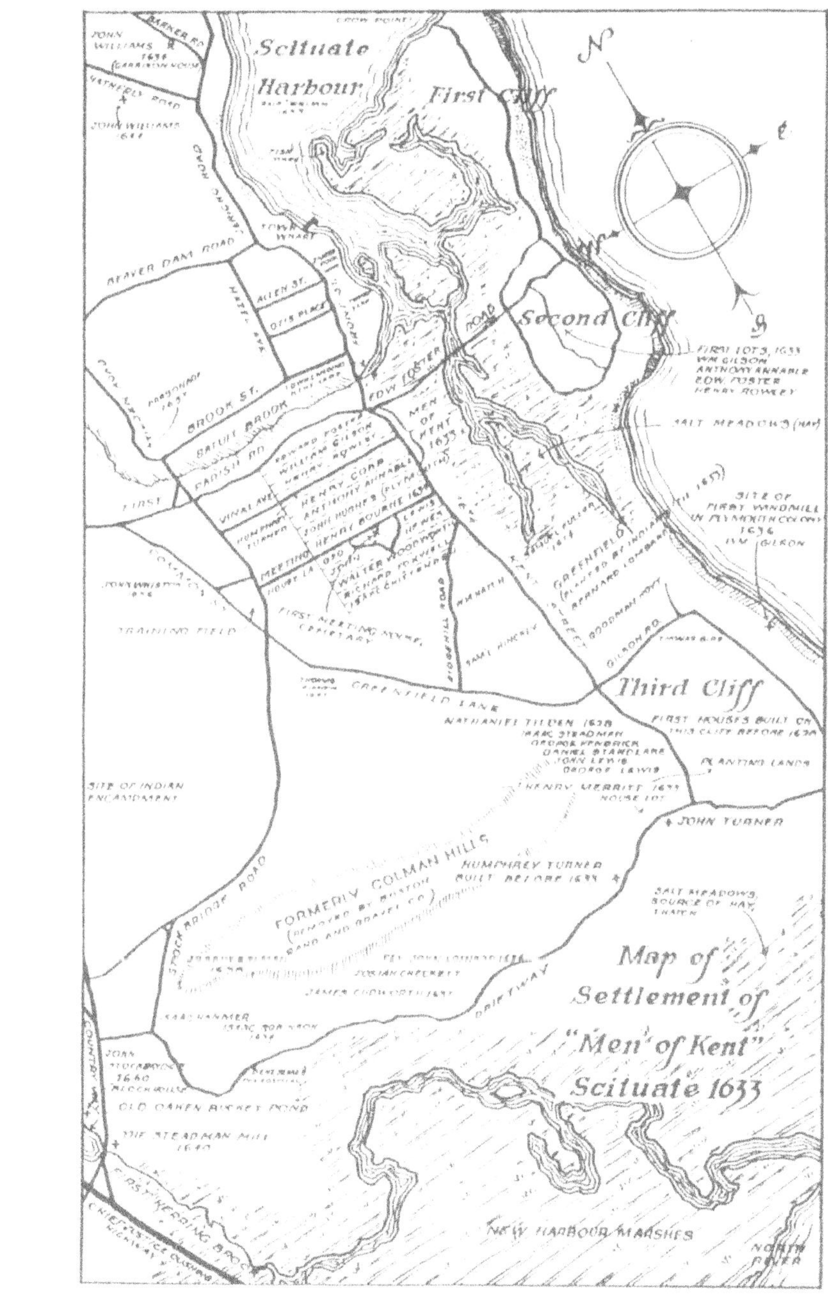

Please note the home of Humphrey Turner

Chapter One

Descendants

of

Nathan S. Leigh

Generation One

1. Nathan S. Leigh was born in 1779 in England and died on 15 Aug 1848 in Tully, New York[1]. He married a woman by the name of Mary Todd[2]. Nathan was listed in the 1840 Tully, New York Census.

Nathan S. Leigh and Mary Todd had the following children:
2.	i.	Elijah Leigh was born on 08 Mar 1802 in New York State[3] and died on 10 Feb 1890 in Minnesota[4].
3.	ii.	William Todd Leigh was born on 30 Jun 1804 in New York State[5] and died on 22 Oct 1888 in Alton, Kansas[6].

---

[1] Genealogy compiled by Rev. Laverne E. Leigh, 414 Washington Ave. East, Albia, Iowa 52531 in the Spring of 1975.
[2] Genealogy compiled by Rev. Laverne E. Leigh, 414 Washington Ave. East, Albia, Iowa 52531 in the Spring of 1975.
[3] Genealogy compiled by Rev. Laverne E. Leigh in 2017.
[4] Genealogy compiled by Rev. Laverne E. Leigh in 2017.
[5] Genealogy compiled by Rev. Laverne E. Leigh, 414 Washington Ave. East, Albia, Iowa 52531 in the Spring of 1975.
[6] Genealogy compiled by Rev. Laverne E. Leigh, 414 Washington Ave. East, Albia, Iowa 52531 in the Spring of 1975.

Generation Two

2. Elijah Leigh[2] (Nathan S.Leigh[1]) was born on 08 Mar 1802 in New York State[7] and died on 10 Feb 1890 in Minnesota[8]. He married Elizabeth Todd. She was born on 11 Apr 1818 in New York State[9] and died on 25 Jul 1892[10].

Elijah Leigh and Elizabeth Todd had the following children:
4.   i.   Mary Abigale Leigh was born on 24 Jan 1836 in New York State[11] and died on 31 Jan 1904 in Money Creek, Minnesota[12].
  ii.   Nathan Leigh was born in 1838 in Omego, New York[13] and died on 16 Nov 1909 in Salem, Oregon[14]. He married Sarah Angeline Halley on 03 May 1861[15]. She was born on 31 May 1846 in Canby, Oregon[16] and died on 27 Mar 1919 in Hayesville, Oregon[17]. Nathan and his wife did not have children.

Sarah Angeline Halley
The funeral services of Mrs. Sarah Angeline Leigh who died March 27, 1919 at the home of her sister, Mrs. L. A. Kelly, and brother, J. C. Halley at Hayesville will be held at the Hayesville Baptist Church Saturday, March 29 at 1:30 o'clock p.m. Mrs. Leigh was the daughter of Barthomew and Agatha Halley who crossed the plains to Oregon in 1843. She was born near Canby, May 31, 1846. On May 3, 1861, she was married to Nathan Leigh who died Nov 16, 1909. The nearest surviving relatives are a sister, Mrs. L. A. Kelly, a brother, J. C. Halley, two nephews, Fred J. and Edward G. Kelly of Portland, Oregon, two nieces, Mrs. G. M. Plummer of San Rafael, California and Mrs. Gertrude VanNuys of Portland, Oregon. Burial will be at Hayesville Cemetery. The services will be conducted by the Rev. Fisher.

---

[7] Genealogy compiled by Rev. Laverne E. Leigh in 2017.
[8] Genealogy compiled by Rev. Laverne E. Leigh in 2017.
[9] Genealogy compiled by Rev. Laverne E. Leigh in 2017.
[10] Genealogy compiled by Rev. Laverne E. Leigh in 2017.
[11] Findagrave.com
[12] Findagrave.com
[13] Ancestry.com, Willamette Valley, Oregon, Death Records, 1838-2006 (Provo, UT, USA, Ancestry.com Operations, Inc., 2012), Ancestry.com, http://www.Ancestry.com, Record for Nathan Leigh.
[14] Ancestry.com, Willamette Valley, Oregon, Death Records, 1838-2006 (Provo, UT, USA, Ancestry.com Operations, Inc., 2012), Ancestry.com, http://www.Ancestry.com, Record for Nathan Leigh.
[15] Obituary from Hayesville, Oregon newspaper.
[16] Obituary from Hayesville, Oregon newspaper.
[17] Obituary from Hayesville, Oregon newspaper.

5.	iii.	Julia Fannie Leigh was born on 16 Sep 1840 in Tully, New York[18] and died on 20 Mar 1920 in Sauk County Poor Farm, Wisconsin[19].

	iv.	Elijah Dide Leigh was born on 18 Jun 1849[20] in New York State and died on 03 Dec 1930 in Houston, Minnesota[21]. He married Lucy Jane Dickens, the daughter of Joe and Mary Dickens on 22 Oct 1871 in Sauk, Wisconsin[22]. In the 1880 Spokane, Washington Census, Elijah was divorced and living with his brother, Nathan. In the 1930 census, he was in a poorhouse in Calidonia Township, Houston, Minnesota.

3. William Todd Leigh[2] (Nathan S.Leigh[1])was born on 30 Jun 1804 in New York State [23] and died on 22 Oct 1888 in Alton, Kansas[24]. He married Sarah M. Whipple in 1834 in Deposit, New York[25]. She was born in 1811 in New York[26] and died on 23 Feb 1840 in Deposit, New York[27]. He later married Lydia M. Webb, the daughter of Henry B. Webb and Mary R. Turner, on 20 Feb 1842 in Chemung, New York[28]. She was born in 1819 in Connecticut or Otsego, New York[29] and died in 5 Sept 1856 in Mexico, New York[30]. William Todd Leigh was buried in Alton, Kansas[31].

William Lee and Lydia were first found in the 1850 Laurens, Otsego County, New York Census. They were found in 1855 in Mexico, Oswego County, New York. William was listed as a shoemaker. According to Sarah Amaria Leigh Harden, she recalled her father and grandfather talking about a general merchandise store they operated at West Laurens, New York together prior to moving to Minnesota in 1867. They made harness and boots, sold groceries and operated the U.S. Post Office. After William's first wife, Sarah passed away, he married Lydia Webb. According to their youngest son, George H. Leigh, Lydia had a drinking problem which eventually caused the marriage to break up. In April of 1896, George H. Leigh, wrote to Minnie Leigh, a daughter of Reuben Harrington Leigh, to say that he had not seen his father since he was 5 years old. He had been separated

---

[18] Genealogy compiled by Rev. Laverne E. Leigh in 2017.

[19] Genealogy compiled by Rev. Laverne E. Leigh in 2017.

[20] Genealogy compiled by Rev. Laverne E. Leigh in 2017.

[21] Minnesota Deaths and Burials, "Minnesota Deaths and Burials, 1835-1990," database, FamilySearch (https://familysearch.org/ark:/61903/1:1:FDZK-626 : 4 December 2014), Elijah Dide Leigh, 03 Dec 1930; citing Houston County, Minn, reference p 178 cn 41; FHL microfilm 1,316,885.

[22] Familysearch.org County marriages, "Wisconsin Marriages, 1836-1930," database, FamilySearch (https://familysearch.org/pal:/MM9.1.1/XRTJ-KHD : 4 December 2014), Elijah Jr. Leigh and Lucy Dickens, 22 Oct 1871; citing reference ; FHL microfilm 1,275,558.

[23] Genealogy compiled by Rev. Laverne E. Leigh, 414 Washington Ave. East, Albia, Iowa 52531 in the Spring of 1975.

[24] Genealogy compiled by Rev. Laverne E. Leigh, 414 Washington Ave. East, Albia, Iowa 52531 in the Spring of 1975.

[25] Familysearch.org family trees.

[26] Genealogy compiled by Rev. Laverne E. Leigh, 414 Washington Ave. East, Albia, Iowa 52531 in the Spring of 1975.

[27] Genealogy compiled by Rev. Laverne E. Leigh, 414 Washington Ave. East, Albia, Iowa 52531 in the Spring of 1975.

[28] Civil War Records on their son, Luman D. Leigh.

[29] Ancestry.com, New York, State Census, 1855 (Provo, UT, USA, Ancestry.com Operations, Inc., 2013), Ancestry.com, http://www.Ancestry.com, Record for William T Leigh.

[30] Civil war records, John H. Leigh, son of Lydia.

[31] Civil War Records on their son, Luman D. Leigh.

from his brothers from the age of eight to twenty-one. This indicates they were either separated or divorced with Lydia taking the children. Then the children must have been separated into at least two groups within about three years after the breakup of the marriage. From my investigation their daughter, Lydia Marie, was sent to live with her Aunt Abigail Webb who was married to George L. Foote. After her Aunt Abigail died, Lydia Marie, married her aunt's husband George L. Foote. In the 1870 Madison, New York Census, two more of William Todd Leigh and Lydia Marie Webb's children were living with their sister in the home of George L. Foote. They were Ann Leigh and John H. Leigh. At that time, Lewis B., Luman D., and Nathan H. Leigh had all died in or as a result of the Civil War. I was never able to determine who raised George H. Leigh and his sister, Agnes. In fact, I know very little about Agnes. Perhaps she died young.

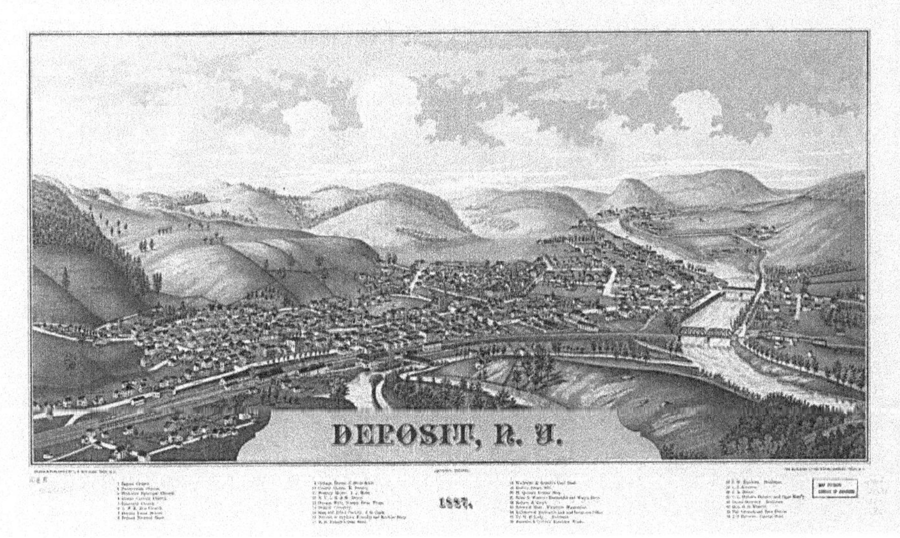

Map of Deposit New York illustrated as the way it looked in 1867.

William Todd was living with his son, William Safford, in Farimont, Minnesota in 1877. William Safford's place was located one half mile from his brother, Reuben Harrington's, farm. In June 7, 1885 William Todd was living with his son, William Safford, in Winnebago City, Minnesota when he wrote a letter to his son, Reuben Harrington, at Alton, Kansas. He was still in Winnebago City in August and then in November of 1885 at which time he wrote again to Reuben. In August, he mentioned the progress of a claim he was making to the US Government for a pension because of the loss of three sons: Luman, Lewis B. and Nathan in the Civil War. His November letter referred to his leg being swollen with poison and infection from May to September and then his slow progress back to being able to use the leg. He mentioned a desire to go to Kansas to join Reuben Harrington and his family.

William Todd did move to Alton in Osborn County, Kansas and purchased a farm with the money he received from the US Government as a pension for the loss of his three sons in the Civil War. His move was probably about 1886. William Todd died suddenly on October 22, 1888 after he had just finished his noon meal and was reclining on the couch. He is buried in Alton, Kansas alongside his son, Reuben Harrington, Reuben's wife, Addie S. and their infant son, Harry Whipple. He was 84. Today there is a marker at the grave for the other three, but no marker for the grave of William Todd.

Sarah M. Whipple died in 1840 of consumption of the marrow of the bone. Before her death, little running sores broke out at her joints according to information related by William Todd to their granddaughter, Sarah Amaria (Leigh) Harden, daughter of William Safford Leigh.

William Todd Leigh and Sarah M. Whipple had the following children:
6.   i.   William Safford Leigh was born on 24 Mar 1835 in Deposit, New York [32] and died on 28 Jul 1902 in Perkins, Oklahoma[33].
7.   ii.   Reuben Harrington Leigh was born on 24 Jan 1837[34] in Deposit, New York and died on 10 Jan 1889 in Alton, Kansas[35].

William Todd Leigh and Lydia M. Webb had the following children:
8.   iii.   Lydia Marie Leigh was born on 30 Jan 1839 in Onondaga County, New York[36] and died on 30 Mar 1886 in Oriskany, New York[37].
       iv.   Lewis B. Leigh was born in 1844 in Cazenovia, New York[38] and died on the way home after being discharged from the Civil War[39]. Lewis enlisted in Company A., New York 157th Infantry Regiment on 19 Sept 1862 at the age of 18 from Madison, New York. He was wounded, a prisoner of war, but survived the war and mustered out 10 July 1865 at Charleston, South Carolina. However, he never made it home. He died of dysentery on the way home and so was a casualty of the Civil War.

---

[32] Findagrave.com.

[33] Findagrave.com.

[34] Ancestry.com, U.S., Civil War Draft Registrations Records, 1863-1865 (Provo, UT, USA, Ancestry.com Operations, Inc., 2010), Ancestry.com, http://www.Ancestry.com, National Archives and Records Administration (NARA); Washington, D.C

[35] Findagrave.com.

[36] Ancestry.com, North America, Family Histories, 1500-2000 (Provo, UT, USA, Ancestry.com Operations, Inc., 2016), Ancestry.com, http://www.Ancestry.com, Book Title: Foote Family : Comprising the Genealogy and History of Nathaniel Foote of Wethersfield, Connecticut, and His Descendants.

[37] Foote Family History & Genealogy, Vol 1.

[38] Historical Data Systems, comp., U.S. Civil War Soldier Records and Profiles (Provo, UT, USA, Ancestry.com Operations Inc, 2009), www.ancestry.com, Record for Lewis B Leigh. http://search.ancestry.com/cgi-bin/sse.dll?db=civilwar_histdatasys&h=2964063&indiv=try.

[39] Civil war records obtained from the National Archives on John H. Leigh.

v.	Luman D. Leigh was born in Dec 1845 in Laurens, Otsego, New York[40] and died on 20 Jun 1864 in Petersburg, Virginia[41]. Luman D. Leigh enlisted 22 Dec 1863 as a Private at Orwell, New York and then into Company G, New York 24th Cavalry Regiment on 07 Jan 1864. He died on 20 June 1864 when he was wounded at Petersburg, Virginia and died in a hospital in Philadelphia, Pennsylvania[42] .

9.	vi.	John H. Leigh was born on 27 Nov 1847[43] in West Laurens, New York and died on 01 Jan 1930 in Sherburne, New York[44].

vii.	Nathan H. Leigh was born on 20 Sep 1848 in Lauren, Otsego, New York[45] and died on 05 Sep 1864 in Madison, New York[46]. Nathan H. Leigh was buried in Sep 1864 in Madison Center, Madison, New York[47]. Nathan died in Madison, New York as a result of injuries in the Civil War. He enlisted in the army Dec 25, 1863 at the same time his brother, Luman enlisted. Nathan was 16 and Luman was 18. On January 7, 1864 he was assigned to Company G of the 24th Regiment NY Cavalry. Nathan died Sep 5, 1864 less than a year later. The Civil War took the lives of Lewis, Nathan and Luman all sons of William Todd and Lydia Webb.

vii.	Mary Ann Leigh was born in 1851 in Otsego, New York[48] and died in before 1896[49]. Mary Ann lived with her sister, Lydia Foote, in the 1865 and 1870 census.

10.	ix.	George Henry Leigh was born in 05 Aug 1855 in Oswego, New York[50] and died on 26 Jun 1927 in Oneida, New York[51].

x.	Agnes Leigh. I have no information on Agnes except she was mentioned in her brother, John H. Leigh's, Civil War record as being his sister[52].

---

[40] Civil War Records on Luman D. Leigh.

[41] Civil War Records on Luman D. Leigh.

[42] Civil War records on John H. Leigh.

[43] Civil War records on John H. Leigh.

[44] Ancestry.com, Web: New York, Find A Grave Index, 1664-2011

[45] Ancestry.com, New York, Town Clerks' Registers of Men Who Served in the Civil War, ca 1861-1865 (Provo, UT, USA, Ancestry.com Operations, Inc., 2011), www.ancestry.com, New York State Archives; Albany, New York; Town Clerks´ Registers of Men Who Served in the Civil War, ca 1861-1865; Collection Number: (N-Ar)13774; Box Number: 43; Roll Number: 25. Record for Nathan Leigh. http://search.ancestry.com/cgi-bin/sse.dll?db=ClerksRegistersCW&h=48173&indiv=try.

[46] Ancestry.com, Headstones Provided for Deceased Union Civil War Veterans, 1879-1903 (Provo, UT, USA, Ancestry.com Operations Inc, 2007), Ancestry.com, http://www.Ancestry.com, Record for Nathan H Leigh. http://search.ancestry.com/cgi-bin/sse.dll?db=CivilWarHeadstones&h=55453&indiv=try.

[47] Ancestry.com, Headstones Provided for Deceased Union Civil War Veterans, 1879-1903 (Provo, UT, USA, Ancestry.com Operations Inc, 2007), Ancestry.com, http://www.Ancestry.com, Record for Nathan H Leigh. http://search.ancestry.com/cgi-bin/sse.dll?db=CivilWarHeadstones&h=55453&indiv=try.

[48] Ancestry.com, New York, State Census, 1855 (Provo, UT, USA, Ancestry.com Operations, Inc., 2013), Ancestry.com, http://www.Ancestry.com, Record for William T Leigh.

[49] civil war records, John H. Leigh.

[50] Obituary, Daily Sentinel, Rome, New York, June 27, 1929, page 5.

[51] Obituary, Daily Sentinel, Rome, New York, June 27, 1929, page 5.

[52] Civil war records, John H. Leigh.

Generation Three

4. Mary Abigale Leigh[3] (Elijah Leigh[2], Nathan S. Leigh[1]) was born on 24 Jan 1836 in New York State[53] and died on 31 Jan 1904 in Money Creek, Minnesota[54]. She married Cyrus Gilbert Berry, the son of Nathan Dolby Berry and Lydia Bosworth, on 02 Aug 1858 in Houston, Minnesota[55]. He was born on 12 Jan 1829 in Newport, Maine[56] and died on 03 Nov 1894 in Money Creek, Minnesota[57]. Mary Abigale Leigh was buried in Money Creek, Minnesota[58]. Cyrus Gilbert Berry married Jane Lemon as a young man. She died fairly young after a short marriage. Cyrus was buried in Money Creek, Minnesota[59].

Mary Abigale Leigh Obituary

Money Creek, Feb. 9. - Died at her home on January 31, 1904, Mrs. Mary Berry aged 67 years. She was born at Mexico, Oswego County, New York, coming to Minnesota in the early fifties with her parents, Mr. & Mrs. Elijah Leigh, and soon afterwards married the late Cyrus Gilbert Berry. She leaves to mourn the great loss five children. They are Cyrus N. Berry, Mrs. Lydia Wood, Edward Berry, Mrs. Jennie Corey and Eugene Berry, the latter living in Western Minnesota, and one sister and two brothers and numerous grand children. The funeral was held at the Union Baptist Church. Rev. J.B. Gidney her pastor, preached and was assisted by Rev. J. B. Utton. The funeral was largely attended considering the severity of the weather. J. Holland was the funeral director. The pall bearers were:. John Campbell, O. G. Robinson and John Jurgensen. The choir rendered excellent and appropriate music for the occasion, which consisted of H. T. Brann, Mrs. George Sinclair, Mrs. Henry Holmes, Miss Anna Warwick, Miss Lucy Campbell and Miss Utton. The remains were laid to rest in the Evergreen Cemetery beside those of her husband and two children who preceded her in death many years ago.

---

[53] Ancestry.com, U.S., Find A Grave Index, 1700s-Current (Provo, UT, USA, Ancestry.com Operations, Inc., 2012), Ancestry.com, http://www.Ancestry.com, Record for Cyrus Gilbert Berry.

[54] Ancestry.com, U.S., Find A Grave Index, 1700s-Current (Provo, UT, USA, Ancestry.com Operations, Inc., 2012), Ancestry.com, http://www.Ancestry.com, Record for Cyrus Gilbert Berry.

[55] Ancestry.com, Minnesota, Marriages Index, 1849-1950 (Provo, UT, USA, Ancestry.com Operations, Inc., 2011), Ancestry.com, http://www.Ancestry.com.

[56] Ancestry.com, U.S., Find A Grave Index, 1700s-Current (Provo, UT, USA, Ancestry.com Operations, Inc., 2012), Ancestry.com, http://www.Ancestry.com, Record for Cyrus Gilbert Berry.

[57] Ancestry.com, U.S., Find A Grave Index, 1700s-Current (Provo, UT, USA, Ancestry.com Operations, Inc., 2012), Ancestry.com, http://www.Ancestry.com, Record for Cyrus Gilbert Berry.

[58] Ancestry.com, U.S., Find A Grave Index, 1700s-Current (Provo, UT, USA, Ancestry.com Operations, Inc., 2012), Ancestry.com, http://www.Ancestry.com, Record for Cyrus Gilbert Berry.

[59] Ancestry.com, U.S., Find A Grave Index, 1700s-Current (Provo, UT, USA, Ancestry.com Operations, Inc., 2012), Ancestry.com, http://www.Fancestry.com, Record for Cyrus Gilbert Berry.

Cyrus Gilbert Berry Obituary
Cyrus Gilbert Berry died in Money Creek, Minnesota. On the evening before his death he retired and appeared in usual health. During the night his wife awakened and thinking something was unusual, spoke to him calling him by name and made an effort to awaken him. As soon as she had obtained a light she looked and to her dismay, he was dead. The Berry family was living in Newport, Maine when Cyrus was born. Cyrus traveled to Wisconsin in 1848 and purchased 40 acres on Sept. 1, 1849 in Winnebago County for cash, planted a crop in preparation for his parents who moved there to take over the farm.

Cyrus Gilbert Berry and Mary Abigale Leigh had the following children:

i. Mary Etta Berry was born in 1860[60] and died on 20 Jun 1891 in Money Creek, Minnesota. She married James Otis Randall, the son of James Randall and Lucy E. Hassen, on 05 Sep 1885 in Lacrosse, Wisconsin[61]. He was born in 1864[62] and died on 14 Dec 1925 in Coos, Oregon[63]. Mary Etta Berry was buried in Money Creek, Minnesota[64].

Photo of Mary Etta Berry and James Otis Randall from the collection of Kathryn Cummings and used with permission.

11. ii. Cyrus Nathan Berry was born on 06 Dec 1862 in Money Creek, Minnesota[65] and died on 27 Jun 1942 in Alma Center, Wisconsin[66].

---

[60] Ancestry.com, U.S., Find A Grave Index, 1700s-Current (Provo, UT, USA, Ancestry.com Operations, Inc., 2012), Ancestry.com, http://www.Ancestry.com, Record for Mary Etta Berry.

[61] Familysearch.org County marriages, "Wisconsin, County Marriages, 1836-1911," database, FamilySearch (https://familysearch.org/ark:/61903/1:1:XRGJ-XSV : 3 June 2016), James Otis Randall and Mary Etta Berry, 05 Sep 1885; citing , Lacrosse, Wisconsin, United States, Wisconsin Historical Society, Madison; FHL microfilm 1,276,058.

[62] Year: *1870;* Census Place: *Trempealeau, Trempealeau, Wisconsin;* Roll: *M593_1737;* Page: *279B;* Family History Library Film: *553236*

[63] Familysearch.org, "Oregon Death Index, 1903-1998," database, FamilySearch (https://familysearch.org/ark:/61903/1:1:VZH1-HGW : 11 December 2014), James Otis Randall, 14 Dec 1925; from "Oregon, Death Index, 1898-2008," database and images, Ancestry (http://www.ancestry.com : 2000); citing Coos, Oregon, certificate number 331, Oregon State Archives and Records Center, Salem.

[64] Ancestry.com, U.S., Find A Grave Index, 1700s-Current (Provo, UT, USA, Ancestry.com Operations, Inc., 2012), Ancestry.com, http://www.Ancestry.com, Record for Mary Etta Berry.

[65] Ancestry.com, Minnesota, Births and Christenings Index, 1840-1980 (Provo, UT, USA, Ancestry.com Operations, Inc., 2011), Ancestry.com, http://www.Ancestry.com, Record for Cyrus Nathan Berry

[66] Ancestry.com, U.S., Find A Grave Index, 1700s-Current (Provo, UT, USA, Ancestry.com Operations, Inc., 2012), Ancestry.com, http://www.Ancestry.com, Record for Cyrus Nathan Berry.

12.   iii.   Edward Ulysses Berry was born on 04 Jul 1865 in Minnesota[67] and died on 26 Oct 1946 in Winona, Minnesota[68].

13.   iv.   Lydia A. Berry was born in 1867[69] and died in 1953[70].

14.   v.   Genevieve Berry was born on 22 May 1869 in Minnesota[71] and died on 15 Sep 1949 in Houston County, Minnesota[72].

15.   vi.   Eugene L. Berry was born on 25 Apr 1871 in Money Creek, Minnesota[73] and died on 06 Nov 1951 in Moose Lake, Minnesota[74].

5. Julia Fannie Leigh (Elijah Leigh[2], Nathan S. Leigh[1]) was born on 16 Sep 1840 in Tully, New York[75] and died on 20 Mar 1920 in Sauk County Poor farm, Wisconsin[76]. She married William A. Todd on 10 Aug 1856 in Money Creek, Minnesota[77]. He was born in 1832[78] and died in 1861 in Vicksburg, Mississippi while in the Civil War[79]. She later married Richard Priest, the son of James Priest and Nancy Ferguson, on 11 Nov 1866 in Reedsburg, Wisconsin[80]. He was born on 29 Sept 1814 in Henry County, Kentucky[81] and died on 28 Mar 1892 in Miltonvale, Kansas[82].

Julia Fannie Leigh Obituary
April 9, 1920, Winona Republican Herald - Mrs. Julia Priest nee Julia Fannie Leigh, daughter of Mr. and Mrs. Elijah Leigh, was born at Tully, New York on Sept 16, 1840. With her parents she moved to Dodge County, from which place they immigrated to Money Creek. At age 16, she became the bride of W. Todd on August 10, 1856, later going to Ironton, Wisconsin to make their home. During their stay there, the Civil War

[67] Ancestry.com, U.S., Find A Grave Index, 1700s-Current (Provo, UT, USA, Ancestry.com Operations, Inc., 2012), Ancestry.com, http://www.Ancestry.com, Record for Edward Ulysses Berry.

[68] Ancestry.com, U.S., Find A Grave Index, 1700s-Current (Provo, UT, USA, Ancestry.com Operations, Inc., 2012), Ancestry.com, http://www.Ancestry.com, Record for Edward Ulysses Berry.

[69] Ancestry.com, Minnesota, Marriages Index, 1849-1950 (Provo, UT, USA, Ancestry.com Operations, Inc., 2011), Ancestry.com, http://www.Ancestry.com, Record for Perry A Wood.

[70] Ancestry.com, U.S., Find A Grave Index, 1700s-Current (Provo, UT, USA, Ancestry.com Operations, Inc., 2012), Ancestry.com, http://www.Ancestry.com, Record for Mary Abigail Berry.

[71] Ancestry.com, U.S., Find A Grave Index, 1700s-Current (Provo, UT, USA, Ancestry.com Operations, Inc., 2012), Ancestry.com, http://www.Ancestry.com, Record for Mary Abigail Berry.

[72] Ancestry.com, U.S., Find A Grave Index, 1700s-Current (Provo, UT, USA, Ancestry.com Operations, Inc., 2012), Ancestry.com, http://www.Ancestry.com, Record for Mary Abigail Berry.

[73] Ancestry.com, Washington, Marriage Records, 1854-2013 (Provo, UT, USA, Ancestry.com Operations, Inc., 2012), Ancestry.com, http://www.Ancestry.com, Washington State Archives; Olympia, Washington; Collection Title: Washington Marriage Records, 1854-2013; Reference Number: easpmr5195. Record for Eugene L Berry.

[74] Ancestry.com, Minnesota, Death Index, 1908-2002 (Provo, UT, USA, Ancestry.com Operations Inc, 2001), Ancestry.com, http://www.Ancestry.com, Record for Eugene L. Berry

[75] Genealogy compiled by Rev. Laverne E. Leigh in 2017.

[76] Genealogy compiled by Rev. Laverne E. Leigh in 2017.

[77] Genealogy compiled by Rev. Laverne E. Leigh in 2017.

[78] Genealogy compiled by Rev. Laverne E. Leigh in 2017.

[79] Genealogy compiled by Rev. Laverne E. Leigh in 2017.

[80] Genealogy compiled by Rev. Laverne E. Leigh in 2017.

[81] Genealogy compiled by Rev. Laverne E. Leigh in 2017.

[82] Genealogy compiled by Rev. Laverne E. Leigh in 2017.

broke out and Mr. Todd enlisted, having to leave his wife and two little children alone, as many other mothers had to remain to look after the comforts of their home at this time. Mr. Todd did not return, but died in 1861. Later she was united in marriage to Richard Priest at Reedsburg, Wisconsin. After residing there for some time, they moved to Topeka, Kansas. Four children were born to them, two sons and two daughters. One daughter, who had grown to womanhood and Mr. Priest were called to the great beyond. Mrs. Priest then returned to Reedsburg and later of Lavallie, Wisconsin at which place she purchased a home for her family, where she spend the rest of her days until death came as a result of the flu.

Richard Priest Obituary
Wednesday, March 30, 1892
THE ADVANCE, Miltonvale, Cloud County, Kansas.
Richard Priest a respected citizen, died with consumption Monday, March 28 at his home four miles north of town. He was aged 77 years. Funeral services were held at the Christian Church today where Elder LeBaron delivered an appropriate sermon, after which his body was interred in the cemetery near town.

April 14, 1892
REEDSBURG FREE PRESS, Reedsburg, Sauk County, WI;
DIED PRIEST.---A his home in Miltonville Kansas. Richard Priest was born in Kentucky in 1814 where he resided until 1846 when he moved to Dane County, this state. In 1852 he moved to Reedsburg, settling 1 1/2 miles east of the city, where he lived until 1885, when he moved to Kansas. Mr. P. was married in 1838 to Miss Ellen Moore, of Indiana, by whom he had four children, three of whom are now living. Mrs. Priest died in 1862. He married again, taking Mrs. Julia Todd, of Ironton, for his wife, by whom he had four children, three of the number surviving him.

Contributed by: Richard Charles Priest (1927-2012), great-grandson of Richard Priest Sr. and Julia F. (Leigh) Todd Priest: June, 2001 - Took the highway north from Interstate 80 toward Concordia, made a right at the designated corner and headed east. Was about to turn around when we came to a small Miltonvale 1 mile sign. The visit to Miltonvale was interesting to say the least. The country was not what I had visualized in my mind--it was hilly and well forested, though that probably was not the case in the 1880's. Miltonvale is a sleepy little village exhibiting little prosperity and few pretty homes. The cemetery wasn't particularly pretty either. It was easy to see that it surely wasn't a very hospitable place back then either. Richard and Millie (Richard's daughter who died at about 17) are both buried in the cemetery, and I located their lot with the help of a map. There was no sign on the lots that anyone was in fact buried there, any type of memorial was long since gone. I also located two Fowler lots--Amanda's family but was unable to locate anything on her father James. I was able to locate James Fowler's land, but alas no buildings remained. Also, I had read where Richard's farm was north of Miltonvale. I can now visualize where it might have been. I guess that sooner or later we all experience a feeling that we have been someplace before when we know that we haven't been there--I had it the whole time there, didn't really want to stay and yet wanted to see for myself. I don't think I'm particularly prone to that type of sensation, but I have to admit, it was a strange feeling. Probably caused by all of the time that I have been involved with Miltonvale over the years, visualizing in my mind all of their hardships and often sad experiences.

When Julie and William Todd were married in 1856, witnesses to their marriage were Stafford William (probably as William Stafford Leigh) and Nathan Vance (probably her brother Nathan who well may have had the middle name, Vance). Their marriage was performed by F.N. Goodrich, Justice of the Peace. William was a casualty of the Civil War.

 William A. Todd and Julia Fannie Leigh had the following children:
16.   i.   Rose Ann Lindel Todd was born in 1858 in Money Creek, Minnesota[83] and died on 14 Mar 1897 in Miltonvale, Kansas[84].
17.   ii.   Ransom William Todd was born on 23 Oct 1860 in Money Creek, Minnesota[85] and died on 27 Oct 1931 in Crandon, Wisconsin[86].

Richard Priest and Julia Fannie Leigh had the following children:
18.   i.   Fred M. Priest was born on 08 Feb 1868 in Reedsburg, Wisconsin[87] and died on 16 Feb 1941 in St. James, Minnesota[88].
19.   ii.   Nora Eleanor Priest was born on 24 Oct 1873 in Reedsburg, Wisconsin[89] and died on 29 Jul 1940[90].
    iii.   Nellie Priest was born in Dec 1874 in Reedsburg, Wisconsin[91].
20.   v.   Richard Priest was born on 02 Dec 1883 in Wisconsin[92] and died on 06 Oct 1950[93].

---

[83] Genealogy compiled by Rev. Laverne E. Leigh in 2017.
[84] Genealogy compiled by Rev. Laverne E. Leigh in 2017.
[85] Ancestry.com, Wisconsin, Births and Christenings Index, 1801-1928 (Provo, UT, USA, Ancestry.com Operations, Inc., 2011), Ancestry.com, http://www.Ancestry.com, Record for Ransom Wm Todd.
[86] Genealogy compiled by Rev. Laverne E. Leigh in 2017.
[87] Genealogy compiled by Rev. Laverne E. Leigh in 2017.
[88] Ancestry.com. *Minnesota, Death Index, 1908-2002* [database on-line]. Provo, UT, USA: Ancestry.com Operations Inc, 2001..
[89] Genealogy compiled by Rev. Laverne E. Leigh in 2017
[90] Genealogy compiled by Rev. Laverne E. Leigh in 2017
[91] Genealogy compiled by Rev. Laverne E. Leigh in 2017
[92] Ancestry.com, World War I Draft Registration Cards, 1917-1918
[93] Ancestry.com. *U.S., Social Security Applications and Claims Index, 1936-2007* [database on-line]. Provo, UT, USA: Ancestry.com Operations, Inc., 2015.

6. William Safford Leigh[3] (William Todd Leigh[2], Nathan S. Leigh[1]) was born on 24 Mar 1835 in Deposit, New York[94] and died on 28 July 1902 in Perkins, Oklahoma[95]. He married Rosetta Lavancia Hathaway, the daughter of John King Hathaway and Polly Amaria Northrup, in 1861 in Deposit, New York[96]. She was born on 05 Mar 1835 in New York[97] and died on 08 Jul 1872 in Fairmont, Minnesota[98]. He later married Priscilla E. Pierson, the daughter of Martin L. Pierson, on 14 Nov 1894 in Stillwater, Oklahoma[99]. She was born in Nov 1852 in Steubenville, Ohio[100]. William Safford Leigh was buried in Pawnee, Oklahoma[101].

William was living in Sanford, Broome County, New York at the time of the 1860 United States Census and was living in Deposit, Broome County, New York in 1861 when he married Rosetta Hathaway. The towns of Sanford and Deposit share a common boundary between them. He operated a general merchandise store with his father, William Todd, in West Laurens, New York prior to their both moving to Minnesota. In the store they made harness and boots, sold groceries and operated the US Post Office. William was appointed postmaster of West Laurens, New York, January 17, 1866. Later, just before his death, he operated a shoe repair shop in Perkins, Oklahoma.

They were living in Fairmont, Minnesota at the time of the 1870 Census and his father, William Todd, was living with them and their daughter, Sarah, age 7. They were living near Fairmont, Minnesota, July 8, 1872 when his wife, Rosetta died. She had sclerosis and had to be carried because one of her legs was shorter than the other one according to their daughter, Sarah Amaria Leigh. William was still living in Fairmont in 1877. His father, William Todd was living with him and his brother, Reuben Harrington, was living on a farm nearby. At the time of the 1880 United States Census, William Safford, age 45, was listed as living in Sherburne, Martin County, Minnesota as a widower with his daughter Sarah, age 17, and his father, William Todd, age 75. He was listed as being a minister.

---

[94]Ancestry.com, U.S., Find A Grave Index, 1700s-Current (Provo, UT, USA, Ancestry.com Operations, Inc., 2012), Ancestry.com, http://www.Ancestry.com, Record for William S Leigh.

[95] Ancestry.com, U.S., Find A Grave Index, 1700s-Current (Provo, UT, USA, Ancestry.com Operations, Inc., 2012), Ancestry.com, http://www.Ancestry.com, Record for William S Leigh.

[96] Genealogy compiled by Rev. Laverne E. Leigh, 414 Washington Ave. East, Albia, Iowa 52531 in the Spring of 1975.

[97] Genealogy compiled by Rev. Laverne E. Leigh, 414 Washington Ave. East, Albia, Iowa 52531 in the Spring of 1975.

[98] Ancestry.com, Oklahoma, County Marriages, 1890-1995 (Lehi, UT, USA, Ancestry.com Operations, Inc., 2016), Ancestry.com, http://www.Ancestry.com, Record for Pricella E Peirson.

[99] Ancestry.com, Oklahoma, County Marriages, 1890-1995 (Lehi, UT, USA, Ancestry.com Operations, Inc., 2016), Ancestry.com, http://www.Ancestry.com, Record for Pricella E Peirson.

[100] Ancestry.com, Oklahoma, County Marriages, 1890-1995 (Lehi, UT, USA, Ancestry.com Operations, Inc., 2016), Ancestry.com, http://www.Ancestry.com, Record for Pricella E Peirson.

[101] Ancestry.com, U.S., Find A Grave Index, 1700s-Current (Provo, UT, USA, Ancestry.com Operations, Inc., 2012), Ancestry.com, http://www.Ancestry.com, Record for William S Leigh.

William Safford and Reuben Harrington operated a creamery for a time. Minnie Leigh, Reuben's daughter wrote a letter on February 5, 1884 and mentioned her father had dissolved his partnership in the creamery with Uncle William Safford.

During 1885 and 1886, William Safford lived in Winnebago City, Minnesota and may have lived there even longer. Part of this time, his father, William Todd, lived with him. The exact time is not known, but during this period at Winnebago City in 1885, William Safford began preaching. He was working for a Bible Society and preaching half time at Mapleton (ed. - this name was not clear in the letter written by his father, William Todd, on November 23, 1885 from Winnebago City to the other brother, Reuben Harrington, at Alton, Kansas).

William Safford, also, owned a store in Winnebago City for a time but we have no record that indicates the type of store. He made a trip to Georgia in 1885 or 1886 with the idea of moving there, but did not like the country. Our information does not indicate when the move was made, but he moved to Kansas some time after Reuben Harrington, his brother, and William Todd, his father, moved there. We know he was preaching at Codell, Kansas on January 5, 1894 at the Shiloh Presbyterian Church. He was not yet affiliated with any church organization, but hoped to be before the winter ended according to a letter he wrote in January of 1894 to Minnie Leigh, his niece.

William Safford became a Free-Will Baptist minister and served churches in Kansas and Oklahoma for many years until his death. He was living in Perkins Oklahoma and both preaching and operating a shoe repair shop at the time of his death. He is buried in Pawnee, Oklahoma.

At the time of the 1880 United States Census, William was listed as living in Sherburne, Minnesota as a widower with his daughter, Sarah A., and his father William Todd. He was listed as being a minister.

William Safford Leigh and Rosetta Lavancia Hathaway had the following child:
21.   i.   Sarah Amaria Leigh was born on 04 Oct 1862 in New York[102] and died on 01 Feb 1947 in Pawnee, Oklahoma[103].

7. Reuben Harrington Leigh[3] (William Todd Leigh[2], Nathan S. Leigh[1]) was born on 24 Jan 1837[104] in Deposit New York and died on 10 Jan 1889 in Alton, Kansas[105]. He

---

[102] Ancestry.com, U.S., Find A Grave Index, 1700s-Current (Provo, UT, USA, Ancestry.com Operations, Inc., 2012), Ancestry.com, http://www.Ancestry.com, Record for Sarah Amaria Harnden.
[103] Ancestry.com, U.S., Find A Grave Index, 1700s-Current (Provo, UT, USA, Ancestry.com Operations, Inc., 2012), Ancestry.com, http://www.Ancestry.com, Record for Sarah Amaria Harnden..
[104] Ancestry.com, U.S., Civil War Draft Registrations Records, 1863-1865 (Provo, UT, USA, Ancestry.com Operations, Inc., 2010), Ancestry.com, http://www.Ancestry.com, National Archives and Records Administration

married Phoebe Amelia Hathaway, the daughter of John King Hathaway and Polly Amaria Northrup, on 15 June 1857[106] in Deposit, New York. She was born on 14 Jun 1841 in New York State[107] and died on 12 Dec 1865 in Saratoga, Minnesota[108]. After the death of Polly, he married her sister, Adelaid Sophrenia Hathaway, the daughter of John King Hathaway and Polly Amaria Northrup, on 09 Jan 1867[109] in West Lauren, New York. She was born on 07 May 1843[110] in West Laurens, New York and died on 22 Feb 1893 in Alton, Kansas[111]. Reuben Harrington Leigh was buried in Alton, Kansas[112].

Phoebe and Reuben moved to Minnesota sometime between August 19, 1862, when Reuben Henry was born and October 9th 1864 when their third child was born, Andrew Lincoln. Reuben moved with his wife and children from Wisconsin to Tilden Township, Osborne County, Kansas in 1885. He died of diabetes and had ten children when he died.

During the next year after Phoebe's death, her brother, Lebbaus Scott Hathaway, came and lived with Reuben Harrington. Mary Jane (Hathaway) Haight, an older sister of Phoebe's, took care of the children in her own home. About a year after Phoebe's death, Reuben took his two children and went back to New York where he courted and married Phoebe's sister, Adelaid Sophrenia. They were married by Rev. E. C. Hodge.

Adelaid and Reuben Harrington returned with his two children to Minnesota to live at Wasioji in Dodge County. Here they homesteaded eighty acres of land and took an adjoining eighty acres as a timer claim. The farm was about seven miles north west of Fairmont in Frazer Township. Lilly Creek runs through the south west corner of the homestead. Reuben Harrington was a real horticulturist. He had a fine fruit orchard on

(NARA); Washington, D.C.; Consolidated Lists of Civil War Draft Registration Records (Provost Marshal General's Bureau; Consolidated Enrollment Lists, 1863-1865); Record Group: 110, Records of the Provost Marshal General's Bureau (Civil War); Collection Name: Consolidated Enrollment Lists, 1863-1865 (Civil War Union Draft Records); NAI: 4213514; Archive Volume Number: 2 of 3. Record for R H Leigh.

[105] Ancestry.com, The New England Historical & Genealogical Register, 1847-2011 (Provo, UT, USA, Ancestry.com Operations, Inc., 2011), Ancestry.com, http://www.Ancestry.com, Record for Reuben H Leigh.

[106] Genealogy compiled by Rev. Laverne E. Leigh, 414 Washington Ave. East, Albia, Iowa 52531 in the Spring of 1975.

[107] Ancestry.com, U.S., Find A Grave Index, 1700s-Current (Provo, UT, USA, Ancestry.com Operations, Inc., 2012), Ancestry.com, http://www.Ancestry.com, Record for Phebe A Leigh.

[108] Ancestry.com, U.S., Find A Grave Index, 1700s-Current (Provo, UT, USA, Ancestry.com Operations, Inc., 2012), Ancestry.com, http://www.Ancestry.com, Record for Phebe A Leigh.

[109] Genealogy compiled by Rev. Laverne E. Leigh, 414 Washington Ave. East, Albia, Iowa 52531 in the Spring of 1975.

[110] Genealogy compiled by Rev. Laverne E. Leigh, 414 Washington Ave. East, Albia, Iowa 52531 in the Spring of 1975.

[111] Genealogy compiled by Rev. Laverne E. Leigh, 414 Washington Ave. East, Albia, Iowa 52531 in the Spring of 1975.

[112] Ancestry.com, U.S., Find A Grave Index, 1700s-Current (Provo, UT, USA, Ancestry.com Operations, Inc., 2012), Ancestry.com, http://www.Ancestry.com, Record for Addie S Leigh.

his homestead. During this time at Fairmont, Reuben Harrington was thrown out of a runaway wagon onto the back of his neck while taking the children to the circus. He was sickly and had a great deal of back trouble from that time until his death.

He operated a creamery in partnership with his brother, William Safford, for a period of time. They dissolved this partnership before February 4, 1884 according to a letter written at that time by his daughter, Minnie Augusta. Hard work and conditions had told on his health. Finally with the approval of the family and Dr. Rice, it was decided to try a change of climate and move to Kansas where the winters were not so cold. A letter written December 8, 1884 by his daughter Phoebe Adella, to his son, Reuben Henry, at Kingsly, Iowa said: "Father has gone to Kansas to buy a farm. He went last Monday, will be gone two or three weeks. He has been to St. Paul to see a doctor. It is the spinal complaint that ails him. Says he has got to go to bed for three months or he can't get well. He must have perfect rest..." (letter in the possession of Minnie (Moore) Canada of Hominy, Oklahoma). Reuben Harrington wrote just before this on April 7, 1884 to Phoebe Adella to say, "...I have earned but little with my back in consequence of my health. I have not got my belt yet. Expect it every day. It will cost $3.00" It is presumed that he did receive this belt and that he probably wore it as a support for his back for the rest of his life.

Reuben did buy land in Alton, Kansas and sold their property at Fairmont for $2,000. They began the five hundred mile trip to Alton, Kansas in the Spring of 1885 and arrived in Alton on Decoration Day, May 30, 1885 where they were met by Ed and Mary Jane (Hathaway) Haight Ives who were already living in Alton. His choice of Alton, Kansas as their new home was probably influenced by part of the family living there already. He tried to grow fruit trees in Kansas as he had in Minnesota. Many fruit trees were planted, but the hot, dry weather in Kansas did not allow them to prosper.

Adelaid the Reuben's eight and last child, Harry Whipple, was born November 24, 1884 at Fairmont, Minnesota and lived less than a year to die October 3, 1885 in Alton, Kansas. He was buried in the cemetery at Alton. The change of climate was not enough and after continued illness Reuben Harrington died January 10, 1889 at the age of 51. He is buried with Harry Whipple, his wife, Adelaid, and his father, William Todd, in the cemetery in Alton. A family marker indicates his final resting place.

Rueben Harrington Leigh and Phoebe Amelia Hathaway had the following children:
22.   i.   Phoebe Adella Leigh was born on 08 Oct 1860 in Deposit, New York[113] and died on 23 Jul 1943 in Hominy, Oklahoma[114].

---

[113] Ancestry.com, U.S., Find A Grave Index, 1700s-Current (Provo, UT, USA, Ancestry.com Operations, Inc., 2012), Ancestry.com, http://www.Ancestry.com, Record for Phebe A Moore.
[114] Ancestry.com, U.S., Find A Grave Index, 1700s-Current (Provo, UT, USA, Ancestry.com Operations, Inc., 2012), Ancestry.com, http://www.Ancestry.com, Record for Phebe A Moore.-

ii.   Reuben Henry Leigh was born on 19 Aug 1862 in Deposit, New York[115] and died on 15 Oct 1886 in Winnebago City, Minnesota[116]. He was about to marry Minnie Reynolds on 08 Sep 1886 in Fairbault, Minnesota[117], but died just prior to the marriage. Reuben Henry Leigh was buried in Fairmont, Minnesota[118].

Reuben Henry moved with his parents at the age of two to Saratoga, Minnesota in time for a baby brother, Andrew Lincoln, to be born there October 9, 1864. In less than a year, Andrew died and their mother, Phoebe died two months after the baby. Early family letters from this period tell of Reuben Henry having blue eyes and that he was a good boy that everyone seemed to like. He loved to rock and sing to his little brother, Andrew and was quite broken up at his death.

After their mother's death, Reuben and Dell lived with Mary Jane Hathaway Haight, an older sister of their mother, in her home for about a year. Then their father, Reuben Harrington, took them both back to New York where he courted, won and married Adelaid Sophrenia Hathaway. This was according to their mother's death-bed wish that if he should marry again that he would marry her sister, Adelaid, if she was willing. Phoebe felt that her sister would do a better job of raising her children than a stranger.

They all went back to Minnesota and settled at Wasioji where a baby sister, Minnie Augusta was born November 6, 1867. Then sometime between Minnie's birth and July of 1871, the family moved to Fairmont, Minnesota. Reuben Henry grew up on the farm at Fairmont, Minnesota. They lived for fourteen years on an eighty acre homestead and an eighty acre timer claim that was seven miles north west of Fairmont. It was here that during these years saw six more brothers born. During this time, Reuben Henry was baptized by Rev. E. A. How at Free-Will Baptist (Open Communion) minister.

When he was 17, he moved five hundred miles with his family from Fairmont to Alton, Kansas. He stayed only a short time at Alton before he began to travel and work elsewhere. From family letters still in existence, we can trace his movements to being in Winnebago City, Minnesota selling trees on June 7, 1885. These were trees that he had cut around February 4, 1874 while working for Will Berry east of Mankato, Minnesota. Before the family moved to Alton, Kansas in the spring of 1885, he had made a trip to

---

[115] Death record, Winnebago City, Minnesota - FHC Film#1,710,732.

[116] Death record, Winnebago City, Minnesota - FHC Film#1,710,732.

[117] Marriage records, "Minnesota, County Marriages, 1860-1949," database with images, FamilySearch (https://familysearch.org/ark:/61903/1:1:VKN2-TJ4 : 13 June 2016), Reuben H Leigh and Minnie Reynolds, 08 Sep 1886, Faribault, Minnesota, United States; citing p. , local historical societies and universities, Minnesota; FHL microfilm 1,673,714.

[118] Genealogy compiled by Rev. Laverne E. Leigh, 414 Washington Ave. East, Albia, Iowa 52531 in the Spring of 1975.

Iowa and was at Kinglsy, Iowa on December 12, 1884. He was again in Winnebago City on March 18, 1886 and was going with a girl named Tilley McCalley.   During this period of time, he was running a feed mill for Haight, his mother and step-mother's sister Mary Jane Hathaway Haight's husband. He wrote February 11, 1886 to his sister Dell to describe the mill, "...I have been running a feed mill for Haight. It is a large one the wheel is thirty feet wide and mounted on a tower fifty five feet wide..."

Sometime during the summer of 1886, he began going with Miss Minnie Reynolds. They became engaged and planned to marry. But this was to never be for Reuben Henry became ill with typhoid fever in the fall of 1886. During his last illness, he was at the home of his uncle, William Safford Leigh, who wrote cards to Reuben Henry's father, Reuben Harrington, to keep him posted. The cards told of how sick Reuben Henry was, the fear for his life and how he was unconscious most of the time at the last. Reuben died Friday, October 15, 1886.

Fairmont Sentinel of October 22, 1886
"R. Henry age 24 years son of Reuben Leigh formally of this county died of typhoid fever at the house of his uncle in Winnebago City last Friday and was buried in the Fairmont Cemetery from the Baptist church on Saturday. He was a bright young man of good habits, industrious disposition and possessing an unusual amount of business ability and self reliance for one of his years. The fact that he had made every arrangement and was about to be married to a daughter of J. C. Reynolds of Easton when stricken down with the disease makes his death unusually sad. A large number of his friends and associates from Winnebago City attended the burial service at this place."

Reuben Henry was a young man of great Christian faith and worked hard in the church where he lived. When he moved from Fairmont to Winnebago City, the church where he served at Fairmont sent a letter to the church in Winnebago City commending him and recommending him to the new church with the firm believe that he would be a real worker in the new congregation. Reuben Henry's death brought much sadness to a family that had already know the death of the youngest brother, Harry Whipple, on October 3, 1885 - the year before.

     iii.   Andrew Lincoln Leigh was born on 09 Oct 1864 in Saratoga, Minnesota[119] and died on 03 Oct 1865 in Saratoga, Minnesota[120]. Andrew is buried beside his mother in the Saratoga, Minnesota Cemetery. In the far NW corner, Laverne and Betty Leigh had a cement pad poured and their tomb stones set in the pad in the 1970's.

---

[119] Ancestry.com, The New England Historical & Genealogical Register, 1847-2011 (Provo, UT, USA, Ancestry.com Operations, Inc., 2011), Ancestry.com, http://www.Ancestry.com, Record for Andrew L Leigh.
[120] Ancestry.com, The New England Historical & Genealogical Register, 1847-2011 (Provo, UT, USA, Ancestry.com Operations, Inc., 2011), Ancestry.com, http://www.Ancestry.com, Record for Andrew L Leigh.

Kent News-Journal, Oct. 21, 1964, p-3
"Services Held for Mrs. Addie Leigh"
Funeral services were held at Edline Chapel Tuesday for Mrs. Addie C. Leigh, 86, 10426 S.E. 244th Street, a resident of Kent for 58 years. Mrs. Leigh died Saturday at Marsolais Manor Nursing Home in Auburn after an illness of more than a month. She was born in Fairmont, Minnesota and came to the Kent Valley from her native state. Her late husband, Charles, was a fruit farmer until his death in 1948. Mrs. Leigh was a charter member of the Helping Hand Circle, organized in Kent in 1910. She also belonged to the Kent Christian Church for many years. Surviving are three sons, Chester Leigh of Camano Island, Otis Leigh of Kent and Ray Leigh of Colfax; three daughters, Mrs. Pearl Harris and Miss Hazel Leigh, both of Kent and Mrs. Dottie Sutherland of Seattle; ten grandchildren and five great-grandchildren."

Photo of Adelaid Sophrenia Hathaway from the collection of Rev. Laverne E. Leigh and used with permission.

Adelaid lived until February 22, 1893 after Reuben's death raising the children and keeping the family together as best she could. Much of this time, she was in bad health herself. Letters from this time written by Adelaid indicate that she was in poor health during the last years of her husband's life. But due to his extreme illness and the necessity of caring for him, she did not mention it. Likely her caring for him and the lifting it entailed shortened her life. Upon her death, she was buried at Alton between her husband and her youngest son, Harry Whipple. She had lived 50 years and they were hard years.

Rueben Harrington Leigh and Adelaid Sophrenia Hathaway had the following children:

    iv.   Minnie Augusta Leigh was born on 06 Nov 1867 in Wasioji, Minnesota[121] and died on 05 Mar 1962 in Eugene, Oregon[122]. Minnie Augusta Leigh was born November 6, 1867 at Wasioji in Dodge County, Minnesota. She was the first child of Reuben Harrington and Adelaid Hathaway Leigh. She had an older half-brother Reuben

---

[121] Ancestry.com, U.S., Find A Grave Index, 1700s-Current (Provo, UT, USA, Ancestry.com Operations, Inc., 2012), Ancestry.com, http://www.Ancestry.com, Record for Minnie A Leigh.
[122] Ancestry.com, U.S., Find A Grave Index, 1700s-Current (Provo, UT, USA, Ancestry.com Operations, Inc., 2012), Ancestry.com, http://www.Ancestry.com, Record for Minnie A Leigh.

Henry, and a half-sister, Dell. The family lived for only a short time in Dodge County before they moved to a farm seven miles north west of Fairmont, Minnesota.

While the family lived at Fairmont, six brothers were born that Minnie and Dell helped their mother care for while they grew up. Minnie was baptized with her brother, Reuben Henry, and Aunt Carrie Hathaway in Buffalo Lake near Fairmont September 19, 1880. The minister was Rev. E.A. How, a Free-Will Baptist (open communion) minister. All through her life Minnie remained a committed Christian.

Photo of Minnie Augusta Leigh from the collection of Rev. Laverne E. Leigh and used with permission.

She moved with the family to Alton, Kansas in the spring of 1885 at the age of 17. Shortly after moving to Kansas, she began to teach in a small rural school. A family letter tells of her teaching in the fall of 1890 the year her sister, Dell, was married. In the summer 1891, she went with her brother, George Asa, to Minnesota to stay with Dell and her husband, George Moore, to help Dell take care of their first child, Guy Rowley, born in May. That fall she returned to Kansas in time to begin teaching school.

After their mother, Adelaide's, death February 22, 1893, Minnie and all of her brothers drifted back to Minnesota. Minnie lived with George and Dell Moore and taught school across Lily Creek in sight of their farm. A family letter indicates that she was at Welcome, Minnesota on January 5, 1894.

Photo of Minnie Augusta Leigh from the collection of Rev. Laverne E. Leigh and used with permission.

Minnie received an inheritance of $2,317.40 in 1885 from the estate of a great aunt, Phebe B. Northup Robertson Hackett, who was born April 9, 1816 and lived in Chautauqua County New York and owned property at Sinclairville, New York. Her will provided that her estate be equally distributed among the female hers of her sister, Polly Northup. There were four female heirs: Minnie Augusta Leigh, Phoebe Adell (Dell) Leigh Moore, Sarah Amaria Leigh Harnden and Mary Jane Hathaway Haight Ives who each received an inheritance of $2,317.40.

Minnie left Minnesota in 1902 and moved to Idaho to live in the Parma, Idaho area until 1934. She taught at the Ten Davis school in the Parma area. She operated with her brother, Jay Noel, the first furniture store in Parma during this time.

During the 1920's she trained to be a foreign missionary in a Bible School in Seattle, Washington. After she graduated with high hopes of being a foreign missionary, she was informed that she was too old to be considered for the mission field. Family members felt strongly that the school had treated her badly in to telling her earlier, but she never seemed to hold it against them.

She moved to Fall Creek, Oregon in 1934. She lived with her brother, George Asa, on a small farm he had purchased from another brother, Jay Noel, whose farm surrounded George's. After several years, George and Minnie left the farm and moved into a small house in the town of Fall Creek. George had to move into a rest home in Eugene, Oregon first and then in 1955 Minnie had to leave the little house in Fall Creek to enter a rest home in Eugene. She was in the rest home until her death March 5, 1962.

Minnie lived to be the last of her generation. She survived all her nine brothers and one sister. Her funeral was conducted by the Rev. Laverne E. Leigh, her great nephew and grandson of her brother, Jay Noel Leigh. She is buried in the West Lawn Memorial Cemetery, Eugene, Oregon.

Photo of Minnie Augusta Leigh and Jay Noel Leigh in their later years from the collection of Rev. Laverne E. Leigh and used with permission.

23.　　v.　　Charles Emery Leigh was born on 14 Jul 1871[123] in Fairmont, Minnesota and died on 24 Aug 1948 in Kent, Washington[124].

24.　　vi.　　Jay Noel Leigh was born on 19 Mar 1873 in Fairmont, Minnesota[125] and died on 06 Dec 1958 in Parma, Idaho[126].

25.　　vii.　　George Asa Leigh was born on 17 Feb 1876 in Fairmont, Minnesota[127] and died on 19 Jan 1949 in Fall Creek, Oregon[128].

26.　　viii.　　William Edson Leigh was born on 03 Aug 1877 in Fairmont, Minnesota[129] and died on 11 Mar 1939 in Parma, Idaho[130].

27.　　ix.　　Nathan Evan Leigh was born on 04 Mar 1879[131] in Fairmont, Minnesota and died on 30 Apr 1954 in Flathead, Montana[132].

---

[123] Ancestry.com, Washington, Select Death Certificates, 1907-1960 (Provo, UT, USA, Ancestry.com Operations, Inc., 2014), Ancestry.com, http://www.Ancestry.com, Record for Charles Emory Leigh.

[124] Ancestry.com, Washington, Select Death Certificates, 1907-1960 (Provo, UT, USA, Ancestry.com Operations, Inc., 2014), Ancestry.com, http://www.Ancestry.com, Record for Charles Emory Leigh.

[125] Ancestry.com, Idaho, Death Index, 1890-1964 (Provo, UT, USA, Ancestry.com Operations Inc, 2003), Ancestry.com, http://www.Ancestry.com, Record for Jay Noel Leigh.

[126] Ancestry.com, Idaho, Death Index, 1890-1964 (Provo, UT, USA, Ancestry.com Operations Inc, 2003), Ancestry.com, http://www.Ancestry.com, Record for Jay Noel Leigh.

[127] Ancestry.com, U.S., Find A Grave Index, 1700s-Current (Provo, UT, USA, Ancestry.com Operations, Inc., 2012), Ancestry.com, http://www.Ancestry.com, Record for George Asa Leigh.

[128] Ancestry.com, U.S., Find A Grave Index, 1700s-Current (Provo, UT, USA, Ancestry.com Operations, Inc., 2012), Ancestry.com, http://www.Ancestry.com, Record for George Asa Leigh.

[129] Ancestry.com, World War I Draft Registration Cards, 1917-1918 (Provo, UT, USA, The Generations Network, Inc., 2005), www.ancestry.com, Registration State: Idaho; Registration County: Canyon; Roll: 1452112. Record for William Edson Leigh.

[130] Ancestry.com, U.S., Find A Grave Index, 1700s-Current (Provo, UT, USA, Ancestry.com Operations, Inc., 2012), Ancestry.com, http://www.Ancestry.com, Record for William Edson Leigh.

[131] Ancestry.com, U.S. World War II Draft Registration Cards, 1942 (Provo, UT, USA, The Generations Network, Inc., 2007), www.ancestry.com, The National Archives at St. Louis; St. Louis, Missouri; Draft Registration Cards for Fourth Registration for Idaho, 04/27/1942 - 04/27/1942; NAI Number: 563870; Record Group Title: Records of the Selective Service System; Record Group Number: 147. Record for Nathan Evan Leigh.

[132] Ancestry.com, U.S., Find A Grave Index, 1700s-Current (Provo, UT, USA, Ancestry.com Operations, Inc., 2012), Ancestry.com, http://www.Ancestry.com, Record for Nathan Evan Leigh.

28.   x.   Mentor Garfield Leigh was born on 13 Mar 1882[133] in Fairmont, Minnesota and died on 14 Mar 1906 in Caldwell, Idaho[134].

xi.   Harry Whipple Leigh was born on 24 Nov 1884 in Fairmont, Minnesota[135] and died on 17 Sep 1885 in Alton, Kansas[136].

8. Lydia Marie Leigh[3] (William Todd Leigh[2], Nathan S. Leigh[1]) was born on 30 Jan 1839 in Onondaga County, New York[137] and died on 30 Mar 1886 in Oriskany, New York[138]. She married George L. Foote Sr., the son of Jesse Selkrigg Foote and Abigail Hosley, on 11 Dec 1859 in Madison, New York[139]. He was born on 15 Jul 1818 in the Town of Eaton, New York[140] and died on 03 Mar 1911 in Madison, New York[141]. Lydia Marie Leigh was buried in Madison , New York[142].

In the 1860 Census, Lydia was 17 years old and had married George within that last year. The1865 Census indicated Lydia was born in Onondaga County and an Ann Lee, age 14, born in Otsego County was living with them. That would be Lydia's younger sister.   In the 1870 Census Lydia was married to George and with them lived John Lee, age 21 and Annie Lee, age 19.   Again, brother and sister of Lydia.

Lydia was alive in the 1880 Census but indicated she was sick at that time with Rheumatism. Lydia sold the Oriskany Hotel to Mr. Carr on May 5, 1884 and moved to Railroad Street in Oriskany, New York. George had apparently left her in 1881 or 1882 as he married again in 1882 in Michigan. Lydia died of consumption and pneumonia.

Obituary - Waterville Times, March 10, 1911
Died at 4:10 PM of Bronchial Pneumonia.
The funeral of George Foote was held at his home Monday afternoon. He was 97 years of age and had been in poor health for some time. He was a member of the G.A.R. Post.

---

[133] Ancestry.com, U.S., Find A Grave Index, 1700s-Current (Provo, UT, USA, Ancestry.com Operations, Inc., 2012), Ancestry.com, http://www.Ancestry.com, Record for Mentor G. Leigh

[134] Ancestry.com, U.S., Find A Grave Index, 1700s-Current (Provo, UT, USA, Ancestry.com Operations, Inc., 2012), Ancestry.com, http://www.Ancestry.com, Record for Mentor G. Leigh

[135] Genealogy compiled by Rev. Laverne E. Leigh in 2017.

[136] Genealogy compiled by Rev. Laverne E. Leigh in 2017.

[137] Place of birth taken from "History of Chenango & Madison Counties" Rome Library, Rome, New York.

[138] Foote Family History & Genealogy Vol 1.

[139] Ancestry.com, North America, Family Histories, 1500-2000 (Provo, UT, USA, Ancestry.com Operations, Inc., 2016), Ancestry.com, http://www.Ancestry.com, Book Title: Foote Family : Comprising the Genealogy and History of Nathaniel Foote of Wethersfield, Connecticut, and His Descendants.

[140] Ancestry.com, North America, Family Histories, 1500-2000 (Provo, UT, USA, Ancestry.com Operations, Inc., 2016), Ancestry.com, http://www.Ancestry.com, Book Title: Foote Family : Comprising the Genealogy and History of Nathaniel Foote of Wethersfield, Connecticut, and His Descendants.

[141] Death Certificate from the Town of Whitestown, New York.

[142] Death Certificate from the Town of Whitestown, New York.

Obituary - Madison County Leader, Morrisville, NY March 9, 1911

George L. Foote of Madison died at his late home on Friday, aged 93 years. He was born in the town of Smithfield in the year 1818, where he lived until early manhood, when he took up his residence at Syracuse where he entered the canal boating traffic between Buffalo and New York over the Erie Canal. A few years later he moved to Madison and went into the butchering and meat business. He followed this vocation for a number of years and when the Civil War broke out he enlisted in the Union forces and served throughout the conflict, and was honorably discharged. He then returned to Madison and purchased a farm at Madison Center, which he conducted for several years, when he sold the property and purchased the Madison Hotel. A few years later he disposed of the hotel and moved to Michigan and again took up farming. After a number of years in Michigan he returned to Madison, some six or seven years since. He has since lived a retired life. He had been three times married, and is survived by his widow and one son William H. Foote, of Madison, and a daughter Mrs. Mary A. Mather of Whitesboro; L.G. Foote of Utica, J.D. Foote of Cooks Falls, Charles Foote and Earl Foote of Canastota. The funeral services were held from his late home on Monday afternoon at 1 o'clock, burial being made in the village cemetery.

Photo of George L. Foote from the collection of Kerry Cannon and used with permission.

Civil War records - George L. Foote, age 44, Enlisted November 5, 1862 at Madison to serve 9 mo. Mustered in as a private Co. A. November 26, 1862. Captured in action June 23, 1863 at Brashear City, LA. His tombstone says he was in CO. A 176th Reg NYSV. Paroled no date, mustered out with company November 20, 1863 a New York City from the 176th Volunteer Infantry. Following his discharge from the Civil War, he lived in Madison, New York for 18 years. In 1881 he moved to Michigan. He stayed in Michigan for 25 years. At the time of his marriage to Catherine Price, they lived in Maple Rapids, Michigan. He then moved back to Madison, New York where he died.

The 1850 Census listed George as a butcher. He was 39 years old, Abigale was 24, William was 4 and Mary A. was 1 year old. The 1855 Census listed George as a butcher. He was married to Abigale and had William age 9 and Mary age 5. They had lived in Madison for 5 years. The 1860 Census said he owned land and was a farmer. The 1880 Madison Census says George Foote was a hotel keeper. In the 1880 Madison Census, it listed the following people living with George and Lydia: Jay D. Foot, Charles Foot, Earl Foot, Mary Hull, (age - 57), Albert Fitch (age 46), Burton Gifford (age 23), William Darrow (age 28) and Nellie Bohan (age 22). This may have been when he was the proprietor of the Madison Hotel. These people were most likely employees.

In the 1900 Census, he lived in Lyons, Ionia, Michigan In the1910 Census, he lived on West Street in Madison.

Taken from Pioneers of Madison Co. ---
George L. Foote born in Madison Co. 1818, proprietor of Foot's Hotel at Eaton 1878. Wife Abigail died 1857. George engaged in farming following the Civil War. He later disposed of his farm and purchased the Madison Hotel, which he ran for number of years. After he sold the hotel, he moved to Michigan where he again took up farming. He lived in Madison, New York after his retirement.

July 27, 1904 - Utica Paper
George L. Foote of Pompeii, Michigan arrived in Madison for a visit with his family. He stayed with his son, William. He had not been home in 18 years.   George apparently left his wife, Lydia and his children and moved to Michigan about 1881.   They were all together in the 1880 census, but he married again in 1882 in Michigan. Lydia did not die until 1886. There was a notice in the Rome Citizen newspaper to serve George as three of his children were minors.

George L. Foote Sr. and Lydia Marie Leigh had the following children:
     i.   Agnes E. Foote was born on 24 Nov 1861[143] and died on 20 Jan 1862[144]. Agnes E. Foote was buried in Madison Village Cemetery, Madison, New York[145].
29.   ii.   George Lynn Foote, Jr. was born on 15 Jan 1863 in Madison, New York[146] and died on 14 Jun 1945 in Utica, New York[147].
     iii.   Jay Dean Foote was born on 07 Jan 1870 in Madison, New York[148] and died on 21 Aug 1923 in Cooks Falls, New York[149]. He married Lizzie Dolaway on 15 Jan 1903 in Jersey City, New Jersey[150]. She was born about 1884 in New York. Jay Dean Foote[151] was buried in Aug 1923 in Canastota, New York[152].

Obituary - The Sullivan County Review, Thursday, August 30, 1923
J.D.Foote - On Tuesday evening, August 21st at 11:30, J.D. Foote of Cooks Falls passed away quietly at his home . People were shocked at this news, for, while it was known that

---

[143] Madison Center Cemetery List, Madison, New York.
[144] Gravestone, Madison Center Cemetery, Madison, New York.
[145] Gravestone, Madison Center Cemetery, Madison, New York.
[146] Ancestry.com, Web: New York, Find A Grave Index, 1664-2011
[147] Ancestry.com, Web: New York, Find A Grave Index, 1664-2011
[148] Obituary, The Sullivan County Review, Sullivan County, New York, August 30, 1923 page 5.
[149] Obituary, The Sullivan County Review, Sullivan County, New York, August 30, 1923 page 5.
[150] New Jersey Marriage Index at Ancestry.com.
[151] Ancestry.com, New York, State Census, 1915 (Provo, UT, USA, Ancestry.com Operations, Inc., 2012), Ancestry.com, http://www.Ancestry.com, New York State Archives; Albany, New York; State Population Census Schedules, 1915; Election District: 02; Assembly District: 01; City: Colchester; County: Delaware; Page: 05. Record for Lezzie M Foote.
[152] Gravestone at Mt. Pleasant Cemetery, Canastota, New York.

Mr. Foote had been ailing for months, his death was unlooked for. Jay Dean Foote was born at Madison, NY January 7th, 1870, the second son of George Foote and Lydia Lee Foote. He is survived by three brothers, a half brother and a stepmother and by his widow Lizzie Dolaway Foote whose former home was South Fallsburgh, and to whom he was married in Jersey City on January 15th, 1903. He has been station agent at Cook's Falls for over sixteen years and was employed by the O. and W. Railroad for approximately twenty-five years. He was a member of the Brotherhood of O.R.T. and a man of sterling qualities who will be sadly missed by hosts of friends. Jay and his wife did not have any children.

30. iv. Charles Lewis Foote was born on 04 Jan 1874 in Madison, New York[153] and died on 17 Dec 1950 in Oneida City Hospital, Oneida, New York[154].

31. v. Earl James Foote was born on 12 Mar 1878 in New York State[155] and died on 20 Nov 1971 in Canastota, New York[156].

9. John H. Leigh[3] (William Todd Leigh[2], Nathan S. Leigh[1]) was born on 27 Nov 1847[157] in West Laurens, New York and died on 01 Jan 1930 in Sherburne, New York[158]. He married Grace Alice Lamphere, the daughter of John and Jane Lamphere on 03 Nov 1887 in Sherburne, New York[159]. She was born on 03 Nov 1860 in Holmesville, New York[160] and died on 18 Nov 1934 at 14 Marshall Street, Sherburne, New York[161]. John H. Leigh was buried on 04 Jan 1930 in theSherburne Episcopal Cemetery, Sherburne, New York[162]. John lived in Gilbertsville, New York in May of 1896 according to the Genealogy compiled by Rev. Laverne E. Leigh. Inscription on his gravestone: Co. G. 24th Regt N. Y. C. along with Civil War marker and flag.

---

[153] Ancestry.com, U.S., Social Security Applications and Claims Index, 1936-2007 (Provo, UT, USA, Ancestry.com Operations, Inc., 2015), Ancestry.com, http://www.Ancestry.com, Record for Charles Lewis Foote. http://search.ancestry.com/cgi-bin/sse.dll?db=Numident&h=1080117&indiv=try.

[154] Obituary, Newspaper in Oneida, New York, Dec. 18, 1950.

[155] Ancestry.com, U.S. World War II Draft Registration Cards, 1942 (Provo, UT, USA, The Generations Network, Inc., 2007), www.ancestry.com, The National Archives at St. Louis; St. Louis, Missouri; Draft Registration Cards for Fourth Registration for New York State, 04/27/1942 - 04/27/1942; NAI Number: 2555973; Record Group Title: Records of the Selective Service System; Record Group Number: 147. Record for Earl James Foote.

[156] Obituary, Utica Daily Press, Utica, New York, November 17, 1959 page 8.

[157] Ancestry.com, U.S., Find A Grave Index, 1700s-Current (Provo, UT, USA, Ancestry.com Operations, Inc., 2012), Ancestry.com, http://www.Ancestry.com, Record for John H Leigh.

[158] Ancestry.com, U.S., Find A Grave Index, 1700s-Current (Provo, UT, USA, Ancestry.com Operations, Inc., 2012), Ancestry.com, http://www.Ancestry.com, Record for John H Leigh.

[159] Civil War Records on John H. Leigh from the National Archives.

[160] Ancestry.com, U.S., Find A Grave Index, 1700s-Current (Provo, UT, USA, Ancestry.com Operations, Inc., 2012), Ancestry.com, http://www.Ancestry.com, Record for John H Leigh.

[161] Ancestry.com, U.S., Find A Grave Index, 1700s-Current (Provo, UT, USA, Ancestry.com Operations, Inc., 2012), Ancestry.com, http://www.Ancestry.com, Record for John H Leigh.

[162] Ancestry.com, U.S., Find A Grave Index, 1700s-Current (Provo, UT, USA, Ancestry.com Operations, Inc., 2012), Ancestry.com, http://www.Ancestry.com, Record for John H Leigh.

John received a gunshot wound in the left hand causing the loss of the first or index finger of the left hand. He was in action at Coal Harbor, Virginia when he was injured. He was sent to the US General Hospital for treatment and about two months afterwards, he returned to duty and remained in duty until he mustered out. John was in good health and physically sound. He was a faithful and efficient soldier.

John enlisted the 7th of January 1864 from Orwell, New York at the age of 17 in Company G of the 24th Calvary just six months before his brother, Luman was fatally wounded. He was transferred to Company G of the 1st Calvary June 17, 1865 and mustered out of the service on July 19, 1865 at Cloud's Mills, Virginia. He returned home at the end of the war and married and lived until 1930. He was the only one of the brothers who went into the Civil War that survived.

Grace Alice died of breast and lung cancer. She was buried on 21 Nov 1934 in Christ Church Cemetery, Sherburne, New York[163].

John H. Leigh and Grace Alice Lamphere Leigh had the following children:
      i.   Raymond Paul Leigh was born on 10 Dec 1885 in Gilbertsville, New York[164] and died on 13 Dec 1919 in Utica , New York[165]. Raymond was paroled from jail and admitted to Inmates in Almshouses and Poorhouse in June 10, 1919.

Cazenovia Republican - July 1, 1919 -
Raymond Leigh, a rag collector, was sent to jail for six months for attempting to hug and kiss Mrs. John Tackabury of Smyrna, while the woman was sorting rags in her barn that she had sold to the junk hugger.

32.   ii.   Earl R. Leigh was born on 26 Sep 1890 in Sherburne, New York[166] and died in Aug 1966 in Norwich, New York[167].
33.   iii.   Anna Elizabeth Leigh was born on 10 Mar 1894 in Gilbertsville, New York[168] and died on 23 Sep 1952 in Syracuse, New York[169].

---

[163] Death Certificate from the State of New York Vital Records.

[164] Ancestry.com, New York, Census of Inmates in Almshouses and Poorhouses, 1830-1920 (Provo, UT, USA, Ancestry.com Operations, Inc., 2011), Ancestry.com, http://www.Ancestry.com, New York State Archives; Albany, New York; Census of Inmates in Almshouses and Poorhouses, 1875-1921; Series: A1978; Reel: A1978:19; Record Number: 1324. Record for Raymond P Leigh

[165] New York State Death Index, at Ancestry.com.

[166] Ancestry.com, U.S., Find A Grave Index, 1700s-Current (Provo, UT, USA, Ancestry.com Operations, Inc., 2012), Ancestry.com, http://www.Ancestry.com, Record for Earl Leigh.

[167] Ancestry.com, U.S., Find A Grave Index, 1700s-Current (Provo, UT, USA, Ancestry.com Operations, Inc., 2012), Ancestry.com, http://www.Ancestry.com, Record for Earl Leigh.

[168] Ancestry.com, U.S., Social Security Applications and Claims Index, 1936-2007 (Provo, UT, USA, Ancestry.com Operations, Inc., 2015), Ancestry.com, http://www.Ancestry.com, Record for Ann Ancestry.com, U.S., Social Security Applications and Claims Index, 1936-2007 Record for Anna E Unger. a E Unger.

[169] Ancestry.com, U.S., Social Security Applications and Claims Index, 1936-2007, Record for Anna E Unger.

10. George Henry Leigh[3] (William Todd Leigh[2], Nathan S. Leigh[1]) was born in 05 Aug 1855 in Oswego, New York[170] and died on 26 Jun 1927 in Oneida, New York[171]. He married Martha Emmaliza Butler, the daughter of Eliza Butler, on 20 Feb 1878 in Morrisville, New York[172]. She was born on 16 Mar 1859 in Morrisville, New York[173] and died on 22 Jul 1941 in Oneida, New York[174]. George Henry Leigh was buried in 1927 in Glenwood Cemetery, Oneida, New York[175].

George Henry Leigh Obituary
Oneida, June 27.-George Henry Leigh, 71, died suddenly from heart disease Saturday night at his home, 420 Randall Avenue. He had been in poor health only recently. For many years he was employed by National Casket Company. He was born at Oswego, August 5, 1855, and had lived In Oneida 50 years. Surviving are his wife, Mrs. Martha Butler Leigh; one son, Claude Leigh of Oneida; two daughters, Edith, of Florida and Mrs. Martha Wotten of Utica and a brother, John Leigh of Sherburne.

Mrs. Martha E. Leigh Obituary
Oneida-Mrs. Martha E. Leigh, 82 whose husband, the late George H. Leigh was a cigar maker, died July 22, 1941 in the home of her daughter, Mrs. Martha Etta Wooton, 813 Waverly Place, Utica. She was born in Morrisviile and spent most of her life in Oneida. She attended the Presbyterian churches of Oneida and Utica. Surviving besides her daughter are one son, Claude J., Oneida; three grandchildren and three great grandchildren. The funeral will be conducted from the home of the son, 655 Fitch St., Oneida, at 2:10 p.m. tomorrow by the Rev. James H. Moreley, associate pastor of the first Presbyterian Church, Utica. Burial will be in Glenwood Cemetery.

George Henry Leigh and Martha Emmaliza Butler had the following children:

      i.   Edith Agnes Leigh was born on 23 Sep 1881 in Madison, New York[176] and died on 13 Jun 1939 in St. Joseph's Hospital, Syracuse, New York[177]. She married Arthur W. Sweatman, the son of Ransom Sweatman and Elizabeth Smith, on 18 Jul 1899 in Constantia, New York[178]. He was born on 13 Apr 1875 in Oneida, New York[179] and

---

[170] Obituary, Daily Sentinel, Rome, New York, June 27, 1927, page 5.

[171] Obituary, Daily Sentinel, Rome, New York, June 27, 1927, page 5.

[172] Family trees at Ancestry.com

[173] Ancestry.com, U.S., Find A Grave Index, 1700s-Current (Provo, UT, USA, Ancestry.com Operations, Inc., 2012), Ancestry.com, http://www.Ancestry.com

[174] Ancestry.com, U.S., Find A Grave Index, 1700s-Current (Provo, UT, USA, Ancestry.com Operations, Inc., 2012), Ancestry.com, http://www.Ancestry.com

[175] Ancestry.com, U.S., Find A Grave Index, 1700s-Current (Provo, UT, USA, Ancestry.com Operations, Inc., 2012), Ancestry.com, http://www.Ancestry.com

[176] Obituary, Utica Daily Press, June 13, 1939, page 16.

[177] Obituary, Utica Daily Press, June 13, 1939, page 16.

[178] New York State Department of Health; Albany, NY, USA; *New York State Marriage Index*

[179] Ancestry.com, World War I Draft Registration Cards, 1917-1918 (Provo, UT, USA, The Generations Network, Inc., 2005), www.ancestry.com, Database online. Registration Location: Oneida County, New York; Roll: ; Draft Board:.

died on 04 Sep 1963 in Oneida , New York[180].   Edith Agnes Leigh was buried in Oneida, New York[181].

Oneida, June 13 - *Taken ill Saturday while alighting from a Watertown train in Syracuse, Mrs. Edith Leigh Sweatman, 57, died in St. Joseph's Hospital, Syracuse, Monday. She was on her way home when she became ill. Mrs. Sweatman suffered a shock four years ago in Orlando, Fla., and since her recovery, she made her home with Mr. and Mrs. Charles Childs, 225 Farrierr Ave. She was born in this city, Sept. 23, 1881 and lived here most of her life. Her parents are the late George Leigh and Martha Butler. Survivors are her husband, Arthur Sweatman, Sylvan Beach a sister, Mrs. Harry Wootton, Utica; a brother, Claude Leigh; two nephews, Claude and Charles Leigh, and a niece, Mrs. Carl Wood.*

ARTHUR W. SWEATMAN Obituary
Oneida - Arthur W. Sweatman, 87, of 112 West St., a retired maintenance man, died Wednesday after a brief illness. Born in Oneida, April 13, 1876, he was the son of the late Ransom and Elizabeth Smith Sweatman. He had resided in Oneida all his life. Before his retirement he was employed at Gary's Hotel, Verona Beach. Surviving are two sisters, Mrs. Anson S. Marsh of Oneida and Mrs. August Flament of Verona Beach and several nieces and nephews. Services will be at 10 a.m. Friday at the Whitford-Edkin Funeral Home, 322 Washington Ave. Burial will be in Fish Creek Cemetery. Friends may call from 2 to 4 and 7 to 9 p.m. Thursday at the funeral home.

34.   ii.   Claude Jay Leigh was born on 25 Sep 1885 in Oneida, New York[182] and died on 19 Sep 1957 in Oneida, New York[183].

       iii.   Martha Etta Leigh was born on 02 Jun 1889 in Madison, New York[184] and died on 22 Jul 1945 in Oneida, New York[185]. She married Harry Charles Wootton on 21 Apr 1911 in Oneida , New York[186]. He was born on 13 Jun 1884[187] and died in 1968. Martha Etta Leigh Wootton was buried in 1945 in Glenwood Cemetery, Oneida, New York[188].

---

[180] Ancestry.com, Social Security Death Index (Provo, UT, USA, The Generations Network, Inc., 2008), www.ancestry.com, Database online. Number: 096-14-8065; Issue State: New York; Issue Date: Before 1951.

[181] Ancestry.com, U.S., Find A Grave Index, 1700s-Current (Provo, UT, USA, Ancestry.com Operations, Inc., 2012), Ancestry.com, http://www.Ancestry.com, Record for Edith A. Sweatman.

[182] Ancestry.com, World War I Draft Registration Cards, 1917-1918 (Provo, UT, USA, The Generations Network, Inc., 2005), www.ancestry.com, Database online. Registration Location: Madison County, New York; Roll: ; Draft Board:.

[183] Obituary, Rome Daily Sentinel, Sept 20, 1957, page 8.

[184] Ancestry.com, U.S., Find A Grave Index, 1700s-Current (Provo, UT, USA, Ancestry.com Operations, Inc., 2012), Ancestry.com, http://www.Ancestry.com, Record for Martha Etta Wootton. .

[185] Ancestry.com, U.S., Find A Grave Index, 1700s-Current Record for Martha Etta Wootton.

[186] Marriage announcement Utica paper, Utica Daily Press, April 22, 1911

[187] Ancestry.com, World War I Draft Registration Cards, 1917..

[188] Ancestry.com, U.S., Find A Grave Index, 1700s-Current (Provo, UT, USA, Ancestry.com Operations, Inc., 2012), Ancestry.com, http://www.Ancestry.com, Record for Martha Etta Wootton.

Martha Wootton, *56, of 813 Waverly PL, Utica, a native of Oneida, died Sunday in City Hospital where she had been a patient since May 18. She was born here June 2, 1889, daughter of George and Martha Leigh, and had resided in Utica about 25 years. She was a member of the First Presbyterian Church of Utica, Daughters of the Nile, Eastern Star and Ladies of the Maccabees, all of Utica. Surviving are a brother, Claude Leigh of Fitch St., Oneida; two nephews, Sgt. Claude Leigh, Jr., in Germany and Lt. Charles J. Leigh, stationed at Geneva, Neb.; and a niece. Mrs. Carl Wood of Niagara Falls.*

iv.	Ada G. Leigh was born in Aug 1891 in United States[189] and died on 15 Mar 1896 in Oneonta, New York[190]. Ada G. Leigh was buried in Mar 1896 in Glenwood Cemetery, Oneida, New York[191].

---

[189] Genealogy compiled by Rev. Laverne E. Leigh, 414 Washington Ave. East, Albia, Iowa 52531 in the Spring of 1975.

[190] New York State Death Index, at Ancestry.com.

[191] Ancestry.com, U.S., Find A Grave Index, 1700s-Current (Provo, UT, USA, Ancestry.com Operations, Inc., 2012), Ancestry.com, http://www.Ancestry.com, Record for Ada Leigh.

Generation Four

11. Cyrus Nathan Berry[4] (Mary Abigale Leigh[3], Elijah Leigh[2], Nathan S. Leigh[1]) was born on 06 Dec 1862 in Money Creek, Minnesota[192] and died on 27 Jun 1942 in Alma Center, Wisconsin[193]. He married Mary Bell Prouty, the daughter of Roderick Prouty and Rose Ann Oiler, in 1885[194]. She was born on 19 Jun 1868 in Reedsburg, Wisconsin[195] and died on 25 Jan 1955 in Black River Falls, Wisconsin[196].   Cyrus Nathan Berry was buried in Money Creek, Minnesota[197].

Photo of Cyrus Nathan Berry from the collection of Kathryn Cummings and used with permission.

Photo of Mary Bell Pouty from the collection of Kathryn Cummings and used with permission.

From the Winona Daily News, April 26, 1955, page 11: Black River Falls, Wis. - *Mrs. Mary Prouty Berry, 85, a former resident of Money Creek, Minn., died Monday morning at the Krohn Hospital here following a brief illness. Funeral services will be held Thursday at 2 p.m. at the Money Creek Baptist church with burial in the church cemetery. The Jenson Funeral Home, Hixton, is in charge of arrangements. Her husband, Nathan Berry, died several years ago. A recent resident of Alma Center, she is survived by two daughters, Mrs. Paul (Gladys) Ledebuhr, Money Creek, and Mrs. Myrtle Norem, Black River Falls; five sons, Gilbert and Ivan, Muskegon, Mich., Clifford and Roy, Taylor, and Francis, Black River Falls, and 22 grandchildren.*

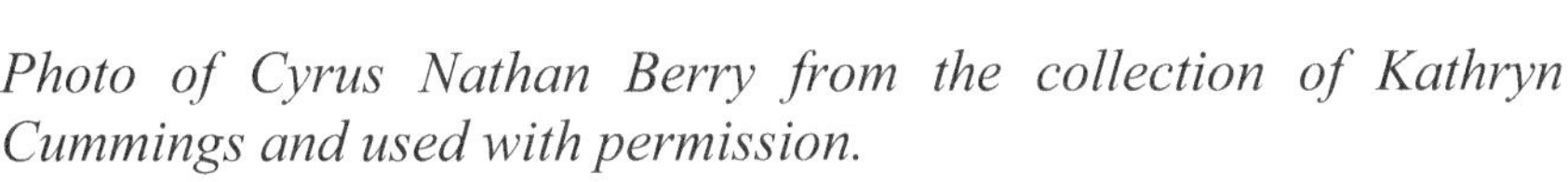

[192]Ancestry.com, U.S., Find A Grave Index, 1700s-Current (Provo, UT, USA, Ancestry.com Operations, Inc., 2012), Ancestry.com, http://www.Ancestry.com, Record for Cyrus Nathan Berry.

[193] Ancestry.com, U.S., Find A Grave Index, 1700s-Current (Provo, UT, USA, Ancestry.com Operations, Inc., 2012), Ancestry.com, http://www.Ancestry.com, Record for Cyrus Nathan Berry.

[194] Ancestry.com, 1900 United States Federal Census (Provo, UT, USA, Ancestry.com Operations Inc, 2004), Ancestry.com, http://www.Ancestry.com, Year: 1900; Census Place: Money Creek, Houston, Minnesota; Roll: 765; Page: 2A; Enumeration District: 0073; FHL microfilm: 1240765. Record for Cyrus Berry.

[195] Ancestry.com, U.S., Find A Grave Index, 1700s-Current (Provo, UT, USA, Ancestry.com Operations, Inc., 2012), Ancestry.com, http://www.Ancestry.com, Record for Mainie B Berry.

[196] Ancestry.com, U.S., Find A Grave Index, 1700s-Current (Provo, UT, USA, Ancestry.com Operations, Inc., 2012), Ancestry.com, http://www.Ancestry.com, Record for Mainie B Berry.

[197] Ancestry.com, U.S., Find A Grave Index, 1700s-Current (Provo, UT, USA, Ancestry.com Operations, Inc., 2012), Ancestry.com, http://www.Ancestry.com, Record for Cyrus Nathan Berry.

Cyrus Nathan Berry and Mary Bell Prouty had the following children:

35. i. Gladys Gertrude Berry was born on 25 May 1886 in Minnesota[198] and died on 26 Jan 1977 in Houston, Minnesota[199].

36. ii. Cyrus Gilbert Berry was born on 22 Oct 1887 in Minnesota[200] and died on 01 Sep 1970 in Muskegon County, Michigan[201].

37. iii. Myrtle Mae Berry was born on 17 Jul 1889 in Pleasant Hill Township, Minnesota[202] and died on 26 Sep 1966 in Wisconsin[203].

38. iv. Ivan Lee Berry was born on 20 Apr 1891 in Pleasant Hill, Winona, Minnesota[204] and died on 13 May 1970 in Muskegon, Michigan[205].

39. v. Alta Irene Berry was born on 29 Sep 1894 in Money Creek, Minnesota[206] and died on 26 Feb 1954 in Yonkers, New York[207].

vi. Beatrice Belle Berry was born in 17 Jul 1894 in Minnesota[208] and died in March 1937. She married Clark Pine

Photo of Myrtle Mae and Alta Irene Berry from the collection of Kathryn Cummings and used with permission.

[198] Ancestry.com, Minnesota, Death Index, 1908-2002 (Provo, UT, USA, Ancestry.com Operations Inc, 2001), Ancestry.com, http://www.Ancestry.com, Record for Gladys Gertrude Ledebuhr.

[199] Ancestry.com, Minnesota, Death Index, 1908-2002 (Provo, UT, USA, Ancestry.com Operations Inc, 2001), Ancestry.com, http://www.Ancestry.com, Record for Gladys Gertrude Ledebuhr.

[200] Ancestry.com, U.S., Find A Grave Index, 1700s-Current (Provo, UT, USA, Ancestry.com Operations, Inc., 2012), Ancestry.com, http://www.Ancestry.com, Record for Cyrus Gilbert Berry.

[201] Ancestry.com, U.S., Find A Grave Index, 1700s-Current (Provo, UT, USA, Ancestry.com Operations, Inc., 2012), Ancestry.com, http://www.Ancestry.com, Record for Cyrus Gilbert Berry.

[202] Ancestry.com, Wisconsin Death Index, 1959-1997 (Provo, UT, USA, Ancestry.com Operations Inc, 2007), Ancestry.com, http://www.Ancestry.com, Record for Myrtle Noren.

[203] Ancestry.com, Wisconsin Death Index, 1959-1997 (Provo, UT, USA, Ancestry.com Operations Inc, 2007), Ancestry.com, http://www..Ancestry.com, Record for Myrtle Noren..

[204] Ancestry.com, U.S., Find A Grave Index, 1700s-Current (Provo, UT, USA, Ancestry.com Operations, Inc., 2012), Ancestry.com, http://www.Ancestry.com, Record for Ivan L Berry.

[205] Ancestry.com, U.S., Find A Grave Index, 1700s-Current (Provo, UT, USA, Ancestry.com Operations, Inc., 2012), Ancestry.com, http://www.Ancestry.com, Record for Ivan L Berry.

[206] Ancestry.com, Minnesota, Marriages Index, 1849-1950 (Provo, UT, USA, Ancestry.com Operations, Inc., 2011), Ancestry.com, http://www.Ancestry.com, Record for Alta Berry.

[207] Obituary, The Winona Republican-Herald, Winona, Minnesota, March 1, 1954, page 9.

[208] Ancestry.com, 1900 United States Federal Census (Provo, UT, USA, Ancestry.com Operations Inc, 2004), Ancestry.com, http://www.Ancestry.com, Year: 1900; Census Place: Money Creek, Houston, Minnesota; Roll: 765; Page: 2A; Enumeration District: 0073; FHL microfilm: 1240765. Record for Cyrus Berry.

Wood, the son of Charles Loren Wood and Minnie Mann, on 11 May 1922 in Money Creek Minnesota. He was born 17 Jan 1894 in Minnesota[209] and died 08 Sep 1962[210].

Photo of Clifford Nathan Berry from the collection of Thomas Coulson and used with permission.

vii.　Clifford Nathan Berry was born on 15 Mar 1898[211] and died on 16 May 1976 in Lack, Wisconsin[212]. He married a woman by the name of Rubie who was born in 1904 in Wisconsin[213].

40.　viii.　Roy Lester Berry was born on 09 Mar 1901[214] and died on 27 Jan 1969 in Hixton, Wisconsin[215].

ix.　Verna Beulah Berry was born on 25 May 1903 in Money Creek, Minnesota[216] and died on 01 Mar 1911 in Money Creek, Minnesota[217].

Photo of Verna Beulah Berry from the collection of Kathryn Cummings and used with permission.

Photo of Beatrice Belle Berry and Clark Pine Wood from the collection of Kathryn Cummings and used with permission.

---

[209] Minnesota Birth Index at Ancestry.com

[210] U.S., Headstone Applications for Military Veterans, 1925-1963

[211] Ancestry.com, World War I Draft Registration Cards, 1917-1918 (Provo, UT, USA, The Generations Network, Inc., 2005), www.ancestry.com, Registration State: Wisconsin; Registration County: Jackson; Record for Clifford Berry.

[212] Ancestry.com, Social Security Death Index (Provo, UT, USA, The Generations Network, Inc., 2008), www.ancestry.com, Number: 389-26-4758;. Record for Clifford Berry.

[213] Ancestry.com, 1940 United States Federal Census (Provo, UT, USA, Ancestry.com Operations, Inc., 2012), www.ancestry.com, Year: 1940; Census Place: Springfield, Jackson, Wisconsin; Roll: T627_4484; Page: 8A; Enumeration District: 27-28. Record for Clifford Berry.

[214] Ancestry.com, U.S., Find A Grave Index, 1700s-Current (Provo, UT, USA, Ancestry.com Operations, Inc., 2012), Ancestry.com, http://www.Ancestry.com, Record for Roy L. Berry.

[215] Ancestry.com, U.S., Find A Grave Index, 1700s-Current (Provo, UT, USA, Ancestry.com Operations, Inc., 2012), Ancestry.com, http://www.Ancestry.com, Record for Roy L. Berry.

[216] Ancestry family trees.

[217] Ancestry family trees.

12. Edward Ulysses Berry[4] (Mary Abigale Leigh[3], Elijah Leigh[2], Nathan S. Leigh[1]) was born on 04 Jul 1865 in Minnesota[218] and died on 26 Oct 1946 in Winona, Minnesota[219]. He married Rosa Ann Gordon. She was born on 01 May 1872[220] and died on 26 Mar 1966 in Winona, Minnesota[221]. Edward Ulysses Berry was buried in Money Creek, Minnesota[222] along with his wife Rosa Ann Gordon[223].

Photo of Edward Ulysses Berry from the collection of Kathryn Cummings and used with permission.

Edward Ulysses Berry and Rosa Ann Gordon had the following children:

41.   i.   Harry Glen Berry was born on 08 Jul 1905 in Houston, Minnesota[224] and died on 17 Apr 1990 in Winona, Minnesota[225].

    ii.   Elva Marie Berry was born on 17 Nov 1910 in Houston, Minnesota[226] and died on 07 Oct 1985 in Winona, Minnesota[227]. Elva married Jack Arthur Moore, the son of William Robert Gile and Rosa R. Molzahn April 25, 1936 in Winona, Minnesota[228]. Jack was born 02 May 1912 in Winona, Minnesota and died 30 October 1957[229]. Elva Marie Berry and her husband were buried in Money Creek, Minnesota[230].

[218] Ancestry.com, U.S., Find A Grave Index, 1700s-Current (Provo, UT, USA, Ancestry.com Operations, Inc., 2012), Ancestry.com, http://www.Ancestry.com, Record for Edward Ulysses Berry.

[219] Ancestry.com, Minnesota, Death Index, 1908-2002 (Provo, UT, USA, Ancestry.com Operations Inc, 2001), Ancestry.com, http://www.Ancestry.com, Record for Edward U. Berry.

[220] Ancestry.com, U.S., Find A Grave Index, 1700s-Current (Provo, UT, USA, Ancestry.com Operations, Inc., 2012), Ancestry.com, http://www.Ancestry.com, Record for Rose A Berry. .

[221] Ancestry.com, U.S., Find A Grave Index, 1700s-Current (Provo, UT, USA, Ancestry.com Operations, Inc., 2012), Ancestry.com, http://www.Ancestry.com, Record for Rose A Berry.

[222] Ancestry.com, U.S., Find A Grave Index, 1700s-Current (Provo, UT, USA, Ancestry.com Operations, Inc., 2012), Ancestry.com, http://www.Ancestry.com, Record for Edward Ulysses Berry.

[223] Ancestry.com, U.S., Find A Grave Index, 1700s-Current (Provo, UT, USA, Ancestry.com Operations, Inc., 2012), Ancestry.com, http://www.Ancestry.com, Record for Rose A Berry.

[224] Ancestry.com, U.S., Find A Grave Index, 1700s-Current (Provo, UT, USA, Ancestry.com Operations, Inc., 2012), Ancestry.com, http://www.Ancestry.com, Record for Harry Glenn Berry.

[225] Ancestry.com, Minnesota, Death Index, 1908-2002 (Provo, UT, USA, Ancestry.com Operations Inc, 2001), Ancestry.com, http://www.Ancestry.com, Record for Harry Glen Berry.

[226] Ancestry.com, Social Security Death Index (Provo, UT, USA, The Generations Network, Inc., 2008), www.ancestry.com, Number: 475-30-3138; Issue State: Minnesota; Issue Date: Before 1951. Record for Elva Moore.

[227] Ancestry.com, Social Security Death Index (Provo, UT, USA, The Generations Network, Inc., 2008), www.ancestry.com, Number: 475-30-3138; Issue State: Minnesota; Issue Date: Before 1951. Record for Elva Moore.

[228] Ancestry.com, Minnesota Death Index.

[229] Ancestry.com, Minnesota Death Index.

[230] Ancestry.com, Web: Minnesota, Find A Grave Index, 1800-2012 (Provo, UT, USA, Ancestry.com Operations, Inc., 2012), Ancestry.com, http://www.Ancestry.com, Record for Elva M Moore.

Photo of Elva Marie Berry and Jack Moore from the collection of Kathryn Cummings and used with permission.

13. Lydia A. Berry[4] (Mary Abigale Leigh[3], Elijah Leigh[2], Nathan S. Leigh[1]) was born in 1867[231] and died in 1953[232]. She married Perry A. Wood, the son of Lorin Wood and Alma Gifford, on 10 Nov 1887 in Money Creek, Minnesota[233]. He was born in 1865 in German Flats, New York[234] and died in 1941 in Money Creek, Minnesota[235]. Lydia A Berry and her husband were buried in Money Creek, Minnesota[236].

Perry A. Wood and Lydia A. Berry had the following children:

  i. Ruby Wood was born in 1902 in Minnesota[237].

42. ii. Harley Berry Wood was born on 07 Dec 1907 in Houston, Minnesota[238] and died on 31 Jan 1968 in Houston, Minnesota[239].

Photo of Lydia A. Berry and Perry A. Wood from the collection of Kathryn Cummings and used with permission.

[231] Ancestry.com, U.S., Find A Grave Index, 1700s-Current (Provo, UT, USA, Ancestry.com Operations, Inc., 2012), Ancestry.com, http://www.Ancestry.com, Record for Mary Abigail Berry

[232] Ancestry.com, U.S., Find A Grave Index, 1700s-Current (Provo, UT, USA, Ancestry.com Operations, Inc., 2012), Ancestry.com, http://www.Ancestry.com, Record for Mary Abigail Berry

[233] Ancestry.com, Minnesota, Marriages Index, 1849-1950 (Provo, UT, USA, Ancestry.com Operations, Inc., 2011), Ancestry.com, http://www.Ancestry.com, Record for Perry A Wood.

[234] Ancestry.com, Minnesota, Marriages Index, 1849-1950 (Provo, UT, USA, Ancestry.com Operations, Inc., 2011), Ancestry.com, http://www.Ancestry.com, Record for Perry A Wood.

[235] U.S., Find A Grave Index, 1700s-Current at Ancestry.com.

[236] U.S., Find A Grave Index, 1700s-Current at Ancestry.com.

[237] Ancestry.com, 1920 United States Federal Census (Online publication - Provo, UT, USA: Ancestry.com Operations Inc, 2010. Images reproduced by FamilySearch.Original data - Fourteenth Census of the United States, 1920. (NARA microfilm publication T625, 2076 rolls). Records of the Bureau of the Census, Reco), Ancestry.com, http://www.Ancestry.com, Year: 1920; Census Place: Money Creek, Houston, Minnesota; Roll: T625_840; Page: 1A; Enumeration District: 70. Record for Wood Perry.

[238] Ancestry.com, Minnesota, Death Index, 1908-2002 (Provo, UT, USA, Ancestry.com Operations Inc, 2001), Ancestry.com, http://www.Ancestry.com, Record for Harley Berry Wood.

[239] Ancestry.com, Minnesota, Death Index, 1908-2002 (Provo, UT, USA, Ancestry.com Operations Inc, 2001), Ancestry.com, http://www.Ancestry.com, Record for Harley Berry Wood.

14. Genevieve Berry[4] (Mary Abigale Leigh[3], Elijah Leigh[2], Nathan S. Leigh[1]) was born on 22 May 1869 in Minnesota[240] and died 15 Sep 1949 in Houston County, Minnesota[241]. She married Charles Gilbert Corey, the son of Sylvester Corey and Caroline Howell, in 1888 [242]. He was born on 24 Jan 1865 in Winona County, Minnesota[243] and died on 21 Nov 1943 in Houston County, Minnesota[244]. Genevieve Berry was buried in Money Creek, Minnesota[245].

Photo of the family of Genevieve Berry and Charles Gilbert Corey from the collection of Thomas Coulson and used with permission. Back row: Lydia Belle, Joseph Sylvester, Edna P., and James Edgar. Front row: Grace Caroline, Charles, Glendon Genevieve, and Jennie.

Charles Gilbert Corey and Genevieve Berry had the following children:
43.   i.   Edna P. Corey was born on 27 Dec 1889 in Minnesota[246] and died on 26 Oct 1961 in La Crosse, Minnesota[247].

[240] Ancestry.com, U.S., Find A Grave Index, 1700s-Current (Provo, UT, USA, Ancestry.com Operations, Inc., 2012), Ancestry.com, http://www.Ancestry.com, Record for Mary Abigail Berry.

[241] Ancestry.com, U.S., Find A Grave Index, 1700s-Current (Provo, UT, USA, Ancestry.com Operations, Inc., 2012), Ancestry.com, http://www.Ancestry.com, Record for Mary Abigail Berry.

[242] Ancestry.com, 1900 United States Federal Census (Provo, UT, USA, The Generations Network, Inc., 2004), www.ancestry.com, Year: 1900; Census Place: Money Creek, Houston, Minnesota; Roll: 765; Page: 2A; Enumeration District: 0073; FHL microfilm: 1240765. Record for Jennie Corey.

[243] U.S., Find A Grave Index, 1700s-Current at Ancestry.com

[244] U.S., Find A Grave Index, 1700s-Current at Ancestry.com

[245] U.S., Find A Grave Index, 1700s-Current at Ancestry.com

[246] Ancestry.com, U.S., Find A Grave Index, 1700s-Current (Provo, UT, USA, Ancestry.com Operations, Inc., 2012), Ancestry.com, http://www.Ancestry.com, Record for Edna P Potter.

[247] Ancestry.com, U.S., Find A Grave Index, 1700s-Current (Provo, UT, USA, Ancestry.com Operations, Inc., 2012), Ancestry.com, http://www.Ancestry.com, Record for Edna P Potter.

ii.   Joseph Sylvester Corey was born on 29 Jan 1891[248] and died on 06 Jun 1975 in Winona, Minnesota[249]. He married Hazel May Mann[250]. She was born on 22 Nov 1896 in Yorktown, Fillmore, Minnesota[251] and died on 24 Feb 1920 in Winona, Minnesota[252]. Joseph Sylvester Corey was buried in Money Creek, Minnesota[253].

44.   iii.   Lydia Belle Corey was born on 23 Oct 1896[254] and died on 24 Aug 1991 in Houston, Minnesota[255].

45.   iv.   James Edgar Corey was born on 12 Aug 1898[256] and died on 19 Jun 1971 in Houston, Minnesota[257].

46.   v.   Grace Caroline Corey was born on 18 Jun 1902 in Houston, Minnesota[258] and died on 16 Sep 1971 in Houston, Minnesota[259].

vi.   Glendon Genevieve Corey was born on 25 Jun 1906 in Houston, Minnesota[260] and died on 26 May 1986 in Wisconsin[261]. She married Gynther Muhle on 25 May 1968 in Houston, Minnesota[262]. He was born on 13 Nov 1913 in Houston,

---

[248] Ancestry.com, U.S., Find A Grave Index, 1700s-Current (Provo, UT, USA, Ancestry.com Operations, Inc., 2012), Ancestry.com, http://www.Ancestry.com, Record for Joseph Corey.

[249] Ancestry.com, U.S., Find A Grave Index, 1700s-Current (Provo, UT, USA, Ancestry.com Operations, Inc., 2012), Ancestry.com, http://www.Ancestry.com, Record for Joseph Corey.

[250] Ancestry.com, U.S., Find A Grave Index, 1700s-Current (Provo, UT, USA, Ancestry.com Operations, Inc., 2012), Ancestry.com, http://www.Ancestry.com, Record for Joseph Corey.

[251] Ancestry.com, Minnesota, Births and Christenings Index, 1840-1980 (Provo, UT, USA, Ancestry.com Operations, Inc., 2011), Ancestry.com, http://www.Ancestry.com, Record for Hazel May Mann.

[252] Ancestry.com, Minnesota, Death Index, 1908-2002 (Provo, UT, USA, Ancestry.com Operations Inc, 2001), Ancestry.com, http://www.Anccstry.com, Rccord for Hazel Corey.

[253] Ancestry.com, U.S., Find A Grave Index, 1700s-Current (Provo, UT, USA, Ancestry.com Operations, Inc., 2012), Ancestry.com, http://www.Ancestry.com, Record for Joseph Corey.

[254] Ancestry.com, Minnesota, Death Index, 1908-2002 (Provo, UT, USA, Ancestry.com Operations Inc, 2001), Ancestry.com, http://Ilwww.Ancestry.com, Record for (Lydia) L. Belle Coulson.

[255] Ancestry.com, Minnesota, Death Index, 1908-2002 (Provo, UT, USA, Ancestry.com Operations Inc, 2001), Ancestry.com, http://www.Ancestry.com, Record for (Lydia) L. Belle Coulson.

[256] Ancestry.com, Minnesota, Death Index, 1908-2002 (Provo, UT, USA, Ancestry.com Operations Inc, 2001), Ancestry.com, http://www.Ancestry.com, Record for James Edgar Corey.

[257] Ancestry.com, Minnesota, Death Index, 1908-2002 (Provo, UT, USA, Ancestry.com Operations Inc, 2001), Ancestry.com, http://www.Ancestry.com, Record for James Edgar Corey.

[258] Ancestry.com, Minnesota, Death Index, 1908-2002 (Provo, UT, USA, Ancestry.com Operations Inc, 2001), Ancestry.com, http://www.Ancestry.com, Record for Grace Caroline Steele.

[259] Ancestry.com, Minnesota, Death Index, 1908-2002 (Provo, UT, USA, Ancestry.com Operations Inc, 2001), Ancestry.com, http://www.Ancestry.com, Record for Grace Caroline Steele.

[260] Ancestry.com, U.S., Find A Grave Index, 1700s-Current (Provo, UT, USA, Ancestry.com Operations, Inc., 2012), Ancestry.com, http://www.Ancestry.com, Record for Glendon G Muhle

[261] Ancestry.com, U.S., Find A Grave Index, 1700s-Current (Provo, UT, USA, Ancestry.com Operations, Inc., 2012), Ancestry.com, http://www.Ancestry.com, Record for Glendon G Muhle

[262] Ancestry.com. Minnesota, Marriage Index, 1958-2001 [database on-line]. Provo, UT, USA: Ancestry.com Operations Inc, 2007.

Minnesota[263] and died on 25 Jul 2008 in Houston, Minnesota[264].   Glendon Genevieve Corey along with her husband were buried in Houston, Minnesota[265].

15. Eugene L. Berry[4] (Mary Abigale Leigh[3], Elijah Leigh[2], Nathan S. Leigh[1]) was born on 25 Apr 1871 in Money Creek, Minnesota[266] and died on 06 Nov 1951 in Moose Lake, Minnesota[267]. He married Susan J. Northrop in Sep 1901[268]. She was born in Jan 1876 in Maine[269] and died in 1953[270]. Next he married Zula M. Hoyt on 31 Aug 1903 in Hillyard, Spokane, Washington[271]. Lastly he married Dora Kingsley on 30 May 1926 in Money Creek, Minnesota[272]. Eugene L Berry was buried in Money Creek, Minnesota[273].

Photo of Eugene L. Berry from the collection of Kathryn Cummings and used with permission.

Winona Republican-Herald, Monday, November 12, 1951:
Funeral services for Mr. Berry were conducted at the Cromwell Methodist church Friday at 2 p.m., the Rev. Paul Langer, MacGregor, officiating. Pallbearers were Clarence Smith, Donald Smith, Ervin Smith, Kenneth Kingsley, Frederick Pelofski, and Peter Svoboda.   Mr. Berry was born at Money Creek April 25, 1871. He married Susan Northrop in September 1901. She died in 1908. He lived at various places in Montana and Minnesota before settling in Houston where he was mail carrier for 15 years. He married Mrs. Dora Kingsley at Money Creek May 30, 1926. He

[263] Ancestry.com, U.S., Find A Grave Index, 1700s-Current (Provo, UT, USA, Ancestry.com Operations, Inc., 2012), Ancestry.com, http://www.Ancestry.com, Record for Gynther Muhle.

[264] Ancestry.com, U.S., Find A Grave Index, 1700s-Current (Provo, UT, USA, Ancestry.com Operations, Inc., 2012), Ancestry.com, http://www.Ancestry.com, Record for Gynther Muhle.

[265] Ancestry.com, U.S., Find A Grave Index, 1700s-Current (Provo, UT, USA, Ancestry.com Operations, Inc., 2012), Ancestry.com, http://www.Ancestry.com, Record for Gynther Muhle.

[266] Ancestry.com, Minnesota, Death Index, 1908-2002 (Provo, UT, USA, Ancestry.com Operations Inc, 2001), Ancestry.com, http://www.Ancestry.com, Record for Eugene L. Berry.

[267] Ancestry.com, Minnesota, Death Index, 1908-2002 (Provo, UT, USA, Ancestry.com Operations Inc, 2001), Ancestry.com, http://www.Ancestry.com, Record for Eugene L. Berry.

[268] Ancestry.com, Washington, Marriage Records, 1854-2013 (Provo, UT, USA, Ancestry.com Operations, Inc., 2012), Ancestry.com, http://www.Ancestry.com, Washington State Archives; Olympia, Washington; Collection Title: Washington Marriage Records, 1854-2013; Reference Number: easpmr5195. Record for Eugene L Berry.

[269] Ancestry.com, 1900 United States Federal Census (Provo, UT, USA, The Generations Network, Inc., 2004), www.ancestry.com, Year: 1900; Census Place: Aldrich, Wadena, Minnesota; Roll: 795; Page: 3B; Enumeration District: 0204; FHL microfilm: 1240795. Record for Susan J Berry

[270] Obituary of Eugene L. Berry, Winona Republican-Herald, Monday, November 12, 1951.

[271] Washington Marriage records, Ancestry.com. Washington, Marriage Records, 1854-2013 [database on-line]. Provo, UT, USA: Ancestry.com Operations, Inc., 2012.
Original data: Washington State Archives. Olympia, Washington: Washington State Archives.

[272] Obituary of Eugene L. Berry, Winona Republican-Herald, Monday, November 12, 1951.

[273] Ancestry.com, U.S., Find A Grave Index, 1700s-Current (Provo, UT, USA, Ancestry.com Operations, Inc., 2012), Ancestry.com, http://www.Ancestry.com, Record for C George Berry.

retired as mail carrier in 1939, and they moved to Comwell.   He became seriously ill in July and was taken to the Moose Lake hospital where he died last Tuesday.   Survivors are his wife; one son George, Butte, Mont.; two daughters, Mrs. Anita Covering, Bemidji, and Mrs. Ethel Kingsley, Cromwell; four stepsons, Orrin and Kenneth Kingsley, Cromwell; Abe Kingsley, Rochester, and Thomas Kingsley, Dover; one stepdaughter, Mrs. Clarence Smith, Cromwell; 41 grandchildren; 44 great-grandchildren, and one sister, Mrs. Lydia Wood, Money Creek.

Eugene L Berry and Susan J. Northrop had the following children:

47.   i.   Cyrus George Berry, Jr. was born on 29 Jan 1893 in Money Creek, Minnesota[274] and died on 18 Dec 1966 in Butte, Montana[275].

48.   ii.   Grace Irene Berry was born on 06 May 1894 in Minnesota[276] and died on 04 Mar 1932 in Butte, Montana[277].

49.   iii.   Anita Susan Berry was born on 14 Dec 1899 in Wadena County, Minnesota[278] and died on 18 Sep 1964 in Beltrami, Minnesota[279].

16. Rose Ann Lindel Todd[4] (Julia Fannie Leigh[3], Elijah Leigh[2], Nathan S. Leigh[1]) was born in 1858 in Money Creek, Minnesota[280] and died on 14 Mar 1897 in Miltonvale, Kansas[281]. She married Francis Fletcher Hirst, the son of James and Harriett Hirst, on 15 May 1883 in Baraboo, Wisconsin[282]. He was born in 1858 in Kansas[283] and died on 24 Mar 1897[284].

Francis Fletcher Hirst and Rose Ann Lindel Todd had the following children:

---

[274] Ancestry.com, Montana, County Births and Deaths, 1830-2011 (Lehi, UT, USA, Ancestry.com Operations, Inc., 2017), Ancestry.com, http://www.Ancestry.com, Montans State Historical Society; Helena, Montana; FHL Roll: 47-114. Record for Cyrus George Berry.

[275] Ancestry.com, Montana, County Births and Deaths, 1830-2011 (Lehi, UT, USA, Ancestry.com Operations, Inc., 2017), Ancestry.com, http://www.Ancestry.com, Montans State Historical Society; Helena, Montana; FHL Roll: 47-114. Record for Cyrus George Berry.

[276] Ancestry.com, Montana, County Births and Deaths, 1830-2011 (Lehi, UT, USA, Ancestry.com Operations, Inc., 2017), Ancestry.com, http://www.Ancestry.com, Montans State Historical Society; Helena, Montana; FHL Roll: 47-102. Record for Grace Irene Thomas.

[277] Ancestry.com, Montana, County Births and Deaths, 1830-2011 (Lehi, UT, USA, Ancestry.com Operations, Inc., 2017), Ancestry.com, http://www.Ancestry.com, Montans State Historical Society; Helena, Montana; FHL Roll: 47-102. Record for Grace Irene Thomas.

[278] Ancestry.com, U.S., Find A Grave Index, 1700s-Current (Provo, UT, USA, Ancestry.com Operations, Inc., 2012),

[279] Ancestry.com, U.S., Find A Grave Index, 1700s-Current (Provo, UT, USA, Ancestry.com Operations, Inc., 2012),

[280] Genealogy compiled by Rev. Laverne E. Leigh in 2017.

[281] Genealogy compiled by Rev. Laverne E. Leigh in 2017.

[282] Genealogy compiled by Rev. Laverne E. Leigh in 2017.

[283] Ancestry.com, 1870 United States Federal Census (Provo, UT, USA, The Generations Network, Inc., 2003), www.ancestry.com, Year: 1870; Census Place: Winfield, Sauk, Wisconsin; Roll: M593_1739; Page: 306B; Family History Library Film: 553238. Record for Fletcher Hirst.

[284] Genealogy compiled by Rev. Laverne E. Leigh in 2017.

50.   i.   Glen James Hirst was born on 20 Jul 1886 in Miltonvale, Kansas[285] and died on 04 Mar 1929 in Salt Lake City, Utah[286].

51.   ii.   Leslie Erwin Hirst was born on 02 Feb 1888 in Kansas[287] and died on 17 Sep 1953 in Wisconsin[288].

        iii.   Hadsia Hirst was born in 1890 in Miltonvale, Kansas[289] and died in 1891 in Miltonvale, Kansas[290].

17. Ransom William Todd[4] (Julia Fannie Leigh[3], Elijah Leigh[2], Nathan S. Leigh[1]) was born on 23 Oct 1860 in Money Creek, Minnesota[291] and died on 27 Oct 1931 in Crandon, Wisconsin[292]. He married Mary Jane Staples, the daughter of Zebulon and Leah Jane Staples, on 31 Mar 1881 in Sauk, Wisconsin[293]. She was born on 14 Jun 1863 in Sandusky, Wisconsin[294] and died on 23 Jun 1887 in Sandusky, Wisconsin[295]. He later married Nora Sawyer Jessup, the daughter of William Jessup and Sarah Elizabeth Keith, in 1891 in Wisconsin[296]. She was born in Oct 1872 in Minnesota[297] and died on 30 Jan 1960 in Ramsey, Minnesota[298]. Mary Jane Staples was buried in Sandusky, Wisconsin[299].

Ransom William Todd and Mary Jane Staples had the following children:

---

[285] Ancestry.com, Salt Lake County, Utah, Death Records, 1908-1949 (Provo, UT, USA, Ancestry.com Operations, Inc., 2014), Ancestry.com, http://www.Ancestry.com, Record for Glen James Hirst.

[286] Ancestry.com, U.S., Find A Grave Index, 1700s-Current (Provo, UT, USA, Ancestry.com Operations, Inc., 2012), Ancestry.com, http://www.Ancestry.com, Record for Leslie Erwin Hirst.

[287] Ancestry.com, U.S., Find A Grave Index, 1700s-Current (Provo, UT, USA, Ancestry.com Operations, Inc., 2012), Ancestry.com, http://www.Ancestry.com, Record for Leslie Erwin Hirst.

[288] Ancestry.com, U.S., Find A Grave Index, 1700s-Current (Provo, UT, USA, Ancestry.com Operations, Inc., 2012), Ancestry.com, http://www.Ancestry.com, Record for Leslie Erwin Hirst.

[289] Genealogy compiled by Rev. Laverne E. Leigh in 2017.

[290] Genealogy compiled by Rev. Laverne E. Leigh in 2017.

[291] Ancestry.com, Wisconsin, Births and Christenings Index, 1801-1928 (Provo, UT, USA, Ancestry.com Operations, Inc., 2011), Ancestry.com, http://www.Ancestry.com, Record for Ransom Wm Todd.

[292] Genealogy compiled by Rev. Laverne E. Leigh in 2017.

[293] Wisconsin Marriage Index, Ancestry.com. Wisconsin, Marriage Index, 1820-1907 [database on-line]. Provo, UT, USA: Ancestry.com Operations, Inc., 2000.

[294] Ancestry.com, U.S., Find A Grave Index, 1700s-Current (Provo, UT, USA, Ancestry.com Oper Ancestry.com, U.S., Find A Grave Index, 1700s-Current (Provo, UT, USA, Ancestry.com Operations, Inc., 2012), Ancestry.com, http://www.Ancestry.com, Record for Mary Jane Todd. ations, Inc., 2012), Ancestry.com, http://www.Ancestry.com, Record for Mary Jane Todd.

[295] Ancestry.com, U.S., Find A Grave Index, 1700s-Current (Provo, UT, USA, Ancestry.com Operations, Inc., 2012), Ancestry.com, http://www.Ancestry.com, Record for Mary Jane Todd.

[296] Ancestry.com, 1900 United States Federal Census (Provo, UT, USA, The Generations Network, Inc., 2004), www.ancestry.com, Year: 1900; Census Place: La Valle, Sauk, Wisconsin; Roll: 1816; Page: 2A; Enumeration District: 0139; FHL microfilm: 1241816. Record for Nellie M Todd.

[297] Ancestry.com, 1900 United States Federal Census (Provo, UT, USA, The Generations Network, Inc., 2004), www.ancestry.com, Year: 1900; Census Place: La Valle, Sauk, Wisconsin; Roll: 1816; Page: 2A; Enumeration District: 0139; FHL microfilm: 1241816. Record for Nellie M Todd.

[298] Family trees at Ancestry.com

[299] Ancestry.com, U.S., Find A Grave Index, 1700s-Current (Provo, UT, USA, Ancestry.com Operations, Inc., 2012), Ancestry.com, http://www.Ancestry.com, Record for Mary Jane Todd.

52.   i.   Leon Staples Todd was born on 09 Jan 1882[300] and died in 1952[301].

    ii.   Willie J. Todd was born in Feb 1887 in Sauk County, Wisconsin[302] and died on 17 Oct 1887 in Sauk County, Wisconsin[303].   Willie J. Todd was buried in Sandusky, Wisconsin[304].

Ransom William Todd and Nora Sawyer Jessup had the following children:

    iii.   Nellie M. Todd was born in Oct 1892 in Kansas[305] and died in 1964[306]. She married a man named Divine.

53.   iv.   Ralph Ransom Todd was born on 18 Feb 1894 in La Valle, Wisconsin[307] and died in Sep 1985 in Madison, Wisconsin[308].

54.   v.   Fred Louis Todd was born on 01 Oct 1896 in La Valle, Wisconsin[309] and died on 08 Aug 1962 in Wisconsin[310].

    vi.   Florence Belle Todd was born on 07 Nov 1897 in Wisconsin[311] and died on 22 Feb 1975 in Ramsey, Minnesota[312].   She married Michael Paul Murtaugh[313].   He was born on 12 Sep 1882 in the United Kingdom[314] and died on 16 Jun 1959 in Alameda, California[315].   Michael Paul was born in England.   He immigrated to the United States in 1887 with his parents at the age of four and was living at home at age 17 in Pomfret,

[300] Ancestry.com, U.S., Find A Grave Index, 1700s-Current (Provo, UT, USA, Ancestry.com Operations, Inc., 2012), Ancestry.com, http://www.Ancestry.com, Record for Leon S Todd.

[301] Ancestry.com, U.S., Find A Grave Index, 1700s-Current (Provo, UT, USA, Ancestry.com Operations, Inc., 2012), Ancestry.com, http://www.Ancestry.com, Record for Leon S Todd.

[302] Ancestry.com, U.S., Find A Grave Index, 1700s-Current (Provo, UT, USA, Ancestry.com Operations, Inc., 2012), Ancestry.com, http://www.Ancestry.com, Record for Mary Jane Todd.

[303] Ancestry.com, U.S., Find A Grave Index, 1700s-Current (Provo, UT, USA, Ancestry.com Operations, Inc., 2012), Ancestry.com, http://www.Ancestry.com, Record for Mary Jane Todd.

[304] Ancestry.com, U.S., Find A Grave Index, 1700s-Current (Provo, UT, USA, Ancestry.com Operations, Inc., 2012), Ancestry.com, http://www.Ancestry.com, Record for Mary Jane Todd.

[305] Ancestry.com, 1900 United States Federal Census (Provo, UT, USA, The Generations Network, Inc., 2004), www.ancestry.com, Year: 1900; Census Place: La Valle, Sauk, Wisconsin; Roll: 1816; Page: 2A; Enumeration District: 0139; FHL microfilm: 1241816. Record for Nellie M Todd.

[306] Genealogy compiled by Rev. Laverne E. Leigh in 2017.

[307] Ancestry.com, Social Security Death Index (Provo, UT, USA, The Generations Network, Inc., 2008), www.ancestry.com, Number: 387-18-4788; Issue State: Wisconsin; Issue Date: Before 1951. Record for Ralph Todd.

[308] Ancestry.com, Social Security Death Index (Provo, UT, USA, The Generations Network, Inc., 2008), www.ancestry.com, Number: 387-18-4788; Issue State: Wisconsin; Issue Date: Before 1951. Record for Ralph Todd.

[309] Ancestry.com, Wisconsin Death Index, 1959-1997 (Provo, UT, USA, Ancestry.com Operations Inc, 2007), Ancestry.com, http://www.Ancestry.com, Record for Fred L Todd.

[310] Ancestry.com, Wisconsin Death Index, 1959-1997 (Provo, UT, USA, Ancestry.com Operations Inc, 2007), Ancestry.com, http://www.Ancestry.com, Record for Fred L Todd.

[311] Ancestry.com, Minnesota, Death Index, 1908-2002 (Provo, UT, USA, Ancestry.com Operations Inc, 2001), Ancestry.com, http://www.Ancestry.com, Record for Florence Belle Todd.

[312] Ancestry.com, Minnesota, Death Index, 1908-2002 (Provo, UT, USA, Ancestry.com Operations Inc, 2001), Ancestry.com, http://www.Ancestry.com, Record for Florence Belle Todd.

[313] Ancestry.com, 1930 United States Federal Census (Provo, UT, USA, The Generations Network, Inc., 2002), www.ancestry.com, Year: 1930; Census Place: St Paul, Ramsey, Minnesota; Roll: 1123; Page: 25B; Enumeration District: 0165; FHL microfilm: 2340858. Record for Paul Murtaugh.

[314] Ancestry.com, California Death Index, 1940-1997 (Provo, UT, USA, The Generations Network, Inc., 2000), www.ancestry.com, Date: 1959-06-16. Record for Michael Paul Murtaugh.

[315] Ancestry.com, California Death Index, 1940-1997 (Provo, UT, USA, The Generations Network, Inc., 2000), www.ancestry.com, Date: 1959-06-16. Record for Michael Paul Murtaugh.

Chautauqua, New York in the 1900 census. In the 1930 Census, he was in St. Paul, Minnesota. He was a naturalized citizen in 1939.

55.   vii.   Everett Clifford Todd, Sr. was born on 19 Mar 1900 in La Valle, Wisconsin[316].

56.   viii.   Royal Leslie Todd was born on 06 Mar 1902 in La Valle, Wisconsin[317] and died on 15 Oct 1988[318].

57.   ix.   Harold (Harley) Walter Todd was born on 04 Jan 1904 in La Valle, Wisconsin[319] and died on 14 Mar 1963 in Keno, Wisconsin[320].

58.   x.   Harvey Gary Todd was born on 04 Jan 1904 in La Valle, Wisconsin[321] and died on 13 Feb 1981 in Ramsey, Minnesota[322].

         xi.   Kenneth Myron Todd, Sr. was born on 26 Apr 1906 in Wisconsin[323] and died on 19 May 1991 in Washington, Minnesota[324].

         xii.   Wayne Robert Todd was born on 31 Aug 1909 in Wisconsin[325] and died on 06 Sep 1991 in Sun Prairie, Wisconsin[326]. He married Nona Marie Belau on 29 Oct 1936 in Dubuque, Iowa[327]. She was born on 29 Jan 1914 in Kingston, Wisconsin[328] and died on 26 Jan 2006 in Stoughton, Wisconsin[329]. Wayne Robert Todd was buried in Monona, Wisconsin along with his wife[330].

[316] Ancestry.com, World War I Draft Registration Cards, 1917-1918 (Provo, UT, USA, The Generations Network, Inc., 2005), www.ancestry.com, Registration State: Wisconsin; Registration County: Forest; Roll: 1674639. Record for Everett Clifford Todd.

[317] Ancestry.com, U.S., Social Security Applications and Claims Index, 1936-2007 (Provo, UT, USA, Ancestry.com Operations, Inc., 2015), Ancestry.com, http://www.Ancestry.com, Record for Royal L Todd.

[318] Ancestry.com, U.S., Social Security Applications and Claims Index, 1936-2007 (Provo, UT, USA, Ancestry.com Operations, Inc., 2015), Ancestry.com, http://www.Ancestry.com, Record for Royal L Todd.

[319] Ancestry.com, Wisconsin Death Index, 1959-1997 (Provo, UT, USA, Ancestry.com Operations Inc, 2007), Ancestry.com, http://www.Ancestry.com, Record for Harley W Todd.

[320] Ancestry.com, Wisconsin Death Index, 1959-1997 (Provo, UT, USA, Ancestry.com Operations Inc, 2007), Ancestry.com, http://www.Ancestry.com, Record for Harley W Todd.

[321] Ancestry.com, Minnesota, Death Index, 1908-2002 (Provo, UT, USA, Ancestry.com Operations Inc, 2001), Ancestry.com, http://www.Ancestry.com, Record for Harvey G Todd.

[322] Ancestry.com, Minnesota, Death Index, 1908-2002 (Provo, UT, USA, Ancestry.com Operations Inc, 2001), Ancestry.com, http://www.Ancestry.com, Record for Harvey G Todd.

[323] Ancestry.com, Minnesota, Death Index, 1908-2002 (Provo, UT, USA, Ancestry.com Operations Inc, 2001), Ancestry.com, http://www.Ancestry.com, Record for Kenneth Myron Sr. Todd.

[324] Ancestry.com, Minnesota, Death Index, 1908-2002 (Provo, UT, USA, Ancestry.com Operations Inc, 2001), Ancestry.com, http://www.Ancestry.com, Record for Kenneth Myron Sr. Todd.

[325] Ancestry.com, U.S., Find A Grave Index, 1700s-Current (Provo, UT, USA, Ancestry.com Operations, Inc., 2012), Ancestry.com, http://www.Ancestry.com, Record for Wayne Robert Todd.

[326] Ancestry.com, U.S., Find A Grave Index, 1700s-Current (Provo, UT, USA, Ancestry.com Operations, Inc., 2012), Ancestry.com, http://www.Ancestry.com, Record for Wayne Robert Todd.

[327] Ancestry.com, Iowa, Marriage Records, 1880-1937 (Lehi, UT, USA, Ancestry.com Operations, Inc., 2014), Ancestry.com, http://www.Ancestry.com, Iowa Department of Public Health; Des Moines, Iowa; Series Title: Iowa Marriage Records, 1923-1937; Record Type: Microfilm Records. Record for Wayne Robert Todd

[328] Ancestry.com, U.S., Find A Grave Index, 1700s-Current (Provo, UT, USA, Ancestry.com Operations, Inc., 2012), Ancestry.com, http://www.Ancestry.com, Record for Wayne Robert Todd.

[329] Ancestry.com, U.S., Find A Grave Index, 1700s-Current (Provo, UT, USA, Ancestry.com Operations, Inc., 2012), Ancestry.com, http://www.Ancestry.com, Record for Wayne Robert Todd.

[330] Ancestry.com, U.S., Find A Grave Index, 1700s-Current (Provo, UT, USA, Ancestry.com Operations, Inc., 2012), Ancestry.com, http://www.Ancestry.com, Record for Wayne Robert Todd.

Wisconsin State Journal - Sunday, September 8, 1991 - 4C
"SUN PRAIRIE/MADISON - Wayne R. Todd, age 82, of 601 Chase Boulevard in Sun Prairie, died on Friday, September 6, 1991, unexpectedly at his residence. He was born on August 31, 1909 in Sand Rock, Wisconsin. He married the former Nona Belau in June of 1936. They had been Madison residents from that time until 1985, when they moved to Sun Prairie."

   xiii. Dorothy Todd was born in 1912 in Wisconsin[331].

59. xiv. Beulah E. Todd was born on 04 Oct 1913 in Wisconsin[332] and died on 22 Dec 1993 in St Paul, Minnesota[333].

   xv. Donald Forest Todd was born on 23 Apr 1915 in Wisconsin[334] and died on 20 May 2005 in Saint Paul, Minnesota[335]. He married Rosella Ann who was born on 07 Jul 1915[336] and died on 07 Jul 1987 in Ramsey, Minnesota[337].

18. Fred M. Priest (Julia Fannie Leigh[3], Elijah Leigh[2], Nathan S. Leigh[1]) was born on 08 Feb 1868 in Reedsburg, Wisconsin[338] and died on 16 Feb 1941 in St. James, Minnesota[339]. He married Amanda Melcina Fowler in 1890 in Kansas[340]. She was born on 02 Feb 1874 in Kansas[341] and died on 24 Jan 1953[342].

Fred M. Priest and Amanda Melcina Fowler had the following children:
60. i. Leo Melvin Priest was born on 26 Oct 1893 in Kansas[343] and died on 02 Aug 1967 in Los Angeles[344].

---

[331] Ancestry.com, 1930 United States Federal Census (Provo, UT, USA, The Generations Network, Inc., 2002), www.ancestry.com, Year: 1930; Census Place: St Paul, Ramsey, Minnesota; Roll: 1123; Page: 25B; Enumeration District: 0165; FHL microfilm: 2340858. Record for Dorothy Todd.

[332] Ancestry.com, U.S., Social Security Applications and Claims Index, 1936-2007 (Provo, UT, USA, Ancestry.com Operations, Inc., 2015), Ancestry.com, http://www.Ancestry.com, Record for Beulah E Fusenig.

[333] Ancestry.com, U.S., Social Security Applications and Claims Index, 1936-2007 (Provo, UT, USA, Ancestry.com Operations, Inc., 2015), Ancestry.com, http://www.Ancestry.com, Record for Beulah E Fusenig.

[334] Ancestry.com, Social Security Death Index (Provo, UT, USA, The Generations Network, Inc., 2008), www.ancestry.com, Issue State: Minnesota; Issue Date: Before 1951. Record for Donald Forest Todd

[335] Ancestry.com, Social Security Death Index (Provo, UT, USA, The Generations Network, Inc., 2008), www.ancestry.com, Issue State: Minnesota; Issue Date: Before 1951. Record for Donald Forest Todd

[336] Ancestry.com, Social Security Death Index (Provo, UT, USA, The Generations Network, Inc., 2008), www.ancestry.com, Number: 474-09-1206; Issue State: Minnesota; Issue Date: Before 1951. Record for Rosella Todd.

[337] Ancestry.com, Social Security Death Index (Provo, UT, USA, The Generations Network, Inc., 2008), www.ancestry.com, Number: 474-09-1206; Issue State: Minnesota; Issue Date: Before 1951. Record for Rosella Todd.

[338] Ancestry.com, Minnesota, Births and Christenings Index, 1840-1980 (Provo, UT, USA, Ancestry.com Operations, Inc., 2011), Ancestry.com, http://www.Ancestry.com, Record for Myrl Frederick Priest.

[339] Ancestry.com. *Minnesota, Death Index, 1908-2002* [database on-line]. Provo, UT, USA: Ancestry.com Operations Inc, 2001.

[340] Genealogy compiled by Rev. Laverne E. Leigh in 2017.

[341] Genealogy compiled by Rev. Laverne E. Leigh in 2017.

[342] Ancestry.com. *Minnesota, Death Index, 1908-2002* [database on-line]. Provo, UT, USA: Ancestry.com Operations Inc, 2001.

[343] Ancestry.com, World War I Draft Registration Cards, 1917-1918, Record for Leo Melvin Priest.

[344] Ancestry.com, California Death Index, 1940-1997 (Provo, UT, USA, The Generations Network, Inc., 2000), www.ancestry.com, Date: 1967-08-02. Record for Leo M Priest.

61.   ii.   Claude Morton Priest was born on 08 May 1896 in Wisconsin[345] and died on 02 Feb 1970 in St James, Watonwan, Minnesota[346].

62.   iii.   Bernice P. Priest was born on 03 Nov 1898[347] and died on 09 May 1967 in Ramsey, Minnesota[348].

iv.   Myrl Frederick Priest was born on 17 Dec 1900 in Windom, Minnesota[349] and died on 07 Nov 1953 in Minneapolis, Minnesota[350]. He married Ruby B. Paulson. She was born on 10 Nov 1906 in Princeton, Illinois[351] and died on 23 Feb 1979 in Broward, Florida[352].   Myrl Frederick Priest and his wife were buried Lakewood Cemetery in Minneapolis, Minnesota[353].   Myrl and Ruby were living in Minneapolis and he was a Claims Agent for an Indemnity and Insurance Company in 1920 at the time of the census.   Then at the 1940 Census, they were living in Minneapolis and he was a Claims Attorney.   Myrl had five plus years of college education.

63.   v.   Ray M. Priest was born on 08 Sep 1905 in Windom, Minnesota[354] and died on 13 Jun 1939 in Watonwan, Minnesota[355].

64.   vi.   Jay Marion Priest was born on 08 Sep 1905 in Windom, Minnesota[356] and died on 06 Nov 1976 in Grove City, Pennsylvania[357].

65.   vii.   Robert Gaylord Priest was born on 16 Mar 1917 in St. James, Minnesota[358] and died in Jul 1994 in Kalispell, Montana[359].

---

[345] Ancestry.com, World War I Draft Registration Cards, 1917-1918 (Provo, UT, USA, The Generations Network, Inc., 2005), www.ancestry.com, Registration State: Minnesota; Registration County: Watonwan; Roll: 1682695. Record for Claud Morton Priest.

[346] Ancestry.com, Minnesota, Death Index, 1908-2002 (Provo, UT, USA, Ancestry.com Operations Inc, 2001), Ancestry.com, http://www.Ancestry.com, Record for Mr. Claude Monroe Priest.

[347] Ancestry.com, Minnesota, Death Index, 1908-2002 (Provo, UT, USA, Ancestry.com Operations Inc, 2001), Ancestry.com, http://www.Ancestry.com, Record for Bernice P. Beatty.

[348] Ancestry.com, Minnesota, Death Index, 1908-2002 (Provo, UT, USA, Ancestry.com Operations Inc, 2001), Ancestry.com, http://www.Ancestry.com, Record for Bernice P. Beatty.

[349] Ancestry.com, U.S., Find A Grave Index, 1700s-Current (Provo, UT, USA, Ancestry.com Operations, Inc., 2012), Ancestry.com, http://www.Ancestry.com, Record for Myrl F Priest.

[350] Ancestry.com, U.S., Find A Grave Index, 1700s-Current (Provo, UT, USA, Ancestry.com Operations, Inc., 2012), Ancestry.com, http://www.Ancestry.com, Record for Myrl F Priest.

[351] Ancestry.com, U.S., Social Security Applications and Claims Index, 1936-2007 (Provo, UT, USA, Ancestry.com Operations, Inc., 2015), Ancestry.com, http://www.Ancestry.com, Record for Ruby Paulson Priest.

[352] Ancestry.com, U.S., Social Security Applications and Claims Index, 1936-2007 (Provo, UT, USA, Ancestry.com Operations, Inc., 2015), Ancestry.com, http://www.Ancestry.com, Record for Ruby Paulson Priest.

[353] Ancestry.com, U.S., Find A Grave Index, 1700s-Current (Provo, UT, USA, Ancestry.com Operations, Inc., 2012), Ancestry.com, http://www.Ancestry.com, Record for Myrl F Priest.

[354] Ancestry.com, U.S., Find A Grave Index, 1700s-Current (Provo, UT, USA, Ancestry.com Operations, Inc., 2012), Ancestry.com, http://www.Ancestry.com, Record for Ray M. Priest.

[355] Ancestry.com, U.S., Find A Grave Index, 1700s-Current (Provo, UT, USA, Ancestry.com Operations, Inc., 2012), Ancestry.com, http://www.Ancestry.com, Record for Ray M. Priest.

[356] Ancestry.com, U.S., Find A Grave Index, 1700s-Current (Provo, UT, USA, Ancestry.com Operations, Inc., 2012), Ancestry.com, http://www.Ancestry.com, Record for Jay M. Priest.

[357] Ancestry.com, U.S., Find A Grave Index, 1700s-Current (Provo, UT, USA, Ancestry.com Operations, Inc., 2012), Ancestry.com, http://www.Ancestry.com, Record for Jay M. Priest .

[358] Ancestry.com, Montana, County Marriages, 1865-1950, Record for Robert Gaylor Priest.

[359] Ancestry.com. *U.S., Social Security Applications and Claims Index, 1936-2007* [database on-line]. Provo, UT, USA: Ancestry.com Operations, Inc., 2015.

19. Nora Eleanor Priest (Julia Fannie Leigh[3], Elijah Leigh[2], Nathan S. Leigh[1]) was born on 24 Oct 1873 in Reedsburg, Wisconsin[360] and died on 29 Jul 1940[361]. She married Loren Walter Johnson, the son of Immer Benjamin Johnson and Rosanna Dawley, in 1890[362]. He was born in Jan 1867 in Michigan[363] and died on 02 Dec 1950[364]. In 1910, Walter ran a hotel in La Valle, Wisconsin.

Loren Walter Johnson and Nora Eleanor Priest had the following children:

66. i. Genevieve Jewel Johnson was born on 16 Feb 1893 in Miltonvale, Kansas[365] and died on 24 Oct 1971 in Rhinelander, Wisconsin[366].

ii. Reuben Merle Johnson was born on 21 Oct 1895 in Wisconsin[367] and died on 09 Apr 1970 in Inyo, California[368]. He married Charolett Llewellyn on 12 Nov 1921 in Crystal Falls, Michigan[369]. She was born in 1902 in Wisconsin[370].

67. iii. Violet Johnson was born on 11 Aug 1897 in Reedsburg, Wisconsin[371] and died on 26 Oct 1959 in Laona, Wisconsin[372].

68. iv. Icell Irving Johnson was born on 16 Jun 1903 in La Valle, Wisconsin[373] and died on 23 Oct 1974 in Deschutes, Oregon, United States[374].

---

[360] Genealogy compiled by Rev. Laverne E. Leigh in 2017.

[361] Ancestry.com. *Minnesota, Death Index, 1908-2002* [database on-line]. Provo, UT, USA: Ancestry.com Operations Inc, 2001..

[362] Ancestry.com, 1900 United States Federal Census (Provo, UT, USA, The Generations Network, Inc., 2004), www.ancestry.com, Year: 1900; Census Place: Money Creek, Houston, Minnesota; Roll: 765; Page: 7B; Enumeration District: 0073; FHL microfilm: 1240765. Record for Walter Johnson.

[363] Ancestry.com, 1900 United States Federal Census (Provo, UT, USA, The Generations Network, Inc., 2004), www.ancestry.com, Year: 1900; Census Place: Money Creek, Houston, Minnesota; Roll: 765; Page: 7B; Enumeration District: 0073; FHL microfilm: 1240765. Record for Walter Johnson.

[364] Genealogy compiled by Rev. Laverne E. Leigh in 2017.

[365] Ancestry.com, U.S., Find A Grave Index, 1700s-Current (Provo, UT, USA, Ancestry.com Operations, Inc., 2012), Ancestry.com, http://www.Ancestry.com, Record for William Martin Schultz.

[366] Ancestry.com, U.S., Find A Grave Index, 1700s-Current (Provo, UT, USA, Ancestry.com Operations, Inc., 2012), Ancestry.com, http://www.Ancestry.com, Record for William Martin Schultz.

[367] Ancestry.com, California Death Index, 1940-1997 (Provo, UT, USA, The Generations Network, Inc., 2000), www.ancestry.com, Date: 1970-04-09. Record for Reuben M Johnson.

[368] Ancestry.com, California Death Index, 1940-1997 (Provo, UT, USA, The Generations Network, Inc., 2000), www.ancestry.com, Date: 1970-04-09. Record for Reuben M Johnson.

[369] Ancestry.com, Michigan, Marriage Records, 1867-1952 (Provo, UT, USA, Ancestry.com Operations, Inc., 2015), Ancestry.com, http://www.Ancestry.com, Record for Reuben M Johnson.

[370] Ancestry.com, Michigan, Marriage Records, 1867-1952 (Provo, UT, USA, Ancestry.com Operations, Inc., 2015), Ancestry.com, http://www.Ancestry.com, Record for Reuben M Johnson.

[371] Ancestry.com. *U.S., Find A Grave Index, 1600s-Current* [database on-line]. Provo, UT, USA: Ancestry.com Operations, Inc., 2012.

[372] Ancestry.com. *Wisconsin, Death Index, 1959-1997* [database on-line]. Provo, UT, USA: Ancestry.com Operations Inc, 2007.

[373] Ancestry.com, Wisconsin, Births and Christenings Index, 1801-1928 (Provo, UT, USA, Ancestry.com Operations, Inc., 2011), Ancestry.com, http://www.Ancestry.com, Record for Icel Irving Johnson.

[374] Ancestry.com, Oregon Death Index, 1903-98 (Provo, UT, USA, Ancestry.com Operations Inc, 2000), www.ancestry.com, Oregon State Library; 1966-1970 Death Index; Reel Title: State of Oregon Death Index; Year Range: 1971-1980. Record for Icel Irv Johnson.

20. Richard Priest[4] ((Julia Fannie Leigh[3], Elijah Leigh[2], Nathan S. Leigh[1]) was born on 02 Dec 1883 in Wisconsin[375] and died on 06 Oct 1950[376]. He married Lydia H. Kanneberg. She was born on 28 Mar 1897[377] and died on 12 Apr 1976 in La Valle, Wisconsin[378].

Richard Priest and Lydia H. Kanneberg had the following child:
    i.   Elaine Priest was born in 1918 in Wisconsin[379].

21. Sarah Amaria Leigh[4] (William Safford Leigh[3], William Todd Leigh[2], Nathan S. Leigh[1]) was born on 04 Oct 1862 in New York[380] and died on 01 Feb 1947 in Pawnee, Oklahoma[381]. She married Florus David Meacham Harnden, the son of George Rising Harnden and Frances Ann Meacham, on 25 Mar 1884 in Sherburn, Minnesota[382]. He was born on 25 Mar 1863 in Illinois[383] and died on 03 Mar 1934 in Stillwater, Oklahoma[384]. Sarah Amaria Leigh and her husband were buried in 1947 in Stillwater, Oklahoma[385].

Photo of Florus David Meacham Harnden from Ancestry.com.

[375] Ancestry.com, World War I Draft Registration Cards, 1917-1918 (Provo, UT, USA, The Generations Network, Inc., 2005), www.ancestry.com, Registration State: Wisconsin; Registration County: Sauk; Roll: 1674982. Record for Richard Priest.

[376] Ancestry.com. *U.S., Social Security Applications and Claims Index, 1936-2007* [database on-line]. Provo, UT, USA: Ancestry.com Operations, Inc., 2015.

[377] Ancestry.com, Social Security Death Index (Provo, UT, USA, The Generations Network, Inc., 2008), www.ancestry.com, Number: 391-20-0444; Issue State: Wisconsin; Issue Date: Before 1951. Record for Lydia Priest.

[378] Ancestry.com, Social Security Death Index (Provo, UT, USA, The Generations Network, Inc., 2008), www.ancestry.com, Number: 391-20-0444; Issue State: Wisconsin; Issue Date: Before 1951. Record for Lydia Priest.

[379] Ancestry.com, 1930 United States Federal Census (Provo, UT, USA, The Generations Network, Inc., 2002), www.ancestry.com, Year: 1930; Census Place: La Valle, Sauk, Wisconsin; Roll: 2609; Page: 2A; Enumeration District: 0020; FHL microfilm: 2342343. Record for Richard Priest.

[380] Ancestry.com, U.S., Find A Grave Index, 1700s-Current (Provo, UT, USA, Ancestry.com Operations, Inc., 2012), Ancestry.com, http://www.Ancestry.com, Record for Sarah Amaria Harnden.

[381] Ancestry.com, U.S., Find A Grave Index, 1700s-Current (Provo, UT, USA, Ancestry.com Operations, Inc., 2012), Ancestry.com, http://www.Ancestry.com, Record for Sarah Amaria Harnden.

[382] Genealogy compiled by Rev. Laverne E. Leigh, 414 Washington Ave. East, Albia, Iowa 52531 in 1975.

[383] Genealogy compiled by Rev. Laverne E. Leigh, 414 Washington Ave. East, Albia, Iowa 52531 in 1975.

[384] Genealogy compiled by Rev. Laverne E. Leigh, 414 Washington Ave. East, Albia, Iowa 52531 in 1975.

[385] Ancestry.com, U.S., Find A Grave Index, 1700s-Current (Provo, UT, USA, Ancestry.com Operations, Inc., 2012), Ancestry.com, http://www.Ancestry.com, Record for Sarah Amaria Harnden.

Sarah Amaria Leigh was the first and only child of William Safford and Rosetta Hathaway Leigh to live beyond infancy. Her early life was spend in New York State part of which was in West Laurens, New York where her father and grandfather, William Todd Leigh, operated a general merchandising store. She moved to Fairmont, Minnesota with her parents around the age of nine. Her mother, Rosetta, died when she was ten in 1872. Sarah lived with her father or near him for a number of years. She was married to Florus D. Harnden before 1885 as their first child, George W., was born January 28, 1885. Florus was a teacher and school principal most of his life. It is not known whether they moved directly to Oklahoma from Minnesota or lived in Kansas for a time near her father while he was in Kansas. They had nine children of which seven lived to reach adulthood.

Florus David Meacham Harnden and Sarah Amaria Leigh had the following children:

69.   i.   George William Harden was born on 28 Jan 1885 in Minnesota[386] and died on 19 Jan 1952 in Stillwater, Oklahoma[387].

70.   ii.   Rosetta Frances Harden was born on 12 Sep 1886 in Winnebago City, Minnesota[388] and died on 16 Nov 1914 in Pawnee, Oklahoma[389].

71.   iii.   Edward Eugene Harnden was born on 02 Apr 1889 in Kansas[390] and died on 26 May 1963 in Oklahoma[391].

72.   iv.   Elsie Ruth Ann Harnden was born on 18 Aug 1891 in Alton, Kansas[392] and died on 17 Sep 1970[393].

73.   v.   Lemuel Meacham Harnden was born on 28 Sep 1893[394] in Stockton, Kansas and died on 27 Feb 1973 in Mamoth Springs, Arkansas[395].

       vi.   Elizabeth Augusta Harnden was born on 28 Mar 1896 and died in infancy[396].

       vii.   Minnie Glenn Harnden was born on 28 Apr 1898 in Oklahoma[397].

---

[386] Ancestry.com, U.S., Social Security Applications and Claims Index, 1936-2007 (Provo, UT, USA, Ancestry.com Operations, Inc., 2015), Ancestry.com, http://www.Ancestry.com, Record for George W Harnden.

[387] Ancestry.com, U.S., Social Security Applications and Claims Index, 1936-2007 (Provo, UT, USA, Ancestry.com Operations, Inc., 2015), Ancestry.com, http://www.Ancestry.com, Record for George W Harnden.

[388] Familysearch.org, "Minnesota Births and Christenings, 1840-1980," database, FamilySearch (https://familysearch.org/ark:/61903/1:1:FD7G-Q8K : 4 December 2014), Rosetta F. Harndon,

[389] Ancestry.com, U.S., Find A Grave Index, 1700s-Current (Provo, UT, USA, Ancestry.com Operations, Inc., 2012), Ancestry.com, http://www.Ancestry.com, Record for Rosetta Doty.

[390] Ancestry.com, U.S., Find A Grave Index, 1700s-Current (Provo, UT, USA, Ancestry.com Operations, Inc., 2012),

[391] Ancestry.com, U.S., Find A Grave Index, 1700s-Current (Provo, UT, USA, Ancestry.com Operations, Inc., 2012),

[392] Ancestry.com, U.S., Find A Grave Index, 1700s-Current (Provo, UT, USA, Ancestry.com Operations, Inc., 2012), Ancestry.com, http://www.Ancestry.com, Record for Elsie Ruth Ann Peirson.

[393] Ancestry.com, U.S., Find A Grave Index, 1700s-Current (Provo, UT, USA, Ancestry.com Operations, Inc., 2012), Ancestry.com, http://www.Ancestry.com, Record for Elsie Ruth Ann Peirson.

[394] Ancestry.com, U.S., Find A Grave Index, 1700s-Current (Provo, UT, USA, Ancestry.com Operations, Inc., 2012), Ancestry.com, http://www.Ancestry.com.

[395] Ancestry.com, U.S., Find A Grave Index, 1700s-Current.

[396] Genealogy compiled by Rev. Laverne E. Leigh in 2017.

[397] Genealogy compiled by Rev. Laverne E. Leigh in 2017.

74.	viii.	Adell Grace Harnden was born on 01 Aug 1904 in Pawnee, Oklahoma[398] and died on 05 Feb 1981[399].

ix.	Charles Harnden was born in lived only one day.

22. Phoebe Adella Leigh[4] (Rueben Harrington Leigh[3], William Todd Leigh[2], Nathan S. Leigh[1]) was born on 08 Oct 1860 in Deposit, New York[400] and died on 23 Jul 1943 in Hominy, Oklahoma[401]. She married George Asro Moore, the son of German Rowley Moore and Elmina Orcutt, on 29 Jul 1890 in Alton, Kansas[402]. He was born on 04 Jul 1857 in Belfast, New York[403] and died on 23 Feb 1917 in Pawnee, Oklahoma[404]. Phoebe Adella Leigh was buried in Pawnee, Pawnee County, Oklahoma[405].

Phoebe Adella Leigh was born October 8, 1860 in Deposit, New York. She was the first child of Reuben Harrington and Phoebe A. Hathaway Leigh. Her name was to be Adell or more often, Dell through the years because of having the same first name as her mother. The family moved to Saratoga, Minnesota in time for her brother, Andrew Lincoln, to be born there on October 9, 1864. Dell knew sorrow early when her baby brother died October 3, 1865 and her mother, Phoebe, died less than three months later of typhoid fever, loneliness and heartbreak.

After her mother's death, Dell and Reuben Henry lived with her Aunt Mary Jane Hathaway Haight, an older sister of her mother, in their home for about a year. Then her father took them back to New York where he courted, won and married their mother's next younger sister, Adelaid Sophrenia Hathaway, January 9, 1867.

Reuben took his new wife and children back to Minnesota to settle first at Wasioji where a baby sister, Minnie Augusta was born November 6, 1867. Then sometime between Minnie's birth in 1867 and July of 1871 they moved to Fairmont, Minnesota. Fairmont was to be the real home Dell know as they lived there until the Spring of 1885. At the age of 24, she moved with her family 500 miles to Alton, Kansas. Dell stayed with them

---

[398] Ancestry.com, U.S., Find A Grave Index, 1700s-Current (Provo, UT, USA, Ancestry.com Operations, Inc., 2012), Ancestry.com, http://www.Ancestry.com, Record for Adell G Henrick.

[399] Ancestry.com, U.S., Find A Grave Index, 1700s-Current (Provo, UT, USA, Ancestry.com Operations, Inc., 2012), Ancestry.com, http://www.Ancestry.com, Record for Adell G Henrick.

[400] Ancestry.com, U.S., Find A Grave Index, 1700s-Current (Provo, UT, USA, Ancestry.com Operations, Inc., 2012), Ancestry.com, http://www.Ancestry.com, Record for Phebe A Moore.

[401] Ancestry.com, U.S., Find A Grave Index, 1700s-Current (Provo, UT, USA, Ancestry.com Operations, Inc., 2012), Ancestry.com, http://www.Ancestry.com, Record for Phebe A Moore.

[402] Genealogy compiled by Rev. Laverne E. Leigh, 414 Washington Ave. East, Albia, Iowa 52531 in the Spring of 1975.

[403] Ancestry.com, U.S., Sons of the American Revolution Membership Applications, 1889-1970 (Provo, UT, USA, Ancestry.com Operations, Inc., 2011), www.ancestry.com, Record for Phebe Adell Leigh.

[404] Ancestry.com, U.S., Sons of the American Revolution Membership Applications, 1889-1970 (Provo, UT, USA, Ancestry.com Operations, Inc., 2011), www.ancestry.com, Record for Phebe Adell Leigh.

[405] Ancestry.com, U.S., Find A Grave Index, 1700s-Current (Provo, UT, USA, Ancestry.com Operations, Inc., 2012), Ancestry.com, http://www.Ancestry.com, Record for Phebe A Moore.

in Alton for a short time and then she traveled a lot during the next few years. Through letters either written to her or by Dell to others, we know that she was in St. Paul, Minnesota on January 3 and February 4, 1884, in Fairmont, Minnesota on December 18, 1884, then at Sioux city June , 1885 and March 1886, and in Alton Kansas April 5, 1886 where her Uncle, William Safford, and her grandfather, William Todd Leigh were living at the time. The letters do not tell either how she traveled or what she was doing that led her to move around so much or as rapidly as she did at times. She lived at Sioux City at 1610 3rd Street and received mail there March 15 and September 15, 1888.

Dell married George Azro Moore in Alton Kansas in 1890. They moved to Minnesota for their first home where they lived on the farm George bought in 1889. This farm was located near Fairmont and was adjacent to the farm owned by her father at the time he lived in Fairmont. The Leighs and the Moores had been neighbors for several years, so that Dell and George played together as children and grew up together as young people.

George Azro Moore was born July 4, 1857 in Belfast, New York. He was the son of German Rowley Moore. His life experience paralleled Dell's life quite closely. For he lived in New York when he was quite young, the he moved to Minnesota with his parents to settle seven miles North West of Fairmont on a farm near Dell's parents farm. Research has not indicated whether the Moores or the Leighs left New York to move to Minnesota first. While a young man in his twenties, George went west into Montana and Wyoming as a sheep shearer. He told, later, of going over the old battle field of "Custers Last Fight." The money he saved while in the west enabled him to purchase his father's homestead in Minnesota from his mother in 1889 for $2,000. A letter he wrote during the time he was in the west on September 5, 1888 told of shearing one hundred sheep a day regularly in a ten hour day and of shearing one hundred twenty six sheep in just less than eleven hours one day. For this, he said that he made eight or nine dollars a day.

George purchased his father's farm before he was married. He paid his mother $1,000 down and $100 a year plus five percent interest. By the time his mother died, he had paid all but $100. He used that to pay his mother's funeral expenses. Then on September 27, 1897, Phoebe A. Moore purchased from Frank H. and Anna Thompson 100.26 acres for $2,200. The deed is recorded in book 74 at page 321, Martin County Deeds in Minnesota. This purchase was made possible by the proceeds of a will her Aunt Phebe B. Northrup left her. This land was in the same county as Fairmont and was probably close to their first farm.

Being tired of the long cold Minnesota winters, they moved with their family to Parma, Idaho. The move was shortly after their son, George Azro was born September 12, 1899 and before 1903 when the next child was born. They secured an "Emigrant Car" and loaded it with household goods, two good draft horses and a cow, a wagon and other implements. Jay Noel Leigh went along in the freight car to care for the livestock. Mentor Garfield Leigh, then a young lad, stowed away in the car and went along. George and Dell purchased a tract of land from a developing company which had dug a ditch to carry the water from the Boise River to the land then known as the "Lower Bench". Jay Noel Leigh was a good carpenter. George hired him to build a house. This six room two story house was still standing in 1928. They sold their land in Minnesota and purchased the land in Idaho.

After clearing 40 acres of land of the sage brush and planting an orchard and sowing the land to alfalfa, George became dissatisfied because of the irregularity and undependability of the water supply. A neighbor whose lateral ditch took off above where George received his supply repeatedly stole the water at night. George declared that he would not live in a country where he had to work all day and sit up all night to keep his neighbors from stealing from him.

So early in the winter of 1901, George went to Oklahoma where he purchased from a Matthew Green land in Pawnee County. During his same winter, he moved his family to Pawnee. On January 15, 192, Phoebe purchased property at Pawnee with the money she received from selling her property in Minnesota. This farm cornered the famous Pawnee Bill Buffalo Ranch.

Their entire family, including the two children born after they moved to Pawnee, were educated in the Pawnee Public Schools. Mr. Moore served as both the Assessor of Fraser Township, Martin County, Minnesota and of Liberty Township, Pawnee County Oklahoma. For several years, he was treasurer of the Farmer's Union Gin Company of Pawnee where his duties brought him into contact with all the farmers who sold their cotton at the mill.

George Moore died of pneumonia on February 23, 1917 at Pawnee just before the outbreak of World War I. He was buried in the cemetery at Pawnee. Dell lived in Pawnee for a time and then moved to Hominy, Oklahoma to be with her daughter, Minnie Marilla Moore Canada. She died July 23, 1943 at Hominy and was buried beside George in Pawnee Cemetery.

George Asro Moore and Phebe Adella Leigh had the following children:
75.   i.   Guy Rowley Moore was born on 14 May 1891 in Fairmont, Minnesota[406] and died on 15 Sep 1991 in Roseburg, Oregon[407].

---

[406] National Cemetery Administration, U.S. Veterans Gravesites, ca.1775-2006 (Provo, UT, USA, The Generations Network, Inc., 2006), www.ancestry.com, Record for Guy R Moore.
[407] National Cemetery Administration, U.S. Veterans Gravesites, ca.1775-2006 (Provo, UT, USA, The Generations Network, Inc., 2006), www.ancestry.com, Record for Guy R Moore.

ii.   Minnie Marilla Moore was born on 29 Sep 1892 in Fairmont, Minnesota[408] and died in Mar 1986 in Hominy, Oklahoma[409]. She married Milo Orlando (Pete) Canada on 16 July 1939 in Pawnee, Oklahoma[410]. He was born on 23 Mar 1892 in Lynn County, Missouri[411] and died on 25 Feb 1964 in Hominy, Oklahoma[412]. Minnie Marilla Moore and her husband were buried in Hominy, Oklahoma[413].

Minnie earned her BA from the University of Kansas and her MA from the University of Oklahoma. Her brother or brothers helped finance her education and then she, in turn, helped finance one or more of their brother's education. She remained single for a number of years while she taught school. After her marriage, they made their home in Hominy, Oklahoma where Pete was a barber and Minnie continued to teach. Minnie taught until retirement in Hominy. She was living in Hominy in 1975 when Laverne E. Leigh compiled his genealogy and contributed much information to it. Minnie and Pete cared for Minnie's mother, Dell Leigh Moore, in their home for a number of years until she

passed away. They also had several of Minnie's nieces in their home for varying periods of time or helped them in other ways. Not having children of their own, they helped the children of others.

Minnie cared for Rosemary Shanklin in her home for a time before she was married. They raised Rosemary during her High School years. During their years together, they had several of Minnie's nieces in their home for a time and helped them in other ways.

Photo of Minnie Marilla Moore Canada from the collection of Rev. Laverne E. Leigh and used with permission.

76.   iii.   Stanley Leigh Moore was born on 21 Dec 1893 in Fairmont, Minnesota[414] and died on 07 Apr 1969 in Norman, Oklahoma[415].

---

[408] Ancestry.com, U.S., Find A Grave Index, 1700s-Current (Provo, UT, USA, Ancestry.com Operations, Inc., 2012), Ancestry.com, http://www.Ancestry.com, Record for Minnie M Canada.

[409] Ancestry.com, U.S., Find A Grave Index, 1700s-Current (Provo, UT, USA, Ancestry.com Operations, Inc., 2012), Ancestry.com, http://www.Ancestry.com, Record for Minnie M Canada.

[410] Genealogy compiled by Rev. Laverne E. Leigh, 414 Washington Ave. East, Albia, Iowa 52531 in the Spring of 1975.

[411] Ancestry.com, U.S., Find A Grave Index, 1700s-Current (Provo, UT, USA, Ancestry.com Operations, Inc., 2012), Ancestry.com, http://www.Ancestry.com, Record for Pfc Milo Orlando Canada.

[412] Ancestry.com, U.S., Find A Grave Index, 1700s-Current (Provo, UT, USA, Ancestry.com Operations, Inc., 2012), Ancestry.com, http://www.Ancestry.com, Record for Pfc Milo Orlando Canada.

[413] Ancestry.com, U.S., Find A Grave Index, 1700s-Current (Provo, UT, USA, Ancestry.com Operations, Inc., 2012), Ancestry.com, http://www.Ancestry.com, Record for Minnie M Canada.

[414] Ancestry.com, World War I Draft Registration Cards, 1917-1918 (Provo, UT, USA, The Generations Network, Inc., 2005), www.ancestry.com, Registration State: Oklahoma; Registration County: Pawnee; Roll: 1852068. Record for Stanley Leigh Moore.

[415] Ancestry.com, Web: RootsWeb Cemetery Index, 1800-2010 (Provo, UT, USA, Ancestry.com Operations, Inc., 2013), Ancestry.com, http://www.Ancestry.com, Record for Stanley Leigh Moore.

77. iv.   Myrtle Elmina Moore was born on 07 Dec 1896 in Fairmont, Minnesota[416] and died on 07 Feb 1990 in Houston, Texas[417].

78. v.   Ethel Adell Moore was born on 30 Oct 1897 in Fairmont, Minnesota[418] and died on 21 Aug 1927 in Enid, Oklahoma[419].

79. vi.   George Asro Moore, Jr. was born on 12 Sep 1899 in Fairmont, Minnesota[420] and died on 17 Nov 1998 in Abilene, Texas[421].

vii.   Nathan Orcutt Moore was born on 20 Jun 1903 in Pawnee, Oklahoma[422] and died on 01 Jul 1927 in Pawnee, Oklahoma[423]. Nathan Orcutt Moore was buried in Pawnee, Oklahoma[424]. He died of osteomyelitis of the bones of his leg (a bone infection) as a result of a football injury to his hip in high school.

viii.   Duane Clinton Moore was born on 25 Aug 1905 in Pawnee, Oklahoma[425] and died 21 Sep 1981 in Multnomah, Oregon[426]. He married Mary Lou Bryant on 23 June 1934 in Corsicana, Texas[427]. She was born 4 July 1907 in Fort Smith, Arkansas[428]. Later he married Viola Laura Marple McDonald on 10 Feb 1941[429]. She was born on 14 Jul 1905 in Coal Hill, Arkansas[430]. He later married Leota Shohlmann Bohlman on 19 Jun 1965 in Rena, Nevada. She was born on 20 Nov 1910[431] and died on 20 Nov 1978 in

---

[416] Ancestry.com, Social Security Death Index (Provo, UT, USA, The Generations Network, Inc., 2008), www.ancestry.com.

[417] Ancestry.com, Social Security Death Index (Provo, UT, USA, The Generations Network, Inc., 2008), www.ancestry.com.

[418] Ancestry.com, U.S., Find A Grave Index, 1700s-Current (Provo, UT, USA, Ancestry.com Operations, Inc., 2012), Ancestry.com, http://www.Ancestry.com, Record for Ethel Shanklin.

[419] Ancestry.com, U.S., Find A Grave Index, 1700s-Current (Provo, UT, USA, Ancestry.com Operations, Inc., 2012), Ancestry.com, http://www.Ancestry.com, Record for Ethel Shanklin.

[420] Ancestry.com, World War I Draft Registration Cards, 1917-1918 (Provo, UT, USA, The Generations Network, Inc., 2005), www.ancestry.com, Registration State: Oklahoma; Registration County: Pawnee; Roll: 1852068. Record for George Azro Moore.

[421] Ancestry.com, Social Security Death Index (Provo, UT, USA, The Generations Network, Inc., 2008), www.ancestry.com, Number: 441-30-7942; Issue State: Oklahoma; Issue Date: Before 1951. Record for Geo A. Moore

[422] Ancestry.com, U.S., Find A Grave Index, 1700s-Current (Provo, UT, USA, Ancestry.com Operations, Inc., 2012), Ancestry.com, http://www.Ancestry.com, Record for Nathan O Moore.

[423] Ancestry.com, U.S., Find A Grave Index, 1700s-Current (Provo, UT, USA, Ancestry.com Operations, Inc., 2012), Ancestry.com, http://www.Ancestry.com, Record for Nathan O Moore.

[424] Ancestry.com, U.S., Find A Grave Index, 1700s-Current (Provo, UT, USA, Ancestry.com Operations, Inc., 2012), Ancestry.com, http://www.Ancestry.com, Record for Nathan O Moore.

[425] Genealogy compiled by Rev. Laverne E. Leigh, 414 Washington Ave. East, Albia, Iowa 52531 in the Spring of 1975.

[426] Oregon State Library; 1966-1970 Death Index; Reel Title: State of Oregon Death Index; Year Range: 1981-1990

[427] Genealogy compiled by Rev. Laverne E. Leigh, 414 Washington Ave. East, Albia, Iowa 52531 in the Spring of 1975.

[428] Genealogy compiled by Rev. Laverne E. Leigh, 414 Washington Ave. East, Albia, Iowa 52531 in the Spring of 1975.

[429] Genealogy compiled by Rev. Laverne E. Leigh, 414 Washington Ave. East, Albia, Iowa 52531 in the Spring of 1975.

[430] Genealogy compiled by Rev. Laverne E. Leigh, 414 Washington Ave. East, Albia, Iowa 52531 in the Spring of 1975.

[431] Ancestry.com, Oregon Death Index, 1903-98 (Provo, UT, USA, Ancestry.com Operations Inc, 2000), www.ancestry.com, Oregon State Library; 1966-1970 Death Index; Reel Title: State of Oregon Death Index; Year Range: 1971-1980. Record for Leota S Moore.

Portland, Oregon [432]. Then he married Nell C. Alloway. She was born on 13 Mar 1905 in Reubens, Idaho[433] and died on 02 Feb 1961 in Portland, Oregon[434]. Nell C. Alloway was buried in Lincoln Park Memorial Cemetery, Portland, Oregon[435].

23. Charles Emery Leigh[4] (Rueben Harrington Leigh[3], William Todd Leigh[2], Nathan S. Leigh[1]) was born on 14 Jul 1871 in Fairmont, Minnesota[436] and died on 24 Aug 1948 in Kent, Washington[437]. He married Addie C. Bailey, the daughter of Edward Bailey and Louisa Carrier, on 08 Dec 1897 in Fairmont, Minnesota[438]. She was born on 28 Aug 1878 in Minnesota[439] and died on 20 Oct 1964[440] in Kent, Washington. Charles Emery Leigh and his wife were buried in Hillcrest Cemetery, Kent Washington[441].

Charles Emery Leigh was the second child of Reuben Harrington and his second wife, Adelaid S. Hathaway Leigh. He grew up on the family farm at Fairmont, Minnesota. He was 13 when the family moved to Alton, Kansas. While living in Alton, the Christian Crusader, an off shoot of the Salvation Army, came to Alton and held a series of meetings. Charley with his brothers, Jay, George and Will, gave his life to the Lord.

While he was growing up in Alton, his brother, Harry Whipple, died October 3, 1885, his grandfather, William Todd Leigh, on October 22, 1888, his father Reuben Harrington on January 10, 1889 and his mother Adelaid, on February 22, 1893. They were all buried in the cemetery in Alton side by side. This made the years at Alton both happy and sad years for Charley.

Charley had left home and was working on a large farm as foreman in 1891. He married Addie C. Bailey on December 8, 1897 at Fairmont, Minnesota. Their first child was born

---

[432] Ancestry.com, Oregon Death Index, 1903-98 (Provo, UT, USA, Ancestry.com Operations Inc, 2000), www.ancestry.com, Oregon State Library; 1966-1970 Death Index; Reel Title: State of Oregon Death Index; Year Range: 1971-1980. Record for Leota S Moore.

[433] Genealogy compiled by Rev. Laverne E. Leigh, 414 Washington Ave. East, Albia, Iowa 52531 in the Spring of 1975

[434] Genealogy compiled by Rev. Laverne E. Leigh, 414 Washington Ave. East, Albia, Iowa 52531 in the Spring of 1975

[435] Genealogy compiled by Rev. Laverne E. Leigh, 414 Washington Ave. East, Albia, Iowa 52531 in the Spring of 1975.

[436] Ancestry.com, Washington, Select Death Certificates, 1907-1960 (Provo, UT, USA, Ancestry.com Operations, Inc., 2014), Ancestry.com, http://www.Ancestry.com, Record for Charles Emory Leigh. http://search.ancestry.com.

[437] Ancestry.com, Washington, Select Death Certificates, 1907-1960 (Provo, UT, USA, Ancestry.com Operations, Inc., 2014), Ancestry.com, http://www.Ancestry.com, Record for Charles Emory Leigh. http://search.ancestry.com.

[438] Marriage application for Charles Leigh and Addie Bailey in Fairmont, Minnesota December 8, 1897.

[439] Ancestry.com, Washington Death Index, 1940-1996 (Provo, UT, USA, The Generations Network, Inc., 2002), www.ancestry.com, Record for Charles E Leigh.

[440] Ancestry.com, Washington Death Index, 1940-1996 (Provo, UT, USA, The Generations Network, Inc., 2002), www.ancestry.com, Record for Charles E Leigh.

[441] Ancestry.com, U.S., Find A Grave Index, 1700s-Current (Provo, UT, USA, Ancestry.com Operations, Inc., 2012), Ancestry.com, http://www.Ancestry.com, Record for Charles Emory.

in Minnesota. Then they moved to Idaho where their second child was born. They then moved back to Fairmont, Minnesota where their third child was born. By 1909, they were living in Kent, Washington where the rest of their eight children were born. They had a small farm in Kent with fruit, truck, gardening and nursery stock. Charles Emery died August 24, 1948 at Kent and was buried in the Hillcrest Cemetery in Kent. Addie lived until October 17, 1964. Several of her last years she lived with their daughter Hazel Marie Leigh in Kent. Addie is buried beside her husband.

According to his Washington State death record, Charles was the son of Ruben H. Leigh and Addie B. Hathaway. His wife was also named Addie.

Obit: Kent News-Journal, Sept. 2, 1948, p-1
"Charles Leigh" Services Held Funeral services for Charles Emory Leigh, age 77, were held Friday at the Kent Funeral Home. Leigh, an East Hill resident, died at his Route 4 home on August 24 following a short illness. Burial followed in Kent cemetery and the Rev. A. A. Harriman officiated. Born July 14, 1871 in Fairmont, Minn., Leigh lived in the Kent area for 42 years. He leaves a multitude of friends in the East Hill and Kent community. Surviving are his widow, Addie Leigh of Kent; four sons, Chester of Stanwood, Edward of Ocean City, Otis of Kent, and Ray of Port Angeles; and three daughters, Miss Hazel Leigh and Mrs. Pearl Harris of Kent, and Mrs. Dottie Sutherland of Seattle. Surviving also are eight grandchildren and two great-grandchildren."

Obit: Kent News-Journal, Oct. 21, 1964, p-3
"Services Held for Mrs. Addie Leigh"
Funeral services were held at Edline Chapel Tuesday for Mrs. Addie C. Leigh, 86, 10426 S.E. 244th Street, a resident of Kent for 58 years. Mrs. Leigh died Saturday at Marsolais Manor Nursing Home in Auburn after an illness of more than a month. She was born in Fairmont, Minnesota and came to the Kent Valley from her native state. Her late husband, Charles, was a fruit farmer until his death in 1948. Mrs. Leigh was a charter member of the Helping Hand Circle, organized in Kent in 1910. She also belonged to the Kent Christian Church for many years. Surviving are three sons, Chester Leigh of Camano Island, Otis Leigh of Kent and Ray Leigh of Colfax; three daughters, Mrs. Pearl Harris and Miss Hazel Leigh, both of Kent and Mrs. Dottie Sutherland of Seattle; ten grandchildren and five great-grandchildren."

Charles Emery Leigh and Addie C. Bailey had the following children:

      i.   Henry Guy Leigh was born on 31 Jul 1898[442] in Fairmont, Minnesota and died on 04 Jul 1924 in Little Port Walter, Alaska[443]. Henry Guy Leigh was buried in Hillcrest Cemetery in Kent, Washington[444].

Dale Biggar kindly added: *"Henry Guy Leigh was the older brother of my uncle Chester Cecil Leigh. Henry was working in Ketchekan, Alaska at the time of his death. He was celebrating July 4th and didn't let go of the stick of dynamite soon enough - he was blown to bits. His remains were sent back to Kent for burial. His parents were Charles E. and Addie C. Bailey Leigh. Both are buried at Hillcrest."*

In his WWI Draft Registration Card, Henry lived in Kent. He worked as a quartermaster for the Puget Sound Nav. Co., in Seattle. His closest relative was listed as Charles Leigh. The card was dated 9/11/1918.

80.   ii.   Chester Cecil Leigh was born on 02 Mar 1901 in Nyssa, Oregon[445] and died on 24 Mar 1970[446] in Camano, Washington.
81.   iii.   Edward Mead Leigh was born on 11 Jul 1906[447] and died on 20 Nov 1961 in Annacortes, Washington[448].
      iv.   Hazel Marie Leigh was born on 01 Sep 1909[449] in Kent, Washington and died on 28 Mar 1982 in Renton, Washington[450]. She married George Leonce Lazzarini, the son of Victor Lazzarini and Margareta Tunbourinii, on 08 May 1970 in Kent,

---

[442] Ancestry.com, World War I Draft Registration Cards, 1917-1918 (Provo, UT, USA, The Generations Network, Inc., 2005), www.ancestry.com, Registration State: Washington; Registration County: King; Roll: 1991649; Draft Board: 01. Record for Henry Guy Leigh.

[443] Ancestry.com, Alaska, Vital Records, 1818 -1963 (Lehi, UT, USA, Ancestry.com Operations, Inc., 2017), Ancestry.com, http://www.Ancestry.com, Alaska State Archives; Juneau, Alaska; Description: Birth, Marriage, and Death Certificates, 1923 - 1925; Reference Number: VS 1257; Volume: Vol. 13, Book 5; Page: 100.

[444] Ancestry.com, U.S., Find A Grave Index, 1700s-Current (Provo, UT, USA, Ancestry.com Operations, Inc., 2012), Ancestry.com, http://www.Ancestry.com, Record for Charles Emory Leigh.

[445] Ancestry.com, Social Security Death Index (Provo, UT, USA, The Generations Network, Inc., 2008), www.ancestry.com, Number: 531-05-4016; Issue State: Washington; Issue Date: Before 1951. Record for Chester Leigh.

[446] Ancestry.com, Social Security Death Index (Provo, UT, USA, The Generations Network, Inc., 2008), www.ancestry.com, Number: 531-05-4016; Issue State: Washington; Issue Date: Before 1951. Record for Chester Leigh.

[447] Ancestry.com, U.S., Find A Grave Index, 1700s-Current (Provo, UT, USA, Ancestry.com Operations, Inc., 2012), Ancestry.com, http://www.Ancestry.com, Record for Edward Meade Leigh.

[448] Ancestry.com, U.S., Find A Grave Index, 1700s-Current (Provo, UT, USA, Ancestry.com Operations, Inc., 2012), Ancestry.com, http://www.Ancestry.com, Record for Edward Meade Leigh.

[449] Ancestry.com, U.S., Find A Grave Index, 1700s-Current (Provo, UT, USA, Ancestry.com Operations, Inc., 2012), Ancestry.com, http://www.Ancestry.com, Record for Hazel Marie Lazzarini.

[450] Ancestry.com, U.S., Find A Grave Index, 1700s-Current (Provo, UT, USA, Ancestry.com Operations, Inc., 2012), Ancestry.com, http://www.Ancestry.com, Record for Hazel Marie Lazzarini.

Washington[451]. He was born on 25 Apr 1913 in Seattle, Washington[452] and died on 07 Apr 1991[453] in Kent, Washington.   Hazel Marie Leigh and her husband were buried in Kent, Washington[454]. Hazel was a companion, housekeeper to her Uncle, Nathan Evan Leigh, a younger brother of her father for several years. She was a clerk and kept a home for her mother for a number years after that until her mother died in 1964. She lived in Kent, Washington in 1975.

   v. Otis Wayne Leigh was born on 21 Dec 1912 in King, Washington[455] and died on 05 Oct 1995 in Kent, Washington[456]. He married Gladys Norman in 1950 in Kent, Washington[457]. She was born on 01 Jun 1901[458] and died on 25 Dec 1963 in Tacoma, Washington[459]. Otis Wayne and his wife were buried in Hillcrest Burial Park, Kent, Washington[460].   Otis has been a logger and is a custodian. He lived in Kent, Washington in 1974.

82. vi. Ray Hugh Leigh was born on 12 May 1915 in Kent, Washington[461] and died on 16 Sep 1989 in Okanogan, Washington[462].

83. vii. Pearl Etta Leigh was born on 14 Mar 1918 in Kent, Washington [463] and died on 28 May 2000 in Belfair, Washington[464].

   viii. Living Leigh

---

[451] Genealogy compiled by Rev. Laverne E. Leigh, 414 Washington Ave. East, Albia, Iowa 52531 in the Spring of 1975.

[452] Ancestry.com, Washington, Birth Records, 1870-1935 (Provo, UT, USA, Ancestry.com Operations Inc, 2010), Ancestry.com, http://www.Ancestry.com, Washington State Archives; Olympia, Washington; Washington Births, 1891-1919; Film Info: Various county birth registers. Microfilm. Record for Geo Leonce Lazzarinii.

[453] Ancestry.com, Social Security Death Index (Provo, UT, USA, The Generations Network, Inc., 2008), www.ancestry.com, Number: 535-07-5690; Issue State: Washington; Issue Date: Before 1951. Record for George L. Lazzarini

[454] Ancestry.com, U.S., Find A Grave Index, 1700s-Current (Provo, UT, USA, Ancestry.com Operations, Inc., 2012), Ancestry.com, http://www.Ancestry.com, Record for Hazel Marie Lazzarini.

[455] Ancestry.com, U.S., Find A Grave Index, 1700s-Current (Provo, UT, USA, Ancestry.com Operations, Inc., 2012), Ancestry.com, http://www.Ancestry.com, Record for Otis W. Leigh.

[456] Ancestry.com, Washington Death Index, 1940-1996 (Provo, UT, USA, The Generations Network, Inc., 2002), www.ancestry.com, Record for Otis W Leigh.

[457] Genealogy compiled by Rev. Laverne E. Leigh, 414 Washington Ave. East, Albia, Iowa 52531 in the Spring of 1975.

[458] Ancestry.com, U.S., Find A Grave Index, 1700s-Current (Provo, UT, USA, Ancestry.com Operations, Inc., 2012), Ancestry.com, http://www.Ancestry.com, Record for Gladys E Leigh.

[459] Ancestry.com, U.S., Find A Grave Index, 1700s-Current (Provo, UT, USA, Ancestry.com Operations, Inc., 2012), Ancestry.com, http://www.Ancestry.com, Record for Gladys E Leigh.

[460] Ancestry.com, U.S., Find A Grave Index, 1700s-Current (Provo, UT, USA, Ancestry.com Operations, Inc., 2012), Ancestry.com, http://www.Ancestry.com, Record for Gladys E Leigh.

[461] Ancestry.com, Washington Death Index, 1940-1996 (Provo, UT, USA, The Generations Network, Inc., 2002), www.ancestry.com, Record for Ray H Leigh.

[462] Ancestry.com, Washington Death Index, 1940-1996 (Provo, UT, USA, The Generations Network, Inc., 2002), www.ancestry.com, Record for Ray H Leigh.

[463] Ancestry.com, Social Security Death Index (Provo, UT, USA, The Generations Network, Inc., 2008), www.ancestry.com, Number: 536-01-2268; Issue State: Washington; Issue Date: Before 1951. Record for Pearl E. Harris

[464] Ancestry.com, Social Security Death Index (Provo, UT, USA, The Generations Network, Inc., 2008), www.ancestry.com, Number: 536-01-2268; Issue State: Washington; Issue Date: Before 1951. Record for Pearl E. Harris

24.   Jay Noel Leigh[4] (Rueben Harrington Leigh[3], William Todd Leigh[2], Nathan S. Leigh[1]) was born on 19 Mar 1873 in Fairmont, Minnesota[465] and died on 06 Dec 1958 in Parma, Idaho[466]. He married Eva P. Paul, the daughter of George Waite Paul and Agnes Arvilla Shipley, on 24 June 1903 in Apple Valley, Idaho[467]. She was born on 09 Jun 1884 in Apple Valley Idaho[468] and died on 05 Jan 1971 in Caldwell Idaho[469]. Jay Noel Leigh and his wife were buried in Parma, Idaho[470].

Photo of Jay Noel Leigh from the collection of Rev. Laverne E. Leigh and used with permission.

Jay spent the first eleven years of his life in Fairmont, Minnesota and then moved with his parents to Alton, Kansas. While in Alton, Jay accepted Christ during a series of evangelistic meetings by the Christian Crusader, an off-shoot of the Salvation Army, at the same time as three of his brothers. He remained a very religious man throughout his life and belonged for many years to the Hard Shelled Baptist church. His father died in 1889 when he was fifteen and his mother in 1893 when he was 19 years old. Shortly after his mother's death, Jay returned to Fairmont, Minnesota where he his sister, Phoebe Adella and her husband George Moore, were living.

In 1898 at the age of twenty-six, Jay rode an "Emigrant Car" on the railroad for his brother-in-law, George Moore, and family to Idaho and cared for the livestock that was on board. Reaching Idaho he settled in the Roswell Community and worked as a carpenter in Roswell and Parma, Idaho for a period of time. He operated with his sister, Minnie, the first furniture store in Parma for a short time. He was in partnership, prior to 1903, in a livery barn with two of his brothers, Will and Nate. Jay and Nate soon left the livery barn business, but Will continued to operate it for many years.

---

[465] Ancestry.com, Idaho, Death Index, 1890-1964 (Provo, UT, USA, Ancestry.com Operations Inc, 2003), Ancestry.com, http://www.Ancestry.com, Record for Jay Noel Leigh.

[466] Ancestry.com, Idaho, Death Index, 1890-1964 (Provo, UT, USA, Ancestry.com Operations Inc, 2003), Ancestry.com, http://www.Ancestry.com, Record for Jay Noel Leigh.

[467] Genealogy compiled by Rev. Laverne E. Leigh, 414 Washington Ave. East, Albia, Iowa 52531 in the Spring of 1975.

[468] Ancestry.com, Idaho, Select Deaths and Burials, 1907-1965 (Provo, UT, USA, Ancestry.com Operations, Inc, 2014), Ancestry.com, http://www.Ancestry.com, Record for Eva Leigh.

[469] Ancestry.com, Idaho, Select Deaths and Burials, 1907-1965 (Provo, UT, USA, Ancestry.com Operations, Inc, 2014), Ancestry.com, http://www.Ancestry.com, Record for Eva Leigh.

[470] Ancestry.com, U.S., Find A Grave Index, 1700s-Current (Provo, UT, USA, Ancestry.com Operations, Inc., 2012), Ancestry.com, http://www.Ancestry.com, Record for Jay N. Leigh.

Photo of Jay Noel Leigh and his wife, Eva P. Paul from the collection of Rev. Laverne E. Leigh and used with permission.

Jay married Eva Paul at her home in the Apple Valley Community just west of Parma. Eva's family were real pioneers in the Boise Valley. Her grandfather Shipley, on her mother's side of the family, owned and operated the first freight line from Salt Lake City, Utah to Boise, Idaho. Her Grandmother Shipley, operated the first hotel in Parma. Her grandfather, George Paul was the first Lieutenant Governor of Idaho. He resigned his office rather than have to hang a man as his position required. Her father was the first settler in Apple Valley and her oldest sister, Birtha Paul, was the first white child born in that area.

Jay and Eva settled on the original Paul homestead on the Boise River near old Fort Boise in Apple Valley. They farmed there from 1903 until 1906. They moved of Kent, Washington in 1906 where Jay's brother, Charley, and family were living. A little less than two years later, they moved back to Apple Valley to farm the homestead. In 1941, with their four children, they drove two teams and wagons to Modesta, California. Before too long, they again returned to the farm in Apple Valley and stayed for several years.

In 1923, they sold the homestead in Idaho and moved to Oregon and stayed twenty years. Settling in Alvidore, Oregon first, Jay worked in Eugene as a finish carpenter. He worked seven years on one square block doing the finish work on, among others, the McDonald and Rex theaters and the Montgomery Ward's Store. He also did much of the finish work on the Catholic Church in Eugene. During this time, their son, Reuben Harold, quit High School and operated the farm at Alvidore so Jay could work in Eugene. Ethel Murriel died April 10, 1925 at the age of eleven. Her body was returned to be buried in Parma, Idaho beside her baby brother, Russell George.

In 1932, Jay and Eva traded their farm at Alvidore for a 1360 acre farm at Fall Creek, Oregon that was twenty miles east of Eugene. The Fall Creek farm was considerably larger and worth more than the Alvidore farm so the additional money was borrowed from the Federal Land Bank. This farm was divided with Jay and Eva farming 700 acres, Cecil 320 acres and Reuben 320 acres. Then in 1934, Cecil returned to Idaho to buy the original homestead back and transferred his 320 acres to Guy R. Moore. Guy kept it for a time and then returned to Jay and Eva and moved away. Jay gave his brother, George Asa, forty acres of land in 1933.

When Jay and Eva came upon hard times and were in danger of losing their portion of the farm, Reuben Harold assumed the Federal Land Bank loan and took over ownership of the farm in 1939. Grace Viola died July 17, 1939 and was buried in Parma beside her brother and sister. Jay and Eva continued to live on the farm and work until 1943 when they moved back to Idaho and bought a farm in the Apple Valley Community about one mile north of the old homestead that Cecil now owned. They farmed this place from 1943 to 1957 when they moved into Parma to live. Jay died December 9, 1958. His funeral was at the Baptist Church in Roswell where they were members. The ministers were the Rev. Irving Frank of Kuna, Idaho and the Rev. G. D. Phipps of Roswell. He was buried in Parma with his three children. Eva lived until January 5, 1971. She lived several years in Parma and then in a rest home first in Roswell and later in Caldwell. She died in Caldwell, Idaho at the age of 86. Her funeral was held in the Funeral Chapel in Parma and she was laid to rest in the Parma Cemetery. She had out lived her husband and four of their six children.

Photo of Jay Noel Paul, his wife Eva P. Paul, and first two children, Cecil Paul and Reuben Harold from the collection of Rev. Laverne E. Leigh and used with permission.

Jay Noel Leigh and Eva P. Paul had the following children:

84.   i.   Cecil Paul Leigh was born on 04 Apr 1904 in Parma, Idaho[471] and died on 30 Oct 1966 in Parma, Idaho[472].

85.   ii.   Reuben Harold Leigh was born on 09 Oct 1905[473] in Parma, Idaho and died on 25 May 1995 in Springfield, Oregon[474].

        iii.   Russell George Leigh was born on 18 Apr 1908 in Parma, Idaho[475] and died of pneumonia on 28 Jul 1908 in Parma, Idaho[476]. Russell George Leigh was buried in Parma Cemetery, Parma, Idaho[477].

86.   iv.   Ruth Arvilla Leigh was born on 22 Apr 1909 in Parma, Idaho[478] and died on 13 Sep 1975 in Salem, Oregon[479].

        v.   Ethel Murriel Leigh was born on 17 Aug 1913 in Parma, Idaho[480] and died on 10 Apr 1925 in Junction City, Oregon[481]. Ethel died as a young girl of typhoid fever that developed into pneumonia. Ethel Murriel Leigh was buried in Parma Cemetery, Parma, Idaho[482].

---

[471] Death certificate from the State of Idaho.

[472] Death certificate from the State of Idaho.

[473] Ancestry.com, U.S., Social Security Applications and Claims Index, 1936-2007.

[474] Ancestry.com, U.S., Social Security Applications and Claims Index, 1936-2007.

[475] Ancestry.com, Idaho, Select Deaths and Burials, 1907-1965

[476] Ancestry.com, Idaho, Select Deaths and Burials, 1907-1965

[477] Ancestry.com, U.S., Find A Grave Index, 1700s-Current (Provo, UT, USA, Ancestry.com Operations, Inc., 2012), Ancestry.com, http://www.Ancestry.com.

[478] Ancestry.com, Oregon Death Index, 1903-98 (Provo, UT, USA, Ancestry.com Operations Inc, 2000), www.ancestry.com, Oregon State Library; 1966-1970 Death Index; Reel Title: State of Oregon Death Index; Year Range: 1971-1980. Record for Ruth Arv Lambert.

[479] Ancestry.com, Oregon Death Index, 1903-98 (Provo, UT, USA, Ancestry.com Operations Inc, 2000), www.ancestry.com, Oregon State Library; 1966-1970 Death Index; Reel Title: State of Oregon Death Index; Year Range: 1971-1980. Record for Ruth Arv Lambert.

[480] Ancestry.com, U.S., Find A Grave Index, 1700s-Current (Provo, UT, USA, Ancestry.com Operations, Inc., 2012), Ancestry.com, http://www.Ancestry.com, Record for Ethel M. Leigh.

[481] Ancestry.com, U.S., Find A Grave Index, 1700s-Current (Provo, UT, USA, Ancestry.com Operations, Inc., 2012), Ancestry.com, http://www.Ancestry.com, Record for Ethel M. Leigh.

[482] Ancestry.com, U.S., Find A Grave Index, 1700s-Current (Provo, UT, USA, Ancestry.com Operations, Inc., 2012), Ancestry.com, http://www.Ancestry.com, Record for Ethel M. Leigh.

vi.   Grace Viola Leigh was born on 12 Sep 1915 in Modesta, California[483] and died on 17 Jul 1939 in Fall Creek, Oregon[484]. Grace Viola Leigh was buried in Parma Cemetery, Parma, Idaho[485].

Grace, while born in Modesta, California, returned with her parents and family to their farm in Apple Valley, Idaho where they were living at the time of the 1920 Census. She was seven years old when the family sold the farm in Apple Valley and moved to a farm in Alvadore, Oregon. Grace lived with her parents all her life and moved with them when they purchased a farm in Fall Creek, Oregon in 1932 when she was 16 years old. Grace developed sugar diabetes and needed to take insulin. She refused to do this saying she would not depend on a shot to live. Add to this, she ate everything she should not eat as a diabetic. She died of complications of diabetes at the age of 23.

Photo of Grace Viola Leigh from the collection of Rev. Laverne E. Leigh and used with permission.

---

[483] Ancestry.com, California Birth Index, 1905-1995 (Provo, UT, USA, Ancestry.com Operations Inc, 2005), Ancestry.com, http://www.Ancestry.com, Birthdate: 12 Sep 1915; Birth County: Stanislaus. Record for Viola G Leigh.

[484] Ancestry.com, Oregon Death Index, 1903-98 (Provo, UT, USA, Ancestry.com Operations Inc, 2000), www.ancestry.com, Oregon State Library; Oregon Death Index 1931-1941; Reel Title: Oregon Death Index M-Z; Year Range: 1931-1941. Record for Viola Leigh.

[485] Ancestry.com, U.S., Find A Grave Index, 1700s-Current (Provo, UT, USA, Ancestry.com Operations, Inc., 2012), Ancestry.com, http://www.Ancestry.com, Record for Grace V. Leigh.

Photo of Jay Noel, is wife, Eva; Cecil Paul and his wife, Lena; Ruth Lambert, Bonnie, Mary and Reuben Leigh. On the ground is Alan Lambert, Laverne Leigh, Stanley and Nova Leigh. Alice Ann Lambert is in Reuben's arms. This photo was from the collection of Rev. Laverne E. Leigh and used with permission.

25.   George Asa Leigh[4] (Rueben Harrington Leigh[3], William Todd Leigh[2], Nathan S. Leigh[1]) was born on 17 Feb 1876 in Fairmont, Minnesota[486] and died on 17 Jan 1949 in Fall Creek, Oregon[487]. He married Edith A. Walburg Horn on 26 Aug 1918 in Parma, Idaho[488]. She was born about 1899 in Utah[489]. George Asa Leigh was buried in Roswell, Idaho[490].

George lived in Fairmont, Minnesota with his parents for the first 10 years of his life and then moved to Kansas with his parents. George walked to Kansas from Minnesota for a bet of $2 in 1885 when he was ten years old. A five hundred mile walk and only rode the ferry boat across the Missouri River at Sioux City, Iowa. He helped to drive the cattle from Minnesota to Kansas. He accepted the lord and joined the church in Alton, Kansas during a series of evangelistic meetings by the Christian Crusader, on off-shoot of the Salvation Army at the same time as three of his brothers. His father, Reuben Harrington,

[486] Ancestry.com, U.S., Find A Grave Index, 1700s-Current (Provo, UT, USA, Ancestry.com Operations, Inc., 2012), Ancestry.com, http://www.Ancestry.com, Record for George Asa Leigh.

[487] Ancestry.com, U.S., Find A Grave Index, 1700s-Current (Provo, UT, USA, Ancestry.com Operations, Inc., 2012), Ancestry.com, http://www.Ancestry.com, Record for George Asa Leigh.

[488] Genealogy compiled by Rev. Laverne E. Leigh, 414 Washington Ave. East, Albia, Iowa 52531 in the Spring of 1975.

[489] Genealogy compiled by Rev. Laverne E. Leigh, 414 Washington Ave. East, Albia, Iowa 52531 in the Spring of 1975.

[490] Ancestry.com, U.S., Find A Grave Index, 1700s-Current (Provo, UT, USA, Ancestry.com Operations, Inc., 2012), Ancestry.com, http://www.Ancestry.com, Record for George Asa Leigh.

died when he was thirteen and his mother died when he was eighteen. Shortly after his mother's death, George returned to Fairmont, Minnesota as did the other brothers and sisters after their parent's deaths. This was not a new experience in Minnesota for he spent his early childhood there and then he had worked for A.W. Ward in Minnesota during the summer of 1891 while his mother was still alive. At the end of the summer, he and his sister, Minnie Augusta, returned to their home in Alton so Minnie could teach school in a nearby community and George could continue his schooling in Alton.

George migrated to Idaho as did his brothers and sisters. The year he went to Idaho is not known. It is known that he was in Idaho in Parma on May 31, 1910. George made several trips back to Kansas from Idaho, during the following years, to work in the corn harvest. He was a prize corn husker averaging 90 bushels a day. George was a hard worker in his youth. He bought a ninety acre ranch in Apple Valley, Idaho from his brother, Nathan, sometime after 1914. His place was on the Snake River next to the farm owned by his brother, Jay, and was a part of the original Paul range-right land.

On August 26, 1918, he married Edith Walburg Horn in Parma, Idaho. They had a son, Roscoe Victor born December 26, 1920 at their home in Apple Valley. While Roscoe was still a small child, Edith left George and took Roscoe when George was away from home. She took all their linens and small items leaving him a note and went to Salt Lake, Utah where her parents lived. George went to Salt Lake to visit her. While there, he took Edith and Roscoe to dinner. On a street car going home (her parents lived at the edge of town and at the end of the street car line) by pre-arrangement, he jumped off the street car with Roscoe under his arm and into a waiting taxi. He took the cab to Green River, Wyoming where he caught a train to Kansas where he lived under a false name for one and a half years so Edith could not find them.

George then moved with Roscoe to Alvidore, Oregon and bought seventy acres near the farm his brother, Jay, owned. George did not believe in paying taxes and finally lost this farm when it was sold for taxes. After that, he lived for a period of time in Eugene, Oregon where he worked for Stein Brothers Contractors. Then in 1933, Jay gave George forty acres of land on the farm he had purchased at Fall Creek, Oregon. Thus for a number of years George lived on this land. Then they moved off the farm and sold it to Jay's boy, Reuben Harold, and moved into a small house in the town of Fall Creek. From there George went to a nursing home in Eugene. George began as a hard worker with a great deal of ambition. Even though he was a little man, he could match most men as a worker. Somewhere along the line while he was living in Oregon, he lost his drive and energy and finished out his years living off others and unwilling to work.

Edith was never heard of by the family after George abducted their son, Roscoe, while she was living in Salt Lake City with her parents. She was remarried before December

31, 1923 according to a letter written on that date by George to his sister, Mrs. George Moore.

George Asa Leigh and Edith A. Wallburg Horn had the following child:

i.   Roscoe Victor Leigh was born on 26 Dec 1920 in Parma, Idaho[491] and died on 21 Jan 1998 in Multnomah, Oregon[492]. He married Margery Swam in 1948[493]. She was born on 28 Mar 1907 in Waushara County, Wisconsin[494] and died on 03 Dec 2003 in Portland, Oregon[495]. Roscoe had quite an ability with electronics and invented an electrical time clock for Lowell High School in Lowell, Oregon while he was in high school. The clock was still working in 1945-1948 when his 1st cousin once removed, Laverne Leigh, attended the school. After high school, Roscoe was in the US Army for a time before he was dishonorably discharged. Later he spend a period of time in the State Penitentiary of Oregon. While there, he invented an instrument that could cut open the bottom of a woman's purse and remove the billfold from within. This was taken from him. Roscoe's life never seemed to jell. He did marry and was last seen by the family when he attended his father's funeral in Springfield, Oregon in January of 1949. At that time, he was living in Roseburg, Oregon. Margery was a hairdresser and homemaker. She moved to Salem in 1950 and later to Portland, Oregon where she died in 2003. She had a sister named Marion J. Thomas. At her death a private service was held and a remembrance to the Oregon Humane Society was suggested.

---

[491] Ancestry.com, Oregon Death Index, 1903-98 (Provo, UT, USA, Ancestry.com Operations Inc, 2000), www.ancestry.com, Oregon State Library; Oregon Death Index 1931-1941; Reel Title: State of Oregon Death Index; Year Range: 1991-2000. Record for Victor Leigh.

[492] Ancestry.com, Oregon Death Index, 1903-98 (Provo, UT, USA, Ancestry.com Operations Inc, 2000), www.ancestry.com, Oregon State Library; Oregon Death Index 1931-1941; Reel Title: State of Oregon Death Index; Year Range: 1991-2000. Record for Victor Leigh.

[493] Oregon State Library; *Oregon Death Indexes, 1971-2008*; Reel Title: *State of Oregon Death Index*; Year Range: *2001-2005*

[494] Ancestry.com. *U.S., Social Security Death Index, 1935-2014* [database on-line]. Provo, UT, USA: Ancestry.com Operations Inc, 2014.

[495] Oregon State Library; *Oregon Death Indexes, 1971-2008*; Reel Title: *State of Oregon Death Index*; Year Range: *2001-2005*

26. William Edson Leigh[4] (Rueben Harrington Leigh[3], William Todd Leigh[2], Nathan S. Leigh[1]) was born on 03 Aug 1877[496] in Fairmont, Minnesota and died on 11 Mar 1939 in Parma, Idaho[497].   He married Marie Elizabeth Wilhelmina Juries, the daughter of Herman Juries and Mary Kitzerow, on 12 Jun 1901 in Welcome, Minnesota[498]. She was born on 06 Nov 1883 in Frankfort, Illinois[499] and died on 05 Mar 1909 in Parma, Idaho[500]. He later married Mary Lois Boyer, the daughter of Richard Haynie Boyer and Delora Lydia Record, on 03 Sep 1917 in Weiser, Idaho[501]. She was born on 25 Aug 1890 in Halfway, Oregon[502] and died on 08 Oct 1960 in Turner, Oregon[503].   William Edson Leigh along with his wife Marie Elizabeth were buried in Parma, Idaho[504].

Photo of Marie Elizabeth Wilhelmina Juries from the collection of Rev. Laverne E. Leigh and used with permission.

William Edison Leigh spent the first seven and a half years of his life in Fairmont, Minnesota and then moved with his parents to Alton, Kansas in the spring of 1885. During the years at Alton, Will accepted Christ during a series of evangelistic meeting by the Christian Crusader, an off shoot of the Salvation Army. Will was eleven and half when his father died in 1889. He continued to live at home with his mother and to attend school in Alton. After his mother died, he drifted back to Minnesota to the Fairmont community with the rest of his brothers and sisters.

[496] Ancestry.com, U.S., Find A Grave Index, 1700s-Current (Provo, UT, USA, Ancestry.com Operations, Inc., 2012), Ancestry.com, http://www.Ancestry.com, Record for William Edson Leigh.

[497] Ancestry.com, U.S., Find A Grave Index, 1700s-Current (Provo, UT, USA, Ancestry.com Operations, Inc., 2012), Ancestry.com, http://www.Ancestry.com, Record for William Edson Leigh.

[498] Genealogy compiled by Rev. Laverne E. Leigh, 414 Washington Ave. East, Albia, Iowa 52531 in the Spring of 1975.

[499] Ancestry.com, U.S., Find A Grave Index, 1700s-Current (Provo, UT, USA, Ancestry.com Operations, Inc., 2012), Ancestry.com, http://www.Ancestry.com, Record for William Edson Leigh.

[500] Ancestry.com, U.S., Find A Grave Index, 1700s-Current (Provo, UT, USA, Ancestry.com Operations, Inc., 2012), Ancestry.com, http://www.Ancestry.com, Record for William Edson Leigh.

[501] Genealogy compiled by Rev. Laverne E. Leigh, 414 Washington Ave. East, Albia, Iowa 52531 in the Spring of 1975.

[502] Ancestry.com, Oregon, Select Births and Christenings, 1868-1929 (Provo, UT, USA, Ancestry.com Operations, Inc, 2014), Ancestry.com, http://www.Ancestry.com, Record for Mary Lois Boyles.

[503] Ancestry.com. *Idaho, County Marriages, 1864-1950* [database on-line]. Provo, UT, USA: Ancestry.com Operations, Inc., 2014.

[504] Ancestry.com, U.S., Find A Grave Index, 1700s-Current (Provo, UT, USA, Ancestry.com Operations, Inc., 2012), Ancestry.com, http://www.Ancestry.com, Record for William Edson Leigh.

Will Leigh became a big, strong man. He appeared to be fat, but there was very little fat on him. Most of his weight was muscle and he was a hard working man. Shortly after his marriage to Mattie, they moved to Parma, Idaho where Will owned and operated a Livery barn with his father-in-law, Herman Juries. The livery barn had thirty head of horses that were comprised of four black horses, draft horses and fancy trotters. They had wagons and buggies to rent with the horses. They owned the town hearse and used the four black horses to pull it. This was the first livery barn in Parma. Will hired a housekeeper, Sally Burger, to do the housework and to take care of the girls while he continues to operate the livery business. Sally left his employment to get married and Will then hired Mrs. Lois Boyer. Then in 1914, Will sold his home in Parma and his interest in the livery business and purchased two farms. The first farm was on the river bottom near Parma and the second ranch was at Ten Davis, Idaho, a nearby community. He milked cows for just a short time and then he turned to raising and running forty horses and beef cattle on the two places.

Will purchased in the East and had shipped to Idaho a purebred Hamiltonian Trotter stallion and several Hamiltonian Trotter mares. His intention was to race the stallion and to raise race horses to sell due to his fame. The stallion's leg was paralyzed, due to an accident with the ten or twelve mares, in the immigrant car while being shipped to Idaho. Not being able to race the stallion, he turned the stallion and the mares out on his ranch to run and raise colts. Will married his housekeeper, Lois Boyles Boyer. Lois divorced her first husband, Jim Boyer, during the years she was keeping house for Will. From all indications, the divorce was not the fault of Will or because anything was happening between Will and Lois. She kept house for him for several years after her divorce before they were married. Lois had a daughter, Betty Boyer, from her first marriage that she and Will raised after they were married.

Will and Lois sold their two ranches about 1922-1923 and purchased property in the west edge of Parma, Idaho on the main east-west highway and built a service station and unit of motel cabins which they operated until Will's death in March of 1939. Will owned the second car bought in the Parma Valley. It was a two cylinder Buick. Louis sold the service station and motel to Mentor Leigh who was the son of Will's brother, Nathan.

William Edson Leigh and Maria Elizabeth Wilhelmina Juries had the following children:
     i.   Myrtle May Leigh was born on 07 Oct 1902 in North Star, Minnesota[505] and died on 05 Jan 2007[506] in Payette, Idaho. She married Jesse R. Wymer, the son of Frank L. Wymer and Essie M. Chrisman, on 04 Jul 1926 in Emmett, Idaho[507]. He was

---

[505] Ancestry.com, Social Security Death Index (Provo, UT, USA, The Generations Network, Inc., 2008), www.ancestry.com, Issue State: Idaho; Issue Date: Before 1951. Record for Myrtle M. Clark

[506] Ancestry.com, Social Security Death Index (Provo, UT, USA, The Generations Network, Inc., 2008), www.ancestry.com, Issue State: Idaho; Issue Date: Before 1951. Record for Myrtle M. Clark

[507] Genealogy compiled by Rev. Laverne E. Leigh in 2017.

born on 29 Jun 1901 in Pomona, Kansas[508] and died on 26 April 1965 in Parma, Idaho[509]. She married John Elwood Clark, the son of Record Clark and Edith George, on 28 Apr 1962 in Reno, Nevada[510]. He was born on 13 Oct 1908 in Siloam Springs, Arkansas[511] and died on 21 May 1967 in Redding, California[512]. Myrtle May Leigh along with John Elwood Clark were buried in Payette, Idaho[513].   Jesse R. Wymer was buried in Glens Ferry, Idaho[514].

Published in the Idaho Statesman on 1/10/2007.
Myrtle May Clark, 104, of Payette, passed away Friday, Jan. 5, 2007 at a local care center in Payette. Funeral services will be held 2 p.m., Thursday, Jan. 11 at Shaffer-Jensen Memory Chapel, Payette with Pastor John Tucker officiating. Interment will

follow at Riverside Cemetery, Payette. A visitation for family and friends will be held from 4-7 p.m., Wednesday, Jan. 10, 2007 at Shaffer-Jensen Memory Chapel, Payette. Condolences may be made to the family at www.shaffer-jensenchapel.com . Myrtle was born Oct. 7, 1902 in North Star, Minn. to William Edson Leigh and Mary Elizabeth Jurries. Her grandparents, Herman and Mary Jurries came from Germany.

Photo of Myrtle May Leigh found on findagrave.com.

An avid writer throughout her life, Myrtle wrote the following chronology when she was 96. *"When I was three months old my mother and her brother Albert Jurries came out on the emigrant train to Parma. We arrived on Christmas Day. My father came in a freight car bringing some stock. He*

[508] Idaho, Death Records, 1890-1966 (Provo, UT, USA, Ancestry.com Operations, Inc., 2014), Ancestry.com, http://www.Ancestry.com, Idaho Bureau of Vital Records and Health Statistics; Boise, Idaho; Death Index and Image, 1911-1966. Record for Jess R. Wymer.

[509] Idaho, Death Records, 1890-1966 (Provo, UT, USA, Ancestry.com Operations, Inc., 2014), Ancestry.com, http://www.Ancestry.com, Idaho Bureau of Vital Records and Health Statistics; Boise, Idaho; Death Index and Image, 1911-1966. Record for Jess R. Wymer.

[510] Genealogy compiled by Rev. Laverne E. Leigh, 414 Washington Ave. East, Albia, Iowa 52531 in the Spring of 1975.

[511] Ancestry.com, California Death Index, 1940-1997 (Provo, UT, USA, The Generations Network, Inc., 2000), www.ancestry.com, Date: 1967-05-21. Record for John E Clark.

[512] Ancestry.com, California Death Index, 1940-1997 (Provo, UT, USA, The Generations Network, Inc., 2000), www.ancestry.com, Date: 1967-05-21. Record for John E Clark.

[513] Ancestry.com, U.S., Find A Grave Index, 1700s-Current (Provo, UT, USA, Ancestry.com Operations, Inc., 2012), Ancestry.com, http://www.Ancestry.com, Record for Myrtle May Clark

[514] Ancestry.com, U.S., Find A Grave Index, 1700s-Current (Provo, UT, USA, Ancestry.com Operations, Inc., 2012), Ancestry.com, http://www.Ancestry.com, Record for Jesse R Wymer.

opened a livery barn and rented teams of horses to different people. He had a pair of roan horses that were real gentle and he let people drive them. Their names were Dutch and Prince. He had a pair of high-strung horses, Joe and Riley, that he drove salesmen around the country and took doctors out on calls. My mother died in 1909 when I was six years old and my sister Frances was two years old. We went back to Minnesota and lived with our grandparents for awhile, then they came out to Idaho and kept house for us. When she was no longer able to keep house and take care of us we stayed with two different families. Then my father got housekeepers to take care of us. He got one housekeeper that had a little girl and he finally married her. We lived right across the street from the church and our father would carry us to Sunday school if he hadn't cleaned the snow off the walks. He sold the livery barn and we moved to a ranch west of Parma. In the winter he would take his saddle horse and take us to Sunday school in a three-seated sled he had made. He milked cows and had a separator and sold cream. My father sold the ranch and opened up a Texaco gas station in town. He operated it for several years until he died of a heart attack in 1939. I worked in the C. C. Anderson store for a lot of years until Mr. Price, the manager, went into business for himself. He asked me to work for him, so I worked for him until he closed his store. Then I worked at the Idaho Department store. I married Jess Wymer and we bought Grandma Shipley's house that had two apartments; we lived in one and rented the other one. We built a little house on part of the lot. We moved to a house on the west side of town and built a little house on the back of the lot that we rented to two girls who worked in the telephone office. Later we sold that house and bought Governor Baldridges home. It was a big two-story house and we made it into four apartments, lived in one and rented the others. After 37 years we divorced. I lived with a friend in Parma until I moved to Roseburg, Ore. and lived with my sister. I worked in the style shop she managed. From there I went to Redding, Calif. John Clark had a plumbing shop and had quite a few men working for him, so I wrote payroll checks. John and I married in 1962 in Reno. We had a lovely home in Redding, and those were the happiest years of my life. We were married just five years when he passed away. I stayed in Redding for two years then came back to Payette to Mother Clark's home and have lived here ever since. I decided to come to Payette rather than going to Parma as Aunt Guila Davis and Helen were both here. Then Aunt Guila passed away and Helen moved to Boise and married. But I got to see Helen every two weeks as she came down for Eastern Star, and I saw Frank and Margaret every once in the while. So that is my story. I graduated from Parma High School in 1921 in a class of eight; four boys and four girls. Special appreciation to Edna Mae Brockman for the unwavering concern and care she gave to Myrtle the last several years of both their lives. Also a heartfelt thank you to Sandi Wonka and Heart-N-Home Hospice."

John had been previously married to Doris Wood. John was a plumber and a plumbing contractor and Myrtle was a sales lady and the store manager for a ladies ready to wear store.

87.   ii.   Frances Mary Leigh was born on 05 Jun 1906 in Parma, Idaho[515] and died on 07 Apr 1997 in Winston, Oregon[516].

William Edson Leigh and Mary Lois Boyles had the following child:
88.   iii.   William Paul Leigh was born on 26 Aug 1918 in Parma, Idaho[517] and died on 29 May 2003 in Baker City, Oregon[518].

27. Nathan Evan Leigh[4] (Rueben Harrington Leigh[3], William Todd Leigh[2], Nathan S. Leigh[1]) was born on 04 Mar 1879[519] in Fairmont, Minnesota and died on 30 Apr 1954 in Flathead, Montana[520]. He married Mary E. Allen, the daughter of Charles H. Allen and Charlotte S. Soper, on 26 Mar 1902 in Roswell, Idaho[521]. She was born on 27 Feb 1884 in Madelia, Minnesota[522] and died on 05 Dec 1963 in Caldwell, Idaho[523]. He later married Grace M. Berry on 24 Oct 1918 in Caldwell, Idaho[524]. She was born in 1897 in Virginia[525]. Nathan Evan Leigh along with his first wife, Mary E. Allen were buried in Parma, Idaho[526].

---

[515] Ancestry.com, U.S., Social Security Applications and Claims Index, 1936-2007 (Provo, UT, USA, Ancestry.com Operations, Inc., 2015), Ancestry.com, http://www.Ancestry.com, Record for Frances Mary Young.

[516] Ancestry.com, U.S., Social Security Applications and Claims Index, 1936-2007 (Provo, UT, USA, Ancestry.com Operations, Inc., 2015), Ancestry.com, http://www.Ancestry.com, Record for Frances Mary Young.

[517] Ancestry.com, U.S., Social Security Applications and Claims Index, 1936-2007 (Provo, UT, USA, Ancestry.com Operations, Inc., 2015), Ancestry.com, http://www.Ancestry.com, Record for William Paul Leigh.

[518] Ancestry.com, U.S., Social Security Applications and Claims Index, 1936-2007 (Provo, UT, USA, Ancestry.com Operations, Inc., 2015), Ancestry.com, http://www.Ancestry.com, Record for William Paul Leigh.

[519] Ancestry.com, U.S. World War II Draft Registration Cards, 1942 (Provo, UT, USA, The Generations Network, Inc., 2007), www.ancestry.com, The National Archives at St. Louis; St. Louis, Missouri; Draft Registration Cards for Fourth Registration for Idaho, 04/27/1942 - 04/27/1942; NAI Number: 563870; Record Group Title: Records of the Selective Service System; Record Group Number: 147. Record for Nathan Evan Leigh.

[520] Ancestry.com, Montana, Death Index, 1868-2011 (Provo, UT, USA, Ancestry.com Operations, Inc., 2001), Ancestry.com, http://www.Ancestry.com, Record for Nathan E Leigh

[521] Genealogy compiled by Rev. Laverne E. Leigh, 414 Washington Ave. East, Albia, Iowa 52531 in the Spring of 1975.

[522] Ancestry.com, Idaho, Birth Index, 1861-1914, Stillbirth Index, 1905-1964 (Provo, UT, USA, Ancestry.com Operations, Inc., 2013), Ancestry.com, http://www.Ancestry.com, Idaho State Department of Health; Boise, Idaho; Idaho Birth and Stillbirth Index, 1913-1964. Record for Mary E. Allen.

[523] Idaho, Death Records, 1890-1966 (Provo, UT, USA, Ancestry.com Operations, Inc., 2014), Ancestry.com, http://www.Ancestry.com, Idaho Bureau of Vital Records and Health Statistics; Boise, Idaho; Death Index and Image, 1911-1966. Record for Mary E. Jones.

[524] Genealogy compiled by Rev. Laverne E. Leigh, 414 Washington Ave. East, Albia, Iowa 52531 in the Spring of 1975.

[525] Genealogy compiled by Rev. Laverne E. Leigh, 414 Washington Ave. East, Albia, Iowa 52531 in the Spring of 1975.

[526] Ancestry.com, U.S., Find A Grave Index, 1700s-Current (Provo, UT, USA, Ancestry.com Operations, Inc., 2012), Ancestry.com, http://www.Ancestry.com, Record for Nathan Evan Leigh.

Nathan Evan Leigh was six years old when his parents moved from their home in Fairmont, Minnesota to Alton, Kansas. During the years in Alton, he was in school. Nate was almost 10 when his father died and almost 14 when his mother died. He returned to Minnesota with his other siblings after his mother's death. Nate was his sister, Minnie Augusta's favorite brother. Minnie, as the oldest child at home, unmarried, sold the family property in Alton after the death of their parents. Minnie used the money to send Nate to college. He did not like college and soon returned home. None of the other children every received any money from the sale of the property at Alton except Minnie and when she spent it on Nate's college education, this caused hard feelings with the other children.

Photo of Nathan Evan Leigh from the collection of Rev. Laverne E. Leigh and used with permission.

The exact time that Nate traveled from Minnesota to Idaho, is not know, but the compiler of this genealogy has a picture of Nate taken on a trip to the Jordan Valley of Idaho on August 14, 1900. Nate and Mary purchased a farm in Apple Valley, Idaho on the old Paul range right in 1903. It was ninety acres and they farmed it until 1914, when they sold it to his brother, George Asa. They bought a building in Parma with a garage and movie house downstairs and living quarters upstairs. It was just down the street from his brother, Will's, livery barn and south of the railroad tracks. Nate operated the picture show at Parma and did carpentry work part time until he and Mary (Mae) were separated and finally divorced.

Members of the family felt that Mae and Nate would have made a go of their union if Mae's mother had not been against the marriage and worked so hard to break it up. Nate was great joker and kidded too much. Between these two, their marriage became more and more difficult. Mae was a fine person and was considered a part of the family until her death in 1963. Mae tried to commit suicide twice before they separated in about 1915. While they were separated and before they divorced, Nate operated the picture show at Parma, built and owned a new show house in Nysia, Oregon, rented a building in Wilder, Idaho and operated a show in it, had a show house in New Plymouth, Idaho that he probably rented and then build a new theater in Parma. He then sold the old theater in Parma. Nate and Mae almost made up twice and then she divorced him.

After the divorce, Nate turned the operation of all his theaters over to his son, Milton, and moved to California and worked as a carpenter at Long Beach, California. He did this to keep from paying, what he thought was, a too large a property settlement to Mary that she was trying to get. He, however, sent money to Mae from California for her support. About 1919, Nate returned from California to Idaho and worked with Milton operating the theaters. In 1922 or 1923, he turned over the operation of the New Plymouth theater to his second son, Mentor. They abandoned the theater at Wilder around 1923. They continued to operate the Parma and Nysia, Oregon theaters until about 1943.

Photo of Nathan Evan Leigh, his wife Mary E. Allen and three of their children from the collection of Rev. Laverne E. Leigh and used with permission.

Nathan Leigh maintained a house in Parma and property at Flathead Lake, Montana with his two sons after the theaters in Parma and Nysia were sold about 1943. He traveled a great amount after this. Hazel Leigh, the daughter of Nate's brother, Charles, kept house for him and was his traveling companion for years. He was in Montana at his property on Flathead Lake at the time of his death. He actually died in Polson, Montana.

Mary had a good life with Howard Jones. They lived in Apple Valley, Idaho. They cared for Mildred until her death in April of 1950.

Nathan Evan Leigh and Mary E. Allen had the following children:
89.   i.   Milton Allen Leigh was born on 28 Feb 1903 in Roswell, Idaho[527] and died on 13 May 1962 in Newport, Oregon[528].
        ii.   Mildred Leigh was born on 25 June 1905 in Seattle, Washington[529] and died on 13 Apr 1950 in Canyon, Idaho[530]. Mildred Leigh was buried in Parma Cemetery,

[527] Ancestry.com, Oregon Death Index, 1903-98 (Provo, UT, USA, Ancestry.com Operations Inc, 2000), www.ancestry.com, Oregon State Library; Oregon Death Index 1931-1941; Reel Title: Oregon Death Index A-Z; Year Range: 1961-1965. Record for Milton A Leigh.
[528] Ancestry.com, Oregon Death Index, 1903-98 (Provo, UT, USA, Ancestry.com Operations Inc, 2000), www.ancestry.com, Oregon State Library; Oregon Death Index 1931-1941; Reel Title: Oregon Death Index A-Z; Year Range: 1961-1965. Record for Milton A Leigh.
[529] Ancestry.com, Idaho, Death Index, 1890-1964 (Provo, UT, USA, Ancestry.com Operations Inc, 2003), Ancestry.com, http://www.Ancestry.com, Record for Mildred Leigh.

Parma, Idaho. Mildred was physically and mentally limited most, if not all, of her life. Her mother kept her after she and Nate were separated. Mildred spent many of her years in bed.

90.   iii.   Mentor G. Leigh was born on 26 Mar 1909 in Parma, Idaho[531] and died on 11 Apr 1965 in Rural, Idaho[532].

    iv.   Della Fern Leigh was born on 26 May 1910 in Parma, Idaho[533] and died on 05 Jun 1910 in Parma, Idaho[534]. Della Fern Leigh was buried in Parma Cemetery, Parma, Idaho[535].

Nathan Evan Leigh and Grace M. Berry had the following child:

    v.   Evelyn Margaret Leigh was born on 06 Nov 1919 in Parma, Idaho[536] and died on 25 May 1938 in Boise, Idaho[537].   Evelyn died at the age of eighteen as a result of an appendicitis operation. Evelyn had graduated from High School in 1937. She was in Boise, Idaho working as a cashier of the Walgreen Drug Company. She was a good student, active in many school activities, a four year letterman in tennis, involved in many music programs in school and a yell leader her senior year. She was a member of Parma Community Church. Evelyn Margaret Leigh was buried in Parma Cemetery, Parma, Idaho[538].

28. Mentor Garfield Leigh[4] (Rueben Harrington Leigh[3], William Todd Leigh[2], Nathan S. Leigh[1]) was born on 13 Mar 1882[539] in Fairmont, Minnesota and died on 14 Mar 1906 in Caldwell, Idaho[540]. He married Carrie Gertrude Odem, the daughter of William B. Odem

---

[530] Ancestry.com, Idaho, Death Index, 1890-1964 (Provo, UT, USA, Ancestry.com Operations Inc, 2003), Ancestry.com, http://www.Ancestry.com, Record for Mildred Leigh.

[531] Idaho, Death Records, 1890-1966 (Provo, UT, USA, Ancestry.com Operations, Inc., 2014), Ancestry.com, http://www.Ancestry.com, Idaho Bureau of Vital Records and Health Statistics; Boise, Idaho; Death Index and Image, 1911-1966. Record for Mentor G. Leigh.

[532] Idaho, Death Records, 1890-1966 (Provo, UT, USA, Ancestry.com Operations, Inc., 2014), Ancestry.com, http://www.Ancestry.com, Idaho Bureau of Vital Records and Health Statistics; Boise, Idaho; Death Index and Image, 1911-1966. Record for Mentor G. Leigh.

[533] Ancestry.com, U.S., Find A Grave Index, 1700s-Current (Provo, UT, USA, Ancestry.com Operations, Inc., 2012), Ancestry.com, http://www.Ancestry.com, Record for Della Fern Leigh.

[534] Ancestry.com, U.S., Find A Grave Index, 1700s-Current (Provo, UT, USA, Ancestry.com Operations, Inc., 2012), Ancestry.com, http://www.Ancestry.com, Record for Della Fern Leigh.

[535] Ancestry.com, U.S., Find A Grave Index, 1700s-Current (Provo, UT, USA, Ancestry.com Operations, Inc., 2012), Ancestry.com, http://www.Ancestry.com, Record for Della Fern Leigh.

[536] Ancestry.com, Idaho, Death Index, 1890-1964 (Provo, UT, USA, Ancestry.com Operations Inc, 2003), Ancestry.com, http://www.Ancestry.com, Record for Evelyn Leigh.

[537] Ancestry.com, Idaho, Death Index, 1890-1964 (Provo, UT, USA, Ancestry.com Operations Inc, 2003), Ancestry.com, http://www.Ancestry.com, Record for Evelyn Leigh.

[538] Ancestry.com, U.S., Find A Grave Index, 1700s-Current (Provo, UT, USA, Ancestry.com Operations, Inc., 2012), Ancestry.com, http://www.Ancestry.com, Record for Evelyn Leigh.

[539] Ancestry.com, U.S., Find A Grave Index, 1700s-Current (Provo, UT, USA, Ancestry.com Operations, Inc., 2012), Ancestry.com, http://www.Ancestry.com, Record for Mentor G. Leigh.

[540] Ancestry.com, U.S., Find A Grave Index, 1700s-Current (Provo, UT, USA, Ancestry.com Operations, Inc., 2012), Ancestry.com, http://www.Ancestry.com, Record for Mentor G. Leigh.

and Ellen A. Myers, in Sep 1903 in Caldwell, Idaho[541]. She was born on 05 Feb 1885 in Idaho[542] and died on 30 Jan 1959 in Oakland, California[543]. Mentor Garfield Leigh was buried in Roswell, Idaho[544].

Mentor was only three years old when the family moved from Minnesota to Alton, Kansas. After the death of his parents, he went with this brothers and sisters to live in Minnesota. It is not known just how he was cared for and by whom during these years he was growing up. It is known that he stowed away on the immigrant car that George and Dell Moore and family used in 1898 to move from Minnesota to Idaho. His brother, Jay was on this car to care for the livestock. It is pretty likely that Jay knew that Mentor was there. Mentor would have been sixteen at this time.

It is not known what he did in Idaho before 1903 at the time he married Carrie Gertrude Odom. They made their home in Caldwell where they had a son in 1905. Then Mentor died suddenly after a short illness. The family, by and large, did not like his wife, Carrie. It is said that she was not friendly at all. It was rumored by several that Mentor had died suddenly because she had poisoned him. Another member of family related to the complier that Mentor had been an alcoholic and had probably died as a result of his drinking. However, neither of these are any more than rumor and are unconfirmed.

After Mentor's death, Carrie took their infant son, Harry Wayne, and left the area. It is known that she married a man named Waters later and that her son married and had a daughter named Patricia. Other than that, this branch of the family has been totally lost.

Mentor Garfield Leigh and Carrie Gertrude Odem had the following child:
91.   i.   Harry Wayne Leigh was born on 29 Apr 1905 in Caldwell, Idaho[545] and died on 02 Jun 1983 in Marin, California[546].

---

[541] Genealogy compiled by Rev. Laverne E. Leigh in 2017.
[542] Ancestry.com. *California, Death Index, 1940-1997* [database on-line]. Provo, UT, USA: Ancestry.com Operations Inc, 2000.
[543] Ancestry.com. *California, Death Index, 1940-1997* [database on-line]. Provo, UT, USA: Ancestry.com Operations Inc, 2000.
[544] Ancestry.com. *U.S., Find A Grave Index, 1600s-Current* [database on-line]. Provo, UT, USA: Ancestry.com Operations, Inc., 2012.
[545] Ancestry.com. *California, Death Index, 1940-1997* [database on-line]. Provo, UT, USA: Ancestry.com Operations
[546] Ancestry.com. *California, Death Index, 1940-1997* [database on-line]. Provo, UT, USA: Ancestry.com Operations

29.   George Lynn Foote, Jr.[4] (Lydia Marie Leigh[3], William Todd Leigh[2], Nathan S. Leigh[1]) was born on 15 Jan 1863 in Madison, New York[547] and died on 14 Jun 1945 in Utica, New York[548]. He married Mary Etta Clancy, the daughter of John H. Clancy and Mary Ann Donovan, on 27 Dec 1888 in Utica, New York[549]. She was born on 09 Aug 1864 in Redfield, New York[550] and died on 11 Jul 1923 in 1210 Churchill Avenue, Utica, New York[551]. George L. Foote, Jr. and his wife are buried in Jun 1945 in Mt. Oliviet Cemetery, Whitesboro, New York[552]. In the 1880 Oneida Census, George was listed as Lynn Foote and lived with the Baker family. He had worked as an Iron molder for many

years. He was a member of Sacred Heart Church. The 1887 Utica Directory listed George as a molder living at 96 Fayette Street, Utica, New York. In the 1920 Census, George was living in Syracuse, New York on Burmet Avenue. Ward 5, with his wife Mary and was working as an Iron Molder. George lived with his daughter, Mary Agnes Emery at time of his death at 1131 Downer Avenue., Utica, New York.

Photos are George Lynn Foote, Jr. and his wife, Mary Etta Clancy. These pictures are from the authors collection.

---

[547] George L. Foote. Jr. Obituary. Utica Daily Press, Utica, New York, June 15, 1945.

[548] George L. Foote. Jr. Obituary. Utica Daily Press, Utica, New York, June 15, 1945.

[549] George L. Foote. Jr. Obituary. Utica Daily Press, Utica, New York, June 15, 1945.

[550] Obituary of Mrs. Mary Clancy Foote, Utica Daily Press, Utica, New York, July 12, 1923.

[551] Obituary of Mrs. Mary Clancy Foote, Utica Daily Press, Utica, New York, July 12, 1923.

[552] Ancestry.com, U.S., Find A Grave Index, 1700s-Current (Provo, UT, USA, Ancestry.com Operations, Inc., 2012), Ancestry.com, http://www.Ancestry.com, Record for George Lynn Foote Jr.

Mary lived with her daughter, Edna Hickey, at time of death at 1210 Churchill Avenue, Utica, New York. She was a member of St. Patrick's Church, Utica, New York. She had lived in Utica for 37 years.

George Lynn Foote and Mary Etta Clancy had the following children:
92.   i.   Mary Agnes Foote was born on 16 Aug 1890 in Utica, New York[553] and died on 27 Mar 1982 in Lakeland Florida[554].
93.   ii.   Isabel Lydia Foote was born on 08 Jan 1894 in Milford, Massachusetts[555] and died on 31 Aug 1973 in New Hartford, New York[556].
       iii.   Edna Cecelia Foote was born on 11 Jan 1897 in Utica, New York[557] and died on 22 Sep 1987 in Lakeland, Florida[558]. She married Edward James Hickey on 12 Jun 1917 in St. Patrick's Church, Utica, New York[559]. He was born on 21 Apr 1892 in New Jersey[560] and died on 03 Aug 1972 in Winter Haven, Florida[561]. Edna Cecelia Foote and her husband, Edward are buried in Mt. Olivet Cemetery, Whitesboro, New York[562]. Edna received her education in the Utica schools and worked as a postal clerk. They lived in Rome, New York until they retired in Florida 30 years before her death. She was a member of St. Joseph's Church, Lakeland, Florida.

Ed attended Utica schools and was employed in the transportation department at Griffiss Air Force Base. He had lived in Florida for 15 years after his retirement. He served in the Army in WW I. He was a member of St. Joseph's Church, Winter Haven, Florida and Sacred Heart Church in Utica. He was also a former member of the Utica Council Knights of Columbus. His obituary mentions a sister, Margaret Whalen of Utica.

---

[553] Death Certificate from the State of Florida.
[554] Death Certificate from the State of Florida.
[555] Ancestry.com, U.S., Find A Grave Index, 1700s-Current (Provo, UT, USA, Ancestry.com Operations, Inc., 2012), Ancestry.com, http://www.Ancestry.com.
[556] Ancestry.com, U.S., Find A Grave Index, 1700s-Current (Provo, UT, USA, Ancestry.com Operations, Inc., 2012), Ancestry.com, http://www.Ancestry.com.
[557] Family Group Sheet.
[558] Obituary, Utica Observer Dispatch, Utica, New York, September 24, 1987, page 6A.
[559] Marriage Record, New York, County Marriages, 1908-1935 for Edna C. Foote, LDS Film.#381750.
[560] Ancestry.com, World War I Draft Registration Cards, 1917-1918 (Provo, UT, USA, The Generations Network, Inc., 2005), www.ancestry.com, Registration State: New York; Registration County: Oneida; Roll: 1819117; Draft Board: 1.
[561] Ancestry.com, Florida Death Index, 1877-1998.
[562] Ancestry.com, U.S., Find A Grave Index, 1700s-Current (Provo, UT, USA, Ancestry.com Operations, Inc., 2012), Ancestry.com, http://www.Ancestry.com.

Photo of the Foote family about 1910. Left to right - Isabel Lydia, George Lynn, Mary Agnes, Mary Etta, and Edna Cecilia Foote. This photo is in the authors collection.

30. Charles Lewis Foote[4] (Lydia Marie Leigh[3], William Todd Leigh[2], Nathan S. Leigh[1]) was born on 04 Jan 1874 in Madison, New York[563] and died on 17 Dec 1950 in Oneida City Hospital, Oneida, New York[564]. He married Zoola Read, the daughter of Edward R. Read and Sarah M. Eldred, on 17 Jan 1895 in Canastota, New York[565]. She was born on 28 Aug 1878 in Canastota, New York[566] and died on 25 Sep 1955 in Community Hospital, Hamilton, New York[567]. Charles Lewis Foote and his wife are buried in Mt. Pleasant Cemetery, Canastota, New York[568]. Charles Lewis Foote was a foreman of the General Aniline & Film Corp., Binghamton, New York and retired in 1944. He was a member of the Morrisville Methodist church and of the Odd Fellows Lodge of Johnson City, New York. He had a granddaughter in 1950 by the name of Mrs. Preben Hensen of Johnson City, New York. At the turn of the century Charles conducted a laundry in the present American Legion dugout in Depot Street.

Zoola was the president of the Madison County Women's Christian Temperance Union. She was also a God Star Mother, a member of the American Legion Auxiliary, the Grange and the Methodist Church of Morrisville.

---

[563] Ancestry.com, World War I Draft Registration Cards, 1917-1918 (Provo, UT, USA, The Generations Network, Inc., 2005),

[564] New York Department of Health; Albany, NY; *NY State Death Index*; Certificate Number: *72912*

[565] Obituary, Canastota, New York newspaper, September 29, 1955.

[566] Obituary, Canastota, New York newspaper, September 29, 1955.

[567] Obituary, Canastota, New York newspaper, September 29, 1955.

[568] Ancestry.com, U.S., Find A Grave Index, 1700s-Current (Provo, UT, USA, Ancestry.com Operations, Inc., 2012), Ancestry.com, http://www.Ancestry.com, Record for Charles L. Foote. http://search.ancestry.com/cgi-

Charles Lewis Foote and Zoola Read Foote had the following children:

      i.   Harold Foote was born on 13 Nov 1895 in Canastota, New York[569] and died on 14 Nov 1895 in Canastota, New York[570]. Harold Foote died as an infant and was buried with his parents in Nov 1895 in Canastota, New York[571].

      ii.   Carl L. Foote was born on 18 Jan 1897[572] and died on 23 Jun 1918 in Chateau Thierry, France while fighting in World War I[573]. Carl L. Foote was buried in Belleau, Department de l'Aisne, Picardie, France[574]. Carl enlisted June 18, 1917 at Utica, New York; Camp Syracuse; branch of service, 9th Infantry, Private 1st Class killed in action at Chateau Thierry June 23, 1918; overseas September 6, 1917.

94.   iii.   Earl E. Foote was born on 28 Feb 1898 in Canastota, New York[575] and died on 16 Nov 1959 in Eaton Road, Morrisville, New York[576].

      iv.   Stewart Jay Foote was born on 22 Mar 1900 in Canastota, New York[577] and died on 30 Apr 1953 in Binghamton City Hospital, Binghamton, New York[578]. He married Ceila G. Walker[579]. She was born 21 March 1901 in Pennsylvania[580] and died 7 Jan 1989 in Binghamton, New York[581]. Stewart Jay Foote was buried on 04 May 1953 in Canastota, New York[582].

Stewart lived in Binghamton in 1950. He was a veteran of WW I. He enlisted August 28, 1917 at Utica, New York. He went to the Great Lakes Training Station, Illinois. He was a Seaman 2nd Class in the US Navy assigned to Sub Chaser 328 at Little Falls;

---

[569] Death Notice of Harold Foote in the Canastota, New York newspaper, Nov 16, 1895.

[570] Death Notice of Harold Foote in the Canastota, New York newspaper, Nov 16, 1895.

[571] Ancestry.com, U.S., Find A Grave Index, 1700s-Current (Provo, UT, USA, Ancestry.com Operations, Inc., 2012), Ancestry.com, http://www.Ancestry.com.

[572] Cuccinello, Karen, Herkimer County, New York Soldiers, 1916-1918 (Provo, UT, USA, Ancestry.com Operations Inc., 1999), Ancestry.com, http://www.Ancestry.com, HERKIMER COUNTY IN THE WORLD WAR. Record for Carl L. Foote.

[573] Ancestry.com, Global, Find A Grave Index for Burials at Sea and other Select Burial Locations, 1300s-Current (Provo, UT, USA, Ancestry.com Operations, Inc., 2012), Ancestry.com, http://www.Ancestry.com, Record for Pvt 1cl Carl L Foote.

[574] Ancestry.com, Global, Find A Grave Index for Burials at Sea and other Select Burial Locations, 1300s-Current (Provo, UT, USA, Ancestry.com Operations, Inc., 2012), Ancestry.com, http://www.Ancestry.com, Record for Pvt 1cl Carl L Foote.

[575] Obituary, Utica Daily Press, Utica, New York, November 17, 1959, page 8.

[576] Obituary, Utica Daily Press, Utica, New York, November 17, 1959, page 8.

[577] Ancestry.com, U.S., Headstone Applications for Military Veterans, 1925-1963 (Provo, UT, USA, Ancestry.com Operations, Inc., 2012), www.ancestry.com, Record for Stewart Jay Foote.

[578] Ancestry.com, U.S., Headstone Applications for Military Veterans, 1925-1963 (Provo, UT, USA, Ancestry.com Operations, Inc., 2012), www.ancestry.com, Record for Stewart Jay Foote.

[579] Ancestry.com, U.S., Find A Grave Index, 1700s-Current (Provo, UT, USA, Ancestry.com Operations, Inc., 2012), Ancestry.com, http://www.Ancestry.com.

[580] Ancestry.com, U.S., Find A Grave Index, 1700s-Current (Provo, UT, USA, Ancestry.com Operations, Inc., 2012), Ancestry.com, http://www.Ancestry.com.

[581] Ancestry.com, U.S., Find A Grave Index, 1700s-Current (Provo, UT, USA, Ancestry.com Operations, Inc., 2012), Ancestry.com, http://www.Ancestry.com.

[582] Ancestry.com, U.S., Headstone Applications for Military Veterans, 1925-1963 (Provo, UT, USA, Ancestry.com Operations, Inc., 2012), www.ancestry.com, Record for Stewart Jay Foote.

Annapolis where 328 was used as training ship. He was discharged February 28, 1919. He had three stepchildren at the time of his death and a granddaughter.

Photo of Carl L, Earl E. and Stewart Jay Foote from the authors collection.

31. Earl James Foote[4] (Lydia Marie Leigh[3], William Todd Leigh[2], Nathan S. Leigh[1]) was born on 12 Mar 1878 in New York State[583] and died on 20 Nov 1971 in Oneida City Hospital, Oneida, New York[584]. He married Claudia C. Baker, the daughter of John H. and Margaret Williams, in 1900 in Hamilton, New York[585]. She was born in 1882 in Pine Woods, New York[586] and died on 09 Apr 1957 in Lenox Memorial Hospital, Lenox, New York[587]. Earl James Foote and his wife are buried in Mt. Pleasant Cemetery, Canastota, New York[588]. Earl was a member of the Canastota Methodist Church. He worked for Niagara Mohawk for many years as a meter reader. Had three grandchildren and 8 great-grandchildren at the time of his death. Claudia moved to Canastota after their marriage and lived there ever since.

Earl James Foote and Claudia C. Baker Foote had the following child:
95.   i.   Hazel E. Foote was born on 29 Apr 1907 in Canastota, New York[589] and died on 29 May 1995 in Oneida City Hospital, Oneida, New York[590].

---

[583] World War I draft registrations at Ancestry.com

[584] Obituary, The Daily Press, Utica, New York, November 22, 1971, page 32.

[585] Obituary, The Daily Press, Utica, New York, November 22, 1971, page 32.

[586] Gravestone at Mt. Pleasant Cemetery, Canastota, New York.

[587] Gravestone at Mt. Pleasant Cemetery, Canastota, New York.

[588] Gravestone at Mt. Pleasant Cemetery, Canastota, New York.

[589] Ancestry.com, Social Security Death Index (Provo, UT, USA, The Generations Network, Inc., 2008), www.ancestry.com, Database online. Record for Hazel E. Rousseau.

[590] Ancestry.com, Social Security Death Index (Provo, UT, USA, The Generations Network, Inc., 2008), www.ancestry.com, Database online. Record for Hazel E. Rousseau.

32. Earl R. Leigh[4] (John H. Leigh[3], William Todd Leigh[2], Nathan S. Leigh[1]) was born on 26 Sep 1890 in Sherburne, New York [591] and died in Aug 1966 in Norwich, New York[592]. He married Nellie L. VanNamee. She was born in 1892 in New York[593] and died in 1967[594] . Earl R Leigh and his wife are buried in Norwich, , New York[595].

Earl R Leigh and Nellie L. VanNamee Leigh had the following children:
    i.   Laurie Jean Leigh was born on 21 Oct 1926 in Norwich, New York[596] and died on 11 Jan 2001 in Norwich, New York[597]. She married a man by the name of Vorhies. Laurie Jean Leigh was buried in Norwich, New York [598].
    ii.   John S. Leigh was born on 31 Jul 1935 in Norwich, New York[599] and died on 02 Sep 1982[600] .

33. Anna Elizabeth Leigh[4] (John H. Leigh[3], William Todd Leigh[2], Nathan S. Leigh[1]) was born on 10 Mar 1894 in Gilbertsville, New York[601] and died on 23 Sep 1952 in Syracuse, New York[602]. She married Fred Helmer Adams, the son of Ervin W. Adams and Sara Coffin, on 13 Jun 1914 in Chenango, New York[603]. He was born on 29 Jan 1882 in

[591] Ancestry.com, U.S., Find A Grave Index, 1700s-Current (Provo, UT, USA, Ancestry.com Operations, Inc., 2012), Ancestry.com, http://www.Ancestry.com, Record for Earl Leigh.
[592] Ancestry.com, U.S., Find A Grave Index, 1700s Current (Provo, UT, USA, Ancestry.com Operations, Inc., 2012), Ancestry.com, http://www.Ancestry.com, Record for Earl Leigh.
[593] Ancestry.com, U.S., Find A Grave Index, 1700s-Current (Provo, UT, USA, Ancestry.com Operations, Inc., 2012), Ancestry.com, http://www.Ancestry.com, Record for Earl Leigh.
[594] Ancestry.com, U.S., Find A Grave Index, 1700s-Current (Provo, UT, USA, Ancestry.com Operations, Inc., 2012), Ancestry.com, http://www.Ancestry.com, Record for Earl Leigh.
[595] Ancestry.com, U.S., Find A Grave Index, 1700s-Current (Provo, UT, USA, Ancestry.com Operations, Inc., 2012), Ancestry.com, http://www.Ancestry.com, Record for Earl Leigh.
[596] Ancestry.com, U.S., Social Security Applications and Claims Index, 1936-2007 (Provo, UT, USA, Ancestry.com Operations, Inc., 2015), Ancestry.com, http://www.Ancestry.com, Record for Laurie Jean Leigh.
[597] Ancestry.com, U.S., Social Security Applications and Claims Index, 1936-2007 (Provo, UT, USA, Ancestry.com Operations, Inc., 2015), Ancestry.com, http://www.Ancestry.com, Record for Laurie Jean Leigh.
[598] Ancestry.com, U.S., Find A Grave Index, 1700s-Current (Provo, UT, USA, Ancestry.com Operations, Inc., 2012), Ancestry.com, http://www.Ancestry.com, Record for Laurie J Vorhies.
[599] Ancestry.com, Social Security Death Index (Provo, UT, USA, The Generations Network, Inc., 2008), www.ancestry.com, Number: 093-26-0621; Issue State: New York; Issue Date: 1951. Record for John Leigh
[600] Ancestry.com, Social Security Death Index (Provo, UT, USA, The Generations Network, Inc., 2008), www.ancestry.com, Number: 093-26-0621; Issue State: New York; Issue Date: 1951. Record for John Leigh
[601] Ancestry.com, U.S., Social Security Applications and Claims Index, 1936-2007 (Provo, UT, USA, Ancestry.com Operations, Inc., 2015), Ancestry.com, http://www.Ancestry.com, Record for Anna E Unger.
[602] Ancestry.com, U.S., Social Security Applications and Claims Index, 1936-2007 (Provo, UT, USA, Ancestry.com Operations, Inc., 2015), Ancestry.com, http://www.Ancestry.com, Record for Anna E Unger.
[603] Ancestry.com, New York, County Marriages, 1847-1849; 1907-1936 (Lehi, UT, USA, Ancestry.com Operations, Inc., 2016), Ancestry.com, http://www.Ancestry.com, Record for Fred H Adams. http://search.ancestry.com/cgi-

Delta, New York[604] and died on 21 Aug 1947[605]. She married Ross E. Unger in 1946[606]. He was born on 10 Aug 1897 in New York State[607] and died in Aug 1967 in Syracuse, New York [608].   Fred Helmer Adams lived in Sherburne in Chenango County, New York when his WWI Draft registration was signed.

Fred Helmer Adams and Anna E Leigh had the following child:

      i.   George H. Adams was born on 21 Feb 1916 in New York[609] and died on 06 Jan 1987 in Santa Clara, California[610].

34. Claude Jay Leigh[4] (George Henry Leigh[3], William Todd Leigh[2], Nathan S. Leigh[1]) was born on 25 Sep 1885 in Oneida, New York[611] and died on 19 Sep 1957 in Oneida, New York[612]. He married Mary Eva Roehm, the daughter of John George Roehm and Maria P Mehl, on 23 Jan 1908 in Oneida, New York[613]. She was born on 11 Jan 1885 in Oneida, New York[614] and died on 10 Sep 1955 in Oneida , New York[615].   Claude Jay Leigh and his wife are buried in Glenwood Cemetery, Oneida, New York[616].   Claude was a retired electro typist and was last employed at the Smith-Lee Bottle Cap Corp. He was a member of St. Paul's Evangelical United Brethren Church and Oneida Lodge, F&AM.

---

[604] Ancestry.com, U.S. World War II Draft Registration Cards, 1942 (Provo, UT, USA, The Generations Network, Inc., 2007), www.ancestry.com. Record for Fred Helner Adams.

[605] Ancestry.com, U.S., Social Security Applications and Claims Index, 1936-2007 (Provo, UT, USA, Ancestry.com Operations, Inc., 2015), Ancestry.com, http://www.Ancestry.com, Record for Fred Helmer Adams.

[606] Obituary of Anna Elizabeth Leigh Unger, in the Chenango Union newspaper, Chenango, New York, September 24, 1952, page 5.

[607] Ancestry.com. *U.S., Social Security Death Index, 1935-2014* [database on-line]. Provo, UT, USA: Ancestry.com Operations Inc, 2014.

[608] Ancestry.com. *U.S., Social Security Death Index, 1935-2014* [database on-line]. Provo, UT, USA: Ancestry.com Operations Inc, 2014.

[609] Ancestry.com, California Death Index, 1940-1997 (Provo, UT, USA, The Generations Network, Inc., 2000), www.ancestry.com, Date: 1987-01-06. Record for George H Adams.

[610] Ancestry.com, California Death Index, 1940-1997 (Provo, UT, USA, The Generations Network, Inc., 2000), www.ancestry.com, Date: 1987-01-06. Record for George H Adams.

[611] Ancestry.com, World War I Draft Registration Cards, 1917-1918 (Provo, UT, USA, The Generations Network, Inc., 2005), www.ancestry.com, Database online. Registration Location: Madison County, New York; Roll: ; Draft Board:.

[612] Obituary, Rome Daily Sentinel, Sept 20, 1957, page 8.

[613] "New York, County Marriages, 1847-1848; 1908-1936," database with images, *FamilySearch* (https://familysearch.org/ark:/61903/1:1:V6H2-1J4 : 25 September 2017), Claude Jay Leigh and Mary Eva Roehm, 13 Feb 1908; citing county clerk's office, Madison, New York, United States; FHL microfilm 1,023,124.

[614] Ancestry.com, U.S., Social Security Applications and Claims Index, 1936-2007 (Provo, UT, USA, Ancestry.com Operations, Inc., 2015), Ancestry.com, http://www.Ancestry.com, Record for Maria E Leigh

[615] Ancestry.com, U.S., Social Security Applications and Claims Index, 1936-2007 (Provo, UT, USA, Ancestry.com Operations, Inc., 2015), Ancestry.com, http://www.Ancestry.com, Record for Maria E Leigh.

[616] Ancestry.com, Web: New York, Find A Grave Index, 1664-2011 (Provo, UT, USA, Ancestry.com Operations, Inc., 2012), www.ancestry.com, Database online.

Claude Jay Leigh and Mary Eva Roehm had the following children:
96.   i.   Doris M. Leigh was born on 27 Mar 1911 in Oneida , New York[617] and died on 02 Jan 2002 in Oneida, New York[618].
97.   ii.   Claude Jay Leigh Jr. was born on 06 Dec 1917 in Oneida, New York[619] and died on 12 Mar 2004 in Oneida, New York[620].
       iii.   Charles J. Leigh was born on 12 Jan 1924[621]. He married Marilyn Joan MacDaniels on 06 Jul 1945 in Fairmont Army Air Field, Geneva, Nebraska[622].

---

[617] Ancestry.com, Social Security Death Index (Provo, UT, USA, The Generations Network, Inc., 2008),
[618] Ancestry.com, Social Security Death Index (Provo, UT, USA, The Generations Network, Inc., 2008),
[619] Ancestry.com, Social Security Death Index (Provo, UT, USA, The Generations Network, Inc., 2008), www.ancestry.com,
[620] Ancestry.com, Social Security Death Index (Provo, UT, USA, The Generations Network, Inc., 2008), www.ancestry.com,
[621] National Archives and Records Administration, U.S. World War II Army Enlistment Records, 1938-1946 (Provo, UT, USA, The Generations Network, Inc., 2005), www.ancestry.com, Record for Charles J Leigh.
[622] Obituary, Madison County Times, Madison, New York, July 20, 1945.

Generation Five

35.   Gladys Gertrude[623] Berry[5] (Cyrus Nathan Leigh[4], Mary Abigale Leigh[3], Elijah Leigh[2], Nathan S. Leigh[1]) was born on 25 May 1886 in Minnesota and died on 26 Jan 1977 in Houston, Minnesota[624]. She married Paul Otto Gustav Ledebuhr[625] He was born on 28 Jul 1885 in Minnesota[626] and died on 16 Sep 1971 in Winona, Minnesota[627].   Gladys Gertrude Berry was buried in Money Creek, Minnesota[628].

Photo of Gladys Gertrude Berry from the collection of Kathryn Cummings and used with permission.

Photo of Paul Otto Gustav Ledebuhr from the collection of Kathryn Cummings and used with permission.

Paul Otto Gustav Ledebuhr and Gladys Gertrude Berry had the following children:
        i.   Lenard Ledebuhr was born on 12 Jan 1907[629] and died on 13 Aug 1995 in Houston, Minnesota[630].   He married Adeline Jane Rouse[631]. She was born on 02 Mar 1910

[623] Ancestry.com, Minnesota, Death Index, 1908-2002 (Provo, UT, USA, Ancestry.com Operations Inc, 2001), Ancestry.com, http://www.Ancestry.com, Record for Gladys Gertrude Ledebuhr. http://search.ancestry.com/cgi-bin/sse.dll?db=7316&h=1512685&indiv=try.

[624] Ancestry.com, Minnesota, Death Index, 1908-2002 (Provo, UT, USA, Ancestry.com Operations Inc, 2001), Ancestry.com, http://www.Ancestry.com, Record for Gladys Gertrude Ledebuhr. http://search.ancestry.com/cgi-bin/sse.dll?db=7316&h=1512685&indiv=try.

[625] Ancestry.com, 1930 United States Federal Census (Provo, UT, USA, The Generations Network, Inc., 2002), www.ancestry.com, Year: 1930; Census Place: Money Creek, Houston, Minnesota; Roll: 1101; Page: 6B; Enumeration District: 0015; Image: 759.0; FHL microfilm: 2340836. Record for Paul G Ledebuhr.

[626] Ancestry.com, World War I Draft Registration Cards, 1917-1918 (Provo, UT, USA, The Generations Network, Inc., 2005), www.ancestry.com, Registration State: Minnesota; Registration County: Houston; Roll: 1675470. Record for Paul Otto Ledebuhr.

[627] Ancestry.com, Minnesota, Death Index, 1908-2002 (Provo, UT, USA, Ancestry.com Operations Inc, 2001), Ancestry.com, http://www.Ancestry.com, Record for Paul Otto Ledebuhr.

[628] Ancestry.com, U.S., Find A Grave Index, 1700s-Current (Provo, UT, USA, Ancestry.com Operations, Inc., 2012), Ancestry.com, http://www.Ancestry.com, Record for Gladys Ledebuhr.

[629] Ancestry.com, Minnesota, Death Index, 1908-2002 (Provo, UT, USA, Ancestry.com Operations Inc, 2001), Ancestry.com, http://www.Ancestry.com, Record for Lenard Ledebuhr.

[630] Ancestry.com, Minnesota, Death Index, 1908-2002 (Provo, UT, USA, Ancestry.com Operations Inc, 2001), Ancestry.com, http://www.Ancestry.com, Record for Lenard Ledebuhr.

[631] Ancestry.com. *U.S., Find A Grave Index, 1600s-Current* [database on-line]. Provo, UT, USA: Ancestry.com Operations, Inc., 2012.

in Minnesota[632] and died on 22 May 1981 in Minnesota[633]. Lenard Ledebuhr was buried in Money Creek, Minnesota[634].

Photo of Lenard Ledebuhr and his wife Adeline Jane Rouse from the collection of Kathryn Cummings and used with permission.

98.   ii.   Victor Ledebuhr was born on 22 Jul 1908 in Houston, Minnesota[635] and died on 25 Oct 1968 in Winona, Minnesota[636].

99.   iii.   August Ledebuhr was born on 19 Aug 1913 in Houston, Minnesota[637] and died on 18 May 1970 in Hennepin, Minnesota[638].

100.   iv.   Goldie L. Ledebuhr was born on 01 Nov 1919[639] and died on 26 Jan 1985[640].

     v.   Eva Ledebuhr was born in August 28, 1925 in Houston, Minnesota[641] and died 4 Jan 2005 in Chatfield, Minnesota[642]. She married a man with the last name of Cummings.

---

[632] Ancestry.com. *U.S., Find A Grave Index, 1600s-Current* [database on-line]. Provo, UT, USA: Ancestry.com Operations, Inc., 2012.

[633] Ancestry.com. *U.S., Find A Grave Index, 1600s-Current* [database on-line]. Provo, UT, USA: Ancestry.com Operations, Inc., 2012.

[634] Ancestry.com. *U.S., Find A Grave Index, 1600s-Current* [database on-line]. Provo, UT, USA: Ancestry.com Operations, Inc., 2012.

[635] Ancestry.com, Minnesota, Death Index, 1908-2002 (Provo, UT, USA, Ancestry.com Operations Inc, 2001), Ancestry.com, http://www.Ancestry.com, Record for Victor Ledebuhr.

[636] Ancestry.com, Minnesota, Death Index, 1908-2002 (Provo, UT, USA, Ancestry.com Operations Inc, 2001), Ancestry.com, http://www.Ancestry.com, Record for Victor Ledebuhr.

[637] Ancestry.com, Minnesota, Death Index, 1908-2002 (Provo, UT, USA, Ancestry.com Operations Inc, 2001), Ancestry.com, http://www.Ancestry.com, Record for August Ledebuhr.

[638] Ancestry.com, Minnesota, Death Index, 1908-2002 (Provo, UT, USA, Ancestry.com Operations Inc, 2001), Ancestry.com, http://www.Ancestry.com, Record for August Ledebuhr.

[639] Ancestry.com, Social Security Death Index (Provo, UT, USA, The Generations Network, Inc., 2008), www.ancestry.com, Number: 503-64-8013; Issue State: South Dakota; Issue Date: 1966. Record for Goldie Kiral.

[640] Ancestry.com, Social Security Death Index (Provo, UT, USA, The Generations Network, Inc., 2008), www.ancestry.com, Number: 503-64-8013; Issue State: South Dakota; Issue Date: 1966. Record for Goldie Kiral.

[641] Ancestry.com. *Web: Minnesota, Birth Index, 1900-1934* [database on-line]. Provo, UT, USA: Ancestry.com Operations, Inc., 2015.

[642] Ancestry.com. *U.S., Social Security Death Index, 1935-2014* [database on-line]. Provo, UT, USA: Ancestry.com Operations Inc, 2014.

36. Cyrus Gilbert Berry[5] (Cyrus Nathan Leigh[4], Mary Abigale Leigh[3], Elijah Leigh[2], Nathan S. Leigh[1]) was born on 22 Oct 1887 in Minnesota[643] and died on 01 Sep 1970 in Muskegon County, Michigan[644]. He married Klea Ione Sovacool on 12 Jan 1912 in Muskegon, Michigan, the daughter of Mr. and Mrs. Delzon B. Sovacool[645]. She was born on 06 Apr 1893 in Nebraska[646] and died on 20 Nov 1990 in North Muskegon, Michigan[647]. Cyrus Gilbert Berry and his wife were buried in North Muskegon, Michigan[648].

Photo of Cyrus Gilbert Berry and his wife, Klea Ione Sovacool, from the collection of Kathryn Cummings and used with permission.

Cyrus Gilbert Berry and Klea Ione Sovacool had the following children:

101. i. Nathan Delzon Berry was born on 10 Aug 1913 in Houston County, Minnesota[649] and died in Jun 1968 in Muskegon County, Michigan[650].

102. ii. Inez Beulah Berry was born in 1915 in Michigan[651] and died in 2002 in Michigan[652].

---

[643] Ancestry.com, U.S., Find A Grave Index, 1700s-Current (Provo, UT, USA, Ancestry.com Operations, Inc., 2012), Ancestry.com, http://www.Ancestry.com, Record for Cyrus Gilbert Berry. http://search.ancestry.com/cgi-bin/sse.dll?db=60525&h=91500307&indiv=try.

[644] Ancestry.com, U.S., Find A Grave Index, 1700s-Current (Provo, UT, USA, Ancestry.com Operations, Inc., 2012), Ancestry.com, http://www.Ancestry.com, Record for Cyrus Gilbert Berry. http://search.ancestry.com/cgi-bin/sse.dll?db=60525&h=91500307&indiv=try.

[645] Familysearch.org, Michigan Marriages, 1822-1995.

[646] Ancestry.com, U.S., Find A Grave Index, 1700s-Current (Provo, UT, USA, Ancestry.com Operations, Inc., 2012), Ancestry.com, http://www.Ancestry.com, Record for Cyrus Gilbert Berry.

[647] Ancestry.com, U.S., Find A Grave Index, 1700s-Current (Provo, UT, USA, Ancestry.com Operations, Inc., 2012), Ancestry.com, http://www.Ancestry.com, Record for Cyrus Gilbert Berry.

[648] Ancestry.com, U.S., Find A Grave Index, 1700s-Current (Provo, UT, USA, Ancestry.com Operations, Inc., 2012), Ancestry.com, http://www.Ancestry.com, Record for Cyrus Gilbert Berry.

[649] Ancestry.com, U.S., Find A Grave Index, 1700s-Current (Provo, UT, USA, Ancestry.com Operations, Inc., 2012), Ancestry.com, http://www.Ancestry.com.

[650] Ancestry.com, U.S., Find A Grave Index, 1700s-Current (Provo, UT, USA, Ancestry.com Operations, Inc., 2012), Ancestry.com, http://www.Ancestry.com.

[651] Ancestry.com, U.S., Find A Grave Index, 1700s-Current (Provo, UT, USA, Ancestry.com Operations, Inc., 2012), Ancestry.com, http://www.Ancestry.com.

[652] Ancestry.com, U.S., Find A Grave Index, 1700s-Current (Provo, UT, USA, Ancestry.com Operations, Inc., 2012), Ancestry.com, http://www.Ancestry.com.

103.   iii.   Florence Stella Berry was born on 13 May 1918 in North Muskegon, Michigan[653] and died on 21 Jan 2006 in Muskegon, Michigan[654].

104.   iv.   Gilbert C. Berry Jr. was born on 31 Jan 1921 in Muskegon, Michigan[655] and died on 25 Oct 2007 in Muskegon, Michigan[656].

v.   Gordon R. Berry was born on 04 Apr 1923 in Muskegon County, Michigan[657] and died on 03 May 1923 in Casnovia, Michigan (He only lived 31 days[658].   Gordon R. Berry was buried in North Muskegon, Michigan[659].

Photo of Cyrus Gilbert Berry, his wife, Klea Ione Sovacool, and their first two children from the collection of Kathryn Cummings and used with permission.

vi.   Helen Irene Berry was born on 28 Oct 1926 in Michigan[660] and died on 27 May 2006 in Michigan[661]. She married Raymond Eugene Puffer, the son of Ira Puffer and Lottie M. Frece, on 20 Jan 1943 in Muskegon, Michigan[662]. He was born on 06 May 1928 in Muskegon, Michigan[663] and died on 20 Feb 2005[664]. Helen Irene Berry was buried in North Muskegon, Michigan[665].

---

[653] Ancestry.com, U.S., Find A Grave Index, 1700s-Current (Provo, UT, USA, Ancestry.com Operations, Inc., 2012), Ancestry.com, http://www.Ancestry.com.

[654] Ancestry.com, U.S., Find A Grave Index, 1700s-Current (Provo, UT, USA, Ancestry.com Operations, Inc., 2012), Ancestry.com, http://www.Ancestry.com.

[655] Ancestry.com, U.S., Find A Grave Index, 1700s-Current (Provo, UT, USA, Ancestry.com Operations, Inc., 2012), Ancestry.com, http://www.Ancestry.com.

[656] Ancestry.com, U.S., Find A Grave Index, 1700s-Current (Provo, UT, USA, Ancestry.com Operations, Inc., 2012), Ancestry.com, http://www.Ancestry.com.

[657] Ancestry.com, U.S., Find A Grave Index, 1700s-Current (Provo, UT, USA, Ancestry.com Operations, Inc., 2012), Ancestry.com, http://www.Ancestry.com.

[658] Ancestry.com, U.S., Find A Grave Index, 1700s-Current (Provo, UT, USA, Ancestry.com Operations, Inc., 2012), Ancestry.com, http://www.Ancestry.com.

[659] Ancestry.com, U.S., Find A Grave Index, 1700s-Current (Provo, UT, USA, Ancestry.com Operations, Inc., 2012), Ancestry.com, http://www.Ancestry.com.

[660] Ancestry.com, U.S., Find A Grave Index, 1700s-Current (Provo, UT, USA, Ancestry.com Operations, Inc., 2012), Ancestry.com, http://www.Ancestry.com.

[661] Ancestry.com, U.S., Find A Grave Index, 1700s-Current (Provo, UT, USA, Ancestry.com Operations, Inc., 2012), Ancestry.com, http://www.Ancestry.com.

[662] Ancestry.com, Michigan, Marriage Records, 1867-1952 (Record for Mr R E Puffer.

[663] Ancestry.com, Michigan, Marriage Records, 1867-1952 (Record for Mr R E Puffer.

[664] Ancestry.com, U.S., Social Security Applications and Claims Index, 1936-2007 (Provo, UT, USA, Ancestry.com Operations, Inc., 2015), Ancestry.com, http://www.Ancestry.com, Record for Raymond Eugene Puffer.

[665] Ancestry.com, U.S., Find A Grave Index, 1700s-Current (Provo, UT, USA, Ancestry.com Operations, Inc., 2012), Ancestry.com, http://www.Ancestry.com.

37. Myrtle Mae Berry[5] (Cyrus Nathan Leigh[4], Mary Abigale Leigh[3], Elijah Leigh[2], Nathan S. Leigh[1]) was born on 17 Jul 1889 in Pleasant Hill Township, Minnesota[666] and died on 26 Sep 1966 in Wisconsin[667]. She married Joseph Francis Kowalewski, the son of Andrew J. Kowalewski and Ida Bartz, on 09 Oct 1911 in Winona, Minnesota[668]. He was born on 27 Nov 1889 in Minnesota[669] and died on 07 Feb 1916 in Winona, Minnesota[670]. She later married John H. Noren on 30 Aug 1928. He was born on 16 Apr 1890[671] and died on 01 Jan 1969 in Wisconsin[672]. John H. Noren was buried in Black River Falls, Wisconsin[673]. Myrtle Mae Berry was buried in Black River Falls, Wisconsin[674]. Joseph Francis Kowalewski was buried in Winona, Minnesota[675].

Photo of Myrtle Mae Berry from the collection of Kathryn Cummings and used with permission.

---

[666] Ancestry.com, Wisconsin Death Index, 1959-1997 (Provo, UT, USA, Ancestry.com Operations Inc, 2007), Ancestry.com, http://www.Ancestry.com, Record for Myrtle Noren.

[667] Ancestry.com, Wisconsin Death Index, 1959-1997 (Provo, UT, USA, Ancestry.com Operations Inc, 2007), Ancestry.com, http://www.Ancestry.com, Record for Myrtle Noren.

[668] Ancestry.com. Minnesota, Marriages Index, 1849-1950 [database on-line]. Provo, UT, USA: Ancestry.com Operations, Inc., 2011.

[669] Ancestry.com, U.S., Find A Grave Index, 1700s-Current (Provo, UT, USA, Ancestry.com Operations, Inc., 2012), Ancestry.com, http://www.Ancestry.com, Record for Joseph Kowalewski.

[670] Ancestry.com, U.S., Find A Grave Index, 1700s-Current (Provo, UT, USA, Ancestry.com Operations, Inc., 2012), Ancestry.com, http://www.Ancestry.com, Record for Joseph Kowalewski.

[671] Ancestry.com, Wisconsin Death Index, 1959-1997 (Provo, UT, USA, Ancestry.com Operations Inc, 2007), Ancestry.com, http://www.Ancestry.com, Record for John Noren.

[672] Ancestry.com, Wisconsin Death Index, 1959-1997 (Provo, UT, USA, Ancestry.com Operations Inc, 2007), Ancestry.com, http://www.Ancestry.com, Record for John Noren.

[673] Ancestry.com, U.S., Find A Grave Index, 1700s-Current (Provo, UT, USA, Ancestry.com Operations, Inc., 2012), Ancestry.com, http://www.Ancestry.com,

[674] Ancestry.com, U.S., Find A Grave Index, 1700s-Current (Provo, UT, USA, Ancestry.com Operations, Inc., 2012), Ancestry.com, http://www.Ancestry.com, Record for Myrtle M Noren.

[675] Ancestry.com, U.S., Find A Grave Index, 1700s-Current (Provo, UT, USA, Ancestry.com Operations, Inc., 2012), Ancestry.com, http://www.Ancestry.com, Record for Joseph Kowalewski.

Joseph Francis Kowalewski and Myrtle Mae Berry had the following children:

      i.   Harry Lester Kowalewski was born on 08 Aug 1912 in Buffalo, Wisconsin[676] and died on 06 Mar 1992 in Volusia, Florida[677]. He married Ethel Mae Pearce on 12 Nov 1943 in Pierce, Washington[678]. She was born on 03 Apr 1908[679] and died on 19 Aug 1983 in Olmsted, Minnesota[680]. Ethel Mae Pearce was buried in Saint Charles, Minnesota[681].

105. ii.   Hazel Kowalewski was born on 18 Dec 1914 in Winona, Minnesota[682] and died on 20 May 1995 in Tomah, Wisconsin[683].

106. iii.   Donald Frank Kowalewski was born on 21 Jun 1917[684] and died on 20 Jun 2003[685].

John H. Noren and Myrtle Mae Berry had the following child:

107. iv.   Violet Noren was born on 01 Mar 1930 in Ettrick, Wisconsin[686] 435 and died on 18 Dec 2012 in Whitehall, Wisconsin[687].

Photo of Joseph Francis Kowalewski from the collection of Kathryn Cummings and used with permission.

[676] Ancestry.com, Florida Death Index, 1877-1998 (Provo, UT, USA, The Generations Network, Inc., 2004), www.ancestry.com, Record for Harry L Kowalewski.

[677] Ancestry.com, Florida Death Index, 1877-1998 (Provo, UT, USA, The Generations Network, Inc., 2004), www.ancestry.com, Record for Harry L Kowalewski.

[678] Ancestry.com, Washington, County Marriages, 1855-2008 (Provo, UT, USA, Ancestry.com Operations, Inc., 2014), Ancestry.com, http://www.Ancestry.com, Record for Ethel Mae Pearce.

[679] Ancestry.com, Minnesota, Death Index, 1908-2002 (Provo, UT, USA, Ancestry.com Operations Inc, 2001), Ancestry.com, http://www.Ancestry.com, Record for Ethel Kowalewski.

[680] Ancestry.com, Minnesota, Death Index, 1908-2002 (Provo, UT, USA, Ancestry.com Operations Inc, 2001), Ancestry.com, http://www.Ancestry.com, Record for Ethel Kowalewski.

[681] Ancestry.com, Minnesota, Death Index, 1908-2002 (Provo, UT, USA, Ancestry.com Operations Inc, 2001), Ancestry.com, http://www.Ancestry.com, Record for Ethel Kowalewski

[682] Ancestry.com, Social Security Death Index (Provo, UT, USA, The Generations Network, Inc., 2008), www.ancestry.com, Number: 395-14-4780; Issue State: Wisconsin; Issue Date: Before 1951. Record for Hazel Harmon.

[683] Ancestry.com, Social Security Death Index (Provo, UT, USA, The Generations Network, Inc., 2008), www.ancestry.com, Number: 395-14-4780; Issue State: Wisconsin; Issue Date: Before 1951. Record for Hazel Harmon.

Ancestry.com, U.S., Find A Grave Index, 1700s-Current (Provo, UT, USA, Ancestry.com Operations, Inc., 2012), Ancestry.com, http://www.Ancestry.com, Record for Donald F Kowalski.

[684] Ancestry.com, U.S., Find A Grave Index, 1700s-Current (Provo, UT, USA, Ancestry.com Operations, Inc., 2012), Ancestry.com, http://www.Ancestry.com, Record for Donald F Kowalski.

[685] Ancestry.com, U.S., Find A Grave Index, 1700s-Current (Provo, UT, USA, Ancestry.com Operations, Inc., 2012), Ancestry.com, http://www.Ancestry.com, Record for Donald F Kowalski.

[686] Ancestry.com, U.S., Find A Grave Index, 1700s-Current (Provo, UT, USA, Ancestry.com Operations, Inc., 2012),

[687] Ancestry.com, U.S., Find A Grave Index, 1700s-Current (Provo, UT, USA, Ancestry.com Operations, Inc., 2012),

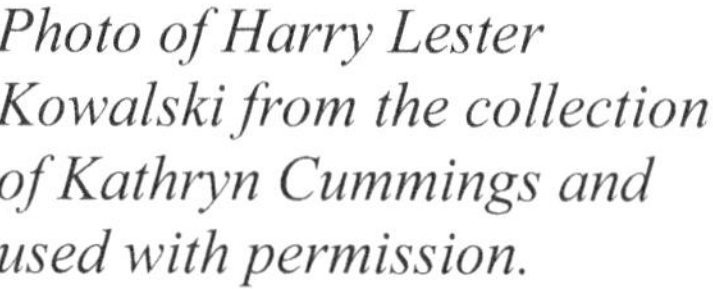

Photo of Violet F. Noren found on Ancestry.com.

Photo of Harry Lester Kowalski from the collection of Kathryn Cummings and used with permission.

38. Ivan Lee Berry[5] (Cyrus Nathan Leigh[4], Mary Abigale Leigh[3], Elijah Leigh[2], Nathan S. Leigh[1]) was born on 20 Apr 1891 in Pleasant Hill, Minnesota[688] and died on 13 May 1970 in Muskegon, Michigan[689]. He married Gladys Irene Horton on 23 Aug 1919 in Muskegon, Michigan[690]. She was born on 07 Aug 1895 in Michigan[691] and died on 06 Apr 1974 in Muskegon, Michigan[692]. Ivan Lee Berry was buried in Muskegon, Michigan[693].

Photo of Ivan Berry, and his wife, Gladys Irene Horton, from the collection of Kathryn Cummings and used with permission.

---

[688] Ancestry.com, U.S., Find A Grave Index, 1700s-Current (Provo, UT, USA, Ancestry.com Operations, Inc., 2012), Ancestry.com, http://www.Ancestry.com, Record for Ivan L Berry.

[689] Ancestry.com, U.S., Find A Grave Index, 1700s-Current (Provo, UT, USA, Ancestry.com Operations, Inc., 2012), Ancestry.com, http://www.Ancestry.com, Record for Ivan L Berry.

[690] Ancestry.com. Michigan, Marriage Records, 1867-1952 [database on-line]. Provo, UT, USA: Ancestry.com Operations, Inc., 2015.

[691] Michigan Department of Vital and Health Records, Michigan, Death Index, 1971-1996 (Provo, UT, USA, Ancestry.com Operations Inc, 1998), Ancestry.com,

[692] Michigan Department of Vital and Health Records, Michigan, Death Index, 1971-1996 (Provo, UT, USA, Ancestry.com Operations Inc, 1998), Ancestry.com, http://www.Ancestry.com, Record for Gladys B Berry.

[693] Ancestry.com, U.S., Find A Grave Index, 1700s-Current (Provo, UT, USA, Ancestry.com Operations, Inc., 2012), Ancestry.com, http://www.Ancestry.com, Record for Ivan L Berry

Ivan Lee Berry and Gladys Irene Horton had the following child:

  i. Melvin Lee Berry was born on 21 Mar 1920 in Laketon Town, Michigan[694] and died on 02 Apr 2006[695]. He married Charlene Durham, the daughter of Charles Roy Durham and Gladie Marsh[696]. She was born on 23 Mar 1933 in Pangburn, Arkansas[697] and died on 18 Jul 2016[698]. Melvin Lee Berry and his wife were buried in Searcy, Arkansas[699].

Melvin Lee Berry, age 86, of Searcy, died Sunday, April 2, 2006. He was born Sunday, March 21, 1920 in Muskegon, Michigan to Ivan and Gladys Horton Berry. He is survived by his wife Charlene and several cousins along with a host of other family and friends. Mr. Berry was a member of the Fraternal Order of Police, a Life Member of the Michigan Mineralogical Society, and a founding member of the Friends of the Museum of Paleontology on the campus of the University of Michigan.

Charlene Durham Berry, 84, of Wilburn, Arkansas passed away July 18, 2016. She was born March 23, 1933 in Pangburn, Arkansas to the late Charles Roy Durham and Gladie Marsh Durham. She was also preceded in death by her husband, Melvin Berry, two brothers and two sisters. Charlene was an armature Paleontologist and enjoyed traveling to discover new and unique areas. She was active in different organizations in this field on the local and national levels. She is survived by her brother Charles H. Durham of Wilburn, Arkansas along with many nieces and nephews and a host of friends.

Photo of Melvin Lee Berry from the collection of Kathryn Cummings and used with permission.

39. Alta Irene Berry[5] (Cyrus Nathan Leigh[4], Mary Abigale Leigh[3], Elijah Leigh[2], Nathan S. Leigh[1]) was born on 29 Sep 1894 in Money Creek, Minnesota[700] and died on 26 Feb

[694] Ancestry.com, U.S., Social Security Applications and Claims Index, 1936-2007 (Provo, UT, USA, Ancestry.com Operations, Inc., 2015), Ancestry.com, http://www.Ancestry.com, Record for Melvin Lee Berry

[695] Ancestry.com, U.S., Social Security Applications and Claims Index, 1936-2007 (Provo, UT, USA, Ancestry.com Operations, Inc., 2015), Ancestry.com, http://www.Ancestry.com, Record for Melvin Lee Berry

[696] Ancestry.com, U.S., Find A Grave Index, 1700s-Current, Record for Charlene Berry.

[697] Ancestry.com, U.S., Find A Grave Index, 1700s-Current, Record for Charlene Berry.

[698] Ancestry.com, U.S., Find A Grave Index, 1700s-Current, Record for Charlene Berry.

[699] Ancestry.com, U.S., Find A Grave Index, 1700s-Current, Record for Charlene Berry.

[700] Ancestry.com, Minnesota, Marriages Index, 1849-1950 (Provo, UT, USA, Ancestry.com Operations, Inc., 2011), Ancestry.com, http://www.Ancestry.com, Record for Alta Berry.

1954 in Yonkers, New York[701]. She married John A. Kowalski on 18 Apr 1911 in Winona, Minnesota[702]. He was born in 1887[703] and died in 1921[704]. She later married C. Tracy[705]. He was born in 1890[706].

John A. Kowalski and Alta Irene Berry had the following children:

108.   i.   Valentine John Kowalewski was born on 04 Jul 1911 in Wisconsin[707] and died on 28 Jan 1998 in Wabasha, Minnesota[708].

    ii.   Ida Mayme Kowalewski born on 07 Nov 1913 in Houston, Minnesota[709] and died on 29 May 1923[710].

    iii.   Mary Kowalewski was born on 18 Jan 1916[711] and died on 28 Jan 1990[712]. She married Mr. Murchie and later Mr. Schleininger. Mary Kowalewski was buried in Money Creek, Minnesota[713].

Photo of Alta Irene Berry from the collection of Kathryn Cummings and used with permission.

---

[701] Obituary, The Winona Republican-Herald, Winona, Minnesota, March 1, 1954, page 9.

[702] Ancestry.com, Minnesota, Marriages Index, 1849-1950 (Provo, UT, USA, Ancestry.com Operations, Inc., 2011), Ancestry.com, http://www.Ancestry.com, Record for Alta Berry.

[703] Ancestry.com, Minnesota, Marriages Index, 1849-1950 (Provo, UT, USA, Ancestry.com Operations, Inc., 2011), Ancestry.com, http://www.Ancestry.com, Record for Alta Berry.

[704] Genealogy compiled by Rev. Laverne E. Leigh in 2017.

[705] Genealogy compiled by Rev. Laverne E. Leigh in 2017.

[706] Genealogy compiled by Rev. Laverne E. Leigh in 2017.

[707] Ancestry.com, Minnesota, Death Index, 1908-2002 (Provo, UT, USA, Ancestry.com Operations Inc, 2001), Ancestry.com, http://www.Ancestry.com, Record for Valentine John Kowalewski.

[708] Ancestry.com, Minnesota, Death Index, 1908-2002 (Provo, UT, USA, Ancestry.com Operations Inc, 2001), Ancestry.com, http://www.Ancestry.com, Record for Valentine John Kowalewski.

[709] Ancestry.com. *Web: Minnesota, Birth Index, 1900-1934* [database on-line]. Provo, UT, USA: Ancestry.com Operations, Inc., 2015.

[710] Ancestry.com, Minnesota, Death Index, 1908-2002

[711] Ancestry.com, U.S., Social Security Applications and Claims Index, 1936-2007 (Provo, UT, USA, Ancestry.com Operations, Inc., 2015), Ancestry.com, http://www.Ancestry.com, Record for Mary Kowalewski Murchie.

[712] Ancestry.com, U.S., Social Security Applications and Claims Index, 1936-2007 (Provo, UT, USA, Ancestry.com Operations, Inc., 2015), Ancestry.com, http://www.Ancestry.com, Record for Mary Kowalewski Murchie.

[713] Ancestry.com, U.S., Find A Grave Index, 1700s-Current (Provo, UT, USA, Ancestry.com Operations, Inc., 2012), Ancestry.com, http://www.Ancestry.com, Record for Mary M Schleininger.

40. Roy Lester Berry[5] (Cyrus Nathan Leigh[4], Mary Abigale Leigh[3], Elijah Leigh[2], Nathan S. Leigh[1]) was born on 09 Mar 1901[714] and died on 27 Jan 1969 in Hixton, Wisconsin[715]. He married Edna Laviola Sonnenberg[716]. She was born on 15 Jan 1904[717] and died on 01 Apr 2000 in Black River Falls, Wisconsin[718]. Roy Lester Berry was buried in Black River Falls, Wisconsin[719]. Edna Laviola Sonnenberg was buried in Melrose, Wisconsin[720].

Photo of Roy Lester Berry and Edna Laviola Sonnenberg from the collection of Kathryn Cummings and used with permission.

Roy Lester Berry and Edna Laviola Sonnenberg had the following children:

i.   Beulah Blanch Berry was born on 10 Sep 1921 in Wisconsin[721] and died on 11 Jun 2017 in Black River Falls, Wisconsin[722]. She married George Sanford Severson[723]. He was

[714] Ancestry.com, Social Security Death Index (Provo, UT, USA, The Generations Network, Inc., 2008), www.ancestry.com, Number: 387-16-5555; Issue State: Wisconsin; Issue Date: Before 1951. Record for Roy Berry.
[715] Ancestry.com, Social Security Death Index (Provo, UT, USA, The Generations Network, Inc., 2008), www.ancestry.com, Number: 387-16-5555; Issue State: Wisconsin; Issue Date: Before 1951. Record for Roy Berry.
[716] Ancestry.com, 1940 United States Federal Census (Provo, UT, USA, Ancestry.com Operations, Inc., 2012), www.ancestry.com, Year: 1940; Census Place: Springfield, Jackson, Wisconsin;
[717] Ancestry.com, Social Security Death Index (Provo, UT, USA, The Generations Network, Inc., 2008), www.ancestry.com, Number: 374-20-2046; Issue State: Michigan; Issue Date: Before 1951. Record for Edna L. Berry.
[718] Ancestry.com, Social Security Death Index (Provo, UT, USA, The Generations Network, Inc., 2008), www.ancestry.com, Number: 374-20-2046; Issue State: Michigan; Issue Date: Before 1951. Record for Edna L. Berry.
[719] Ancestry.com, U.S., Find A Grave Index, 1700s-Current (Provo, UT, USA, Ancestry.com Operations, Inc., 2012), Ancestry.com, http://www.Ancestry.com, Record for Roy L. Berry.
[720] Ancestry.com, U.S., Find A Grave Index, 1700s-Current (Provo, UT, USA, Ancestry.com Operations, Inc., 2012), Ancestry.com, http://www.Ancestry.com, Record for Beulah Blanche Severson.
[721] Ancestry.com, U.S., Find A Grave Index, 1700s-Current (Provo, UT, USA, Ancestry.com Operations, Inc., 2012), Ancestry.com, http://www.Ancestry.com, Record for Beulah Blanche Severson
[722] Ancestry.com, U.S., Find A Grave Index, 1700s-Current (Provo, UT, USA, Ancestry.com Operations, Inc., 2012), Ancestry.com, http://www.Ancestry.com, Record for Beulah Blanche Severson
[723] Ancestry.com, U.S., Find A Grave Index, 1700s-Current (Provo, UT, USA, Ancestry.com Operations, Inc., 2012), Ancestry.com, http://www.Ancestry.com, Record for George Sanford Severson.

born on 29 Sep 1909 in Jackson County, Wisconsin[724] and died on 24 Nov 1997 in Black River Falls, Wisconsin[725]. Beulah Blanch Berry and her husband were buried in Black River Falls, Wisconsin[726].

Beulah Blanche (Berry) Severson, 95, of Black River Falls passed away peacefully, surrounded by her family on June 11, 2017 at the Pine View Care Center. Funeral services will be held Friday, June 16, 2017, 10:30 a.m., at the United Methodist Church, Black River Falls, WI. Reverend Kathleen Jury will be officiating. Burial will follow in Riverside Cemetery, Black River Falls. Family and friends are invited for visitation Thursday, June 15, 2017, from 5:00 p.m. until 7:00 p.m., at Buswell Funeral Home, Black River Falls, and again Friday, from 9:30 a.m. until the time of the service at the church. Buswell Funeral Home of Black River Falls is assisting the family with arrangements

ii.   Alice Berry was born on 14 Jun 1924[727] and died on 26 Sep 2009 in Black River Falls, Wisconsin[728]. She married John Martin Hagen[729].

iii.   Living Berry.

iv.   Living Berry.

Photo of Harry Glen Berry from Ancestry.com.

41.   Harry Glen Berry[5] (Edward Ulysses Berry[4], Mary Abigale Leigh[3], Elijah Leigh[2], Nathan S. Leigh[1]) was born on 08 Jul 1905 in Houston, Minnesota[730] and died on 17 Apr 1990 in Winona, Minnesota[731]. He married Mabel Celia Holtzclaw[732]. She was born on 05 May 1909 in Amherst,

[724] Ancestry.com, Social Security Death Index (Provo, UT, USA, The Generations Network, Inc., 2008), www.ancestry.com, Number: 397-14-9535; Issue State: Wisconsin; Issue Date: Before 1951. Record for George S. Severson.

[725] Ancestry.com, Social Security Death Index (Provo, UT, USA, The Generations Network, Inc., 2008), www.ancestry.com, Number: 397-14-9535; Issue State: Wisconsin; Issue Date: Before 1951. Record for George S. Severson.

[726] Ancestry.com, U.S., Find A Grave Index, 1700s-Current (Provo, UT, USA, Ancestry.com Operations, Inc., 2012), Ancestry.com, http://www.Ancestry.com, Record for Beulah Blanche Severson

[727] Ancestry.com, Social Security Death Index (Provo, UT, USA, The Generations Network, Inc., 2008), www.ancestry.com, Issue State: Michigan; Issue Date: Before 1951. Record for Alice Hagen.

[728] Ancestry.com, Social Security Death Index (Provo, UT, USA, The Generations Network, Inc., 2008), www.ancestry.com, Issue State: Michigan; Issue Date: Before 1951. Record for Alice Hagen.

[729] Ancestry.com, Social Security Death Index (Provo, UT, USA, The Generations Network, Inc., 2008), www.ancestry.com, Issue State: Michigan; Issue Date: Before 1951. Record for Alice Hagen.

[730] Ancestry.com, Minnesota, Death Index, 1908-2002, Record for Harry Glen Berry.

[731] Ancestry.com, Minnesota, Death Index, 1908-2002, Record for Harry Glen Berry.

[732] Ancestry.com, U.S., Find A Grave Index, 1700s-Current (Provo, UT, USA, Ancestry.com Operations, Inc., 2012), Ancestry.com, http://www.Ancestry.com, Record for Harry Glenn Berry

Minnesota[733] and died on 10 Sep 1996 in Winona, Minnesota[734]. He later married Ellen Muller[735]. She was born in 1909 in Minnesota[736]. Harry Glen Berry and his wife Mabel were buried in Lanesboro, Minnesota[737]. Harry Glen Berry and Ellen Muller had two children who may still be living.

42. Harley Berry Wood[5] (Lydia A. Berry[4], Mary Abigale Leigh[3], Elijah Leigh[2], Nathan S. Leigh[1]) was born on 07 Dec 1907 in Houston, Minnesota[738] and died on 31 Jan 1968 in Houston, Minnesota[739]. He married Alyce Benora Lauritzen, the daughter of Olaf Lauritzen and Kari Kolstad, on 05 Oct 1936 in Money Creek, Minnesota[740]. She was born on 05 Jul 1916 in Spring Grove, Minnesota[741] and died on 06 Mar 1995[742]. Alyce B Wood was buried in Money Creek, Minnesota[743]. Harley Berry Wood and Alyce Benora Lauritzen had one daughter who may still be living.

Wedding photo of Harley Berry Wood and Alyce Benora Lauritzen from Ancestry.com.

---

[733] Ancestry.com, U.S., Find A Grave Index, 1700s-Current (Provo, UT, USA, Ancestry.com Operations, Inc., 2012), Ancestry.com, http://www.Ancestry.com, Record for Harry Glenn Berry

[734] Ancestry.com, U.S., Find A Grave Index, 1700s-Current (Provo, UT, USA, Ancestry.com Operations, Inc., 2012), Ancestry.com, http://www.Ancestry.com, Record for Harry Glenn Berry

[735] Ancestry.com, 1940 United States Federal Census (Provo, UT, USA, Ancestry.com Operations, Inc., 2012), www.ancestry.com, Year: 1940; Census Place: Winona, Winona, Minnesota; Roll: T627_1969; Page: 2A; Enumeration District: 85-28A. Record for Rosellen Berry

[736] Ancestry.com, 1940 United States Federal Census (Provo, UT, USA, Ancestry.com Operations, Inc., 2012), www.ancestry.com, Year: 1940; Census Place: Winona, Winona, Minnesota; Roll: T627_1969; Page: 2A; Enumeration District: 85-28A. Record for Rosellen Berry

[737] Ancestry.com, U.S., Find A Grave Index, 1700s-Current (Provo, UT, USA, Ancestry.com Operations, Inc., 2012), Ancestry.com, http://www.Ancestry.com, Record for Harry Glenn Berry

[738] Ancestry.com, Minnesota, Death Index, 1908-2002 (Provo, UT, USA, Ancestry.com Operations Inc, 2001), Ancestry.com, http://www.Ancestry.com, Record for Harley Berry Wood.

[739] Ancestry.com, Minnesota, Death Index, 1908-2002 (Provo, UT, USA, Ancestry.com Operations Inc, 2001), Ancestry.com, http://www.Ancestry.com, Record for Harley Berry Wood.

[740] Ancestry.com, 1940 United States Federal Census (Provo, UT, USA, Ancestry.com Operations, Inc., 2012), www.ancestry.com, Year: 1940; Census Place: Money Creek, Houston, Minnesota; Roll: T627_1927; Page: 3A; Enumeration District: 28-16. Record for Harley B Wood.

[741] Ancestry.com, U.S., Social Security Applications and Claims Index, 1936-2007 (Provo, UT, USA, Ancestry.com Operations, Inc., 2015), Ancestry.com, http://www.Ancestry.com, Record for Alyce Benora Wood.

[742] Ancestry.com, U.S., Social Security Applications and Claims Index, 1936-2007 (Provo, UT, USA, Ancestry.com Operations, Inc., 2015), Ancestry.com, http://www.Ancestry.com, Record for Alyce Benora Wood.

[743] Ancestry.com, U.S., Find A Grave Index, 1700s-Current (Provo, UT, USA, Ancestry.com Operations, Inc., 2012), Ancestry.com, http://www.Ancestry.com, Record for Alyce B Wood.

43. Edna P. Corey[5] (Genevieve Berry[4], Mary Abigale Leigh[3], Elijah Leigh[2], Nathan S. Leigh[1]) was born on 27 Dec 1889 in Minnesota[744] and died on 26 Oct 1961 in La Crosse, Minnesota[745]. She married Cushman Kellogg Potter on 24 Nov 1918[746], the son of

Frederick M. Potter and Mary Libby. He was born in 29 Oct 1890 in Minnesota[747] and died 24 Jun 1965 in Houston, Minnesota[748]. Edna P. Corey and her husband were buried in Money Creek, Minnesota[749].

Cushman Kellogg Potter and Edna P. Corey had the following child:

109. i. Wanda Geneva Potter was born on 22 May 1922 in Money Creek, Minnesota[750] and died on 21 Jan 2001 in Key West, Florida[751].

Photo of Edna P. and Lydia Belle Corey from the collection of Thomas Coulson and used with permission.

44. Lydia Belle Corey[5] (Genevieve Berry[4], Mary Abigale Leigh[3], Elijah Leigh[2], Nathan S. Leigh[1]) was born on 23 Oct 1896[752] and died on 24 Aug 1991 in Houston, Minnesota[753]. She married Charles Edgar Coulson, the son of Lewis Coulson and Nancy Jane Cochran on 01 Dec 1917 in Houston, Minnesota[754]. He was born on 26 Jan 1892 in

[744] Ancestry.com, U.S., Find A Grave Index, 1700s-Current (Provo, UT, USA, Ancestry.com Operations, Inc., 2012), Ancestry.com, http://www.Ancestry.com, Record for Edna P Potter.

[745] Ancestry.com, U.S., Find A Grave Index, 1700s-Current (Provo, UT, USA, Ancestry.com Operations, Inc., 2012), Ancestry.com, http://www.Ancestry.com, Record for Edna P Potter.

[746] Ancestry.com, U.S., Find A Grave Index, 1700s-Current (Provo, UT, USA, Ancestry.com Operations, Inc., 2012), Ancestry.com, http://www.Ancestry.com, Record for Edna P Potter

[747] Ancestry.com. *Minnesota, Death Index, 1908-2002* [database on-line]. Provo, UT, USA: Ancestry.com Operations Inc, 2001.

[748] Ancestry.com. *Minnesota, Death Index, 1908-2002* [database on-line]. Provo, UT, USA: Ancestry.com Operations Inc, 2001.

[749] Ancestry.com, U.S., Find A Grave Index, 1700s-Current (Provo, UT, USA, Ancestry.com Operations, Inc., 2012), Ancestry.com, http://www.Ancestry.com, Record for Edna P Potter.

[750] Ancestry.com, U.S., Social Security Applications and Claims Index, 1936-2007 (Provo, UT, USA, Ancestry.com Operations, Inc., 2015), Ancestry.com, http://www.Ancestry.com, Record for Wanda Potter Holter.

[751] Ancestry.com, U.S., Social Security Applications and Claims Index, 1936-2007 (Provo, UT, USA, Ancestry.com Operations, Inc., 2015), Ancestry.com, http://www.Ancestry.com, Record for Wanda Potter Holter.

[752] Ancestry.com, Minnesota, Death Index, 1908-2002 (Provo, UT, USA, Ancestry.com Operations Inc, 2001), Ancestry.com, http://www.Ancestry.com, Record for (Lydia) L. Belle Coulson.

[753] Ancestry.com, Minnesota, Death Index, 1908-2002 (Provo, UT, USA, Ancestry.com Operations Inc, 2001), Ancestry.com, http://www.Ancestry.com, Record for (Lydia) L. Belle Coulson.

[754] Ancestry.com, U.S., Find A Grave Index, 1700s-Current (Provo, UT, USA, Ancestry.com Operations, Inc., 2012), Ancestry.com, http://www.Fancestry.com, Record for L Belle Coulson.

Mahaska, Iowa[755] and died on 25 Dec 1945 in Houston, Minnesota[756]. Lydia Belle Corey and her husband were buried in Money Creek, Minnesota[757].

Charles was a mailman who drove a model T that was converted for winter with skis and tracks.

Photo of Charles Edgar Coulson and Lydia Belle Corey from the collection of Kathryn Cummings and used with permission.

Charles Edgar Coulson and Lydia Belle Corey had the following children:

110. i.   Dorothy Ruth Coulson was born on 21 Oct 1918 in Houston, Minnesota[758] and died on 20 Feb 1990 in Hidalgo, Texas[759].

111. ii.   June Genevieve Coulson was born on 05 Jun 1920 in Winona County, Minnesota[760] and died on 30 Apr 2000 in Houston, Minnesota[761].

112. iii.   Dwight Edward Coulson was born on 28 Nov 1921 in Houston, Minnesota[762] and died on 19 Feb 2009 in Springfield, Missouri[763].

113. iv.   Joseph Lewis Coulson was born on 18 Feb 1924[764] and died on 19 Dec 1999[765].

---

[755] Ancestry.com, U.S. World War II Draft Registration Cards, 1942 (Provo, UT, USA, The Generations Network, Inc., 2007), www.ancestry.com, The National Archives at St. Louis; St. Louis, Missouri; World War II Draft Cards, Record for Charles Edgar Coulson.

[756] Ancestry.com, Minnesota, Death Index, 1908-2002 (Provo, UT, USA, Ancestry.com Operations Inc, 2001), Ancestry.com, http://www.Ancestry.com, Record for Charles Edgar Coulson.

[757] Ancestry.com, U.S., Find A Grave Index, 1700s-Current (Provo, UT, USA, Ancestry.com Operations, Inc., 2012), Ancestry.com, http://www.Ancestry.com, Record for L Belle Coulson.

[758] Ancestry.com, U.S., Social Security Applications and Claims Index, 1936-2007 (Provo, UT, USA, Ancestry.com Operations, Inc., 2015), Ancestry.com, http://www.Ancestry.com, Record for Dorothy Ruth Chapel.

[759] Ancestry.com, U.S., Social Security Applications and Claims Index, 1936-2007 (Provo, UT, USA, Ancestry.com Operations, Inc., 2015), Ancestry.com, http://www.Ancestry.com, Record for Dorothy Ruth Chapel.

[760] Ancestry.com, U.S., Find A Grave Index, 1700s-Current (Provo, UT, USA, Ancestry.com Operations, Inc., 2012), Ancestry.com, http://www.Ancestry.com, Record for Charles E Coulson.

[761] Ancestry.com, U.S., Find A Grave Index, 1700s-Current (Provo, UT, USA, Ancestry.com Operations, Inc., 2012), Ancestry.com, http://www.Ancestry.com, Record for Charles E Coulson.

[762] Ancestry.com, U.S., Find A Grave Index, 1700s-Current (Provo, UT, USA, Ancestry.com Operations, Inc., 2012), Ancestry.com, http://www.Ancestry.com, Record for Dwight Edward Coulson.

[763] Ancestry.com, U.S., Find A Grave Index, 1700s-Current (Provo, UT, USA, Ancestry.com Operations, Inc., 2012), Ancestry.com, http://www.Ancestry.com, Record for Dwight Edward Coulson.

[764] Ancestry.com, U.S., Social Security Applications and Claims Index, 1936-2007 (Provo, UT, USA, Ancestry.com Operations, Inc., 2015), Ancestry.com, http://www.Ancestry.com, Record for Joseph Lewis Coulson.

114. v. Carol Beth Coulson was born on 27 Feb 1926 in Houston, Minnesota[766] and died on 25 Jan 2014 in Houston, Minnesota[767].

vi. David Allen Coulson was born on 02 Mar 1933 in Houston County, Minnesota[768] and died on 11 Jun 1998[769]. He married Julia A. Olson, the daughter of Theodore E. Olson and Myrtle E. Hoff, on 22 Aug 1959 in Houston, Minnesota[770]. She was born on 07 Dec 1941 in Fillmore, Minnesota[771] and died on 11 Dec 2001[772].

Photo of David Allen Coulson from the collection of genie67rn and used with permission.

45. James Edgar Corey[5] (Genevieve Berry[4], Mary Abigale Leigh[3], Elijah Leigh[2], Nathan S. Leigh[1]) was born on 12 Aug 1898[773] and died on 19 Jun 1971 in Houston, Minnesota[774]. He married Pearl Ann Ullan[775]. She was born on 29 Aug 1901[776] and died on 03 Dec 1989[777]. James Edgar Corey and his wife were buried in Money Creek, Minnesota[778].

[765] Ancestry.com, U.S., Social Security Applications and Claims Index, 1936-2007 (Provo, UT, USA, Ancestry.com Operations, Inc., 2015), Ancestry.com, http://www.Ancestry.com, Record for Joseph Lewis Coulson.

[766] Ancestry.com, Web: Minnesota, Birth Index, 1900-1934 (Provo, UT, USA, Ancestry.com Operations, Inc., 2015), Ancestry.com, http://www.Ancestry.com, Record for Carol Beth Coulson

[767] Ancestry.com, U.S., Find A Grave Index, 1700s-Current (Provo, UT, USA, Ancestry.com Operations, Inc., 2012),

[768] Ancestry.com, U.S., Social Security Applications and Claims Index, 1936-2007 (Provo, UT, USA, Ancestry.com Operations, Inc., 2015), Ancestry.com, http://www.Ancestry.com, Record for David Allen Coulson.

[769] Ancestry.com, U.S., Social Security Applications and Claims Index, 1936-2007 (Provo, UT, USA, Ancestry.com Operations, Inc., 2015), Ancestry.com, http://www.Ancestry.com, Record for David Allen Coulson.

[770] Ancestry.com, Minnesota, Marriage Index, 1958-2001 (Provo, UT, USA, Ancestry.com Operations Inc, 2007), Ancestry.com, http://www.Ancestry.com, Record for Julia A Olson

[771] Minnesota Department of Health, Minnesota Birth Index, 1935-1995 (Provo, UT, USA, Ancestry.com Operations Inc, 2004), Ancestry.com, http://www.Ancestry.com, Record for Julia Ann Olson.

[772] Ancestry.com, U.S., Social Security Applications and Claims Index, 1936-2007 (Provo, UT, USA, Ancestry.com Operations, Inc., 2015), Ancestry.com, http://www.Ancestry.com, Record for Julia Ann Coulson.

[773] Ancestry.com, Minnesota, Death Index, 1908-2002 (Provo, UT, USA, Ancestry.com Ope Ancestry.com, Minnesota, Death Index, 1908-2002 (Provo, UT, USA, Ancestry.com Operations Inc, 2001), Ancestry.com, http://www.Ancestry.com, Record for James Edgar Corey. rations Inc, 2001), Ancestry.com, http://www.Ancestry.com, Record for James Edgar Corey.

[774] Ancestry.com, Minnesota, Death Index, 1908-2002 (Provo, UT, USA, Ancestry.com Ope Ancestry.com, Minnesota, Death Index, 1908-2002 (Provo, UT, USA, Ancestry.com Operations Inc, 2001), Ancestry.com, http://www.Ancestry.com, Record for James Edgar Corey. rations Inc, 2001), Ancestry.com, http://www.Ancestry.com, Record for James Edgar Corey

[775] Ancestry.com, U.S., Find A Grave Index, 1700s-Current (Provo, UT, USA, Ancestry.com Operations, Inc., 2012), Ancestry.com, http://www.Ancestry.com, Record for Pearly A Corey.

[776] Ancestry.com, U.S., Find A Grave Index, 1700s-Current (Provo, UT, USA, Ancestry.com Operations, Inc., 2012), Ancestry.com, http://www.Ancestry.com, Record for Pearly A Corey.

[777] Ancestry.com, U.S., Find A Grave Index, 1700s-Current (Provo, UT, USA, Ancestry.com Operations, Inc., 2012), Ancestry.com, http://www.Ancestry.com, Record for Pearly A Corey.

James Edgar Corey and Pearl Ann Ullan had the following children:

    i   Bernice Irene Corey was born on 17 Nov 1921 in Houston, Minnesota[779] and died 14 May 2013 in Houston Minnesota[780]. She married Herman Martin Forsyth on 31 Aug 1940 in Kahoka, Missouri[781]. He was born on 14 Sep 1916 in Houston Minnesota[782] and died 04 Jan 1999 in Houston, Minnesota[783].

Photo of Bernice Irene Corey and Herman Martin Forsyth found on Ancestry.com.

    ii.   Betty Marie Corey was born 29 Mar 1923 in Houston, Minnesota[784] and died 22 Jan 2015 in Houston, Minnesota[785]. She married Ole Arnold Thorson, the son of Theodore Thorson and Bertha Karlsbraten on 29 Aug 1940 in Decorah, Iowa[786]. He was born 29 Dec 1915 in Houston,

Photo of Betty Marie Corey found on Ancestry.com.

---

[778] Ancestry.com, U.S., Find A Grave Index, 1700s-Current (Provo, UT, USA, Ancestry.com Operations, Inc., 2012), Ancestry.com, http://www.Ancestry.com, Record for Pearly A Corey.

[779] Minnesota Department of Health, Minnesota Birth Index, 1935-1995.

[780] Ancestry.com, U.S., Find A Grave Index, 1700s-Current (Provo, UT, USA, Ancestry.com Operations, Inc., 2012), Ancestry.com, http://www.Ancestry.com,

[781] Ancestry.com, U.S., Find A Grave Index, 1700s-Current (Provo, UT, USA, Ancestry.com Operations, Inc., 2012), Ancestry.com, http://www.Ancestry.com,

[782] Minnesota Department of Health, Minnesota Death Index, 1935-1995.

[783] Ancestry.com, U.S., Find A Grave Index, 1700s-Current (Provo, UT, USA, Ancestry.com Operations, Inc., 2012), Ancestry.com, http://www.Ancestry.com,

[784] Minnesota Department of Health, Minnesota Birth Index, 1935-1995.

[785] Ancestry.com, U.S., Find A Grave Index, 1700s-Current (Provo, UT, USA, Ancestry.com Operations, Inc., 2012), Ancestry.com, http://www.Ancestry.com,

[786] Iowa Department of Public Health; Des Moines, Iowa; Series Title: Iowa Marriage Records, 1923–1937; Record Type: Microfilm Records

Minnesota[787] and died 08 Oct 1986 in Houston, Minnesota[788].

115. iii. Illa May Corey was born on 31 May 1926 in Houston, Minnesota[789]. and died on 16 Dec 2016[790]. She married Lyle Sweet in 1947[791]. He was born on 05 Mar 1925 in Minnesota[792] and died on 06 Jan 1968 in Caledonia, Minnesota[793].

iv. Living Corey

v. Jeanette Elaine Corey was born 13 Oct 1931 in Houston, Minnesota[794] and died 06 Mar 2010 in Houston, Minnesota[795]. She married Clifton Bernard Johnston on 31 Mar 1987 in Florida[796]. He was born 30 Sep 1921[797] and died 30 Nov 1995[798].

Photo of Jeanette Elaine Corey found on Ancestry.com. →

Photo of Grace Caroline Corey and daughter, Genevieve, found on Ancestry.com.

←

46. Grace Caroline Corey[5] (Genevieve Berry[4], Mary Abigale Leigh[3], Elijah Leigh[2], Nathan S. Leigh[1]) was born on 18 Jun 1902 in Houston, Minnesota[799] and died on 16 Sep 1971 in Houston, Minnesota[800]. She married

---

[787] Minnesota Department of Health, Minnesota Birth Index, 1935-1995.

[788] U.S., Department of Veterans Affairs BIRLS Death File, 1850-2010.

[789] Ancestry.com, Web: Minnesota, Birth Index, 1900-1934 (Provo, UT, USA, Ancestry.com Operations, Inc., 2015), Ancestry.com, http://www.Ancestry.com, Record for Illa Mae Corey

[790] Ancestry.com, U.S., Find A Grave Index, 1700s-Current (Provo, UT, USA, Ancestry.com Operations, Inc., 2012), Ancestry.com, http://www.Ancestry.com, Record for Lyle Sweet.

[791] Ancestry.com, U.S., Find A Grave Index, 1700s-Current (Provo, UT, USA, Ancestry.com Operations, Inc., 2012), Ancestry.com, http://www.Ancestry.com, Record for Lyle Sweet.

[792] Ancestry.com, U.S., Find A Grave Index, 1700s-Current (Provo, UT, USA, Ancestry.com Operations, Inc., 2012), Ancestry.com, http://www.Ancestry.com, Record for Lyle Sweet.

[793] Ancestry.com, U.S., Find A Grave Index, 1700s-Current (Provo, UT, USA, Ancestry.com Operations, Inc., 2012), Ancestry.com, http://www.Ancestry.com, Record for Lyle Sweet.

[794] Minnesota Department of Health, Minnesota Birth Index, 1935-1995.

[795] Ancestry.com, Social Security Death Index, Issue State: Minnesota; Issue Date: Before 1951

[796] Ancestry.com, Florida Marriage Index

[797] Ancestry.com, U.S., Find A Grave Index, 1700s-Current (Provo, UT, USA, Ancestry.com Operations, Inc., 2012),

[798] Ancestry.com, U.S., Find A Grave Index, 1700s-Current (Provo, UT, USA, Ancestry.com Operations, Inc., 2012),

[799] Ancestry.com, Minnesota, Death Index, 1908-2002 (Provo, UT, USA, Ancestry.com Operations Inc, 2001), Ancestry.com, http://www.Ancestry.com, Record for Grace Caroline Steele.

[800] Ancestry.com, Minnesota, Death Index, 1908-, Record for Grace Caroline Steele.

James Tyler Steele[801].   He was born on 02 Dec 1896[802] and died on 13 Oct 1957 in Houston, Minnesota[803].   James Tyler Steele was buried in Money Creek, Minnesota[804].

James Tyler Steele and Grace Caroline Corey had the following children:
116.   i.   Wayne Howard Steele was born on 30 Jun 1922 in Minnesota[805] and died on 03 Oct 1974[806].
        ii.   Keith Kenneth Steele was born on 17 Nov 1924 in Houston, Minnesota[807] and died on 22 Jun 1998[808].   Keith Kenneth Steele was buried in Riverside, California[809].
        iii.   Living Steele

Photo of James Tyler Steele found on Ancestry.com.

[801] Ancestry.com, U.S., Find A Grave Index, 1700s-Current, Record for James Tyler Steele.

[802] Ancestry.com, U.S., Find A Grave Index, 1700s-Current (Provo, UT, USA, Ancestry.com Operations, Inc., 2012), Ancestry.com, http://www.Ancestry.com, Record for James Tyler Steele.

[803] Ancestry.com, U.S., Find A Grave Index, 1700s-Current (Provo, UT, USA, Ancestry.com Operations, Inc., 2012), Ancestry.com, http://www.Ancestry.com, Record for James Tyler Steele.

[804] Ancestry.com, U.S., Find A Grave Index, 1700s-Current (Provo, UT, USA, Ancestry.com Operations, Inc., 2012), Ancestry.com, http://www.Ancestry.com, Record for James Tyler Steele.

[805] Ancestry.com, Social Security Death Index (Provo, UT, USA, The Generations Network, Inc., 2008), www.ancestry.com, Number: 475-16-0502; Issue State: Minnesota; Issue Date: Before 1951. Record for Wayne Steele.

[806] Ancestry.com, Social Security Death Index (Provo, UT, USA, The Generations Network, Inc., 2008), www.ancestry.com, Number: 475-16-0502; Issue State: Minnesota; Issue Date: Before 1951. Record for Wayne Steele.

[807] Ancestry.com, U.S., Find A Grave Index, 1700s-Current (Provo, UT, USA, Ancestry.com Operations, Inc., 2012), Ancestry.com, http://www.Ancestry.com, Record for Keith K Steele.

[808] Ancestry.com, U.S., Find A Grave Index, 1700s-Current (Provo, UT, USA, Ancestry.com Operations, Inc., 2012), Ancestry.com, http://www.Ancestry.com, Record for Keith K Steele.

[809] Ancestry.com, U.S., Find A Grave Index, 1700s-Current (Provo, UT, USA, Ancestry.com Operations, Inc., 2012), Ancestry.com, http://www.Ancestry.com, Record for Keith K Steele.

47. Cyrus George Berry[5], Jr. (Eugene L. Berry[4], Mary Abigale Leigh[3], Elijah Leigh[2], Nathan S. Leigh[1])was born on 29 Jan 1893 in Money Creek, Minnesota[810] and died on 18 Dec 1966 in Butte, Montana[811]. He married Mary Ellen Ronan, the daughter of Patrick Ronan and Mary Cullinan.[812]. She was born 15 August 1894 in Montana[813] and died 9 July 1974 in Butte, Montana[814]. Cyrus George Berry Jr. and his wife were buried in Butte, Montana[815].

Cyrus George Berry Jr. and Mary Ellen Ronan had the following children:
     i.   Jean Depaul Marin Berry was born 02 Oct 1918[816] in Butte, Montana and died 29 Jul 1996 in Billings, Montana[817].
     ii.   Kathryn A. Berry was born 13 June 1920 in Butte, Montana[818] and died 06 Dec 2015 in Bozeman, Montana[819].

Photo of Kathryn A. Berry McKay found in her obituary.

Obituary, Bozeman, Montana
Kathryn "Kay" McKay, 95, of Bozeman, passed away Sunday, Dec. 6, 2015. She was born June 13, 1920, in Butte, Montana, to George and Mary (Ronan) Berry. She graduated from Butte High in 1937 and from St. James Hospital School of Nursing in 1941. Kay completed her Master's Degree in Nursing from Montana State University. She received her certification as a cardiac care nurse from the University of Utah. Kay married Joseph McKay on Dec. 12, 1942, in San Francisco, California. Kay lived in Butte, Montana, San Francisco, New London, Connecticut, Idaho Falls, Idaho, and settled in Bozeman, Montana, after World War II. Kay was a nurse for 70

[810] Ancestry.com, Montana, County Births and Deaths, 1830-2011 (Lehi, UT, USA, Ancestry.com Operations, Inc., 2017), Ancestry.com, http://www.Ancestry.com, Montans State Historical Society; Helena, Montana; FHL Roll: 47-114. Record for Cyrus George Berry.
[811] Ancestry.com, Montana, County Births and Deaths, 1830-2011 (Lehi, UT, USA, Ancestry.com Operations, Inc., 2017), Ancestry.com, http://www.Ancestry.com, Montans State Historical Society; Helena, Montana; FHL Roll: 47-114. Record for Cyrus George Berry.
[812] Ancestry.com, Montana County Marriages.
[813] Ancestry.com. *U.S., Find A Grave Index, 1600s-Current* [database on-line]. Provo, UT, USA: Ancestry.com Operations, Inc., 2012.
[814] Ancestry.com. *U.S., Find A Grave Index, 1600s-Current* [database on-line]. Provo, UT, USA: Ancestry.com Operations, Inc., 2012.
[815] Ancestry.com, U.S., Find A Grave Index, 1700s-Current (Provo, UT, USA, Ancestry.com Operations, Inc., 2012), Ancestry.com, http://www.Ancestry.com, Record for C George Berry.
[816] Ancestry.com. *U.S., Social Security Applications and Claims Index, 1936-2007* [database on-line]. Provo, UT, USA: Ancestry.com Operations, Inc., 2015.
[817] Ancestry.com. *U.S., Social Security Applications and Claims Index, 1936-2007* [database on-line]. Provo, UT, USA: Ancestry.com Operations, Inc., 2015.
[818] Obituary in Bozeman, Montana newspaper.
[819] Obituary in Bozeman, Montana newspaper.

years, worked in local clinics and Bozeman Deaconess Hospital, and retired from active nursing duty in 1984. Kay gave of her time and talent freely, volunteering with the American Red Cross blood donor program and the Retired Senior Volunteer Program. Kay was a devout Catholic and loved her Catholic Community of Holy Rosary. At Holy Rosary she was a member of the Foresters, served as an officer in the Altar Society, and was a Eucharist Minister to the Sick for 14 years. Quote from Kay: "I could never do fancy work (like crochet), but I could sew when necessary. My family said "but you could talk," which was an advantage to teaching as a cardiac nurse specialist and very often I was asked to be the Mistress of Ceremony. These special times were a great joy for me. I was blessed with a sense of humor - which made my life easier". She was preceded in death by her husband, Joseph, her brothers, Robert and Walter Berry, and her sister, Marion Berry of The Sisters of Charity. She was also preceded in death by her daughter, Mary Eileen Knoll. Survivors include her sister, Eileen Tourikis, and sister in-law, Carol Berry, both of Butte, Montana, sons and daughters-in-law, Robert Joseph and Sharon McKay of Stockton, California, Kenneth Patrick and Sandy McKay of Pittsburg, Pennsylvania, George Timothy and Deanna of Columbus, Montana, James Anthony and Diana McKay of Corvallis, Montana, son in law, Kary Knoll, of Baraboo, Wisconsin, and her devoted friend and companion, Sandy McKay. Kay was blessed with 18 grandchildren, 16 great-grandchildren and one great-great-grandchild. Kay was also blessed with many nieces and nephews from both the McKay and Berry families. A Rosary Service will be held on Wednesday, Dec. 9 at 5 p.m. at Dahl Funeral Chapel followed by a Vigil Service at 5:30 p.m. The Funeral Mass will be on Thursday, Dec. 10, at 10 a.m. at Holy Rosary Catholic Church. Interment will follow the Mass at Sunset Hills Cemetery. All are invited to a reception and lunch, sponsored by the Foresters, at the Church after interment. An additional celebration of Kay's life will be held next summer. Memorials may be made to the "Burn the Mortgage Campaign" at Holy Rosary Catholic Church, P.O. Box 96, Bozeman, MT 59771.

     iii.   Eugene Robert Berry was born 08 Jun 1925 in Butte, Montana[820] and died 15 Aug 2007 in Butte, Montana[821].
     iv.   Living Berry

---

[820] Ancestry.com. *U.S., Social Security Death Index, 1935-2014* [database on-line]. Provo, UT, USA: Ancestry.com Operations Inc, 2011.
[821] Ancestry.com. *U.S., Social Security Death Index, 1935-2014* [database on-line]. Provo, UT, USA: Ancestry.com Operations Inc, 2011.

v.   Walter G. Berry was born 16 May 1934 in Butte, Montana[822] and died 31 Jan 2005 in Butte, Montana[823].

Photo of Walter G. Berry found in findagrave.com.

48.   Grace Irene Berry[5] (Eugene L. Berry[4], Mary Abigale Leigh[3], Elijah Leigh[2], Nathan S. Leigh[1]) was born on 06 May 1894 in Minnesota[824] and died on 04 Mar 1932 in Butte, Montana[825]. She married Arthur Casper Thomas on 25 Feb 1910 in Sandpoint, Idaho[826]. He was born on 07 Jun 1883 in Maine[827] and died on 10 Jan 1940 in Butte, Montana[828].

Arthur Casper Thomas and Grace Irene Berry had the following children:

i.   Melvin A. Thomas was born on 07 Jul 1914 in Thompson Falls, Montana[829] and died on 12 Sep 1988 in Butte, Montana[830]. He married Jean Alma Fritzlan, the daughter of Winslow Homer and Myrtle Rebecca Fritzlan, on 21 Oct 1936 in Helena, Montana[831]. She was born on 17 Jan 1916 in Anaconda, Montana[832] and died on

---

[822] Ancestry.com. *U.S., Find A Grave Index, 1600s-Current* [database on-line]. Provo, UT, USA: Ancestry.com Operations, Inc., 2012.

[823] Ancestry.com. *U.S., Find A Grave Index, 1600s-Current* [database on-line]. Provo, UT, USA: Ancestry.com Operations, Inc., 2012.

[824] Ancestry.com, Montana, County Births and Deaths, 1830-2011 (Lehi, UT, USA, Ancestry.com Operations, Inc., 2017), Ancestry.com, http://www.Ancestry.com, Montans State Historical Society; Helena, Montana; FHL Roll: 47-102. Record for Grace Irene Thomas.

[825] Ancestry.com, Montana, County Births and Deaths, 1830-2011 (Lehi, UT, USA, Ancestry.com Operations, Inc., 2017), Ancestry.com, http://www.Ancestry.com, Montans State Historical Society; Helena, Montana; FHL Roll: 47-102. Record for Grace Irene Thomas.

[826] Ancestry.com. Idaho, County Marriages, 1864-1950 [database on-line]. Provo, UT, USA: Ancestry.com Operations, Inc., 2014.

[827] Ancestry.com, Montana, County Births and Deaths, 1830-2011 (Lehi, UT, USA, Ancestry.com Operations, Inc., 2017), Ancestry.com, http://www.Ancestry.com, Montans State Historical Society; Helena, Montana; FHL Roll: 47-105. Record for Arthur C Thomas.

[828] Ancestry.com, Montana, County Births and Deaths, 1830-2011 (Lehi, UT, USA, Ancestry.com Operations, Inc., 2017), Ancestry.com, http://www.Ancestry.com, Montans State Historical Society; Helena, Montana; FHL Roll: 47-105. Record for Arthur C Thomas.

[829] Ancestry.com, Montana, County Births and Deaths, 1830-2011 (Lehi, UT, USA, Ancestry.com Operations, Inc., 2017), Ancestry.com, http://www.Ancestry.com, Montans State Historical Society; Helena, Montana; FHL Roll: 47-119. Record for Melvin Thomas.

[830] Ancestry.com, Montana, County Births and Deaths, 1830-2011 (Lehi, UT, USA, Ancestry.com Operations, Inc., 2017), Ancestry.com, http://www.Ancestry.com, Montans State Historical Society; Helena, Montana; FHL Roll: 47-119. Record for Melvin Thomas.

[831] Ancestry.com. Montana, County Marriages, 1865-1950 [database on-line]. Provo, UT, USA: Ancestry.com Operations, Inc., 2014.

[832] Ancestry.com, U.S., Social Security Applications and Claims Index, 1936-2007 (Provo, UT, USA, Ancestry.com Operations, Inc., 2015), Ancestry.com, http://www.Ancestry.com, Record for Jean Fritzlan Thomas.

14 Oct 1997 in Carbon County, Montana[833].   Melvin A. Thomas and his wife were buried in Mount Moriah Cemetery, Butte, Montana[834].

ii.   Myrtle June Thomas was born on 23 June 1919 in Thompson Falls, Montana[835] and died on 02 Oct 2006 in Buxton, Montana[836]. She married Paul Leo Dougherty on 30 June 1937 in Silver Bow, Montana[837]. He was born in 1909 in Utah[838]. She later married Alexander Lee Christie, the son of Colon and Ruth Christie, on 14 Feb 1948 in Butte, Montana[839]. He was born on 09 May 1916 in Butte, Montana[840] and died on 09 May 2000 in Butte, Montana[841]. Myrtle June Thomas was buried in Butte Montana[842].

Myrtle June Christie, 87 of Buxton died there Monday, Oct. 2, 2006, after a brief illness. Myrtle was born June 23, 1919, in Thompson Falls to Arthur C. and Grace I. (Berry) Thomas. She moved to Butte with her family as a young child and attended local schools, graduating from Butte High in 1937. During World War II she worked with the U.S.O. to meet the troops passing through Butte on the trains and established her own business at the Grand Silver, repairing silk stockings, due to the shortage of silk during the war.
Myrtle married Alex Christie on Valentine's Day in 1948 at which time she began her career in jewelry sales at Leys Jewelry, the family business, and she began raising her family. After the family business closed in 1965, Myrtle worked from home, restringing beads for various Butte jewelry stores and reupholstering furniture. During the 1970s, she worked for Hannifin Jewelry, Alma's Smart Shop, and Hord's Jewelry. She was an active volunteer in Ramsay PTA, Girl Scouts, Cub Scouts, and 4-H activities. She was preceded in death by her husband of 52 years, Alex; her sister, Adeline; her brothers, Eugene and Melvin; and her brother-in-law, Duane Willis.

---

[833] Ancestry.com, U.S., Social Security Applications and Claims Index, 1936-2007 (Provo, UT, USA, Ancestry.com Operations, Inc., 2015), Ancestry.com, http://www.Ancestry.com, Record for Jean Fritzlan Thomas.

[834] Ancestry.com. *U.S., Find A Grave Index, 1600s-Current* [database on-line]. Provo, UT, USA: Ancestry.com Operations, Inc., 2012.

[835] Ancestry.com, Montana, Death Index, 1868-2011 (Provo, UT, USA, Ancestry.com Operations, Inc., 2001), Ancestry.com, http://www.Ancestry.com, Record for Myrtle June Christie.

[836] Ancestry.com, Montana, Death Index, 1868-2011 (Provo, UT, USA, Ancestry.com Operations, Inc., 2001), Ancestry.com, http://www.Ancestry.com, Record for Myrtle June Christie.

[837] Ancestry.com, Montana, County Marriages, 1865-1950 (Provo, UT, USA, Ancestry.com Operations, Inc., 2014), Ancestry.com, http://www.Ancestry.com, Record for Myrtle June Thomas.

[838] Ancestry.com, Montana, County Marriages, 1865-1950 (Provo, UT, USA, Ancestry.com Operations, Inc., 2014), Ancestry.com, http://www.Ancestry.com, Record for Myrtle June Thomas.

[839] Ancestry.com, Montana, County Marriages, 1865-1993 (Lehi, UT, USA, Ancestry.com Operations, Inc., 2016), Ancestry.com, http://www.Ancestry.com, Record for Alexander Lee Christie.

[840] Ancestry.com, Montana, County Births and Deaths, 1830-2011 (Lehi, UT, USA, Ancestry.com Operations, Inc., 2017), Ancestry.com, http://www.Ancestry.com, Montans State Historical Society; Helena, Montana; FHL Roll: 47-122. Record for Alexander Lee Christie.

[841] Ancestry.com, Montana, County Births and Deaths, 1830-2011 (Lehi, UT, USA, Ancestry.com Operations, Inc., 2017), Ancestry.com, http://www.Ancestry.com, Montans State Historical Society; Helena, Montana; FHL Roll: 47-122. Record for Alexander Lee Christie.

[842] Ancestry.com, U.S., Find A Grave Index, 1700s-Current (Provo, UT, USA, Ancestry.com Operations, Inc., 2012), Ancestry.com, http://www.Ancestry.com, Record for Myrtle June Christie.

Myrtle is survived by her daughter and son-in-law, Jan and Doug Torpey of Buxton; sons and daughters-in-law, Jim and Jamey Christie of West Wendover, Nev., Kristal and Bill Christie of St. Helens, Ore., and Bob Christie and Kerianne Sitzabee of Washougal, Wash.; grandchildren, Michael and Lindsay Torpey, Malia Christie, Brad Brooks, Robby and Brent Greene, Ezra Holmes, and Jacob and Nicole Christie; sister, Frances Willis of Kalispell, and numerous nieces and nephews.

Graveside funeral services will be conducted Saturday at 11 a.m. in Mount Moriah Cemetery with the Rev. Jim Heikes officiating. Memorials may be made to the Butte Special Riders, c/o Joani Kissock, 1179 Beacon Road, Butte, MT 59701, Our Lady of the Rockies. or to Highlands Hospice.

iii.   Frances Marie Thomas was born on 27 Apr 1927 in Butte, Montana[843] and died on 07 Aug 2013 in Kalispell, Montana[844]. She married Bernard Duane Willis, the son of Leland D. Willis and Agatha S. Behm, on 11 Jun 1949 in Butte, Montana[845]. He was born on 05 Feb 1928 in Lansford, North Dakota[846] and died on 07 Mar 2006 in Kalispell, Montana[847].

49. Anita Susan Berry[5] (Eugene L. Berry[4], Mary Abigale Leigh[3], Elijah Leigh[2], Nathan S. Leigh[1]) was born on 14 Dec 1899 in Wadena County, Minnesota[848] and died on 18 Sep 1964 in Beltrami County, Minnesota[849]. She married Ralph Steven Lovering, the son of Albert Warren Lovering, on 16 Aug 1916 in Bemidji, Minnesota[850]. He was born in 1888 in Minneapolis, Minnesota[851] and died in 1953[852]. Anita Susan Berry and her husband were buried in Blackduck, Minnesota[853].

---

[843] Ancestry.com, Montana, County Births and Deaths, 1830-2011 (Lehi, UT, USA, Ancestry.com Operations, Inc., 2017), Ancestry.com, http://www.Ancestry.com, Montana State Historical Society; Helena, Montana; FHL Roll: 47-69. Record for Frances Marie Thomas.

[844] Ancestry.com, Montana, County Births and Deaths, 1830-2011 (Lehi, UT, USA, Ancestry.com Operations, Inc., 2017), Ancestry.com, http://www.Ancestry.com, Montana State Historical Society; Helena, Montana; FHL Roll: 47-69. Record for Frances Marie Thomas.

[845] Ancestry.com. Montana, County Marriages, 1865-1950 [database on-line]. Provo, UT, USA: Ancestry.com Operations, Inc., 2014.

[846] Ancestry.com, Montana, County Births and Deaths, 1830-2011 (Lehi, UT, USA, Ancestry.com Operations, Inc., 2017), Ancestry.com, http://www.Ancestry.com, Montans State Historical Society; Helena, Montana. Record for Bernard Duane Willis.

[847] Ancestry.com, Montana, County Births and Deaths, 1830-2011 (Lehi, UT, USA, Ancestry.com Operations, Inc., 2017), Ancestry.com, http://www.Ancestry.com, Montans State Historical Society; Helena, Montana. Record for Bernard Duane Willis.

[848] Ancestry.com, U.S., Find A Grave Index, 1700s-Current (Provo, UT, USA, Ancestry.com Op Ancestry.com, U.S., Find A Grave Index, 1700s-Current (Provo, UT, USA, Ancestry.com Operations, Inc., 2012), erations, Inc., 2012),

[849] Ancestry.com, U.S., Find A Grave Index, 1700s-Current (Provo, UT, USA, Ancestry.com Operations, Inc., 2012),

[850] Ancestry.com, U.S., Find A Grave Index, 1700s-Current (Provo, UT, USA, Ancestry.com Operations, Inc., 2012),

[851] Ancestry.com, U.S., Find A Grave Index, 1700s-Current (Provo, UT, USA, Ancestry.com Operations, Inc., 2012),

[852] Ancestry.com, U.S., Find A Grave Index, 1700s-Current (Provo, UT, USA, Ancestry.com Operations, Inc., 2012),

[853] Ancestry.com, U.S., Find A Grave Index, 1700s-Current (Provo, UT, USA, Ancestry.com Operations, Inc., 2012),

Bemidji Daily Pioneer, Nov. 10, 1966 Obituary
Ralph Steven Lovering, 78, died at his home at 2712 Minnesota Ave., Bemidji. He was born at Minneapolis and moved with his parents, Mr. and Mrs. Albert Warren to Northfield as a child, later lived in Washington state and moved to Birch township, Beltrami county, in 1917. In 1932 he moved into Blackduck and since 1937 had lived in Bemidji. Mr. Lovering is survived by a son, Steven of Bemidji; two daughters, Mrs. Jack White (Lois) of Mason City, Ia., and Mrs. Donald Dickinson (Mae) of Green Bay, Wis.; 11 grandchildren, two great grandchildren; a sister, Mrs. Al Schulties of Superior, Wis. His wife, the former Anita Berry to whom he was married at Bemidji Aug 16, 1916, died Sept 18, 1964. Funeral services will be held at the Olson Funeral Home. Burial in Lakeview Cemetery at Blackduck.

Ralph Steven Lovering and Anita Susan Berry had the following children:
     i.   Living Lovering
     ii.   Steven Warren Lovering was born 22 Nov 1919[854] and died 29 Dec 1972 in Beltrami, Minnesota[855]. Steven Lovering served in the US Army: January 7 1942 - November 17 1945.
117.   iii.   Mae Mina Lovering was born on 27 Jun 1924 in Beltrami, Minnesota[856] and died on 31 Dec 2015[857].

50. Glen James Hirst[5] (Rose Ann Lindel Todd[4], Julia Fannie Leigh[3], Elijah Leigh[2], Nathan S. Leigh[1]) was born on 20 Jul 1886 in Miltonvale, Kansas[858] and died on 04 Mar 1929 in Salt Lake City, Utah[859]. He married Chrystal Vivian Darby on 09 Mar 1911 in Kansas City, Missouri[860]. She was born on 05 Jul 1887 in Independence, Missouri[861]. She

[854] Ancestry.com, Minnesota, Death Index, 1908-2002 (Provo, UT, USA, Ancestry.com Operations Inc, 2001), Ancestry.com, http://www.Ancestry.com, Record for Steven Warren Lovering.

[855] Ancestry.com, Minnesota, Death Index, 1908-2002 (Provo, UT, USA, Ancestry.com Operations Inc, 2001), Ancestry.com, http://www.Ancestry.com, Record for Steven Warren Lovering.

[856] Ancestry.com, U.S., Find A Grave Index, 1700s-Current (Provo, UT, USA, Ancestry.com Operations, Inc., 2012), Ancestry.com, http://www.Ancestry.com, Record for Mae M. Dickinson.

[857] Ancestry.com, U.S., Find A Grave Index, 1700s-Current (Provo, UT, USA, Ancestry.com Operations, Inc., 2012), Ancestry.com, http://www.Ancestry.com, Record for Mae M. Dickinson.

[858] Ancestry.com, Salt Lake County, Utah, Death Records, 1908-1949 (Provo, UT, USA, Ancestry.com Operations, Inc., 2014), Ancestry.com, http://www.Ancestry.com, Record for Glen James Hirst.

[859] Ancestry.com, Salt Lake County, Utah, Death Records, 1908-1949 (Provo, UT, USA, Ancestry.com Operations, Inc., 2014), Ancestry.com, http://www.Ancestry.com, Record for Glen James Hirst.

[860] Marriage Record, Ancestry.com. Missouri, Marriage Records, 1805-2002 [database on-line]. Provo, UT, USA: Ancestry.com Operations, Inc., 2007.

[861] Ancestry.com, Salt Lake County, Utah, Death Records, 1908-1949 (Provo, UT, USA, Ancestry.com Operations, Inc., 2014), Ancestry.com, http://www.Ancestry.com, Record for Glen James Hirst.

died on 17 Jun 1948 in Salt Lake City, Utah[862]. Glen James Hirst and his wife were buried in Salt Lake City, Utah [863].

Glen James Hirst and Chrystal Vivian Darby had the following children:
118.   i.   Erwin Glenn Hirst was born on 25 Jan 1912 in South Jordan, Utah[864] and died on 30 Mar 1959[865].

Photos   of   Glen James   Hirst   and Chyrstal   Vivial Darby   found   on familysearch.org.

ii.   Laura Rose Hirst was born on 27 Sep 1913 in Utah[866] and died on 07 May 1927 in Utah[867]. Laura Rose Hirst was buried in Salt Lake City, Utah[868].
iii.   Blythe Samuel Hirst was born on 19 Jul 1915[869] and died on 29 Jul 1984[870].

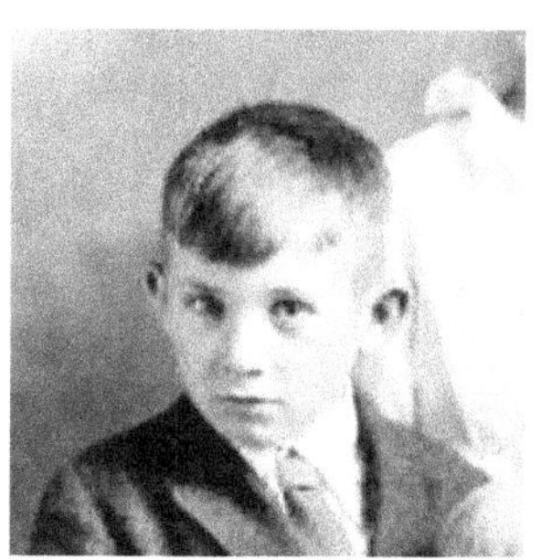

Photo of Blythe Samuel Hirst found on familysearch.org.

iv.   Grant Darby Hirst was born on 19 Oct 1916 in Utah[871] and died on 30 Jul 1918 in Utah[872]. Grant Darby Hirst

---

[862] Ancestry.com, Salt Lake County, Utah, Death Records, 1908-1949 (Provo, UT, USA, Ancestry.com Operations, Inc., 2014), Ancestry.com, http://www.Ancestry.com, Record for Glen James Hirst.

[863] Ancestry.com, Salt Lake County, Utah, Death Records, 1908-1949 (Provo, UT, USA, Ancestry.com Operations, Inc., 2014), Ancestry.com, http://www.Ancestry.com, Record for Glen James Hirst.

[864] Ancestry.com, U.S., Find A Grave Index, 1700s-Current (Provo, UT, USA, Ancestry.com Operations, Inc., 2012), Ancestry.com, http://www.Ancestry.com, Record for Erwin Glenn Hirst.

[865] Ancestry.com, U.S., Find A Grave Index, 1700s-Current (Provo, UT, USA, Ancestry.com Operations, Inc., 2012), Ancestry.com, http://www.Ancestry.com, Record for Erwin Glenn Hirst.

[866] Ancestry.com, U.S., Find A Grave Index, 1700s-Current (Provo, UT, USA, Ancestry.com Operations, Inc., 2012),

[867] Ancestry.com, U.S., Find A Grave Index, 1700s-Current (Provo, UT, USA, Ancestry.com Operations, Inc., 2012),

[868] Ancestry.com, U.S., Find A Grave Index, 1700s-Current (Provo, UT, USA, Ancestry.com Operations, Inc., 2012),

[869] Ancestry.com, Social Security Death Index ,Record for Blythe Hirst.

[870] Ancestry.com, Social Security Death Index ,Record for Blythe Hirst.

[871] Ancestry.com, U.S., Find A Grave Index, 1700s-Current (Provo, UT, USA, Ancestry.com Operations, Inc., 2012),

[872] Ancestry.com, U.S., Find A Grave Index, 1700s-Current (Provo, UT, USA, Ancestry.com Operations, Inc., 2012),

was buried in Salt Lake City, Utah[873].

      v.   James Warren Hirst was born on 18 Jul 1922 in Salt Lake City, Utah[874] and died on 07 Nov 1973 in Utah[875]. James Warren Hirst was buried in Millcreek, Utah[876].

Photo of James Warren Hirst found on familysearch.org.

51.   Leslie Erwin Hirst[5] (Rose Ann Lindel Todd[4], Julia Fannie Leigh[3], Elijah Leigh[2], Nathan S. Leigh[1]) was born on 02 Feb 1888 in Kansas[877] and died on 17 Sep 1953 in Wisconsin[878]. He married a woman by the name of Alice Belle. She was born on 04 Jun 1893 in Wisconsin[879] and died on 26 Oct 1973 in Reedsburg, Wisconsin[880]. Leslie Erwin Hirst and his wife were buried in Reedsburg, Wisconsin, United States of America[881].

Leslie Erwin Hirst and Alice Belle had the following children:
119.   i.   Francis Alva Hirst was born on 24 Jul 1915 in Sauk County, Wisconsin[882] and died on 02 Sep 1998 in Reedsburg, Wisconsin[883].
120.   ii.   Melbourne Clyde Hirst was born on 19 Jun 1920 in Lyndon Station, Wisconsin[884] and died on 27 Sep 1987 in Reedsburg, Wisconsin[885].

52.   Leon Staples Todd[5] (Ransom William Todd[4], Julia Fannie Leigh[3], Elijah Leigh[2], Nathan S. Leigh[1]) was born on 09 Jan 1882[886] and died in 1952[887]. He married Maude I.

---

[873] Ancestry.com, U.S., Find A Grave Index, 1700s-Current (Provo, UT, USA, Ancestry.com Operations, Inc., 2012),

[874] Ancestry.com, U.S. WWII Draft Cards Young Men, 1940-1947 (Lehi, UT, USA, Ancestry.com Operations, Inc., 2011), Ancestry.com, http://www.Ancestry.com, The National Archives in St. Louis, Missouri; St. Louis, Missouri; WWII Draft Registration Cards for Utah, 10/16/1940 - 03/31/1947; Record Group: Records of the Selective Service System, 147; Box: 041. Record for James Warren Hirst.

[875] Ancestry.com, Social Security Death Index (Provo, UT, USA, The Generations Network, Inc., 2008), www.ancestry.com, Number: 528-12-5420; Issue State: Utah; Issue Date: Before 1951. Record for James Hirst.

[876] Ancestry.com, U.S., Find A Grave Index, 1700s-Current (Provo, UT, USA, Ancestry.com Operations, Inc., 2012), Ancestry.com, http://www.Ancestry.com, Record for James Warren Hirst.

[877] Ancestry.com, U.S., Find A Grave Index, 1700s-Current, Record for Leslie Erwin Hirst.

[878] Ancestry.com, U.S., Find A Grave Index, 1700s-Current, Record for Leslie Erwin Hirst.

[879] Ancestry.com, U.S., Find A Grave Index, 1700s-Current, Record for Leslie Erwin Hirst.

[880] Ancestry.com, U.S., Find A Grave Index, 1700s-Current, Record for Leslie Erwin Hirst.

[881] Ancestry.com, U.S., Find A Grave Index, 1700s-Current, Record for Leslie Erwin Hirst.

[882] Ancestry.com, U.S., Find A Grave Index, 1700s-Current (Provo, UT, USA, Ancestry.com Operations, Inc., 2012),

[883] Ancestry.com, U.S., Find A Grave Index, 1700s-Current (Provo, UT, USA, Ancestry.com Operations, Inc., 2012),

[884] Ancestry.com, U.S., Find A Grave Index, 1700s-Current (Provo, UT, USA, Ancestry.com Operations, Inc., 2012),

[885] Ancestry.com, U.S., Find A Grave Index, 1700s-Current (Provo, UT, USA, Ancestry.com Operations, Inc., 2012),

[886] Ancestry.com, U.S., Find A Grave Index, 1700s-Current (Provo, UT, USA, Ancestry.com Operations, Inc., 2012), Ancestry.com, http://www.Ancestry.com, Record for Leon S Todd.

[887] Ancestry.com, U.S., Find A Grave Index, 1700s-Current (Provo, UT, USA, Ancestry.com Operations, Inc., 2012), Ancestry.com, http://www.Ancestry.com, Record for Leon S Todd.

"Lettie" Robinson[888]. She was born on 08 Feb 1888 in Waukesha, Wisconsin[889] and died in 1947[890]. Leon Staples Todd and his wife were buried in Sauk City, Wisconsin, United States of America[891].

Leon Staples Todd and Maude I. "Lettie" Robinson had the following children:

    i.   Gordon L. Todd was born on 05 Feb 1920 in Wisconsin[892] and died on 27 Feb 1969 in Los Angeles[893]. He married Ione E. Mahnke.

    ii.   Raymond Cecil Todd was born on 19 Jun 1923 in Sandusky, Wisconsin[894] and died on 19 Oct 1995[895].

53.   Ralph Ransom Todd[5] (Ransom William Todd[4], Julia Fannie Leigh[3], Elijah Leigh[2], Nathan S. Leigh[1]) was born on 18 Feb 1894 in La Valle, Wisconsin[896] and died in Sep 1985 in Madison, Wisconsin[897]. He married Ethel Amelia Luberg[898]. She was born on 02 May 1896 in River Falls, Wisconsin[899] and died on 30 May 1989 in South Holland, Illinois[900].   Ralph Ransom Todd and Ethel Amelia Luberg had one child who may still be living.

54.   Fred Louis Todd[5] (Ransom William Todd[4], Julia Fannie Leigh[3], Elijah Leigh[2], Nathan S. Leigh[1]) was born on 01 Oct 1896 in La Valle, Wisconsin[901] and died on 08

---

[888] Ancestry.com, U.S., Find A Grave Index, 1700s-Current (Provo, UT, USA, Ancestry.com Operations, Inc., 2012), Ancestry.com, http://www.Ancestry.com, Record for Lettie Todd.

[889] Ancestry.com, Wisconsin, Births and Christenings Index, 1801-1928 (Provo, UT, USA, Ancestry.com Operations, Inc., 2011), Ancestry.com, http://www.Ancestry.com, Record for Maud Robinson.

[890] Ancestry.com, U.S., Find A Grave Index, 1700s-Current (Provo, UT, USA, Ancestry.com Operations, Inc., 2012), Ancestry.com, http://www.Ancestry.com, Record for Lettie Todd.

[891] Ancestry.com, U.S., Find A Grave Index, 1700s-Current (Provo, UT, USA, Ancestry.com Operations, Inc., 2012), Ancestry.com, http://www.Ancestry.com, Record for Lettie Todd.

[892] Ancestry.com, California Death Index, 1940-1997 (Provo, UT, USA, The Generations Network, Inc., 2000), ww.w.ancestry.com, Date: 1969-02-27. Record for Gordon L Todd.

[893] Ancestry.com, California Death Index, 1940-1997 (Provo, UT, USA, The Generations Network, Inc., 2000), www.ancestry.com, Date: 1969-02-27. Record for Gordon L Todd.

[894] Ancestry.com, U.S., Social Security Applications and Claims Index, 1936-2007 (Provo, UT, USA, Ancestry.com Operations, Inc., 2015), Ancestry.com, http://www.Ancestry.com, Record for Letty Robinson.

[895] Ancestry.com, U.S., Social Security Applications and Claims Index, 1936-2007 (Provo, UT, USA, Ancestry.com Operations, Inc., 2015), Ancestry.com, http://www.Ancestry.com, Record for Letty Robinson.

[896] Ancestry.com, Social Security Death Index (Provo, UT, USA, The Generations Network, Inc., 2008), www.ancestry.com, Number: 387-18-4788; Issue State: Wisconsin; Issue Date: Before 1951. Record for Ralph Todd.

[897] Ancestry.com, Social Security Death Index (Provo, UT, USA, The Generations Network, Inc., 2008), www.ancestry.com, Number: 387-18-4788; Issue State: Wisconsin; Issue Date: Before 1951. Record for Ralph Todd.

[898] Ancestry.com, 1940 United States Federal Census (Provo, UT, USA, Ancestry.com Operations, Inc., 2012), Ancestry.com, http://www.Ancestry.com, Year: 1940; Census Place: Madison, Dane, Wisconsin; Roll: T627_4470; Page: 7B; Enumeration District: 13-66. Record for Ralph Todd.

[899] Ancestry.com, Wisconsin, Births and Christenings Index, 1801-1928 (Provo, UT, USA, Ancestry.com Operations, Inc., 2011), Ancestry.com, http://www.Ancestry.com, Record for Ethel Amelia Luberg.

[900] Ancestry.com, U.S., Social Security Applications and Claims Index, 1936-2007 (Provo, UT, USA, Ancestry.com Operations, Inc., 2015), Ancestry.com, http://www.Ancestry.com, Record for Ethel A Todd.

[901] Ancestry.com, Wisconsin Death Index, 1959-1997 (Provo, UT, USA, Ancestry.com Operations Inc, 2007), Ancestry.com, http://www.Ancestry.com, Record for Fred L Todd.

Aug 1962 in Wisconsin[902]. He married Mabel Eliz Lubert[903]. She was born in Dec 1893 in River Falls, Wisconsin[904] and died on 17 Jan 1972 in Madison, Wisconsin[905]. Fred Louis Todd and Mabel Eliz Luberg had one child who may still be alive.

55. Everett Clifford Todd[5] (Ransom WilliamTodd[4], Julia Fannie Leigh[3], Elijah Leigh[2], Nathan S. Leigh[1]) was born on 19 Mar 1900 in La Valle, Wisconsin[906] and married Evelyn Catherine Freeman[907]. She was born on 15 Jun 1906[908].

Everett Clifford Todd Sr. and Evelyn Catherine Freeman had the following children:
      i. Robert Clifford Todd was born on 23 Dec 1923 in Laona, Wisconsin[909]. and died on 04 Mar 1991 in Kingman, Arizona[910].
121. ii. Jocelyn Dawn Todd was born on 09 Jul 1927 in Crandon, Wisconsin[911] and died on 13 Nov 2006[912].
      iii. Patricia Faye Todd was born on 17 Mar 1931 in Laona, Wisconsin[913] and died on 05 Aug 2003[914]. She married Mr. Blalock[915]. Patricia Faye Todd was buried in Birnamwood, Wisconsin[916].

[902] Ancestry.com, Wisconsin Death Index, 1959-1997 (Provo, UT, USA, Ancestry.com Operations Inc, 2007), Ancestry.com, http://www.Ancestry.com, Record for Fred L Todd..

[903] Ancestry.com, 1930 United States Federal Census (Provo, UT, USA, Ancestry.com Operations Inc, 2002), Ancestry.com, http://www.Ancestry.com, Year: 1930; Census Place: Madison, Dane, Wisconsin; Roll: 2567; Page: 5A; Enumeration District: 0051; FHL microfilm: 2342301. Record for Fred L Todd.

[904] Ancestry.com, 1930 United States Federal Census (Provo, UT, USA, Ancestry.com Operations Inc, 2002), Ancestry.com, http://www.Ancestry.com, Year: 1930; Census Place: Madison, Dane, Wisconsin; Roll: 2567; Page: 5A; Enumeration District: 0051; FHL microfilm: 2342301. Record for Fred L Todd.

[905] I have no documentation for this fact.

[906] Ancestry.com, World War I Draft Registration Cards, 1917 1918 (Provo, UT, USA, The Generations Network, Inc., 2005), www.ancestry.com, Registration State: Wisconsin; Registration County: Forest; Roll: 1674639. Record for Everett Clifford Todd.

[907] Ancestry.com, 1940 United States Federal Census (Provo, UT, USA, Ancestry.com Operations, Inc., 2012), Ancestry.com, http://www.Ancestry.com, Year: 1940; Census Place: Crandon, Forest, Wisconsin; Roll: T627_4480; Page: 21A; Enumeration District: 21-8. Record for Evelyn Todd.

[908] Ancestry.com. *Wisconsin, Births and Christenings Index, 1801-1928* [database on-line]. Provo, UT, USA: Ancestry.com Operations, Inc., 2011.

[909] Ancestry.com, Social Security Death Index (Provo, UT, USA, The Generations Network, Inc., 2008), www.ancestry.com, Number: 355-12-6367; Issue State: Illinois; Issue Date: Before 1951. Record for Robert C. Todd.

[910] Ancestry.com, Social Security Death Index (Provo, UT, USA, The Generations Network, Inc., 2008), www.ancestry.com, Number: 355-12-6367; Issue State: Illinois; Issue Date: Before 1951. Record for Robert C. Todd.

[911] Ancestry.com, U.S., Social Security Applications and Claims Index, 1936-2007 (Provo, UT, USA, Ancestry.com Operations, Inc., 2015), Ancestry.com, http://www.Ancestry.com, Record for Joyce Dawn Shufelt.

[912] Ancestry.com, U.S., Social Security Applications and Claims Index, 1936-2007 (Provo, UT, USA, Ancestry.com Operations, Inc., 2015), Ancestry.com, http://www.Ancestry.com, Record for Joyce Dawn Shufelt.

[913] Ancestry.com, U.S., Social Security Applications and Claims Index, 1936-2007 (Provo, UT, USA, Ancestry.com Operations, Inc., 2015), Ancestry.com, http://www.Ancestry.com, Record for Patricia Faye Finley.
Ancestry.com, U.S., Social Security Applications and Claims Index, 1936-2007 (Provo, UT, USA, Ancestry.com Operations, Inc., 2015), Ancestry.com, http://www.Ancestry.com, Record for Patricia Faye Finley[914]

[915] Ancestry.com, U.S., Find A Grave Index, 1700s-Current (Provo, UT, USA, Ancestry.com Operations, Inc., 2012), Ancestry.com, http://www.Ancestry.com, Record for Patricia Blalock.

[916] Ancestry.com, U.S., Find A Grave Index, 1700s-Current (Provo, UT, USA, Ancestry.com Operations, Inc., 2012), Ancestry.com, http://www.Ancestry.com, Record for Patricia Blalock.

iv.   Living Todd.

v.   Everett Clifford Todd Jr. was born on 27 Jul 1933 in Laona, Wisconsin[917] and died on 07 Mar 2002[918].

vi.   Delhart Romain Todd was born on 26 Apr 1938[919] and died on 08 Aug 2004 in Deerbrook, Wisconsin[920]. Delhart Romain Todd/Evans was buried in Birnamwood, Wisconsin[921].

vii.   Living Todd.

56. Royal Leslie Todd[5] (Ransom William Todd[4], Julia Fannie Leigh[3], Elijah Leigh[2], Nathan S. Leigh[1]) was born on 06 Mar 1902 in La Valle, Wisconsin[922] and died on 15 Oct 1988[923]. He married Margaret Rose Snaith[924]. She was born on 08 Nov 1902[925] and died on 22 Aug 1987 in Wisconsin[926]. Margaret Rose Snaith was buried in Rhinelander, Wisconsin[927].

Royal Leslie Todd and Margaret Rose Snaith had the following children:

i.   Richard Leslie Todd was born on 14 Oct 1926 in Rhinelander, Wisconsin[928] and died on 04 Apr 1995[929]. He married Vera F. McClain[930]. She was born on 21 May 1926 in Rhinelander, Wisconsin[931] and died on 29 Jul 2015[932].

---

[917] Ancestry.com, U.S., Department of Veterans Affairs BIRLS Death File, 1850-2010 (Provo, UT, USA, Ancestry.com Operations, Inc., 2011), www.ancestry.com, Record for Everett.

[918] Ancestry.com, U.S., Department of Veterans Affairs BIRLS Death File, 1850-2010 (Provo, UT, USA, Ancestry.com Operations, Inc., 2011), www.ancestry.com, Record for Everett.

[919] Ancestry.com, Social Security Death Index (Provo, UT, USA, The Generations Network, Inc., 2008), www.ancestry.com, Number: 391-36-2189; Issue State: Wisconsin; Issue Date: 1955. Record for Delhart R. Evans

[920] Ancestry.com, Social Security Death Index (Provo, UT, USA, The Generations Network, Inc., 2008), www.ancestry.com, Number: 391-36-2189; Issue State: Wisconsin; Issue Date: 1955. Record for Delhart R. Evans

[921] Ancestry.com, U.S., Find A Grave Index, 1700s-Current (Provo, UT, USA, Ancestry.com Operations, Inc., 2012), Ancestry.com, http://www.Ancestry.com, Record for Delhart Evans.

[922] Ancestry.com, U.S., Social Security Applications and Claims Index, 1936-2007 (Provo, UT, USA, Ancestry.com Operations, Inc., 2015), Ancestry.com, http://www.Ancestry.com, Record for Royal L Todd.

[923] Ancestry.com, U.S., Social Security Applications and Claims Index, 1936-2007 (Provo, UT, USA, Ancestry.com Operations, Inc., 2015), Ancestry.com, http://www.Ancestry.com, Record for Royal L Todd.

[924] Ancestry.com, Social Security Death Index (Provo, UT, USA, The Generations Network, Inc., 2008), www.ancestry.com, Number: 387-50-8202; Issue State: Wisconsin; Issue Date: 1964. Record for Margaret Todd

[925] Ancestry.com, Social Security Death Index (Provo, UT, USA, The Generations Network, Inc., 2008), www.ancestry.com, Number: 387-50-8202; Issue State: Wisconsin; Issue Date: 1964. Record for Margaret Todd

[926] Ancestry.com, Social Security Death Index (Provo, UT, USA, The Generations Network, Inc., 2008), www.ancestry.com, Number: 387-50-8202; Issue State: Wisconsin; Issue Date: 1964. Record for Margaret Todd

[927] Ancestry.com, U.S., Find A Grave Index, 1700s-Current (Provo, UT, USA, Ancestry.com Operations, Inc., 2012), Ancestry.com, http://www.Ancestry.com, Record for Royal L. Todd.

[928] Ancestry.com, U.S., Social Security Applications and Claims Index, 1936-2007 (Provo, UT, USA, Ancestry.com Operations, Inc., 2015), Ancestry.com, http://www.Ancestry.com, Record for Richard Leslie Todd.

[929] Ancestry.com, U.S., Social Security Applications and Claims Index, 1936-2007 (Provo, UT, USA, Ancestry.com Operations, Inc., 2015), Ancestry.com, http://www.Ancestry.com, Record for Richard Leslie Todd.

[930] Obituary included on this page.

[931] Obituary included on this page.

[932] Obituary included on this page.

Vera F. Todd, age 89, of Rhinelander, passed away Wednesday, July 29, 2015, at Rennes Health and Rehab. She was born May 21, 1926, in Rhinelander, to Joseph and Martha Belgard. Vera attended school in Rhinelander and later married Roy Gilbert who preceded her in death in 1959. She married Richard Todd in 1964 and together they raised their large family. In addition to caring for her family, Vera enjoyed gardening, fishing (especially fly fishing for trout), and berry picking. She was also an accomplished seamstress and will be fondly remembered for the beautiful Christmas gifts she created each year. She was a member of Nativity of Our Lord Catholic Church. Vera is survived by two sons, Brian (Laura) Gilbert of Rhinelander and John Todd of Roscoe, Ill.; four daughters, Frances Sackett of Waukesha, Corrine (George) Krzmarcik of Mosinee, Laurie Gilbert of Rhinelander, and JoAnn (Greg) Trouller of Pulaski; a son-in-law, Paul Hanse of Tomahawk; many grandchildren and great-grandchildren, a great-great-grandchild and other relatives and friends. She was preceded in death by her parents; her husbands, Roy and Richard; a daughter, Linda Hanse; and a sister, Antonia Urban. Interment will be in Nativity of Our Lord Catholic Cemetery.

      ii.   Living Todd.
      iii.   Living Todd.

57. Harold (Harley) Walter Todd[5] (Ransom William Todd[4], Julia Fannie Leigh[3], Elijah Leigh[2], Nathan S. Leigh[1]) was born on 04 Jan 1904 in La Valle, Wisconsin[933] and died on 14 Mar 1963 in Keno, Wisconsin[934]. He married Cornelia T. Kessner[935]. She was born on 02 Jun 1903[936] and died on 16 Feb 2000 in Kenosha, Wisconsin [937].
Harold (Harley) Walter Todd and Cornelia T. Kessner had the following child:

      i.   Lorraine Joy Todd was born on 15 Apr 1924 in Laona Forest, Wisconsin[938] and died on 03 Sep 1989 in Wisconsin, Kenosha[939]. She married Mr. Jelleson.

---

[933] Ancestry.com, Wisconsin Death Index, 1959-1997 (Provo, UT, USA, Ancestry.com Operations Inc, 2007), Ancestry.com, http://www.Ancestry.com, Record for Harley W Todd.

[934] Ancestry.com, Wisconsin Death Index, 1959-1997 (Provo, UT, USA, Ancestry.com Operations Inc, 2007), Ancestry.com, http://www.Ancestry.com, Record for Harley W Todd.

[935] Ancestry.com, Social Security Death Index (Provo, UT, USA, The Generations Network, Inc., 2008), www.ancestry.com, Number: 390-03-5869; Issue State: Wisconsin; Issue Date: Before 1951. Record for Cornelia Todd.

[936] Ancestry.com, Social Security Death Index (Provo, UT, USA, The Generations Network, Inc., 2008), www.ancestry.com, Number: 390-03-5869; Issue State: Wisconsin; Issue Date: Before 1951. Record for Cornelia Todd.

[937] Ancestry.com, Social Security Death Index (Provo, UT, USA, The Generations Network, Inc., 2008), Number: 390-03-5869; Issue State: Wisconsin; Issue Date: Before 1951. Record for Cornelia Todd.

[938] Ancestry.com, U.S., Social Security Applications and Claims Index, 1936-2007 (Provo, UT, USA, Ancestry.com Operations, Inc., 2015), Ancestry.com, http://www.Ancestry.com, Record for Lorraine Joy Todd.

[939] Ancestry.com, U.S., Social Security Applications and Claims Index, 1936-2007 (Provo, UT, USA, Ancestry.com Operations, Inc., 2015), Ancestry.com, http://www.Ancestry.com, Record for Lorraine Joy Todd.

58. Harvey Gary Todd[5] (Ransom William Todd[4], Julia Fannie Leigh[3], Elijah Leigh[2], Nathan S. Leigh[1]) was born on 04 Jan 1904 in La Valle, Wisconsin[940] and died on 13 Feb 1981 in Ramsey, Minnesota[941]. He married Annabelle Minton on 23 Sep 1923 in La Valle, Wisconsin[942], the daughter of Alfred Edmond Minton and Christina Maren Jensen. She was born in 23 Dec 1904 in Marville, Wisconsin[943] and died 14 Mar 1939 in Ironwood Michigan[944]. At the time of her death she was married to Sidney A. Chaney[945].

Harvey Gary Todd and Annabelle Minton had the following child:
    i.   Daniel Harvey Todd was born on 10 Jan 1924 in Wisconsin[946] and died on 13 Jan 1924 in Wisconsin[947]. Daniel Harvey Todd was buried in Crandon, Wisconsin[948].

59. Beulah E. Todd[5] (Ransom William Todd[4], Julia Fannie Leigh[3], Elijah Leigh[2], Nathan S. Leigh[1]) was born on 04 Oct 1913 in Wisconsin[949] and died on 22 Dec 1993 in St Paul, Minnesota[950]. She married Nicholas Joseph Fusenig Jr.[951]. He was born on 28 Oct 1914 in St Paul, Minnesota[952] and died on 19 Sep 1977 in Ramsey, Minnesota[953]. Nicholas Joseph Fusenig Jr. was buried in Vermillion, Minnesota[954].

Nicholas Joseph Fusenig Jr. and Beulah E. Todd had the following child:

---

[940] Ancestry.com, Minnesota, Death Index, 1908-2002 (Provo, UT, USA, Ancestry.com Operations Inc, 2001), Ancestry.com, http://www.Ancestry.com, Record for Harvey G Todd.

[941] Ancestry.com, Minnesota, Death Index, 1908-2002 (Provo, UT, USA, Ancestry.com Operations Inc, 2001), Ancestry.com, http://www.Ancestry.com, Record for Harvey G Todd.

[942] Genealogy compiled by Rev. Laverne E. Leigh in 2017.

[943] Michigan, Death Records, 1867-1950.

[944] Michigan, Death Records, 1867-1950.

[945] Michigan, Death Records, 1867-1950.

[946] Ancestry.com, U.S., Find A Grave Index, 1700s-Current (Provo, UT, USA, Ancestry.com Operations, Inc., 2012), Ancestry.com, http://www.Ancestry.com, Record for Donald Harvey Todd.

[947] Ancestry.com, U.S., Find A Grave Index, 1700s-Current (Provo, UT, USA, Ancestry.com Operations, Inc., 2012), Ancestry.com, http://www.Ancestry.com, Record for Donald Harvey Todd.

[948] Ancestry.com, U.S., Find A Grave Index, 1700s-Current (Provo, UT, USA, Ancestry.com Operations, Inc., 2012), Ancestry.com, http://www.Ancestry.com, Record for Donald Harvey Todd.

[949] Ancestry.com, U.S., Social Security Applications and Claims Index, 1936-2007 (Provo, UT, USA, Ancestry.com Operations, Inc., 2015), Ancestry.com, http://www.Ancestry.com, Record for Beulah E Fusenig.

[950] Ancestry.com, U.S., Social Security Applications and Claims Index, 1936-2007 (Provo, UT, USA, Ancestry.com Operations, Inc., 2015), Ancestry.com, http://www.Ancestry.com, Record for Beulah E Fusenig.

[951] Year: *1940;* Census Place: *St Paul, Ramsey, Minnesota;* Roll: *m-t0627-01995;* Page: *9A;* Enumeration District: *90-35.*

[952] Ancestry.com, Minnesota, Death Index, 1908-2002 (Provo, UT, USA, Ancestry.com Operations Inc, 2001), Ancestry.com, http://www.Ancestry.com, Record for Nicholas Joseph Fusenig.

[953] Ancestry.com, Minnesota, Death Index, 1908-2002 (Provo, UT, USA, Ancestry.com Operations Inc, 2001), Ancestry.com, http://www.Ancestry.com, Record for Nicholas Joseph Fusenig.

[954] Ancestry.com, U.S., Find A Grave Index, 1700s-Current (Provo, UT, USA, Ancestry.com Operations, Inc., 2012), Ancestry.com, http://www.Ancestry.com, Record for Nicholas J Fusenig.

i.   Nicholas Dudley Fusenig was born on 29 Mar 1941 in St Paul, Minnesota[955] and died on 06 Jun 1998 in Glynn County, Georgia[956]. Nicholas Dudley Fusenig was buried in Bushnell, Florida [957].

60. Leo Melvin Priest[5] (Fred M. Priest[4], Julia Fannie Leigh[3], Elijah Leigh[2], Nathan S. Leigh[1]) was born on 26 Oct 1893 in Kansas[958] and died on 02 Aug 1967 in Los Angeles, California[959]. He married Thelma Ragnhild Olson[960]. She was born on 30 Dec 1901 in Minnesota[961] and died on 13 May 1978 in Orange County, California[962]. Leo Melvin Priest and his wife were buried in Cypress, Orange County, California[963].

Leo Melvin Priest and Thelma Ragnhild Olsen had the following children:
122.   i.   Bruce Robert Priest was born on 15 Dec 1927 in Watonwan, Minnesota[964] and died on 10 Sep 1963 in Hennepin, Minnesota[965].
ii.   Patricia Louise Priest was born on 28 Mar 1930 in Watonwan, Minnesota[966] and died on 25 March 1997 in Orange County, California[967]. Patricia Louise Priest was buried in Cypress, California[968].

61. Claude Morton Priest[5] (Fred M. Priest[4], Julia Fannie Leigh[3], Elijah Leigh[2], Nathan S. Leigh[1]) was born on 08 May 1896 in Wisconsin[969] and died on 02 Feb 1970 in St James,

[955] Ancestry.com, U.S., Social Security Applications and Claims Index, 1936-2007 (Provo, UT, USA, Ancestry.com Operations, Inc., 2015), Ancestry.com, http://www.Ancestry.com, Record for Nicholas Dudly Fusenig.
[956] Ancestry.com, U.S., Social Security Applications and Claims Index, 1936-2007 (Provo, UT, USA, Ancestry.com Operations, Inc., 2015), Ancestry.com, http://www.Ancestry.com, Record for Nicholas Dudly Fusenig.
[957] Ancestry.com, U.S., Find A Grave Index, 1700s-Current (Provo, UT, USA, Ancestry.com Operations, Inc., 2012), Ancestry.com, http://www.Ancestry.com, Record for Nicholas D Fusenig.
[958] Ancestry.com, World War I Draft Registration Cards, 1917-1918 (Provo, UT, USA, The Generations Network, Inc., 2005), www.ancestry.com, Registration State: Minnesota; Registration County: Watonwan; Roll: 1682695. Record for Leo Melvin Priest.
[959] Ancestry.com, California Death Index, 1940-1997 (Provo, UT, USA, The Generations Network, Inc., 2000), www.ancestry.com, Date: 1967-08-02. Record for Leo M Priest.
[960] Ancestry.com, California Death Index, 1940-1997 (Provo, UT, USA, The Generations Network, Inc., 2000), www.ancestry.com, Date: 1978-05-13. Record for Thelma R Priest.
[961] Ancestry.com, California Death Index, 1940-1997 (Provo, UT, USA, The Generations Network, Inc., 2000), www.ancestry.com, Date: 1978-05-13. Record for Thelma R Priest.
[962] Ancestry.com, California Death Index, 1940-1997 (Provo, UT, USA, The Generations Network, Inc., 2000), www.ancestry.com, Date: 1978-05-13. Record for Thelma R Priest.
[963] Ancestry.com, U.S., Find A Grave Index, 1700s-Current (Provo, UT, USA, Ancestry.com Operations, Inc., 2012), Ancestry.com, http://www.Ancestry.com, Record for Leo Melvin Priest.
[964] Ancestry.com, Web: Minnesota, Birth Index, 1900-1934 (Provo, UT, USA, Ancestry.com Operations, Inc., 2015), Ancestry.com, http://www.Ancestry.com, Record for Bruce Robert Priest.
[965] Ancestry.com, Minnesota, Death Index, 1908-2002 (Provo, UT, USA, Ancestry.com Operations Inc, 2001), Ancestry.com, http://www.Ancestry.com, Record for Bruce Robert Priest.
[966] Ancestry.com. Web: Minnesota, Birth Index, 1900-1934.
[967] Ancestry.com, U.S., Find A Grave Index, 1700s-Current.
[968] Ancestry.com, U.S., Find A Grave Index, 1700s-Current.
[969] Ancestry.com, World War I Draft Registration Cards, 1917-1918 (Provo, UT, USA, The Generations Network, Inc., 2005), www.ancestry.com, Registration State: Minnesota; Registration County: Watonwan; Roll: 1682695. Record for Claud Morton Priest.

Minnesota[970]. He married Rose Melvina Fjelsta, the daughter of Nils Fjelsta and Rachel Ellertson[971]. She was born on 22 Mar 1899[972] and died on 01 Sep 1991[973]. Claude was the owner of a produce house.

Claude Morton Priest and Rose Melvina Fjelsta had the following children:
123.   i.   Joan Alicia Priest was born on 07 Mar 1922 in Madelia Wato, Minnesota[974] and died on 02 Jun 1995 in Las Vegas, Nevada[975].
124.   ii.   Richard Charles Priest was born on 17 May 1927 in Watonwan, Minnesota[976] and died on 02 Feb 2012[977].

62.   Bernice P. Priest[5] (Fred M. Priest[4], Julia Fannie Leigh[3], Elijah Leigh[2], Nathan S. Leigh[1]) was born on 03 Nov 1898[978] and died on 09 May 1967 in Ramsey, Minnesota[979]. She married Grover C. Beatty[980]. He was born on 24 Jul 1892 in Dryden Township, Minnesota[981] and died on 08 Dec 1961 in Minnesota[982]. Bernice P. Priest and her husband were buried in Mendota Heights, Minnesota[983].

---

[970] Ancestry.com, Minnesota, Death Index, 1908-2002 (Provo, UT, USA, Ancestry.com Operations Inc, 2001), Ancestry.com, http://www.Ancestry.com, Record for Mr. Claude Monroe Priest.
[971] Ancestry.com, 1930 United States Federal Census (Provo, UT, USA, The Generations Network, Inc., 2002), www.ancestry.com, Year: 1930; Census Place: St James, Watonwan, Minnesota; Roll: 1134; Page: 26A; Enumeration District: 0018; FHL microfilm: 2340869. Record for Claude M Priest.
[972] Ancestry.com. *Minnesota, Death Index, 1908-2002* [database on-line]. Provo, UT, USA: Ancestry.com Operations Inc, 2001.
[973] Ancestry.com. *Minnesota, Death Index, 1908-2002* [database on-line]. Provo, UT, USA: Ancestry.com Operations Inc, 2001.
[974] Ancestry.com, U.S., Social Security Applications and Claims Index, 1936-2007 (Provo, UT, USA, Ancestry.com Operations, Inc., 2015), Ancestry.com, http://www.Ancestry.com, Record for Joan Alicia Priest
[975] Ancestry.com, U.S., Social Security Applications and Claims Index, 1936-2007 (Provo, UT, USA, Ancestry.com Operations, Inc., 2015), Ancestry.com, http://www.Ancestry.com, Record for Joan Alicia Priest
[976] Ancestry.com, U.S., Find A Grave Index, 1700s-Current (Provo, UT, USA, Ancestry.com Operations, Inc., 2012), Ancestry.com, http://www.Ancestry.com, Record for Richard C. Priest.
[977] Ancestry.com, U.S., Find A Grave Index, 1700s-Current (Provo, UT, USA, Ancestry.com Operations, Inc., 2012), Ancestry.com, http://www.Ancestry.com, Record for Richard C. Priest.
[978] Ancestry.com, Minnesota, Death Index, 1908-2002 (Provo, UT, USA, Ancestry.com Operations Inc, 2001), Ancestry.com, http://www.Ancestry.com, Record for Bernice P. Beatty.
[979] Ancestry.com, Minnesota, Death Index, 1908-2002 (Provo, UT, USA, Ancestry.com Operations Inc, 2001), Ancestry.com, http://www.Ancestry.com, Record for Bernice P. Beatty.
[980] Ancestry.com, U.S., Find A Grave Index, 1700s-Current (Provo, UT, USA, Ancestry.com Operations, Inc., 2012), Ancestry.com, http://www.Ancestry.com, Record for Bernice Beatty.
[981] Ancestry.com, U.S., Find A Grave Index, 1700s-Current (Provo, UT, USA, Ancestry.com Operations, Inc., 2012), Ancestry.com, http://www.Ancestry.com, Record for Bernice Beatty.
[982] Ancestry.com, U.S., Find A Grave Index, 1700s-Current (Provo, UT, USA, Ancestry.com Operations, Inc., 2012), Ancestry.com, http://www.Ancestry.com, Record for Bernice Beatty.
[983] Ancestry.com, U.S., Find A Grave Index, 1700s-Current (Provo, UT, USA, Ancestry.com Operations, Inc., 2012), Ancestry.com, http://www.Ancestry.com, Record for Bernice Beatty.

Grover C. Beatty and Bernice P. Priest had the following children:
125.   i.   Marilyn Grace Beatty was born on 30 Jul 1926 in Sibley, Minnesota[984] and died on 01 Dec 2001[985].
        ii.   Living Beatty.

63.   Ray M. Priest[5] (Fred M. Priest[4], Julia Fannie Leigh[3], Elijah Leigh[2], Nathan S. Leigh[1]) was born on 08 Sep 1905 in Windom, Minnesota[986] and died on 13 Jun 1939 in Watonwan, Minnesota[987]. He married Gladys Louise Wold[988]. She was born on 05 Feb 1906 in Fillmore, Minnesota[989] and died on 18 Apr 1971 in Saint James, Minnesota[990]. Ray M. Priest and his wife were buried in Saint James, Minnesota[991]. Ray M. Priest and Gladys Louise Wold had one child who may still be living.

64.   Jay Marion Priest[5] (Fred M. Priest[4], Julia Fannie Leigh[3], Elijah Leigh[2], Nathan S. Leigh[1]) was born on 08 Sep 1905 in Windom, Minnesota[992] and died on 06 Nov 1976 in Grove City, Pennsylvania[993]. He married Winifred Lucille Cooper[994]. She was born on 23 Jan 1908 in Montford, Wisconsin[995] and died on 16 Apr 1992 in Dallas, Texas[996]. Jay Marion Priest and his wife were buried in Crestview Memorial Park, Grove City, Pennsylvania[997]. Jay was a twin to Ray. Jay was listed as a teacher and a Principal in the

---

[984] Ancestry.com, U.S., Social Security Applications and Claims Index, 1936-2007 (Provo, UT, USA, Ancestry.com Operations, Inc., 2015), Ancestry.com, http://www.Ancestry.com, Record for Marilyn Grace Beatty
[985] Ancestry.com, U.S., Social Security Applications and Claims Index, 1936-2007 (Provo, UT, USA, Ancestry.com Operations, Inc., 2015), Ancestry.com, http://www.Ancestry.com, Record for Marilyn Grace Beatty
[986] Ancestry.com, U.S., Find A Grave Index, 1700s-Current (Provo, UT, USA, Ancestry.com Operations, Inc., 2012), Ancestry.com, http://www.Ancestry.com, Record for Ray M. Priest.
[987] Ancestry.com, U.S., Find A Grave Index, 1700s-Current (Provo, UT, USA, Ancestry.com Operations, Inc., 2012), Ancestry.com, http://www.Ancestry.com, Record for Ray M. Priest.
[988] Genealogy compiled by Rev. Laverne E. Leigh in 2017.
[989] Ancestry.com, Web: Minnesota, Birth Index, 1900-1934 (Provo, UT, USA, Ancestry.com Operations, Inc., 2015), Ancestry.com, http://www.Ancestry.com, Record for Gladys Louise Wold.
[990] Ancestry.com, U.S., Find A Grave Index, 1700s-Current (Provo, UT, USA, Ancestry.com Operations, Inc., 2012), Ancestry.com, http://www.Ancestry.com, Record for Glady Louise Stradtman.
[991] Ancestry.com, U.S., Find A Grave Index, 1700s-Current (Provo, UT, USA, Ancestry.com Operations, Inc., 2012), Ancestry.com, http://www.Ancestry.com, Record for Glady Louise Stradtman.
[992] Ancestry.com, U.S., Find A Grave Index, 1700s-Current (Provo, UT, USA, Ancestry.com Operations, Inc., 2012), Ancestry.com, http://www.Ancestry.com, Record for Jay M. Priest.
[993] Ancestry.com, U.S., Find A Grave Index, 1700s-Current (Provo, UT, USA, Ancestry.com Operations, Inc., 2012), Ancestry.com, http://www.Ancestry.com, Record for Jay M. Priest.
[994] Ancestry.com, 1940 United States Federal Census (Provo, UT, USA, Ancestry.com Operations, Inc., 2012), Ancestry.com, http://www.Ancestry.com, Year: 1940; Census Place: Versailles, Allegheny, Pennsylvania; Roll: T627_3420; Page: 16A; Enumeration District: 2-577. Record for Jay Priest.
[995] Ancestry.com, U.S., Social Security Applications and Claims Index, 1936-2007 (Provo, UT, USA, Ancestry.com Operations, Inc., 2015), Ancestry.com, http://www.Ancestry.com, Record for Winifred Lucille Priest.
[996] Ancestry.com, U.S., Social Security Applications and Claims Index, 1936-2007 (Provo, UT, USA, Ancestry.com Operations, Inc., 2015), Ancestry.com, http://www.Ancestry.com, Record for Winifred Lucille Priest.
[997] Ancestry.com, U.S., Find A Grave Index, 1700s-Current (Provo, UT, USA, Ancestry.com Operations, Inc., 2012), Ancestry.com, http://www.Ancestry.com, Record for Winifred L. Priest.

1940 Census. He went to college and finished the fifth year. Jay Marion Priest and Winifred Lucille Cooper had one child who may still be living.

65. Robert Gaylord Priest[5] (Fred M. Priest[4], Julia Fannie Leigh[3], Elijah Leigh[2], Nathan S. Leigh[1]) was born on 16 Mar 1917 in St. James, Minnesota[998] and died in Jul 1994 in Kalispell, Montana[999]. He married Eileen Kathryn Roche, the daughter of Bernard Charles Roche and Ida Mae Drinkard, on 29 Oct 1938 in Kalispell, Montana[1000]. She was born on 23 Feb 1917 in North Dakota[1001] and died on 21 Feb 2009 in Burnsville, Minnesota[1002]. Robert Gaylord Priest and Eileen Kathryn Roche had one child who may still be living.

66. Genevieve Jewel Johnson[5] (Nora Eleanor Priest[4], Julia Fannie Leigh[3], Elijah Leigh[2], Nathan S. Leigh[1]) was born on 16 Feb 1893 in Miltonvale, Kansas[1003] and died on 24 Oct 1971 in Rhinelander, Wisconsin[1004]. She married William Martin Michael Schultz, the son of William F. Schultz and Louise Kulka, on 19 Jul 1937 in Crystal Falls, Michigan[1005]. He was born on 06 Sep 1882 in Stettin, Federal Republic of Germany[1006] and died on 26 Jan 1968[1007]. Genevieve Jewel Johnson and her husband were buried in Crandon, Wisconsin[1008].

---

[998] Ancestry.com, Montana, County Marriages, 1865-1950 (Provo, UT, USA, Ancestry.com Operations, Inc., 2014), Ancestry.com, http://www.Ancestry.com, Record for Robert Gaylor Priest.

[999] Ancestry.com. *U.S., Social Security Applications and Claims Index, 1936-2007* [database on-line]. Provo, UT, USA: Ancestry.com Operations, Inc., 2015.

[1000] Ancestry.com, Montana, County Marriages, 1865-1950 (Provo, UT, USA, Ancestry.com Operations, Inc., 2014), Ancestry.com, http://www.Ancestry.com, Record for Robert Gaylor Priest.

[1001] Ancestry.com, Social Security Death Index (Provo, UT, USA, The Generations Network, Inc., 2008), www.ancestry.com, Issue State: Montana; Issue Date: Before 1951. Record for Eileen Kathryn Priest.

[1002] Ancestry.com, Social Security Death Index (Provo, UT, USA, The Generations Network, Inc., 2008), www.ancestry.com, Issue State: Montana; Issue Date: Before 1951. Record for Eileen Kathryn Priest.

[1003] Ancestry.com, U.S., Find A Grave Index, 1700s-Current (Provo, UT, USA, Ancestry.com Operations, Inc., 2012), Ancestry.com, http://www.Ancestry.com, Record for William Martin Schultz.

[1004] Ancestry.com, U.S., Find A Grave Index, 1700s-Current (Provo, UT, USA, Ancestry.com Operations, Inc., 2012), Ancestry.com, http://www.Ancestry.com, Record for William Martin Schultz.

[1005] Ancestry.com, Michigan, Marriage Records, 1867-1952 (Provo, UT, USA, Ancestry.com Operations, Inc., 2015), Ancestry.com, http://www.Ancestry.com, Record for Mr William M Schultz.

[1006] Ancestry.com, U.S., Find A Grave Index, 1700s-Current (Provo, UT, USA, Ancestry.com Operations, Inc., 2012), Ancestry.com, http://www.Ancestry.com, Record for William Martin Schultz.

[1007] Ancestry.com, U.S., Find A Grave Index, 1700s-Current (Provo, UT, USA, Ancestry.com Operations, Inc., 2012), Ancestry.com, http://www.Ancestry.com, Record for William Martin Schultz.

[1008] Ancestry.com, U.S., Find A Grave Index, 1700s-Current (Provo, UT, USA, Ancestry.com Operations, Inc., 2012), Ancestry.com, http://www.Ancestry.com, Record for William Martin Schultz.

Photo of Genevieve Jewel Johnson and William Martin Michael Schultz found on familysearch.org.

William Martin Michael Schultz and Genevieve Jewel Johnson had the following children:
126.   i.   Wilfred Wine Schultz was born on 18 Jul 1909 in Argonne, Wisconsin[1009] and died on 24 Feb 1983 in Rhinelander, Wisconsin[1010].

Photo of Genevieve Jewel Johnson and William Martin Michael Schultz found on familysearch.org.

127.   ii.   Irvin Michael Anthony Schultz was born on 29 Jul 1911 in Argonne, Wisconsin[1011] and died on 14 Dec 1999 in Iron River, Michigan[1012].

67. Violet R. Johnson[5] (Nora Eleanor Priest[4], Julia Fannie Leigh[3], Elijah Leigh[2], Nathan S. Leigh[1]) was born on 11 Aug 1897 in Reedsburg, Wisconsin[1013] 216-216 and died on 26 Oct 1959 in Laona, Wisconsin[1014]. She married Francis McGregor on 30 Sep 1918[1015]. This was a brief marriage lasting only a couple of years.

Thursday, October 29, 1969 - THE FOREST REPUBLICAN, Crandon, Forest County, WI; Page 1:
Violet McGregor of Crandon Dies. Mrs. Violet R. McGregor, 62, of Crandon died at 8:10 Monday evening at the Ovitz Hospital, Laona, after being seriously ill for three

[1009] Ancestry.com. *U.S., Find A Grave Index, 1600s-Current* [database on-line]. Provo, UT, USA: Ancestry.com Operations, Inc., 2012.

[1010] Ancestry.com. *U.S., Find A Grave Index, 1600s-Current* [database on-line]. Provo, UT, USA: Ancestry.com Operations, Inc., 2012.

[1011] Ancestry.com. *U.S., Find A Grave Index, 1600s-Current* [database on-line]. Provo, UT, USA: Ancestry.com Operations, Inc., 2012.

[1012] Ancestry.com. *U.S., Find A Grave Index, 1600s-Current* [database on-line]. Provo, UT, USA: Ancestry.com Operations, Inc., 2012.

[1013] Ancestry.com. *U.S., Find A Grave Index, 1600s-Current* [database on-line]. Provo, UT, USA: Ancestry.com Operations, Inc., 2012.

[1014] Ancestry.com. *Wisconsin, Death Index, 1959-1997* [database on-line]. Provo, UT, USA: Ancestry.com Operations Inc, 2007.

[1015] Obituary, The Forest Republican, Crandon, Forest County, Wisconsin, October 29, 1969, page 1.

days. Death resulted suddenly from a heart attack. Mrs. McGregor suffered a stroke, while at the NuRoc Home in Blackwell and pneumonia set in. She was admitted to the hospital Friday afternoon. Funeral services were held at 2 o'clock this afternoon at the Halverson Funeral Home here with the Rev. Howard Ott, Crandon Methodist pastor, officiating. Pallbearers were Fay Marsh, Jack Netzel, Vern Russell, Lynn Paul, Lyle Jackson and John Kuss. Burial was in the Lakeside cemetery here. Deceased was born Aug. 11, 1897 in Reedsburg, Wis., the daughter of Walter and Nora (should be Nona) Johnson. She was married to Francis McGregor on Sept. 30, 1918. Mrs. McGregor entered the NuRoc Home on June 18, 1956. Among the survivors are a son, Jack McGregor, address unknown, a sister, Mrs. Wm. M. Schulz, of Argonne; two brothers, Reuben Johnson of Bishop, Calif., and Icel Johnson of Medford, Ore., and one grandchild. Her parents and a son, Thomas, preceded her in death.

Francis McGregor and Violet R Johnson had the following child:

  i. Jack McGregor was born 27 Feb 1919 in Wisconsin[1016] and died on 07 Mar 1957 in Wisconsin[1017].

68. Icel Irving Johnson[5] (Nora Eleanor Priest[4], Julia Fannie Leigh[3], Elijah Leigh[2], Nathan S. Leigh[1]) was born on 16 Jun 1903 in La Valle, Wisconsin[1018] and died on 23 Oct 1974 in Deschutes, Oregon[1019]. He married Vila C. Thompson[1020]. She was born on 09 Feb 1903 in Brillion, Wisconsin[1021] and died on 25 Nov 1995 in Redmond, Oregon[1022]. Icel Irving Johnson and his wife were buried in Medford, Oregon[1023].

Icel Irving Johnson and Vila C. Thompson had the following children:

  i. Calvin Frederick Johnson was born on 07 Jul 1926 in Crandon, Wisconsin[1024] and died on 08 Jan 1927 in Crandon, Wisconsin[1025]. Calvin Fredrick Johnson was buried in Crandon, Wisconsin[1026].

[1016] U.S., Find A Grave Index, 1700s-Current at Ancestry.com.

[1017] U.S., Find A Grave Index, 1700s-Current at Ancestry.com.

[1018] Ancestry.com, Wisconsin, Births and Christenings Index, 1801-1928 (Provo, UT, USA, Ancestry.com Operations, Inc., 2011), Ancestry.com, http://www.Ancestry.com, Record for Icel Irving Johnson.

[1019] Ancestry.com, Oregon Death Index, 1903-98 (Provo, UT, USA, Ancestry.com Operations Inc, 2000), www.ancestry.com, Oregon State Library; 1966-1970 Death Index; Reel Title: State of Oregon Death Index; Year Range: 1971-1980. Record for Icel Irv Johnson.

[1020] Ancestry.com, U.S., Find A Grave Index, 1700s-Current (Provo, UT, USA, Ancestry.com Operations, Inc., 2012), Ancestry.com, http://www.Ancestry.com, Record for Icel Irving Johnson.

[1021] Ancestry.com, U.S., Find A Grave Index, 1700s-Current (Provo, UT, USA, Ancestry.com Operations, Inc., 2012), Ancestry.com, http://www.Ancestry.com, Record for Icel Irving Johnson.

[1022] Ancestry.com, U.S., Find A Grave Index, 1700s-Current (Provo, UT, USA, Ancestry.com Operations, Inc., 2012), Ancestry.com, http://www.Ancestry.com, Record for Icel Irving Johnson.

[1023] Ancestry.com, U.S., Find A Grave Index, 1700s-Current (Provo, UT, USA, Ancestry.com Operations, Inc., 2012), Ancestry.com, http://www.Ancestry.com, Record for Icel Irving Johnson.

[1024] Ancestry.com, U.S., Find A Grave Index, 1700s-Current (Provo, UT, USA, Ancestry.com Operations, Inc., 2012), Ancestry.com, http://www.Ancestry.com, Record for Icel Irving Johnson.

[1025] Ancestry.com, U.S., Find A Grave Index, 1700s-Current (Provo, UT, USA, Ancestry.com Operations, Inc., 2012), Ancestry.com, http://www.Ancestry.com, Record for Icel Irving Johnson.

ii.   William Lee Johnson was born on 04 Jan 1938 in Crandon, Wisconsin[1027] and died on 28 Jan 1938 in Crandon, Wisconsin[1028]. William Lee Johnson was buried in Crandon, Wisconsin[1029].

69. George William Harnden[5] (Sarah Amaria Leigh[4], William Safford Leigh[3], William Todd Leigh[2], Nathan S. Leigh[1]) was born on 28 Jan 1885 in Minnesota[1030] and died on 19 Jan 1952 in Stillwater, Oklahoma[1031]. He married Rosabelle Breedlove[1032]. She was born in 1885 in Missouri[1033]. He later married Sylvia Fern Pratt[1034].   She was born on 14 Nov 1894 in Oklahoma[1035] and died on 14 Sep 1988 in Fairfield, California[1036]. George William Harnden and his wife Sylvia Fern Pratt were buried in 1952 in Stillwater, Oklahoma[1037].

Photo of George William Harnden found on ancestry.com.

[1026] Ancestry.com, U.S., Find A Grave Index, 1700s-Current (Provo, UT, USA, Ancestry.com Operations, Inc., 2012), Ancestry.com, http://www.Ancestry.com, Record for Icel Irving Johnson.

[1027] Ancestry.com, U.S., Find A Grave Index, 1700s-Current (Provo, UT, USA, Ancestry.com Operations, Inc., 2012), Ancestry.com, http://www.Ancestry.com, Record for Icel Irving Johnson.

[1028] Ancestry.com, U.S., Find A Grave Index, 1700s-Current (Provo, UT, USA, Ancestry.com Operations, Inc., 2012), Ancestry.com, http://www.Ancestry.com, Record for Icel Irving Johnson.

[1029] Ancestry.com, U.S., Find A Grave Index, 1700s-Current (Provo, UT, USA, Ancestry.com Operations, Inc., 2012), Ancestry.com, http://www.Ancestry.com, Record for Icel Irving Johnson.

[1030] Ancestry.com, U.S., Social Security Applications and Claims Index, 1936-2007 (Provo, UT, USA, Ancestry.com Operations, Inc., 2015), Ancestry.com, http://www.Ancestry.com, Record for George W Harnden.

[1031] Ancestry.com, U.S., Social Security Applications and Claims Index, 1936-2007 (Provo, UT, USA, Ancestry.com Operations, Inc., 2015), Ancestry.com, http://www.Ancestry.com, Record for George W Harnden.

[1032] Ancestry.com, 1920 United States Federal Census (Online publication - Provo, UT, USA: Ancestry.com Operations Inc, 2010. Images reproduced by FamilySearch.Original data - Fourteenth Census of the United States, 1920. (NARA microfilm publication T625, 2076 rolls). Records of the Bureau of the Census, Reco), Ancestry.com, http://www.Ancestry.com, Year: 1920; Census Place: Stillwater Ward 2, Payne, Oklahoma; Roll: T625_1482; Page: 19A; Enumeration District: 190. Record for George W Harnden.

[1033] Ancestry.com, 1920 United States Federal Census (Online publication - Provo, UT, USA: Ancestry.com Operations Inc, 2010. Images reproduced by FamilySearch.Original data - Fourteenth Census of the United States, 1920. (NARA microfilm publication T625, 2076 rolls). Records of the Bureau of the Census, Reco), Ancestry.com, http://www.Ancestry.com, Year: 1920; Census Place: Stillwater Ward 2, Payne, Oklahoma; Roll: T625_1482; Page: 19A; Enumeration District: 190. Record for George W Harnden.

[1034] Year: *1940;* Census Place: *Stillwater, Payne, Oklahoma;* Roll: *m-t0627-03323;* Page: *4B;* Enumeration District: *60-30.*

[1035] Ancestry.com, U.S., Find A Grave Index, 1700s-Current (Provo, UT, USA, Ancestry.com Operations, Inc., 2012), Ancestry.com, http://www.Ancestry.com, Record for Sylvia F Harnden.

[1036] Ancestry.com, U.S., Find A Grave Index, 1700s-Current (Provo, UT, USA, Ancestry.com Operations, Inc., 2012), Ancestry.com, http://www.Ancestry.com, Record for Sylvia F Harnden.

[1037] Ancestry.com, U.S., Find A Grave Index, 1700s-Current (Provo, UT, USA, Ancestry.com Operations, Inc., 2012), Ancestry.com, http://www.Ancestry.com, Record for Sylvia F Harnden.

George William Harnden and Rosabelle Breedlove had the following children:

128.   i.   Mrytle Rozette Harnden was born on 24 Apr 1908 in Oklahoma[1038] and died on 10 Dec 1974[1039].

       ii.   Robert Francis Harnden was born on 12 Nov 1912 in Mammoth, Arkansas[1040] and died in Dec 1976 in Norman, Oklahoma[1041]. He married Genevieve Mae Packer on 11 Sep 1937 in Jackson, Missouri[1042]. She was born on 05 May 1916 in Webb City, Missouri[1043] and died in 1970[1044]. Robert Francis was buried in Pawnee, Oklahoma[1045].

Photo of Genevieve Mae Packer found on Ancestry.com.

       iii.   Georgiabell Harnden was born on 04 Jun 1915 in Pawnee, Oklahoma[1046] and died on 03 Oct 1991 in Stillwater, Oklahoma[1047]. She married Vern Gilbert Nelson on 08 Sep 1934[1048]. He was born on 17 Jul 1900 in Kansas[1049] and died on 09 Dec 1988 in Stillwater, Oklahoma[1050]. Georgiabell Harnden and her husband were buried in Stillwater, Oklahoma[1051].

[1038] Ancestry.com, Social Security Death Index (Provo, UT, USA, The Generations Network, Inc., 2008), www.ancestry.com, Number: 445-54-8483; Issue State: Oklahoma; Issue Date: 1967. Record for Myrtle Dodson.

[1039] Ancestry.com, Social Security Death Index (Provo, UT, USA, The Generations Network, Inc., 2008), www.ancestry.com, Number: 445-54-8483; Issue State: Oklahoma; Issue Date: 1967. Record for Myrtle Dodson.

[1040] Ancestry.com, U.S., Find A Grave Index, 1700s-Current (Provo, UT, USA, Ancestry.com Operations, Inc., 2012), Ancestry.com, http://www.Ancestry.com, Record for Robert F. L. Harnden.

[1041] Ancestry.com, U.S., Find A Grave Index, 1700s-Current (Provo, UT, USA, Ancestry.com Operations, Inc., 2012), Ancestry.com, http://www.Ancestry.com, Record for Robert F. L. Harnden.

[1042] Ancestry.com, Missouri, Marriage Records, 1805-2002 (Provo, UT, USA, Ancestry.com Operations, Inc., 2007), Ancestry.com, http://www.Ancestry.com, Record for Genevieve Packer.

[1043] Genealogy compiled by Rev. Laverne E. Leigh in 2017.

[1044] Genealogy compiled by Rev. Laverne E. Leigh in 2017.

[1045] Ancestry.com, U.S., Find A Grave Index, 1700s-Current (Provo, UT, USA, Ancestry.com Operations, Inc., 2012), Ancestry.com, http://www.Ancestry.com, Record for Robert F. L. Harnden.

[1046] Ancestry.com, U.S., Find A Grave Index, 1700s-Current (Provo, UT, USA, Ancestry.com Operations, Inc., 2012), Ancestry.com, http://www.Ancestry.com, Record for Georgebell Nelson.

[1047] Ancestry.com, U.S., Find A Grave Index, 1700s-Current (Provo, UT, USA, Ancestry.com Operations, Inc., 2012), Ancestry.com, http://www.Ancestry.com, Record for Georgebell Nelson.

[1048] Genealogy compiled by Rev. Laverne E. Leigh in 2017.

[1049] Ancestry.com, World War I Draft Registration Cards, 1917-1918 (Provo, UT, USA, The Generations Network, Inc., 2005), www.ancestry.com, Registration State: Oklahoma; Registration County: Payne; Roll: 1852069. Record for Vernie Gilbert Nelson.

[1050] Ancestry.com, U.S., Social Security Applications and Claims Index, 1936-2007 (Provo, UT, USA, Ancestry.com Operations, Inc., 2015), Ancestry.com, http://www.Ancestry.com, Record for Vern Nelson.

[1051] Ancestry.com, U.S., Find A Grave Index, 1700s-Current (Provo, UT, USA, Ancestry.com Operations, Inc., 2012), Ancestry.com, http://www.Ancestry.com, Record for Vern Nelson.

70. Rosetta Frances Harnden[5] (Sarah Amaria Leigh[4], William Safford Leigh[3], William Todd Leigh[2], Nathan S. Leigh[1]) was born on 12 Sep 1886 in Winnebago City, Minnesota[1052] and died on 16 Nov 1914 in Pawnee, Oklahoma[1053]. She married Lemuel Elmer Doty[1054] He was born on 22 Aug 1878[1055]. Rosetta Frances Harnden was buried in Pawnee, Oklahoma[1056].

Lemuel Elmer Doty and Rosetta Frances Harnden had the following children:

    i.   Lola Rosebelle Doty was born on 10 Jan 1906 in Oklahoma[1057] and died on 28 Jun 1994 in Montgomery, Texas[1058]. She married Ollie W Harrison, the son of Wilburn H. Harrison and Alice Peacock, on 24 Mar 1969 in Harris, Texas[1059]. He was born on 15 Jul 1910 in Texas[1060] and died on 18 Jun 1982 in Lufkin, Texas[1061].

129. ii.   Charles E. M. Doty was born on 24 Jun 1910 in Oklahoma[1062] and died on 30 Aug 1984[1063].

    iii.   Nellie Doty was born in 1913[1064].

    iv.   Evelyn Doty was born on 04 Sep 1914 in Oklahoma[1065] and died on 21 Mar 1996 in Tulsa, Oklahoma[1066]. She married Oliver Clinton Reed[1067]. He was born on 29 Dec 1907 in Fulton, Arkansas[1068].

[1052] Familysearch.org, "Minnesota Births and Christenings, 1840-1980," database, FamilySearch (https://familysearch.org/ark:/61903/1:1:FD7G-Q8K : 4 December 2014), Rosetta F. Harndon,

[1053] Ancestry.com, U.S., Find A Grave Index, 1700s-Current (Provo, UT, USA, Ancestry.com Operations, Inc., 2012), Ancestry.com, http://www.Ancestry.com, Record for Rosetta Doty.

[1054] Ancestry.com, U.S., Find A Grave Index, 1700s-Current (Provo, UT, USA, Ancestry.com Operations, Inc., 2012), Ancestry.com, http://www.Ancestry.com, Record for Rosetta Doty.

[1055] U.S., World War I Draft Registration Cards, 1917-1918.

[1056] Ancestry.com, U.S., Find A Grave Index, 1700s Current (Provo, UT, USA, Ancestry.com Operations, Inc., 2012), Ancestry.com, http://www.Ancestry.com, Record for Rosetta Doty.

[1057] Ancestry.com, Social Security Death Index (Provo, UT, USA, The Generations Network, Inc., 2008), www.ancestry.com, Number: 459-38-9306; Issue State: Texas; Issue Date: Before 1951. Record for Lola R. Harrison.

[1058] Ancestry.com, Social Security Death Index (Provo, UT, USA, The Generations Network, Inc., 2008), www.ancestry.com, Number: 459-38-9306; Issue State: Texas; Issue Date: Before 1951. Record for Lola R. Harrison

[1059] Ancestry.com, Texas, Marriage Index, 1814-1909 and 1966-2011 (Provo, UT, USA, Ancestry.com Operations Inc, 2005), Ancestry.com, http://www.Ancestry.com, Record for Lola R Doty.

[1060] Ancestry.com, Texas, Death Certificates, 1903-1982 (Provo, UT, USA, Ancestry.com Operations, Inc., 2013), Ancestry.com, http://www.Ancestry.com, Record for Ollie Wilburn Harrison.

[1061] Ancestry.com, Texas, Death Certificates, 1903-1982 (Provo, UT, USA, Ancestry.com Operations, Inc., 2013), Ancestry.com, http://www.Ancestry.com, Record for Ollie Wilburn Harrison.

[1062] Ancestry.com, Web: Kansas, Find A Grave Index, 1854-2012 (Provo, UT, USA, Ancestry.com Operations, Inc., 2012), Ancestry.com, http://www.Ancestry.com, Record for Charles E Doty.

[1063] Ancestry.com, Web: Kansas, Find A Grave Index, 1854-2012 (Provo, UT, USA, Ancestry.com Operations, Inc., 2012), Ancestry.com, http://www.Ancestry.com, Record for Charles E Doty.

[1064] Ancestry.com. *1920 United States Federal Census* [database on-line]. Provo, UT, USA: Ancestry.com Operations, Inc., 2010. Images reproduced by FamilySearch.

[1065] Ancestry.com, U.S., Social Security Applications and Claims Index, 1936-2007 (Provo, UT, USA, Ancestry.com Operations, Inc., 2015), Ancestry.com, http://www.Ancestry.com, Record for Evelyn L Reed.

[1066] Ancestry.com, U.S., Social Security Applications and Claims Index, 1936-2007 (Provo, UT, USA, Ancestry.com Operations, Inc., 2015), Ancestry.com, http://www.Ancestry.com, Record for Evelyn L Reed.

[1067] Ancestry.com, U.S., Social Security Applications and Claims Index, 1936-2007 (Provo, UT, USA, Ancestry.com Operations, Inc., 2015), Ancestry.com, http://www.Ancestry.com, Record for Evelyn L Reed.

71. Edward Eugene Harnden[5] (Sarah Amaria Leigh[4], William Safford Leigh[3], William Todd Leigh[2], Nathan S. Leigh[1]) was born on 02 Apr 1889 in Kansas[1069] and died on 26 May 1963 in Oklahoma[1070]. He married Leona M. Craig on 18 Jul 1923 in the Methodist Episcopal Church, Red Rock, Oklahoma[1071]. She was born on 27 May 1901 in Oklahoma[1072] and died on 13 Oct 1978 in Stillwater, Oklahoma[1073]. Edward Eugene Harnden and his wife were buried in Stillwater, Oklahoma[1074]. Edward was on the faculty of Oklahoma State University for several years. He taught Entomology - a branch of Zoology that deals with insects. He was a doctor of refinery medicine and taught Bacteriology. Leona was well known throughout Oklahoma for her candle making.

Wedding photo of Edward Eugene Harnden and Leona M. Craig found on Ancestry.com.

Edward Eugene Harnden and Leona M. Craig had the following children:

    i.   Gerald E. Harnden was born on 11 Feb 1925[1075] and died in Oct 1978 in Sipsey, Alabama[1076].

130. ii.   Roger Louis Harnden was born on 13 Mar 1928[1077] and died on 04 Jul 2006 in Houston, Texas[1078].

[1068] "Arkansas First Draft Registration Cards, 1940-1945," database with images, *FamilySearch*

[1069] Ancestry.com, U.S., Find A Grave Index, 1700s-Current (Provo, UT, USA, Ancestry.com Operations, Inc., 2012),

[1070] Ancestry.com, U.S., Find A Grave Index, 1700s-Current (Provo, UT, USA, Ancestry.com Operations, Inc., 2012),

[1071] Familysearch.org County marriages, "Oklahoma, County Marriages, 1890-1995", database with images, FamilySearch (https://familysearch.org/ark:/61903/1:1:QVP6-WHDW : 3 December 2014), Edward E Harnden and Leona M Craig,

[1072] Ancestry.com, Social Security Death Index (Provo, UT, USA, The Generations Network, Inc., 2008), www.ancestry.com, Number: 441-46-3922; Issue State: Oklahoma; Issue Date: 1962. Record for Leona Harnden

[1073] Ancestry.com, Social Security Death Index (Provo, UT, USA, The Generations Network, Inc., 2008), www.ancestry.com, Number: 441-46-3922; Issue State: Oklahoma; Issue Date: 1962. Record for Leona Harnden

[1074] Ancestry.com, U.S., Find A Grave Index, 1700s-Current (Provo, UT, USA, Ancestry.com Operations, Inc., 2012), Ancestry.com, http://www.Ancestry.com, Record for Leona M Harnden.

[1075] Ancestry.com, U.S., Department of Veterans Affairs BIRLS Death File, 1850-2010 (Provo, UT, USA, Ancestry.com Operations, Inc., 2011), www.ancestry.com, Record for Gerald Harnden.

[1076] Ancestry.com, U.S., Department of Veterans Affairs BIRLS Death File, 1850-2010 (Provo, UT, USA, Ancestry.com Operations, Inc., 2011), www.ancestry.com, Record for Gerald Harnden.

[1077] Ancestry.com, Social Security Death Index (Provo, UT, USA, The Generations Network, Inc., 2008), www.ancestry.com, Issue State: Oklahoma; Issue Date: Before 1951. Record for Roger Louis Harnden

[1078] Ancestry.com, Social Security Death Index (Provo, UT, USA, The Generations Network, Inc., 2008), www.ancestry.com, Issue State: Oklahoma; Issue Date: Before 1951. Record for Roger Louis Harnden

131. iii.   Lloyd Wayne Harnden was born on 19 Jun 1932 in Stillwater, Oklahoma[1079] and died on 01 Feb 2005 in Edmond, Oklahoma[1080].

Photo of Lloyd Wayne, Roger Lewis and Gerald E. Harnden found on Ancestry.com.

72. Elsie Ruth Ann Harnden[5] (Sarah Amaria Leigh[4], William Safford Leigh[3], William Todd Leigh[2], Nathan S. Leigh[1]) was born on 18 Aug 1891 in Alton, Kansas[1081] and died on 17 Sep 1970[1082]. She married Edward Garfield Peirson on 29 Jan 1911 in Payne, Oklahoma[1083]. He was born on 27 Feb 1883 in Jefferson, Nebraska[1084] and died on 10

[1079] Ancestry.com, Social Security Death Index (Provo, UT, USA, The Generations Network, Inc., 2008), www.ancestry.com, Issue State: Oklahoma; Issue Date: Before 1951. Record for Lloyd W. Harnden.

[1080] Ancestry.com, Social Security Death Index (Provo, UT, USA, The Generations Network, Inc., 2008), www.ancestry.com, Issue State: Oklahoma; Issue Date: Before 1951. Record for Lloyd W. Harnden.

[1081] Ancestry.com, U.S., Find A Grave Index, 1700s-Current (Provo, UT, USA, Ancestry.com Operations, Inc., 2012), Ancestry.com, http://www.Ancestry.com, Record for Elsie Ruth Ann Peirson.

[1082] Ancestry.com, U.S., Find A Grave Index, 1700s-Current (Provo, UT, USA, Ancestry.com Operations, Inc., 2012), Ancestry.com, http://www.Ancestry.com, Record for Elsie Ruth Ann Peirson.

[1083] Ancestry.com, Oklahoma, County Marriages, 1890-1995 (Lehi, UT, USA, Ancestry.com Operations, Inc., 2016), Ancestry.com, http://www.Ancestry.com, Record for Elsie Ruth Ann Harnden.

[1084] Ancestry.com, Social Security Death Index (Provo, UT, USA, The Generations Network, Inc., 2008), www.ancestry.com, Number: 506-46-8616; Issue State: Nebraska; Issue Date: 1955. Record for Edward Peirson.

Nov 1967[1085]. Elsie Ruth Ann Harnden and her husband were buried in Broken Bow, Nebraska[1086].

Edward Garfield Peirson and Elsie Ruth Ann Harnden had the following children:

      i.   Maude Edwina Peirson was born on 09 Feb 1912 in Nebraska[1087] and died on 31 Oct 1966 in Grand Island, Nebraska[1088]. She married Ralph Edward Cooper on 03 Sep 1932[1089]. He was born on 15 Oct 1910 in Illinois[1090] and died 27 Apr 1997 in Lincoln, Nebraska[1091]. Ralph Edward Cooper is buried in Lincoln Memorial Park, Lincoln Nebraska along with his second wife, LaVerne Maxine Cooper[1092].

      ii.   Charles William Peirson was born on 07 Jul 1915 in Alexandria, Nebraska[1093] and died in 1992 in Nebraska[1094]. He married Winona K. Souders[1095]. She was born on 06 Jan 1920 in Merna Custer, Nebraska[1096] and died on 04 May 2002 in Grand Island, Nebraska[1097]. Charles William Peirson and his wife were buried in Grand Island, Nebraska[1098].

132.   iii.   May Sarah Peirson was born on 16 May 1917 in Gilead Thaye, Nebraska[1099] and died on 19 Feb 2005[1100].

[1085] Ancestry.com, Social Security Death Index (Provo, UT, USA, The Generations Network, Inc., 2008), www.ancestry.com, Number: 506-46-8616; Issue State: Nebraska; Issue Date: 1955. Record for Edward Peirson.

[1086] Ancestry.com, U.S., Find A Grave Index, 1700s-Current (Provo, UT, USA, Ancestry.com Operations, Inc., 2012), Ancestry.com, http://www.Ancestry.com, Record for Elsie Ruth Ann Peirson.

[1087] Genealogy compiled by Rev. Laverne E. Leigh in 2017.

[1088] Genealogy compiled by Rev. Laverne E. Leigh in 2017.

[1089] Familysearch.org County marriages, "Nebraska Marriages, 1855-1995", database, FamilySearch (https://familysearch.org/ark:/61903/1:1:Q298-8CNH : 18 April 2016), Ralph Edward Cooper and Maude Edwina Peirson, 1932.

[1090] Ancestry.com. *U.S., Find A Grave Index, 1600s-Current* [database on-line]. Provo, UT, USA: Ancestry.com Operations, Inc., 2012.

[1091] Ancestry.com. *U.S., Find A Grave Index, 1600s-Current* [database on-line]. Provo, UT, USA: Ancestry.com Operations, Inc., 2012.

[1092] Ancestry.com. *U.S., Find A Grave Index, 1600s-Current* [database on-line]. Provo, UT, USA: Ancestry.com Operations, Inc., 2012.

[1093] Ancestry.com, U.S., Social Security Applications and Claims Index, 1936-2007 (Provo, UT, USA, Ancestry.com Operations, Inc., 2015), Ancestry.com, http://www.Ancestry.com, Record for Charles William Peirson.

[1094] Ancestry.com, U.S., Social Security Applications and Claims Index, 1936-2007 (Provo, UT, USA, Ancestry.com Operations, Inc., 2015), Ancestry.com, http://www.Ancestry.com, Record for Charles William Peirson.

[1095] Ancestry.com. *U.S., Find A Grave Index, 1600s-Current* [database on-line]. Provo, UT, USA: Ancestry.com Operations, Inc., 2012.

[1096] Ancestry.com, U.S., Social Security Applications and Claims Index, 1936-2007 (Provo, UT, USA, Ancestry.com Operations, Inc., 2015), Ancestry.com, http://www.Ancestry.com, Record for Winona Kathleen Peirson.

[1097] Ancestry.com, U.S., Social Security Applications and Claims Index, 1936-2007 (Provo, UT, USA, Ancestry.com Operations, Inc., 2015), Ancestry.com, http://www.Ancestry.com, Record for Winona Kathleen Peirson.

[1098] Ancestry.com. *U.S., Find A Grave Index, 1600s-Current* [database on-line]. Provo, UT, USA: Ancestry.com Operations, Inc., 2012.

[1099] Ancestry.com. *U.S., Social Security Applications and Claims Index, 1936-2007* [database on-line]. Provo, UT, USA: Ancestry.com Operations, Inc., 2015.

[1100] Ancestry.com. *U.S., Social Security Applications and Claims Index, 1936-2007* [database on-line]. Provo, UT, USA: Ancestry.com Operations, Inc., 2015.

73. Lemuel Meacham Harnden[5] (Sarah Amaria Leigh[4], William Safford Leigh[3], William Todd Leigh[2], Nathan S. Leigh[1]) was born on 28 Sep 1893[1101] in Stockton, Kansas and died on 27 Feb 1973 in Mamoth Springs, Arkansas[1102]. He married Lella B. Spencer. She was born in Arkansas[1103]. He later married Ollie McClasky on 04 Jul 1927 in Howell, Missouri[1104]. She was born in 1898[1105]. He then married Clara Mae Griffith on 09 Jan 1938 in Fulton, Arkansas, the daughter of John William Griffith and Virgie Minnie Jones[1106]. She was born 20 Oct 1902 in Arkansas[1107] and died on 24 Aug1972.[1108] Lemuel Meacham Harnden and his wife Clara Mae Griffith were buried in Pilot Church Cemetery Mammoth Spring, Arkansas[1109].

Photo of Lemuel Meacham Harnden found on Ancestry.com.

Lemuel Meacham Harnden and Lella B. Spencer had the following child:

133.   i.   Veralyne Nalhama Harnden was born on 10 June 1921 in Oklahoma[1110] and died on 01 Jan 2011 in Cheyenne, Wyoming[1111].

Lemuel Meacham Harnden and Ollie McClasky had one child who may still be living. Lemuel Meacham Harnden and Clara Griffith had three children who may still be living.

74. Adell Grace Harnden[5] (Sarah Amaria Leigh[4], William Safford Leigh[3], William Todd Leigh[2], Nathan S. Leigh[1]) was born on 01 Aug 1904 in Pawnee, Oklahoma[1112] and died

[1101] Ancestry.com. *U.S., Find A Grave Index, 1600s-Current* [database on-line]. Provo, UT, USA: Ancestry.com Operations, Inc., 2012.

[1102] Ancestry.com. *U.S., Find A Grave Index, 1600s-Current* [database on-line]. Provo, UT, USA: Ancestry.com Operations, Inc., 2012.

[1103] Genealogy compiled by Rev. Laverne E. Leigh in 2017.

[1104] Missouri Marriage records at Ancestry.com.

[1105] Genealogy compiled by Rev. Laverne E. Leigh in 2017.

[1106] Arkansas, County Marriages Index, 1837-1957.

[1107] Ancestry.com. *U.S., Find A Grave Index, 1600s-Current* [database on-line]. Provo, UT, USA: Ancestry.com Operations, Inc., 2012.

[1108] Ancestry.com. *U.S., Find A Grave Index, 1600s-Current* [database on-line]. Provo, UT, USA: Ancestry.com Operations, Inc., 2012.

[1109] Ancestry.com. *U.S., Find A Grave Index, 1600s-Current* [database on-line]. Provo, UT, USA: Ancestry.com Operations, Inc., 2012.

[1110] Ancestry.com, U.S., Find A Grave Index, 1700s-Current (Provo, UT, USA, Ancestry.com Operations, Inc., 2012), Ancestry.com, http://www.Ancestry.com, Record for Veralyne Sutherland.

[1111] Ancestry.com, U.S., Find A Grave Index, 1700s-Current (Provo, UT, USA, Ancestry.com Operations, Inc., 2012), Ancestry.com, http://www.Ancestry.com, Record for Veralyne Sutherland.

on 05 Feb 1981[1113]. She married Floyd Francis Henrick, the son of Benjamin Franklin Henrick and Mary Elizabeth Eyler, on 24 Jul 1924 in Noble, Oklahoma[1114]. He was born on 16 Jan 1896 in Illinois[1115] and died on 16 Jan 1964 in Missouri[1116]. Adell Grace Harden and her husband were buried in Jefferson Barracks National Cemetery, Lemay, Missouri[1117].

Floyd Francis Henrick and Adell Grace Harden Henrick had the following children:
134.   i.   Florus Frederick Henrick was born on 22 Jun 1925 in Stillwater, Oklahoma[1118] and died on 31 Dec 2005 in Greenbrier, Tennessee[1119].
        ii.   Mary Louise Henrick was born on 28 Jul 1926 in Stillwater, Oklahoma[1120] and died on 15 Dec 2003[1121]. She married Walter Smith on 12 Jun 1948[1122]. He died on 19 Jan 1950[1123]. She later married James Woodward 25 Jul 1953[1124]. After James, she married Thomas Madden Stacey[1125]. He was born on 01 May 1911[1126] and died on 16 Dec 1999 in Cottontown, Tennessee[1127]. Mary Louise Henrick and her husband, Thomas Madden Stacey, were buried in Robertson County, Tennessee[1128].

[1112] Ancestry.com, U.S., Find A Grave Index, 1700s-Current (Provo, UT, USA, Ancestry.com Operations, Inc., 2012), Ancestry.com, http://www.Ancestry.com, Record for Adell G Henrick

[1113] Ancestry.com, U.S., Find A Grave Index, 1700s-Current (Provo, UT, USA, Ancestry.com Operations, Inc., 2012), Ancestry.com, http://www.Ancestry.com, Record for Adell G Henrick

[1114] Ancestry.com, Oklahoma, County Marriages, 1890-1995 (Lehi, UT, USA, Ancestry.com Operations, Inc., 2016), Ancestry.com, http://www.Ancestry.com, Record for Adell Harnden.

[1115] Ancestry.com, World War I Draft Registration Cards, 1917-1918 (Provo, UT, USA, The Generations Network, Inc., 2005), www.ancestry.com, Registration State: Oklahoma; Registration County: Payne; Roll: 1852069. Record for Floyd Francis Henrick.

[1116] Ancestry.com, Social Security Death Index (Provo, UT, USA, The Generations Network, Inc., 2008), www.ancestry.com, Number: 432-14-0192; Issue State: Arkansas; Issue Date: Before 1951. Record for Floyd Henrick.

[1117] Ancestry.com, U.S., Find A Grave Index, 1700s-Current

[1118] Ancestry.com, Social Security Death Index (Provo, UT, USA, The Generations Network, Inc., 2008), www.ancestry.com, Issue State: Missouri; Issue Date: Before 1951. Record for Florus F. Henrick.

[1119] Ancestry.com, Social Security Death Index (Provo, UT, USA, The Generations Network, Inc., 2008), www.ancestry.com, Issue State: Missouri; Issue Date: Before 1951. Record for Florus F. Henrick.

[1120] Ancestry.com, U.S., Find A Grave Index, 1700s-Current (Provo, UT, USA, Ancestry.com Operations, Inc., 2012), Ancestry.com, http://www.Ancestry.com, Record for Thomas M Stacey.

[1121] Ancestry.com, U.S., Find A Grave Index, 1700s-Current (Provo, UT, USA, Ancestry.com Operations, Inc., 2012), Ancestry.com, http://www.Ancestry.com, Record for Thomas M Stacey.

[1122] Genealogy compiled by Rev. Laverne E. Leigh, 414 Washington Ave. East, Albia, Iowa 52531 in the Spring of 1975.

[1123] Genealogy compiled by Rev. Laverne E. Leigh, 414 Washington Ave. East, Albia, Iowa 52531 in the Spring of 1975.

[1124] Genealogy compiled by Rev. Laverne E. Leigh, 414 Washington Ave. East, Albia, Iowa 52531 in the Spring of 1975.

[1125] Ancestry.com, U.S., Find A Grave Index, 1700s-Current (Provo, UT, USA, Ancestry.com Operations, Inc., 2012), Ancestry.com, http://www.Ancestry.com, Record for Thomas M Stacey.

[1126] Ancestry.com, U.S., Find A Grave Index, 1700s-Current (Provo, UT, USA, Ancestry.com Operations, Inc., 2012), Ancestry.com, http://www.Ancestry.com, Record for Thomas M Stacey.

[1127] Ancestry.com, U.S., Find A Grave Index, 1700s-Current (Provo, UT, USA, Ancestry.com Operations, Inc., 2012), Ancestry.com, http://www.Ancestry.com, Record for Thomas M Stacey.

[1128] Ancestry.com, U.S., Find A Grave Index, 1700s-Current (Provo, UT, USA, Ancestry.com Operations, Inc., 2012), Ancestry.com, http://www.Ancestry.com, Record for Thomas M Stacey.

135.   iii.   Francis Otto Henrick was born on 04 Jul 1928 in Stillwater, Oklahoma[1129] and died on 14 Jun 2007 in Columbia, South Carolina[1130].

136.   iv.   Allen Elwood Henrick was born on 24 Jun 1932 in Stillwater, Oklahoma[1131] and died on 29 Aug 1982 in St. Louis, Missouri[1132].

        v.   Living Henrick.

137.   vi.   Bobbie Eugene Henrick was born on 07 Aug 1938[1133] and died on 02 Jul 2015[1134].

        vii.   Living Henrick.

        viii.   Living Henrick

138.   ix.   David Leon Henrick was born on 05 Dec 1946 in Cadiz, Philippines[1135] and died on 10 Dec 2009 in Vanderbilt University Medical Center, Nashville, Tennessee[1136].

75. Guy Rowley Moore[5] (Phebe Adella Leigh[4], Rueben Harrington Leigh[3], William Todd Leigh[2], Nathan S. Leigh[1]) was born on 14 May 1891 in Fairmont, Minnesota[1137] and died on 15 Sep 1991 in Roseburg, Oregon[1138]. He married Edith Almyra Taylor on 03 Aug 1921 in Pawnee, Oklahoma[1139]. She was born on 17 Jul 1903 in Hallet, Oklahoma[1140] and died on 24 Dec 1995[1141]. He later married Ruby Pearl Miller, the daughter of Edward Elmer Miller and Martha Susannah Forgey, on 06 Sep 1936 in Roseburg, Oregon[1142].

[1129] Ancestry.com. *U.S., Social Security Death Index, 1935-2014* [database on-line]. Provo, UT, USA: Ancestry.com Operations Inc, 2014.

[1130] Ancestry.com. *U.S., Social Security Death Index, 1935-2014* [database on-line]. Provo, UT, USA: Ancestry.com Operations Inc, 2014.

[1131] Ancestry.com, Social Security Death Index (Provo, UT, USA, The Generations Network, Inc., 2008), www.ancestry.com, Number: 492 34 3538; Issue State: Missouri; Issue Date: Before 1951. Record for Allen Henrick.

[1132] Ancestry.com, Social Security Death Index (Provo, UT, USA, The Generations Network, Inc., 2008), www.ancestry.com, Number: 492-34-3538; Issue State: Missouri; Issue Date: Before 1951. Record for Allen Henrick.

[1133] Ancestry.com, U.S. Cemetery and Funeral Home Collection (Provo, UT, USA, Ancestry.com Operations Inc, 2011),

[1134] Ancestry.com, U.S. Cemetery and Funeral Home Collection (Provo, UT, USA, Ancestry.com Operations Inc, 2011),

[1135] Newspaper: Bowling Green Daily News; Publication Date: 12/ 12/ 2009; Publication Place: Bowling Green, Kentucky, USA; Web edition: http://bgdailynews.com/articles/2009/12/12/obituaries/obit2.txt.

[1136] Newspaper: Bowling Green Daily News; Publication Date: 12/ 12/ 2009; Publication Place: Bowling Green, Kentucky, USA; Web edition: http://bgdailynews.com/articles/2009/12/12/obituaries/obit2.txt.

[1137] National Cemetery Administration, U.S. Veterans Gravesites, ca.1775-2006 (Provo, UT, USA, The Generations Network, Inc., 2006), www.ancestry.com, Record for Guy R Moore.

[1138] National Cemetery Administration, U.S. Veterans Gravesites, ca.1775-2006 (Provo, UT, USA, The Generations Network, Inc., 2006), www.ancestry.com, Record for Guy R Moore.

[1139] Genealogy compiled by Rev. Laverne E. Leigh, 414 Washington Ave. East, Albia, Iowa 52531 in the Spring of 1975.

[1140] Genealogy compiled by Rev. Laverne E. Leigh, 414 Washington Ave. East, Albia, Iowa 52531 in the Spring of 1975.

[1141] Genealogy compiled by Rev. Laverne E. Leigh, 414 Washington Ave. East, Albia, Iowa 52531 in the Spring of 1975.

[1142] Genealogy compiled by Rev. Laverne E. Leigh, 414 Washington Ave. East, Albia, Iowa 52531 in the Spring of 1975. Ancestry.com, U.S., Find A Grave Index, 1700s-Current (Provo, UT, USA, Ancestry.com Operations, Inc., 2012), Ancestry.com, http://www.Ancestry.com, Record for Guy R Moore.

She was born on 21 Mar 1890 in Nortonville, Illinois[1143] and died on 26 Oct 1972 in Roseburg, Oregon[1144]. Guy Rowley Moore was buried on 19 Sep 1991 in Willamette National Cemetery, Portland, Oregon, Section M Site 1918[1145].

Guy served fourteen months in the US Army during World War I and was in France with Base Hospital No. 85 for ten of these months. His service extended from May 29, 1918 to August 2, 1919. After returning home, he earned a BA Degree from the University of Kansas and a MA Degree from the University of Oklahoma. He taught for a time in an Indian School in Montana. He and Edith made their home in Oklahoma City where three of their children were born. They moved to Pocatello, Idaho where their fourth and last child was born. After this, they moved to Fall Creek, Oregon where they were living at the time of their separation and eventual divorce.

Guy married Ruby Pearl Norton after his divorce. They lived in Camas Valley, Oregon for several years. After Ruby's death, Guy's children persuaded him to sell his farm in Camas Valley and move to Roseburg, Oregon.

Guy Rowley Moore and Edith Almyra Taylor had the following children:
139.   i.   Ellen Genevieve Moore was born on 21 Nov 1922 in Oklahoma City, Oklahoma[1146] and died on 30 Jul 2009 in Medford, Oregon[1147].
        ii.   Guy Rowley Moore, Jr. was born on 01 Mar 1925 in Oklahoma City, Oklahoma[1148] and died on 03 Jan 1963 in VA Hospital, North Little Rock, Arkansas[1149]. Guy Rowley Moore Jr. was buried in National Cemetery, Little Rock, Arkansas[1150]. Guy served during World War II on a PT Boat. He was an emotional victim of World War II from serving as a sonar operator on a sea going tug. He spent a number of years at the V.A. Hospital in North Little Rock, Arkansas.

[1143] Ancestry.com, U.S., Find A Grave Index, 1700s-Current (Provo, UT, USA, Ancestry.com Operations, Inc., 2012), Ancestry.com, http://www.Ancestry.com, Record for Guy R Moore.

[1144] Ancestry.com, U.S., Find A Grave Index, 1700s-Current (Provo, UT, USA, Ancestry.com Operations, Inc., 2012), Ancestry.com, http://www.Ancestry.com, Record for Guy R Moore.

[1145] Ancestry.com, U.S., Find A Grave Index, 1700s-Current (Provo, UT, USA, Ancestry.com Operations, Inc., 2012), Ancestry.com, http://www.Ancestry.com, Record for Guy R Moore.

[1146] Ancestry.com, U.S., Find A Grave Index, 1700s-Current (Provo, UT, USA, Ancestry.com Operations, Inc., 2012), Ancestry.com, http://www.Ancestry.com, Record for Genevieve M Ashenberner.

[1147] Ancestry.com, U.S., Find A Grave Index, 1700s-Current (Provo, UT, USA, Ancestry.com Operations, Inc., 2012), Ancestry.com, http://www.Ancestry.com, Record for Genevieve M Ashenberner.

[1148] Ancestry.com, Little Rock, Arkansas, Little Rock National Cemetery, 1868-2010 (Provo, UT, USA, Ancestry.com Operations, Inc., 2011), Ancestry.com, http://www.Ancestry.com, Little Rock National Cemetery; Section: 14. Record for Guy Rowley Jr Moore.

[1149] Ancestry.com, Little Rock, Arkansas, Little Rock National Cemetery, 1868-2010 (Provo, UT, USA, Ancestry.com Operations, Inc., 2011), Ancestry.com, http://www.Ancestry.com, Little Rock National Cemetery; Section: 14. Record for Guy Rowley Jr Moore.

[1150] Ancestry.com, Little Rock, Arkansas, Little Rock National Cemetery, 1868-2010 (Provo, UT, USA, Ancestry.com Operations, Inc., 2011), Ancestry.com, http://www.Ancestry.com, Little Rock National Cemetery; Section: 14. Record for Guy Rowley Jr Moore.

      iii.   Living Moore

140.   iv.   Phoebe Anne Moore was born on 25 Mar 1934 in Pocatello, Idaho[1151] and died on 01 Nov 2007 in Visalia, California[1152].

76. Stanley Leigh Moore[5] (Phebe Adella Leigh[4], Rueben Harrington Leigh[3], William Todd Leigh[2], Nathan S. Leigh[1]) was born on 21 Dec 1893 in Fairmont, Minnesota[1153] and died on 07 Apr 1969 in Norman, Oklahoma[1154]. He married Elizabeth Louise Acree, the daughter of Jesse McDonald Acree and Nancy J. McCall, on 02 Nov 1918 in Louisville, Kentucky[1155]. She was born on 16 Feb 1894 in West Plains, Missouri[1156] and died in Jan 1985 in Norman, Oklahoma[1157]. Stanley Leigh Moore and his wife were buried in Norman, Oklahoma[1158].

Photo of Stanley Leigh Moore found on findagrave.com.

Stanley and Bess first lived in Jennings, Oklahoma for a time and then moved to Norman, Oklahoma where he owned and operated a carburetor and electric company until he took an early retirement and sold out. He then attended college and received his BA Degree in General Engineering from Oklahoma University in 1957. He was hired as an instructor in Civil Engineering by Oklahoma University where he received his degree. He taught there until his retirement in 1964 at the age of 70. Stanley did the original genealogy work on the Moore family and related families of which the Leigh family was one. This genealogy is much indebted to the work he did and his son, Stanley Leigh Moore II shared with a distant relative, Laverne E. Leigh.

[1151] Ancestry.com, U.S., Find A Grave Index, 1700s-Current (Provo, UT, USA, Ancestry.com Operations, Inc., 2012), Ancestry.com, http://www.Ancestry.com, Record for Phoebe Anne Bailey.

[1152] Ancestry.com, U.S., Find A Grave Index, 1700s-Current (Provo, UT, USA, Ancestry.com Operations, Inc., 2012), Ancestry.com, http://www.Ancestry.com, Record for Phoebe Anne Bailey.

[1153] Ancestry.com, World War I Draft Registration Cards, 1917-1918 (Provo, UT, USA, The Generations Network, Inc., 2005), www.ancestry.com, Registration State: Oklahoma; Registration County: Pawnee; Roll: 1852068. Record for Stanley Leigh Moore.

[1154] Ancestry.com, Web: RootsWeb Cemetery Index, 1800-2010 (Provo, UT, USA, Ancestry.com Operations, Inc., 2013), Ancestry.com, http://www.Ancestry.com, Record for Stanley Leigh Moore.

[1155] Ancestry.com. *U.S., Sons of the American Revolution Membership Applications, 1889-1970* [database on-line]. Provo, UT, USA: Ancestry.com Operations, Inc., 2011.
Original data: *Sons of the American Revolution Membership Applications, 1889-1970*. Louisville, Kentucky: National Society of the Sons of the American Revolution. Microfilm, 508 rolls.

[1156] Ancestry.com, U.S., Find A Grave Index, 1700s-Current (Provo, UT, USA, Ancestry.com Operations, Inc., 2012), Ancestry.com, http://www.Ancestry.com, Record for Stanley Leigh Moore.

[1157] Ancestry.com, U.S., Find A Grave Index, 1700s-Current (Provo, UT, USA, Ancestry.com Operations, Inc., 2012), Ancestry.com, http://www.Ancestry.com, Record for Stanley Leigh Moore.

[1158] Ancestry.com, U.S., Find A Grave Index, 1700s-Current (Provo, UT, USA, Ancestry.com Operations, Inc., 2012), Ancestry.com, http://www.Ancestry.com, Record for Stanley Leigh Moore.

Stanley Leigh Moore and Elizabeth Louise Acree had the following children:
141. i. Stanley Leigh Moore was born on 28 Jun 1920 in Jennings, Oklahoma[1159] and died on 08 Jan 2004 in Lubbock, Texas[1160].
 ii. Living Moore

77. Myrtle Elmina Moore[5] (Phebe Adella Leigh[4], Rueben Harrington Leigh[3], William Todd Leigh[2], Nathan S. Leigh[1]) was born on 07 Dec 1896 in Fairmont, Minnesota[1161] and died on 07 Feb 1990 in Houston, Texas[1162]. She married Fred Andrew Jackson, the son of C. E. Jackson and Alpha Jack, on 09 Jun 1921 in Pawnee, Oklahoma[1163]. He was born on 15 Oct 1896 in Viola, Arkansas[1164] and died on 28 Aug 1936 in Corsicana, Texas[1165]. Myrtle Elmina Moore and her husband were buried in Corsicana, Texas[1166].

Myrtle and Fred lived first in Jenning, Oklahoma and then moved to Tonkiwa, Oklahoma where their third and last child was born. Myrtle lived in Corsicana, Texas in 1975.

Fred Andrew Jackson and Myrtle Elmina Moore had the following children:
 i. Maurice C. Jackson was born on 26 Mar 1922 in Texas[1167] and died on 09 Mar 1943in Corsicana, Texas[1168]. Maurice C. Jackson was buried in Corsicana, Texas[1169].
142. ii. Milton Lawrence Jackson was born on 26 Mar 1922 in Oklahoma[1170] and died on 22 Dec 2015 in Fort Bend County, Texas[1171].

[1159] Ancestry.com, U.S., Find A Grave Index, 1700s-Current (Provo, UT, USA, Ancestry.com Operations, Inc., 2012), Ancestry.com, http://www.Ancestry.com, Record for Stanley Leigh Moore.

[1160] Ancestry.com, U.S., Find A Grave Index, 1700s-Current (Provo, UT, USA, Ancestry.com Operations, Inc., 2012), Ancestry.com, http://www.Ancestry.com, Record for Stanley Leigh Moore.

[1161] Ancestry.com, Social Security Death Index (Provo, UT, USA, The Generations Network, Inc., 2008), www.ancestry.com.

[1162] Ancestry.com, Social Security Death Index (Provo, UT, USA, The Generations Network, Inc., 2008), www.ancestry.com.

[1163] Ancestry.com, U.S., Find A Grave Index, 1700s-Current (Provo, UT, USA, Ancestry.com Operations, Inc., 2012), Ancestry.com, http://www.Ancestry.com, Record for Elmina Jackson.

[1164] Ancestry.com, U.S., Find A Grave Index, 1700s-Current (Provo, UT, USA, Ancestry.com Operations, Inc., 2012), Ancestry.com, http://www.Ancestry.com, Record for Elmina Jackson.

[1165] Ancestry.com, U.S., Find A Grave Index, 1700s-Current (Provo, UT, USA, Ancestry.com Operations, Inc., 2012), Ancestry.com, http://www.Ancestry.com, Record for Elmina Jackson.

[1166] Ancestry.com, U.S., Find A Grave Index, 1700s-Current (Provo, UT, USA, Ancestry.com Operations, Inc., 2012), Ancestry.com, http://www.Ancestry.com, Record for Elmina Jackson.

[1167] Ancestry.com, U.S., Find A Grave Index, 1700s-Current (Provo, UT, USA, Ancestry.com Operations, Inc., 2012), Ancestry.com, http://www.Ancestry.com, Record for Maurice C Jackson.

[1168] Ancestry.com, U.S., Find A Grave Index, 1700s-Current (Provo, UT, USA, Ancestry.com Operations, Inc., 2012), Ancestry.com, http://www.Ancestry.com, Record for Maurice C Jackson.

[1169] Ancestry.com, U.S., Find A Grave Index, 1700s-Current (Provo, UT, USA, Ancestry.com Operations, Inc., 2012), Ancestry.com, http://www.Ancestry.com, Record for Maurice C Jackson.

[1170] Ancestry.com, U.S., Find A Grave Index, 1700s-Current (Provo, UT, USA, Ancestry.com Operations, Inc., 2012), Ancestry.com, http://www.Ancestry.com, Record for Milton Lawrence Jackson

[1171] Ancestry.com, U.S., Find A Grave Index, 1700s-Current (Provo, UT, USA, Ancestry.com Operations, Inc., 2012), Ancestry.com, http://www.Ancestry.com, Record for Milton Lawrence Jackson

143.   iii.   Patricia Alma Jackson was born on 17 Mar 1925 in Tonkawa, Oklahoma[1172] and died on 31 May 1965 in Pasadena, Texas of cancer[1173].

78.   Ethel Adell Moore[5] (Phebe Adella Leigh[4], Rueben Harrington Leigh[3], William Todd Leigh[2], Nathan S. Leigh[1]) was born on 30 Oct 1897 in Fairmont, Minnesota[1174] and died on 21 Aug 1927 in Enid, Oklahoma[1175]. She married Roscoe McKinley Shanklin, the son of William Ulyssis Shanklin and Elizabeth Florence Guthrie, on 24 Aug 1921 in Stillwater, Oklahoma[1176]. He was born on 04 Jun 1898 in Harrisburg, Iowa[1177] and died on 06 Jun 1963 in Medford, Oklahoma[1178]. Ethel Adell Moore was buried in Stillwater, Oklahoma[1179]. Roscoe McKinley Shanklin was buried in Medford, Oklahoma[1180]. Ethel died while giving birth to a baby girl, Rosemary. Roscoe McKinley Shanklin and Ethel Adell Moore had one child who may still be living.

79.   George Asro Moore Jr.[5] (Phebe Adella Leigh[4], Rueben Harrington Leigh[3], William

Photo of George Asro Moore, Jr. from the collection of Susie Jones and used with permission.

[1172] Ancestry.com, Texas, Death Certificates, 1903-1982 (Provo, UT, USA, Ancestry.com Operations, Inc., 2013), Ancestry.com, http://www.Ancestry.com, Record for Patricia A Haver.

[1173] Ancestry.com, Texas, Death Certificates, 1903-1982 (Provo, UT, USA, Ancestry.com Operations, Inc., 2013), Ancestry.com, http://www.Ancestry.com, Record for Patricia A Haver.

[1174] Ancestry.com, U.S., Find A Grave Index, 1700s-Current (Provo, UT, USA, Ancestry.com Operations, Inc., 2012), Ancestry.com, http://www.Ancestry.com, Record for Ethel Shanklin.

[1175] Ancestry.com, U.S., Find A Grave Index, 1700s-Current (Provo, UT, USA, Ancestry.com Operations, Inc., 2012), Ancestry.com, http://www.Ancestry.com, Record for Ethel Shanklin.

[1176] Ancestry.com, Oklahoma, County Marriages, 1890-1995 (Lehi, UT, USA, Ancestry.com Operations, Inc., 2016), Ancestry.com, http://www.Ancestry.com, Record for Ethel Dell Moore.

[1177] Ancestry.com, U.S., Find A Grave Index, 1700s-Current (Provo, UT, USA, Ancestry.com Operations, Inc., 2012), Ancestry.com, http://www.Ancestry.com, Record for Roscoe M. Shanklin.

[1178] Ancestry.com, U.S., Find A Grave Index, 1700s-Current (Provo, UT, USA, Ancestry.com Operations, Inc., 2012), Ancestry.com, http://www.Ancestry.com, Record for Roscoe M. Shanklin.

[1179] Ancestry.com, U.S., Find A Grave Index, 1700s-Current (Provo, UT, USA, Ancestry.com Operations, Inc., 2012), Ancestry.com, http://www.Ancestry.com, Record for Ethel Shanklin.

[1180] Ancestry.com, U.S., Find A Grave Index, 1700s-Current (Provo, UT, USA, Ancestry.com Operations, Inc., 2012), Ancestry.com, http://www.Ancestry.com, Record for Roscoe M. Shanklin.

Todd Leigh[2], Nathan S. Leigh[1]) was born on 12 Sep 1899 in Fairmont, Minnesota[1181] and died on 17 Nov 1998 in Abilene, Texas[1182]. He married Doris Leone Becknell, the daughter of Charles Becknell and Jane Dodd, on 18 Aug 1923 in Neosho, Missouri[1183]. S he was born on 24 Jun 1902 in Oklahoma City, Oklahoma[1184] and died on 11 Jan 1933 in Stillwater, Oklahoma[1185]. He later married Leah Murphy, the daughter of Kennel Murphy and Esther Fisher, on 14 Jun 1934 in Shawnee, Oklahoma[1186]. She was born on 05 Jan 1907 in Shawnee, Oklahoma[1187] and died on 16 Oct 1994 in Abilene, Texas[1188]. George Asro Moore Jr. and his wife, Leah Murphy, were buried in Stillwater,

Oklahoma[1189]. George earned a BS Degree from Oklahoma A M, a MS from the University of Oklahoma and his PHD from the University of Michigan. He was a professor of Biology at Oklahoma A & M until his retirement in August of 1965.

George Asro Moore Jr and Doris Leone Becknell had the following child:

144. i.   Betty Jean Moore was born on 08 Jul 1925 in Neosho, Missouri[1190] and died on 15 Mar 2010 in Buhl, Idaho[1191].

Photo of Doris Leone Becknell from the collection of Susie Jones and used with permission.

[1181] Ancestry.com, World War I Draft Registration Cards, 1917-1918 (Provo, UT, USA, The Generations Network, Inc., 2005), www.ancestry.com, Registration State: Oklahoma; Registration County: Pawnee; Roll: 1852068. Record for George Azro Moore.

[1182] Ancestry.com, Social Security Death Index (Provo, UT, USA, The Generations Network, Inc., 2008), www.ancestry.com, Number: 441-30-7942; Issue State: Oklahoma; Issue Date: Before 1951. Record for Geo A. Moore

[1183] Ancestry.com. *Missouri, Marriage Records, 1805-2002* [database on-line].

[1184] Ancestry.com. *Iowa, Births and Christenings Index, 1800-1999* [database on-line]. Provo, UT, USA: Ancestry.com Operations, Inc., 2011.

[1185] Ancestry.com. *Web: Oklahoma, Find A Grave Index, 1800-2012* [database on-line]. Provo, UT, USA: Ancestry.com Operations, Inc., 2012.

[1186] Ancestry.com. *Oklahoma, County Marriage Records, 1890-1995* [database on-line]. Lehi, UT, USA: Ancestry.com Operations, Inc., 2016.

[1187] Ancestry.com. *U.S., Find A Grave Index, 1600s-Current* [database on-line]. Provo, UT, USA: Ancestry.com Operations, Inc., 2012.

[1188] Ancestry.com. *U.S., Find A Grave Index, 1600s-Current* [database on-line]. Provo, UT, USA: Ancestry.com Operations, Inc., 2012.

[1189] Ancestry.com. *U.S., Find A Grave Index, 1600s-Current* [database on-line]. Provo, UT, USA: Ancestry.com Operations, Inc., 2012.

[1190] Ancestry.com, United States Obituary Collection (Provo, UT, USA, The Generations Network, Inc., 2006), www.ancestry.com, Newspaper: Moscow-Pullman Daily News; Publication Date: 03/ 17/ 2010; Publication Place: Moscow, Idaho, USA; Web edition: http://www.dnews.com/story/obituaries/50058/. Record for Betty Jean Valder.

[1191] Ancestry.com, United States Obituary Collection (Provo, UT, USA, The Generations Network, Inc., 2006), www.ancestry.com, Newspaper: Moscow-Pullman Daily News; Publication Date: 03/ 17/ 2010; Publication Place: Moscow, Idaho, USA; Web edition: http://www.dnews.com/story/obituaries/50058/. Record for Betty Jean Valder.

George Asro Moore Jr and Leah Murphy had the following children:

  ii. Mary Alice Moore was born on 05 Mar 1939 in Stillwater, Oklahoma[1192]. and died on 30 Mar 1944 in Stillwater, Oklahoma[1193]. Mary Alice Moore was buried in Fairlawn Cemetery, Stillwater, Oklahoma[1194]. Mary died in an auto accident.

  iii. Living Moore

  iv. Living Moore

Photo of Chester Cecil Leigh from the collection of Dale and Biggar and used with permission.

80. Chester Cecil Leigh[5] (Charles Emery Leigh[4], Rueben Harrington Leigh[3], William Todd Leigh[2], Nathan S. Leigh[1]) was born on 02 Mar 1901 in Nyssa, Oregon[1195] and died on 24 Mar 1970[1196] in Camano, Washington. He married Marguerite Elizabeth Biggar, the daughter of Alonzo James and Mable May Biggar, on 25 Oct 1922 in Kent, Washington[1197]. She was born on 24 Apr 1903 in Vancouver, British Columbia, Canada[1198] and died on 25 Jun 1985 in Salem, Oregon[1199]. Chester Cecil Leigh and his wife were buried in Hillcrest Cemetery, Kent, Washington[1200]. Chester was a machinist.

Photo of Marguerite Elizabeth Biggar from the collection of Dale and Biggar and used with permission.

Photo of Doris Elizabeth Leigh from the collection of Virginia Holm and used with permission.

[1192] Ancestry.com, U.S., Find A Grave Index, 1700s-Current (Provo, UT, USA, Ancestry.com Operations, Inc., 2012), Ancestry.com, http://www.Ancestry.com, Record for Mary Alice Moore.

[1193] Ancestry.com, U.S., Find A Grave Index, 1700s-Current (Provo, UT, USA, Ancestry.com Operations, Inc., 2012), Ancestry.com, http://www.Ancestry.com, Record for Mary Alice Moore.

[1194] Ancestry.com, U.S., Find A Grave Index, 1700s-Current (Provo, UT, USA, Ancestry.com Operations, Inc., 2012), Ancestry.com, http://www.Ancestry.com, Record for Mary Alice Moore.

[1195] Ancestry.com, Social Security Death Index (Provo, UT, USA, The Generations Network, Inc., 2008), www.ancestry.com, Number: 531-05-4016; Issue State: Washington; Issue Date: Before 1951. Record for Chester Leigh.

[1196] Ancestry.com, Social Security Death Index (Provo, UT, USA, The Generations Network, Inc., 2008), www.ancestry.com, Number: 531-05-4016; Issue State: Washington; Issue Date: Before 1951. Record for Chester Leigh.

[1197] Genealogy compiled by Rev. Laverne E. Leigh, 414 Washington Ave. East, Albia, Iowa 52531 in the Spring of 1975.

[1198] Ancestry.com, U.S., Find A Grave Index, 1700s-Current (Provo, UT, USA, Ancestry.com Operations, Inc., 2012), Ancestry.com, http://www.Ancestry.com, Record for Marguerite Elizabeth Leigh.

[1199] Ancestry.com, U.S., Find A Grave Index, 1700s-Current (Provo, UT, USA, Ancestry.com Operations, Inc., 2012), Ancestry.com, http://www.Ancestry.com, Record for Marguerite Elizabeth Leigh.

[1200] Ancestry.com, U.S., Find A Grave Index, 1700s-Current (Provo, UT, USA, Ancestry.com Operations, Inc., 2012), Ancestry.com, http://www.Ancestry.com, Record for Marguerite Elizabeth Leigh.

Chester Cecil Leigh and Marguerite Elizabeth Biggar had the following child:
145.   i.   Doris Elizabeth Leigh was born on 28 Sep 1923[1201]   in Auburn, Washington and died on 07 Feb 1975[1202] in Salem, Oregon.

81. Edward Meade Leigh[5] (Charles Emery Leigh[4], Rueben Harrington Leigh[3], William Todd Leigh[2], Nathan S. Leigh[1]) was born on 11 Jul 1906[1203] in Fairmont, Minnesota and died on 20 Nov 1961 in Annacortes, Washington[1204]. He married Marguerite E. Wyatt, the daughter of John Ewing Wyatt, on 26 Jan 1938 in Montesano, Washington[1205]. She was born on 24 Apr 1903 in Washington[1206] and died on 23 Sep 1965 in Seattle, Washington[1207].   Edward Meade Leigh was buried in Hillcrest Burial Park, Seattle, Washington[1208]. Marguerite E. Wyatt was buried in Auburn, Washington[1209]. Edward was a seaman and a machinist. He was separated from Marguerite when he died.
Edward Meade Leigh and Marguerite E. Wyatt had one child who may still be living.

82. Ray Hugh Leigh[5] (Charles Emery Leigh[4], Rueben Harrington Leigh[3], William Todd Leigh[2], Nathan S. Leigh[1]) was born on 12 May 1915 in Kent, Washington[1210] and died on 16 Sep 1989 in Okanogan, Washington[1211]. He married Evagene Hatch, the daughter of Wendell P. Hatch and Eva O. Robertson, on 26 Dec 1934 in Seattle, Washington[1212]. She was born on 22 Jul 1915 in Ridgefield, Washington[1213] and died on 12 Nov 2005 in

---

[1201] Ancestry.com, U.S., Find A Grave Index, 1700s-Current (Provo, UT, USA, Ancestry.com Operations, Inc., 2012), Ancestry.com, http://www.Ancestry.com, Record for Doris Elizabeth Jackson

[1202] Ancestry.com, U.S., Find A Grave Index, 1700s-Current (Provo, UT, USA, Ancestry.com Operations, Inc., 2012), Ancestry.com, http://www.Ancestry.com, Record for Doris Elizabeth Jackson

[1203] Ancestry.com, U.S., Find A Grave Index, 1700s-Current (Provo, UT, USA, Ancestry.com Operations, Inc., 2012), Ancestry.com, http://www.Ancestry.com, Record for Edward Meade Leigh.

[1204] Ancestry.com, U.S., Find A Grave Index, 1700s-Current (Provo, UT, USA, Ancestry.com Operations, Inc., 2012), Ancestry.com, http://www.Ancestry.com, Record for Edward Meade Leigh.

[1205] Ancestry.com, Washington, Marriage Records, 1854-2013 (Provo, UT, USA, Ancestry.com Operations, Inc., 2012), Ancestry.com, http://www.Ancestry.com, Washington State Archives; Olympia, Washington; Marriage Affidavits. Record for Edward M Leigh.

[1206] Ancestry.com, Social Security Death Index (Provo, UT, USA, The Generations Network, Inc., 2008), www.ancestry.com, Number: 533-50-5015; Issue State: Washington; Issue Date: 1965. Record for Marguerite Leigh.

[1207] Ancestry.com, Oregon Death Index, 1903-98 (Provo, UT, USA, Ancestry.com Operations Inc, 2000), www.ancestry.com, Oregon State Library; 1966-1970 Death Index; Reel Title: State of Oregon Death Index; Year Range: 1981-1990. Record for Marguerit Eli Leigh.

[1208] Ancestry.com, U.S., Find A Grave Index, 1700s-Current (Provo, UT, USA, Ancestry.com Operations, Inc., 2012),

[1209] Ancestry.com, U.S., Find A Grave Index, 1700s-Current (Provo, UT, USA, Ancestry.com Operations, Inc., 2012), Ancestry.com, http://www.Ancestry.com, Record for Marguerite Leigh.

[1210] Ancestry.com, Washington Death Index, 1940-1996 (Provo, UT, USA, The Generations Network, Inc., 2002), www.ancestry.com, Record for Ray H Leigh.

[1211] Ancestry.com, Washington Death Index, 1940-1996 (Provo, UT, USA, The Generations Network, Inc., 2002), www.ancestry.com, Record for Ray H Leigh.

[1212] Washington State Archives; Olympia, Washington; Collection Title: *Washington Marriage Records, 1854-2013;* Reference Number: *kingcoarchmcvol50_267.*

[1213] Ancestry.com, Washington Death Index, 1940-1996 (Provo, UT, USA, The Generations Network, Inc., 2002), www.ancestry.com, Record for Evagene L Gidlof.

Pierce, Washington[1214]. He also married Roberta Short on 04 Aug 1946[1215]. Ray was a seaman and lived in Wauconda, Washington in 1975. He divorced both his wives. Ray Hugh Leigh and Evagene Hatch had one child who may still be living. Ray Hugh Leigh and Roberta Short had one child who may still be living.

83. Pearl Etta Leigh[5] (Charles Emery Leigh[4], Rueben Harrington Leigh[3], William Todd Leigh[2], Nathan S. Leigh[1]) was born on 14 Mar 1918 in Kent, Washington[1216] and died on 28 May 2000 in Belfair, Washington[1217]. She married Frank Harris, the son of Robert Harris and Florence Rutledge, on 28 Jan 1945 in Federal Way, Washington[1218]. He was born on 24 Sep 1906 in Kent, Washington[1219] and died on 30 Jul 1977 in Renton, Washington[1220].   Frank Harris was buried in Kent, Washington[1221].   Frank Harris and Pearl Etta Leigh had four children who may still be living.

84. Cecil Paul Leigh[5] (Jay Noel Leigh[4], Rueben Harrington Leigh[3], William Todd Leigh[2], Nathan S. Leigh[1]) was born on 04 Apr 1904 in Parma, Idaho[1222] and died on 30 Oct 1966 in Parma, Idaho[1223].   He married Leona Leota Fretwell, the daughter of William L. Fretwell and Fannie Sparks Ramsey, on 24 Jul 1924 in Roswell, Idaho[1224]. She was born on 04

Photo of Cecil Paul Leigh from the collection of Rev. Laverne E. Leigh and used with permission.

[1214] Ancestry.com, Washington Death Index, 1940-1996 (Provo, UT, USA, The Generations Network, Inc., 2002), www.ancestry.com, Record for Evagene L Gidlof.

[1215] Washington State Archives; Olympia, Washington; *Marriage Certificates;* Collection Title: *Washington Marriage Records, 1854-2013.*

[1216] Ancestry.com, Social Security Death Index (Provo, UT, USA, The Generations Network, Inc., 2008), www.ancestry.com, Number: 536-01-2268; Issue State: Washington; Issue Date: Before 1951. Record for Pearl E. Harris.

[1217] Ancestry.com, Social Security Death Index (Provo, UT, USA, The Generations Network, Inc., 2008), www.ancestry.com, Number: 536-01-2268; Issue State: Washington; Issue Date: Before 1951. Record for Pearl E. Harris

[1218] Ancestry.com. *Washington, County Marriages, 1855-2008* [database on-line]. Provo, UT, USA: Ancestry.com Operations, Inc., 2014.

[1219] Ancestry.com, Washington Death Index, 1940-1996 (Provo, UT, USA, The Generations Network, Inc., 2002), www.ancestry.com, Record for Frank Harris.

[1220] Ancestry.com, Washington Death Index, 1940-1996 (Provo, UT, USA, The Generations Network, Inc., 2002), www.ancestry.com, Record for Frank Harris.

[1221] Ancestry.com, U.S., Find A Grave Index, 1700s-Current (Provo, UT, USA, Ancestry.com Operations, Inc., 2012), Ancestry.com, http://www.Ancestry.com, Record for Frank Harris.

[1222] Death certificate from the State of Idaho.

[1223] Death certificate from the State of Idaho.

[1224] Upper Snake River Family History Center and Ricks College; Rexburg, Idaho; *Idaho Marriages, 1842-1996.*

Dec 1903[1225] in Parma, Idaho and died on 08 Dec 1983 in Parma, Idaho[1226]. Cecil Paul Leigh and his wife were buried in Parma Cemetery, Parma, Idaho[1227].

Cecil and Lena moved to Alvidore, Oregon to operate his father's farm for a short time and then moved back to Idaho. Then in 1929 they again moved to Alvidore, Oregon and took over the running of his father's farm from his brother, Reuben, who moved with his wife, Mary, to Modesto, California. in 1932, Cecil and Lena assumed the responsibility for 320 acres of the farm his father purchased at Fall Creek, Oregon. They built a home and worked the farm until 1934 when the sold their 320 acres to Guy R. Moore and moved back to Idaho to purchase the old original Paul homestead that Jay had sold when they left Idaho. Cecil and Lena farmed and lived on this farm for the rest of Cecil's life except for a short time that they lived in Arizona for Cecil's health. He had asthma. Cecil was in very poor health for a number of years, had more than one stroke and then died October 30, 1966. He is buried in Parma. Lena was still living on the farm in 1975.

Cecil Paul Leigh and Leona Leota Fretwell had the following children:
      i.   Living Leigh.
146. ii.   Stanley Donovan Leigh was born on 21 Jul 1930 in Eugene, Oregon[1228] and died on 11 Nov 2011 in Parma, Idaho[1229].
      iii.   Living Leigh

85. Reuben Harold Leigh[5] (Jay Noel Leigh[4], Rueben Harrington Leigh[3], William Todd Leigh[2], Nathan S. Leigh[1]) was born on 09 Oct 1905[1230] in Parma, Idaho and died on 25 May 1995 in Springfield, Oregon[1231]. He married Mary Elizabeth Bachman Harp, the daughter of John Bachman and Ella Grace Still, on 28 Nov 1928 in Junction City, Oregon[1232]. She was born on 19 May 1805 in Steubenville, Ohio[1233] and died on 24 Nov 1998 in Creswell, Oregon[1234].

[1225] Ancestry.com, U.S., Find A Grave Index, 1700s-Current (Provo, UT, USA, Ancestry.com Operations, Inc., 2012), Ancestry.com, http://www.Ancestry.com, Record for Lena L. Leigh.

[1226] Ancestry.com, U.S., Find A Grave Index, 1700s-Current (Provo, UT, USA, Ancestry.com Operations, Inc., 2012), Ancestry.com, http://www.Ancestry.com, Record for Lena L. Leigh.

[1227] Ancestry.com, U.S., Find A Grave Index, 1700s-Current (Provo, UT, USA, Ancestry.com Operations, Inc., 2012), Ancestry.com, http://www.Ancestry.com, Record for Lena L. Leigh.

[1228] Ancestry.com, U.S., Find A Grave Index, 1700s-Current (Provo, UT, USA, Ancestry.com Operations, Inc., 2012),

[1229] Ancestry.com, U.S., Find A Grave Index, 1700s-Current (Provo, UT, USA, Ancestry.com Operations, Inc., 2012),

[1230] Ancestry.com, U.S., Social Security Applications and Claims Index, 1936-2007.

[1231] Ancestry.com, U.S., Social Security Applications and Claims Index, 1936-2007.

[1232] Genealogy compiled by Rev. Laverne E. Leigh, 414 Washington Ave. East, Albia, Iowa 52531 in the Spring of 1975.

[1233] Ancestry.com, U.S., Social Security Applications and Claims Index, 1936-2007 (Provo, UT, USA, Ancestry.com Operations, Inc., 2015), Ancestry.com, http://www.Ancestry.com, Record for Mary Elizabeth Leigh.

[1234] Ancestry.com, U.S., Social Security Applications and Claims Index, 1936-2007 (Provo, UT, USA, Ancestry.com Operations, Inc., 2015), Ancestry.com, http://www.Ancestry.com, Record for Mary Elizabeth Leigh.

Reuben grew up and attended school in Apple Valley, Idaho. Although he moved with his parents first to Kent, Washington and then to Modesto, California, they always returned to the home place in Apple Valley. Then in 1924, Reuben drove a team and wagon from Nyssa, Oregon to Alvidore, Oregon. Nyssa is only three miles from the farm in Apple Valley that his father sold in 1923. With a friend, Reuben drove the wagon by way of Vale, Burns and Bend, Oregon. At Bend, he discovered that the direct route to the Willamete Valley and Alvidore was snowed full so that a wagon could not pass.

Photo of Reuben Harold Leigh and Mary Elizabeth Bachman Harp from the collection of Rev. Laverne E. Leigh and used with permission.

The friend became homesick and returned to Idaho. Reuben almost sold the team and wagon and tried to walk across the mountains. This would have likely cost him his life. Fortunately, he decided to drive the team and wagon north to the Columbia River and follow the river to Portland, Oregon before then driving to Alvidore near Eugene, Oregon. This he did driving from Bend to Eugene and Alvidore by the much longer but safer route without any companion but the animals. He arrived before his nineteenth birthday.

He attended High School in Eugene, Oregon through his freshman and part of his sophomore years. Part way through his sophomore year he told his father that he could not farm the place in Alvidore and go to school too. There was not time to do both. His father said "Well, the farm work had to be done." So Reuben quit High School to farm so that his father could work as a finish carpenter in Eugene. He married in 1928 Mary Harp. When his brother, Cecil Paul, moved back from Idaho to Alvidore to take over the farming, they moved in 1929 to Modesto, California. While in California during the depression times, he worked on ranches. Their first child, Laverne, was born while they lived in Modesto.

In January of 1931, they moved back to Oregon to rent a farm north of Junction City. Then in 1932, they moved to Fall Creek to farm 320 acres of the 1360 acre place that his father bought. During 1939, Reuben went to work in the woods for the West Fir Logging Company in West Fir, Oregon and they assumed the entire farm from his father and mother with the money that was owed at the Federal Land Bank. He then bought the forty acres from his uncle, George Asa Leigh, that his father had given George in 1933. They moved to Oakridge, Oregon in 1939 for about two years while Reuben continued to work for West Fir Logging Company. In 1941, they moved back to the farm at Fall Creek. Then in 1943, they bought a logging outfit and moved to Eugene, Oregon from 1943 to 1945 when they moved back to the farm to log on the farm. For a number of years, Reuben logged and raised Hereford cattle.

In 1950, their son, Laverne went into partnership with them in both the farm and the

logging business. Shortly afterwards, their son-in-law, Kenneth Parks, joined the business to form a three party partnership. They built an experimental sawmill invented by Reuben that they operated for about a year. The idea was good, but they lacked enough capital to iron the bugs out of it and so the converted the experimental mill to a conventional mill and finished cutting all the timber on the farm. Then for a period of time, Laverne and Reuben continued logging in the Loraine, Oregon area while Kenneth and Nova Parks took over the logging truck and hauled their logs. Kenneth and Nova were no longer in the partnership.

Photo of Reuben Harold Leigh and Mary Elizabeth Bachman Harp from the collection of Rev. Laverne E. Leigh and used with permission.

In 1953, Reuben and Mary bought fifty calves, Laverne and Betty bought one hundred calves and Kenneth and Nova bought twenty-five calves. These calves were three days old when purchased and came from a well known dairy in the edge of Springfield, Oregon. Laverne and his mother, Mary, raised the calves while Reuben continued to operate the logging business. In 1955 when the calves freshened, the logging business closed out so that Reuben and Mary and Laverne and Betty could operate the Grade A milking business they had grown into from baby calves. This business only lasted two years before they were starved out due to the quota system monopoly that forced them to sell two-thirds of their milk at a profit making Grade-A price. The dairy animals were sold in the spring of 1956. Reuben began selling dairy products on the Oregon Coast and Reuben and Mary moved to Coquille, Oregon in March of 1959 to purchase a home and be close to the dairy supply area he served. After working at the dairy supply business for about three years, Reuben went to work for the Coquille School system driving a bus half time and working as a janitor in the High School half time. Reuben worked up steadily until he was full time janitor and then to head janitor in the High School until his retirement in 1967 at the age of 62. In retirement, Reuben and Mary continue to live in Coquille in the home they purchased approximately two years after moving to Coquille. Mary keeps house and tends her flowers while Reuben divides his time between an active practice of Fishing and enough small jobs as a carpenter to earn all that Social Security will allow. Reuben and Mary with their new pickup truck and travel trailer have enjoyed seeing much of the United States and part of Canada during a number of trips they have taken since their retirement.

Mary's mother, Ella Still, died after she and John had four children. John, her father, kept the two oldest children, John and Sarah. The other two children, Mary and James, were too small for a single father to take care of and work. So he allowed William Jennings and Annie Bell Hughes Harp to care for Mary and the Newtons to care of James. Later he allowed the families to adopt Mary and James. So Mary was raised as a Harp and James as a Newton. The Harps moved to Junction City, Oregon while Mary was quite young. She attended school there and graduated from Junction City High School in 1924. She began working at the cannery in Junction City when she was 16. Her son, Rev. Laverne Leigh officiated at her funeral and six of the grandchildren were pallbearers.

Reuben Harold Leigh and Mary Elizabeth Bachman Harp had the following children:

147.　i.　　　Laverne Leigh was born on in Modesto, California..
　　　ii.　　　Living Leigh

86. Ruth Arvilla Leigh[5] (Jay Noel Leigh[4], Rueben Harrington Leigh[3], William Todd Leigh[2], Nathan S. Leigh[1]) was born on 22 Apr 1909 in Parma, Idaho[1235] and died on 13 Sep 1975 in Salem, Oregon[1236]. She married Jerome Delmas Lambert, the son of John William Lambert and Ella Parker, on 12 Jun 1932 in Eugene, Oregon[1237]. He was born on 08 Feb 1907 in Illinois[1238] and died on 08 Feb 1988 in Santa Cruz, California[1239]. Ruth and Jerome made their home slightly north and in between Springfield and Eugene, Oregon for several years while Jerry worked for the Southern Pacific railroad. They then bought and lived in three separate homes in Eugene for a number of years until Jerry

---

[1235] Ancestry.com, Oregon Death Index, 1903-98 (Provo, UT, USA, Ancestry.com Operations Inc, 2000), www.ancestry.com, Oregon State Library; 1966-1970 Death Index; Reel Title: State of Oregon Death Index; Year Range: 1971-1980. Record for Ruth Arv Lambert.

[1236] Ancestry.com, Oregon Death Index, 1903-98 (Provo, UT, USA, Ancestry.com Operations Inc, 2000), www.ancestry.com, Oregon State Library; 1966-1970 Death Index; Reel Title: State of Oregon Death Index; Year Range: 1971-1980. Record for Ruth Arv Lambert.

[1237] Ancestry.com, California, Marriage Index, 1960-1985 (Provo, UT, USA, Ancestry.com Operations Inc, 2007), Ancestry.com, http://www.Ancestry.com, Record for Jerome D Lambert.

[1238] Ancestry.com, California Death Index, 1940-1997 (Provo, UT, USA, The Generations Network, Inc., 2000), www.ancestry.com, Date: 1988-02-08. Record for Jerome Delmas Lambert.

[1239] Ancestry.com, California Death Index, 1940-1997 (Provo, UT, USA, The Generations Network, Inc., 2000), www.ancestry.com, Date: 1988-02-08. Record for Jerome Delmas Lambert.

retired from the railroad. Jerry worked in the Southern Pacific shops and on the wrecker. After retirement, they had a home built in a retirement development on Cascade Drive in Woodburn, Oregon where they have already spent a number of happy years. Jerome Delmas Lambert and Ruth Arvilla Leigh had two children who may still be living.

87. Frances Mary Leigh[5] (William Edson Leigh[4], Rueben Harrington Leigh[3], William Todd Leigh[2], Nathan S. Leigh[1]) was born on 05 June 1906 in Parma, Idaho[1240] and died on 07 Apr 1997 in Winston, Oregon[1241]. She married Fred Leslie Uran, the son of Frank Uran, on 13 Sep 1927 in Vancouver, Washington[1242]. He was born on 07 Dec 1903 in Wisconsin[1243] and died in June 1982 in Chugiak, Alaska[1244]. She later married Delmer Dwight Young, the son of John Young and Studebaker, on 18 May 1941 in Klamath Falls, Oregon[1245]. He was born on 07 Sept 1899 in Hooper, Nebraska[1246] and died on 27 Sep 1968 in Roseburg, Oregon[1247]. Frances Mary Leigh and her husband Delmer Dwight Young were buried in Roseburg, Oregon[1248]. Francis was a sales lady and a store manager in a ladies ready to wear store. Francis was living in Roseburg in 1975. Delmer worked in a lumber mill.

Fred Leslie Uran and Frances Mary Leigh had the following child:
     i.   James Leigh Uran was born on 07 Sep 1938 in Portland, Oregon[1249] and died on 10 Sep 1938 in Portland, Oregon[1250].

88. William Paul Leigh[5] (William Edson Leigh[4], Rueben Harrington Leigh[3], William Todd Leigh[2], Nathan S. Leigh[1]) was born on 26 Aug 1918 in Parma, Idaho[1251] and died

---

[1240] Ancestry.com, U.S., Social Security Applications and Claims Index, 1936-2007 (Provo, UT, USA, Ancestry.com Operations, Inc., 2015), Ancestry.com, http://www.Ancestry.com, Record for Frances Mary Young.

[1241] Ancestry.com, U.S., Social Security Applications and Claims Index, 1936-2007 (Provo, UT, USA, Ancestry.com Operations, Inc., 2015), Ancestry.com, http://www.Ancestry.com, Record for Frances Mary Young.

[1242] Washington State Archives; Olympia, Washington; *Marriage Certificates*; Collection Title: *Washington Marriage Records, 1854-2013*.

[1243] Ancestry.com, Social Security Death Index (Provo, UT, USA, The Generations Network, Inc., 2008), www.ancestry.com, Number: 541-03-6800; Issue State: Oregon; Issue Date: Before 1951. Record for Fred Uran.

[1244] Ancestry.com, Social Security Death Index (Provo, UT, USA, The Generations Network, Inc., 2008), www.ancestry.com, Number: 541-03-6800; Issue State: Oregon; Issue Date: Before 1951. Record for Fred Uran.

[1245] Ancestry.com, U.S., Find A Grave Index, 1700s-Current (Provo, UT, USA, Ancestry.com Operations, Inc., 2012), Ancestry.com, http://www.Ancestry.com, Record for Delmer D Young.

[1246] Ancestry.com, U.S., Find A Grave Index, 1700s-Current (Provo, UT, USA, Ancestry.com Operations, Inc., 2012), Ancestry.com, http://www.Ancestry.com, Record for Delmer D Young.

[1247] Ancestry.com, U.S., Find A Grave Index, 1700s-Current (Provo, UT, USA, Ancestry.com Operations, Inc., 2012), Ancestry.com, http://www.Ancestry.com, Record for Delmer D Young.

[1248] Ancestry.com, U.S., Find A Grave Index, 1700s-Current (Provo, UT, USA, Ancestry.com Operations, Inc., 2012), Ancestry.com, http://www.Ancestry.com, Record for Delmer D Young.

[1249] Genealogy compiled by Rev. Laverne E. Leigh, 414 Washington Ave. East, Albia, Iowa 52531 in the Spring of 1975.

[1250] Genealogy compiled by Rev. Laverne E. Leigh, 414 Washington Ave. East, Albia, Iowa 52531 in the Spring of 1975.

[1251] Ancestry.com, U.S., Social Security Applications and Claims Index, 1936-2007 (Provo, UT, USA, Ancestry.com Operations, Inc., 2015), Ancestry.com, http://www.Ancestry.com, Record for William Paul Leigh.

on 29 May 2003 in Baker City, Oregon[1252]. He married Charlotte Bernice Thompson, the daughter of Charlie Thompson and Wordna Vanoyer, on 14 Feb 1937 in Weiser, Idaho[1253]. She was born in 1916 in Halfway, Oregon[1254]. He married for the second time to Elaine Betty Lewis Ingram, the daughter of Percy Huston Lewis and Thelma Alice Petersen, on 07 Jun 1947 in Winnemucca, Nevada[1255]. She was born on 27 Apr 1921 in Baker City, Oregon[1256] and died on 05 May 2005 in Baker City, Oregon[1257].

Billie, as he was called, married Charlotte Bernice Thompson in 1937. Charlotte's father, Charles Thompson, was the brother of Fae Leigh, Milton Leigh's wife. They were divorced. Billie married second to Elaine Betty Lewis who was a widow with three children, Lyle Chester, Judy Diane and Carl Lewis. Elaine's first husband, Chester Peterson, had been killed in 1953 in an accident. Bill was a farmer-logger (maintenance mechanic) who had a heart attack and was semi-retired in 1975. Elaine worked as a cook in a restaurant. They were living on a farm just east of Baker, Oregon in 1975.

Elaine Betty Leigh, 84, of Baker City, who was nicknamed Happy; by a close friend, died May 5, 2005, at St. Elizabeth Nursing Home. There will be a Celebration of Life service at 1 p.m. Saturday at Gray's West an Damp; Co., 1500 Dewey Ave. Pastor Monte Lloyd of Harvest Church will officiate. There will be a reception afterward at the home of Bill and Cindy Leigh. Elaine was born on April 27, 1921, at Wingville to Percy Huston Lewis and Thelma Alice Petersen-Lewis. She was born a twin with Adele Lewis-Williams. She lived most of her life in the Baker City area. She also spent a short time in Pendleton and the Portland area. Elaine married Chester Ingram on July 5, 1938. They had three children, Lyle Chester Ingram, Judy Diane Ingram and Carl Lewis Ingram. She married William Paul Leigh on June 7, 1947. They had two children, William Paul Leigh Jr. and Mary Alice Leigh. Elaine worked as a waitress, a farm hand and a cook. She enjoyed going on picnics with friends and family, traveling to the mountains and the Snake River area, camping, fishing, cooking, knitting, crocheting and she had an enormous love for animals. She was a loving person with a very kind heart. She will be missed by her friends and family. She had a sense of humor and livened things up wherever she was. Survivors include two sisters, Zena Edwards and Faye Edge, both of Baker City; a son,

---

[1252] Ancestry.com, U.S., Social Security Applications and Claims Index, 1936-2007 (Provo, UT, USA, Ancestry.com Operations, Inc., 2015), Ancestry.com, http://www.Ancestry.com, Record for William Paul Leigh.

[1253] Ancestry.com, Idaho, County Marriages, 1864-1950 (Provo, UT, USA, Ancestry.com Operations, Inc., 2014), Ancestry.com, http://www.Ancestry.com, Record for Charolet Thompson.

[1254] Ancestry.com, Idaho, County Marriages, 1864-1950 (Provo, UT, USA, Ancestry.com Operations, Inc., 2014), Ancestry.com, http://www.Ancestry.com, Record for Charolet Thompson.

[1255] Genealogy compiled by Rev. Laverne E. Leigh, 414 Washington Ave. East, Albia, Iowa 52531 in the Spring of 1975.

[1256] Ancestry.com, U.S., Social Security Applications and Claims Index, 1936-2007 (Provo, UT, USA, Ancestry.com Operations, Inc., 2015), Ancestry.com, http://www.Ancestry.com, Record for Elaine Betty Ingram.

[1257] Ancestry.com, U.S., Social Security Applications and Claims Index, 1936-2007 (Provo, UT, USA, Ancestry.com Operations, Inc., 2015), Ancestry.com, http://www.Ancestry.com, Record for Elaine Betty Ingram.

Lyle Ingram of San Diego; daughter, Judy Ingram of Baker City; son and daughter-in-law, Bill and Cindy Leigh of Baker City; daughter and son-in-law, Mary and Lon Nalder of Oxbow; 12 grandchildren; and 11 great-grandchildren.

She was preceded in death by her husband, William P. Leigh; a son, Carl Lewis Ingram; a sister, Adele Williams; and a granddaughter, Diana Francis-Hulick.

William Paul Leigh and Elaine Betty Lewis Ingram had the following children:

 i. William Paul Leigh, Jr. was born on 01 Jan 1949 in Baker City, Oregon[1258] and died in Baker City, Oregon on 26 Dec 2013[1259].

 ii. Living Leigh.

Photo of William Paul, Jr. from the collection of Rev. Laverne E. Leigh and used with permission.

89. Milton Allen Leigh[5] (Nathan Evan Leigh[4], Rueben Harrington Leigh[3], William Todd Leigh[2], Nathan S. Leigh[1]) was born on 28 Feb 1903 in Roswell, Idaho[1260] and died on 13 May 1962 in Newport, Oregon[1261]. He married Leora Fae Thompson, the daughter of Robert H. Thompson and Elizabeth L. Webb, on 14 Jul 1924 in Baker City, Oregon[1262]. She was born on 24 Sep 1902 in Promise Wall, Oregon[1263] and died on 25 Oct 2002 in Moscow, Montana[1264]. Milton Allen Leigh and his wife were buried in Parma Cemetery, Parma, Idaho[1265].

[1258] Ancestry.com, Social Security Death Index (Provo, UT, USA, The Generations Network, Inc., 2008), www.ancestry.com, Issue State: Oregon; Issue Date: 1963. Record for William P Leigh.

[1259] Ancestry.com, Social Security Death Index (Provo, UT, USA, The Generations Network, Inc., 2008), www.ancestry.com, Issue State: Oregon; Issue Date: 1963. Record for William P Leigh.

[1260] Ancestry.com, Oregon Death Index, 1903-98 (Provo, UT, USA, Ancestry.com Operations Inc, 2000), www.ancestry.com, Oregon State Library; Oregon Death Index 1931-1941; Reel Title: Oregon Death Index A-Z; Year Range: 1961-1965. Record for Milton A Leigh.

[1261] Ancestry.com, Oregon Death Index, 1903-98 (Provo, UT, USA, Ancestry.com Operations Inc, 2000), www.ancestry.com, Oregon State Library; Oregon Death Index 1931-1941; Reel Title: Oregon Death Index A-Z; Year Range: 1961-1965. Record for Milton A Leigh.

[1262] Ancestry.com, Oregon, County Marriages, 1851-1975 (Lehi, UT, USA, Ancestry.com Operations, Inc., 2016), Ancestry.com, http://www.Ancestry.com, Record for Milton Leigh.

[1263] Ancestry.com, U.S., Social Security Applications and Claims Index, 1936-2007 (Provo, UT, USA, Ancestry.com Operations, Inc., 2015), Ancestry.com, http://www.Ancestry.com, Record for Leora Fae Leigh.

[1264] Ancestry.com, U.S., Social Security Applications and Claims Index, 1936-2007 (Provo, UT, USA, Ancestry.com Operations, Inc., 2015), Ancestry.com, http://www.Ancestry.com, Record for Leora Fae Leigh.

[1265] Ancestry.com, U.S., Find A Grave Index, 1700s-Current (Provo, UT, USA, Ancestry.com Operations, Inc., 2012), Ancestry.com, http://www.Ancestry.com, Record for Milton Leigh.

Milton first operated his father's show houses in Nysia, Oregon, Wilder, New Plymouth and Parma, Idaho while his father was in California. He then continued to operate the show houses with his father after Nate returned from California around 1919. After he and his father sold out the show businesses in 1942 and 1943, Milton was involved in several business ventures. One of these was a charter boat and boat supply at Depot Bay, Oregon. Then they sold the boat and business and purchased a motel and operated it for a time in Newport, Oregon. While operating this, Milton died May 13, 1962 in Newport, Oregon. He was buried in Parma, Idaho. Fae sold the motel and moved back to Idaho and was living in Moscow, Idaho in 1975.

LeOra Fae Leigh Obituary · 27 February 2015
Wallowa County Chieftain, Nov 27, 2002
LeOra Fae Thompson Leigh, the oldest living graduate of Wallowa High School at the time of her death at the age of 100, died Oct. 25, 2002, in Moscow, Idaho. She was born Sept. 24, 1902, in a log cabin at Promise to Henry and Louise Thompson. In 1920, the family moved to Halfway where she went to school until her senior year when she transferred to Wallowa High School for health reasons and lived with the John Wray family. Mrs. Leigh graduated with the class of 1921, the first class to take a senior sneak and the first to wear caps and gowns.

After graduation, she returned to Halfway where she worked in a dairy and a bank before marrying Milton Leigh and moving to Parma, Idaho. After the death of her husband, LeOra moved to Moscow, Idaho. She was active in the First Methodist Church, Eastern Star, Daughters of the Nile and the Moscow Garden Club. She is survived by a daughter, LaDena, and a son, Phil. Milton Allen Leigh and Leora Fae Thompson had two children who may still be living.

90. Mentor G. Leigh[5] (Nathan Evan Leigh[4], Rueben Harrington Leigh[3], William Todd Leigh[2], Nathan S. Leigh[1]) was born 25 Mar 1909 in Parma, Idaho[1266] and died 11 Apr 1965 in Rural Canyon, Idaho[1267]. He married Nellie Magini, the daughter of August Magini and Virginia Ambrogi on 22 Aug 1942 in Boston, Massachusetts[1268]. She was

[1266] Idaho, Death Records, 1890-1966 (Provo, UT, USA, Ancestry.com Operations, Inc., 2014), Ancestry.com, http://www.Ancestry.com, Idaho Bureau of Vital Records and Health Statistics; Boise, Idaho; Death Index and Image, 1911-1966. Record for Mentor G. Leigh.
[1267] Idaho, Death Records, 1890-1966 (Provo, UT, USA, Ancestry.com Operations, Inc., 2014), Ancestry.com, http://www.Ancestry.com, Idaho Bureau of Vital Records and Health Statistics; Boise, Idaho; Death Index and Image, 1911-1966. Record for Mentor G. Leigh.
[1268] Genealogy compiled by Rev. Laverne E. Leigh, 414 Washington Ave. East, Albia, Iowa 52531 in the Spring of 1975.

born on 12 Jul 1918 in North Judson, Indiana[1269] and died on 23 Apr 2009 in Parma, Idaho [1270]. Mentor G. Leigh was buried in Parma, Idaho[1271].

Mentor took over the New Plymouth Theater from his father in about 1922 after graduating from high school. During World War II, Mentor was a Machinist Mate 2/c in the Navy when he met Nellie and they were married.

Photo of Mentor G. Leigh from the collection of Rev. Laverne E. Leigh and used with permission.

They made their home in Parma, Idaho after he was discharged from the Navy. Later he purchased the service station and motel from his uncle, William Edson Leigh, that was in the west edge of Parma, Idaho. Mentor was a very successful businessman all his life. Nellie lived in Parma in 1975.Nellie's parents, August and Virginia Maginis, emigrated from Italy to the U.S. through Ellis Island and were indentured servants in Mississippi until they were able to pay for their passage and living expenses. The family then moved west. Nellie was born in North Judson, Indiana. She was the 8th of 9 children. The family eventually moved to Stevensville, Montana where Nellie graduated from High School in 1936 and graduated from business college in Missoula in 1938. When her parents moved to Roswell, Idaho in 1939, Nellie and her youngest brother, Frank, went with them. It was while she was working for Idaho Power in New Plymouth that Nellie met Mentor Leigh. They were married in August of 1942 in Boston, Massachusetts where Mentor was stationed in the Navy. After the war, Mentor and Nellie settled in Parma. Nellie was employed by Idaho Power before their marriage. She moved from the rural home west of Parma to a home in Parma after Mentor died. She became very involved in the community of Parma. Mentor G. Leigh and Nellie Magini had two children who may still be living.

[1269] Ancestry.com, Social Security Death Index (Provo, UT, USA, The Generations Network, Inc., 2008), www.ancestry.com, Issue State: Montana; Issue Date: Before 1951. Record for Nelle Leigh.
[1270] Ancestry.com, Social Security Death Index (Provo, UT, USA, The Generations Network, Inc., 2008), www.ancestry.com, Issue State: Montana; Issue Date: Before 1951. Record for Nelle Leigh.
[1271] Ancestry.com, U.S., Find A Grave Index, 1700s-Current (Provo, UT, USA, Ancestry.com Operations, Inc., 2012), Ancestry.com, http://www.Ancestry.com, Record for Mentor G. Leigh.

Mentor G. Leigh and his "Roadster" from the collection of Rev. Laverne E. Leigh and used with permission.

91. Harry Wayne Leigh[5] (Mentor Garfield Leigh[4], Rueben Harrington Leigh[3], William Todd Leigh[2], Nathan S. Leigh[1]) was born on 29 Apr 1905 in Caldwell, Idaho[1272] and died born on 16 Mar 1907 in Washington[1273]. He married Grace McConnell on 28 May 1926 in Seattle, Washington[1274]. She was born on 16 Mar 1907 in Washington[1275] and died on 30 Jan 1959 in Oakland, California[1276]. He later had a child with a lady by the name of Emma.   There is no information suggesting Harry and Emma were ever actually married. .

92.   Mary Agnes Foote[5] (George L. Foote Jr.[4], Lydia Marie Leigh[3] , William Todd Leigh[2], Nathan S. Leigh[1]) was born on 16 Aug 1890 in Utica, New York[1277] and died on 27 Mar 1982 in Lakeland, Florida[1278].   She married Alcide F. Emery, the son of Jean (John) Baptist Emery and Celina Gagnier, on 14 Jul 1909 in St. Patrick's Church, Utica, New York [1279]. He was born on 18 May 1885 in Stoney Point, Canada[1280] and died on 12

[1272] Ancestry.com. *California, Death Index, 1940-1997* [database on-line]. Provo, UT, USA: Ancestry.com Operations
[1273] Ancestry.com. *California, Death Index, 1940-1997* [database on-line]. Provo, UT, USA: Ancestry.com Operations
[1274] *Washington Marriage Records, 1854-2013;* Reference Number: *kingcoarchmcvol11_909*
[1275] Ancestry.com, 1940 United States Federal Census (Provo, UT, USA, Ancestry.com Operations, Inc., 2012), www.ancestry.com, Year: 1940; Census Place: Oakland, Alameda, California; Roll: T627_437; Page: 4A; Enumeration District: 61-218. Record for Graci Leigh.
[1276] Genealogy compiled by Rev. Laverne E. Leigh in 2017.
[1277] Death Certificate from the State of Florida.
[1278] Death Certificate from the State of Florida.
[1279] Familysearch.org, Oneida County Marriages 1908 to 1935.
[1280] Obituary, Utica Daily Press, Utica, New York, July 14, 1961, page 21.

Jul 1961 in Utica, New York[1281]. Mary Agnes Foote and her husband were buried in Mt. Oliviet Cemetery, Whitesboro, New York[1282].

Photo of Mary Agnes Foote from the authors collection.

Alcide F. Emery was baptized in L'annoanciation De Pointe-aux-r, Catholic. Baptism name was Joseph Philias Alcide. He came with his family on the Grand Trunk Railroad from St. Clair, Canada to Massachusetts where the family first settled. Later they moved to New York Mills, New York. At time of his Naturalization, Alcide Emery lived at 1701 Erie St., Utica, New York.

Alicide (Fred) was my grandfather. What I remember about him is that he was an usher at Sacred Heart Church. He worked at the Utica and Mohawk Cotton Mills and retired in 1952. His occupation was listed as a loom fixer, and a mill hand. He was also a carpenter. I remember the doll house he built for his granddaughters to play with. When my father built our house, my grandfather was there every day sweeping up and organizing the tools so my dad could start working again as soon as he finished work.

Photo Alcide F. Emery and Mary Agnes Foote from the authors collection.

Alcide F. Emery and Mary Agnes Foote had the following children:
148.	i.	Harold Alcide Emery was born on 21 Jul 1913 in Utica, New York[1283] and died on 11 Dec 1989 in New Hartford, New York[1284].
149.	ii.	Gordon Charles Emery was born on 29 Mar 1915 in Utica, New York[1285] and died on 09 Oct 1981 in Utica, New York[1286].

[1281] Obituary, Utica Daily Press, Utica, New York, July 14, 1961, page 21.

[1282] Ancestry.com, U.S., Find A Grave Index, 1700s-Current (Provo, UT, USA, Ancestry.com Operations, Inc., 2012),

[1283] Ancestry.com, Social Security Death Index (Provo, UT, USA, The Generations Network, Inc., 2008), www.ancestry.com, Database online. Number: 115-05-0037; Issue State: New York; Issue Date: Before 1951. Record for Harold A. Emery.

[1284] Ancestry.com, Social Security Death Index (Provo, UT, USA, The Generations Network, Inc., 2008), www.ancestry.com, Database online. Number: 115-05-0037; Issue State: New York; Issue Date: Before 1951. Record for Harold A. Emery.

[1285] Ancestry.com, Social Security Death Index, Record for Gordon Emery.

[1286] Ancestry.com, Social Security Death Index, Record for Gordon Emery.

Photo of Harold Alcide Emery and Gordon Charles Emery taken about 1917.   This photo was in the authors collection.

93.   Isabel Lydia Foote[5] (George L. Foote Jr.[4], Lydia Marie Leigh[3] , William Todd Leigh[2], Nathan S. Leigh[1]) was born on 08 Jan 1894 in Milford, Massachusetts[1287] and died on 31 Aug 1973 in New Hartford, New York[1288]. She married Bert Raynor Hart, the son of John Hart and Helen Arnst, on 19 Apr 1911 in Morrisville, New York[1289]. He was born on 06 Nov 1885 in New York[1290] and died on 23 Feb 1927[1291]. She married Arthur Jay Light, the son of Edward Light and Hannah Delon, on 01 Aug 1925 in Lincoln, Ontario, Canada[1292]. He was born 24 Jul 1896 in Utica, New York[1293] and died in Sept 1973 in Miami, Florida[1294]. She married Claude L. Earley, the son of Fred G. Earley and Lizzie M. Hugill, in 1941 in Massena, New York[1295]. He was born on 04 May 1904 in Vernon Center, New York[1296] and died on 16 Apr 1986 in the Sitrin Nursing Home, New

[1287] Ancestry.com, U.S., Find A Grave Index, 1700s-Current (Provo, UT, USA, Ancestry.com Operations, Inc., 2012),

[1288] Ancestry.com, U.S., Find A Grave Index, 1700s-Current (Provo, UT, USA, Ancestry.com Operations, Inc., 2012),

[1289] Marriage Record, New York, County Marriages, 1908-1935 for Isabel C. Foote, LDS Film #381748.

[1290] Ancestry.com. *New York, Abstracts of World War I Military Service, 1917-1919* [database on-line]. Provo, UT, USA: Ancestry.com Operations, Inc., 2013.

[1291] Will of Burt H. Hart found at the County Clerk's office, Madison, County, New York.

[1292] Ancestry.com and Genealogical Research Library (Brampton, Ontario, Canada), Ontario, Canada Marriages, 1801-1928 (Online publication - Provo, UT, USA: Ancestry.com Operations, Inc., 2010.Original data - Ontario, Canada. Registrations of Marriages, 1869-1928. MS932, Reels 1-833, 850-880. Archives of Ontario, Toronto.Ontario, Canada. Marriage License Books, 1907-1910. M), Ancestry.com, http://www.Ancestry.com, Archives of Ontario; Series: MS932; Reel: 721.

[1293] Ancestry.com. *New York, Abstracts of World War I Military Service, 1917-1919* [database on-line]. Provo, UT, USA: Ancestry.com Operations, Inc., 2013.

[1294] Ancestry.com. *U.S., Social Security Death Index, 1935-2014* [database on-line]. Provo, UT, USA: Ancestry.com Operations Inc, 2014.

[1295] Obituary, Utica Observer Dispatch, Utica, New York, April 17, 1986.

[1296] Ancestry.com. *U.S., Social Security Death Index, 1935-2014* [database on-line]. Provo, UT, USA: Ancestry.com Operations Inc, 2014.

Hartford, New York [1297]. Claude was a graduate of Westmoreland High School. He was a self employed electrician in the Utica area for many years. He was of the Methodist Faith. Isabel Lydia Foote and Claude Earley were buried in Sep 1973 in the Greenlawn Cemetery, New Hartford, New York.

Photo of Isabel Lydia Foote from the author's collection.

Isabel was married to a Mr. Light in 1927 when her first husband, Burt Hart passed away. She was listed as the legal guardian for her children in his will. Isabel lived at 2218 Highland Ave. at time of her death. She was a member of Sacred Heart Church.

Bert Raynor Hart and Isabel Lydia Foote Hart Earley had the following children:
150.   i.   Hazel Hart was born on 10 May 1912 in Morrisville, New York[1298] and died on 10 Jul 1949 in Memorial Hospital, Utica, New York[1299].
151.   ii.   Howard John Hart was born on 16 Sep 1914 in Eaton, New York[1300] and died on 25 Feb 1990 in St. Elizabeth Hospital, Utica, New York[1301].

94.   Earl E. Foote[5] (Charles Lewis Foote[4], Lydia Marie Leigh[3] , William Todd Leigh[2], Nathan S. Leigh[1]) was born on 28 Feb 1898 in Canastota, New York[1302] and died on 16 Nov 1959 in Eaton Road, Morrisville, New York[1303]. He married Hazel J. Dailey, the daughter of Austin J. Dailey and Cora Card, on 19 Jun 1920 in Broome County, New York[1304]. She was born in Apr 1897 in Pennsylvania[1305] and died on 24 Jan 1963 in Greene Hospital, Greene, New York[1306]. Earl E. Foote was buried in Nov 1959 in Mt Pleasant Cemetery, Canastota, New York[1307].
Earl lived in Morrisville in 1950 and Eaton in 1953. He was found dead at his home and had been dead about two days. He was an employee of Henney Motors Co. He was a veteran of World War I and a member of the Munnsville American Legion Post. He

---

[1297] Ancestry.com. *U.S., Social Security Death Index, 1935-2014* [database on-line]. Provo, UT, USA: Ancestry.com Operations Inc, 2014.
[1298] Obituary, Utica Observer Dispatch, Utica, New York, July 11, 1949, page 2A.
[1299] Obituary, Utica Observer Dispatch, Utica, New York, July 11, 1949, page 2A.
[1300] Obituary, Utica Observer Dispatch, Utica, New York, February 27, 1990, page 5A.
[1301] Obituary, Utica Observer Dispatch, Utica, New York, February 27, 1990, page 5A.
[1302] Obituary, Utica Daily Press, Utica, New York, November 17, 1959, page 8.
[1303] Obituary, Utica Daily Press, Utica, New York, November 17, 1959, page 8.
[1304] Ancestry.com. *New York, County Marriage Records, 1847-1849, 1907-1936* [database on-line]. Lehi, UT, USA: Ancestry.com Operations, Inc., 2016.
[1305] Ancestry.com. *1900 United States Federal Census* [database on-line]. Provo, UT, USA: Ancestry.com
[1306] Obituary, Press, Binghamton, New York, January 25, 1963, page 42.
[1307] Obituary, Utica Daily Press, Utica, New York, November 17, 1959, page 8.

enlisted September 16   Ft. Slocum, Taylorbranch of service, 5th infantry.   He was discharged November 1919. He had three grandchildren at the time of his death.

Brookville Courier, October 26, 1921
Earl E Foote, 23, a former resident of Canastota was arrested in Louisville, Kentucky, charged with stealing $9,000 in two packages from the Binghamton post office where he had been employed for the past two years. He still had $5,740 left.

Hazel lived at 224 Harrison Street, Johnson City, New York at the time of her death. She was a member of the Primitive Methodist Church and the Sunshine Scatters Class of Sunday School. She was a retired employee of Ansco having worked for over 40 years.

Earl E. Foote and Hazel J. Dailey had the following child:
      i.   Sarah E. Foote was born on 17 Apr 1921 in New York State[1308] and died on 25 Dec 1987 in Clallam Bay, Washington[1309]. She married Preben M. Hansen, the son of Martin Frederick Schou and Brodil Kirstine Marie Hansen. He was born in Denmark on 11 Jan 1919[1310] and died on 20 Jul 1998 in Suquamish, Washington[1311].

95.   Hazel E. Foote[5] (Earl James Foote[4], Lydia Marie Leigh[3] , William Todd Leigh[2], Nathan S. Leigh[1]) was born on 29 Apr 1907 in Canastota, New York[1312] and died on 29 May 1995 in Oneida City Hospital, Oneida, New York[1313]. She married Raymond A. Rousseau on 25 Apr 1926 in New Hartford, New York[1314]. He was born on 23 Apr 1904[1315] and died on 31 Dec 1956[1316]. Hazel E. Foote and her husband were buried in Mount Pleasant Cemetery, Canastota, New York[1317]. Hazel lived in the Canastota area most of her live, moving to Oneida in 1972. She was a bookkeeper at the former Avon Theater in Canastota more than twenty years, retiring in 1952. She was a Protestant. Raymond A. Rousseau and Hazel E. Foote had the following children:

[1308] Ancestry.com, Social Security Death Index (Provo, UT, USA, The Generations Network, Inc., 2008),

[1309] Ancestry.com, Social Security Death Index (Provo, UT, USA, The Generations Network, Inc., 2008).

[1310] Ancestry.com, Social Security Death Index (Provo, UT, USA, The Generations Network, Inc., 2008),

[1311] Ancestry.com, Social Security Death Index (Provo, UT, USA, The Generations Network, Inc., 2008),

[1312] Ancestry.com, Social Security Death Index (Provo, UT, USA, The Generations Network, Inc., 2008), www.ancestry.com, Database online. Record for Hazel E. Rousseau.

[1313] Ancestry.com, Social Security Death Index (Provo, UT, USA, The Generations Network, Inc., 2008), www.ancestry.com, Database online. Record for Hazel E. Rousseau.

[1314] Obituary, Oneida Daily Dispatch, May 30, 1995.

[1315] Ancestry.com, Social Security Death Index (Provo, UT, USA, The Generations Network, Inc., 2008), www.ancestry.com, Number: 093-03-9160; Issue State: New York; Issue Date: Before 1951. Record for Raymond Rousseau.

[1316] Ancestry.com, Social Security Death Index (Provo, UT, USA, The Generations Network, Inc., 2008), www.ancestry.com, Number: 093-03-9160; Issue State: New York; Issue Date: Before 1951. Record for Raymond Rousseau.

[1317] Ancestry.com, U.S., Find A Grave Index, 1700s-Current (Provo, UT, USA, Ancestry.com Operations, Inc., 2012),

152.   i.   Richard C. Rousseau was born on 30 Sep 1928 in Canastota, New York[1318] and died on 21 Oct 1999 in Stonehedge Health and Rehabilitation Center, Chittenango, New York[1319].

153.   ii.   Judith Rousseau was born on 18 Jul 1941[1320] and died on 30 Nov 1983.

   iii.   Living Rousseau

96.   Doris M. Leigh[5] (Claude Jay Leigh[4], George Henry Leigh[3] , William Todd Leigh[2], Nathan S. Leigh[1]) was born on 27 Mar 1911 in Oneida, New York[1321] and died on 02 Jan 2002 in Oneida, New York[1322]. She married Carl LaVerne Wood on 05 Dec 1931 in St. Paul's Evangelist Church, Oneida, New York[1323]. He was born on 12 May 1907 in Bernards Bay, Oswego, New York[1324] and died on 20 Apr 1995 in Oneida, New York[1325]. Doris M. Leigh and her husband were buried in Oneida, New York[1326]. Carl LaVerne Wood and Doris M Leigh had two children who may still be alive.

Photo of Doris M. Leigh
← and Carl LaVerne Wood →
from the collection of Robert Wood and used with permission.

97.   Claude Jay Leigh Jr.[5] (Claude Jay Leigh[4], George Henry Leigh[3], William Todd

[1318] Ancestry.com, U.S., Social Security Applications and Claims Index, 1936-2007 (Provo, UT, USA, Ancestry.com Operations, Inc., 2015), Ancestry.com, http://www.Ancestry.com, Record for Richard Carl Rousseau

[1319] Ancestry.com, U.S., Social Security Applications and Claims Index, 1936-2007 (Provo, UT, USA, Ancestry.com Operations, Inc., 2015), Ancestry.com, http://www.Ancestry.com, Record for Richard Carl Rousseau.

[1320] Ancestry.com, Social Security Death Index (Provo, UT, USA, The Generations Network, Inc., 2008), www.ancestry.com, Database online. Number: 099-32-4788; Issue State: New York; Issue Date: 1957-1959. Record for Judith Depasquale.

[1321] Ancestry.com, U.S., Find A Grave Index, 1700s-Current (Provo, UT, USA, Ancestry.com Operations, Inc., 2012), Ancestry.com, http://www.Ancestry.com, Record for Doris L. Wood.

[1322] Ancestry.com, U.S., Find A Grave Index, 1700s-Current (Provo, UT, USA, Ancestry.com Operations, Inc., 2012), Ancestry.com, http://www.Ancestry.com, Record for Doris L. Wood.

[1323] Marriage announcement, Rome newspaper, December 7, 1931.

[1324] Ancestry.com, U.S., Find A Grave Index, 1700s-Current (Provo, UT, USA, Ancestry.com Operations, Inc., 2012), Ancestry.com, http://www.Ancestry.com, Record for Carl L. Wood.

[1325] Ancestry.com, U.S., Find A Grave Index, 1700s-Current (Provo, UT, USA, Ancestry.com Operations, Inc., 2012), Ancestry.com, http://www.Ancestry.com, Record for Carl L. Wood.

[1326] A Ancestry.com, U.S., Find A Grave Index, 1700s-Current (Provo, UT, USA, Ancestry.com Operations, Inc., 2012), Ancestry.com, http://www.Ancestry.com, Record for Doris L. Wood.

Leigh[2], Nathan S. Leigh[1]) was born on 06 Dec 1917 in Oneida, Madison, New York[1327] and died on 12 Mar 2004 in Oneida, New York [1328]. He married Christine Irene Webb on 26 Jan 1946 in Oneida, New York[1329]. She was born on 12 Jul 1921 in Syracuse, New York[1330] and died on 15 Aug 1994 in Oneida, New York[1331]. Claude Jay Leigh Jr. and his wife were buried in Verona, New York[1332]. Claude was a chauffeur having finished high school at the time of the 1940 census.

CHRISTINE I. LEIGH Syracuse Herald-Journal (NY) - Tuesday, August 16, 1994
Christine I. Leigh, 73, of 5274 Oneida St. died Monday at home after a long illness. A native of Syracuse, Mrs. Leigh had lived in Durhamville for 45 years. She was once employed with Syracuse Supply Co. Surviving are her husband, Claude "Bud"; two daughters, Carol Swetmon and Mary Cochran, both of Durhamville; six grandchildren; two great-grandchildren; and several nieces and nephews. Services will be at 11 a.m. Wednesday at Coolican-McSweeney Funeral Home, Oneida. Burial will be in West Verona Cemetery. Calling hours will be 2 to 4 and 7 to 9 p.m. today at the funeral home, 322 Washington Ave. Contributions may be made to Hospice Care Inc. or the Sclero Derma Foundation

Claude Jay Leigh Jr and Christine Irene Webb had two children who may still be living.

[1327] Ancestry.com, Web: New York, Find A Grave Index, 1664-2011 (Provo, UT, USA, Ancestry.com Operations, Inc., 2012), www.ancestry.com, Database online.

[1328] Ancestry.com, Web: New York, Find A Grave Index, 1664-2011 (Provo, UT, USA, Ancestry.com Operations, Inc., 2012), www.ancestry.com, Database online.

[1329] New York State Department of Health; Albany, NY, USA; *New York State Marriage Index.*

[1330] Ancestry.com, U.S., Social Security Applications and Claims Index, 1936-2007 (Provo, UT, USA, Ancestry.com Operations, Inc., 2015), Ancestry.com, http://www.Ancestry.com, Record for Christine Irene Webb.

[1331] Ancestry.com, U.S., Social Security Applications and Claims Index, 1936-2007 (Provo, UT, USA, Ancestry.com Operations, Inc., 2015), Ancestry.com, http://www.Ancestry.com, Record for Christine Irene Webb.

[1332] Ancestry.com, Web: New York, Find A Grave Index, 1664-2011 (Provo, UT, USA, Ancestry.com Operations, Inc., 2012),

Generation Six

98.   Victor Ledebuhr[6] (Gladys Gertrude Berry[5], Cyrus Nathan Leigh[4], Mary Abigale Leigh[3], Elijah Leigh[2], Nathan S. Leigh[1]) was born on 22 Jul 1908 in Houston, Minnesota[1333] and died on 25 Oct 1968 in Winona, Minnesota[1334]. He married Clara B. Gaustad, the son of Oscar Gaustad and Annie Jordshaugen. She was born on 12 June 1912 in Houston County, Minnesota[1335] and died on 22 Dec 2004 in Houston, Minnesota[1336]. Victor Ledebuhr and his wife were buried in Money Creek, Minnesota[1337].

Photo of Victor Ledebuhr from the collection of Kathryn Cummings and used with permission.

***HOUSTON, Minn**. - Clara B. Ledebuhr, 92, of Houston died Wednesday, Dec. 22, 2004, at Valley View Nursing Home in Houston. Clara was born June 12, 1912, in Houston County to Oscar and Annie (Jordshaugen) Gaustad. She grew up in the Houston area. On Nov. 9, 1935, she married Victor Ledebuhr in Winona. She and Victor lived in Money Creek, Minn. Clara worked at St. Francis Hospital in La Crosse, Wis., in housekeeping for 20 years. She enjoyed gardening and flowers. Clara grew strawberries and truck farmed them to La Crosse. Crocheting was a big part of her life. She would crochet afghans and doilies. Every friend and relative were given at least one doily. She was a member of Money Creek United Methodist Church. Shortly after retiring she moved to Valley View Manor in Houston, where she lived for 25 years and was a resident at Valley View Nursing Home for the past three years. She was a loving mother, grandmother and great-grandmother and leaves with them many great memories. Clara is survived by one daughter, Darlene (LeRoy) Dockter of Houston; four grandchildren, Douglas (Sue) Dockter of Houston, Timothy Dockter of North St. Paul, Minn., Thomas Dockter of Money Creek and Darcy (Lowell) Papenfuss of Bangor, Wis.; five great-grandchildren, Anthony, David, Jared,*

[1333] Ancestry.com, Minnesota, Death Index, 1908-2002 (Provo, UT, USA, Ancestry.com Operations Inc, 2001), Ancestry.com, http://www.Ancestry.com, Record for Victor Ledebuhr.
[1334] Ancestry.com, Minnesota, Death Index, 1908-2002 (Provo, UT, USA, Ancestry.com Operations Inc, 2001), Ancestry.com, http://www.Ancestry.com, Record for Victor Ledebuhr.
[1335] Ancestry.com, U.S., Find A Grave Index, 1700s-Current (Provo, UT, USA, Ancestry.com Operations, Inc., 2012), Ancestry.com, http://www.Ancestry.com, Record for Victor Ledebuhr.
[1336] Ancestry.com, U.S., Find A Grave Index, 1700s-Current (Provo, UT, USA, Ancestry.com Operations, Inc., 2012), Ancestry.com, http://www.Ancestry.com, Record for Victor Ledebuhr.
[1337] Ancestry.com, U.S., Find A Grave Index, 1700s-Current (Provo, UT, USA, Ancestry.com Operations, Inc., 2012), Ancestry.com, http://www.Ancestry.com, Record for Victor Ledebuhr.

Hunter and Cole; three sisters, Agnes Mierau of Rushford, Minn., Violet Traff of Houston and Lillian Collins of Sun City, Ariz.; and one sister-in-law, Dorothy Gaustad of Houston. She was preceded in death by her husband in 1968; two brothers, Jerry and Odin; and one sister, Gladys Rostad. The funeral service will be at 1 p.m. Friday, Dec. 24, at Money Creek United Methodist Church, with the Rev. Fauntie Wilcoxon officiating. Burial will be in Money Creek Cemetery. Friends may call from 5 to 7 p.m. today at Hoff Funeral Homes n Houston Chapel and one hour prior to the service Friday at the church. The family prefers memorials to be directed to the Money Creek United Methodist Church.

Photo of Clara B. Gaustad Ledebuhr from the collection of Kathryn Cummings and used with permission.

Victor Ledebuhr and Clara B. Gaustad had the following child:

154.   i.   Darlene M. Ledebuhr was born on 27 Oct 1936[1338] and died on 31 Jan 2012[1339].

99. August Ledebuhr[6] (Gladys Gertrude Berry[5], Cyrus Nathan Leigh[4], Mary Abigale Leigh[3], Elijah Leigh[2], Nathan S. Leigh[1]) was born on 19 Aug 1913 in Houston, Minnesota[1340] and died on 18 May 1970 in Hennepin, Minnesota[1341]. He married Elsie Mierau. She was born on 11 Jul 1913[1342] and died in Aug 1983 in Houston, Minnesota[1343].   August Ledebuhr and his wife were buried in Money Creek, Minnesota[1344].

August Ledebuhr and Elsie Mierau had the following child:

[1338] Ancestry.com, U.S., Find A Grave Index, 1700s-Current (Provo, UT, USA, Ancestry.com Operations, Inc., 2012), Ancestry.com, http://www.Ancestry.com, Record for Leroy Dockter.

[1339] Ancestry.com, U.S., Find A Grave Index, 1700s-Current (Provo, UT, USA, Ancestry.com Operations, Inc., 2012), Ancestry.com, http://www.Ancestry.com, Record for Leroy Dockter.

[1340] Ancestry.com, Minnesota, Death Index, 1908-2002 (Provo, UT, USA, Ancestry.com Operations Inc, 2001), Ancestry.com, http://www.Ancestry.com, Record for August Ledebuhr.

[1341] Ancestry.com, Minnesota, Death Index, 1908-2002 (Provo, UT, USA, Ancestry.com Operations Inc, 2001), Ancestry.com, http://www.Ancestry.com, Record for August Ledebuhr.

[1342] Ancestry.com, U.S., Find A Grave Index, 1700s-Current (Provo, UT, USA, Ancestry.com Operations, Inc., 2012), Ancestry.com, http://www.Ancestry.com, Record for August Ledebuhr.

[1343] Ancestry.com, U.S., Find A Grave Index, 1700s-Current (Provo, UT, USA, Ancestry.com Operations, Inc., 2012), Ancestry.com, http://www.Ancestry.com, Record for August Ledebuhr.

[1344] Ancestry.com, U.S., Find A Grave Index, 1700s-Current (Provo, UT, USA, Ancestry.com Operations, Inc., 2012), Ancestry.com, http://www.Ancestry.com, Record for August Ledebuhr.

i.　　Gerald August Ledebuhr was born on 08 Mar 1938 in Lacrosse Lac, Wisconsin[1345] and died on 09 Oct 2005[1346]. Gerald August Ledebuhr was buried in La Crescent, Minnesota[1347].

Photo of August Ledebuhr from the collection of Kathryn Cummings and used with permission.

100.　Goldie L. Ledebuhr[6] (Gladys Gertrude Berry[5], Cyrus Nathan Leigh[4], Mary Abigale Leigh[3], Elijah Leigh[2], Nathan S. Leigh[1]) was born on 01 Nov 1919[1348] and died on 26 Jan 1985[1349]. She married George Frank Kiral. He was born on 31 Mar 1909 in Minnesota[1350] and died on 06 Jul 2000 in Mexico, Missouri[1351]. Goldie L. Ledebuhr and her husband were buried in Jefferson City, Missouri[1352]. George Frank Kiral and Goldie L. Ledebuhr had one child who may still be living.

101. Nathan Delonz Berry[6] (Cyrus Gilbert Berry[5], Cyrus Nathan Leigh[4], Mary Abigale Leigh[3], Elijah Leigh[2], Nathan S. Leigh[1]) was born on 10 Aug 1913 in Houston County, Minnesota[1353] and died in Jun 1968 in Muskegon County, Michigan[1354]. He married Minnie Leona Lohmeyer, the daughter of Albert Lohmeyer and Mary Whelan, on 17 Jul 1937 in Montague, Michigan[1355]. She was born on 04 Nov 1915[1356] and died in Jan

[1345] Ancestry.com, U.S., Social Security Applications and Claims Index, 1936-2007 (Provo, UT, USA, Ancestry.com Operations, Inc., 2015), Ancestry.com, http://www.Ancestry.com, Record for Gerald August Ledebuhr.

[1346] Ancestry.com, U.S., Social Security Applications and Claims Index, 1936-2007 (Provo, UT, USA, Ancestry.com Operations, Inc., 2015), Ancestry.com, http://www.Ancestry.com, Record for Gerald August Ledebuhr.

[1347] Ancestry.com, U.S., Find A Grave Index, 1700s-Current (Provo, UT, USA, Ancestry.com Operations, Inc., 2012), Ancestry.com, http://www.Ancestry.com, Record for Gerald A Ledebuhr.

[1348] Ancestry.com, Social Security Death Index (Provo, UT, USA, The Generations Network, Inc., 2008), www.ancestry.com, Number: 503-64-8013; Issue State: South Dakota; Issue Date: 1966. Record for Goldie Kiral.

[1349] Ancestry.com, Social Security Death Index (Provo, UT, USA, The Generations Network, Inc., 2008), www.ancestry.com, Number: 503-64-8013; Issue State: South Dakota; Issue Date: 1966. Record for Goldie Kiral

[1350] Ancestry.com, U.S., Find A Grave Index, 1700s-Current (Provo, UT, USA, Ancestry.com Operations, Inc., 2012), Ancestry.com, http://www.Ancestry.com, Record for George F Kiral.

[1351] Ancestry.com, U.S., Find A Grave Index, 1700s-Current (Provo, UT, USA, Ancestry.com Operations, Inc., 2012), Ancestry.com, http://www.Ancestry.com, Record for George F Kiral.

[1352] Ancestry.com, U.S., Find A Grave Index, 1700s-Current (Provo, UT, USA, Ancestry.com Operations, Inc., 2012), Ancestry.com, http://www.Ancestry.com, Record for Goldie Kiral.

[1353] Ancestry.com, U.S., Find A Grave Index, 1700s-Current (Provo, UT, USA, Ancestry.com Operations, Inc., 2012), Ancestry.com, http://www.Ancestry.com.

[1354] Ancestry.com, U.S., Find A Grave Index, 1700s-Current (Provo, UT, USA, Ancestry.com Operations, Inc., 2012), Ancestry.com, http://www.Ancestry.com.

[1355] Ancestry.com, Michigan, Marriage Records, 1867-1952 (Provo, UT, USA, Ancestry.com Operations, Inc., 2015), Ancestry.com, http://www.Ancestry.com, Record for Minnie Lohmeyer.

[1356] Ancestry.com, U.S., Find A Grave Index, 1700s-Current (Provo, UT, USA, Ancestry.com Operations, Inc., 2012), Ancestry.com, http://www.Ancestry.com, Record for Minnie L Berry.

1982[1357].   Nathan Delzon Berry and his wife were   buried in North Muskegon, Michigan[1358]. Nathan Delzon Berry and Minnie Leona Lohmeyer had one child who may still be living.

102.   Inez Beulah Berry[6] (Cyrus Gilbert Berry[5], Cyrus Nathan Leigh[4], Mary Abigale Leigh[3], Elijah Leigh[2], Nathan S. Leigh[1]) was born in 1915 in Michigan[1359] and died in 2002   in   Michigan[1360].   She   married Clifford Harold Yonkers, the son of Gerritt H. and Florence May Yonkers, on 06   Jun   1936   in   Grand   Haven, Michigan[1361].   He was born on 06 Mar 1906 in Grand Haven, Michigan[1362] and died on 08 Apr 1994 in Bloomington, Indiana[1363].   Inez Beulah Berry was buried in North Muskegon, Michigan[1364].

Photo of Inez Beulah Berry and Clifford Harold Yonkers from the collection of Kathryn Cummings and used with permission.

Clifford Harold Yonkers and Inez Beulah Berry had the following children:
155.   i.   Russell C. Yonkers was born in 1937[1365] and died on 10 Dec 2013[1366] .
        ii.   Carol Arlene Yonkers was born on 25 Jun 1939 in Muskegon, Michigan[1367] and died on 26 Dec 2016 in San Tan, Arizona[1368]. She married on 18 Jun 1966[1369].

[1357] Ancestry.com, U.S., Find A Grave Index, 1700s-Current (Provo, UT, USA, Ancestry.com Operations, Inc., 2012), Ancestry.com, http://www.Ancestry.com, Record for Minnie L Berry.

[1358] Ancestry.com, U.S., Find A Grave Index, 1700s-Current (Provo, UT, USA, Ancestry.com Operations, Inc., 2012), Ancestry.com, http://www.Ancestry.com.

[1359] Ancestry.com, U.S., Find A Grave Index, 1700s-Current (Provo, UT, USA, Ancestry.com Operations, Inc., 2012), Ancestry.com, http://www.Ancestry.com.

[1360] Ancestry.com, U.S., Find A Grave Index, 1700s-Current (Provo, UT, USA, Ancestry.com Operations, Inc., 2012), Ancestry.com, http://www.Ancestry.com.

[1361] Michigan Department of Community Health, Division of Vital Records and Health Statistics; Lansing, MI, USA; *Michigan, Marriage Records, 1867-1952;* Film: *165;* Film Description: *Muskegon (1936 - 1940).*

[1362] Ancestry.com. *Indiana, Death Certificates, 1899-2011.*

[1363] Ancestry.com. *Indiana, Death Certificates, 1899-2011.*

[1364] Ancestry.com, U.S., Find A Grave Index, 1700s-Current (Provo, UT, USA, Ancestry.com Operations, Inc., 2012),

[1365] Obituary, The Indianapolis Star, Indianapolis, Indiana, Dec. 12, 2013.

[1366] Obituary, The Indianapolis Star, Indianapolis, Indiana, Dec. 12, 2013.

[1367] Public Member Tree at Ancestry.com.

[1368] Public Member Tree at Ancestry.com.

[1369] Public Member Tree at Ancestry.com.

103. Florence Estella Berry[6] (Cyrus Gilbert Berry[5], Cyrus Nathan Leigh[4], Mary Abigale Leigh[3], Elijah Leigh[2], Nathan S. Leigh[1]) was born on 13 May 1918 in North Muskegon, Michigan[1370] and died on 21 Jan 2006 in Muskegon, Michigan[1371]. She married Ray Glenn Race, the son of John Charles Race and Minnie Reinsberger, on 26 Jun 1937 in Muskegon, Michigan[1372]. He was born on 24 May 1918 in Staples, Michigan[1373] and died on 27 Jan 1994 in Muskegon, Michigan[1374]. Florence Estella Race was buried in North Muskegon, Michigan[1375]. Ray Glenn Race and Florence Estella Race had two children who may still be living.

Photo of Florence Estella Berry and Ray Glenn Race found on findagrave.com.

104. Gilbert C. Berry[6] (Cyrus Gilbert Berry[5], Cyrus Nathan Leigh[4], Mary Abigale Leigh[3], Elijah Leigh[2], Nathan S. Leigh[1]) was born on 31 Jan 1921 in Muskegon, Michigan[1376] and died on 25 Oct 2007 in Muskegon, Michigan[1377]. He married Catherine Ann St. Amour on 08 Nov 1941 in Muskegon, Michigan[1378]. She was born on 21 May 1921 in Muskegon, Michigan[1379] and died on 12 Sep 2007 in Muskegon,

[1370] Ancestry.com, U.S., Find A Grave Index, 1700s-Current (Provo, UT, USA, Ancestry.com Operations, Inc., 2012), Ancestry.com, http://www.Ancestry.com.

[1371] Ancestry.com, U.S., Find A Grave Index, 1700s-Current (Provo, UT, USA, Ancestry.com Operations, Inc., 2012), Ancestry.com, http://www.Ancestry.com.

[1372] Ancestry.com, Michigan, Marriage Records, 1867-1952 (Provo, UT, USA, Ancestry.com Operations, Inc., 2015), Ancestry.com, http://www.Ancestry.com, Record for Florence Estella Berry.

[1373] Michigan Department of Vital and Health Records, Michigan, Death Index, 1971-1996 (Provo, UT, USA, Ancestry.com Operations Inc, 1998), Ancestry.com, http://www.Ancestry.com, Record for Raymond G. Race.

[1374] Michigan Department of Vital and Health Records, Michigan, Death Index, 1971-1996 (Provo, UT, USA, Ancestry.com Operations Inc, 1998), Ancestry.com, http://www.Ancestry.com, Record for Raymond G. Race.

[1375] Ancestry.com, U.S., Find A Grave Index, 1700s-Current (Provo, UT, USA, Ancestry.com Operations, Inc., 2012), Ancestry.com, http://www.Ancestry.com.

[1376] Ancestry.com, U.S., Find A Grave Index, 1700s-Current (Provo, UT, USA, Ancestry.com Operations, Inc., 2012), Ancestry.com, http://www.Ancestry.com.

[1377] Ancestry.com, U.S., Find A Grave Index, 1700s-Current (Provo, UT, USA, Ancestry.com Operations, Inc., 2012), Ancestry.com, http://www.Ancestry.com.

[1378] Ancestry.com, Michigan, Marriage Records, 1867-1952 (Provo, UT, USA, Ancestry.com Operations, Inc., 2015), Ancestry.com, http://www.Ancestry.com, Record for Mr Gilbert C Jr Berry.

[1379] Ancestry.com, U.S., Find A Grave Index, 1700s-Current (Provo, UT, USA, Ancestry.com Operations, Inc., 2012), Ancestry.com, http://www.Ancestry.com, Record for Catherine A Berry.

Michigan[1380]. Gilbert C. Berry and his wife were buried in Laketon Township Cemetery, North Muskegon, Michigan[1381].

Muskegon Chronicle, October 27, 2007
Mr. Gilbert C. Berry, age 86, died Thursday, October 25, 2007. He was born in Muskegon, MI on January 31, 1921 to Cyrus Gilbert & Klea (Sovacol) Berry & married the former Catherine A. St. Amour on November 8, 1941 in Muskegon, MI. Mr. Berry served his country in the U.S. Army during WWII in Europe under Patton. He had been employed as a machine operator at Anaconda for 37 years until retiring in 1980. He was a member of Prince of Peace Catholic Church, a life time member of V.F.W. and former member of the Vikings. Gilbert enjoyed fishing and camping, but foremost was his family. SURVIVORS Wife, Catherine A.; 1 son, John Berry of Muskegon; 1 daughter, Joan (Jerry) MacPhee of Battle Creek; 13 grandchildren; 26 great-grandchildren; 1 brother, Walter (Bernice) Berry of Grant; and 2 sons-in-law, Robert Allen of Holton and Robert Ruppel of Clarkdale, AZ. He was preceded in death by 2 daughters, Sandra Ruppel and Donna Allen; brother, Nathan Berry; and 3 sisters, Inez Yonkers, Florence Race, and Helen Puffer. SERVICE Monday, October 29, 2007, 11:00 AM, at Prince of Peace Catholic Church with Fr. Phil Sliwinski officiating. Interment at Laketon Township Cemetery with a veterans service under the Auspices of Don Rea V.F.W. #8846.

Muskegon Chronicle, September 15, 2008
Mrs. Catherine A. Berry, age 87, died Friday, September 12, 2008. She was born in Muskegon, MI on May 21, 1921 to Fred & Ann (Buckley) St. Amour & married Gilbert Berry on November 8, 1941 in Muskegon, MI. Mrs. Berry had been employed as a executive secretary at Clark Floor Machine for 20 years until retiring. She was a member of Prince of Peace Catholic Church. Mrs. Berry enjoyed cooking, boating & camping, but foremost was always her family.
SURVIVORS 1 son, John Berry of Muskegon; 1 daughter, Joan (Jerry) MacPhee of Battle Creek; 13 grandchildren; many great grandchildren; 1 brother, Art (Letty) St. Amour of Muskegon; numerous nieces & nephews She was preceded in death by her husband, Gil in 2007; 2 daughters, Sandra Ruppel & Donna Allen; siblings, Tom, Sam, Jerry, Bill, Jean & Marie. SERVICE Tuesday, September 16, 2008, 11:00 AM at Prince of Peace Catholic Church with Fr. Robert Hart officiating. Interment at Laketon Township Cemetery.

Gilbert C. Berry Jr and Catherine Ann St Amour had the following children:
156.   i.   Sandra Kay Berry was born on 22 Sep 1946 in Muskegon, Michigan[1382] and died on 27 Feb 2007 in Clarkdale, Arizona[1383].

[1380] Ancestry.com, U.S., Find A Grave Index, 1700s-Current (Provo, UT, USA, Ancestry.com Operations, Inc., 2012), Ancestry.com, http://www.Ancestry.com, Record for Catherine A Berry.
[1381] Ancestry.com, U.S., Find A Grave Index, 1700s-Current (Provo, UT, USA, Ancestry.com Operations, Inc., 2012), Ancestry.com, http://www.Ancestry.com, Record for Catherine A Berry.

ii.   Living Berry
iii.   Living Berry
iv.   Living Berry

105.   Hazel Kowlewski[6] (Myrtle Mae Berry[5], Cyrus Nathan Leigh[4], Mary Abigale Leigh[3], Elijah Leigh[2], Nathan S. Leigh[1]) was born on 18 Dec 1914 in Winona, Minnesota[1384] and died on 20 May 1995 in Tomah, Wisconsin[1385]. She married Wayne Eugene Harmon[1386]. He was born on 14 Nov 1914[1387] and died on 15 Mar 1978 in Warrens, Wisconsin[1388]. Hazel Kowlewski and Wayne Eugene Harmon are buried in Shamrock Union Cemetery, Shamrock, Wisconsin along with their infant son, Allen Gene Harmon[1389]. Wayne Eugene Harmon and Hazel Kowlewski had the one child who died as an infant.

106.   Donald Frank Kowleski[6] (Myrtle Mae Berry[5], Cyrus Nathan Leigh[4], Mary Abigale Leigh[3], Elijah Leigh[2], Nathan S. Leigh[1]) was born on 21 Jun 1917[1390] and died on 20 Jun 2003[1391]. He married Irene Matilda Kieler on 07 Jun 1938 in Immaculate Conception Church, Kieler, Wisconsin[1392]. She was born on 08 Apr 1919 in Wisconsin 930 and died on 03 Oct 2006 in Lancaster, Wisconsin[1393]. Donald Frank Kowaleski and his wife were buried in Cassville, Wisconsin[1394].

***CASSVILLE** - Irene M. Kowalski, age 87, of Cassville, died on Tuesday, Oct. 3, 2006, at the Grant Regional Health Center in Lancaster. She was born on April 8, 1919, in Paris*

[1382] Obituary of Sandra Kay Ruppel, Muskegon Chronicle, Muskegon, Michigan newspaper.

[1383] Obituary of Sandra Kay Ruppel, Muskegon, Chronicle, Muskegon, Michigan newspaper.

[1384] Ancestry.com, Social Security Death Index (Provo, UT, USA, The Generations Network, Inc., 2008), www.ancestry.com, Number: 395-14-4780; Issue State: Wisconsin; Issue Date: Before 1951. Record for Hazel Harmon.

[1385] Ancestry.com, Social Security Death Index (Provo, UT, USA, The Generations Network, Inc., 2008), www.ancestry.com, Number: 395-14-4780; Issue State: Wisconsin; Issue Date: Before 1951. Record for Hazel Harmon.

[1386] Findagrave.com, Shamrock Union Cemetery, Shamrock, Wisconsin.

[1387] Ancestry.com, Social Security Death Index (Provo, UT, USA, The Generations Network, Inc., 2008), www.ancestry.com, Number: 391-16-3853; Issue State: Wisconsin; Issue Date: Before 1951. Record for Wayne Harmon.

[1388] Ancestry.com, Social Security Death Index (Provo, UT, USA, The Generations Network, Inc., 2008), www.ancestry.com, Number: 391-16-3853; Issue State: Wisconsin; Issue Date: Before 1951. Record for Wayne Harmon.

[1389] Findagrave.com, Shamrock Union Cemetery, Shamrock, Wisconsin.

[1390] Ancestry.com, U.S., Find A Grave Index, 1700s-Current (Provo, UT, USA, Ancestry.com Operations, Inc., 2012), Ancestry.com, http://www.Ancestry.com, Record for Donald F Kowalski.

[1391] Ancestry.com, U.S., Find A Grave Index, 1700s-Current (Provo, UT, USA, Ancestry.com Operations, Inc., 2012), Ancestry.com, http://www.Ancestry.com, Record for Donald F Kowalski.

[1392] Obituary of Irene M. Kowalski of Cassville, Wisconsin included on page 141.

[1393] Ancestry.com, U.S., Find A Grave Index, 1700s-Current (Provo, UT, USA, Ancestry.com Operations, Inc., 2012), Ancestry.com, http://www.Ancestry.com, Record for Donald F Kowalski.

[1394] Ancestry.com, U.S., Find A Grave Index, 1700s-Current (Provo, UT, USA, Ancestry.com Operations, Inc., 2012), Ancestry.com, http://www.Ancestry.com, Record for Donald F Kowalski.

Township, daughter of Arthur and Elizabeth (Loeffelholz) Kieler. On June 7, 1938, she married Donald F. "Doc" Kowalski at Immaculate Conception Catholic Church in Kieler. Irene was the original bookkeeper for Kowalski-Kieler, Inc., which her husband co-founded with her brother, Lester Kieler, in 1946. Irene was a member of St. Charles Catholic Church and the National Council of Catholic Women. She loved spending time with her family and she enjoyed reading, cooking, sewing, and traveling. Irene is survived by seven children, Mary Jane (Roger) Droessler, Dickeyville, Julaine (Wilfred) Udelhofen, Cassville, Betty Lou (Wayne) Kruser, Dickeyville, James (Charlotte) Kowalski, Dickeyville, Donna Jean (Larry) Bernhardt, Cassville, Collette (the Rev. Tom Hallowell) Kowalski, Schuyler, Neb., and Colleen Kowalski, Cassville; 23 grandchildren; 33 great-grandchildren; two sisters, Orpha Schneider, Cuba City, and Sr. Genesia Ginter, OSF, Milwaukee; a brother, Arthur (Kathleen) Kieler, Hazel Green; and many nieces and nephews. In addition to her parents and her husband, Doc, Irene was preceded in death by her brothers, Lester (Shirley) Kieler and Gene Ginter; and a brother-in-law, Francis Schneider. Funeral services will be held on Saturday, Oct. 7, 2006, at 10 a.m. at ST. CHARLES CATHOLIC CHURCH in Cassville with Father John Norder officiating. Burial will be in the church cemetery.

Donald Frank Kowaleski and Irene Matilda Kieler had seven children who may still be living.

107. Violet F. Noren[6] (Myrtle Mae Berry[5], Cyrus Nathan Leigh[4], Mary Abigale Leigh[3], Elijah Leigh[2], Nathan S. Leigh[1]) was born 01 Mar 1930 in Wisconsin[1395] and died 18 Dec 2012 in Wisconsin[1396]. She married Floyd Pratt. Violet is buried in Black River Falls, Wisconsin with her daughter[1397].

Floyd Pratt and Violet F. Noren had one child:
     i.   Ann M. Pratt was born 27 Jul 1951[1398] and died 14 Jan 2008[1399] in Wisconsin. She is buried in Black River Falls, Wisconsin with her mother[1400].

[1395] Ancestry.com, U.S., Find A Grave Index, 1700s-Current (Provo, UT, USA, Ancestry.com Operations, Inc., 2012), Ancestry.com, http://www.Ancestry.com.
[1396] Ancestry.com, U.S., Find A Grave Index, 1700s-Current (Provo, UT, USA, Ancestry.com Operations, Inc., 2012), Ancestry.com, http://www.Ancestry.com.
[1397] Ancestry.com, U.S., Find A Grave Index, 1700s-Current (Provo, UT, USA, Ancestry.com Operations, Inc., 2012), Ancestry.com, http://www.Ancestry.com.
[1398] Ancestry.com, U.S., Find A Grave Index, 1700s-Current (Provo, UT, USA, Ancestry.com Operations, Inc., 2012), Ancestry.com, http://www.Ancestry.com.
[1399] Ancestry.com, U.S., Find A Grave Index, 1700s-Current (Provo, UT, USA, Ancestry.com Operations, Inc., 2012), Ancestry.com, http://www.Ancestry.com.
[1400] Ancestry.com, U.S., Find A Grave Index, 1700s-Current (Provo, UT, USA, Ancestry.com Operations, Inc., 2012), Anccstry.com, http://www.Anccstry.com.

108.   Valentine John Kowalewski[6] (Alta Irene Berry[5], Cyrus Nathan Leigh[4], Mary Abigale Leigh[3], Elijah Leigh[2], Nathan S. Leigh[1]) was born on 04 Jul 1911 in Wisconsin[1401] and died on 28 Jan 1998 in Wabasha, Minnesota[1402]. He married Charlotte Gallagher. She was born on 02 Jun 1919[1403] and died on 05 Jun 1969 in Winona, Minnesota[1404].

Valentine John Kowalewski and Charlotte Gallagher had the following children:
157.   i.   Donald Roger Kowalewski was born on 20 May 1937[1405] and died on 08 Sep 2012[1406].
       ii.   Living Kowalewski

109.   Wanda Geneva Potter[6] (Edna P. Corey[5], Genevieve Berry[4], Mary Abigale Leigh[3], Elijah Leigh[2], Nathan S. Leigh[1]) was born on 22 May 1922 in Money Creek, Minnesota[1407] and died on 21 Jan 2001 in Key West, Florida[1408]. She married Arnold Garnet Holter. He was born on 27 Jul 1917 in Houston, Minnesota[1409] and died on 01 Feb 1999 in La Crosse, Wisconsin[1410]. She later married Charles Leroy Wilcox. He was born on 28 Oct 1922[1411] and died on 01 Feb 1994 in Miami, Florida[1412].   Arnold Garnet Holter was buried in La Crosse, Wisconsin[1413].

[1401] Ancestry.com, Minnesota, Death Index, 1908-2002 (Provo, UT, USA, Ancestry.com Operations Inc, 2001), Ancestry.com, http://www.Ancestry.com, Record for Valentine John Kowalewski.

[1402] Ancestry.com, Minnesota, Death Index, 1908-2002 (Provo, UT, USA, Ancestry.com Operations Inc, 2001), Ancestry.com, http://www.Ancestry.com, Record for Valentine John Kowalewski.

[1403] Minnesota Department of Health, Minnesota Birth Index, 1935-1995 (Provo, UT, USA, Ancestry.com Operations Inc, 2004), Ancestry.com, http://www.Ancestry.com, Record for Charlene Catherine Kowalewski

[1404] Minnesota Department of Health, Minnesota Birth Index, 1935-1995 (Provo, UT, USA, Ancestry.com Operations Inc, 2004), Ancestry.com, http://www.Ancestry.com, Record for Charlene Catherine Kowalewski

[1405] Ancestry.com, Social Security Death Index (Provo, UT, USA, The Generations Network, Inc., 2008), www.ancestry.com, Issue State: Minnesota; Issue Date: 1951. Record for Donald R Kowalewski.

[1406] An Ancestry.com, Social Security Death Index (Provo, UT, USA, The Generations Network, Inc., 2008), www.ancestry.com, Issue State: Minnesota; Issue Date: 1951. Record for Donald R Kowalewski.

[1407] Ancestry.com, U.S., Social Security Applications and Claims Index, 1936-2007 (Provo, UT, USA, Ancestry.com Operations, Inc., 2015), Ancestry.com, http://www.Ancestry.com, Record for Wanda Potter Holter.

[1408] Ancestry.com, U.S., Social Security Applications and Claims Index, 1936-2007 (Provo, UT, USA, Ancestry.com Operations, Inc., 2015), Ancestry.com, http://www.Ancestry.com, Record for Wanda Potter Holter.

[1409] Ancestry.com, Web: Minnesota, Birth Index, 1900-1934 (Provo, UT, USA, Ancestry.com Operations, Inc., 2015), Ancestry.com, http://www.Ancestry.com, Record for Arnold Garnet Holter.

[1410] Ancestry.com, U.S., Find A Grave Index, 1700s-Current (Provo, UT, USA, Ancestry.com Operations, Inc., 2012), Ancestry.com, http://www.Ancestry.com, Record for Arnold Garnet Holter.

[1411] Ancestry.com, Social Security Death Index (Provo, UT, USA, The Generations Network, Inc., 2008), www.ancestry.com, Number: 341-14-8410; Issue State: Illinois; Issue Date: Before 1951. Record for Charles L. Wilcox.

[1412] Ancestry.com, Social Security Death Index (Provo, UT, USA, The Generations Network, Inc., 2008), www.ancestry.com, Number: 341-14-8410; Issue State: Illinois; Issue Date: Before 1951. Record for Charles L. Wilcox.

[1413] Ancestry.com, U.S., Find A Grave Index, 1700s-Current (Provo, UT, USA, Ancestry.com Operations, Inc., 2012), Ancestry.com, http://www.Ancestry.com, Record for Arnold Garnet Holter.

Arnold Garnet Holter and Wanda Geneva Potter had the following children:

     i.   Jerry Arnold Holter was born on 27 Apr 1938 in Houston, Minnesota[1414] and died on 16 Oct 1973 in Wabasha County, Minnesota[1415]. Jerry Arnold Holter was buried in Money Creek, Minnesota[1416].

     ii.   Living Holter

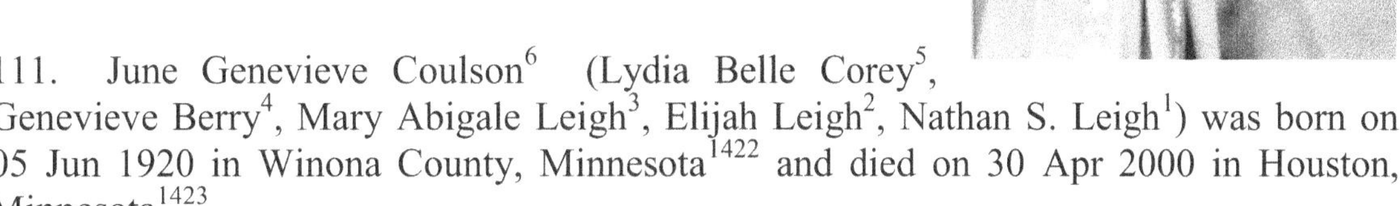

110.   Dorothy Ruth Coulson[6] (Lydia Belle Corey[5], Genevieve Berry[4], Mary Abigale Leigh[3], Elijah Leigh[2], Nathan S. Leigh[1]) was born on 21 Oct 1918 in Houston, Minnesota[1417] and died on 20 Feb 1990 in Hidalgo, Texas[1418]. She married Kenneth Allan Chapel. He was born on 02 Jan 1916 in Fillmore, Minnesota[1419] and died on 22 Jan 2006 in Houston, Minnesota[1420]. Dorothy Ruth Coulson and her husband were buried in Money Creek, Minnesota[1421]. Kenneth Allan Chapel and Dorothy Ruth Coulson had one child who may still be living.

Photo of Dorothy Coulson found on Ancestry.com.

111.   June Genevieve Coulson[6] (Lydia Belle Corey[5], Genevieve Berry[4], Mary Abigale Leigh[3], Elijah Leigh[2], Nathan S. Leigh[1]) was born on 05 Jun 1920 in Winona County, Minnesota[1422] and died on 30 Apr 2000 in Houston, Minnesota[1423].

[1414] Ancestry.com, U.S., Find A Grave Index, 1700s-Current (Provo, UT, USA, Ancestry.com Operations, Inc., 2012), Ancestry.com, http://www.Ancestry.com, Record for Arnold Garnet Holter.

[1415] Ancestry.com, U.S., Find A Grave Index, 1700s-Current (Provo, UT, USA, Ancestry.com Operations, Inc., 2012), Ancestry.com, http://www.Ancestry.com, Record for Arnold Garnet Holter.

[1416] Ancestry.com, U.S., Find A Grave Index, 1700s-Current (Provo, UT, USA, Ancestry.com Operations, Inc., 2012), Ancestry.com, http://www.Ancestry.com, Record for Arnold Garnet Holter.

[1417] Ancestry.com, U.S., Social Security Applications and Claims Index, 1936-2007 (Provo, UT, USA, Ancestry.com Operations, Inc., 2015), Ancestry.com, http://www.Ancestry.com, Record for Dorothy Ruth Chapel.

[1418] Ancestry.com, U.S., Social Security Applications and Claims Index, 1936-2007 (Provo, UT, USA, Ancestry.com Operations, Inc., 2015), Ancestry.com, http://www.Ancestry.com, Record for Dorothy Ruth Chapel.

[1419] Ancestry.com, Minnesota, Births and Christenings Index, 1840-1980 (Provo, UT, USA, Ancestry.com Operations, Inc., 2011), Ancestry.com, http://www.Ancestry.com, Record for Kenneth Allan Chapel.

[1420] Ancestry.com, U.S., Find A Grave Index, 1700s-Current (Provo, UT, USA, Ancestry.com Operations, Inc., 2012), Ancestry.com, http://www.Ancestry.com, Record for Kenneth A Chapel.

[1421] Ancestry.com, U.S., Find A Grave Index, 1700s-Current (Provo, UT, USA, Ancestry.com Operations, Inc., 2012), Ancestry.com, http://www.Ancestry.com, Record for Kenneth A Chapel.

[1422] Ancestry.com, U.S., Find A Grave Index, 1700s-Current (Provo, UT, USA, Ancestry.com Operations, Inc., 2012), Ancestry.com, http://www.Ancestry.com, Record for Charles E Coulson.

[1423] Ancestry.com, U.S., Find A Grave Index, 1700s-Current (Provo, UT, USA, Ancestry.com Operations, Inc., 2012), Ancestry.com, http://www.Ancestry.com, Record for Charles E Coulson.

Photo of June Genevieve Coulson and her husband, Henry Noal Eaton and, I believe, one of their children from the collection of Cheryl Boyum Eaton and used with permission.

She married Henry Noal Eaton. He was born on 09 May 1913 in Wayne County, Missouri[1424] and died on 20 Mar 1984 in La Crosse, Wisconsin[1425]. June Genevieve Coulson and her husband were buried in Money Creek, Minnesota[1426].

Henry Noal Eaton and June Genevieve Coulson had the following children:

    i.   Michael Gilbert Eaton was born on 01 Dec 1943 in Winona, Minnesota[1427] and died on 29 Jan 2002[1428]. He married Sharon K. Murphy on 25 Apr 1964 in Houston, Minnesota[1429].

    ii.   Living Eaton

112. Dwight Edward Coulson[6] (Lydia Belle Corey[5], Genevieve Berry[4], Mary Abigale Leigh[3], Elijah Leigh[2], Nathan S. Leigh[1]) was born on 28 Nov 1921 in Houston, Minnesota[1430] and died on 19 Feb 2009 in Springfield, Missouri[1431]. He married Patricia Ann Corey, the daughter of Hamden Alvin Corey and Mary Frances Gallagher, on 24 Nov 1945 in Ridgeway, Minnesota[1432]. She was born on 30 Aug 1924 in Winona, Minnesota[1433] and died on 09 Jun 2003 in Macomb, Missouri[1434]. Dwight Edward Coulson was buried in Money Creek, Minnesota[1435].

[1424] Ancestry.com, U.S., Find A Grave Index, 1700s-Current Ancestry.com, Record for Henry N Eaton.

[1425] Ancestry.com, U.S., Find A Grave Index, 1700s-Current Ancestry.com, Record for Henry N Eaton.

[1426] Ancestry.com, U.S., Find A Grave Index, 1700s-Current Ancestry.com, Record for Henry N Eaton.

[1427] Ancestry.com, U.S., Social Security Applications and Claims Index, 1936-2007 (Provo, UT, USA, Ancestry.com Operations, Inc., 2015), Ancestry.com, http://www.Ancestry.com, Record for Michael Gilbert Eaton.

[1428] Ancestry.com, U.S., Social Security Applications and Claims Index, 1936-2007 (Provo, UT, USA, Ancestry.com Operations, Inc., 2015), Ancestry.com, http://www.Ancestry.com, Record for Michael Gilbert Eaton.

[1429] Marriage Index, 1958-1995. Minnesota Center for Health Statistics, Office of the State Registrar, St. Paul, Minnesota., Ancestry.com. Minnesota, Marriage Index, 1958-2001.

[1430] Ancestry.com, U.S., Find A Grave Index, 1700s-Current (Provo, UT, USA, Ancestry.com Operations, Inc., 2012), Ancestry.com, http://www.Ancestry.com, Record for Dwight Edward Coulson.

[1431] Ancestry.com, U.S., Find A Grave Index, 1700s-Current (Provo, UT, USA, Ancestry.com Operations, Inc., 2012), Ancestry.com, http://www.Ancestry.com, Record for Dwight Edward Coulson.

[1432] Obituary of Dwight Edward Coulson included in this book on page 144.

[1433] Ancestry.com, U.S., Social Security Applications and Claims Index, 1936-2007 (Provo, UT, USA, Ancestry.com Operations, Inc., 2015), Ancestry.com, http://www.Ancestry.com, Record for Patricia Ann Coulson.

[1434] Ancestry.com, U.S., Social Security Applications and Claims Index, 1936-2007 (Provo, UT, USA, Ancestry.com Operations, Inc., 2015), Ancestry.com, http://www.Ancestry.com, Record for Patricia Ann Coulson.

[1435] Ancestry.com, U.S., Find A Grave Index, 1700s-Current (Provo, UT, USA, Ancestry.com Operations, Inc., 2012), Ancestry.com, http://www.Ancestry.com, Record for Dwight Edward Coulson.

Photo of Dwight Edward Coulson from the collection of Thomas Coulson and used with permission.

Dwight was a marine and was on Guadalcanal, the 1st major battle in the pacific and encountered the Battle at sea between the battleships he observed while guarding the perimeter of Henderson airfield. He was highly decorated and interviewed of his experience. Dwight Edward Coulson and Patricia Ann Corey had three children who may still be living.

Photo of Patricia Ann Corey, wife of Dwight Edward Coulson, from the collection of Thomas Coulson and used with permission.

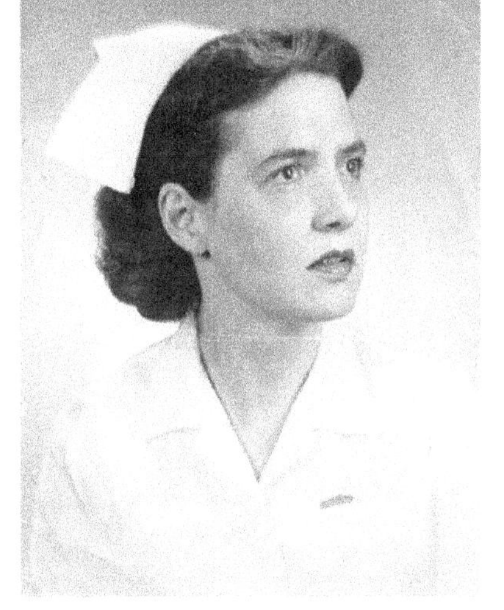

Monday, Feb 23, 2009
Dwight Edward Coulson, 87, of Mt. Vernon, died at 1:20 p.m. February 19 at Cox Medical Center South in Springfield. Mr. Coulson was born November 28, 1921, in Houston, Minnesota, the son of Charles Edward and Lydia Belle Corey Coulson. He was a Marine Corps veteran of World War II. He was a retired construction worker and farmer. He married Ann Corey on November 24, 1945, in Ridgeway, Minnesota, and she preceded him in death. Survivors include two daughters, Maureen Christopher of Marshfield and Barbara Jungblut of Bellview, Iowa; one son, Thomas Coulson of Thailand; one sister, Carol Thompson of Houston, Minnesota; three grandchildren, 17 great grandchildren, and 19 great great grandchildren. He was preceded in death by two brothers, David and Joseph Coulson; and two sisters, Dorothy Chape and June Eaton. Memorial services will be held at a later date in Money Creek Cemetery in Houston, Minnesota. Local arrangements under the direction of Fossett-Mosher Funeral Home of Mt. Vernon.

113.   Joseph Lewis Coulson[6] (Lydia Belle Corey[5], Genevieve Berry[4], Mary Abigale Leigh[3], Elijah Leigh[2], Nathan S. Leigh[1]) was born on 18 Feb 1924[1436] and died on 19 Dec 1999[1437]. He married Eleanor Virginia Rogers[1438]. She was born on 17 Jul 1918[1439] and died on 01 Mar 2006[1440]. Joseph Lewis Coulson and his wife were buried in Money Creek, Minnesota[1441].

Joseph Lewis Coulson and Eleanor Virginia Rogers had the following children:

158.   i.   Susan B. Coulson was born in 1948 in Saint Petersburg, Florida[1442] and died on 03 Feb 2016 in Anchorage, Alaska[1443].

   ii.   Charles Edgar Coulson was born on 28 Dec 1951 in Fillmore, Minnesota[1444] and died on 25 Sep 1975[1445]. Charles Edgar Coulson was buried in Money Creek, Minnesota[1446].

Photo of Joseph Lewis Coulson found on Ancestry.com.

114.   Carol Beth Coulson[6] (Lydia Belle Corey[5], Genevieve Berry[4], Mary Abigale Leigh[3], Elijah Leigh[2], Nathan S. Leigh[1]) was born on 27 Feb 1926 in Houston, Minnesota[1447] and died on 25 Jan 2014 in Houston,

---

[1436] Ancestry.com, U.S., Social Security Applications and Claims Index, 1936-2007 (Provo, UT, USA, Ancestry.com Operations, Inc., 2015), Ancestry.com, http://www.Ancestry.com, Record for Joseph Lewis Coulson.

[1437] Ancestry.com, U.S., Social Security Applications and Claims Index, 1936-2007 (Provo, UT, USA, Ancestry.com Operations, Inc., 2015), Ancestry.com, http://www.Ancestry.com, Record for Joseph Lewis Coulson.

[1438] Ancestry.com, U.S., Find A Grave Index, 1700s-Current (Provo, UT, USA, Ancestry.com Operations, Inc., 2012), Ancestry.com, http://www.Ancestry.com, Record for Eleanor V Coulson.

[1439] Ancestry.com, U.S., Find A Grave Index, 1700s-Current (Provo, UT, USA, Ancestry.com Operations, Inc., 2012), Ancestry.com, http://www.Ancestry.com, Record for Eleanor V Coulson.

[1440] Ancestry.com, U.S., Find A Grave Index, 1700s-Current (Provo, UT, USA, Ancestry.com Operations, Inc., 2012), Ancestry.com, http://www.Ancestry.com, Record for Eleanor V Coulson.

[1441] Ancestry.com, U.S., Find A Grave Index, 1700s-Current (Provo, UT, USA, Ancestry.com Operations, Inc., 2012), Ancestry.com, http://www.Ancestry.com, Record for Eleanor V Coulson.

[1442] Ancestry.com, U.S., Find A Grave Index, 1700s-Current (Provo, UT, USA, Ancestry.com Operations, Inc., 2012), Ancestry.com, http://www.Ancestry.com, Record for Joseph L Coulson.

[1443] Ancestry.com, U.S., Find A Grave Index, 1700s-Current (Provo, UT, USA, Ancestry.com Operations, Inc., 2012), Ancestry.com, http://www.Ancestry.com, Record for Joseph L Coulson.

[1444] Ancestry.com, U.S., Find A Grave Index, 1700s-Current (Provo, UT, USA, Ancestry.com Operations, Inc., 2012), Ancestry.com, http://www.Ancestry.com, Record for Charles Edgar Coulson.

[1445] Ancestry.com, U.S., Find A Grave Index, 1700s-Current (Provo, UT, USA, Ancestry.com Operations, Inc., 2012), Ancestry.com, http://www.Ancestry.com, Record for Charles Edgar Coulson.

[1446] Ancestry.com, U.S., Find A Grave Index, 1700s-Current (Provo, UT, USA, Ancestry.com Operations, Inc., 2012), Ancestry.com, http://www.Ancestry.com, Record for Charles Edgar Coulson.

[1447] Ancestry.com, Web: Minnesota, Birth Index, 1900-1934 (Provo, UT, USA, Ancestry.com Operations, Inc., 2015), Ancestry.com, http://www.Ancestry.com, Record for Carol Beth Coulson

Minnesota[1448]. She married Dale Million Thompson on 17 Aug 1946[1449]. He was born on 02 Nov 1920[1450] and died in Feb 1972. Carol Beth Coulson and her husband were buried in Money Creek, Minnesota[1451]. Dale Million Thompson and Carol Beth Coulson had four children who may still be living.

Carol Beth Coulson Thompson died at Valley View Healthcare and Rehab. She was born to Charles and L. Belle (Corey) Coulson. She was a lifelong resident of the Money Creek and Houston area. She married Dale M. Thompson on August 17, 1946. Carol was a wife, mother, homemaker, and retired employee of Rush Products (TRW), Rushford, Minnesota. Carol was survived by a son, Joel (Sue) Thompson of Winona; and daughters Linda (Rick) Thrune of Winona, Beth (Allen) Klinski of Caledonia, and Sheila Chapel (Howie Wiedman) of La Crescent; Grandchildren Dale (Patti) Kelso of Winona, Jen (Lawrence) Johnson of Duluth, Theresa (Dave) Longhorn of O'Fallon, Illinois, Amanda (Rob) Monk of Minnesota City, Jeremy (Dawn) Klinski of La Crescent, Kevin (Aimee) Klinski of Winona, Brandon (Jackie) Van Gundy of Kansas City, Missouri, Tim (finance' Tammy Enge) Thrune of Winona, and Korto Thrune of Winona; 17 great-grandchildren and many cousins, nieces and nephews. She was preceded in death by her parents; husband, Dale; 3 brothers Dwight (Pat), Joseph (Eleanor), and David (Julie); and sisters Dorothy (Kenneth) Chapel and June (Henry) Eaton.

Photo of Carol Beth Coulson found on Ancestry.com.

115.   Illa May Corey[6] (James Edgar Corey[5], Genevieve Berry[4], Mary Abigale Leigh[3], Elijah Leigh[2], Nathan S. Leigh[1]) was born on 31 May 1926 in Houston, Minnesota[1452] and died on 16 Dec 2016[1453]. She married Lyle Sweet in 1947[1454]. He was born on 05 Mar 1925 in Minnesota[1455] and died on 06 Jan 1968 in

---

[1448] Ancestry.com, U.S., Find A Grave Index, 1700s-Current (Provo, UT, USA, Ancestry.com Operations, Inc., 2012),

[1449] Obituary of Carol Beth Coulson included on page 167 of this book.

[1450] Ancestry.com, U.S., Social Security Applications and Claims Index, 1936-2007 (Provo, UT, USA, Ancestry.com Operations, Inc., 2015), Ancestry.com, http://www.Ancestry.com, Record for Dale M Thompson.

[1451] Ancestry.com, U.S., Find A Grave Index, 1700s-Current (Provo, UT, USA, Ancestry.com Operations, Inc., 2012), Ancestry.com, http://www.Ancestry.com, Record for Dale Million Thompson.

[1452] Ancestry.com, Web: Minnesota, Birth Index, 1900-1934 (Provo, UT, USA, Ancestry.com Operations, Inc., 2015), Ancestry.com, http://www.Ancestry.com, Record for Illa Mae Corey.

[1453] Ancestry.com, U.S., Find A Grave Index, 1700s-Current (Provo, UT, USA, Ancestry.com Operations, Inc., 2012), Ancestry.com, http://www.Ancestry.com, Record for Lyle Sweet.

[1454] Obituary of Illa May Sweet included on page 168 of this book.

[1455] Ancestry.com, U.S., Find A Grave Index, 1700s-Current (Provo, UT, USA, Ancestry.com Operations, Inc., 2012), Ancestry.com, http://www.Ancestry.com, Record for Lyle Sweet.

Caledonia, Minnesota[1456]. Illa May Corey and her husband were buried in Money Creek, Minnesota[1457].

Illa was born on May 31, 1926, in Money Creek, MN to James and Pearly (Ullan) Corey. She was raised at Money Creek where she attended country school. She was a 1944

graduate of Houston High School. Illa married James "Kenny" Botcher. They were later divorced. She married Lyle "Pete" Sweet in 1947. Lyle died in 1968. Illa worked at the Valley View Nursing Home, Houston Library, and Ace Telephone. She was a member of the Houston Legion Auxiliary and the Eastern Star. In her spare time, Illa enjoyed knitting, crocheting, playing cards, flea markets, rummage sales, gardening, reading, and drinking her morning coffee - all day.

Photo of Illa May Corey found on Ancestry.com.

Lyle Sweet and Illa May Corey had the following child:
> i.   Thomas James Sweet was born on 12 Jun 1948 in La Crosse, Wisconsin[1458] and died on 16 Apr 1975 in Winona, Minnesota[1459]. Thomas James Sweet was buried in Money Creek, Minnesota[1460].

[1456] Ancestry.com, U.S., Find A Grave Index, 1700s-Current (Provo, UT, USA, Ancestry.com Operations, Inc., 2012), Ancestry.com, http://www.Ancestry.com, Record for Lyle Sweet.

[1457] Ancestry.com, U.S., Find A Grave Index, 1700s-Current (Provo, UT, USA, Ancestry.com Operations, Inc., 2012), Ancestry.com, http://www.Ancestry.com, Record for Lyle Sweet.

[1458] Ancestry.com, U.S., Find A Grave Index, 1700s-Current (Provo, UT, USA, Ancestry.com Operations, Inc., 2012), Ancestry.com, http://www.Ancestry.com, Record for Lyle Sweet.

[1459] Ancestry.com, U.S., Find A Grave Index, 1700s-Current (Provo, UT, USA, Ancestry.com Operations, Inc., 2012), Ancestry.com, http://www.Ancestry.com, Record for Lyle Sweet.

[1460] Ancestry.com, U.S., Find A Grave Index, 1700s-Current (Provo, UT, USA, Ancestry.com Operations, Inc., 2012), Ancestry.com, http://www.Ancestry.com, Record for Lyle Sweet.

116. Wayne Howard Steele[6] (Grace Caroline Corey[5], Genevieve Berry[4], Mary Abigale Leigh[3], Elijah Leigh[2], Nathan S. Leigh[1]) was born on 30 Jun 1922 in Minnesota[1461] and died on 03 Oct 1974[1462]. He married Bernice Carolyn Slinde. She was born on 19 Feb 1927 in Stanton Merc, North Dakota[1463] and died on 21 Aug 2007[1464]. Wayne Howard Steele and his wife were buried in Everett, Washington[1465] 983.

Wayne Howard Steele and Bernice Carolyn Slinde had the following child:
> i.   James S. Steele was born in 1946[1466] and died in 1976[1467]. James S. Steele was buried in Everett, Washington[1468].

117. Mae Mina Lovering[6] (Anita Susan Berry[5], Eugene L. Berry[4], Mary Abigale Leigh[3], Elijah Leigh[2], Nathan S. Leigh[1]) was born on 27 June 1924 in Beltrami, Minnesota[1469] and died on 31 Dec 2015[1470].

Photo of Mae Mina Lovering found on Ancestry.com.

She married Donald Dickinson. He was born on 01 July 1924 in Bemidji, Minnesota[1471] and died on 20 Oct 1976[1472]. Mae Mina Lovering was buried in Sun Prairie, Wisconsin[1473]. Donald Dickinson was buried in Appleton, Wisconsin[1474].

[1461] Ancestry.com, Social Security Death Index (Provo, UT, USA, The Generations Network, Inc., 2008), www.ancestry.com, Number: 475-16-0502; Issue State: Minnesota; Issue Date: Before 1951. Record for Wayne Steele.
[1462] Ancestry.com, Social Security Death Index (Provo, UT, USA, The Generations Network, Inc., 2008), www.ancestry.com, Number: 475-16-0502; Issue State: Minnesota; Issue Date: Before 1951. Record for Wayne Steele.
[1463] Ancestry.com, U.S., Social Security Applications and Claims Index, 1936-2007 (Provo, UT, USA, Ancestry.com Operations, Inc., 2015), Ancestry.com, http://www.Ancestry.com, Record for Berenice Carolyn Slinde.
[1464] Ancestry.com, U.S., Social Security Applications and Claims Index, 1936-2007 (Provo, UT, USA, Ancestry.com Operations, Inc., 2015), Ancestry.com, http://www.Ancestry.com, Record for Berenice Carolyn Slinde.
[1465] Ancestry.com, U.S., Find A Grave Index, 1700s-Current (Provo, UT, USA, Ancestry.com Operations, Inc., 2012), Ancestry.com, http://www.Ancestry.com, Record for Bernice C. Steele.
[1466] Ancestry.com, U.S., Find A Grave Index, 1700s-Current (Provo, UT, USA, Ancestry.com Operations, Inc., 2012), Ancestry.com, http://www.Ancestry.com, Record for James S. Steele.
[1467] Ancestry.com, U.S., Find A Grave Index, 1700s-Current (Provo, UT, USA, Ancestry.com Operations, Inc., 2012), Ancestry.com, http://www.Ancestry.com, Record for James S. Steele.
[1468] Ancestry.com, U.S., Find A Grave Index, 1700s-Current, Record for James S. Steele.
[1469] Ancestry.com, U.S., Find A Grave Index, 1700s-Current, Record for Mae M. Dickinson.
[1470] Ancestry.com, U.S., Find A Grave Index, 1700s-Current, Record for Mae M. Dickinson.
[1471] Ancestry.com, U.S., Find A Grave Index, 1700s-Current, Record for Mae M. Dickinson.
[1472] Ancestry.com, U.S., Find A Grave Index, 1700s-Current, Record for Mae M. Dickinson.
[1473] Ancestry.com, U.S., Find A Grave Index, 1700s-Current, Record for Mae M. Dickinson.
[1474] Ancestry.com, U.S., Find A Grave Index, 1700s-Current, Record for Mae M. Dickinson.

Sun Prairie - *Mae M. Dickinson, age 91, passed away on Thursday, December 31, 2015 at the Sun Prairie HealthCare Center. She was born in 1924 to Ralph and Anita Lovering in Birch Township, MN. She attended grade school in Black Duck, MN and high school in Bemidji, MN. Mae was an accomplished seamstress, avid gardener and homemaker. In 1944, Mae married Donald Dickinson of Bemidji, who passed away in 1976. She then married Glenn Wolf of Sun Prairie in 1984 and he preceded her in death in 2005. Mae is survived by her daughter; Diane Watson, grandson; Brad Krebs, sister-in-law; Emily Lovering, special nieces and good friend Marlene Konopacki. Mae was preceded in death by her son, Steven Dickinson, brother Steven Lovering and sister Lois White. At Mae's request, there will be no services. Cremation has taken place and her final resting will be held at Sun Prairie Memory Gardens Cemetery, Sun Prairie, Wisconsin. Special thanks to the skilled and caring people at the HealthCare Center for making her last month's comfortable. Cress Funeral & Cremation Services 1310 Emerald Terrace, Sun Prairie 608-837-9054*

Donald Dickinson and Mae Mina Lovering had the following children:

    i.   Steven Michael Dickson was born on 28 Jul 1945 in Beltrami, Minnesota[1475] and died on 03 Sep 1976 in San Joaquin, California[1476].

    ii.   Living Dickinson

118. Erwin Glenn Hirst[6] (Glen James Hirst[5], Rose Ann Lindel Todd[4], Julia Fannie Leigh[3], Elijah Leigh[2], Nathan S. Leigh[1]) was born on 25 Jan 1912 in South Jordan, Utah [1477] and died on 30 Mar 1959[1478]. He married Lyla Holder. She was born on 03 Feb 1916 in Salt Lake City, Utah [1479] and died on 01 Aug 2008 in Murray, Utah[1480]. Erwin Glenn Hirst and his wife were buried in Millcreek, Utah[1481].

[1475] Minnesota Department of Health, Minnesota Birth Index, 1935-1995 (Provo, UT, USA, Ancestry.com Operations Inc, 2004), Ancestry.com, http://www.Ancestry.com, Record for Steven Michael Dickinson.

[1476] Ancestry.com, California Death Index, 1940-1997 (Provo, UT, USA, The Generations Network, Inc., 2000), www.ancestry.com, Date: 1976-09-03. Record for Steven M Dickinson.

[1477] Ancestry.com, U.S., Find A Grave Index, 1700s-Current (Provo, UT, USA, Ancestry.com Operations, Inc., 2012), Ancestry.com, http://www.Ancestry.com, Record for Erwin Glenn Hirst.

[1478] Ancestry.com, U.S., Find A Grave Index, 1700s-Current (Provo, UT, USA, Ancestry.com Operations, Inc., 2012), Ancestry.com, http://www.Ancestry.com, Record for Erwin Glenn Hirst.

[1479] Ancestry.com, U.S., Find A Grave Index, 1700s-Current (Provo, UT, USA, Ancestry.com Operations, Inc., 2012), Ancestry.com, http://www.Ancestry.com, Record for Erwin Glenn Hirst.

[1480] Ancestry.com, U.S., Find A Grave Index, 1700s-Current (Provo, UT, USA, Ancestry.com Operations, Inc., 2012), Ancestry.com, http://www.Ancestry.com, Record for Erwin Glenn Hirst.

[1481] Ancestry.com, U.S., Find A Grave Index, 1700s-Current (Provo, UT, USA, Ancestry.com Operations, Inc., 2012), Ancestry.com, http://www.Ancestry.com, Record for Erwin Glenn Hirst.

Photo of Erwin Glenn Hirst found on familysearch.org.

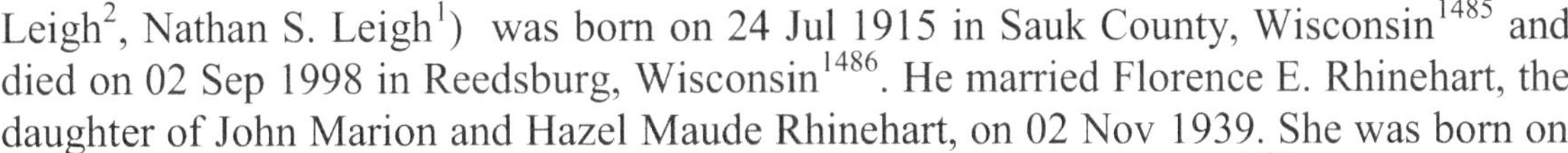

Erwin Glenn Hirst and Lyla Holder had the following child:

      i.   Glen Louis Hirst was born on 21 Dec 1938 in Salt Lake City, Utah[1482] and died on 07 Dec 1953[1483]. Glen Louis Hirst1was buried in Millcreek, Utah[1484].

119. Francis Alva Hirst[6] (Leslie Erwin Hirst[5], Rose Ann Lindel Todd[4], Julia Fannie Leigh[3], Elijah Leigh[2], Nathan S. Leigh[1]) was born on 24 Jul 1915 in Sauk County, Wisconsin[1485] and died on 02 Sep 1998 in Reedsburg, Wisconsin[1486]. He married Florence E. Rhinehart, the daughter of John Marion and Hazel Maude Rhinehart, on 02 Nov 1939. She was born on 19 Feb 1923 in Sauk County, Wisconsin[1487] and died on 02 Dec 2014 in Reedsburg, Wisconsin[1488]. Francis Alva Hirst and his wife were buried in Reedsburg, Wisconsin[1489]. Francis Alva Hirst and Florence E. Rhinehart had three children who may still be living.

Photo of Florence E. Rhinehart found on findagrave.com.

Florence E. Hirst, age 91, of Reedsburg, died on Tuesday, December 2, 2014 at the Sauk County Health Care Center. She was born on February 19, 1923 in the Town of Dellona, Sauk County, the daughter of John and Hazel (Otto) Rhinehart. On November 2, 1939, she was married

[1482] Ancestry.com, U.S., Find A Grave Index, 1700s-Current (Provo, UT, USA, Ancestry.com Operations, Inc., 2012), Ancestry.com, http://www.Ancestry.com, Record for Erwin Glenn Hirst.

[1483] Ancestry.com, U.S., Find A Grave Index, 1700s-Current (Provo, UT, USA, Ancestry.com Operations, Inc., 2012), Ancestry.com, http://www.Ancestry.com, Record for Erwin Glenn Hirst.

Ancestry.com, U.S., Find A Grave Index, 1700s-Current (Provo, UT, USA, Ancestry.com Operat Ancestry.com, U.S., Find A Grave Index, 1700s-Current (Provo, UT, USA, Ancestry.com Operations, Inc., 2012), Ancestry.com, http://www.Ancestry.com, Record for Erwin Glenn Hirst. ions, Inc., 2012), Ancestry.com, http://www.Ancestry.com, Record for Erwin Glenn Hirst. [1484]

[1485] Ancestry.com, U.S., Find A Grave Index, 1700s-Current (Provo, UT, USA, Ancestry.com Operations, Inc., 2012),

[1486] Ancestry.com, U.S., Find A Grave Index, 1700s-Current (Provo, UT, USA, Ancestry.com Operations, Inc., 2012),

[1487] Ancestry.com, U.S., Find A Grave Index, 1700s-Current (Provo, UT, USA, Ancestry.com Operations, Inc., 2012), Ancestry.com, http://www.Ancestry.com, Record for Florence E Hirst.

[1488] Ancestry.com, U.S., Find A Grave Index, 1700s-Current (Provo, UT, USA, Ancestry.com Operations, Inc., 2012), Ancestry.com, http://www.Ancestry.com, Record for Florence E Hirst.

[1489] Ancestry.com, U.S., Find A Grave Index, 1700s-Current (Provo, UT, USA, Ancestry.com Operations, Inc., 2012), Ancestry.com, http://www.Ancestry.com, Record for Florence E Hirst.

to Francis A. Hirst. Florence worked as head cook at Camp Chi in Lake Delton for over eighteen years. She enjoyed quilting, hunting, fishing, cooking, playing cards, gardening, crocheting and spending time at the lake in Birchwood. Florence also collected ceramic chickens and loons. She was a member of the United Methodist Church and a past member of the Eagles Auxiliary, Dell-Aire Homemakers and the Reedsburg Senior Citizens. Survivors include her three children: Beverly Hirst, of Birchwood; Bernard (Agnes) Hirst, of Reedsburg and Brenda (Michael) Hendricks, of Lyndon Station; five grandchildren: Connie (Duane) Cook, Kevin (Kristin) Hirst, Stephanie (Marvin) Kroeger, Leslie Hendricks and Lucas Hendricks; eight great grandchildren; three sisters-in-law: Janice Rhinehart, Edye Rhinehart and Grace Cook; many nieces and nephews. She was preceded in death by her husband, Francis, on September 2, 1998, as well as twelve brothers and sisters. Funeral services will be held at 11:00 A.M. on Saturday, December 6, 2014 at the United Methodist Church in Reedsburg with Pastor Marvin Singh officiating. Interment will be in Butterfield Cemetery. There will be a visitation from 4:00 P.M. to 7:00 P.M. on Friday at the Hoof Funeral Home in Reedsburg and from 10:00 to 11:00 A.M. on Saturday at the church. In lieu of flowers, memorials to the Reedsburg United Methodist Church or the Sauk County Health Care Center would be appreciated. Special thanks to the staff and nurses at the Sauk County Health Care Center and the Reedsburg Area Medical Center for the wonderful care given to Florence. The Hoof Funeral Home is serving the family.

120. Melbourne Clyde Hirst[6] (Leslie Erwin Hirst[5], Rose Ann Lindel Todd[4], Julia Fannie Leigh[3], Elijah Leigh[2], Nathan S. Leigh[1]) was born on 19 Jun 1920 in Lyndon Station, Wisconsin[1490]. He died on 27 Sep 1987 in Reedsburg, Wisconsin[1491] and married Grace Marie Coolidge, the daughter of Clifford and Marie Coolidge, on 21 Dec 1946[1492]. She was born on 12 Feb 1925 in Baraboo, Wisconsin[1493] and died on 28 Jul 2015 in Reedsburg, Wisconsin[1494]. Melbourne Clyde Hirst and his wife were buried in Baraboo, Wisconsin[1495].

Thurs., Oct. 1, 1987 - THE REEDSBURG TIMES-PRESS, Reedsburg, Sauk County, WI; Page 2:
Melbourne C. Hirst, 67, Reedsburg, died on Sunday, September 27, 1987 at his home after a short illness. He was born on June 19, 1920, in Lyndon Station, the son of Leslie and Alice (Hawes) Hirst. On December 21, 1946 , he was married to the former Grace Coolidge in Reedsburg, where they made their home for the past 40 years. Melbourne worked at Hankscraft for 31 years, before retiring in 1985. He was a longtime member of

[1490] Ancestry.com, U.S., Find A Grave Index, 1700s-Current (Provo, UT, USA, Ancestry.com Operations, Inc., 2012),

[1491] Ancestry.com, U.S., Find A Grave Index, 1700s-Current (Provo, UT, USA, Ancestry.com Operations, Inc., 2012),

[1492] Obituary, The Reedsburg Times-Press, Reedsburg, Wisconsin, October 1, 1987, page 2.

[1493] Ancestry.com, U.S., Find A Grave Index, 1700s-Current (Provo, UT, USA, Ancestry.com Operations, Inc., 2012),

[1494] Ancestry.com, U.S., Find A Grave Index, 1700s-Current (Provo, UT, USA, Ancestry.com Operations, Inc., 2012),

[1495] Ancestry.com, U.S., Find A Grave Index, 1700s-Current (Provo, UT, USA, Ancestry.com Operations, Inc., 2012),

the First Church of the Nazarene in Baraboo and a charter member of the Reedsburg Community Church of the Nazarene. He is survived by his wife, Grace; three sons, Donald (Marge), Baraboo, David (Sue), Morrisonville, Milton (Pam), Denver, CO; two daughters, Esther (Richard) Helley, Reedsburg, Kathy (William) Moe, Wichita, KS; 10 grandchildren; one brother, Francis, Reedsburg; one sister, Rosella Ramburg, Verona; many other relatives and friends. He was preceded in death by his parents and a granddaughter, Dawn Marie Hirst, in 1975. Funeral services were held at 1:30 p.m. on Wednesday, September 30, at the First Church of the Nazarene, Baraboo, with Rev. Daniel Wiese and Rev. Leonard Budd officiating. Interment was in Walnut Hill cemetery, Baraboo. The family received friends after 4 p.m. on Tuesday at the Hammer Funeral Home. In lieu of flowers, memorials would be appreciated. The Hammer Funeral Home is serving the family.

Melbourne Clyde Hirst and Grace Marie Coolidge had five children who may still be living.

121. Joycelyn Dawn Todd[6] (Everett Clifford Todd Sr.[5], Ransom William Todd[4], Julia Fannie Leigh[3], Elijah Leigh[2], Nathan S. Leigh[1])was born on 09 Jul 1927 in Crandon, Wisconsin[1496] and died on 13 Nov 2006[1497]. She married Elmer Shufelt, the son of Hanson J. and Ella Shufelt, in Jul 1946 in Antigo, Wisconsin[1498]. He was born on 15 Nov 1920 in Antigo, Wisconsin[1499] and died on 08 Nov 2006[1500]. Joycelyn Dawn Todd and her husband were buried in Clintonville, Wisconsin[1501]. Elmer Shufelt and Joycelyn Dawn Todd had seven children who may still be living.

Joyce D. Shufelt, age 79, of 223 S. Main Street, Clintonville, passed away Monday, November 13, 2006 at her home, following a battle with cancer. The former Joyce Dawn Todd was born July 7, 1927 at Crandon, WI., and was the daughter of the late Evert and Evelyn (Freeman) Todd. In July of 1946, Joyce was united in marriage to Elmer Shufelt at Antigo, WI. The couple lived in the Split Rock/Tigerton until the mid-1970's, when they moved to Clintonville. Mr. Shufelt passed away November 8, 2006. Joyce is survived by seven children, a son, Robert (April) Shufelt, Clintonville, a son Ronald Shufelt, Manawa, a daughter, Jackie (Bret) Moder, Clintonville, a daughter, Sandra (Marlyn) Jepson,

---

[1496] Ancestry.com, U.S., Social Security Applications and Claims Index, 1936-2007 (Provo, UT, USA, Ancestry.com Operations, Inc., 2015), Ancestry.com, http://www.Ancestry.com, Record for Joyce Dawn Shufelt.

[1497] Ancestry.com, U.S., Social Security Applications and Claims Index, 1936-2007 (Provo, UT, USA, Ancestry.com Operations, Inc., 2015), Ancestry.com, http://www.Ancestry.com, Record for Joyce Dawn Shufelt.

[1498] Obituary of Joyce D. Shufelt included in this book, page 173.

[1499] Ancestry.com, U.S., Social Security Applications and Claims Index, 1936-2007 (Provo, UT, USA, Ancestry.com Operations, Inc., 2015), Ancestry.com, http://www.Ancestry.com, Record for Elmer Shufelt.

[1500] Ancestry.com, U.S., Social Security Applications and Claims Index, 1936-2007 (Provo, UT, USA, Ancestry.com Operations, Inc., 2015), Ancestry.com, http://www.Ancestry.com, Record for Elmer Shufelt.

[1501] Ancestry.com, U.S., Find A Grave Index, 1700s-Current (Provo, UT, USA, Ancestry.com Operations, Inc., 2012), Ancestry.com, http://www.Ancestry.com, Record for Elmer Shufelt.

Clintonville, a daughter, Cheryl (Dion) Rice, Twin Lakes, a son Brett (Linda) Shufelt, Clintonville, and a son Bart Shufelt, Clintonville. There are 18 grandchildren, and 11 great-grandchildren. One brother, Jerry (Mary Ann) Todd, Utah, a sister-in-law, Shirley Todd, Milwaukee, half sisters, Connie Riddle, Kentucky, Mary Ann Plaedrael, Kimberly, and Sandy (Larry) Drews, Ringle. One half brother, Larry (Betty) Evans, Antigo, half brother-in-law, Bob Blalock, Marengo, IL., half sister-in-law, Bette Evens, Antigo. Joyce was preceded in death by her husband, Elmer, a granddaughter, Fawn Moder, two brothers, Evert "Bugs" Todd, and Robert Todd, one half sister Patricia Blalock, and one half brother, Del Evans.

Elmer Shufelt, age 85, of 223 S. Main Street, Clintonville, passed away Wednesday, November 8, 2006 at the Wisconsin Veterans Home, King, WI. The former Elmer Shufelt was born November 15, 1920 at Antigo, WI., and was the son of the late Hanson and Ella (Gee) Shufelt. Elmer was raised in the Antigo area, and served in the U.S. Army at the rank of Sergeant, during WW2. In July of 1946, he was united in marriage to Joyce D. Todd at Antigo, WI. The couple made their home in the Tigerton/Split Rock area until the mid 1970's, when they moved to Clintonville. Elmer worked in auto body repair. He was a member of the Disabled American Veterans of Manawa, and was a good handyman, and did home repair work. Survivors include his wife, Joyce, and seven children; a son Robert (April) Shufelt, Clintonville, a son Ronald Shufelt, Manawa, a daughter, Jacki (Bret) Moder, Clintonville, a daughter, Sandra (Marlyn) Jepson, Clintonville, a daughter, Cheryl (Dion) Rice, Twin Lakes, a son Brett (Linda) Shufelt, Clintonville, and a son, Bart Shufelt, Clintonville. There are 18 grandchildren and 11 great grandchildren. One sister, Esther Jensen, Wausau, one brother, Edward Steffen, Milwaukee, many other relatives and friends. He was preceded in death by 5 brothers, Harvey, Art, John, Bob, and Harry, and 2 sisters, Lila Vaughn & Beatrice Virute, and a granddaughter, Fawn Moder. Funeral services will be held on Saturday, November 11, 2006 at 1:30 p.m. at the Beil-Didier Funeral Home, Clintonville. Rev. Willard L. Hager will officiate and burial will follow at Graceland Cemetery, Clintonville. Military honors will be provided at the cemetery by members of the American Legion Post #63 and V.F.W. Post #664, both of Clintonville. Friends may call from 6:00 to 8:00 p.m. on Friday at the funeral home, and on Saturday from 11:00 a.m. until the time of the services.

122. Bruce Robert Priest[6] (Leo Melvin Priest[5], Fred M. Priest[4], Julia Fannie Leigh[3], Elijah Leigh[2], Nathan S. Leigh[1]) was born on 15 Dec 1927 in Watonwan, Minnesota[1502] and died on 10 Sep 1963 in Hennepin, Minnesota[1503]. He married Marian May Taylor. Bruce served in the US Navy during WWII having enlisted May 24, 1945.

[1502] Ancestry.com, Minnesota, Birth Index, 1908-2002 (Provo, UT, USA, Ancestry.com Operations Inc, 2001), Ancestry.com, http://www.Ancestry.com, Record for Bruce Robert Priest.
[1503] Ancestry.com, Minnesota, Death Index, 1908-2002 (Provo, UT, USA, Ancestry.com Operations Inc, 2001), Ancestry.com, http://www.Ancestry.com, Record for Bruce Robert Priest.

Bruce Robert Priest was buried in Minneapolis, Minnesota[1504].

Bruce Robert Priest and Marian May Taylor had the following children:
    i.   Living Priest
    ii.   Kathryn Joan Priest was born on 20 Aug 1957 in Minneapolis, Minnesota[1505] and died on 07 Sep 2013 in Apple Valley, Minnesota[1506].

Kathryn J. "Katy" Priest age 56, of Apple Valley, passed away on Sept. 7, 2013 after a courageous 10 yr. battle with cancer. She is preceded in death by her father, Bruce Priest; her grandparents; 2 aunts; and 2 uncles. Katy is survived by her 2 daughters, Rachel and Elizabeth; her mother, Marian Priest; a brother, David (Laura) Priest; uncle, Richard (Lois) Taylor; aunt, Gail Taylor; Bob and Piper Burghduf; special friends, Dan Tini and Deb Dyslin; nieces, nephews, other family and friends. A "Very Special Thank You" to Lori, Shannon, Tammy, Susan, and Jenny for all of your help over the years! Katy's funeral service will be held on Saturday, Sept. 14 at 10:30 AM at Shepherd of the Valley Lutheran Church, 12650 Johnny Cake Ridge Road, Apple Valley with her visitation to take place one hour prior to the service at the church. Internment at a later date. Memorials are preferred to her daughters custodial fund, the church or the American Cancer Society.

123. Joan Alicia Priest[6] (Claude Morton Priest[5], Fred M. Priest[4], Julia Fannie Leigh[3], Elijah Leigh[2], Nathan S. Leigh[1]) was born on 07 Mar 1922 in Madelia Wato, Minnesota[1507] and died on 02 Jun 1995 in Las Vegas, Nevada[1508]. She married Donald Leroy Barclay Sr. Donald Leroy Barclay Sr. and Joan Alicia Priest had one child who may still be living.

124. Richard Charles Priest[6] (Claude Morton Priest[5], Fred M. Priest[4], Julia Fannie Leigh[3], Elijah Leigh[2], Nathan S. Leigh[1]) was born on 17 May 1927 in Watonwan, Minnesota[1509] and died 02 Feb 2012[1510]. He married Pearl Vila Hansen. She was born on 23 Aug 1928[1511] and died on 02 Mar 2008[1512] in Las Vegas, Nevada. Richard Charles

[1504] Ancestry.com, U.S., Find A Grave Index, 1700s-Current (Provo, UT, USA, Ancestry.com Operations, Inc., 2012), Ancestry.com, http://www.Ancestry.com, Record for Bruce Robert Priest.
[1505] Obituary of Kathryn J. Priest included in this book, page. 175.
[1506] Obituary of Kathryn J. Priest included in this book, page. 175.
[1507] Ancestry.com, U.S., Social Security Applications and Claims Index, 1936-2007 (Provo, UT, USA, Ancestry.com Operations, Inc., 2015), Ancestry.com, http://www.Ancestry.com, Record for Joan Alicia Priest
[1508] Ancestry.com, U.S., Social Security Applications and Claims Index, 1936-2007 (Provo, UT, USA, Ancestry.com Operations, Inc., 2015), Ancestry.com, http://www.Ancestry.com, Record for Joan Alicia Priest
[1509] Ancestry.com, Web: Minnesota, Birth Index, 1900-1934 (Provo, UT, USA, Ancestry.com Operations, Inc., 2015), Ancestry.com, http://www.Ancestry.com, Record for Richard Charles Priest
[1510] Ancestry.com, U.S., Find A Grave Index, 1700s-Current.
[1511] Ancestry.com, U.S., Find A Grave Index, 1700s-Current.
[1512] Ancestry.com, U.S., Find A Grave Index, 1700s-Current.

Priest and Pearl Vila Hansen had children who may still be living. Richard Charles Priest and his wife were buried in Las Vegas, Nevada[1513].

Published in Las Vegas Review-Journal from February 4 to February 5, 2012
Richard C. Priest, 84, of Las Vegas, passed away Feb. 2, 2012. He was a retired educator and long-time middle school principal. He was honored by having Richard C. Priest Elementary School named after him. He served his country honorably in the U.S. Navy. He was preceded in death by his sweet young bride, Pearl; and his sister, Joan Barclay. He is survived by his sons, Richard and Frederick Priest; and his daughter, Peggy Young. He had nine grandchildren, Ryan and Jeremy Young, Brysyn, Juna, Madison, and Morgan Priest, Julie Jackson, and Sheri Ann Shelton. Richard's hobbies included hunting, fishing, gardening, genealogy, traveling, and reading. He is a former member of The National Association of Secondary School Principals, Kiwanis Club, Southwest Rotary, The American Legion, and the Elks. Services will be Memorial services will be at 2 p.m. Saturday, Feb. 11, at Palm Mortuary, 6701 N. Jones Blvd. Graveside services will follow at Palm Memorial Park - Northwest. Richard Priest was a loving father and grandfather and will be missed by family, friends, and his school.

Richard Charles Priest and Pearl Vila Hanson had two children who may still be living.

125. Marilyn Grace Beatty[6] (Bernice P. Priest[5], Fred M. Priest[4], Julia Fannie Leigh[3], Elijah Leigh[2], Nathan S. Leigh[1]) was born on 30 Jul 1926 in Gaylord, Minnesota[1514] and died on 01 Dec 2001[1515]. She married Robert Richard Donlin on 18 Jun 1949 in Sibley, Minnesota[1516]. He was born on 24 Nov 1921 in Minneapolis, Minnesota[1517] and died on 23 Sep 1990 in Maplewood, Minnesota[1518]. Marilyn Grace Beatty and her husband were buried in Minneapolis, Minnesota[1519]. Robert Richard Donlin and Marilyn Grace Beatty had six children who may still be living.

126. Wilfred Wine Schultz[6] (Genevieve Jewel Johnson[5], Nora Eleanor Priest[4], Julia Fannie Leigh[3], Elijah Leigh[2], Nathan S. Leigh[1]) was born on 18 Jul 1909 in Argonne,

---

[1513] Ancestry.com, U.S., Find A Grave Index, 1700s-Current (Provo, UT, USA, Ancestry.com Operations, Inc., 2012), Ancestry.com, http://www.Ancestry.com, Record for Richard C. Priest.

[1514] Ancestry.com, U.S., Social Security Applications and Claims Index, 1936-2007 (Provo, UT, USA, Ancestry.com Operations, Inc., 2015), Ancestry.com, http://www.Ancestry.com, Record for Marilyn Grace Beatty

[1515] Ancestry.com, U.S., Social Security Applications and Claims Index, 1936-2007 (Provo, UT, USA, Ancestry.com Operations, Inc., 2015), Ancestry.com, http://www.Ancestry.com, Record for Marilyn Grace Beatty

[1516] Minnesota, County Marriages, 1860-1949," database with images, FamilySearch, (https://familysearch.org/ark:/61903/1:1:Q2M5-1MFW : 13 June 2016), Robert Richard Donlin and Marilyn Grace Beatty, 18 Jun 1949, Sibley, Minnesota

[1517] Ancestry.com, U.S., Find A Grave Index, 1700s-Current (Provo, UT, USA, Ancestry.com Operations, Inc., 2012), Ancestry.com, http://www.Ancestry.com, Record for Marilyn Grace Donlin.

[1518] Ancestry.com, U.S., Find A Grave Index, 1700s-Current (Provo, UT, USA, Ancestry.com Operations, Inc., 2012), Ancestry.com, http://www.Ancestry.com, Record for Marilyn Grace Donlin.

[1519] Ancestry.com, U.S., Find A Grave Index, 1700s-Current (Provo, UT, USA, Ancestry.com Operations, Inc., 2012), Ancestry.com, http://www.Ancestry.com, Record for Marilyn Grace Donlin.

Wisconsin[1520] and died on 24 Feb 1983 in Rhinelander, Wisconsin[1521]. He married Ella Anna Marie Pfeifer[1522]. She was born on 03 May 1913 in Gillett, Wisconsin[1523] and died on 10 Jan 2003 in Crandon, Wisconsin[1524]. Wilfred Wine Schultz and his wife were buried in Crandon, Wisconsin[1525].   Wilfred Wine Schultz and Ella Anna Marie Pfeiffer had three children who may still be living.

127. Irvin Michael Anthony Schultz[6] (Genevieve Jewel Johnson[5], Nora Eleanor Priest[4], Julia Fannie Leigh[3], Elijah Leigh[2], Nathan S. Leigh[1]) was born on 29 Jul 1911 in Argonne, Wisconsin[1526] and died on 14 Dec 1999 in Iron River, Michigan[1527]. He married Marie Dascola, the daughter of Antonio D. Dascola and Amelia Amarela, on 26 Sep 1933 in Crystal Falls, Michigan[1528]. She was born on 18 Sep 1915 in Stambaugh, Michigan[1529] and died on 25 Nov 2003 in Pontiac, Michigan[1530]. Irvin Michael Anthony and his wife were buried in Crandon, Forest County, Wisconsin, United States of America[1531].

OBITUARY Iron County Reporter Dec 3 2003
IRON RIVER - Marie Dascola Schultz Walker, 88, died Nov. 25 at Pontiac Osteopathic Hospital in Pontiac.
She was born Sept. 18, 1915 in Stambaugh, daughter of the late Tony and Amelia (Amarela) Dascola. In August of 1933 she married Irwin Anthony Schultz in Crystal Falls. She later married Edward Walker of Antioch, Ill. on March 24, 1973. She was a member of St. Cecilia Catholic Church in Caspian and the Mothers Club in Caspian. She will be greatly missed by her friends and family whom she loved so much. She was

[1520] Ancestry.com. *U.S., Find A Grave Index, 1600s-Current* [database on-line]. Provo, UT, USA: Ancestry.com Operations, Inc., 2012.

[1521] Ancestry.com. *U.S., Find A Grave Index, 1600s-Current* [database on-line]. Provo, UT, USA: Ancestry.com Operations, Inc., 2012.

[1522] Ancestry.com. *U.S., Find A Grave Index, 1600s-Current* [database on-line]. Provo, UT, USA: Ancestry.com Operations, Inc., 2012.

[1523] Ancestry.com. *U.S., Find A Grave Index, 1600s-Current* [database on-line]. Provo, UT, USA: Ancestry.com Operations, Inc., 2012.

[1524] Ancestry.com. *U.S., Find A Grave Index, 1600s-Current* [database on-line]. Provo, UT, USA: Ancestry.com Operations, Inc., 2012.

[1525] Ancestry.com. *U.S., Find A Grave Index, 1600s-Current* [database on-line]. Provo, UT, USA: Ancestry.com Operations, Inc., 2012.

[1526] Ancestry.com. *U.S., Find A Grave Index, 1600s-Current* [database on-line]. Provo, UT, USA: Ancestry.com Operations, Inc., 2012.

[1527] Ancestry.com. *U.S., Find A Grave Index, 1600s-Current* [database on-line]. Provo, UT, USA: Ancestry.com Operations, Inc., 2012.

[1528] Ancestry.com, U.S., Find A Grave Index, 1700s-Current (Provo, UT, USA, Ancestry.com Operations, Inc., 2012), Ancestry.com, http://www.Ancestry.com, Record for Marie Walker.

[1529] Ancestry.com, U.S., Find A Grave Index, 1700s-Current (Provo, UT, USA, Ancestry.com Operations, Inc., 2012), Ancestry.com, http://www.Ancestry.com, Record for Marie Walker.

[1530] Ancestry.com, U.S., Find A Grave Index, 1700s-Current (Provo, UT, USA, Ancestry.com Operations, Inc., 2012), Ancestry.com, http://www.Ancestry.com, Record for Marie Walker.

[1531] Ancestry.com, U.S., Find A Grave Index, 1700s-Current (Provo, UT, USA, Ancestry.com Operations, Inc., 2012), Ancestry.com, http://www.Ancestry.com, Record for William Martin Schultz.

preceded in death by a daughter Delores Johnson; brothers, Roosevelt, Ernest and Patsy Dascola; a sister Doris Jacobs; and a son-in-law Jack Gagnea. She is survived by her husband; nine children, Bonnie (John) Baldwin of Iron River, CeCe (Murray) Lance of Atlanta, Ga., Mary Lee (Jim)Baldwin of Clarkston, Mike (Sonya) Schultz of Atlanta, Irvin (Sheila) Schultz of Palatine, Ill. Betty Lou McArthur (Bob Johnson) of Crystal Falls, Bootsie (Donald) Toti of Marquette and Clarice Gagnea of Kingsford; six step-children, Linda (Lloyd) of Salt Lake City, Utah, Pam (Pat) of Waukegan, Ill., Jim (Sue) of Rolling Meadows, Ill., Cindy (Glenn) of Palatine, Ill., Robert and Michael Walker of Waukegan Ill.; two brothers, Joseph (Dorothy) and Domenic Dascola, all of Ann Arbor; many grandchildren, Vicki Lynn, Jaime Lynn, Jennifer Lynn, Robie, Mike, Christopher, Colleen, Cora, Kelly, Mike, Pat, Cindy, Sean, Eric, Gina, Joey, Gloria, Mary, Jan, Carol, Doody, John Michael, Charlie, Charliesun, Shayla, Christopher, Colleen, Cara and Kelly; a son-in-law Ronald Johnson of Zion, Ill.; a special niece Patsy Ann Cederna of South Carolina; special nephews, Donald, Paul and Jack Jacobs; a brother-in-law Thornton (Helen) Schultz of Argonne, Wis.; a very special friend for 85 years, Mary Johns; and many great-grandchildren and great-great-grandchildren. Visitation will be held Friday, Dec. 5 from 5 p.m. to 7 p.m. at the Jacobs-Plowe Funeral Home in Crystal Falls. Prayers will be recited at 5:30 p.m. at the funeral home. The Mass of Christian Burial will be held Saturday, Dec. 6 at 9:30 a.m. at St. Cecilia's Catholic Church in Caspian with Fr. Norman Clisch to officiate. Burial will be in Stambaugh Cemetery. The Jacobs-Plowe Funeral Home of Crystal Falls is serving the family.

Irvin Michael Anthony Schultz and Marie Dascola had the following child:

     i.   Delores Marie Schultz was born on 09 Aug 1942 in Caspian, Michigan[1532] and died on 12 Jun 1999 in Zion, Illinois[1533]. Delores Marie Johnson1063 was buried in Iron River, Michigan[1534]. She married Ronald Roy Johnson.

128. Myrtle Rozette Harnden[6] (George William Harnden[5], Sarah Amaria Leigh[4], William Safford Leigh[3], William Todd Leigh[2], Nathan S. Leigh[1]) was born on 24 Apr 1908 in Oklahoma[1535] and died on 10 Dec 19741[1536]. She married William Cleao Dodson on 27 Dec 1926 in Stillwater, Oklahoma[1537]. He was born on 30 May 1906 in Altus, Oklahoma[1538] and died on 06 Dec 1965 in Knox, Ohio[1539].   Myrtle Rozette Harnden

---

[1532] Ancestry.com, U.S., Find A Grave Index, 1700s-Current, Record for Marie Walker.

[1533] Ancestry.com, U.S., Find A Grave Index, 1700s-Current, Record for Marie Walker.

[1534] Ancestry.com, U.S., Find A Grave Index, 1700s-Current, Record for Marie Walker.

[1535] Ancestry.com, Social Security Death Index, Record for Myrtle Dodson..

[1536] Ancestry.com, Social Security Death Index, Record for Myrtle Dodson.

[1537] Ancestery.com, Ancestry.com. Oklahoma, County Marriages, 1890-1995 [database on-line]. Lehi, UT, USA: Ancestry.com Operations, Inc., 2016.

[1538] Ancestry.com and Ohio Department of Health, Ohio, Deaths, 1908-1932, 1938-2007, Certificate: 93542; Volume: 18295. Record for William C Dodson.

[1539] Ancestry.com and Ohio Department of Health, Ohio, Deaths, 1908-1932, 1938-2007, Certificate: 93542; Volume: 18295. Record for William C Dodson.

and her husband were buried in Oklahoma City, Oklahoma[1540].   William Cleao Dodson and Myrtle Rozette Harnden had three children who may still be living.

129.   Charles E. Doty[6] (Rosetta Frances Harnden[5], Sarah Amaria Leigh[4], William Safford Leigh[3], William Todd Leigh[2], Nathan S. Leigh[1]) was born on 24 Jun 1910 in Oklahoma[1541] and died on 30 Aug 1984[1542]. He married Ruth Maxine Patterson. She was born on 21 Nov 1913[1543] and died on 06 Aug 1982[1544].   Charles E. M. Doty and his wife were buried in Buffalo, Kansas[1545].

Charles E. M. Doty and Ruth Maxine Patterson had the following children:
      i.   Charlene Marie Doty was born on 23 Jan 1935 in Gray, Texas[1546] and died on 10 Feb 1996[1547]. Charlene Marie Doty was buried in Buffalo, Kansas[1548].
      ii.   Mary Joyce Doty was born on 13 Jul 1939 in Gray, Texas[1549] and died on 24 Feb 1998 in Chanute, Kansas[1550]. She married John Sidney Houston, the son of Oren S. Houston and Lola Spencer, on 28 Dec 1961 in Tulsa, Oklahoma[1551]. He was born on 26 May 1937 in Wichita, Kansas[1552] and died on 25 Apr 1999. Mary Joyce Doty and her husband were buried in Buffalo, Kansas[1553].

[1540] Ancestry.com, U.S., Find A Grave Index, 1700s-Current (Provo, UT, USA, Ancestry.com Operations, Inc., 2012), Ancestry.com, http://www.Ancestry.com, Record for Myrtle Dodson.

[1541] Ancestry.com, Web: Kansas, Find A Grave Index, 1854-2012 (Provo, UT, USA, Ancestry.com Operations, Inc., 2012), Ancestry.com, http://www.Ancestry.com, Record for Charles E Doty.

[1542] Ancestry.com, Web: Kansas, Find A Grave Index, 1854-2012 (Provo, UT, USA, Ancestry.com Operations, Inc., 2012), Ancestry.com, http://www.Ancestry.com, Record for Charles E Doty.

[1543] Ancestry.com, Social Security Death Index (Provo, UT, USA, The Generations Network, Inc., 2008), www.ancestry.com, Number: 464-22-8497; Issue State: Texas; Issue Date: Before 1951. Record for Ruth Doty.

[1544] Ancestry.com, Social Security Death Index (Provo, UT, USA, The Generations Network, Inc., 2008), www.ancestry.com, Number: 464-22-8497; Issue State: Texas; Issue Date: Before 1951. Record for Ruth Doty.

[1545] Ancestry.com, Web: Kansas, Find A Grave Index, 1854-2012 (Provo, UT, USA, Ancestry.com Operations, Inc., 2012), Ancestry.com, http://www.Ancestry.com, Record for Charles E Doty.

[1546] Ancestry.com, Texas Birth Index, 1903-1997 (Provo, UT, USA, Ancestry.com Operations Inc, 2005), www.ancestry.com, Record for Charlene Marie Doty.

[1547] Ancestry.com, U.S., Find A Grave Index, 1700s-Current (Provo, UT, USA, Ancestry.com Operations, Inc., 2012), Ancestry.com, http://www.Ancestry.com, Record for Charlene M Doty.

[1548] Ancestry.com, U.S., Find A Grave Index, 1700s-Current (Provo, UT, USA, Ancestry.com Operations, Inc., 2012), Ancestry.com, http://www.Ancestry.com, Record for Charlene M Doty.

[1549] Ancestry.com, Texas Birth Index, 1903-1997 (Provo, UT, USA, Ancestry.com Operations Inc, 2005), www.ancestry.com, Record for Mary Joyce Doty.

[1550] Ancestry.com, U.S., Social Security Applications and Claims Index, 1936-2007 (Provo, UT, USA, Ancestry.com Operations, Inc., 2015), Ancestry.com, http://www.Ancestry.com, Record for Mary Joyce Doty.

[1551] Ancestry.com, Oklahoma, County Marriages, 1890-1995 (Lehi, UT, USA, Ancestry.com Operations, Inc., 2016), Ancestry.com, http://www.Ancestry.com, Record for Mary Joyce Doty.

[1552] Ancestry.com, U.S., Social Security Applications and Claims Index, 1936-2007 (Provo, UT, USA, Ancestry.com Operations, Inc., 2015), Ancestry.com, http://www.Ancestry.com, Record for John Sidney Houston.

[1553] Ancestry.com, U.S., Social Security Applications and Claims Index, 1936-2007 (Provo, UT, USA, Ancestry.com Operations, Inc., 2015), Ancestry.com, http://www.Ancestry.com, Record for John Sidney Houston.

130. Roger Louis Harnden[6] (Edward Eugene Harnden[5], Sarah Amaria Leigh[4], William Safford Leigh[3], William Todd Leigh[2], Nathan S. Leigh[1]) was born on 13 Mar 1928[1554] and died on 04 Jul 2006 in Houston, Texas[1555]. He married Patricia Donna Schloffman, the daughter of John R. Schloffman and Carrie Maddox, on 29 Dec 1950 in Muskingum, Ohio[1556]. She was born on 04 Sep 1929[1557] and died on 15 Nov 2010 in Katy, Texas[1558].

Published in The Oklahoman on 7/10/2006
Roger Harnden, 78, passed away peacefully on July 4, 2006. He was born March 13, 1928 in Stillwater, Oklahoma. He lived in Stillwater and graduated from Oklahoma A and M College in May of 1951 with a Bachelor of Science Degree. Survivors include Pat, his wife, two daughters, Penny Prestwick of Snohomish, Washington, and Paula Evans of Katy, Texas; and four grandchildren, Earl and Eric Hartline, and Kristin and Joe Evans and his wife Crystal. Roger Louis and Patricia Donna 'Pat' (Schloffman) Harnden were married for 56 years. They lived in Oklahoma City, Tulsa, Tripoli, Libya, Springville, Alabama, Bellevue, Washington, Fort Worth Texas, and Houston, Texas. He worked for various industries during his life including oil, and aviation. He was a CPIM, and had been a speaker at their conventions. Memorial services will be held on July 15 at 11:00 AM at Southern Hills United Methodist Church. Interment will be under the direction of Memorial Oaks Funeral Home in Houston, Texas. Memorials may be made to Southern Hills United Methodist Church, 8200 South Pennsylvania, Oklahoma City, Oklahoma 73159.

Roger Louis Harnden and Patricia Donna Schloffman had two children who may still be living.

131. Lloyd Wayne Harnden[6] (Edward Eugene Harnden[5], Sarah Amaria Leigh[4], William Safford Leigh[3], William Todd Leigh[2], Nathan S. Leigh[1]) was born on 19 Jun 1932 in Stillwater, Oklahoma[1559] and died on 01 Feb 2005 in Edmond, Oklahoma[1560]. He married Jane Ellen Amstutz, the daughter of Dillman R. Amstutz and Esther Moore, on 02 Jun 1956 in First Christian Church, Geary, Oklahoma[1561]. She was born on 07 June 1934 in

[1554] Ancestry.com, Social Security Death Index (Provo, UT, USA, The Generations Network, Inc., 2008), www.ancestry.com, Issue State: Oklahoma; Issue Date: Before 1951. Record for Roger Louis Harnden
[1555] Ancestry.com, Social Security Death Index (Provo, UT, USA, The Generations Network, Inc., 2008), www.ancestry.com, Issue State: Oklahoma; Issue Date: Before 1951. Record for Roger Louis Harnden
[1556] Ancestry.com, Ohio, County Marriages, 1774-1993 (Lehi, UT, USA, Ancestry.com Operations, Inc., 2016), Ancestry.com, http://www.Ancestry.com, Record for Patricia Donna Schloffman.
[1557] Ancestry.com, Social Security Death Index (Provo, UT, USA, The Generations Network, Inc., 2008), www.ancestry.com, Issue State: Ohio; Issue Date: Before 1951. Record for Patricia D. Harnden
[1558] Ancestry.com, Social Security Death Index (Provo, UT, USA, The Generations Network, Inc., 2008), www.ancestry.com, Issue State: Ohio; Issue Date: Before 1951. Record for Patricia D. Harnden.
[1559] Ancestry.com, Social Security Death Index (Provo, UT, USA, The Generations Network, Inc., 2008), www.ancestry.com, Issue State: Oklahoma; Issue Date: Before 1951. Record for Lloyd W. Harnden.
[1560] Ancestry.com, Social Security Death Index (Provo, UT, USA, The Generations Network, Inc., 2008), www.ancestry.com, Issue State: Oklahoma; Issue Date: Before 1951. Record for Lloyd W. Harnden.
[1561] Obituary of Lloyd Wayne Harnden, Edmond, Oklahoma newspaper.

Geary, Oklahoma[1562] and died on 23 May 2001 in Edmond, Oklahoma[1563] 1138. Lloyd Wayne Harnden and his wife were buried in Oklahoma[1564].

Lloyd Wayne Harnden "Pa-pa"
June 19, 1932 - February 1, 2005
Born in Stillwater, Oklahoma, the youngest of 3 sons of Leona Mae Josephine (Craig) and Edward Eugene Harnden, D.V.M. Served in the U.S. Navy aboard the destroyer U.S.S. Mullany DD-528, from Feb. 1952 - Dec. 1953, on which Seaman Harnden was a Radar man 3rd/Class. Graduated from Oklahoma A & M College (now Oklahoma State University), where his father was a professor & Head Emeritus of Veterinary Bacteriology, with a Bachelor of Electrical Engineering in 1957. At A & M he met his future wife, Jane , of Geary, Oklahoma, at the campus Disciples of Christ Center. They married at First Christian Church, Geary, Oklahoma, on June 2, 1956. Lloyd worked at Southwestern Bell Telephone Co./ AT&T for his entire career. During that time, he earned a Master of Business Administration from Oklahoma City University in the late 1960's. While most of his career was spent in Oklahoma, it eventually took him to Bell corporate headquarters in St. Louis, Missouri in 1969. Lloyd and Jane's Oklahoma roots, however, called them back to Oklahoma for good when, in 1972, they returned to Edmond. He retired from AT&T in March 1989, after 32 years of service. Lloyd's avocation was always to serve the local Christian Church (Disciples of Christ) wherever he lived. Among his many roles were Elder, church choir tenor, and sound technician. Perhaps his most crucial role was as helpmate to his wife, Jane, enabling her to serve church women's, children's, and youth groups for 45 years. They led the "New Creation", an Edmond, Oklahoma interdenominational youth choir, from 1974-1980 on local, national, and international choir trips. The choir sang at the World Convention of Christian Churches (DOC) in Mexico City (1974) and in Hawaii (1980). In recognition and gratitude for the Harnden's many years of service, Southern Hills Christian Church dedicated the Harnden Memorial Chapel in 2002. Lloyd was preceded in death by his wife (5/23/01), his parents, and his oldest brother, Gerald Eugene. Survived by his children and their families: Dianne Ellen (Eric Alan Overby), Jason Eric and Jennifer Dianne Overby of Utah; Laurie Lynn (Anthony Michael Matthews), Nicholas Craig and Samuel Bennett Matthews of Texas; David Wayne (Sidney Jean Custar) Harnden of Oklahoma; Robert Ray (Virginia Ann Dean), Sarah Virginia and Emily Bohuan Harnden of California. Survived also by his brother, Roger Louis (Patricia "Pat" Donna Schloffman) Harnden; 3 nieces and 1 nephew. The family thanks the Southern Hills Christian Church community for their loving care of Lloyd; for always being a

---

[1562] Ancestry.com, U.S., Social Security Applications and Claims Index, 1936-2007 (Provo, UT, USA, Ancestry.com Operations, Inc., 2015), Ancestry.com, http://www.Ancestry.com, Record for Jane Ellen Amstutz

[1563] Ancestry.com, U.S., Social Security Applications and Claims Index, 1936-2007 (Provo, UT, USA, Ancestry.com Operations, Inc., 2015), Ancestry.com, http://www.Ancestry.com, Record for Jane Ellen Amstutz

[1564] National Cemetery Administration, U.S. Veterans Gravesites, ca.1775-2006 (Provo, UT, USA, The Generations Network, Inc., 2006), www.ancestry.com, Record for Lloyd W Harnden.

welcoming place where he could be of service and know that he was loved. We know that you grieve with us, but also rejoice with us because, through the Grace of God, Lloyd is in the eternal heavenly embrace of our Lord, Jesus Christ, where He is saying "well done, good and faithful servant" - and where Jane is surely waiting for Lloyd to help her with yet another new project! Funeral services will be on Saturday, February 19, 2005 at Southern Hills Christian Church, 3207 South Boulevard, Edmond, Oklahoma, at 3:00 p.m. Lloyd's ashes will be laid to rest during a private ceremony at Plum Canyon, the family's heritage farm, held by Jane's family since 1909

Lloyd Wayne Harnden and Jane Ellen Amstutz had four children who may still be living.

132. May Sarah Peirson[6] (Elsie Ruth Harnden[5], Sarah Amaria Leigh[4], William Safford Leigh[3], William Todd Leigh[2], Nathan S. Leigh[1]) was born on 16 May 1917 in Gilead Thaye, Nebraska[1565] and died on 19 Feb 2005[1566]. She married James Reed, the son of James Reed and Nancy Ditson, 30 Nov 1940[1567]. He was born on 10 Sep 1920 in Broken Bow, Nebraska[1568] and died on 06 Jun 2012 in Jennie Melham Medical Center, Broken Bow, Nebraska[1569].   James Reed and May Sarah Peirson had one child who may still be living.

James E. Reed age 91 of Broken Bow died June 6, 2012 at Jennie Melham Medical Center in Broken Bow. Funeral services will be held Monday June 11, 2012 at 2:00 p.m. at Govier Brothers Mortuary with Floyd Ditson officiating. Interment will be in the Custer Center Cemetery. Mr. Reed was born September 10, 1920 at Broken Bow to James and Nancy (Ditson) Reed. He grew up in Custer County and moved to Dunning in May of 1940. He married May Peirson November 30, 1940. They lived in the Dunning area until 1954 when they moved twenty five miles north of Thedford. They later lived west of Wood Lake before moving back to Dunning. They later moved to Maxwell in 1957, the Pressey Park area in 1961, Cumro 1963 until 1966, lived at Dunning from 1966 until 1981 when they moved to Broken Bow. He was a member of the Custer Campers, Golden Wheels, National Hikers and Campers Association, card club, he enjoyed playing pitch and loved to play pool. Survivors include one daughter Nelda (Willis) Russell of Broken Bow, four grandchildren, Gena (Thomas) Sprague of Loveland, CO. Brandon Russell of Broken Bow, Sarah Russell of Broken Bow and James (Kelley) Russell of Thorton, CO. ,two great grandchildren Annamarie May Russell and Danica Diane Russell both of Thorton, CO. , step grandchildren Joseph and Isaiah Sprague of Loveland, CO. James also claims Peggy (Glen) Birney and children, Micky

---

[1565] Ancestry.com. *U.S., Social Security Applications and Claims Index, 1936-2007* [database on-line]. Provo, UT, USA: Ancestry.com Operations, Inc., 2015.

[1566] Ancestry.com. *U.S., Social Security Applications and Claims Index, 1936-2007* [database on-line]. Provo, UT, USA: Ancestry.com Operations, Inc., 2015.

[1567] Obituary on this page for James E. Reed, Kearney, Nebraska, newspaper.

[1568] Obituary on this page for James E. Reed, Kearney, Nebraska, newspaper.

[1569] Obituary on this page for James E. Reed, Kearney, Nebraska, newspaper.

(Tony) and children and Jeffrey McDermott and children. One sister Edna Schear of Gordon, NE and one brother Harlan Reed of Reedsburg, WI., many cousins, nephews and nieces.

133. Veralyne Nalhama Harnden[6] (Lemuel Meacham Harnden[5], Sarah Amaria Leigh[4], William Safford Leigh[3], William Todd Leigh[2], Nathan S. Leigh[1]) was born on 10 Jun 1921 in Oklahoma[1570] and died on 01 Jan 2011 in Cheyenne, Wyoming[1571]. She married Russell Eugene Sutherland[1572]. He was born on 06 Jun 1919 in Leola, South Dakota[1573] . and died on 10 Nov 1971 in Cheyenne, Wyoming[1574]. Veralyne Nalhama Harnden and her husband were buried in Torrington, Wyoming[1575].

Veralyne "Lyne" Sutherland, 89, of Cheyenne died Jan. 1 in Cheyenne. She was born June 10, 1921, in Yale, Okla., the daughter of Lemuel and Leila (Spencer) Harnden. She grew up in Oklahoma, and graduated high school in Odessa, Texas. She attended Nursing School in San Angelo, Texas, and served in the U.S. Army Nurse Corps during World War II. She married Russell Sutherland at Fort Hood Texas on Aug. 10, 1946. They lived in Torrington from 1956 until 1967, while she worked as a nurse at the Torrington Hospital. The couple moved to Cheyenne in 1967, and she worked as a nurse at DePaul Hospital and also Pershing Memorial Hospital. She was a 50-year member of Order of Eastern Star and a 50-year member of the American Legion Auxiliary. She is survived by her son, Rusty Sutherland of Torrington; daughter, Kathleen Landers of Cheyenne; seven grandchildren; six great-grandchildren; a step-brother, Donald Powell; two half brothers, J.D. and Jim Harnden: and a half sister, Elsie Stone. In addition to her parents and her husband, she was preceded in death by her daughter, Karen Johnson. Visitation hours will be 3-6 p.m. today at the funeral home. Funeral services will be 10 a.m. Thursday at Colyer Funeral Home Chapel with Guy Landers officiating. Burial will follow at Valley View Cemetery. Friends may contribute to the Order of Eastern Star Torrington Chapter No. 22. Funeral arrangements are under direction of the Colyer Funeral Home and friends are invited to send condolences to the family at www.colyerfuneralhome.com.

[1570] Ancestry.com, U.S., Find A Grave Index, 1700s-Current (Provo, UT, USA, Ancestry.com Operations, Inc., 2012), Ancestry.com, http://www.Ancestry.com, Record for Veralyne Sutherland.

[1571] Ancestry.com, U.S., Find A Grave Index, 1700s-Current (Provo, UT, USA, Ancestry.com Operations, Inc., 2012), Ancestry.com, http://www.Ancestry.com, Record for Veralyne Sutherland.

[1572] Ancestry.com, U.S., Find A Grave Index, 1700s-Current (Provo, UT, USA, Ancestry.com Operations, Inc., 2012), Ancestry.com, http://www.Ancestry.com, Record for Veralyne Sutherland.

[1573] Ancestry.com, U.S., Find A Grave Index, 1700s-Current (Provo, UT, USA, Ancestry.com Operations, Inc., 2012), Ancestry.com, http://www.Ancestry.com, Record for Veralyne Sutherland.

[1574] Ancestry.com, U.S., Find A Grave Index, 1700s-Current (Provo, UT, USA, Ancestry.com Operations, Inc., 2012), Ancestry.com, http://www.Ancestry.com, Record for Veralyne Sutherland.

[1575] Ancestry.com, U.S., Find A Grave Index, 1700s-Current (Provo, UT, USA, Ancestry.com Operations, Inc., 2012), Ancestry.com, http://www.Ancestry.com, Record for Veralyne Sutherland.

Russell Eugene Sutherland and Veralyne Nalhama Harnden had the following children:

  i. Karen M. Sutherland was born on 01 Oct 1947[1576] 1146 and died on 11 May 1988[1577]. Karen M. Sutherland was buried in Torrington, Wyoming.

  ii. Living Sutherland

  iii. Living Sutherland

134. Florus Frederick Henrick[6] (Adell Grace Harnden[5], Sarah Amaria Leigh[4], William Safford Leigh[3], William Todd Leigh[2], Nathan S. Leigh[1]) was born on 22 Jun 1925 in Stillwater, Oklahoma[1578] and died on 31 Dec 2005 in Greenbrier, Tennessee[1579]. He married Lucy Christine Sellers, the daughter of John Sellers and Rosey E Chaplin, on 09 Jun 1946 in Charleston, Missouri[1580]. She was born on 23 Oct 1924 in Reynolds, Missouri[1581] and died on 07 May 2003 in Greenbrier, Tennessee[1582]. Florus Frederick Henrick and Lucy Christine Sellers had six children who may still be living.

135. Francis Otto Henrick[6] (Adell Grace Harnden[5], Sarah Amaria Leigh[4], William Safford Leigh[3], William Todd Leigh[2], Nathan S. Leigh[1]) was born on 04 Jul 1928 in Stillwater, Oklahoma[1583] and died on 14 Jun 2007 in Columbia, South Carolina[1584]. He married Mitsey in Apr 1956[1585]. She was born in Japan[1586]. Francis Otto Henrick and Mitsey had one child who may still be living.

136. Allen Elwood Henrick[6] (Adell Grace Harnden[5], Sarah Amaria Leigh[4], William Safford Leigh[3], William Todd Leigh[2], Nathan S. Leigh[1]) was born on 24 Jun 1932 in Stillwater, Oklahoma[1587] and died on 29 Aug 1982 in St. Louis, Missouri[1588]. He married

---

[1576] Ancestry.com, U.S., Find A Grave Index, 1700s-Current (Provo, UT, USA, Ancestry.com Operations, Inc., 2012).

[1577] Ancestry.com, U.S., Find A Grave Index, 1700s-Current (Provo, UT, USA, Ancestry.com Operations, Inc., 2012).

[1578] Ancestry.com, Social Security Death Index (Provo, UT, USA, The Generations Network, Inc., 2008), www.ancestry.com, Issue State: Missouri; Issue Date: Before 1951. Record for Florus F. Henrick.

[1579] Ancestry.com, Social Security Death Index (Provo, UT, USA, The Generations Network, Inc., 2008), www.ancestry.com, Issue State: Missouri; Issue Date: Before 1951. Record for Florus F. Henrick.

[1580] Ancestry.com, Missouri, Marriage Records, 1805-2002 (Provo, UT, USA, Ancestry.com Operations, Inc., 2007), Ancestry.com, http://www.Ancestry.com, Record for Lecy E Sellers.

[1581] Ancestry.com, U.S., Social Security Applications and Claims Index, 1936-2007 (Provo, UT, USA, Ancestry.com Operations, Inc., 2015), Ancestry.com, http://www.Ancestry.com, Record for Lecy Elizabeth Sellers.

[1582] Ancestry.com, U.S., Social Security Applications and Claims Index, 1936-2007 (Provo, UT, USA, Ancestry.com Operations, Inc., 2015), Ancestry.com, http://www.Ancestry.com, Record for Lecy Elizabeth Sellers.

[1583] Ancestry.com. *U.S., Social Security Death Index, 1935-2014* [database on-line]. Provo, UT, USA: Ancestry.com Operations Inc, 2014.

[1584] Ancestry.com. *U.S., Social Security Death Index, 1935-2014* [database on-line]. Provo, UT, USA: Ancestry.com Operations Inc, 2014.

[1585] Genealogy compiled by Rev. Laverne E. Leigh, 414 Washington Ave. East, Albia, Iowa 52531 in the Spring of 1975.

[1586] Genealogy compiled by Rev. Laverne E. Leigh, 414 Washington Ave. East, Albia, Iowa 52531 in 1975.

[1587] National Cemetery Administration, U.S. Veterans Gravesites, ca.1775-2006 (Provo, UT, USA, The Generations Network, Inc., 2006), www.ancestry.com, Record for Allen E Henrick.

[1588] National Cemetery Administration, U.S. Veterans Gravesites, ca.1775-2006 (Provo, UT, USA, The Generations Network, Inc., 2006), www.ancestry.com, Record for Allen E Henrick.

three times. Allen Elwood Henrick was buried on 01 Sep 1982 in Missouri[1589].   Allen Elwood Henrick had three children who may still be living.

137. Bobbie Eugene Henrick[6] (Adell Grace Harnden[5], Sarah Amaria Leigh[4], William Safford Leigh[3], William Todd Leigh[2], Nathan S. Leigh[1]) was born on 07 Aug 1938[1590] in Arkansas and died in Lexington, Kentucky on 02 Jul 2015[1591]. He married Lynda Bright on 05 Jan 1959 in Taylor, Texas[1592]. Bobbie Eugene Henrick and Lynda Bright had two children who may still be living.

138. David Leon Henrick[6] (Adell Grace Harnden[5], Sarah Amaria Leigh[4], William Safford Leigh[3], William Todd Leigh[2], Nathan S. Leigh[1]) was born on 05 Dec 1946 in Cadiz, Philippines[1593] and died on 10 Dec 2009 in Vanderbilt University Medical Center, Nashville, Tennessee[1594]. He married Loretta Bell in 1966[1595]. David Leon Henrick and Loretta Bell had three children who may still be living.

David Leon Henrick, 63, of Bowling Green, died at 6:30 p.m. Dec. 10, 2009, at Vanderbilt University Medical Center in Nashville. The Bertrand, Mo., native was born Dec. 5, 1946. He was retired from the paint repair department at the General Motors Bowling Green Assembly Plant. He was a Baptist, an avid outdoorsman and loved to camp and fish. He was a member of the UAW Local 2164. He and his wife were campground hosts at the Wrangler Campground in Cadiz. He was a son of the late Floyd Henrick and Adell Grace Harnden Henrick. He was preceded in death by several brothers and sisters. Funeral is at 1 p.m. Monday at J.C. Kirby & Son Funeral Home, Broadway Avenue chapel, with burial in Fairview Cemetery No. 2. Visitation is from 3 p.m. to 8 p.m. Sunday at the funeral home. Survivors include his wife of 44 years, Loretta Henrick; three daughters, Edith Henrick, of Bowling Green, Brenda Wynn, of Madison, Tenn., and Amanda Haynes and her husband, Chad, of Auburn; six grandchildren, Brandon Wynn, Robert Henrick, Christopher Wynn, Arik Haynes, Wesley Haynes and

---

[1589] Ancestry.com, U.S., Find A Grave Index, 1700s-Current (Provo, UT, USA, Ancestry.com Operations, Inc., 2012), Ancestry.com, http://www.Ancestry.com, Record for Allen E Henrick.

[1590] Ancestry.com, U.S. Cemetery and Funeral Home Collection (Provo, UT, USA, Ancestry.com Operations Inc, 2011), www.ancestry.com, Publication Place: Lexington, Kentucky, USA; Web edition: Record for Bobbie Eugene Henrick.

[1591] Ancestry.com, U.S. Cemetery and Funeral Home Collection (Provo, UT, USA, Ancestry.com Operations Inc, 2011), www.ancestry.com, Publication Place: Lexington, Kentucky, USA; Web edition: Record for Bobbie Eugene Henrick.

[1592] Ancestry.com. *Texas, Select County Marriage Records, 1837-2015* [database on-line]. Provo, UT, USA: Ancestry.com Operations, Inc., 2014.

[1593] Newspaper: Bowling Green Daily News; Publication Date: 12/ 12/ 2009; Publication Place: Bowling Green, Kentucky, USA; Web edition: http://bgdailynews.com/articles/2009/12/12/obituaries/obit2.txt.

[1594] Newspaper: Bowling Green Daily News; Publication Date: 12/ 12/ 2009; Publication Place: Bowling Green, Kentucky, USA; Web edition: http://bgdailynews.com/articles/2009/12/12/obituaries/obit2.txt.

[1595] Newspaper: Bowling Green Daily News; Publication Date: 12/ 12/ 2009; Publication Place: Bowling Green, Kentucky, USA; Web edition: http://bgdailynews.com/articles/2009/12/12/obituaries/obit2.txt.

Rebecca Haynes; a sister, Jeannie Fontaine, of LaVergne, Tenn.; two brothers, Bob Henrick, of Lexington, and Everette Henrick, of Cahokia, Ill.; and several nieces, nephews, great-nieces and great-nephews.

139.   Ellen Genevieve Moore[6] (Guy RowleyMoore[5], Phebe Adella Leigh[4], Rueben Harrington Leigh[3], William Todd Leigh[2], Nathan S. Leigh[1]) was born on 21 Nov 1922 in Oklahoma City, Oklahoma[1596] and died on 30 Jul 2009 in Medford, Oregon[1597]. She married Robert Samuel Ashenberner, the son of John Ashenberner and Catherine Conley, on 11 Apr 1944 in Portland, Oregon[1598]. He was born on 17 Feb 1925 in Portland, Oregon[1599] and died on 01 Nov 2012 in Jackson County, Oregon[1600]. Ellen Genevieve Moore and her husband were buried in Eagle Point National Cemetery, Eagle Point, Oregon[1601]. Robert Samuel Ashenberner and Ellen Genevieve Moore had five children who may still be living.

Photo of Ellen Genevieve Moore and Robert Samuel Ashenberner found with her obituary.

Published in the Mail Tribune on 8/4/2009
Genevieve M. Ashenberner, 86, of Medford, Ore., passed away Thursday, July 30, 2009 in Medford. Genevieve was born Nov. 21, 1922 in Oklahoma City, Okla. to Guy R. and Edith Moore. She attended SOU and received a B.A. degree in art. She married Robert S. Ashenberner on April 11, 1944 in Portland, Ore. She was a homemaker. She is survived by her husband, Robert; daughter Robbin Botting and her husband, Jim; son, Sam and his wife, Dolores, son, Alan and his wife, Susan, son, David and his wife, Linda; and daughter, Catherine. A viewing will be held at Hillcrest Memorial Park, Medford, Tuesday, Aug. 4th at 3-7:00 p.m. graveside service will be held Wednesday, Aug. 5, 2009 at 11:00 a.m. at Eagle Point National Cemetery. In lieu of flowers the family requests donations be made to Red Cross. Arrangements by Hillcrest Memorial Park and Mortuary, Medford, Ore. 773-6162. www.hillcrestmortuary.com

---

[1596] Ancestry.com, U.S., Find A Grave Index, 1700s-Current (Provo, UT, USA, Ancestry.com Operations, Inc., 2012), Ancestry.com, http://www.Ancestry.com, Record for Genevieve M Ashenberner.

[1597] Ancestry.com, U.S., Find A Grave Index, 1700s-Current (Provo, UT, USA, Ancestry.com Operations, Inc., 2012), Ancestry.com, http://www.Ancestry.com, Record for Genevieve M Ashenberner.

[1598] Genealogy compiled by Rev. Laverne E. Leigh, 414 Washington Ave. East, Albia, Iowa 52531 in the Spring of 1975.

[1599] Ancestry.com, U.S., Find A Grave Index, 1700s-Current (Provo, UT, USA, Ancestry.com Operations, Inc., 2012), Ancestry.com, http://www.Ancestry.com, Record for Genevieve M Ashenberner.

[1600] Ancestry.com, U.S., Find A Grave Index, 1700s-Current (Provo, UT, USA, Ancestry.com Operations, Inc., 2012), Ancestry.com, http://www.Ancestry.com, Record for Genevieve M Ashenberner.

[1601] Ancestry.com, U.S., Find A Grave Index, 1700s-Current (Provo, UT, USA, Ancestry.com Operations, Inc., 2012), Ancestry.com, http://www.Ancestry.com, Record for Genevieve M Ashenberner.

Published in The Oregonian on Nov. 11, 2012

Ashenberner, Robert S. 87 Feb. 17, 1925 Nov. 01, 2012 Robert S. Ashenberner was born on Feb.17, 1925 in Portland, the son of John and Catherine Ashenberner. He married Genevieve Ashenberner on April 8, 1943 and they enjoyed 65 years together until Genevieve's death in 2009. Robert served with distinction in the United States military in World War II and fought in the Battle of the Bulge. He was awarded many medals: the European African Middle Eastern Service Medal, the Good Conduct Medal, the American Theater Service Medal, the Bronze Service Arrowhead, the Victory Medal, the Parachutist's Badge and the Purple Heart. Robert founded Ashenberner Moulding Company in 1960. The company name was subsequently changed to Ashenberner Lumber and then to Southern Oregon Lumber. In 2006, Robert retired and liquidated the company. Robert was a skilled woodworker and expert gardener; he enjoyed both hobbies during his retirement. Robert and Genevieve were long-standing members of Sacred Heart Catholic Church in Medford. Robert is survived by his children, Robbin Botting (Jim) of Los Angeles, Samuel Ashenberner (Dolores) of Beaverton, Alan Ashenberner (Susan) of Portland, David Ashenberner (Linda) of Medford, Catherine Ashenberner of San Diego, Calif. Robert is also survived by 10 grandchildren and eight great-grandchildren. Robert will be remembered as a successful businessman and loving husband, father and grandfather. He was a fan of John Wayne and these words of the actor best describe the reasons for Robert's business success: "Talk low, talk slow and don't say too much." Viewing will be at the Hillcrest Mortuary, 2201 N. Phoenix Rd., Medford. Hours will be from 11 a.m. to 3 p.m., Sunday, Nov. 11, 2012. Interment will be at the Eagle Point National Cemetery, 2763 Riley Rd, Eagle Point at 2 p.m. Tuesday. Memorial contributions may be made to Sacred Heart Catholic Church Medford.

140.   Phoebe Anne Moore[6] (Guy Rowley Moore[5], Phebe Adella Leigh[4], Rueben Harrington Leigh[3], William Todd Leigh[2], Nathan S. Leigh[1]) was born on 25 Mar 1934 in Pocatello, Idaho[1602] and died on 01 Nov 2007 in Visalia, California[1603]. She married William Simpson Grant Bailey, the son of Alexander Grant and Isabel Simpson, on 29 Aug 1954 in Tulare, California[1604]. He was born on 27 Jul 1932 in Scotland[1605] and died on 17 Apr 1995 in Visalia, California[1606]. Phoebe Anne Moore and her husband were buried in Visalia, California[1607]. William was educated in Edinburgh, Scotland.

[1602] Ancestry.com, U.S., Find A Grave Index, 1700s-Current (Provo, UT, USA, Ancestry.com Operations, Inc., 2012), Ancestry.com, http://www.Ancestry.com, Record for Phoebe Anne Bailey.

[1603] Ancestry.com, U.S., Find A Grave Index, 1700s-Current (Provo, UT, USA, Ancestry.com Operations, Inc., 2012), Ancestry.com, http://www.Ancestry.com, Record for Phoebe Anne Bailey.

[1604] Ancestry.com, California, Marriage Index, 1949-1959 (Provo, UT, USA, Ancestry.com Operations, Inc., 2013), Ancestry.com, http://www.Ancestry.com, Record for Phoebe A Moore.

[1605] Ancestry.com, U.S., Find A Grave Index, 1700s-Current (Provo, UT, USA, Ancestry.com Operations, Inc., 2012), Ancestry.com, http://www.Ancestry.com, Record for Phoebe Anne Bailey.

[1606] Ancestry.com, California Death Index, 1940-1997 (Provo, UT, USA, The Generations Network, Inc., 2000), www.ancestry.com, Date: 1995-04-17. Record for William Grant simpson Bailey.

[1607] Ancestry.com, U.S., Find A Grave Index, 1700s-Current (Provo, UT, USA, Ancestry.com Operations, Inc., 2012), Ancestry.com, http://www.Ancestry.com, Record for Phoebe Anne Bailey.

William Simpson Grant Bailey and Phoebe Anne Moore had four children who may still be living.

141. Stanley Leigh Moore, Jr.[6] (Stanley Leigh Moore[5], Phebe Adella Leigh[4], Rueben Harrington Leigh[3], William Todd Leigh[2], Nathan S. Leigh[1]) was born on 28 Jun 1920 in Jennings, Oklahoma[1608] and died on 08 Jan 2004 in Lubbock, Texas[1609]. He married Carol Enid Barquero, the daughter of Nereo Barquero and Victoria Acunna, on 05 Aug 1948 in Changuinola, Bocas del Toro, Panama[1610]. She was born on 03 Dec 1911 in Alejuela, Costa Rica[1611].

Stanley was in the submarine service during World War II and was stationed in the Canal Zone. After the war, he returned to Norman, Oklahoma where he earned his BA and MA degrees from the University of Oklahoma in Civil Engineering. Stanley went to work for Dowell Oil Service in Tulsa after graduation. Moves for the company subsequently took them to Easton, Pennsylvania, to Kansas City, Kansas and then to Lubbock, Texas where they lived in 1975. Stanley Leigh II Moore and Carol Enid Barquero had two children who may still be living.

Obituary - *Stanley Leigh Moore II, born June 28, 1920, died Jan. 7, 2004. He was in the submarine service during WWII and was stationed in the Canal Zone. While serving in the Canal Zone, he married Clara Enid Barquero in Changuinola, Republic of Panama. After the war, they returned to Norman, Okla., where he earned his B.A. and M.A. in engineering from the University of Oklahoma.*

142. Milton Lawrence Jackson[6] (Myrtle Elmina Moore[5], Phebe Adella Leigh[4], Rueben Harrington Leigh[3], William Todd Leigh[2], Nathan S. Leigh[1]) was born on 26 Mar 1922 in Oklahoma[1612] and died on 22 Dec 2015 in Fort Bend County, Texas[1613]. He married Renee Elizabeth Johnson on 04 Feb 1955 in El Dorado, Arkansas[1614]. Milton Lawrence Jackson and Renee Elizabeth Johnson had five children who may still be living.

[1608] Ancestry.com. *U.S., World War I Draft Registration Cards, 1917-1918* [database on-line]. Provo, UT, USA: Ancestry.com Operations Inc, 2005.

[1609] Ancestry.com. *U.S., Sons of the American Revolution Membership Applications, 1889-1970* [database on-line]. Provo, UT, USA: Ancestry.com Operations, Inc., 2011.

[1610] Ancestry.com. *U.S., Sons of the American Revolution Membership Applications, 1889-1970* [database on-line]. Provo, UT, USA: Ancestry.com Operations, Inc., 2011.

[1611] Genealogy compiled by Rev. Laverne E. Leigh, 414 Washington Ave. East, Albia, Iowa 52531 in the Spring of 1975.

[1612] Ancestry.com, U.S., Find A Grave Index, 1700s-Current (Provo, UT, USA, Ancestry.com Operations, Inc., 2012), Ancestry.com, http://www.Ancestry.com, Record for Milton Lawrence Jackson

[1613] Ancestry.com, U.S., Find A Grave Index, 1700s-Current (Provo, UT, USA, Ancestry.com Operations, Inc., 2012), Ancestry.com, http://www.Ancestry.com, Record for Milton Lawrence Jackson

[1614] Obituary of Milton Lawrence Jackson as listed on this page.

Milton Lawrence Jackson 1922-2015
Having lived for 93 years, Milton Lawrence Jackson passed away after a brief illness in the early hours of December 22, 2015. Milton Lawrence Jackson was born to Elmina and Fred Jackson in Jennings, Oklahoma on March 26, 1922. The family moved to Corsicana, Texas in 1929 where they owned and operated a grocery store. Milton's father died when he was just 13 years old, leaving his mother to bravely carry on in caring for him, his fraternal twin brother, Maurice, and his sister, Patricia. Before his eighteenth year, Milton began his military service with the Texas National Guard, which he joined to help the family make ends meet. Milton continued his military service during World War II. His brother, Maurice, died as Milton was shipping out from New York to Ireland where he and thousands of other young men made preparations to engage and defeat the Nazis. Having landed in France on D-Day plus 33, he and his fellow soldiers engaged the enemy and fought their way across Europe. Milton was awarded the Bronze Star and the French Legion of Honor for his service. Milton was honorably discharged from the U.S. Army with the rank of Sergeant First Class. He then returned to his home state where he attended the University of Texas at Austin. Following graduation with a degree in Electrical Engineering, he began his career with the Federal Aviation Administration. However, he spent the vast majority of his career with Fluor Corporation, where he designed processing equipment. Milton specialized in analytical detectors and held several patents. His work remained in such demand that he worked through three retirements until the age of 86. Thereafter, he continued to work as the head of Analytical Detectors, Inc. until selling it in 2014 at the age of 92. Milton chronicled his family history and his mind was sharp until the end. He was a patient, loving husband father, and grandfather. He was also a follower of Christ and reassured his children that he knew where he was going before he passed. Milton was a member of the First United Methodist Church Fulshear. Milton married his one and only love, Rene Elizabeth (nee Johnson) Jackson on February 4, 1955. Milton and Rene have four children whom he also loved greatly and was so very proud. Milton is survived by the love of his life of 60 years, Rene; son, James and his wife, Gail; son, William and his wife, Margaret and their son, Bryan; daughter, Joan and her husband Daniel Linebaugh and their children, Sarah and husband, Nick Rivero, Christopher and his wife Emily, Carolyn, and Alexander; and daughter Jane and her husband, James Recer, and their children, Robert, Katherine, and Victoria. Funeral services will be held at 2:00 p.m. on Saturday, December 26, 2015 at the First United Methodist Church, in Fulshear, with Dr. Mark Welshimer officiating.   Condolences may be expressed at www.SchmidtFuneralHome.net.

143.   Patricia Alma Jackson[6] (Myrtle Elmina Moore[5], Phebe Adella Leigh[4], Rueben Harrington Leigh[3], William Todd Leigh[2], Nathan S. Leigh[1]) was born on 17 Mar 1925 in Tonkawa, Oklahoma[1615] and died of cancer on 31 May 1965 in Pasadena, Texas[1616]. She married Charles Donald Hauver, the son of William J. and Letha A. Hauver, on 01 Jan 1944 in Abilene, Texas[1617]. He was born on 23 Feb 1923 in Bloomsburg, Pennsylvania[1618] and died on 26 Nov 2001 in Paris, Texas[1619]. Patricia Alma Jackson was buried in Corsicana, Texas[1620]. Charles enlisted as an Aviation Cadet during WW II on January 7, 1943 in San Antonio, Texas. He had four years of high school and was working as a waiter. Charles was a Lieutenant when he was married. He retired as a Major February 1, 1963.

Charles Donald Hauver and Patricia Alma Jackson had the following children:

i.   Charles Donald Hauver, Jr. was born on 26 Mar 1946 in Navarro, Texas[1621] and died on 22 Sep 1951 in Sewickley, Pennsylvania[1622]. Charles was killed when he lost control of his tricycle and ran into the street where a car hit him.

ii.   Living Hauver

iii.   Kenrick Jackson Hauver was born on 07 Sep 1957 in United States of America[1623] and died on 25 Feb 1975[1624]. Kenrick Jackson Hauver was buried in Corsicana, Texas[1625]. Kenrick committed suicide by hanging himself from a tree house because he had lost his mother by cancer in 1965 and he could not get along with his father.

[1615] Ancestry.com, Texas, Death Certificates, 1903-1982 (Provo, UT, USA, Ancestry.com Operations, Inc., 2013), Ancestry.com, http://www.Ancestry.com, Record for Patricia A Haver.

[1616] Ancestry.com, Texas, Death Certificates, 1903-1982 (Provo, UT, USA, Ancestry.com Operations, Inc., 2013), Ancestry.com, http://www.Ancestry.com, Record for Patricia A Haver.

[1617] Genealogy compiled by Rev. Laverne E. Leigh, 414 Washington Ave. East, Albia, Iowa 52531 in the Spring of 1975.

[1618] National Archives and Records Administration, U.S. World War II Army Enlistment Records, 1938-1946 (Provo, UT, USA, The Generations Network, Inc., 2005), www.ancestry.com, Record for Charles D Hauver.

[1619] Ancestry.com. *U.S., Social Security Death Index, 1935-2014* [database on-line]. Provo, UT, USA: Ancestry.com Operations Inc, 2014.

[1620] Ancestry.com, U.S., Find A Grave Index, 1700s-Current (Provo, UT, USA, Ancestry.com Operations, Inc., 2012),

[1621] Ancestry.com, Pennsylvania, Death Certificates, 1906-1963 (Provo, UT, USA, Ancestry.com Operations, Inc., 2014), Ancestry.com, http://www.Ancestry.com, Pennsylvania Historic and Museum Commission; Pennsylvania, USA; Certificate Number Range: 075001-077550. Record for Charles Donald II Hauver.

[1622] Ancestry.com, Pennsylvania, Death Certificates, 1906-1963 (Provo, UT, USA, Ancestry.com Operations, Inc., 2014), Ancestry.com, http://www.Ancestry.com, Pennsylvania Historic and Museum Commission; Pennsylvania, USA; Certificate Number Range: 075001-077550. Record for Charles Donald II Hauver.

[1623] Ancestry.com, U.S., Find A Grave Index, 1700s-Current (Provo, UT, USA, Ancestry.com Operations, Inc., 2012), Ancestry.com, http://www.Ancestry.com, Record for Kenrick Jackson Hauver.

[1624] Ancestry.com, U.S., Find A Grave Index, 1700s-Current (Provo, UT, USA, Ancestry.com Operations, Inc., 2012), Ancestry.com, http://www.Ancestry.com, Record for Kenrick Jackson Hauver.

[1625] Ancestry.com, U.S., Find A Grave Index, 1700s-Current (Provo, UT, USA, Ancestry.com Operations, Inc., 2012), Ancestry.com, http://www.Ancestry.com, Record for Kenrick Jackson Hauver.

144. Betty Jean Moore[6] (George Asro Moore[5], Phebe Adella Leigh[4], Rueben Harrington Leigh[3], William Todd Leigh[2], Nathan S. Leigh[1]) was born on 08 Jul 1925 in Neosho, Missouri[1626] and died on 15 Mar 2010 in Buhl, Idaho[1627]. She married David Clarence Valder, the son of Clayton Stephenson Valder and Sarah Emily Bassett, on 12 May 1942 in Stillwater, Oklahoma[1628]. He was born on 08 Sep 1924 in Lexington, Nebraska[1629] and died on 29 May 1983 in Moscow, Idaho[1630]. David Clarence Valder and Betty Jean Moore had three children who may still be living.

Betty Jean Valder, 85, of Buhl, Idaho, passed away peacefully Monday, March 15, 2010, at Twin Falls Care Center in Twin Falls, Idaho. Betty was born July 8, 1924, in Neosho, Mo., to Doris and George Moore. Betty grew up exploring the wonders of nature while her parents were in graduate school studying ichthyology at Friday Harbor in Washington state's Puget Sound. Betty lost her mother at the age of 13 to tuberculosis and was then raised by her loving stepmother, Leah Moore. While attending high school in Stillwater, Okla., Betty met the love of her life, David Valder. Betty and Dave were married, May 12, 1942, shortly before Dave was deployed to the South Pacific in World War II. After the war Betty supported Dave as a stenographer in the local hospital while Dave attended medical school in Oklahoma City. After completing school Betty and Dave chose Moscow, Idaho, to settle down and raise their family. Betty was an integral part in their family-run surgical practice. She was the CEO, bookkeeper, receptionist, scheduler and public relations officer, keeping Dave on track. Betty was active within the Moscow Presbyterian Church, Camp Fire Girls, and later the Methodist Church in Buhl where she led Bible study. She enjoyed many summers at the family cabin on Lake Coeur d'Alene. She enjoyed backyard barbecues and volleyball games, along with musical and theatrical extravaganzas put on by her children, neighbor children and grandchildren, and numerous gatherings with dear lifelong friends. Betty played an active part in the raising of her grandchildren. When she lost Dave she became a central part to all her daughters' families, living with each family for some part of the grandchildren's lives. Betty taught each child by reading tirelessly to them every night. She enjoyed working in the yard, raising flowers and raspberries, and taking Sunday drives looking for flora and fauna. Betty also was quite the adventurer, accompanying Dave on canoe trips in

[1626] Ancestry.com, United States Obituary Collection (Provo, UT, USA, The Generations Network, Inc., 2006), www.ancestry.com, Newspaper: Moscow-Pullman Daily News; Publication Date: 03/ 17/ 2010; Publication Place: Moscow, Idaho, USA; Web edition: http://www.dnews.com/story/obituaries/50058/. Record for Betty Jean Valder.
[1627] Ancestry.com, United States Obituary Collection (Provo, UT, USA, The Generations Network, Inc., 2006), www.ancestry.com, Newspaper: Moscow-Pullman Daily News; Publication Date: 03/ 17/ 2010; Publication Place: Moscow, Idaho, USA; Web edition: http://www.dnews.com/story/obituaries/50058/. Record for Betty Jean Valder.
[1628] Ancestry.com, United States Obituary Collection (Provo, UT, USA, The Generations Network, Inc., 2006), www.ancestry.com, Newspaper: Moscow-Pullman Daily News; Publication Date: 03/ 17/ 2010; Publication Place: Moscow, Idaho, USA; Web edition: http://www.dnews.com/story/obituaries/50058/. Record for Betty Jean Valder.
[1629] Ancestry.com, U.S., Department of Veterans Affairs BIRLS Death File, 1850-2010 (Provo, UT, USA, Ancestry.com Operations, Inc., 2011), www.ancestry.com, Record for David Valder.
[1630] Ancestry.com, U.S., Department of Veterans Affairs BIRLS Death File, 1850-2010 (Provo, UT, USA, Ancestry.com Operations, Inc., 2011), www.ancestry.com, Record for David Valder.

Canada, Alaska and down the Snake River in the Tetons. Betty traveled with Dave to Africa and spent several vacations in Hawaii. She also was an accomplished knitter and seamstress, sewing for all three daughters and grandchildren. Betty was an active reader and crossword fiend. Ever gracious, Betty always acknowledged birthdays and special occasions to friends, family and acquaintances. Betty was preceded in death by her parents, husband and one sister. Survivors include daughters Salli Valder of Buhl, Susie (Doug) Jones of Buhl, and Kathy (Quinn) Davidson of Orofino; eight grandchildren; four great-grandchildren; and sisters Marti (Joe) White of Tucson, Arizona, and Patty (Bob) Martin of Fort Davis, Texas. A celebration of Betty's life will be Memorial Day weekend in Buhl. Betty will be cremated and her ashes blended with Dave's. Cremation is under the direction of Serenity Funeral Chapel, Twin Falls.

David enlisted in the Army October 12, 1942 in Stillwater, Oklahoma. He had four years of High School and one year of college. His home at that time was in Payne, Oklahoma. He was in the medical corps during World War II. Betty went with him until he was stationed in Luzon in the Philippines. After the war, David earned his MD at the University of Oklahoma, then did his internship and residency at the University of Michigan Medical Center. After graduation, he joined a clinic in Corvallis, Oregon. Later they moved to Moscow, Idaho where he worked as a surgeon. They were living there in May of 1983 when David died.

145. Doris Elizabeth Leigh[6] (Chester Cecil Leigh[5], Charles Emery Leigh[4], Rueben Harrington Leigh[3], William Todd Leigh[2], Nathan S. Leigh[1]) was born on 28 Sep 1923[1631] in Auburn, Washington and died on 07 Feb 1975[1632] in Salem, Oregon. She married William Albert Jackson, the son of Fred P. Jackson and Mary Sue Duncan, on 29 Jul 1944 in Mt Vernon, Washington[1633]. He was born on 22 Dec 1922 in Burlington Washington [1634] and died on 01 Sep 2008 in Salem, Oregon[1635]. Doris Elizabeth Leigh and her husband were buried in Salem, Oregon[1636]. William Albert Jackson and Doris Elizabeth Leigh had three children who may still be living.

William "Bill" A. Jackson December 22, 1922 - September 1, 2008 SALEM
Bill passed away on Sunday September 1, 2008. He was born in Burlington, Wash. and was raised and educated in Mt. Vernon, Wash. Upon graduation, he enlisted in the Navy.

[1631] Ancestry.com, U.S., Find A Grave Index, 1700s-Current (Provo, UT, USA, Ancestry.com Operations, Inc., 2012), Ancestry.com, http://www.Ancestry.com, Record for Doris Elizabeth Jackson.

[1632] Ancestry.com, U.S., Find A Grave Index, 1700s-Current (Provo, UT, USA, Ancestry.com Operations, Inc., 2012), Ancestry.com, http://www.Ancestry.com, Record for Doris Elizabeth Jackson.

[1633] Ancestry.com. *Washington, Marriage Records, 1854-2013* [database on-line]. Provo, UT, USA: Ancestry.com Operations, Inc., 2012.

[1634] Web: RootsWeb Obituary Index (RootsWeb), www.ancestry.com, Record for William A Jackson.

[1635] Web: RootsWeb Obituary Index (RootsWeb), www.ancestry.com, Record for William A Jackson.

[1636] Ancestry.com, U.S., Find A Grave Index, 1700s-Current (Provo, UT, USA, Ancestry.com Operations, Inc., 2012), Ancestry.com, http://www.Ancestry.com, Record for Doris Elizabeth Jackson.

Bill was honorably discharged in October of 1945. He was married to Doris Leigh in 1944. He then married Virginia Hockett in 1975. He was preceded in death by both his wives; and by a son, Bill Jr. in 1999. Bill then married Charlotte Bingenheimer in 1988. Bill worked as an Evangelistic gospel singer. He toured many places singing in churches and concerts. Survivors include his wife, Charlotte of Salem; sons, Steve (Carol) Jackson of Dallas, John (Nancy) Jackson of Tigard; a daughter, Ruby (Steve) Atchison of Bremerton, Wash.; stepsons, Steve (Dee) Bingenheimer of Albany, and Brad (Tami) Bingenheimer of Salem; 10 grandchildren; and 19 great-grandchildren. A memorial service will be held at 10 a.m. on Friday September 5, 2008 at Calvary Baptist Church, 1230 Liberty St. SE., Salem. In Lieu of flowers, contributions may be made to the Calvary Baptist Church Music Department. Arrangements are in care of Keizer Funeral Chapel.

146. Stanley Donovan Leigh[6] (Cecil Paul Leigh[5], Jay Noel Leigh[4], Rueben Harrington Leigh[3], William Todd Leigh[2], Nathan S. Leigh[1]) was born 21 Jul 1930 in Eugene, Oregon[1637] and died on 11 Nov 2011 in Parma, Idaho[1638]. He married Ella Mae Cox, the daughter of Wilford L. Cox and Clara M. Howell, on 12 Jun 1949 in Emmett, Idaho[1639]. She was born on 04 Aug 1931 in Boise, Idaho[1640] and died on 08 Feb 2005 in Clark, Washington[1641]. He married Coralee Ann Rath on 25 May 1957 in Reno, Nevada[1642]. He married Joanne Palmero McCoy, the daughter of Joseph Palermo and Elam Marie Esmond, on 07 May 1958 in Winnemucca, Nevada. He married Julie Mitchell Hammond on 22 Jul 1961 in Winnemucca, Nevada[1643]. He married Mary Merrick McBride, the daughter of Clarence Hebert Merrick and Emma Palestine Fillman, on 08 Jun 1968 in Reno, Nevada[1644]. He married Joanne Akers Thornton, the daughter of Aubrey Herrel and Lois E. Akers, on 05 Apr 1981 in Parma, Idaho[1645]. She was born on 03 Jul 1939 in Waverly, Iowa[1646] and died on 02 Dec 2008 in Parma, Idaho[1647]. Stanley Donovan Leigh and his wife Joanne Akers were buried in Parma, Idaho[1648]. Stanley Donovan Leigh and Ella Mae Cox had four children who may still be living.

[1637] Ancestry.com, U.S., Find A Grave Index, 1700s-Current (Provo, UT, USA, Ancestry.com Operations, Inc., 2012),

[1638] Ancestry.com, U.S., Find A Grave Index, 1700s-Current (Provo, UT, USA, Ancestry.com Operations, Inc., 2012),

[1639] Idaho Department of Health and Welfare, Bureau of Vital Records and Health Statistics; Boise, Idaho; *Marriage Index for Years 1947-1962*

[1640] Ancestry.com, U.S., Social Security Applications and Claims Index, 1936-2007 (Provo, UT, USA, Ancestry.com Operations, Inc., 2015), Ancestry.com, http://www.Ancestry.com, Record for Ella Mae Leigh.

[1641] Ancestry.com, U.S., Social Security Applications and Claims Index, 1936-2007 (Provo, UT, USA, Ancestry.com Operations, Inc., 2015), Ancestry.com, http://www.Ancestry.com, Record for Ella Mae Leigh.

[1642] Genealogy compiled by Rev. Laverne E. Leigh, 414 Washington Ave. East, Albia, Iowa 52531 in 1975.

[1643] Genealogy compiled by Rev. Laverne E. Leigh, 414 Washington Ave. East, Albia, Iowa 52531 in 1975.

[1644] Genealogy compiled by Rev. Laverne E. Leigh, 414 Washington Ave. East, Albia, Iowa 52531 in 1975.

[1645] Obituary of Stanley Leigh on page 194 of this book.

[1646] Ancestry.com, U.S., Find A Grave Index, 1700s-Current (Provo, UT, USA, Ancestry.com Operations, Inc., 2012), Ancestry.com,

[1647] Ancestry.com, U.S., Find A Grave Index, 1700s-Current (Provo, UT, USA, Ancestry.com Operations, Inc., 2012), Ancestry.com,

[1648] Ancestry.com, U.S., Find A Grave Index, 1700s-Current (Provo, UT, USA, Ancestry.com Operations, Inc., 2012), Ancestry.com,

Stanley (Stan) Leigh, of Parma, died Friday, November 11, 2011 at home at the age 81.

At Stan's request, immediate burial will take place at the Parma Cemetery next to his beloved Jo Anne under the direction of Dakan Funeral Chapel, with no formal services to be held.   Stanley Donovan Leigh was born July 21, 1930 to Cecil Leigh and Lena Fretwell Leigh in Eugene, Oregon. In 1933, Stanley, along with his father, mother and older sister, Bonita, moved to the Parma area in Idaho. After about two years, his father was able to acquire that portion of the original homestead in Apple Valley that had been inherited by his mother, Eva Paul Leigh. Stan grew up there, attending grade school in Apple Valley and high school in Parma. During that time his younger sister, Beulah was born. In 1949, Stan married Ella Mae Cox of Emmett, Idaho. To that union four children were born, Sandra (Andy) Marrical, Steven (Jan) Leigh, Sidney Leigh and Sherri (Curt) Garrett. He and Ella later divorced. Although these are the only children Stan actually fathered, in the years that followed he was father to many wonderful children. He was occasionally heard to say "I helped raise 15 kids". Several of whom still call him Dad. In addition to all of these, there are many grandchildren and great-grandchildren that he loves very much! Stan loved to work and held too many different jobs to list here. Although he always thought of Idaho as home, he lived in several other states, Florida, California, Nevada, Utah and Oregon with trips back to Idaho in between some. His last trip back to Idaho was in 1976 and he has lived here since then. Wherever he lived he was much happier if he had a garden spot where he could grow some veggies and some wild game nearby that he could hunt to help put food on the table. In 1981 Stan married "His Angel" Jo Anne Akers Thornton of Parma. They enjoyed 27 wonderful years together before she passed away in 2008. Stan is a child of God (read john 1:12-14) and is anxiously looking forward to the promise given in First Thessalonians 4:13-18, "The Lord himself shall descend from heaven with a shout, with the voice of the Archangel, and with the trump of God: and the dead in Christ shall rise first; then we which are alive and remain shall be caught up together with them in the clouds, to meet the Lord in the air; and so shall we ever be with the Lord!". Please join him in this wonderful hope!

147. Laverne E. Leigh[6] (Reuben Harold Leigh[5], Jay Noel Leigh[4], Rueben Harrington Leigh[3], William Todd Leigh[2], Nathan S. Leigh[1]) was born in Modesto, California. He married Betty Jean Hendryx, the daughter of Dean Clyde Hendryx and Hazel Elizabeth Zwicker, on 19 June 1949 in Fall Creek, Oregon[1649]. She was born on 11 Aug 1930 in Omaha, Nebraska[1650] and died on 30 Apr 2016 in Lane County, Oregon[1651]. Betty Jean Hendryx was buried in Oakridge, Oregon[1652]. Laverne Edward Leigh and Betty Jean Hendryx had four children who may still be living.

Laverne attended grade school at both Fall Creek and Oakridge, Oregon, Junior High in Eugene, Oregon and High School at Lowell, Oregon where he graduated in 1948. Betty moved to Fall Creek during her Junior year and Laverne's Senior year in High School from Springfield, Oregon. She had lived previously in Nebraska, Wyoming, Montana and Idaho before moving to Springfield while her father, Herb Pierce, followed the construction business.

Betty and Laverne were married in June of 1949 a month after Betty graduated from Lowell High School. They made their first home from 1949 until August of 1957 on the Fall creek Farm. Betty kept house while Laverne worked for one year for the Lowell Lumber Company and then went into partnership with his father in logging and farming.

Wedding photo of Laverne E. Leigh and his wife, Betty Jean Hendryx, from the collection of Rev. Laverne E. Leigh and used with permission.

[1649] Genealogy compiled by Rev. Laverne E. Leigh, 414 Washington Ave. East, Albia, Iowa 52531 in the Spring of 1975.

[1650] Ancestry.com, U.S., Find A Grave Index, 1700s-Current (Provo, UT, USA, Ancestry.com Operations, Inc., 2012), Ancestry.com, http://www.Ancestry.com, Record for Betty Jean Leigh.

[1651] Ancestry.com, U.S., Find A Grave Index, 1700s-Current (Provo, UT, USA, Ancestry.com Operations, Inc., 2012), Ancestry.com, http://www.Ancestry.com, Record for Betty Jean Leigh.

[1652] Ancestry.com, U.S., Find A Grave Index, 1700s-Current (Provo, UT, USA, Ancestry.com Operations, Inc., 2012), Ancestry.com, http://www.Ancestry.com, Record for Betty Jean Leigh.

In the fall of 1956, Laverne and Betty made the decision that they would answer the call to Christian ministry. Laverne began his training for the ministry at Northwest Christian College in September of 1957 and graduated with a B.Th. Degree in June of 1962. During this time of schooling, they moved to Springfield, Oregon and bought a home. Laverne worked for Weirhauser Timber Company a forty hour week at night and went to school during the day for the six years he was in undergraduate school and for one year after he graduated.

In January of 1959, Laverne and Betty and family became the minister and wife of the Deadwood Community Church at Deadwood, Oregon. This was a Sunday church that they drove sixty miles one way each Sunday to serve until the last day of May 1961. On June 1, 1961, Laverne and Betty took the pastorate of the Glenwood Christian Church in between Eugene and Springfield, Oregon. The Glenwood church was a half-time church that Laverne served while attending school and working full time at night for Weirhauser Company.

Laverne and Betty resigned the Glenwood church pastorate the last Sunday of May in 1963 to move to Oklahoma to attend graduate school. They purchased a truck, loaded their furniture and left their home in Springfield the second week of July. During June a real sadness entered their life when Melalee Sittner, a daughter of Betty's sister, Billie Louise, went to live with her father after having been a part of the Leigh household and family for a little over three years. She went to a good home and a loving family, but it was like a loss of one of their own children.

The family arrived in Oklahoma and camped at the Great Salt Plains State Park in northern Oklahoma for a month while they were being considered by and then called to minister the Oxford Christian Church at Oxford, Kansas. Laverne began seminary at the Graduate Seminary of Phillips University in September of 1963 and his family lived in Oxford, Kansas one hundred miles away. The Oxford Church was a half-time student charge. Laverne lived in Enid and attended school from Tuesday morning until Friday afternoon. Then he served the church from Friday evening through Monday night. Betty did much of the work at the church during the week

Photo of Laverne E. Leigh and his wife, Betty Jean Hendryx, from the collection of Rev. Laverne E. Leigh and used with permission.

They moved to Eureka, Kansas in January of 1967 after Laverne had finished his course of study that January to take the First Christian Church of Eureka. This was their first full-time ministry. They moved to take the First Christian Church of Albia, Iowa in February of 1972 just a month over five years later. During the pastorate at Eureka, Brenda and Neil graduated from High School and Elaine stayed in Eureka to finish her High School in May of 1972.

Photo of Laverne E. Leigh and his wife, Betty Jean Hendryx, and their children, Brenda, Neil, Elaine and Jolene from the collection of Rev. Laverne E. Leigh and used with permission. Also in the picture is Melanee who stayed with them for a time.

In 1975, Laverne, Betty and Jolene were still in Albia serving the Albia Christian Church with Neil being in the US Navy at Emporia, Kansas. Elaine and her husband, Jerry Cook, live in the edge of Wichita, Kansas.

Betty Jean Hendryx was born August 11, 1930, the first child of Clyde Dean and Hazel Elizabeth Hutcheson Hendryx in Omaha, Nebraska. The family moved to Wyoming in the Casper area where Billie, Harold, and Dorothy were born before the parents divorced.

Betty and the other three children spent about two years in a Catholic orphanage at Torrington, Wyoming as a result of parent disagreement. Betty's mother Hazel reclaimed her children and they lived at Edgerten, Wyoming. Hazel married Herbert Pierce who worked in construction. They lived in Butte, Montana and later moved to Springfield, Oregon.   Betty attended Springfield High School her freshman and sophomore years and the family moved to Fall Creek in December 1947, her junior year. She began attending Lowell High School and graduated from Lowell in 1949.

Photo of four generations, Reuben Harold, Laverne E., Neil and Steven Leigh from the collection of Rev. Laverne E. Leigh and used with permission.

Laverne Edward Leigh was a senior when they met in December of 1947. They became engaged in June 1948 and were married on June 19, 1949 after Betty graduated.

Betty and Laverne made their home on the Leigh ranch where he was in partnership with his parents in farming and logging. Born to their union were four children; Brenda, Neil, Elaine, and Jolene. In 1957, having made a decision to train for the Christian ministry, Lavern started training at Northwest Christian College in Eugene and graduated from there in June 1962.   They moved to Springfield and Betty raised their children while he went to school and worked a 40-hour week at night in the plywood division of Weyerhauser in Springfield.

 The family moved to Oxford, Kansas in 1963 where they served the Christian church and Lavern attended Phillips Graduate Seminary in Enid, Oklahoma to graduate in June of 1967.

From 1967 until June 1996 the family served as pastoral family at Eureka, Kansas Christian Church six years; Albia, Iowa Christian Church seven years; Marysville, Kansas Christian Church six years; and the Shenandoah, Iowa Christian Church nine years.

Betty wore many hats as she was a mother and pastor's wife. She worked as a teacher's aide in Eureka and Albia, was a Brownie leader in Springfield, and a Girl Scout District Chairman at Albia. She served one year as a clerk and three years as a lecturer for Weight Watchers while in Shenandoah. She worked as a clerk for the PAMIDA Discount Store in Shenandoah while serving as an elder and head of the CWF kitchen for several years. She was a true helpmate for the church, husband, and family. In retirement Betty worked as an activity director for the LaMirada RV Camp in Harlingen, Texas for 15 years in a part time position where the family camped for four months each winter. Betty is survived by her husband Lavern; four children Brenda Addison of Frisco, Texas, Neil Leigh of Oakridge, Elaine and Jim Whitman of Bandon, and Jolene Thurber of Frisco, Texas; seven grandchildren; nine great-grandchildren; four sisters, Billie (Jim) Harris of Henderson, Nevada, Dorothy Smith of Old Station, California, Patti (Lyle) Loffer of Meridian, Idaho, Sherri Mangum of Norwalk, California; and a brother Jerry (Donna) Hendryx of Seaside.   A celebration of life will be held Saturday, June 11 at 1:00 p.m. at Northwood Christian Church in Springfield. Graveside service follow at 4:00 p.m. at Forestvale Memorial Cemetery. Major Family Funeral Home is in care of arrangements

148.   Harold Alcide Emery[6] (Mary Agnes Foote[5], George L. Foote Jr.[4], Lydia Marie Leigh[3], William Todd Leigh[2], Nathan S. Leigh[1]) was born on 21 Jul 1913 in Utica, New York[1653] and died on 11 Dec 1989 in New Hartford, New York[1654]. He married Marie Longtin, the daughter of Paul H. Longtin and Amelia F. Fletcher, on 08 Jan 1938 in Utica, New York[1655]. She was born on 29 Jan 1916 in Norristown, Pennsylvania and died

---

[1653] Ancestry.com, Social Security Death Index (Provo, UT, USA, The Generations Network, Inc., 2008), www.ancestry.com, Database online. Number: 115-05-0037; Issue State: New York; Issue Date: Before 1951. Record for Harold A. Emery.

[1654] Ancestry.com, Social Security Death Index (Provo, UT, USA, The Generations Network, Inc., 2008), www.ancestry.com, Database online. Number: 115-05-0037; Issue State: New York; Issue Date: Before 1951. Record for Harold A. Emery.

[1655] Ancestry.com. *New York State, Marriage Index, 1881-1967* [database on-line]. Lehi, UT, USA: Ancestry.com Operations, Inc., 2017.

on 01 Jan 1990 in New Hartford, New York[1656]. Harold Alcide Emery and his wife were buried in Calvary Cemetery in Utica, New York[1657]. Harold was a graduate of Utica Free Academy and the Philadelphia College of Pharmacy and Science. He was the founder of Emery Pharmacy on the corner of James and Neilson Streets in Utica, New York. He served his country as a Lieutenant in the U.S. Navy during World War II. He and his wife were members of St. John the Evangelist Church in New Hartford, New York. Harold was past president of the Mohawk Valley Pharmaceutical Society and a member of the American Society of Consultant Pharmacist, the Utica Elks Lodge #31 and honorary life member of the William E. Burke Utica Council #189 Knights of Columbus.

Harold Alcide Emery and Marie Longtin Emery had the following children:

      i.   Living Emery

159. ii.   Susan Emery born on 23 Jun 1947 in Utica, New York[1658] and died on 17 Jan 2013 in Winchester Medical Center, Winchester, Virginia[1659].

Photo of Harold Alcide Emery from the authors collection.

149. Gordon Charles Emery[6] (Mary Agnes Foote[5], George L. Foote Jr.[4], Lydia Marie Leigh[3], William Todd Leigh[2], Nathan S. Leigh[1]) was born on 29 Mar 1915 in Utica, New York[1660] and died on 09 Oct 1981 in Utica, New York[1661]. He married Gertrude Marie Bowman, the daughter of George Francis Bowman and Susanna Etta Sifer, on 26 Apr 1941 in St. Joseph's Church, Utica, New York[1662]. Gordon Charles Emery was buried 12 Oct 1981 in St. Mary's Cemetery, Clayville, New York[1663]. Gordon served in the US Navy in World War II. He worked for Chicago Pneumatic Tool Company for many years retiring in 1973. He lived in Florida and Sauquoit until he died.

[1656] Ancestry.com, Social Security Death Index (Provo, UT, USA, The Generations Network, Inc., 2008), www.ancestry.com, Database online. Number: 075-01-6225; Issue State: New York; Issue Date: Before 1951. Record for Marie L. Emery

[1657] Obituary, Utica Observer Dispatch, Utica, New York December 12, 1989.

[1658] Ancestry.com. *U.S., Obituary Collection, 1930-2018* [database on-line]. Lehi, UT, USA: Ancestry.com Operations Inc, 2006.

[1659] Ancestry.com. *U.S., Obituary Collection, 1930-2018* [database on-line]. Lehi, UT, USA: Ancestry.com Operations Inc, 2006.

[1660] Ancestry.com, Social Security Death Index (Provo, UT, USA, The Generations Network, Inc., 2008), www.ancestry.com, Database online. Record for Gordon Emery.

[1661] Ancestry.com, Social Security Death Index (Provo, UT, USA, The Generations Network, Inc., 2008), www.ancestry.com, Database online. Record for Gordon Emery.

[1662] Verbal from Gertrude Bowman Emery.

[1663] Ancestry.com, Web: New York, Find A Grave Index, 1660-2012 (Provo, UT, USA, Ancestry.com Operations, Inc., 2012),

hoto of Gordon Charles Emery and Gertrude Marie Bowman from the authors collection.

Gordon Charles Emery and Gertrude Bowman had the following children:

160.   i.   Karen Susanne Emery.   She married Martin Jay Dwyer, the son of James Eckland Dwyer and Eleanor Pratt in St. Patrick's Church, Clayville, New York.

161.   ii.   Gaile Joyce Emery.   She married Michael John Shimon, the son of Casper and Edna Shimon.

150.   Hazel Hart[6] (Isabel Lydia Foote[5], George L. Foote Jr.[4], Lydia Marie Leigh[3], William Todd Leigh[2], Nathan S. Leigh[1]) was born on 10 May 1912 in Morrisville, New York[1664] and died on 10 Jul 1949 in Memorial Hospital, Utica, New York[1665]. She married Ivan Jay Collins, the son of Robert N. Collins and Eliza Marie Shaw, on 29 Apr 1932 in[1666]. He was born on 04 Nov 1904 in Norwood, New York[1667] and died on 03 Mar 1964 at 1138 Conkling Avenue, Utica, New York[1668]. Hazel moved to Utica with her family in 1919 and attended local schools graduating from Utica Free Academy in 1930. She was a member of the Calvary Episcopal Church and it's Circle L. Ivan Jay Collins was buried on 07 Mar 1964 in Geenlawn Cemetery, New Hartford, New York[1669].

Photo of Hazel Hart from the authors collection.

Ivan was a Linotype operator for the Utica Observer Dispatch for 40 years. He attended school in Norwood, New York. He worked for the Ogdensburg Journal before coming to Utica. He was a member of the International Typographical Union.

[1664] Obituary, Utica Observer Dispatch, Utica, New York, July 11, 1949, page 2A.
[1665] Obituary, Utica Observer Dispatch, Utica, New York, July 11, 1949, page 2A.
[1666] Obituary, Utica Observer Dispatch, Utica, New York, July 11, 1949, page 2A.
[1667] Obituary, Utica Observer Dispatch, Utica, New York, March 4, 1964, page 12.
[1668] Obituary, Utica Observer Dispatch, Utica, New York, March 4, 1964, page 12.
[1669] Obituary, Utica Observer Dispatch, Utica, New York, March 4, 1964, page 12.

Ivan Jay Collins and Hazel Hart Collins had the following children:

  i. Kathleen Isabel Collins was born on 26 Aug 1936[1670] and died on 20 Mar 2010 in Pinellas Park, Florida[1671]. She married Lowell Edward Odit, the son of Amos C. Odit and Alice C. Paul, on 09 July 1953 in Utica, New York[1672]. He was born on 26 Jan 1934[1673] and died on 18 May 1999 in Pinellas Park, Florida[1674]. Lowell Edward Odit was buried in May 1999 in Bay Pines National Cemetery, Florida[1675].

  ii. Living Collins

151. Howard John Hart[6] (Isabel Lydia Foote[5], George L. Foote Jr.[4], Lydia Marie Leigh[3], William Todd Leigh[2], Nathan S. Leigh[1]) was born on 16 Sep 1914 in Eaton, New York[1676] and died on 25 Feb 1990 in St. Elizabeth Hospital, Utica, New York[1677]. He married Elizabeth Marie Mahlman, 211, the daughter of Harry C. Mahlman and Amelia Kroutch, on 31 Mar 1938 in the home of Rev. Walter Leo Bailey, Utica, New York [1678]. She was born on 05 Dec 1918 in Utica, New York[1679] and died on 02 Oct 2008 in the Presbyterian Home, New Hartford, New York[1680]. Howard John Hart and his wife were buried in Forest Hill Cemetery, Utica, New York[1681]. Howard retired from Utica Daily Press June 1, 1974 after 37 years of service as typographical staff. He served 22 of those years as Chapel Chairman of the International Typographical Union, Local 62 Newspaper Chapel. For 35 years he operated a linotype machine. He lived at 6 Oatley Ave. Yorkville at the time of his death. He graduated from Utica Free Academy.

Photo of Howard John Hart from the collection of his son, Howard Hart, and used with permission.

[1670] Ancestry.com, Social Security Death Index (Provo, UT, USA, The Generations Network, Inc., 2008),

[1671] Ancestry.com, Social Security Death Index (Provo, UT, USA, The Generations Network, Inc., 2008),

[1672] Ancestry.com. *New York State, Marriage Index, 1881-1967* [database on-line]. Lehi, UT, USA: Ancestry.com Operations, Inc., 201

[1673] Ancestry.com, Web: Florida, Find A Grave Index, 1819-2011 (Provo, UT, USA, Ancestry.com Operations, Inc., 2012), www.ancestry.com, Database online.

[1674] Ancestry.com, Web: Florida, Find A Grave Index, 1819-2011 (Provo, UT, USA, Ancestry.com Operations, Inc., 2012), www.ancestry.com, Database online.

[1675] Ancestry.com, Web: Florida, Find A Grave Index, 1819-2011 (Provo, UT, USA, Ancestry.com Operations, Inc., 2012), www.ancestry.com, Database online.

[1676] Obituary, Utica Observer Dispatch, Utica, New York, February 27, 1990, page 5A.

[1677] Obituary, Utica Observer Dispatch, Utica, New York, February 27, 1990, page 5A.

[1678] Ancestry.com. *New York State, Marriage Index, 1881-1967* [database on-line]. Lehi, UT, USA: Ancestry.com Operations, Inc., 2017.

[1679] Obituary, Utica Observer Dispatch, Utica, New York online.

[1680] Obituary, Utica Observer Dispatch, Utica, New York online.

[1681] Obituary, Utica Observer Dispatch, Utica, New York online.

Elizabeth was a graduate of Utica Free Academy. She worked for over 30 years for the Whitesboro School System, retiring as cafeteria manager. She was a member of the Order of Eastern Star and the Yorkville Presbyterian Church for over 50 years. She spend and enjoyed summers at Sand Bay, Clayton, New York for over 50 years and her family camp. She had seven great grandchildren at the time of her death.

Howard John Hart and Elizabeth Marie Mahlmann had two children who may still be living.

152. Richard C. Rousseau[6] (Hazel E. Foote[5], Earl James Foote[4], Lydia Marie Leigh[3], William Todd Leigh[2], Nathan S. Leigh[1]) was born on 30 Sep 1928 in Canastota, New York[1682] and died on 21 Oct 1999 in Stonehedge Health and Rehabilitation Center, Chittenango, New York[1683]. He married Jeanne Murdough. She was born on 03 Aug 1935 in Camden, New York[1684] and died on 09 Jun 2001 in Oneida, New York[1685]. He later married Esther Cook on 27 Apr 1985 in Canastota, New York.   Richard C. Rousseau was buried on 25 Oct 1999 in Verona, New York[1686].

Richard had spend his early years in Canastota, attending the Canastota Schools. He later lived in Verona for 28 years, moving to Florida in 1994. He had spent summers at his camp in Old Forge since 1965. Richard was an avid Lionel train collector and he loved biking. He had worked for the New York State Thruway Maintenance Department for 33 years, retiring in 1985. He had been a member of the Loyal Order of Moose #421 of Oneida, the Verona Volunteer Fire Department, William Russell American Legion Post #404 of Vernon, and UFW Post #6811 of Verona. He was a Veteran of the Korean Conflict, serving overseas with the US Army. Jeanne Murdough was buried in Camden, New York[1687].   Richard C. Rousseau and Jeanne Murdough had three children who may still be living.

153. Judith Rousseau[6] (Hazel E. Foote[5], Earl James Foote[4], Lydia Marie Leigh[3], William Todd Leigh[2], Nathan S. Leigh[1]) was born on 18 Jul 1941[1688] and died on 30

[1682] Ancestry.com, U.S., Social Security Applications and Claims Index, 1936-2007 (Provo, UT, USA, Ancestry.com Operations, Inc., 2015), Ancestry.com, http://www.Ancestry.com, Record for Richard Carl Rousseau

[1683] Ancestry.com, U.S., Social Security Applications and Claims Index, 1936-2007 (Provo, UT, USA, Ancestry.com Operations, Inc., 2015), Ancestry.com, http://www.Ancestry.com, Record for Richard Carl Rousseau

[1684] Ancestry.com, U.S., Social Security Applications and Claims Index, 1936-2007 (Provo, UT, USA, Ancestry.com Operations, Inc., 2015), Ancestry.com, http://www.Ancestry.com, Record for Jeanne Helen Murdough.

[1685] Ancestry.com, U.S., Social Security Applications and Claims Index, 1936-2007 (Provo, UT, USA, Ancestry.com Operations, Inc., 2015), Ancestry.com, http://www.Ancestry.com, Record for Jeanne Helen Murdough.

[1686] National Cemetery Administration, U.S. Veterans Gravesites, ca.1775-2006 (Provo, UT, USA, The Generations Network, Inc., 2006), www.ancestry.com, Database online.

[1687] Ancestry.com, U.S., Find A Grave Index, 1700s-Current (Provo, UT, USA, Ancestry.com Operations, Inc., 2012), Ancestry.com, http://www.Ancestry.com, Record for Jeanne M. Rousseau.

[1688] Ancestry.com, Social Security Death. Record for Judith Depasquale.

Nov 1983[1689]. She married Daniel DePassquale. Daniel DePassquale and Judith Rousseau DePassquale three children who may still be living.

[1689] Ancestry.com, Social Security Death Index (Provo, UT, USA, The Generations Network, Inc., 2008), www.ancestry.com, Database online. Number: 099-32-4788; Issue State: New York; Issue Date: 1957-1959. Record for Judith Depasquale.

Generation Seven

154. Darlene M. Ledebuhr[7] (Victor Ledebuhr[6], Gladys Gertrude Berry[5], Cyrus Nathan Leigh[4], Mary Abigale Leigh[3], Elijah Leigh[2], Nathan S. Leigh[1]) was born on 27 Oct 1936[1690] and died on 31 Jan 2012[1691]. She married Leroy Dockter on 09 Nov 1956[1692]. He was born on 08 Nov 1931[1693] and died on 09 Feb 2008[1694]. Darlene M. Ledebuhr was buried in Money Creek, Minnesota[1695].

HOUSTON, Minn. - Darlene M. Dockter, 75, of Houston, Minn. *passed away peacefully surrounded by her family on Tuesday, Jan. 31, 2012, at Gundersen Lutheran Medical Center in La Crosse, Wis., surrounded by her family. Darlene was born on Oct. 27, 1936, in La Crosse, to Victor and Clara (Gaustad) Ledebuhr. She was raised in Money Creek, Minn., and attended Money Creek Country School. Darlene graduated from Houston High School in 1954. On Nov. 9, 1956, she married Leroy Dockter. Darlene was a loving wife, mother, mother-in-law and grandmother and enjoyed her family and grandchildren. Darlene lived in the Houston area all of her married life. She worked at the Houston State Bank and the Company Store in La Crosse, Wis. Darlene enjoyed crocheting, bowling, antiques, social networking and games on her computer, rummage sales, spending summers on*

Photo of Darlene M. Ledebuhr found on findagrave.com.

[1690] Ancestry.com, U.S., Find A Grave Index, 1700s-Current (Provo, UT, USA, Ancestry.com Operations, Inc., 2012), Ancestry.com, http://www.Ancestry.com, Record for Leroy Dockter.

[1691] Ancestry.com, U.S., Find A Grave Index, 1700s-Current (Provo, UT, USA, Ancestry.com Operations, Inc., 2012), Ancestry.com, http://www.Ancestry.com, Record for Leroy Dockter.

[1692] Obituary of Darlene M. Dockter, Houston, Minnesota on page 204 of this book.

[1693] Ancestry.com, U.S., Find A Grave Index, 1700s-Current (Provo, UT, USA, Ancestry.com Operations, Inc., 2012), Ancestry.com, http://www.Ancestry.com, Record for Leroy Dockter.

[1694] Ancestry.com, U.S., Find A Grave Index, 1700s-Current (Provo, UT, USA, Ancestry.com Operations, Inc., 2012), Ancestry.com, http://www.Ancestry.com, Record for Leroy Dockter.

[1695] Ancestry.com, U.S., Find A Grave Index, 1700s-Current (Provo, UT, USA, Ancestry.com Operations, Inc., 2012), Ancestry.com, http://www.Ancestry.com, Record for Leroy Dockter.

the Mississippi at Brownsville, weekend adventures with her grandchildren, family holiday traditions and was a huge Willy Nelson fan. She was a member of the Money Creek United Methodist Church. She will be greatly missed by her family and friends. Darlene is survived by four children, Douglas (Sue) Dockter of Houston, Tim (Lee Elson) Dockter of Roseville, Minn., Thomas Dockter of Money Creek and Darcy Papenfuss of Bangor, Wis.; six grandchildren, Anthony Dockter, David Dockter, Jared Papenfuss, Hunter Dockter, Cole Papenfuss and Lauren Elson. She was preceded in death by her parents; and husband. The funeral service will be at 11 a.m. on Saturday, Feb. 4 at Money Creek United Methodist Church with the Rev. James Strom officiating. Burial will be in the Money Creek Cemetery. Visitation will be from 5 to 7 p.m. today at Hoff Funeral and Cremation Service in Houston and one hour prior to the service on Saturday at the church.

Darlene's family prefers memorials to be directed to the Money Creek United Methodist Church or to the donor's choice.

Photo of Leroy Dockter from his obituary.

Leroy Dockter, 76, died Saturday, February 9, 2008, *at Gundersen Lutheran Hospital in LaCrosse, WI, surrounded by his family. Leroy was born November 8, 1931, in Trail City, SD to Theodore and Magdalena (Schrenk) Dockter. Leroy grew up in Ashley, ND and served in the U.S. Air Force during the Korean War. In 1956 he came to Houston, MN where he married Darlene Ledebuhr on November 9, 1956. Leroy worked for Ace Communications for 36 years. Leroy was a member of Money Creek Methodist Church and the American Legion in Houston. Leroy was a loving husband, father and especially enjoyed his grandchildren. Leroy was a member of the Antique Car Club, collected antique telephones, enjoyed hunting and fishing, playing cards and bowling. He will be missed by his family and friends. Survivors include his wife, Darlene; four children, Douglas (Sue) Dockter of Houston, MN, Timothy (Lee Elson) Dockter of Roseville, MN, Thomas Dockter of Money Creek, MN and Darcy (Lowell) Papenfuss of Bangor, WI; five grandchildren, Anthony Dockter, David Dockter, Jared Papenfuss, Hunter Dockter and Cole Papenfuss; and two sisters, Atlanda Dockter and Myrdis Heupel both of Ashley, ND. He was preceded in death by his parents, twin sister, Lenora and three brothers, Reinhold, Clifford and Lenhard. Funeral services will be held on Tuesday, February 12, 2008, at 1:00pm at Money Creek Methodist Church with the Reverend James Strom officiating. Burial will be in the Money Creek Cemetery. Friends may call at Hoff Funeral Homes ? Houston Chapel on Monday from 4-7:00pm and also one hour prior to the service at the church on Tuesday. The family suggests* *memorials may be directed to Money Creek Methodist Church or the donor's choice. Please share a memory of Leroy with the family or view his video tribute at: www.hofffuneral.com*

Leroy Dockter and Darlene M. Ledebuhr had the following children:
      i.   Living Dockter
      ii.   Living Dockter
162. iii.   Thomas Victor Dockter was born on 04 Feb 1961 in Caledonia, Minnesota[1696] and died on 01 Aug 2016 in Houston County, Minnesota[1697].
      iv.   Living Dockter

155. Russell C. Yonkers[7] (Inez Beulah Berry[6], Cyrus Gilbert Berry[5], Cyrus Nathan Leigh[4], Mary Abigale Leigh[3], Elijah Leigh[2], Nathan S. Leigh[1]) was born in 1937 in Michigan[1698] and died on 10 Dec 2013[1699]. He married Carol Brandt. Russell C. Yonkers was buried in Tallmadge, Michigan[1700].

Published in The Indianapolis Star on Dec. 12, 2013
Russell C. Yonkers aged 76, went to be with his Lord on Tuesday, December 10, 2013. He was preceded in death by his parents Clifford and Inez (Berry) Yonkers. He is survived by his wife of 54 years, Carol (Brandt) Yonkers, son, Russell (Karen) Yonkers, daughter, Lynn (John) Boyer; 13 grandchildren; 7 great grandchildren; his sister, Carol Johnson; two nephews and one niece. Russell graduated from Hope College in 1959. He worked for seven years as an executive with the Boy Scouts and 26 years for Deere and Co. He was very active with the Presbyterian Church by serving as lay pastor for seven years and by holding the offices of Elder, Treasurer, and Moderator. Russell was also an Exalted Ruler of the Elks in Bedford, IN. Funeral services will be held Saturday 2:00 p.m. at the Zaagman Memorial Chapel , 2800 Burton St. SE, Grand Rapids, MI with Rev. Mike Abma officiating. Interment Rosedale Memorial Park. Visitation will be held Friday 7 to 9 p.m. and Saturday from 1 to 2 p.m. prior to the service. Memorial contributions may be made to Hope College.

Russell C. Yonkers and Carol Brandt Yonkers had two children who may still be living.

[1696] Ancestry.com, U.S., Find A Grave Index, 1700s-Current (Provo, UT, USA, Ancestry.com Operations, Inc., 2012), Ancestry.com, http://www.Ancestry.com, Record for Leroy Dockter.
[1697] Ancestry.com, U.S., Find A Grave Index, 1700s-Current (Provo, UT, USA, Ancestry.com Operations, Inc., 2012), Ancestry.com, http://www.Ancestry.com, Record for Leroy Dockter.
[1698] Obituary, The Indianapolis Star, Indianapolis, Indiana, Dec. 12, 2013.
[1699] Obituary, The Indianapolis Star, Indianapolis, Indiana, Dec. 12, 2013.
[1700] Ancestry.com, U.S., Find A Grave Index, 1700s-Current (Provo, UT, USA, Ancestry.com Operations, Inc., 2012), Ancestry.com, http://www.Ancestry.com, Record for Russell C. Yonkers.

156. Sandra Kay Berry[7] (Gilbert C. B Berry, Jr.[6], Cyrus Gilbert Berry[5], Cyrus Nathan Leigh[4], Mary Abigale Leigh[3], Elijah Leigh[2], Nathan S. Leigh[1]) was born on 22 Sep 1946 in Muskegon, Michigan[1701] and died on 27 Feb 2007 in Clarkdale, Arizona[1702]. She married Robert Ruppel. He was born on 31 May 1945 in Muskegon, Michigan[1703] and died on 23 Mar 2015 in Clarkdale, Arizona[1704]. Robert Ruppel and Sandra Kay Berry had three children who may still be living.

***RUPPEL, SANDRA KAY Clarkdale, AZ Formerly of Muskegon** Sandra Kay Ruppel, age 60, passed Tuesday, Feb. 27, 2007 in Clarkdale, AZ. She is survived by her husband, Robert Ruppel, her parents Gil and Kate Berry of Muskegon, MI; her sister, Joan and Jerry MacPhee of Battle Creek, MI, her brother, John. It is with great sorrow that we report the passing of our amazing father, Robert (Bob) R. Ruppel, who, at the age 69, died in his Clarkdale, AZ home on March 23, 2015. Bob was born on May 31, 1945 in Muskegon, MI to Rosswell and Ruth Ruppel. Bob was a great person. He was one of those people that everyone liked and wanted to be around. He always had a helping hand when one was needed-he was a "light" on this earth. Bob was a great husband, father, grandfather and uncle, always making time to get on the floor and play or let his little girl nieces braid and brush his long hair and beard; and what a beard it was! As all of us know, Bob was a one of a kind. He was like a toasted marshmallow, Hard on the outside but warm and gooey within. He loved his family and friends with all he had and nothing less. Bob was a U.S. Navy Veteran and he has played Santa Claus for many, many years. He worked at Clark Floor Machine, Howmet and, in Arizona, Phelps and Sons, but in 2007 Bob and his friend Stan Wokow started Verde River Hold 'Em, an area Texas Hold 'Em game held at many area restaurants and bars. Of all the many things he has done, the poker game, and all the great people he met through it, has been his most favorite "job". Bob was preceded in death by his loving wife, Sandra K. Ruppel in 2007. He is survived by his children, Deanna (Tim) Todaro, Robert A. Ruppel and Brian A. Ruppel; his brother, Olin C. Ruppel; his sisters, Mary (Bruce) Faulkner and Jeanine (Raulph) Spencer; ten grandchildren; two great-grandchildren; many nieces and nephews and many great friends. Memorial donations in Bob's name may be made to the American Legion, Post 25, in Cottonwood, AZ. He is going to be greatly missed. We love you Dad! RIP Poker Bob*

157. Donald Roger Kowalewski[7] (Valentine JohnKowalewski[6], Alta Irene Berry[5], Cyrus Nathan Leigh[4], Mary Abigale Leigh[3], Elijah Leigh[2], Nathan S. Leigh[1]) was born on 20 May 1937[1705] and died on 08 Sep 2012[1706]. He married Judith Ann Kobus on 22 Nov

---

[1701] Obituary of Sandra Kay Ruppel, Muskegon, Michigan newspaper.

[1702] Obituary of Sandra Kay Ruppel, Muskegon, Michigan newspaper.

[1703] Obituary of Robert R. Ruppel, Muskegon, Michigan newspaper.

[1704] Obituary of Robert R. Ruppel, Muskegon, Michigan newspaper.

[1705] Ancestry.com, Social Security Death Index, Record for Donald R Kowalewski.

1958 in Winona, Minnesota[1707]. Donald Roger Kowalewski and Judith Ann Kobus four children who may still be living.

158. Susan B. Coulson[7] (Joseph Lewis Coulson[6], Lydia Belle Corey[5], Genevieve Berry[4], Mary Abigale Leigh[3], Elijah Leigh[2], Nathan S. Leigh[1]) was born in 1948 in St. Petersburg, Florida[1708] and died on 03 Feb 2016 in Anchorage, Alaska[1709]. She married David Kilpatrick on 27 Oct 1973[1710]. They had two children who may still be living. Susan B. Coulson was buried in Money Creek, Minnesota[1711].

Published in The Alaska Dispatch News, 02/06/2016:
Susan B. Kilpatrick, 67, passed peacefully in her Anchorage, Alaska, home to meet her Lord and Savior Jesus Christ on Feb. 3, 2016. Susan enjoyed serving her Lord by ministering to children, teen and adult groups and greeting newcomers at her place of worship - Rabbit Creek Community Church. Susan's generosity, compassion and willingness of spirit endeared her to family, friends, colleagues, acquaintances and strangers alike. Above all, Susan loved spending time with her husband, family and friends. She was the center-pin of holidays and weekly gatherings. Susan and her husband, David, recently celebrated their 42nd wedding anniversary on Oct. 27, 2015, surrounded by their children and grandchildren. Susan was born in St. Petersburg, Fla. She is survived by her husband, David; children, Brice (Kelly) Kilpatrick and Sunny (Ruben) Medina; grandchildren, Tyler, Harmony and Sebastian; sisters, Nancy Hemenway and Peggy Coulson; and brother, Corey Coulson. Susan was preceded in death by her parents, Joseph and Eleanor Coulson; and brother, Charles Coulson all of Houston, Minn. There will be a Celebration of Life at Rabbit Creek Community Church on Feb. 9, 2016, at 10 a.m. Flowers are welcome; should contributions be made, please address them to the Susan Kilpatrick Memorial Fund, care of Rabbit Creek Church.

[1706] Ancestry.com, Social Security Death Index, Record for Donald R Kowalewski.

[1707] Ancestry.com, Minnesota, Marriage Index, 1958-2001 (Provo, UT, USA, Ancestry.com Operations Inc, 2007), Ancestry.com, http://www.Ancestry.com, Record for Donald R Kowalewski.

[1708] Ancestry.com. *U.S., Find A Grave Index, 1600s-Current* [database on-line]. Provo, UT, USA: Ancestry.com Operations, Inc., 2012.

[1709] Ancestry.com. *U.S., Find A Grave Index, 1600s-Current* [database on-line]. Provo, UT, USA: Ancestry.com Operations, Inc., 2012.

[1710] Obituary of Susan B. Kilpatrick from The Alaska Dispatch News, February 2, 2016 and listed in this book on page 208.

[1711] Ancestry.com. *U.S., Find A Grave Index, 1600s-Current* [database on-line]. Provo, UT, USA: Ancestry.com Operations, Inc., 2012.

159. Susan E. Emery[7] (Harold Alcide Emery[6], Mary Agnes Foote[5], George L. Foote, Jr.[4], Lydia Marie Leigh[3], William Todd Leigh[2], Nathan S. Leigh[1]) was born on 23 Jun 1947 in Utica, New York[1712] and died on 17 Jan 2013 in Winchester Medical Center, Winchester, Virginia[1713]. She married Alan K. Ellinwood on 29 Mar 1969 in New Hartford, New York. Susan Emery was buried on 21 Jan 2013 in Gerald B.H. Solomon Saratoga National Cemetery, Saratoga, New York[1714]. Susan was a graduate of Utica Catholic Academy and Utica College where she received a Bachelor's Degree in English. She dedicated her life to her children and grandchildren as a homemaker. She was a devout Catholic. Alan K. Ellinwood and Susan Emery had three children who may still be living.

160. Karen Susanne Emery[7] (Gordon Charles Emery[6], Mary Agnes Foote[5], George L. Foote, Jr.[4], Lydia Marie Leigh[3], William Todd Leigh[2], Nathan S. Leigh[1]) was born in Faxton Hospital, Utica, New York. She married Martin Jay Dwyer, the son of James Eckland Dwyer and Eleanor Pratt, on 24 Feb 1968 in St. Patrick's Church, Clayville, New York.

Martin Jay Dwyer and Karen Susanne Emery Dwyer had the following child:

163. i. Shari Lynn Dwyer born in New Hartford, New York.

Photo of Karen Susanne Emery and Martin Jay Dwyer taken on their 50th wedding anniversary. Photo in the authors collection.

[1712] Ancestry.com. *U.S., Obituary Collection, 1930-2018* [database on-line]. Lehi, UT, USA: Ancestry.com Operations Inc, 2006.
[1713] Ancestry.com. *U.S., Obituary Collection, 1930-2018* [database on-line]. Lehi, UT, USA: Ancestry.com Operations Inc, 2006.
[1714] Ancestry.com. *U.S., Find A Grave Index, 1600s-Current* [database on-line]. Provo, UT, USA: Ancestry.com Operations, Inc., 2012.

161. Gaile Joyce Emery[7] (Gordon Charles Emery[6], Mary Agnes Foote[5], George L. Foote, Jr.[4], Lydia Marie Leigh[3], William Todd Leigh[2], Nathan S. Leigh[1]) was born in Faxton Hospital, Utica, New York. She married Michael Shimon, the son of Casper and Edna Shimon, on 27 Jan 1979 in Gilmore City, Iowa.

Gaile Joyce Emery had the following child:
164.   i.   John Joseph Williams was born in Syracuse, New York.

Michael Shimon and Gaile Joyce Emery Shimon had the following child:
        i.   Alexandra   Danielle Shimon was born in Joplin, Missouri.

Photo of Gaile Joyce Emery and Michael John Shimon from the authors collection.

Generation Eight

162.   Thomas Victor Dockter[8] (Darlene M. Ledebuhr[7], Victor Ledebuhr[6], Gladys Gertrude Berry[5], Cyrus Nathan Berry[4], Mary Abigale Leigh[3], Elijah Leigh[2], Nathan S. Leigh[1]) was born on 04 Feb 1961 in Caledonia, Minnesota[1715] and died on 01 Aug 2016 in Houston County, Minnesota[1716]. He married Denise Meeker on 12 May 1984[1717].
 Thomas Victor Dockter and Denise Meeker had two children who may still be living.

MONEY CREEK, Minn. - *Thomas "Tom" Victor Dockter, 55, of Money Creek passed away Monday, Aug. 1, 2016. He was born Feb. 4, 1961, to LeRoy and Darlene (Ledebuhr) Dockter, in Caledonia. Tom graduated in 1979 from Houston High School, then attended the technical school in Winona, where he received his associate's degree. While traveling to Michigan for work, he met Denise Meeker. They were married May 12, 1984, and had two boys, Anthony and David, but later divorced. He spent most of his career working for Wenonah Canoe doing trim work. Tom was a man who loved the outdoors. He spent his free time camping, hunting, fishing, four-wheeling, road tripping, searching for Indian artifacts, gardening, cooking, and wood working, but most of all he loved his boys, grandchildren, and family. Tom is survived by his sons, Anthony (Tanya)*

Dockter and David (Kelly) Dockter; grandchildren, Braelee, Blakelyn, and Kip; siblings, Doug (Sue) Dockter, Tim (Lee Elson) Dockter, and Darcy Dockter; niece, Lauren Elson; and nephews, Jared and Cole Papenfuss, and Hunter Dockter. He was preceded in death by his parents. A funeral service will be 10 a.m. Saturday, Aug. 6, at Money Creek United Methodist Church, with the Reverend James Strom officiating. Visitation will be 4 to 7 p.m. Friday at Hoff Funeral Home, Houston, and one hour prior to the service at the church. Hoff Funeral and Cremation Service, Houston, is assisting the family with arrangements.

Photo of Thomas Victor Dockter found in his obituary.

[1715] Ancestry.com, U.S., Find A Grave Index, 1700s-Current (Provo, UT, USA, Ancestry.com Operations, Inc., 2012), Ancestry.com, http://www.Ancestry.com, Record for Leroy Dockter.
[1716] Ancestry.com, U.S., Find A Grave Index, 1700s-Current (Provo, UT, USA, Ancestry.com Operations, Inc., 2012), Ancestry.com, http://www.Ancestry.com, Record for Leroy Dockter.
[1717] Obituary of Thomas Victor Dockter from the Money Creek, Minnesota newspaper in this book on page 211.

163. Shari Lynn Dwyer[8] (Karen Susanne Emery[7], Gordon Charles Emery[6], Mary Agnes Foote[5], George L. Foote, Jr.[4], Lydia Marie Leigh[3], William Todd Leigh[2], Nathan S. Leigh[1]) was born New Hartford, New York. She married Douglas Charles Phillips, the son of Claude Charles Phillips and Sybil Elaine Sprague, on 06 Mar 2006 at Dawn Beach, St. Maarten, Netherlands Antilles.

Douglas Charles Phillips is the father of the following children. Shari Lynn Dwyer is their step mother.
> i.   Ryan Leonard Phillips was born in Syracuse, New York.
> ii.   Tyler Phillips was born in Syracuse, New York.

Douglas Charles Phillips and Shari Lynn Dwyer had the following children:
> iii.   Johnathon Martin Phillips was born in St. Joseph's Hospital, Syracuse, New York weighing 8 lbs. 5 oz. and was 20 inches long[1718].
> iv.   Harrison James Phillips was born in Crouse Hospital, Syracuse, New York weighing 9 lbs. 1 oz. and was 21 inches long[1719].
> v.   Parker Scott Phillips was born in Crouse Hospital, Syracuse, New York weighing 8. lbs 15 oz[1720].

Photo of Douglas Charles Phillips, Shari Lynn Dwyer, Johnathon Martin Phillips, Harrison James Phillips and Parker Scott Phillips from the authors collection. Photo taken April 2017.

164. John Joseph Williams[8] (Gaile Joyce Emery[7], Gordon Charles Emery[6], Mary Agnes Foote[5], George L. Foote, Jr.[4], Lydia Marie Leigh[3], William Todd Leigh[2], Nathan S. Leigh[1]) was born in Syracuse, New York. John Joseph Williams has one child named Kristyn Williams.

[1718] Family information from myself, Karen Emery Dwyer.
[1719] Family information from myself, Karen Emery Dwyer.
[1720] Family information from myself, Karen Emery Dwyer.

Chapter Two

Descendants

of

HENRY B. WEBB

Generation One

1. Henry B. Webb was born in 1784 in Connecticut[1] and died in 1864 in Madison, New York[2]. He married Mary R. Turner. She was born on 23 Dec 1789 in Massachusetts[3] and died on 06 May 1869 in Madison, New York[4]. Henry B. Webb and his wife, Mary R. Turner were buried in the Madison Village Cemetery, Madison, New York[5].

Henry B. Webb and Mary R. Turner had the following children:
2.   i.   John H. Webb was born on 09 Jun 1817[6] and died on 01 Feb 1910 in Willard, New York[7].
3.   ii.   Lydia M. Webb was born in 1819 in Connecticut or Otsego, New York[8] and died in 1856 in Mexico, New York[9].
4.   iii.   Abigail Webb was born on 22 Jan 1824[10] and died on 20 Jul 1858 in Madison, New York[11].
5.   iv.   Heneretta Webb was born on 25 Sep 1826 in Kortright, New York[12] and died on 09 Jan 1892[13].
6.   v.   Samantha Martha Webb was born on 11 Jul 1828 in Kortright, New York[14] and died on 04 Jun 1887 in Madison, New York[15].
7.   vi.   Lafayette Webb was born on 07 Jul 1830[16] and died on 02 Aug 1882 in Winnebago, Minnesota[17].

---

[1] Ancestry.com, U.S., Find A Grave Index, 1700s-Curren , Record for Henry B. Webb.

[2] Ancestry.com, U.S., Find A Grave Index, 1700s-Curren , Record for Henry B. Webb.

[3] Ancestry.com, U.S., Find A Grave Index, 1700s-Current, Record for Mary R. Webb.

[4] Ancestry.com, U.S., Find A Grave Index, 1700s-Current, Record for Mary R. Webb.

[5] Ancestry.com, U.S., Find A Grave Index, 1700s-Curren , Record for Henry B. Webb.

[6] Willard Cemetery Listing, http://www.suvcw.org/ny/camps/caywood/Willard.htm.

[7] Willard Cemetery Listing, http://www.suvcw.org/ny/camps/caywood/Willard.htm.

[8] Ancestry.com, New York, State Census, 1855 (Provo, UT, USA, Ancestry.com Operations, Inc., 2013), Ancestry.com, http://www.Ancestry.com, Record for William T Leigh.

[9] Civil war records, John H. Leigh, son of Lydia M. Webb.

[10] Civil War records for George Foote, husband of Abigail Webb.

[11] Civil War records for George Foote, husband of Abigail Webb.

[12] Ancestry.com, U.S., Find A Grave Index, 1700s-Current (Provo, UT, USA, Ancestry.com Operations, Inc., 2012),

[13] Ancestry.com, U.S., Find A Grave Index, 1700s-Current (Provo, UT, USA, Ancestry.com Operations, Inc., 2012),

[14] Ancestry.com, 1860 United States Census, Year: 1860; Census Place: Madison, Madison, New York; Roll: M653_781; Page: 1061; Family History Library Film: 803781. Record for Charles Lovejoy.

[15] NYS Death Index, Ancestry.com. New York, Death Index, 1880-1956 Lehi, UT, USA: Ancestry.com.

[16] Ancestry.com, U.S., Find A Grave Index, 1700s-Current (Provo, UT, USA, Ancestry.com Operations, Inc., 2012).

[17] Ancestry.com, U.S., Find A Grave Index, 1700s-Current (Provo, UT, USA, Ancestry.com Operations, Inc., 2012).

8.   vii.   Adelia M. Webb was born on 17 Dec 1832[18] and died on 12 Jun 1903 in Sherburne, New York[19].

9.   viii.   Thomas H. Webb was born on 01 Oct 1834 in Kortright, New York[20] and died in 1907 in Blue Earth, Minnesota[21].

Photo of gravestone of Henry B. Webb and Mary R. Turner taken by the author. This stone was found in the Madison Village Cemetery, Madison, New York.

[18] Ancestry.com, New York, Wills and Probate Records, 1659-1999 (Provo, UT, USA, Ancestry.com Operations, Inc., 2015), Ancestry.com, http://www.Ancestry.com, Probate Records, 1798-1970; Author: New York. Surrogate's Court (Chenango County); Probate Place: Chenango, New York. Record for Adelia M Fagin

[19] Ancestry.com, New York, Wills and Probate Records, 1659-1999 (Provo, UT, USA, Ancestry.com Operations, Inc., 2015), Ancestry.com, http://www.Ancestry.com, Probate Records, 1798-1970; Author: New York. Surrogate's Court (Chenango County); Probate Place: Chenango, New York. Record for Adelia M Fagin

[20] Ancestry.com, U.S., Find A Grave Index, 1700s-Current (Provo, UT, USA, Ancestry.com Operations, Inc., 2012), Ancestry.com, http://www.Ancestry.com, Record for Thomas H. Webb.

[21] Ancestry.com, U.S., Find A Grave Index, 1700s-Current (Provo, UT, USA, Ancestry.com Operations, Inc., 2012), Ancestry.com, http://www.Ancestry.com, Record for Thomas H. Webb.

Generation Two

2. John H. Webb[2] (Henry B. Webb[1]) was born on 09 Jun 1817[22] and died on 01 Feb 1910 in Willard, New York[23]. He married Roena E. Penny[24]. She was born in 1836 in Pennsylvania[25].

John was 93 and for a very long time had been disabled from spinal injuries suffered during his service in the Civil War. He apparently spent the end of his life in the Willard New York Asylum, and is buried there in the Willard Cemetery

John H. Webb and Roena E. Penny had the following children:

10.	i.	Mary H. Webb was born in June 1855 in Harmony Township, Pennsylvania[26] and died in Friendship, New York[27].

11.	ii.	Adelia M. Webb was born on 14 Apr 1858 in Harmony Township, Pennsylvania[28] and died in 09 Jan1914[29].

12.	iii.	Ellen M. Webb was born in Dec 1859 in Harmony Township, Pennsylvania[30] and died on 18 Oct 1942[31].

	iv.	William B. Webb was born in Jul 1865 in New York[32] and died on 29 May 1951 in Tioga, New York[33]. He married Eva B. Woodward in 1898[34]. She was born

---

[22] Willard Cemetery Listing, http://www.suvcw.org/ny/camps/caywood/Willard.htm

[23] Willard Cemetery Listing, http://www.suvcw.org/ny/camps/caywood/Willard.htm

[24] Ancestry.com, New York, State Census, 1875 (Provo, UT, USA, Ancestry.com Operations, Inc., 2013), Ancestry.com, http://www.Ancestry.com, Record for Roena Web.

[25] Ancestry.com, New York, State Census, 1875 (Provo, UT, USA, Ancestry.com Operations, Inc., 2013), Ancestry.com, http://www.Ancestry.com, Record for Roena Web.

[26] Ancestry.com, 1900 United States Federal Census (Provo, UT, USA, The Generations Network, Inc., 2004), www.ancestry.com, Year: 1900; Census Place: Waterloo, Seneca, New York; Roll: 1162; Page: 10B; Enumeration District: 0101; FHL microfilm: 1241162. Record for Mary Pool.

[27] Ancestry.com, U.S., Find A Grave Index, 1700s-Current (Provo, UT, USA, Ancestry.com Operations, Inc., 2012), Ancestry.com, http://www.Ancestry.com, Record for Mary H. Poole.

[28] Ancestry.com, Web: New York, Find A Grave Index, 1660-2012 (Provo, UT, USA, Ancestry.com Operations, Inc., 2012), Ancestry.com, http://www.Ancestry.com, Record for Adelia M. Benjamin.

[29] New York Department of Health; Albany, NY; *NY State Death Index*; Certificate Number: *332*

[30] Ancestry.com, 1900 United States Federal Census (Provo, UT, USA, The Generations Network, Inc., 2004), www.ancestry.com, Year: 1900; Census Place: Friendship, Allegany, New York; Roll: 1008; Page: 6A; Enumeration District: 0016; FHL microfilm: 1241008. Record for Muser A Baker.

[31] City directories, Ancestry.com. U.S. City Directories, 1822-1995 [database on-line]. Provo, UT, USA: Ancestry.com operations, Inc., 2011.

[32] Ancestry.com, 1900 United States Federal Census (Provo, UT, USA, The Generations Network, Inc., 2004), www.ancestry.com, Year: 1900; Census Place: Greene, Chenango, New York; Roll: 1017; Page: 1A; Enumeration District: 0061; FHL microfilm: 1241017. Record for William B Webb

[33] NYS Death Index, Ancestry.com. New York, Death Index, 1880-1956.

[34] Ancestry.com, 1900 United States Federal Census (Provo, UT, USA, The Generations Network, Inc., 2004), www.ancestry.com, Year: 1900; Census Place: Greene, Chenango, New York; Roll: 1017; Page: 1A; Enumeration District: 0061; FHL microfilm: 1241017. Record for William B Webb

in Jun 1866[35] and died on 28 Aug 1946 in Binghamton, New York[36].
      v.   Susan Webb was born in 1869 in Broome County, New York[37] and died on 31 Mar 1950 in Goshen, New York[38].

3. Lydia M. Webb[2] (Henry B. Webb[1]) was born in 1819 in Connecticut or Otsego, New York[39] and died on 05 Sep 1856 in Mexico, New York[40]. She married William Todd Leigh, the son of Nathan S. Leigh and Mary Todd, on 20 Feb 1842 in Chemung, New York[41]. He was born on 30 Jun 1804 in New York State[42] and died on 22 Oct 1888 in Alton, Kansas[43].

FOR MORE ON LYDIA M. WEBB AND HER DESCENDANTS, PLEASE SEE CHAPTER ONE.

4. Abigail Webb[2] (Henry B. Webb[1]) was born on 22 Jan 1824[44] and died on 20 Jul 1858 in Madison, New York[45]. She married George L. Foote Sr., the son of Jesse Selkrigg Foote and Abigail Hosley, on 21 Jan 1841[46]. He was born on 15 Jul 1818 in Town of Eaton, New York[47] and died on 03 Mar 1911 in Madison, New York[48].

---

[35] Ancestry.com, 1900 United States Federal Census (Provo, UT, USA, The Generations Network, Inc., 2004), www.ancestry.com, Year: 1900; Census Place: Greene, Chenango, New York; Roll: 1017; Page: 1A; Enumeration District: 0061; FHL microfilm: 1241017. Record for William B Webb

[36] NYS Death Index, Ancestry.com. New York, Death Index, 1880-1956 [database on-line]. Lehi, UT, USA· Ancestry.com Operations, Inc., 2017.

[37] Ancestry.com, New York, Death Index, 1880-1956 (Lehi, UT, USA, Ancestry.com Operations, Inc., 2017), Ancestry.com, http://www.Ancestry.com, New York Department of Health; Albany, NY; NY State Death Index; Certificate Number: 17357. Record for Susan Webb.

[38] Ancestry.com, New York, Death Index, 1880-1956 (Lehi, UT, USA, Ancestry.com Operations, Inc., 2017), Ancestry.com, http://www.Ancestry.com, New York Department of Health; Albany, NY; NY State Death Index; Certificate Number: 17357. Record for Susan Webb.

[39] Ancestry.com, New York, State Census, 1855 (Provo, UT, USA, Ancestry.com Operations, Inc., 2013), Ancestry.com, http://www.Ancestry.com, Record for William T Leigh.

[40] Civil war records, Luman D. Leigh, son of Lydia M. Webb.

[41] Civil war records, Luman D. Leigh, son of Lydia M. Webb.

[42] Genealogy compiled by Rev. Laverne E. Leigh, 414 Washington Ave. East, Albia, Iowa 52531 in the Spring of 1975.

[43] Genealogy compiled by Rev. Laverne E. Leigh, 414 Washington Ave. East, Albia, Iowa 52531 in the Spring of 1975.

[44] Civil War records for George L. Foote, husband of Abigail Webb.

[45] Civil War records for George L. Foote, husband of Abigail Webb.

[46] Ancestry.com, North America, Family Histories, 1500-2000 (Provo, UT, USA, Ancestry.com Operations, Inc., 2016), Ancestry.com, http://www.Ancestry.com, Book Title: Foote Family : Comprising the Genealogy and History of Nathaniel Foote of Wethersfield, Connecticut, and His Descendants : also a partial record of Descendants of Pasco Foote of Salem, Massachusetts : Richard Foote of Stafford County, Virginia, and John Foote of New York City : Volume 1. Record for Abigail A Webb.

[47] Civil War records for George L. Foote.

[48] Ancestry.com, Web: New York, Find A Grave Index, 1664-2011 (Online publication - Provo, UT, USA: Ancestry.com Operations, Inc.,

George L. Foote , Sr. and Abigail Webb had the following children:
13.   i.   William H. Foote was born on 03 Apr 1846 in Syracuse, New York[49] and died on 21 Mar 1938 in 117 Central Avenue, Cortland, New York[50].
14.   ii.   Mary Abigail Foote was born on 26 Jun 1849 in Syracuse, New York[51] and died on 03 Mar 1913 in Whitesboro, New York[52].

Article found in the Syracuse Herald, Sunday, July 26, 1908. In the center, 90 year old George L. Foote. To his right, his oldest daughter, Mrs. Mary Abigail Mather, her daughter, Mrs. Annie Rudd, and her daughter, Iva. To Mr. Foote's left; his oldest son, William H. Foote, and his daughter, Mrs. Millie O'Connell and her daughter, Helene.

---

[49] Ancestry.com, North America, Family Histories, 1500-2000 (Provo, UT, USA, Ancestry.com Operations, Inc., 2016), Ancestry.com, http://www.Ancestry.com, Book Title: Foote Family : Comprising the Genealogy and History of Nathaniel Foote of Wethersfield, Connecticut, and His Descendants : also a partial record of Descendants of Pasco Foote of Salem, Massachusetts : Richard Foote of Stafford County, Virginia, and John Foote of New York

[50] New York State Death Records at Ancestry.com.

[51] Ancestry.com, North America, Family Histories, 1500-2000 (Provo, UT, USA, Ancestry.com Operations, Inc., 2016), Ancestry.com, http://www.Ancestry.com, Book Title: Foote Family : Comprising the Genealogy and History of Nathaniel Foote of Wethersfield, Connecticut, and His Descendants : also a partial record of Descendants of Pasco Foote of Salem, Massachusetts : Richard Foote of Stafford County, Virginia, and John Foote of New York.

[52] Obituary, Utica Daily Press, Utica, New York, March 4, 1913.

5. Henretta Webb[2] (Henry B. Webb[1]) was born on 25 Sep 1826 in Kortright, New York[53] and died on 09 Jan 1892[54]. She married Daniel Stilwell[55]. He was born on 18 Jul 1820 in Summit, New York[56] and died on 21 May 1890[57].

Daniel Stilwell and Heneretta Webb had the following child:

    i.   Fanny M. Stilwell was born on 15 Mar 1865 in Harpersfield, New York[58] and died on 16 Feb 1911 in Otsego County, New York[59]. She married Homer Clark. He was born in 1868 in the United States[60].

The Otsego Farmer and Republican (Cooperstown, NY), Feb 14, 1911 page 7.
"After ten days illness of acute bronchitis, Mrs. Fanny Stilwell Clark died at her home near Elk Creek, Thursday Morning, February 16th. She was born in the town of Harpersfield, March 15, 1865, the daughter of Daniel and Henrietta Stilwell. Twenty-three years ago she became the wife of Homer Clark, who with the three sisters, Mrs. Adelbert Shelley, of Davenport Center and Mrs. Jackson VanWie of Schenevus and two brothers, S.B. Stilwell of Elk Creek and F. L. Stilwell of Hartwick, survive her. For fifteen years she has been confined to her bed and although a shut-in, she was cheerful and hopeful, an inspiration and blessing to all who were privileged to know her. The funeral was held from the Methodist Episcopal church at Elk Creek, Sunday 2 p.m. and was largely attended. Interment in the Elk Creek Cemetery. Relatives and friends from away who attended were: F.L. Stilwell and son, William Hartwick; Mrs. Adelbert Shelley of Davenport Centre; Mr. and Mrs. Clark and Mr. Fagen of Hamilton; Mr. and Mrs. L. P. VanHoesen, Mrs. Grant, Oneonta; Mrs. Beach and daughters; Mr. and Mrs. John VanWie and Mr. and Mrs. Jackson VanWie."

---

[53] Ancestry.com, Public Member Trees (Provo, UT, USA, Ancestry.com Operations Inc, 2006), www.ancestry.com, Record for Henry B Sr Webb family.

[54] Ancestry.com, U.S., Find A Grave Index, 1700s-Current (Provo, UT, USA, Ancestry.com Operations, Inc., 2012), Ancestry.com, http://www.Ancestry.com, record for Henretta Stilwell.

[55] Ancestry.com, U.S., Find A Grave Index, 1700s-Current (Provo, UT, USA, Ancestry.com Operations, Inc., 2012), Ancestry.com, http://www.Ancestry.com, record for Daniel Stilwell.

[56] Ancestry.com, U.S., Find A Grave Index, 1700s-Current (Provo, UT, USA, Ancestry.com Operations, Inc., 2012), Ancestry.com, http://www.Ancestry.com, record for Daniel Stilwell.

[57] Ancestry.com, U.S., Find A Grave Index, 1700s-Current (Provo, UT, USA, Ancestry.com Operations, Inc., 2012), Ancestry.com, http://www.Ancestry.com, record for Daniel Stilwell.

[58] Ancestry.com, U.S., Find A Grave Index, 1700s-Current (Provo, UT, USA, Ancestry.com Operations, Inc., 2012), Ancestry.com, http://www.Ancestry.com, record for Fanny Clark.

[59] Ancestry.com, U.S., Find A Grave Index, 1700s-Current (Provo, UT, USA, Ancestry.com Operations, Inc., 2012), Ancestry.com, http://www.Ancestry.com, record for Fanny Clark.

[60] Ancestry.com, 1910 United States Federal Census (Online publication - Provo, UT, USA: Ancestry.com Operations Inc, 2006.Original data - Thirteenth Census of the United States, 1910 (NARA microfilm publication T624, 1,178 rolls). Records of the Bureau of the Census, Record Group 29. National Archives, Was), Ancestry.com, http://www.Ancestry.com, Year: 1910; Census Place: Maryland, Otsego, New York; Roll: T624_949; Page: 10B; Enumeration District: 0051; FHL microfilm: 1374962. Record for Homer S Clark.

6. Samantha Martha Webb[2] (Henry B. Webb[1]) was born on 11 Jul 1828 in Kortright, New York[61] and died on 04 Jun 1887 in Madison, New York[62]. She married Charles Lovejoy. He was born in 1828 in New York[63] and died on 21 Sep 1888[64].

Charles Lovejoy and Samantha Martha Webb had the following children:
    i.   William A. Lovejoy was born in 1859 in New York[65].
    ii.   Charles Lovejoy was born in Jan 1860 in New York[66] and died on 30 Dec 1948 in Oneida, New York[67].
15.   iii.   Frederick M. Lovejoy was born in Aug 1861 in New York[68] and died in 1905[69].

7. LaFayette Webb[2] (Henry B. Webb[1]) was born on 07 Jul 1830[70] and died on 02 Aug 1882 in Winnebago, Minnesota[71]. He married Rhoda E. Ward[72]. She was born in 1835[73]

[61] Ancestry.com, 1860 United States Federal Census (Provo, UT, USA, The Generations Network, Inc., 2004), www.ancestry.com, Year: 1860; Census Place: Madison, Madison, New York; Roll: M653_781; Page: 1061; Family History Library Film: 803781. Record for Charles Lovejoy.

[62] NYS Death Index, Ancestry.com. New York, Death Index, 1880-1956 [database on-line]. Lehi, UT, USA: Ancestry.com Operations, Inc., 2017.

[63] Ancestry.com, 1860 United States Federal Census (Provo, UT, USA, The Generations Network, Inc., 2004), www.ancestry.com, Year: 1860; Census Place: Madison, Madison, New York; Roll: M653_781; Page: 1061; Family History Library Film: 803781. Record for Charles Lovejoy.

[64] *Minutes, Order and Decrees, 1830-1902, and Miscellaneous Minutes, Orders and Decrees, 1854-1900 (Madison County, New York);* Author: *New York. Surrogate's Court (Madison County);* Probate Place: *Madison, New York.*

[65] Ancestry.com, 1860 United States Federal Census (Provo, UT, USA, The Generations Network, Inc., 2004), www.ancestry.com, Year: 1860; Census Place: Madison, Madison, New York; Roll: M653_781; Page: 1061; Family History Library Film: 803781. Record for William A. Lovejoy.

[66] Ancestry.com, 1860 United States Federal Census (Provo, UT, USA, The Generations Network, Inc., 2004), www.ancestry.com, Year: 1860; Census Place: Madison, Madison, New York; Roll: M653_781; Page: 1061; Family History Library Film: 803781. Record for Charles Lovejoy.

[67] NYS Death Index, Ancestry.com. New York, Death Index, 1880-1956 [database on-line]. Lehi, UT, USA: Ancestry.com Operations, Inc., 2017.

[68] Ancestry.com, U.S., Find A Grave Index, 1700s-Current (Provo, UT, USA, Ancestry.com Operations, Inc., 2012), Ancestry.com, http://www.Ancestry.com, Record for Fred M. Lovejoy.

[69] Ancestry.com, U.S., Find A Grave Index, 1700s-Current (Provo, UT, USA, Ancestry.com Operations, Inc., 2012), Ancestry.com, http://www.Ancestry.com, Record for Fred M. Lovejoy.

[70] Ancestry.com, U.S., Find A Grave Index, 1700s-Current (Provo, UT, USA, Ancestry.com Operations, Inc., 2012).

[71] Ancestry.com, U.S., Find A Grave Index, 1700s-Current (Provo, UT, USA, Ancestry.com Operations, Inc., 2012).

[72] Ancestry.com, 1910 United States Federal Census (Online publication - Provo, UT, USA: Ancestry.com Operations Inc, 2006.Original data - Thirteenth Census of the United States, 1910 (NARA microfilm publication T624, 1,178 rolls). Records of the Bureau of the Census, Record Group 29. National Archives, Was), Ancestry.com, http://www.Ancestry.com, Year: 1910; Census Place: Winnebago, Faribault, Minnesota; Roll: T624_696; Page: 5A; Enumeration District: 0091; FHL microfilm: 1374709. Record for Myron D Webb.

[73] Ancestry.com, 1910 United States Federal Census (Online publication - Provo, UT, USA: Ancestry.com Operations Inc, 2006.Original data - Thirteenth Census of the United States, 1910 (NARA microfilm publication T624, 1,178 rolls). Records of the Bureau of the Census, Record Group 29. National Archives, Was), Ancestry.com, http://www.Ancestry.com, Year: 1910; Census Place: Winnebago, Faribault, Minnesota; Roll: T624_696; Page: 5A; Enumeration District: 0091; FHL microfilm: 1374709. Record for Myron D Webb.

and died on 13 Jun 1914 in Fairbault, Minnesota[74].   Lafayette moved to Winnebago, Minnesota between 1860 and 1870.

LaFayette Webb and Rhoda E. Ward had the following children:
      i.   George Henry Webb was born in 1855[75] and died on 25 Jan 1877 in Fairbault, Minnesota[76].
16. ii.   Myron D. Webb was born in 1859 in New York[77] and died on 19 Feb 1916 in Fairbault, Minnesota[78].
      iii.   Alice Ann Webb was born in 1860 [79] and died on 27 Apr 1888 in Fairbault, Minnesota[80].

Tombstone photo of LaFayette Webb found on Findagrave.com. Hillside Cemetery in Winnebago, Minnesota.

8. Adelia M. Webb[2] (Henry B. Webb[1]) was born on 17 Dec 1832[81] and died on 12 Jun 1903 in Sherburne, New York[82]. She married John Fagin[83]. He was born in 1831 in New York[84] and died on 30 Mar 1900[85].   John was a private in the Civil War. Adelia M. Webb and John Fagin were buried in the Madison Village Cemetery, Madison, New York.

---

74 Familysearch.org, "Minnesota Death Index, 1908-2002," database, FamilySearch (https://familysearch.org/ark:/61903/1:1:V4HM-L5M : 4 December 2014), Rhoda E Webb, 13 Jun 1914.

75 Ancestry.com, U.S., Find A Grave Index, 1700s-Current (Provo, UT, USA, Ancestry.com Operations, Inc., 2012), Ancestry.com, http://www.Ancestry.com, Record for Henry Webb.

76 Ancestry.com, U.S., Find A Grave Index, 1700s-Current (Provo, UT, USA, Ancestry.com Operations, Inc., 2012), Ancestry.com, http://www.Ancestry.com, Record for Henry Webb.

77 Ancestry.com, 1860 United States Federal Census (Provo, UT, USA, The Generations Network, Inc., 2004), www.ancestry.com, Year: 1860; Census Place: Madison, Madison, New York; Roll: M653_781; Page: 1092; Family History Library Film: 803781. Record for Myron Webb.

78 Familysearch.org, "Minnesota Death Index, 1908-2002," database, FamilySearch (https://familysearch.org/ark:/61903/1:1:V4CM-BRL : 4 December 2014), Myron Webb, 19 Feb 1916

79 Ancestry.com and The Church of Jesus Christ of Latter-day Saints, 1880 United States Federal Census (Provo, UT, USA, The Generations Network, Inc., 2005), www.ancestry.com, Year: 1880; Census Place: Winnebago City, Faribault, Minnesota; Roll: 619; Family History Film: 1254619; Page: 131D; Enumeration District: 063. Record for Alice Webb

80 Ancestry.com, U.S., Find A Grave Index, 1700s-Current (Provo, UT, USA, Ancestry.com Operations, Inc., 2012), Ancestry.com, http://www.Ancestry.com, Record for Alice Ann Webb.

81 Ancestry.com, U.S., Find A Grave Index, 1700s-Current (Provo, UT, USA, Ancestry.com Operations, Inc., 2012), Ancestry.com, http://www.Ancestry.com, Record for Adelia M. Fagin.

82 Ancestry.com, U.S., Find A Grave Index, 1700s-Current (Provo, UT, USA, Ancestry.com Operations, Inc., 2012), Ancestry.com, http://www.Ancestry.com, Record for Adelia M. Fagin.

83 Ancestry.com, New York, State Census, 1875 (Provo, UT, USA, Ancestry.com Operations, Inc., 2013), Ancestry.com, http://www.Ancestry.com, Record for John Fagan.

84 Ancestry.com, New York, State Census, 1875 (Provo, UT, USA, Ancestry.com Operations, Inc., 2013), Ancestry.com, http://www.Ancestry.com, Record for John Fagan.

85 Ancestry.com, U.S., Find A Grave Index, 1700s-Current (Provo, UT, USA, Ancestry.com Operations, Inc., 2012), Ancestry.com, http://www.Ancestry.com, Record for John W. Fagin

John Fagin and Adelia M. Webb had the following children:

17.   i.   Sally Foliett "Ettie" Fagan was born in May 17, 1859[86] and died in 1942[87].

18.   ii.   George H. Fagin was born in Feb 1866 in New York[88] and died on 30 Apr 1951 in Sherburne, New York[89].

       iii.   Anna Fagin was born in 1872 and died in 1875[90].

19.   iv.   Charles Read Fagan was born on 04 May 1874[91] and died on 03 Nov 1952 in Sherburne, New York[92].

9.   Thomas H. Webb[2] (Henry B. Webb[1]) was born on 01 Oct 1834 in Kortright, New York[93] and died in 1907 in Blue Earth, Minnesota[94]. He married Mary Elizabeth Crandall in 1861[95]. She was born in Oct 1842 in New York[96] and died 24 Feb 1937 in

Los Angeles County, California[97]. Thomas enlisted in the Civil War in Norwich, New York and mustered in 12 Aug 1862 at the age of 27 into Company G of the 114th New York Infantry. He was transferred to Co. G, 10 VRC as Sgt., on 28 Apr 1864.

Thomas H. Webb and Mary Elizabeth Crandall had the following children:

       i.   Iva Mabel Webb was born on 10 Oct 1861[98] in New York State and died on 29 Mar 1864 in

Photo of the gravestone of Iva Mabel Webb from the authors collection.

---

[86] New York State Archives; Albany, New York; *New York State Veterans' Home. Resident Case Files, 1897-1963;* Series Number: *A0710;* Box Number: *10*

[87] Findagrave at Ancestry.com.

[88] Ancestry.com, 1900 United States Federal Census (Provo, UT, USA, The Generations Network, Inc., 2004), www.ancestry.com, Year: 1900; Census Place: Hamilton, Madison, New York; Roll: 1071; Page: 9A; Enumeration District: 0013; FHL microfilm: 1241071. Record for George F Fagin.

[89] Ancestry.com, New York, Death Index, 1880-1956 (Lehi, UT, USA, Ancestry.com Operations, Inc., 2017),

[90] Findagrave.com. Madison Village Cemetery, Madison, New York.

[91] Ancestry.com, U.S., Social Security Applications and Claims Index, 1936-2007 (Provo, UT, USA, Ancestry.com Operations, Inc., 2015), Ancestry.com, http://www.Ancestry.com, Record for Charles Read Fagan.

[92] ancestery.com, Ancestry.com. New York, Death Index, 1880-1956 [database on-line]. Lehi, UT, USA: Ancestry.com Operations, Inc., 2017.

[93] Ancestry.com, U.S., Find A Grave Index, 1700s-Current (Provo, UT, USA, Ancestry.com Operations, Inc., 2012),

[94] Ancestry.com, U.S., Find A Grave Index, 1700s-Current (Provo, UT, USA, Ancestry.com Operations, Inc., 2012),

[95] Ancestry.com, 1900 United States Federal Census (Provo, UT, USA, Ancestry.com Operations Inc, 2004), Ancestry.com, http://www.Ancestry.com, Year: 1900; Census Place: Blue Earth, Faribault, Minnesota; Roll: 762; Page: 13A; Enumeration District: 0080; FHL microfilm: 1240762. Record for Thomas H Webb.

[96] Ancestry.com, 1900 United States Federal Census (Provo, UT, USA, Ancestry.com Operations Inc, 2004), Ancestry.com, http://www.Ancestry.com, Year: 1900; Census Place: Blue Earth, Faribault, Minnesota; Roll: 762; Page: 13A; Enumeration District: 0080; FHL microfilm: 1240762. Record for Thomas H Webb.

[97] Ancestry.com, U.S., Find A Grave Index, 1700s-Current (Provo, UT, USA, Ancestry.com Operations, Inc., 2012),

[98] Ancestry.com, U.S., Find A Grave Index, 1700s-Current (Provo, UT, USA, Ancestry.com Operations, Inc., 2012),

New York State[99]. She was buried in Madison Village Cemetery, Madison, New York.
20.   ii.   Ina Elizabeth Webb was born on 25 Dec 1866 in Minnesota[100] and died on 20 Sep 1940 in Los Angeles County, California[101].

---

[99] Ancestry.com, U.S., Find A Grave Index, 1700s-Current (Provo, UT, USA, Ancestry.com Operations, Inc., 2012),
[100] Ancestry.com, California Death Index, 1940-1997 (Provo, UT, USA, The Generations Network, Inc., 2000), www.ancestry.com, Date: 1940-09-20. Record for Ina Webb Palmer.
[101] Ancestry.com, California Death Index, 1940-1997 (Provo, UT, USA, The Generations Network, Inc., 2000), www.ancestry.com, Date: 1940-09-20. Record for Ina Webb Palmer.

Generation Three

10. Mary H. Webb[3] (John H. Webb[2], Henry B. Webb[1]) was born in Jun 1855 in Harmony Township, Pennsylvania[102] and died in Friendship, New York[103]. She first married Samuel H. Poole. He was born in 1845 and died in 1880. She later married William Augustus Poole. He was born in 1857 in New York [104] and died in 1918[105].

Samuel H. Poole and Mary H. Webb had the following children:

    i.   Franklin Daniel Poole was born on 16 Nov 1873[106] and died in 11 Dec 1926 in Ithaca, New York[107].

    ii.   Charles A. Poole was born in 1875.

21.   iii.   William Ellsworth Poole was born on 13 Aug 1878 in Windsor, New York[108] and died in 1959 in El Dorado, Kansas[109].

Photo of Mary H. Webb and her husband, Samuel H. Poole, on their wedding day found on Ancestry.com.

---

[102] Ancestry.com, U.S., Find A Grave Index, 1700s-Current (Provo, UT, USA, Ancestry.com Operations, Inc., 2012), Ancestry.com, http://www.Ancestry.com, Record for Mary H. Poole.

[103] Ancestry.com, U.S., Find A Grave Index, 1700s-Current (Provo, UT, USA, Ancestry.com Operations, Inc., 2012), Ancestry.com, http://www.Ancestry.com, Record for Mary H. Poole.

[104] Ancestry.com, U.S., Find A Grave Index, 1700s-Current (Provo, UT, USA, Ancestry.com Operations, Inc., 2012), Ancestry.com, http://www.Ancestry.com, Record for Mary H. Poole.

[105] Ancestry.com, U.S., Find A Grave Index, 1700s-Current (Provo, UT, USA, Ancestry.com Operations, Inc., 2012), Ancestry.com, http://www.Ancestry.com, Record for Mary H. Poole.

[106] Ancestry.com, World War I Draft Registration Cards, 1917-1918 (Provo, UT, USA, The Generations Network, Inc., 2005), www.ancestry.com, Registration State: New York; Registration County: Allegany; Roll: 1711955. Record for Frank Daniel Poole.

[107] New York Department of Health; Albany, NY; *NY State Death Index*; Certificate Number: *75549*

[108] Ancestry.com, World War I Draft Registration Cards, 1917-1918 (Provo, UT, USA, The Generations Network, Inc., 2005), www.ancestry.com, Registration State: New York; Registration County: Allegany; Roll: 1711955. Record for William Ellsworth Poole.

[109] Ancestry.com, U.S., Find A Grave Index, 1700s-Current (Provo, UT, USA, Ancestry.com Operations, Inc., 2012).

William Augustus Poole and Mary H. Webb had the following children:

       i.   Bert Poole was born on 03 Sep 1882[110] and died in Oct 1967 in Tucson, Arizona[111].

22.   ii.   Pansey Maude Poole was born on 25 Jul 1886 in Friendship, New York[112] and died in 1985 in Friendship, New York[113].

      iii.   Pearl Mae Poole was born on 25 Jul 1887[114] in Friendship, New York and died in Jan 1973 in Friendship, New York[115]. She married George H. Henry, the son of Maximillian Henry, on 17 Jan 1931 in Rochester, New York[116]. He was born in 17 Jul 1881 in Cleveland, Ohio[117].

11. Adelia M. Webb[3] (John H. Webb[2], Henry B. Webb[1]) was born on 14 Apr 1858 in Harmony Township, Pennsylvania[118] and died in Jan 9, 1914[119]. She first married Albert Casper Niver. He was born on 29 Nov 1843 and died on 01 Mar 1877. She later married Francis Marion Benjamin in 1882[120]. He was born in 09 Oct 1847 in New York[121] and died 09 Sept 1932[122]. Adelia M. Webb and her husband, Francis Marion Benjamin, were both buried in the Maple Grove Cemetery, Friendship, New York[123].

Photo of Adelia M. Webb from the collection of Norma Dwyer and used with permission.

---

[110] Ancestry.com, World War I Draft Registration Cards, 1917-1918 (Provo, UT, USA, The Generations Network, Inc., 2005), www.ancestry.com, Registration State: New York; Registration County: Allegany; Roll: 1711955. Record for William Ellsworth Poole.

[111] Ancestry.com, Social Security Death Index (Provo, UT, USA, The Generations Network, Inc., 2008), www.ancestry.com, Number: 071-14-6478; Issue State: New York; Issue Date: Before 1951. Record for Bert Poole.

[112] Ancestry.com, U.S., Find A Grave Index, 1700s-Current (Provo, UT, USA, Ancestry.com Operations, Inc., 2012),

[113] Ancestry.com, U.S., Find A Grave Index, 1700s-Current (Provo, UT, USA, Ancestry.com Operations, Inc., 2012),

[114] New York, County Marriages, 1847-1848; 1908-1936

[115] Ancestry.com, Social Security Death Index (Provo, UT, USA, The Generations Network, Inc., 2008), www.ancestry.com, Number: 098-18-5107; Issue State: New York; Issue Date: Before 1951. Record for Pearl Henry.

[116] New York, County Marriages, 1847-1848; 1908-1936.

[117] New York, County Marriages, 1847-1848; 1908-1936.

[118] Ancestry.com, Web: New York, Find A Grave Index, 1660-2012 (Provo, UT, USA, Ancestry.com Operations, Inc., 2012), Ancestry.com, http://www.Ancestry.com, Record for Adelia M. Benjamin.

[119] New York Department of Health; Albany, NY; *NY State Death Index*; Certificate Number: *332*

[120] Ancestry.com, 1900 United States Federal Census (Provo, UT, USA, Ancestry.com Operations Inc, 2004), Ancestry.com, http://www.Ancestry.com, Year: 1900; Census Place: Friendship, Allegany, New York; Roll: 1008; Page: 6B; Enumeration District: 0016; FHL microfilm: 1241008.

[121] Ancestry.com, U.S., Find A Grave Index, 1700s-Current (Provo, UT, USA, Ancestry.com Operations, Inc., 2012),

[122] Ancestry.com, U.S., Find A Grave Index, 1700s-Current (Provo, UT, USA, Ancestry.com Operations, Inc., 2012),

[123] Ancestry.com, U.S., Find A Grave Index, 1700s-Current (Provo, UT, USA, Ancestry.com Operations, Inc., 2012),

Albert Casper Niver and Adelia M. Webb had the following child:
23.   i.   Charles Albert Niver Sr. was born on 31 Aug 1876 in Friendship, New York[124] and died on 27 Jan 1957[125].

Photo of Albert Casper Niver found on Ancestry.com.

Francis Marion Benjamin and Adelia M. Webb had the following children:
        ii.   Arthur George Benjamin was born in 24 Dec 1883 in New York[126]. He married Cora Belle Clark on 26 Feb 1926 in Monroe, New York[127]. She was born in 1881[128].

Photo taken in the Summer of 1907 found on ancestry.com. Seated at far left may be John Webb, father of Adelia, Nell and Mary Webb. Back Frank Benjamin Adelia Webb Niver Benjamin Arthur Benjamin; third row Nell Webb Baker, with Hazel Niver; Edith Niver, Cora Niver and son Harold; Pansey Poole Perkins and daughter Vera; front: Laura and Lola Niver.

---

[124] Ancestry.com, U.S., Social Security Applications and Claims Index, 1936-2007 (Provo, UT, USA, Ancestry.com Operations, Inc., 2015), Ancestry.com, http://www.Ancestry.com, Record for Charles A Sr Niver.
[125] Ancestry.com, U.S., Social Security Applications and Claims Index, 1936-2007 (Provo, UT, USA, Ancestry.com Operations, Inc., 2015), Ancestry.com, http://www.Ancestry.com, Record for Charles A Sr Niver.
[126] Ancestry.com, 1900 United States Federal Census (Provo, UT, USA, Ancestry.com Operations Inc, 2004), Ancestry.com, http://www.Ancestry.com, Year: 1900; Census Place: Friendship, Allegany, New York; Roll: 1008; Page: 6B; Enumeration District: 0016; FHL microfilm: 1241008. Record for Arthur G Benjamin.
[127] NY County Marriages, Ancestry.com. New York, County Marriages, 1847-1849; 1907-1936 [database on-line]. Lehi, UT, USA: Ancestry.com Operations, Inc., 2016.
[128] NY County Marriages, Ancestry.com. New York, County Marriages, 1847-1849; 1907-1936 [database on-line]. Lehi, UT, USA: Ancestry.com Operations, Inc., 2016.

12. Ellen M. Webb[3] (John H. Webb[2], Henry B. Webb[1]) was born in Dec 1859 in Harmony Township, Pennsylvania[129] and died on 18 Oct 1942[130]. She married John W. Baker about 1880. He was born in Jun 1856[131] and died in 1930.

John W. Baker and Ellen M. Webb had the following children:
24. i.   Miner A. Baker was born on 01 Dec 1881[132].
25. ii.   Robert Oney Baker was born on 31 Oct 1883 in Friendship, New York[133] and died on 21 Jun 1945[134].
     iii.   Edward E. Baker was born in Sep 1886[135].
     iv.   Frederick James Baker was born on 01 Aug 1887 in New York[136].
26. v.   Ernest Leroy Baker was born on 09 Mar 1890 in Friendship, New York[137] and died in Nov 1973 in Rochester, New York[138].
     vi.   Warren E. Baker was born on 11 Jul 1897 in Friendship, New York[139] and died on 30 Apr 1950[140]. He married Helen Weaver on 28 Mar 1930 in Monroe, New York [141]. She was born in 1900 in Canada[142].

---

[129] Ancestry.com, 1900 United States Federal Census (Provo, UT, USA, The Generations Network, Inc., 2004), www.ancestry.com, Year: 1900; Census Place: Friendship, Allegany, New York; Roll: 1008; Page: 6A; Enumeration District: 0016; FHL microfilm: 1241008.

[130] City directories, Ancestry.com. U.S. City Directories, 1822-1995 [database on-line]. Provo, UT, USA: Ancestry.com Operations, Inc., 2011.

[131] Ancestry.com, 1900 United States Federal Census (Provo, UT, USA, The Generations Network, Inc., 2004), www.ancestry.com, Year: 1900; Census Place: Friendship, Allegany, New York; Roll: 1008; Page: 6A; Enumeration District: 0016; FHL microfilm: 1241008. Record for Muser A Baker.

[132] Ancestry.com, World War I Draft Registration Cards, 1917-1918 (Provo, UT, USA, The Generations Network, Inc., 2005), www.ancestry.com, Registration State: New York; Registration County: Monroe; Roll: 1818811; Draft Board: 8. Record for Miner Baker.

[133] Ancestry.com, U.S. World War II Draft Registration Cards, 1942 (Provo, UT, USA, The Generations Network, Inc., 2007), www.ancestry.com, The National Archives at St. Louis; St. Louis, Missouri; World War II Draft Cards (Fourth Registration) for the State of New York; Record Group Title: Records of the Selective Service System, 1926-1975; Record Group Number: 147; Box or Roll Number: 23. Record for Robert Oney Baker.

[134] Ancestry.com, U.S., Social Security Applications and Claims Index, 1936-2007 (Provo, UT, USA, Ancestry.com Operations, Inc., 2015), Ancestry.com, http://www.Ancestry.com, Record for Robert Oney Baker

[135] Year: 1900; Census Place: Friendship, Allegany, New York; Roll: 1008; Page: 6A; Enumeration District: 0016; FHL microfilm: 1241008

[136] Ancestry.com, World War I Draft Registration Cards, 1917-1918 (Provo, UT, USA, The Generations Network, Inc., 2005), www.ancestry.com, Registration State: New York; Registration County: Monroe; Roll: 1818807; Draft Board: 6. Record for Frederick James Baker.

[137] Ancestry.com, World War I Draft Registration Cards, 1917-1918 (Provo, UT, USA, The Generations Network, Inc., 2005), www.ancestry.com, Registration State: New York; Registration County: Monroe; Roll: 1818807; Draft Board: 6. Record for Ernest Le Roy Baker.

[138] Ancestry.com, Social Security Death Index (Provo, UT, USA, The Generations Network, Inc., 2008), www.ancestry.com, Number: 071-01-8528; Issue State: New York; Issue Date: Before 1951. Record for Ernest Baker.

[139] Ancestry.com, U.S., Social Security Applications and Claims Index, 1936-2007 (Provo, UT, USA, Ancestry.com Operations, Inc., 2015), Ancestry.com, http://www.Ancestry.com, Record for Warren Ernest Baker.

[140] Ancestry.com, U.S., Social Security Applications and Claims Index, 1936-2007 (Provo, UT, USA, Ancestry.com Operations, Inc., 2015), Ancestry.com, http://www.Ancestry.com, Record for Warren Ernest Baker.

[141] Ancestry.com, New York, County Marriages, 1847-1849; 1907-1936, Record for Warren C Baker.

[142] Ancestry.com, New York, County Marriages, 1847-1849; 1907-1936, Record for Warren C Baker.

13. William H. Foote[3] (Abigail Webb[2], Henry B. Webb[1]) was born 03 Apr 1846 in Syracuse, New York[143] and died on 21 Mar 1938 at 117 Central Avenue, Cortland, New York[144]. He married Anna Mariah Weaver on 25 Feb 1875[145]. She was born in 1845 in Stockbridge, New York [146] and died on 26 Dec 1905 in Madison, New York[147]. He later married Mary L. O'Dell, the daughter of Benjamin O'Dell and Maria Brace, on 06 Apr 1908 in Utica, New York[148]. She was born on 17 Sept 1846[149] and died on 05 Dec 1924 in Madison, New York[150]. Mary L. O'Dell was buried in New Forest Cemetery, Utica, New York[151]. William H. Foote and Anna Mariah Weaver were buried in Madison Village Cemetery, Madison, New York[152].

The 1910 Census showed William had been married twice. Mary S. was his second wife. At that time they lived on Solsville Road, Madison, New York. William was a carpenter by trade.

Taken from his Obituary

William H. Foote, 93, former resident of Utica and Madison and veteran of 46 engagements in the Civil War, died Monday at his home in Cortland. He lived in Utica and Madison until about a year ago when he removed to Cortland. Foote was in many important battles and several horses were shot under him, yet he never was wounded. He was at the siege of Harper's Ferry, Antietam, Fredericksburg, Gettysburg and Brandy Station and participated in the review of the Grand Army in Washington in May 1865. He was honorable discharged June 27, 1865 at Alexandria, Virginia. He was born at a small settlement near Syracuse, the son of the late Mr. & Mrs. George Foote. He enlisted in Utica in December 1861 in Company I, New York Cavalry.

William H. Foote and Anna Mariah Weaver Foote had the following children:

---

[143] Ancestry.com, North America, Family Histories, 1500-2000 (Provo, UT, USA, Ancestry.com Operations, Inc., 2016), Ancestry.com, http://www.Ancestry.com, Book Title: Foote Family : Comprising the Genealogy and History of Nathaniel Foote of Wethersfield, Connecticut, and His Descendants : also a partial record of Descendants of Pasco Foote of Salem, Massachusetts : Richard Foote of Stafford County, Virginia, and John Foote of New York

[144] New York State Death Records at Ancestry.com.

[145] Death Certificate on William H. Foote found at the New York State Vital Records, Albany, New York.

[146] Ancestry.com, Web: New York, Find A Grave Index, 1664-2011 (Provo, UT, USA, Ancestry.com Operations, Inc., 2012), www.ancestry.com, Database online.

[147] Civil War pension records on William H. Foot.

[148] Ancestry.com. *New York, County Marriage Records, 1847-1849, 1907-1936* [database on-line]. Lehi, UT, USA: Ancestry.com Operations, Inc., 2016. Original data: *Marriage Records. New York Marriages.* Various New York County Clerk offices.

[149] Ancestry.com, Web: New York, Find A Grave Index, 1664-2011 (Provo, UT, USA, Ancestry.com Operations, Inc., 2012), www.ancestry.com, Database online.

[150] Ancestry.com, Web: New York, Find A Grave Index, 1664-2011 (Provo, UT, USA, Ancestry.com Operations, Inc., 2012), www.ancestry.com, Database online.

[151] Ancestry.com. *U.S., Find A Grave Index, 1600s-Current* [database on-line]. Provo, UT, USA: Ancestry.com Operations, Inc., 2012.

[152] Ancestry.com. *U.S., Find A Grave Index, 1600s-Current* [database on-line]. Provo, UT, USA: Ancestry.com Operations, Inc., 2012.

  i. Clarence E. Foote was born on 21 Feb 1876[153] and died on 04 Mar 1880[154].

  ii. Clara E. Foote was born on 29 Oct 1878 in Michigan[155] and died on 23 Oct 1930 in Cortland, New York[156]. An obituary for Clara was not found in the Cortland paper. A death notice was found stating she was the daughter of William.

  iii. George Henry Foote was born on 17 Jan 1881[157] and died on 23 Mar 1923[158]. He married Alice Henry on 16 Sep 1903[159]. She was born on 11 Apr 1881 in Madison, New York[160]. George was found in the 1910 Census living at 154 Carroll St., Binghamton, New York. He was listed as a mail carrier. He had been married for six years and had no children at that time. He was still living in Binghamton in 1920 and had no children listed. Alice was listed in the Binghamton Census in 1930 was a widow.

27. iv. Mildred E. Foote was born on 10 Jun 1884 in Madison , New York[161] and died on 19 Dec 1964 in Utica , New York[162].

14. Mary Abigal Foote[3] (Abigail Webb[2], Henry B. Webb[1]) was born on 26 Jun 1849 in Syracuse, New York[163] and died on 03 Mar 1913 in Whitesboro, New York[164]. She married Herman D. Mather on 12 June 1873 in Utica, New York[165]. He was born in 1845 in Augusta, New York[166] and died on 11 Apr 1926 in a G.A.R. Home, St. Johnsville, New York[167]. Abby Foote worked as a servant for the Julius Tucker family in 1865 in

---

[153] Civil War pension records on William H. Foot.

[154] Civil War pension records on William H. Foot.

[155] Ancestry.com, Web: New York, Find A Grave Index, 1664-2011 (Provo, UT, USA, Ancestry.com Operations, Inc., 2012), www.ancestry.com, Database online.

[156] Ancestry.com, Web: New York, Find A Grave Index, 1664-2011 (Provo, UT, USA, Ancestry.com Operations, Inc., 2012), www.ancestry.com, Database online.

[157] Ancestry.com, World War I Draft Registration Cards, 1917-1918 (Provo, UT, USA, The Generations Network, Inc., 2005), www.ancestry.com, Registration State: New York; Registration County: Broome; Roll: 1712043.

[158] Ancestry.com. *New York, Death Index, 1880-1956* [database on-line]. Lehi, UT, USA: Ancestry.com Operations, Inc., 2017.

[159] Ancestry.com, North America, Family Histories, 1500-2000 (Provo, UT, USA, Ancestry.com Operations, Inc., 2016), Ancestry.com, http://www.Ancestry.com, Book Title: Foote Family : Comprising the Genealogy and History of Nathaniel Foote of Wethersfield, Connecticut, and His Descendants

[160] Ancestry.com, North America, Family Histories, 1500-2000 (Provo, UT, USA, Ancestry.com Operations, Inc., 2016), Ancestry.com, http://www.Ancestry.com, Book Title: Foote Family : Comprising the Genealogy and History of Nathaniel Foote of Wethersfield, Connecticut, and His Descendants

[161] Obituary, Utica Observer Dispatch, Utica, New York December 21, 1964, page 29.

[162] Obituary, Utica Observer Dispatch, Utica, New York December 21, 1964, page 29.

[163] Ancestry.com, North America, Family Histories, 1500-2000 (Provo, UT, USA, Ancestry.com Operations, Inc., 2016), Ancestry.com, http://www.Ancestry.com, Book Title: Foote Family : Comprising the Genealogy and History of Nathaniel Foote of Wethersfield, Connecticut, and His Descendants : also a partial record of Descendants of Pasco Foote of Salem, Massachusetts : Richard Foote of Stafford County, Virginia, and John Foote of New York

[164] Obituary, Utica Daily Press, Utica, New York, March 4, 1913.

[165] Ancestry.com. *North America, Family Histories, 1500-2000* [database on-line]. Provo, UT, USA: Ancestry.com Operations, Inc., 2016.

[166] Tombstone, Mt. Pleasant Cemetery, Canastota, New York.

[167] Death announcement Utica Daily Press, Utica, New York paper April 16, 1926.

Madison, New York. She was a servant for Edwin R. Barker in Madison County, Town of Eaton in 1870. Mary and Herman D. lived in Utica, New York in 1880. Mary lived on Powell Road in Whitesboro in the 1910 Whitestown Census. That census indicated she had three children, two living. Her obituary said she had two children and two grandchildren. In the 1900 Census, she lived with her daughter Anna in Lenox, Madison County, New York.

Photo of Mary Abigal Foote Mather from the authors collection.

Herman fought in the Civil War. Co. E., 16 Regiment US Infantry. The Canastota Directory for 1887 and 1888 said Herman was a night policeman and lived at Stocking Lane in Canastota.

Herman D. Mather and Mary Abigal Foote had the following children:
28.	i.	Lydia Anna Mather was born on 26 Apr 1875 in Madison, New York[168] and died on 15 Mar 1969 at 9 West Street, Whitesboro, New York[169].

Photo of Lydia Anna Mather from the authors collection.

29.	ii.	Gertrude M. Mather was born on 19 Nov 1876 in Oneida, New York[170] and died on 06 May 1963 in St. Luke's Memorial Hospital, New Hartford, New York[171].
	iii.	George F. Mather was born on 09 Apr 1879 in New York State[172] and died on 13 Jul 1888[173]. George F. Mather was buried in the Mt. Pleasant Cemetery, Canastota, New York.

---

[168] Foote Family History & Genealogy Vol 1.
[169] Obituary, Utica Daily Press, Utica, New York, March 18, 1969, page 12.
[170] Foote Family History & Genealogy Vol 1.
[171] Obituary, Utica Daily Press, Utica, New York, May 7, 1963.
[172] Foote Family History & Genealogy Vol 1.
[173] Gravestone, Mt. Pleasant Cemetery, Canastota, New York.

15. Frederick M. Lovejoy[3] (Samantha Martha Webb[2], Henry B. Webb[1]) was born in Aug 1861 in New York[174] and died in 1905[175]. He married Alice M. Dixon, the daughter of Robert C. Dixon and Polly Wiltsy, in 1896[176]. She was born in Feb 1870 in New York[177] and died on 09 Jun 1925 in Syracuse, New York[178].

Frederick M. Lovejoy and Alice M. Dixon had the following children:

     i.   Raymond G. Lovejoy was born in May 1897 in New York[179] and died in 1918[180]. Raymond may have been a casualty of World War I.

     ii.   Edna Lovejoy was born in Dec 1898 in Madison, New York[181].

16. Myron D. Webb[3] (LaFayette Webb[2], Henry B. Webb[1]) was born in 1859 in New York[182] and died on 19 Feb 1916 in Fairbault, Minnesota[183]. He married Catherine Corcoran on 04 Dec 1882 in Blue Earth, Minnesota.[184]. She was born in Apr 1857 in Wisconsin[185] and died in 1928.

---

[174] Ancestry.com, U.S., Find A Grave Index, 1700s-Current (Provo, UT, USA, Ancestry.com Operations, Inc., 2012), Ancestry.com, http://www.Ancestry.com, Record for Fred M. Lovejoy

[175] Ancestry.com, U.S., Find A Grave Index, 1700s-Current (Provo, UT, USA, Ancestry.com Operations, Inc., 2012), Ancestry.com, http://www.Ancestry.com, Record for Fred M. Lovejoy

[176] Ancestry.com, 1900 United States Federal Census (Provo, UT, USA, The Generations Network, Inc., 2004), www.ancestry.com, Year: 1900; Census Place: Madison, Madison, New York; Roll: 1072; Page: 4B; Enumeration District: 0022; FHL microfilm: 1241072. Record for Fred M Lovejoy.

[177] Ancestry.com, 1900 United States Federal Census (Provo, UT, USA, The Generations Network, Inc., 2004), www.ancestry.com, Year: 1900; Census Place: Madison, Madison, New York; Roll: 1072; Page: 4B; Enumeration District: 0022; FHL microfilm: 1241072. Record for Fred M Lovejoy.

[178] Ancestry.com. New York, Death Index, 1880-1956 [database on-line]. Lehi, UT, USA: Ancestry.com Operations, Inc., 2017.

[179] Ancestry.com, 1900 United States Federal Census (Provo, UT, USA, The Generations Network, Inc., 2004), www.ancestry.com, Year: 1900; Census Place: Madison, Madison, New York; Roll: 1072; Page: 4B; Enumeration District: 0022; FHL microfilm: 1241072. Record for Fred M Lovejoy.

[180] Ancestry.com, U.S., Find A Grave Index, 1700s-Current (Provo, UT, USA, Ancestry.com Operations, Inc., 2012), Ancestry.com, http://www.Ancestry.com, Record for Raymond G. Lovejoy

[181] Ancestry.com, 1900 United States Federal Census (Provo, UT, USA, The Generations Network, Inc., 2004), www.ancestry.com, Year: 1900; Census Place: Madison, Madison, New York; Roll: 1072; Page: 4B; Enumeration District: 0022; FHL microfilm: 1241072. Record for Fred M Lovejoy.

[182] Ancestry.com, 1860 United States Federal Census (Provo, UT, USA, The Generations Network, Inc., 2004), www.ancestry.com, Year: 1860; Census Place: Madison, Madison, New York; Roll: M653_781; Page: 1092; Family History Library Film: 803781. Record for Myron Webb.

[183] Familysearch.org, "Minnesota Death Index, 1908-2002," database, FamilySearch (https://familysearch.org/ark:/61903/1:1:V4CM-BRL : 4 December 2014), Myron Webb, 19 Feb 1916.

[184] Ancestry.com. *Minnesota, Marriages Index, 1849-1950* [database on-line]. Provo, UT, USA: Ancestry.com Operations, Inc., 2011.

[185] Ancestry.com, 1900 United States Federal Census (Provo, UT, USA, The Generations Network, Inc., 2004), www.ancestry.com, Year: 1900; Census Place: Blue Earth, Faribault, Minnesota; Roll: 762; Page: 12A; Enumeration District: 0081; FHL microfilm: 1240762. Record for M D Webb.

Myron D. Webb and Catherine Corcoran had the following children:

30.   i.   Frank Joseph Webb was born on 06 Jun 1882 in Blue Earth City, Minnesota[186] and died on 28 Sep 1965[187].

31.   ii.   Rhoda Ann Webb was born on 29 Sep 1884 in Minnesota[188] and died on 28 Feb 1976 in Benton, Oregon[189].

32.   iii.   Julia Catherine Webb was born on 27 Dec 1886 in Blue Earth City, Minnesota[190] and died in May 1968 in Conrad, Montana[191].

       iv.   Bessie Webb was born in Sep 1890 in Minnesota[192].

33.   v.   Hazel Mary Webb was born on 15 Aug 1894 in Blue Earth, Minnesota[193] and died on 02 Jul 1976 in Havre, Montana[194].

17. Sally Foliett "Ettie" Fagan was born in May 17, 1859[195] and died in May 1942[196]. She married Walter Chrispell in 17 Feb 1878[197]. He was born in Aug 1848 in New York[198] and died on 01 Mar 1925 in Sherburne, New York[199].

[186] Ancestry.com, U.S. World War II Draft Registration Cards, 1942 (Provo, UT, USA, The Generations Network, Inc., 2007), www.ancestry.com, The National Archives at St. Louis; St. Louis, Missouri; World War II Draft Cards (Fourth Registration) for the State of Iowa; Record Group Title: Records of the Selective Service System, 1926-1975; Record Group Number: 147; Box or Roll Number: 242. Record for Frank Joseph Webb.

[187] Ancestry.com, Social Security Death Index (Provo, UT, USA, The Generations Network, Inc., 2008), www.ancestry.com, Number: 517-12-5901; Issue State: Montana; Issue Date: Before 1951. Record for Frank Webb.

[188] Ancestry.com, Social Security Death Index (Provo, UT, USA, The Generations Network, Inc., 2008), www.ancestry.com, Number: 550-52-3206; Issue State: California; Issue Date: 1955. Record for Rhoda Palmer

[189] Ancestry.com, Oregon Death Index, 1903-98 (Provo, UT, USA, Ancestry.com Operations Inc, 2000), www.ancestry.com, Oregon State Library; 1966-1970 Death Index; Reel Title: State of Oregon Death Index; Year Range: 1971-1980. Record for Rhoda Ann Palmer.

[190] Ancestry.com, Social Security Death Index (Provo, UT, USA, The Generations Network, Inc., 2008), www.ancestry.com, Number: 516-05-3489; Issue State: Montana; Issue Date: Before 1951. Record for Julia Porter.

[191] Ancestry.com, Social Security Death Index (Provo, UT, USA, The Generations Network, Inc., 2008), www.ancestry.com, Number: 516-05-3489; Issue State: Montana; Issue Date: Before 1951. Record for Julia Porter.

[192] Ancestry.com, 1900 United States Federal Census (Provo, UT, USA, The Generations Network, Inc., 2004), www.ancestry.com, Year: 1900; Census Place: Blue Earth, Faribault, Minnesota; Roll: 762; Page: 12A; Enumeration District: 0081; FHL microfilm: 1240762. Record for M D Webb

[193] Ancestry.com, Minnesota, Births and Christenings Index, 1840-1980 (Provo, UT, USA, Ancestry.com Operations, Inc., 2011), Ancestry.com, http://www.Ancestry.com, Record for Hazel Mary Webb.

[194] Ancestry.com, Montana, Death Index, 1868-2011 (Provo, UT, USA, Ancestry.com Operations, Inc., 2001), Ancestry.com, http://www.Ancestry.com, Record for Hazel M Atwood.

[195] New York State Archives; Albany, New York; *New York State Veterans' Home. Resident Case Files, 1897-1963;* Series Number: *A0710;* Box Number: *10*

[196] Findagrave at Ancestry.com.

[197] New York State Archives; Albany, New York; *New York State Veterans' Home. Resident Case Files, 1897-1963;* Series Number: *A0710;* Box Number: *10*

[198] Ancestry.com, 1900 United States Federal Census (Provo, UT, USA, The Generations Network, Inc., 2004), www.ancestry.com, Year: 1900; Census Place: Sherburne, Chenango, New York; Roll: 1017; Page: 15A; Enumeration District: 0081; FHL microfilm: 1241017. Record for Walter Crisfield

[199] Ancestery.com, Ancestry.com. New York, Death Index, 1880-1956 [database on-line]. Lehi, UT, USA: Ancestry.com Operations, Inc., 2017.

Walter Chrispell and Sally Foliett Fagan had the following child:
34.   i.   Peter Henry Crispell was born 17 Dec 1900 in New York State[200] and died 17 June 1978 in Sherburne, New York[201].

18. George H. Fagin[3] (Adelia M. Webb[2], Henry B. Webb[1]) was born in Feb 1866 in New York[202] and died on 30 Apr 1951 in Sherburne, New York[203]. He married Cora Aylesworth[204]. She was born in Sep 1870 in New York[205] and died on 24 May 1929 in Sherburne, New York[206]. George H. Fagin and Cora Aylesworth were buried in Graham Cemetery, Hubbardsville, New York.

George H. Fagin and Cora Aylesworth had the following child:
        i.   Anna Maude Fagan was born in Jul 1889 in New York[207] and died in 1962[208]. She married Frank Madison Williams, the son of Arton Williams and Clara Bugbee, on 30 Oct 1912 in Chenango, New York[209]. He was born on 18 Nov 1887 in New York[210] died on 27 Dec 1946 in Utica, New York[211]. Anna Maude Fagin and Frank Madison Williams were buried in Graham Cemetery, Hubbardsville, New York[212].

19. Charles Read Fagan[3] (Adelia M. Webb[2], Henry B. Webb[1]) was born in Madison, New York on 04 May 1874[213] and died on 03 Nov 1952 in Sherburne, New York[214]. He

---

[200] Ancestry.com. Social Security Death Index, Number: 105-14-4623; Issue State: New York; Issue Date: Before 1951.

[201] Ancestry.com. Social Security Death Index, Number: 105-14-4623; Issue State: New York; Issue Date: Before 1951.

[202] Ancestry.com, 1900 United States Federal Census (Provo, UT, USA, The Generations Network, Inc., 2004), www.ancestry.com, Year. 1900; Census Place: Hamilton, Madison, New York; Roll: 1071; Page: 9A; Enumeration District: 0013; FHL microfilm: 1241071. Record for George F Fagin.

[203] Ancestry.com, New York, Death Index, 1880-1956 (Lehi, UT, USA, Ancestry.com Operations, Inc., 2017),

[204] Ancestry.com, 1900 United States Federal Census (Provo, UT, USA, The Generations Network, Inc., 2004), www.ancestry.com, Year: 1900; Census Place: Hamilton, Madison, New York; Roll: 1071; Page: 9A; Enumeration District: 0013; FHL microfilm: 1241071. Record for George F Fagin.

[205] Ancestry.com, 1900 United States Federal Census (Provo, UT, USA, The Generations Network, Inc., 2004), www.ancestry.com, Year: 1900; Census Place: Hamilton, Madison, New York; Roll: 1071; Page: 9A; Enumeration District: 0013; FHL microfilm: 1241071. Record for George F Fagin.

[206] Ancestry.com, New York, Death Index, 1880-1956 (Lehi, UT, USA, Ancestry.com Operations, Inc., 2017),

[207] Ancestry.com, 1900 United States Federal Census (Provo, UT, USA, The Generations Network, Inc., 2004), www.ancestry.com, Year: 1900; Census Place: Hamilton, Madison, New York; Roll: 1071; Page: 9A; Enumeration District: 0013; FHL microfilm: 1241071. Record for George F Fagin.

[208] Findagrave.com. Graham Cemetery, Hubbardsville, New York.
Ancestry.com, New York, County Marriages, 1847-1849; 1907-1936 (Lehi, UT, USA, Ancestry.com Operations, Inc., 2016), Ancestry.com, http://www.Ancestry.com, Record for Frank M Williams. [209]

[210] Ancestry.com, World War I Draft Registration Cards, 1917-1918 (Provo, UT, USA, The Generations Network, Inc., 2005), www.ancestry.com, Registration State: New York; Registration County: Madison; Roll: 1753843; Draft Board: 1. Record for Frank Madison Williams

[211] Ancestry.com. New York, Death Index, 1880-1956 Lehi, UT, USA: Ancestry.com Operations, Inc., 2017.

[212] Findagrave.com. Graham Cemetery, Hubbardsville, New York.

[213] Ancestry.com, U.S., Social Security Applications and Claims Index, 1936-2007 (Provo, UT, USA, Ancestry.com Operations, Inc., 2015), Ancestry.com, http://www.Ancestry.com, Record for Charles Read Fagan.

[214] Ancestry.com. New York, Death Index, 1880-1956.

married Alice F. in 1898[215]. She was born in Oct 1874 in New York[216] and died on 03 Aug 1928 in Sherburne[217].

Charles Read and Alice F. Fagan had the following children:

     i.   Francis J. Fagin was born in Aug 1899 in New York[218] and died on 29 Sep 1904 in Sherburne, New York[219].

     ii.   Kenneth P. Fagan was born on 17 May 1903[220] and died on 24 Sep 1992 in Sherburne, New York [221]. He married Ann H.[222]. She was born on 04 Sep 1903[223] and died in Dec 1985 in Sherburne, New York[224].

     iii.   Hazel A. Fagan was born in 1905 in New York[225]. She married Frederick F. Howe on 21 Sep 1928 in Susquehanna, Pennsylvania[226]. He was born in 1904[227].

     iv.   Clifford Fagin was born in 1908 in New York[228] and died 02 Jul 1965 in Sherburne, New York[229].

---

[215] Ancestry.com, 1900 United States Federal Census (Provo, UT, USA, The Generations Network, Inc., 2004), www.ancestry.com, Year: 1900; Census Place: Sherburne, Chenango, New York; Roll: 1017; Page: 16A; Enumeration District: 0081; FHL microfilm: 1241017. Record for Charles Fagin.

[216] Ancestry.com, 1900 United States Federal Census (Provo, UT, USA, The Generations Network, Inc., 2004), www.ancestry.com, Year: 1900; Census Place: Sherburne, Chenango, New York; Roll: 1017; Page: 16A; Enumeration District: 0081; FHL microfilm: 1241017. Record for Charles Fagin.

[217] ancestery.com, Ancestry.com. New York, Death Index, 1880-1956 [database on-line]. Lehi, UT, USA: Ancestry.com Operations, Inc., 2017.

[218] Ancestry.com, 1900 United States Federal Census (Provo, UT, USA, The Generations Network, Inc., 2004), www.ancestry.com, Year: 1900; Census Place: Sherburne, Chenango, New York; Roll: 1017; Page: 16A; Enumeration District: 0081; FHL microfilm: 1241017. Record for Charles Fagin.

[219] ancestery.com, Ancestry.com. New York, Death Index, 1880-1956 [database on-line]. Lehi, UT, USA: Ancestry.com Operations, Inc., 2017.

[220] Ancestry.com, Social Security Death Index (Provo, UT, USA, The Generations Network, Inc., 2008), www.ancestry.com, Number: 093-09-7797; Issue State: New York; Issue Date: Before 1951. Record for Kenneth P. Fagan

[221] Ancestry.com, Social Security Death Index (Provo, UT, USA, The Generations Network, Inc., 2008), www.ancestry.com, Number: 093-09-7797; Issue State: New York; Issue Date: Before 1951. Record for Kenneth P. Fagan

[222] Ancestry.com, 1940 United States Federal Census (Provo, UT, USA, Ancestry.com Operations, Inc., 2012), Ancestry.com, http://www.Ancestry.com, Year: 1940; Census Place: Sherburne, Chenango, New York; Roll: T627_2515; Page: 10A; Enumeration District: 9-41. Record for Kenneth P Fagan.

[223] Ancestry.com, Social Security Death Index (Provo, UT, USA, The Generations Network, Inc., 2008), www.ancestry.com, Number: 093-09-7798; Issue State: New York; Issue Date: Before 1951. Record for Ann Fagan.

[224] Ancestry.com, Social Security Death Index (Provo, UT, USA, The Generations Network, Inc., 2008), www.ancestry.com, Number: 093-09-7798; Issue State: New York; Issue Date: Before 1951. Record for Ann Fagan.

[225] Ancestry.com, Pennsylvania, Marriages, 1852-1968 (Lehi, UT, USA, Ancestry.com Operations, Inc., 2016), Ancestry.com, http://www.Ancestry.com, Record for Frederick F Howe.

[226] Ancestry.com, Pennsylvania, Marriages, 1852-1968 (Lehi, UT, USA, Ancestry.com Operations, Inc., 2016), Ancestry.com, http://www.Ancestry.com, Record for Frederick F Howe.

[227] Ancestry.com, Pennsylvania, Marriages, 1852-1968 (Lehi, UT, USA, Ancestry.com Operations, Inc., 2016), Ancestry.com, http://www.Ancestry.com, Record for Frederick F Howe.

[228] Ancestry.com, 1910 United States Federal Census (Provo, UT, USA, The Generations Network, Inc., 2006), www.ancestry.com, Year: 1910; Census Place: Sherburne, Chenango, New York; Roll: T624_924; Page: 5B; Enumeration District: 0102; FHL microfilm: 1374937. Record for Charles Fagan

[229] New York State Death Index, 1957 to 1968.

20. Ina Elizabeth Webb[3] (Thomas H. Webb[2], Henry B. Webb[1]) was born on 25 Dec 1866 in Minnesota[230] and died on 20 Sep 1940 in Los Angeles County, California[231]. She married Dr. Ford Norman Palmer on 29 Oct 1888 in Fairbault, Minnesota[232]. He was born on 22 Apr 1860 in New York[233] and died on 17 Jul 1949 in Los Angeles, California[234].

Dr. Ford Norman Palmer and Ina Elizabeth Webb had the following children:

      i.   Iva Nanette Palmer was born on 21 Sep 1890 in South Dakota[235] and died on 27 Feb 1955 in Los Angeles County, California[236].

35.   ii.   Pearle Marguerite Palmer was born on 21 Sep 1890 in South Dakota[237] and died on 15 Apr 1952 in Los Angeles, California[238].

---

[230] Ancestry.com, California Death Index, 1940-1997 (Provo, UT, USA, The Generations Network, Inc., 2000), www.ancestry.com, Date: 1940-09-20. Record for Ina Webb Palmer.

[231] Ancestry.com, California Death Index, 1940-1997 (Provo, UT, USA, The Generations Network, Inc., 2000), www.ancestry.com, Date: 1940-09-20. Record for Ina Webb Palmer.

[232] Familysearch.org County marriages, "Minnesota, County Marriages, 1860-1949," database with images, FamilySearch (https://familysearch.org/ark:/61903/1:1:VKN2-88Y : 13 June 2016), Ford N Palmer and Ina E Webb, 29 Oct 1888, Faribault, Minnesota, United States; citing p. , local historical societies and universities, Minnesota; FHL microfilm 1,673,573.

[233] Ancestry.com, U.S., Find A Grave Index, 1700s-Current (Provo, UT, USA, Ancestry.com Operations, Inc., 2012), Ancestry.com, http://www.Ancestry.com, Record for Ina Palmer.

[234] Ancestry.com, U.S., Find A Grave Index, 1700s-Current (Provo, UT, USA, Ancestry.com Operations, Inc., 2012), Ancestry.com, http://www.Ancestry.com, Record for Ina Palmer.

[235] Ancestry.com, U.S., Find A Grave Index, 1700s-Current (Provo, UT, USA, Ancestry.com Operations, Inc., 2012), Ancestry.com, http://www.Ancestry.com, Record for Dr Ford Norman Palmer

[236] Ancestry.com, U.S., Find A Grave Index, 1700s-Current (Provo, UT, USA, Ancestry.com Operations, Inc., 2012), Ancestry.com, http://www.Ancestry.com, Record for Dr Ford Norman Palmer

[237] Ancestry.com, South Dakota, Birth Index, 1856-1917 (Provo, UT, USA, Ancestry.com Operations Inc, 2003), Ancestry.com, http://www.Ancestry.com, South Dakota Department of Health; Pierre, South Dakota; South Dakota, Birth Index, 1856-1917.

[238] Ancestry.com, California Death Index, 1940-1997 (Provo, UT, USA, The Generations Network, Inc., 2000), www.ancestry.com, Date: 1952-04-15. Record for Pearl Palmer Holley.

Generation Four

21. William Ellsworth Poole[4] (Mary H. Webb[3], John H. Webb[2], Henry B. Webb[1]) was born on 13 Aug 1878 in Windsor, New York[239] and died in 1959 in El Dorado, Kansas[240]. He married Jessie Gorton Mastin, the daughter of Alonzo and Pheoby F.Mastin[241]. She was born in 1882 in New York State[242] and died in 1964 in Eldorado, Kansas[243].

William Ellsworth Poole and Jessie Gorton Mastin had the following children:
36.   i.   Larue Mastin Poole was born on 14 Mar 1904 in Friendship, New York[244] and died in 1962[245].
37.   ii.   William Alonzo Poole was born on 15 Nov 1909 in Friendship, New York[246] and died on 12 May 1990 in Eldorado, Kansas[247].

22. Pansey Maude Poole[4] (Mary H. Webb[3], John H. Webb[2], Henry B. Webb[1]) was born on 25 Jul 1886 in Friendship, New York[248] and died in 1985 in Friendship, New York[249]. She married Lyle Delette Perkins[250]. He was born on 20 Aug 1877 in Friendship, New York[251] and died on 02 Sep 1941 in Friendship, New York [252].

---

[239] Ancestry.com, World War I Draft Registration Cards, 1917-1918 (Provo, UT, USA, The Generations Network, Inc., 2005), www.ancestry.com, Registration State: New York; Registration County: Allegany; Roll: 1711955. Record for William Ellsworth Poole.

[240] Ancestry.com, U.S., Find A Grave Index, 1700s-Current (Provo, UT, USA, Ancestry.com Operations, Inc., 2012), Ancestry.com, http://www.Ancestry.com, Record for Jessie G. Poole.

[241] Ancestry.com, U.S., Find A Grave Index, 1700s-Current (Provo, UT, USA, Ancestry.com Operations, Inc., 2012), Ancestry.com, http://www.Ancestry.com, Record for Jessie G. Poole.

[242] Ancestry.com, U.S., Find A Grave Index, 1700s-Current (Provo, UT, USA, Ancestry.com Operations, Inc., 2012), Ancestry.com, http://www.Ancestry.com, Record for Jessie G. Poole.

[243] Ancestry.com, U.S., Find A Grave Index, 1700s-Current (Provo, UT, USA, Ancestry.com Operations, Inc., 2012), Ancestry.com, http://www.Ancestry.com, Record for Jessie G. Poole.

[244] Ancestry.com, U.S., Find A Grave Index, 1700s-Current (Provo, UT, USA, Ancestry.com Operations, Inc., 2012), Ancestry.com, http://www.Ancestry.com, Record for Larue M. Poole.

[245] Ancestry.com, U.S., Find A Grave Index, 1700s-Current (Provo, UT, USA, Ancestry.com Operations, Inc., 2012), Ancestry.com, http://www.Ancestry.com, Record for Larue M. Poole.

[246] Ancestry.com, Social Security Death Index (Provo, UT, USA, The Generations Network, Inc., 2008), www.ancestry.com, Number: 442-07-4779; Issue State: Oklahoma; Issue Date: Before 1951. Record for W. A. Poole.

[247] Ancestry.com, Social Security Death Index (Provo, UT, USA, The Generations Network, Inc., 2008), www.ancestry.com, Number: 442-07-4779; Issue State: Oklahoma; Issue Date: Before 1951. Record for W. A. Poole.

[248] Ancestry.com, U.S., Find A Grave Index, 1700s-Current (Provo, UT, USA, Ancestry.com Operations, Inc., 2012), Ancestry.com, http://www.Ancestry.com, Record for Mary H. Poole.

[249] Ancestry.com, U.S., Find A Grave Index, 1700s-Current (Provo, UT, USA, Ancestry.com Operations, Inc., 2012), Ancestry.com, http://www.Ancestry.com, Record for Mary H. Poole.

[250] Ancestry.com, U.S., Find A Grave Index, 1700s-Current, Record for Mary H. Poole and Lyle Perkins..

[251] Ancestry.com, U.S., Find A Grave Index, 1700s-Current, Record for Mary H. Poole and Lyle Perkins.

[252] Ancestry.com, U.S., Find A Grave Index, 1700s-Current, Record for Mary H. Poole and Lyle Perkins.

Photo of Pansey Maude Poole Perkins found on Ancestry.com.

Lyle Delette Perkins and Pansey Maude Poole had the following children:

      i.   Lyle Nathaniel Perkins was born on 29 Nov 1915 in Friendship, New York[253] and died on 20 Jun 2005 in Myrtle Beach, South Carolina[254]. He married Dorothy E. Wilson. She was born on 20 Sep 1917[255] and died on 17 Aug 996 in Myrtle Beach, South Carolina[256].

    38.   ii.   Vera Louise Perkins was born Feb 11, 1908[257] in Friendship, New York and died Jan 8, 2001 in Friendship, New York[258].

      iii.   Erva E. Perkins was born 21 Oct 1909[259] in Friendship, New York and died Feb 12, 2003 in Friendship, New York[260]. She married Cerell Birtcil Schram on 01 Jan 1936 in Genesee, Pennsylvania[261]. He was born 06 Oct 1907[262] in Allegany, New York and died 21 June 1992 in Bolivar, New York[263].

Photo of Lyle Nathaniel Perkins and his wife, Dorothy E. Wilson from Ancestry.com.

[253] Ancestry.com, Social Security Death Index (Provo, UT, USA, The Generations Network, Inc., 2008), www.ancestry.com, Issue State: New York; Issue Date: Before 1951. Record for Lyle Nathaniel Perkins.

[254] Ancestry.com, Social Security Death Index (Provo, UT, USA, The Generations Network, Inc., 2008), www.ancestry.com, Issue State: New York; Issue Date: Before 1951. Record for Lyle Nathaniel Perkins.

[255] Ancestry.com, Social Security Death Index (Provo, UT, USA, The Generations Network, Inc., 2008), www.ancestry.com, Number: 121-05-8497; Issue State: New York; Issue Date: Before 1951. Record for Dorothy W. Perkins.

[256] Ancestry.com, Social Security Death Index (Provo, UT, USA, The Generations Network, Inc., 2008), www.ancestry.com, Number: 121-05-8497; Issue State: New York; Issue Date: Before 1951. Record for Dorothy W. Perkins.

[257] Ancestry.com, U.S., Find A Grave Index, 1700s-Current (Provo, UT, USA, Ancestry.com Operations, Inc., 2012).

[258] Ancestry.com, U.S., Find A Grave Index, 1700s-Current (Provo, UT, USA, Ancestry.com Operations, Inc., 2012).

[259] Obituary as described in this book. page 238.

[260] Obituary as described in this book. page 238.

[261] Obituary as described in this book. page 238.

[262] Ancestry.com, U.S., Find A Grave Index, 1700s-Current (Provo, UT, USA, Ancestry.com Operations, Inc., 2012),

[263] Ancestry.com, U.S., Find A Grave Index, 1700s-Current (Provo, UT, USA, Ancestry.com Operations, Inc., 2012),

Friendship - *Erva E. Perkins Schram, 93, of 16 South Branch Road died Wednesday (Feb. 12, 2003) at her home following a lengthy illness. Born Oct 21, 1909 in Friendship, she was the daughter of Lyle DeLette and Pansey Maude Poole Perkins. On Jan 1, 1936, in Genesee, PA, she married Cerell Birtcil Schram who died June 21, 1992. Mrs. Schram had resided most over life in Friendship and was a graduate of Friendship High School, class of 1925. She later graduated from Buffalo State Teachers College and had done post graduate work at the John Huntington Polytechnic Institute in Cleveland, Ohio, and St. Bonaventure College in Allegany, majoring in drafting technique. She taught at Ashford Hollow and in 1954 became a draftsman at Worthington Corp. in Wellsville, retiring in 1974. Mrs. Schram resided in Brazil for two years. She was a member of Alpha Sigma Tau sorority of Buffalo State Teachers College and the DAR Catherine Schuyler Chapter of Friendship. She enjoyed reading and her three cats. Surviving are a brother, Lyle Nathaniel Perkins of Myrtle Beach, S.C., a niece Shirley McGough Shelley of Friendship, two grand nephews, Michael (Wannetta) Shelley and Mark (Jeanine) Shelley, both of Olean and dear friends, Bernice and Bud Wereley of Friendship. She was predeceased by as sister, Vera Sanborn. Burial will be in Maple Grove Cemetery, Friendship. Arrangements are under direction of the Treusdell Funeral Home, Friendship.*

23. Charles Albert Niver[4] Sr. (Adelia M. Webb[3], John H. Webb[2], Henry B. Webb[1]) was born on 31 Aug 1876 in Friendship, New York[264] and died on 27 Jan 1957[265]. He married Cora Potter[266]. She was born on 04 Aug 1877 in Friendship, New York[267] and died on 06 May 1929 in Friendship, New York[268].

Charles Albert Niver Sr. and Cora Potter had the following children:

39.　i.　Laura Belle Niver was born on 17 Jan 1903 in Denver, Colorado [269] and died on 25 Apr 1990[270].

40.　ii.　Harold Cosper Niver was born on 02 Mar 1907 in Friendship, New York[271] and died in Oct 1985 in Commack, New York[272].

---

[264] Ancestry.com, U.S., Social Security Applications and Claims Index, 1936-2007 (Provo, UT, USA, Ancestry.com Operations, Inc., 2015), Ancestry.com, http://www.Ancestry.com, Record for Charles A Sr Niver.

[265] Ancestry.com, U.S., Social Security Applications and Claims Index, 1936-2007 (Provo, UT, USA, Ancestry.com Operations, Inc., 2015), Ancestry.com, http://www.Ancestry.com, Record for Charles A Sr Niver.

[266] Ancestry.com, U.S., Find A Grave Index, 1700s-Current (Provo, UT, USA, Ancestry.com Operations, Inc., 2012), Ancestry.com, http://www.Ancestry.com, Record for Charles Albert Niver.

[267] Ancestry.com, U.S., Find A Grave Index, 1700s-Current (Provo, UT, USA, Ancestry.com Operations, Inc., 2012), Ancestry.com, http://www.Ancestry.com, Record for Charles Albert Niver.

[268] Ancestry.com, U.S., Find A Grave Index, 1700s-Current (Provo, UT, USA, Ancestry.com Operations, Inc., 2012), Ancestry.com, http://www.Ancestry.com, Record for Charles Albert Niver.

[269] Ancestry.com, U.S., Find A Grave Index, 1700s-Current (Provo, UT, USA, Ancestry.com Operations, Inc., 2012), Ancestry.com, http://www.Ancestry.com, Record for Charles Albert Niver.

[270] Ancestry.com, U.S., Find A Grave Index, 1700s-Current (Provo, UT, USA, Ancestry.com Operations, Inc., 2012), Ancestry.com, http://www.Ancestry.com, Record for Charles Albert Niver.

41.   iii.   Glenn W. Niver was born on 17 Nov 1910[273] and died on 03 Mar 1994 in Olean, New York[274].

Photo of Glenn W. Niver found on Ancestry.com.

iv.   Charles Albert Niver, Jr. was born in 1916 in New York[275] and died on 28 Jan 2009 in Island, Washington[276]. He married Dorothy G. Brader, the daughter of Harris Brader and Rose Martin, on 04 Mar 1939 in Vancouver, Washington[277]. She was born in 1919 in Washington[278] and died on 16 Jan 2004 in Marysville, Washington[279].

v.   Cora Alzetta Niver was born on 05 Apr 1918 in Perry, New York[280] and died on 07 Jan 1994 in Pinellas, Florida[281]. She married Mr. Brown.

24. Miner A. Baker[4] (Ellen M. Webb[3], John H. Webb[2], Henry B. Webb[1]) was born on 01 Dec 1881[282]. The 1925 Rochester, New

[271] Ancestry.com, Social Security Death Index, Record for Harold Niver.

[272] Ancestry.com, Social Security Death Index, Record for Harold Niver.

[273] Ancestry.com, Social Security Death Index, Number: 079-07-2132; Issue State: New York; Issue Date: Before 1951. Record for Glenn W. Niver.

[274] Ancestry.com, Social Security Death Index, Number: 079-07-2132; Issue State: New York; Issue Date: Before 1951. Record for Glenn W. Niver.

[275] Ancestry.com, Washington Death Index, 1940-1996 (Provo, UT, USA, The Generations Network, Inc., 2002), www.ancestry.com, Record for Charles A Niver.

[276] Ancestry.com, Washington Death Index, 1940-1996 (Provo, UT, USA, The Generations Network, Inc., 2002), www.ancestry.com, Record for Charles A Niver.

[277] Ancestry.com, http://www.Ancestry.com, Ancestry.com. Washington, Marriage Records, 1854-2013 [database on-line]. Provo, UT, USA: Ancestry.com Operations, Inc., 2012.

[278] Ancestry.com, Social Security Death Index (Provo, UT, USA, The Generations Network, Inc., 2008), www.ancestry.com, Number: 538-38-8415; Issue State: Washington; Issue Date: 1957-1958. Record for Dorothy G. Niver

[279] Ancestry.com, Washington Death Index, 1940-1996 (Provo, UT, USA, The Generations Network, Inc., 2002), www.ancestry.com, Record for Dorothy G Niver.

[280] Ancestry.com, U.S., Social Security Applications and Claims Index, 1936-2007 (Provo, UT, USA, Ancestry.com Operations, Inc., 2015), Ancestry.com, http://www.Ancestry.com, Record for Cora Alzetta Niver

[281] Ancestry.com, Florida Death Index, 1877-1998 (Provo, UT, USA, The Generations Network, Inc., 2004), www.ancestry.com, Record for Cora A Brown.

[282] Ancestry.com, World War I Draft Registration Cards, 1917-1918 (Provo, UT, USA, The Generations Network, Inc., 2005), www.ancestry.com, Registration State: New York; Registration County: Monroe; Roll: 1818811; Draft Board: 8. Record for Miner Baker.

York Census listed Miner as living in the Rochester State Hospital. I could not find an additional record on him after that date. He married Blanche L. Cobe[283]. She was born in 1887 in New York[284].

Miner A. Baker and Blanche L. Cobe had the following children:
    i.   Gladys B. Baker was born in 1908 [285]. She married Ralph Hendricks on 26 Sep 1932 in Rochester, New York[286].
    ii.   Glen M. Baker was born in New York State in 1910[287].
    iii.   John L. Baker was born in New York State in 1913[288].

25. Robert Oney Baker[4] (Ellen M. Webb[3], John H. Webb[2], Henry B. Webb[1]) was born on 31 Oct 1883 in Friendship, New York[289] and died on 21 Jun 1945[290]. He married Lillian M. Ross[291]. She was born in 1883 in United States[292].

Robert Oney Baker and Lillian M. Ross had the following child:
42.   i.   Dorothy M. Baker was born in 1906 in the United States[293] and married John A Logan on 25 Aug 1923 in Rochester, New York[294].

[283] Ancestry.com. *New York, State Census, 1915* [database on-line]. Provo, UT, USA: Ancestry.com Operations, Inc., 2012.

[284] Ancestry.com, 1910 United States Federal Census (Online publication - Provo, UT, USA: Ancestry.com Operations Inc, 2006.Original data - Thirteenth Census of the United States, 1910 (NARA microfilm publication T624, 1,178 rolls). Records of the Bureau of the Census, Record Group 29. National Archives, Was), Ancestry.com, http://www.Ancestry.com, Year: 1910; Census Place: Rochester Ward 11, Monroe, New York; Roll: T624_991; Page: 3B; Enumeration District: 0111; FHL microfilm: 1375004. Record for Miner A Baker.

[285] Ancestry.com. New York, County Marriages, 1847-1849; 1907-1936

[286] Ancestry.com. New York, County Marriages, 1847-1849; 1907-1936

[287] Ancestry.com. *New York, State Census, 1915* [database on-line]. Provo, UT, USA: Ancestry.com Operations, Inc., 2012.

[288] Ancestry.com. *New York, State Census, 1915* [database on-line]. Provo, UT, USA: Ancestry.com Operations, Inc., 2012.

[289] Ancestry.com, U.S. World War II Draft Registration Cards, 1942 (Provo, UT, USA, The Generations Network, Inc., 2007), www.ancestry.com, The National Archives at St. Louis; St. Louis, Missouri; World War II Draft Cards (Fourth Registration) for the State of New York; Record Group Title: Records of the Selective Service System, 1926-1975; Record Group Number: 147; Box or Roll Number: 23. Record for Robert Oney Baker.

[290] Ancestry.com, U.S., Social Security Applications and Claims Index, 1936-2007 (Provo, UT, USA, Ancestry.com Operations, Inc., 2015), Ancestry.com, http://www.Ancestry.com, Record for Robert Oney Baker

[291] Ancestry.com, New York, State Census, 1915 (Provo, UT, USA, Ancestry.com Operations, Inc., 2012), www.ancestry.com, New York State Archives; Albany, New York; State Population Census Schedules, 1915; Election District: 03; Assembly District: 05; City: Rochester Ward 20; County: Monroe; Page: 06. Record for Robert O Baker.

[292] Ancestry.com, New York, State Census, 1915 (Provo, UT, USA, Ancestry.com Operations, Inc., 2012), www.ancestry.com, New York State Archives; Albany, New York; State Population Census Schedules, 1915; Election District: 03; Assembly District: 05; City: Rochester Ward 20; County: Monroe; Page: 06. Record for Robert O Baker.

[293] Ancestry.com, New York, County Marriages, 1847-1849; 1907-1936 (Lehi, UT, USA, Ancestry.com Operations, Inc., 2016), Ancestry.com, http://www.Ancestry.com, Record for Dorothy M Baker.

[294] Ancestry.com, New York, County Marriages, 1847-1849; 1907-1936 (Lehi, UT, USA, Ancestry.com Operations, Inc., 2016), Ancestry.com, http://www.Ancestry.com, Record for Dorothy M Baker.

6. Ernest Leroy Baker[4] (Ellen M. Webb[3], John H. Webb[2], Henry B. Webb[1]) was born on 09 Mar 1890 in Friendship, New York[295] and died in Nov 1973 in Rochester, New York[296]. He married Lilia May Norton on 02 Sep 1917 in Allegany, New York[297]. She was born in 1896[298]. According to the 1930 Census, Ernest was married in 1917, his son was born in 1921 and he was listed in the 1925 Census as a widow living with his mother.

Photo of Lilia May Norton Baker found on findagrave.com.

Ernest LeRoy Baker and Lilia May Norton had the following child:
 i. James Ernest Baker was born on 18 Jun 1920[299] in Rochester, New York and died on 26 Apr 1995[300]. He married Mildred Marie Dorman Knight[301]. She was born 04 Jun 1927 in Desoto County, Florida[302] and died 12 Feb 2012 in Lakeland, Florida[303].

27. Mildred E. Foote[4] (William H. Foote[3], Abigail Webb[2], Henry B. Webb[1]) was born on 10 Jun 1884 in Madison , New York[304] and died on 19 Dec 1964 in Utica , New York[305]. She married Maurice John O'Connell on 18 Jun 1901 in Utica, New York[306]. He was born on 18 Feb 1876[307] and died in 1953[308]. Mildred attended Madison and Cortland, New York, schools. She was employed by the Cortland Standard, the city's newspaper.

[295] Ancestry.com, World War I Draft Registration Cards, 1917-1918 (Provo, UT, USA, The Generations Network, Inc., 2005), www.ancestry.com, Registration State: New York; Registration County: Monroe; Roll: 1818807; Draft Board: 6. Record for Ernest Le Roy Baker.

[296] Ancestry.com, Social Security Death Index (Provo, UT, USA, The Generations Network, Inc., 2008), www.ancestry.com, Number: 071-01-8528; Issue State: New York; Issue Date: Before 1951. Record for Ernest Baker.

[297] Ancestry.com, New York, County Marriages, 1847-1849; 1907-1936 (Lehi, UT, USA, Ancestry.com Operations, Inc., 2016), Ancestry.com, http://www.Ancestry.com, Record for Ernest Leroy Baker.

[298] Ancestry.com, New York, County Marriages, 1847-1849; 1907-1936 (Lehi, UT, USA, Ancestry.com Operations, Inc., 2016), Ancestry.com, http://www.Ancestry.com, Record for Ernest Leroy Baker.

[299] Ancestry.com. *U.S., Social Security Applications and Claims Index, 1936-2007* [database on-line]. Provo, UT, USA: Ancestry.com Operations, Inc., 2015.

[300] Ancestry.com. *U.S., Social Security Applications and Claims Index, 1936-2007* [database on-line]. Provo, UT, USA: Ancestry.com Operations, Inc., 2015.

[301] Findagrave.com.

[302] Findagrave.com.

[303] Findagrave.com.

[304] Obituary, Utica Observer Dispatch, Utica, New York, December 21, 1964, page 29.

[305] Obituary, Utica Observer Dispatch, Utica, New York, December 21, 1964, page 29.

[306] Obituary, Utica Observer Dispatch, Utica, New York, December 21, 1964, page 29.

[307] Ancestry.com, World War I Draft Registration Cards, 1917-Record for Maurice John O'Connell.

[308] Ancestry.com. *U.S., Find A Grave Index, 1600s-Current* [database on-line]. Provo, UT, USA: Ancestry.com Operations, Inc., 2012.

Maurice John O'connell and Mildred E. Foote had the following children:

43.   i.   Helen L. O'Connell was born on 04 Apr 1902 in Cortland, New York[309] and died on 08 May 1986 in Rome Hospital, Rome, New York[310].

44.   ii.   Robert Daniel O'Connell was born on 01 Sep 1910 in Cortland, New York[311] and died on 22 Jun 1998 in Bloomfield, Connecticut[312].

28. Lydia Anna Mather[4] (Mary Abigail Foote[3], Abigail Webb[2], Henry B. Webb[1]) was born on 26 Apr 1875 in Madison, New York[313] and died on 15 Mar 1969 at 9 West Street, Whitesboro, New York[314]. She married Frank W. Rudd on 15 Apr 1896 in Canastota, New York[315]. He was born in July 1873 in New York State[316] and died on 17 Oct 1906 in Greenway, New York[317]. In the 1880 Madison County Census, he was six years old and lived in the Madison County Children's Home. After Mr. Rudd died, Lydia married Emery C. Inman, the son of George Inman and Ellen House, on 17 Jun 1910 in the home of her mother, Mary Mather on Powell Avenue, Whitesboro, New York[318]. He was born on 16 Jul 1875 in Fenner, New York[319] and died on 17 June 1937 in Rome Hospital, Rome, New York[320]. Lydia Anna was listed as "Annie" in 1908 at the birthday party for her grandfather. She attended school in Madison, New York. She moved to Canastota at an early age. She lived with her daughter, Laura Dillon starting in 1936. She was a Protestant.

Canastota Newspaper, October 21, 1905 - *Frank Rudd, a New York Central freight brakeman living at East Syracuse, was struck by the westbound Empire State Express at Greenway Tuesday afternoon and instantly killed. Engineman George Gilbert of the Empire saw the man sitting on the rail of Track No. 2 upon which the Empire was approaching. Gilbert sounded the whistle several times. He noticed that the man did not leave the track. Before he could stop his engine the unfortunate man had been thrown high in the air, his skull crushed and the head nearly severed from the body. It was said that Rudd was on his way to flag for a stalled freight train and he had fallen asleep sitting on the track. Upon instruction from New York City the engine and caboose of Rudd's train conveyed the body to East Syracuse. Undertaker Andrew Behr, of East Syracuse, went to Greenway and accompanied the remains home.*

---

[309] Obituary, Rome Sentinel, Rome, New York, May 9, 1986.
[310] Obituary, Rome Sentinel, Rome, New York, May 9, 1986.
[311] Obituary, The Hartford Courant, Hartford, Connecticut, June 24, 1998 on line.
[312] Obituary, The Hartford Courant, Hartford, Connecticut, June 24, 1998 on line.
[313] Foote Family History & Genealogy Vol 1.
[314] Obituary, Utica Daily Press, Utica, New York, March 18, 1969, page 12.
[315] Ancestry.com, New York State Marriage Index, certificate #6685.
[316] Ancestry.com, 1900 Federal Census for Lenox, New York.
[317] Obituary, Canastota Newspaper, October 21, 1905 included in this book on page 242.
[318] Wedding Announcement, Utica Newspaper, Utica, New York.
[319] Obituary, Utica Daily Press, Utica, New York, July 18, 1937.
[320] Obituary, Utica Daily Press, Utica, New York, July 18, 1937.

Frank W. Rudd and Lydia Anna Mather had the following child:
45.   i.   Laura Abigail Rudd was born on 18 Feb 1898 in New York State[321] and died on 15 Dec 1993 in Rome, New York[322].

Photo of Lydia Anna Mather, her husband, Frank W. Rudd and daughter, Laura Abigail Rudd from the authors collection.

Emery C. Inman and Lydia Anna Mather had the following child:
       i.   Ruth Helen Inman was born on 29 Jul 1912 in Whitesboro, New York[323] and died on 08 Aug 1936 in St. Luke's Hospital, Utica, New York[324]. Ruth committed suicide by taking poison. She took the poison Friday night and died the next day in the hospital. Ruth has resided in Whitesboro until two years ago, when she moved with her family to Utica. She had been employed by J. B. Wells & Son Company store for six years, having been assigned to the receiving room. She attended the Methodist Church and was a member of the Queen Esther Society of the Methodist Church of Whitesboro.

---

[321] Ancestry.com, Social Security Death Index (Provo, UT, USA, The Generations Network, Inc., 2008), www.ancestry.com, Database online. Number: 081-14-6242; Issue State: New York; Issue Date: Before 1951. Record for Laura Dillon.
[322] Ancestry.com, Social Security Death Index (Provo, UT, USA, The Generations Network, Inc., 2008), www.ancestry.com, Database online. Number: 081-14-6242; Issue State: New York; Issue Date: Before 1951. Record for Laura Dillon.
[323] Obituary, Utica Daily Press, Utica, New York, July 30, 1936.
[324] Obituary, Utica Daily Press, Utica, New York, July 30, 1936.

29. Gertrude M. Mather[4] (Mary Abigail Foote[3], Abigail Webb[2], Henry B. Webb[1]) was born on 19 Nov 1876 in Oneida, New York[325] and died on 06 May 1963 in St. Luke's Memorial Hospital, New Hartford, New York[326]. She married Dayton R. Mallette, the son of Charles Mallette and Sarah Joret, on 1 Jul 1914 in Oneida, New York[327]. He was born in 1852 in New York State[328] and died 12 Dec 1928 in Canajoharie, New York[329]. He was buried in Ames Cemetery, Ames, New York[330]. She later married George

Moore, the son of Lyman Moore and Mary Gage, on 11 Apr 1930 in Canajoharie, New York[331]. He died in 1958[332].

Gertrude lived in Whitesboro in 1913 and on 1 Powell Ave. in 1914. Not found thereafter. The 1910 Census for Whitestown said she was a buttonholer in the knitting mills. Gertrude was educated in Canastota Schools. She later moved to Whitesboro where she had been employed by the Alliance Knitting Mill. For the past five years she had lived with her niece, Mrs. Laura Dillon. Gertrude was of the Baptist faith.

Photo of Lydia Anna Mather and her sister, Gertrude M. Mather, from the authors collection.

Dayton R. Mallette and Gertrude M. Mather had the following child:
46.   i.   Lee J. Mallette was born on 02 Mar 1916 in New York State[333] and died on 23 Nov 1999 in Hemet, California[334]. He married Alida Ann Conrad, the daughter of Kenneth Conrad and Hazel L. Ward[335]. She was born 10 May 1928[336] and died 18 Oct 2006[337].

---

[325] Foote Family History & Genealogy Vol 1.

[326] Obituary, Utica Daily Press, Utica, New York, May 7, 1963.

[327] Ancestry.com. *New York, County Marriage Records, 1847-1849, 1907-1936* [database on-line]. Lehi, UT, USA: Ancestry.com Operations, Inc., 2016.

[328] Ancestry.com, findagrave.com.

[329] Ancestry.com. *New York, Death Index, 1880-1956* [database on-line]. Lehi, UT, USA: Ancestry.com Operations, Inc., 2017.

[330] Ancestry.com, findagrave.com.

[331] Obituary, Utica Daily Press, Utica, New York, May 7, 1963.

[332] Obituary, Utica Daily Press, Utica, New York, May 7, 1963.

[333] New York State Death Index, at Ancestry.com.

[334] New York State Death Index, at Ancestry.com.

[335] Ancestry.com. *U.S., Social Security Applications and Claims Index, 1936-2007* [database on-line]. Provo, UT, USA: Ancestry.com Operations, Inc., 2015.

[336] Ancestry.com. *U.S., Social Security Applications and Claims Index, 1936-2007* [database on-line]. Provo, UT, USA: Ancestry.com Operations, Inc., 2015.

[337] Ancestry.com. *U.S., Social Security Applications and Claims Index, 1936-2007* [database on-line]. Provo, UT, USA: Ancestry.com Operations, Inc., 2015.

30. Frank Joseph Webb[4] (Myron D Webb[3], LaFayette Webb[2], Henry B. Webb[1]) was born on 06 Jun 1882 in Blue Earth City, Minnesota[338] and died on 28 Sep 1965[339]. He married Lura Luella McFarland, the daughter of Robert L. and Ada McFarland, on 16 Sep 1903 in Hardin, Iowa[340]. She was born in Mar 1885 in Decorah, Iowa[341] and died on 14 Sep 1910[342]. He later married Margaret Anna Mulanney Mizener on 05 Jan 1937 in Iowa[343]. She was born on 05 Jul 1872[344] and died on 05 May 1971[345].

Frank Joseph Webb and Lura Luella McFarland had the following child:
      i.   Luella Belle Webb was born in 1905[346] and died on 19 Feb 1911[347].

31. Rhoda Ann Webb[4] (Myron D Webb[3], LaFayette Webb[2], Henry B. Webb[1]was born on 29 Sep 1884 in Minnesota[348] and died on 28 Feb 1976 in Benton, Oregon[349]. She married Walter T. Reeder 27 Nov 1901 in Blue Earth City, Minnesota. Walter was born in 1881[350] in Minnesota and died 12 Jan 1943 in Snohomish, Washington[351]. Later she

---

[338] Ancestry.com, U.S. World War II Draft Registration Cards, 1942 (Provo, UT, USA, The Generations Network, Inc., 2007), www.ancestry.com, The National Archives at St. Louis; St. Louis, Missouri; World War II Draft Cards (Fourth Registration) for the State of Iowa; Record Group Title: Records of the Selective Service System, 1926-1975; Record Group Number: 147; Box or Roll Number: 242. Record for Frank Joseph Webb.

[339] Ancestry.com, Social Security Death Index (Provo, UT, USA, The Generations Network, Inc., 2008), www.ancestry.com, Number: 517-12-5901; Issue State: Montana; Issue Date: Before 1951. Record for Frank Webb.

[340] Ancestry.com, Iowa, Marriage Records, 1880-1937 (Lehi, UT, USA, Ancestry.com Operations, Inc., 2014), Ancestry.com, http://www.Ancestry.com, Iowa Department of Public Health; Des Moines, Iowa; Series Title: Iowa Marriage Records, 1923-1937; Record Type: Microfilm Records. Record for Frank Joseph Webb.

[341] Ancestry.com, U.S., Find A Grave Index, 1700s-Current (Provo, UT, USA, Ancestry.com Operations, Inc., 2012), Ancestry.com, http://www.Ancestry.com, Record for Lura Luella Webb

[342] Ancestry.com, U.S., Find A Grave Index, 1700s-Current (Provo, UT, USA, Ancestry.com Operations, Inc., 2012), Ancestry.com, http://www.Ancestry.com, Record for Lura Luella Webb

[343] Ancestry.com, Iowa Marriage Record.

[344] Ancestry.com, U.S., Find A Grave Index, 1700s-Current (Provo, UT, USA, Ancestry.com Operations, Inc., 2012), Ancestry.com, http://www.Ancestry.com, Record for Margaret A. Webb.

[345] Ancestry.com, U.S., Find A Grave Index, 1700s-Current (Provo, UT, USA, Ancestry.com Operations, Inc., 2012), Ancestry.com, http://www.Ancestry.com, Record for Margaret A. Webb.

[346] Ancestry.com, U.S., Find A Grave Index, 1700s-Current (Provo, UT, USA, Ancestry.com Operations, Inc., 2012), Ancestry.com, http://www.Ancestry.com, Record for Lura Luella Webb.

[347] Ancestry.com, U.S., Find A Grave Index, 1700s-Current (Provo, UT, USA, Ancestry.com Operations, Inc., 2012), Ancestry.com, http://www.Ancestry.com, Record for Lura Luella Webb.

[348] Ancestry.com, Social Security Death Index (Provo, UT, USA, The Generations Network, Inc., 2008), www.ancestry.com, Number: 550-52-3206; Issue State: California; Issue Date: 1955. Record for Rhoda Palmer.

[349] Ancestry.com, Oregon Death Index, 1903-98 (Provo, UT, USA, Ancestry.com Operations Inc, 2000), www.ancestry.com, Oregon State Library; 1966-1970 Death Index; Reel Title: State of Oregon Death Index; Year Range: 1971-1980. Record for Rhoda Ann Palmer.

[350] Ancestry.com. *Washington, Select Death Certificates, 1907-1960* [database on-line]. Provo, UT, USA: Ancestry.com Operations, Inc., 2014.

[351] Ancestry.com. *Washington, Select Death Certificates, 1907-1960* [database on-line]. Provo, UT, USA: Ancestry.com Operations, Inc., 2014.

married PVT. Gus Palmer. He was born in Greece on 21 Mar 1895[352] and died on 04 Mar 1951 in Benton, Oregon[353].

Walter T. Reeder and Rhoda Ann Webb had the following children:

  i. Harry Reeder was born in Minnesota in 18 Mar 1902[354] and died 17 Feb 1971 in Polk County, Oregon[355]. He married Dorothy Isolene Martin[356]. She was born 04 Jul 1896[357] and died 9 Jul 1979 in Lane County, Oregon[358].

  ii. Zilda Luella Reeder was born 19 Feb 1903 in Blue Earth City, Minnesota[359] and died 28 Dec 1987[360]. She married William Watson Wooddy, the son of Lemuel Dale and Fannie Wooddy, on 30 Jun 1927 in Benton, Oregon[361]. He was born 09 Apr 1892 in Arkansas and died 25 Jul 1963 in Benton County, Oregon[362].

Photo of Rhoda Ann Webb found on Ancestry.com.

  iii. Rex Joseph Reeder was born in 10 Dec 1906 in Iowa[363] and died 4 Feb 1929 in Mason City, Iowa[364].

32. Julia Catherine Webb[4] (Myron D Webb[3], LaFayette Webb[2], Henry B. Webb[1]) was born on 27 Dec 1886 in Blue Earth City, Minnesota[365] and died in May 1968 in Conrad,

[352] Ancestry.com, U.S. World War II Draft Registration Cards, 1942 (Provo, UT, USA, The Generations Network, Inc., 2007), www.ancestry.com, The National Archives at St. Louis; St. Louis, Missouri; World War II Draft Cards (Fourth Registration) for the State of Iowa; Record Group Title: Records of the Selective Service System, 1926-1975; Record Group Number: 147; Box or Roll Number: 175. Record for Gus D Palmer

[353] Ancestry.com, Oregon Death Index, 1903-98 (Provo, UT, USA, Ancestry.com Operations Inc, 2000), www.ancestry.com, Oregon State Library; Oregon Death Index 1931-1941; Reel Title: Oregon Death Index L-Z; Year Range: 1951-1960. Record for Gus D Palmer.

[354] memorial page for Harry Bowen Reeder (18 Mar 1902–17 Feb 1971), Find A Grave Memorial no. 140493226,

[355] memorial page for Harry Bowen Reeder (18 Mar 1902–17 Feb 1971), Find A Grave Memorial no. 140493226,

[356] Find A Grave Memorial no. 140493181.

[357] Find A Grave Memorial no. 140493181.

[358] Find A Grave Memorial no. 140493181.

[359] Ancestry.com. *U.S., Social Security Applications and Claims Index, 1936-2007* [database on-line]. Provo, UT, USA: Ancestry.com Operations, Inc., 2015.

[360] Ancestry.com. *U.S., Social Security Applications and Claims Index, 1936-2007* [database on-line]. Provo, UT, USA: Ancestry.com Operations, Inc., 2015.

[361] Ancestry.com. *Oregon, Marriage Indexes, 1906-2009* [database on-line]. Provo, UT, USA: Ancestry.com Operations, Inc, 2000.

[362] Ancestry.com, Findagrave.com.

[363] Ancestry.com., Iowa death records.

[364] Ancestry.com., Iowa death records.

[365] Ancestry.com, Social Security Death Index (Provo, UT, USA, The Generations Network, Inc., 2008), www.ancestry.com, Number: 516-05-3489; Issue State: Montana; Issue Date: Before 1951. Record for Julia Porter.

Montana[366]. She married William T. Porter, the son of Charles H. Porter and Helen Thompson, on 04 Jan 1916 in Helena, Montana[367]. He was born in 1888 in New York[368] and died on 05 Feb 1920 in Spokane, Washington[369].

William T Porter and Julia Catherine Webb had the following child:
47.   i.   Helen K. Porter was born on 05 Jul 1916 in Lewiston, Idaho[370] and died on 13 Mar 1996 in Conrad, Montana[371].

33. Hazel Mary Webb[4] (Myron D Webb[3], LaFayette Webb[2], Henry B. Webb[1]) was born on 15 Aug 1894 in Blue Earth, Minnesota[372] and died on 02 Jul 1976 in Havre, Montana[373]. She married Chester Ely Atwood in Montana[374]. He was born in 1885 in Michigan[375] and died on 06 Dec 1953 in Pondera County, Montana[376].

Chester Ely Atwood and Hazel Mary Webb had the following children:
       i.   Chester J. Atwood was born on 20 Apr 1914[377] and died on 04 May 1981[378].
       ii.   Jack R. Atwood was born in 1917 in Montana[379] and died on 14 Feb 1929 in Pondera County, Montana[380].

---

[366] Ancestry.com, Social Security Death Index (Provo, UT, USA, The Generations Network, Inc., 2008), www.ancestry.com, Number: 516-05-3489; Issue State: Montana; Issue Date: Before 1951. Record for Julia Porter.
[367] Ancestry.com, Montana, County Marriages, 1865-1950 (Provo, UT, USA, Ancestry.com Operations, Inc., 2014), Ancestry.com, http://www.Ancestry.com, Record for William T. Porter.
[368] Ancestry.com, Montana, County Marriages, 1865-1950 (Provo, UT, USA, Ancestry.com Operations, Inc., 2014), Ancestry.com, http://www.Ancestry.com, Record for William T. Porter.
[369] Ancestry.com, Washington, Select Death Certificates, 1907-1960 (Provo, UT, USA, Ancestry.com Operations, Inc., 2014), Ancestry.com, http://www.Ancestry.com, Record for William Porter.
[370] Ancestry.com, U.S., Social Security Applications and Claims Index, 1936-2007 (Provo, UT, USA, Ancestry.com Operations, Inc., 2015), Ancestry.com, http://www.Ancestry.com, Record for Helen Kathryn Berland.
[371] Ancestry.com, U.S., Social Security Applications and Claims Index, 1936-2007 (Provo, UT, USA, Ancestry.com Operations, Inc., 2015), Ancestry.com, http://www.Ancestry.com, Record for Helen Kathryn Berland.
[372] Familysearch.org, "Minnesota Births and Christenings, 1840-1980," database, FamilySearch (https://familysearch.org/ark:/61903/1:1:FD7G-SM6 : 4 December 2014), Webb, 27 Dec 1886;
[373] Ancestry.com, Montana, Death Index, 1868-2011 (Provo, UT, USA, Ancestry.com Operations, Inc., 2001), Ancestry.com, http://www.Ancestry.com, Record for Hazel M Atwood.
[374] Ancestry.com, U.S., Find A Grave Index, 1700s-Current (Provo, UT, USA, Ancestry.com Operations, Inc., 2012), Ancestry.com, http://www.Ancestry.com, Record for Hazel Mary Atwood.
[375] Ancestry.com, U.S., Find A Grave Index, 1700s-Current (Provo, UT, USA, Ancestry.com Operations, Inc., 2012), Ancestry.com, http://www.Ancestry.com, Record for Hazel Mary Atwood.
[376] Ancestry.com, U.S., Find A Grave Index, 1700s-Current (Provo, UT, USA, Ancestry.com Operations, Inc., 2012), Ancestry.com, http://www.Ancestry.com, Record for Hazel Mary Atwood.
[377] National Archives and Records Administration, U.S. World War II Army Enlistment Records, 1938-1946 (Provo, UT, USA, The Generations Network, Inc., 2005), www.ancestry.com, Record for Chester J Atwood.
[378] Ancestry.com, Social Security Death Index (Provo, UT, USA, The Generations Network, Inc., 2008), www.ancestry.com, Number: 533-01-0057; Issue State: Washington; Issue Date: Before 1951. Record for Chester Atwood.
[379] Ancestry.com, U.S., Find A Grave Index, 1700s-Current (Provo, UT, USA, Ancestry.com Operations, Inc., 2012), Ancestry.com, http://www.Ancestry.com, Record for Hazel Mary Atwood.

iii.   Henry Dwight Atwood was born on 10 Apr 1917 in Montana[381] and died on 14 May 1968[382].

iv.   Catherine Atwood was born in 1924 in Montana[383].

v.   Robert Eugene Atwood was born on 19 Aug 1925 in Great Falls, Montana[384] and died in Apr 1979[385]. He married Jennie Lou Olson, the daughter of Sam A. Olson and Georgia Johnson, on 27 Oct 1949 in Great Falls, Montana[386]. She was born on 15 Dec 1932 in Valier, Montana[387] and died on 02 Sep 2016 in Arizona[388].

34. Peter Henry Chrispell[4] (Sally Folliett Fagan[3], Adelia Webb[2], Henry B. Webb[1]) was born 17 Dec 1900 in New York State[389] and died 17 June 1978 in Sherburne, New York[390]. He married Dora Ellen Wightman on 20 Oct 1919 in Sidney, New York[391]. She was born in 1902[392]. They were divorced. He married Gladys Burton, the daughter of John Burton and Harriet Newman, on 18 Apr 1923 in Susquehanna, Pennsylvania[393]. She was born in 1901 in Gilford, New York[394]. Later he married Grace A. Miller on 24 Nov

---

[380] Ancestry.com, U.S., Find A Grave Index, 1700s-Current (Provo, UT, USA, Ancestry.com Operations, Inc., 2012), Ancestry.com, http://www.Ancestry.com, Record for Hazel Mary Atwood.

[381] National Cemetery Administration, U.S. Veterans Gravesites, ca.1775-2006 (Provo, UT, USA, The Generations Network, Inc., 2006), www.ancestry.com, Record for Henry Dwight Atwood.

[382] National Cemetery Administration, U.S. Veterans Gravesites, ca.1775-2006 (Provo, UT, USA, The Generations Network, Inc., 2006), www.ancestry.com, Record for Henry Dwight Atwood.

[383] Ancestry.com, 1940 United States Federal Census (Provo, UT, USA, Ancestry.com Operations, Inc., 2012), www.ancestry.com, Year: 1940; Census Place: Valier, Pondera, Montana; Roll: T627_2227; Page: 5A; Enumeration District: 37-15. Record for Hazel Atwood.

[384] Ancestry.com, U.S., Social Security Applications and Claims Index, 1936-2007 (Provo, UT, USA, Ancestry.com Operations, Inc., 2015), Ancestry.com, http://www.Ancestry.com, Record for Robert Eugene Atwood

[385] Ancestry.com, U.S., Social Security Applications and Claims Index, 1936-2007 (Provo, UT, USA, Ancestry.com Operations, Inc., 2015), Ancestry.com, http://www.Ancestry.com, Record for Robert Eugene Atwood

[386] Ancestry.com, Montana, County Marriages, 1865-1950 (Provo, UT, USA, Ancestry.com Operations, Inc., 2014), Ancestry.com, http://www.Ancestry.com, Record for Robert E. Atwood.

[387] Ancestry.com, Montana, County Marriages, 1865-1950 (Provo, UT, USA, Ancestry.com Operations, Inc., 2014), Ancestry.com, http://www.Ancestry.com, Record for Robert E. Atwood.

[388] Information found on familysearch.org family trees. Not sourced.

[389] Ancestry.com. Social Security Death Index, Number: 105-14-4623; Issue State: New York; Issue Date: Before 1951.

[390] Ancestry.com. Social Security Death Index, Number: 105-14-4623; Issue State: New York; Issue Date: Before 1951.

[391] Ancestry.com. New York, County Marriage Records, 1847-1849, 1907-1936 [database on-line]. Lehi, UT, USA: Ancestry.com Operations, Inc., 2016. Original data: Marriage Records. New York Marriages. Various New York County Clerk offices.

[392] Ancestry.com. New York, County Marriage Records, 1847-1849, 1907-1936 [database on-line]. Lehi, UT, USA: Ancestry.com Operations, Inc., 2016. Original data: Marriage Records. New York Marriages. Various New York County Clerk offices.

[393] "Pennsylvania, County Marriages, 1885-1950", database with images, FamilySearch (https://familysearch.org/ark:/61903/1:1:VF4X-7TS : 23 September 2017), Peter Chrispell and Gladys Burton, 1923.

[394] "Pennsylvania, County Marriages, 1885-1950", database with images, FamilySearch (https://familysearch.org/ark:/61903/1:1:VF4X-7TS : 23 September 2017), Peter Chrispell and Gladys Burton, 1923.

1943 in Susquehanna, Pennsylvania[395]. She was born in 1885[396] and died in 1971[397]. Lastly he married Marjorie Ewen on 03 Sep 1972[398].

Peter Henry Chrispell and Dora Ellen Wightman had the following children:

    i.   John K. Chrispell was born 10 Jan 1920[399] and died 10 Apr 1945 in Okinawa, Japan under enemy fire[400].

    ii.   Lulu Bernice Chrispell was born 01 Oct 1921[401] in Sherburne, New York and died 26 Sep 1993 in Greene, New York[402]. She married Richard Eugene Harrington. He was born 08 Jan 1923[403] in Green, New York and died 11 May 1992[404].

Peter H. Chrispell was born Dec. 16, 1900 in Sherburne, son of Walter and Sallyette (Fagan) Chrispell. He was a member of the Lutheran Church, American Legion Post 876 of Sherburne, Christy Rock Post 278 of the Veterans of Foreign Wars of Norwich, Disabled America Veterans Chapter 59 of Norwich, Chenango County Law Enforcement Association, White Tail Deer Association of Cole Brook, and the Midstate Arms Association. He was a veteran of both world wars, serving in the United States Army Air Corps with 20th Troop Carrier Squadron in World War II. He was married Dec. 27, 1943 to Grace Miller. She died in 1971. He was married Sept 3, 1972 to Marjorie Ewen. He is survived by his widow, Marjorie, of Sherburne; a daughter, Mrs. Richard (Lula) Harrington of Greene; two stepsons, Jack Ewen of Oneonta and Bruce Ewen of Detroit, Michigan, two step daughters; Mrs. Lee (Mildred) Park of Norwich and Mrs. Ronald (Sandra) Cleveland of Earlville. Funeral services will be held Wednesday at 2:00 p.m. at the William W. Kehoe Funeral Home with the Rev. John Joslyn officiating. Buries will be in Sherburne's West Hill Cemetery. Calling hours are Tuesday from 2 to 4 and 7 to 9.

Body of Fallen Hero to be Returned for Burial Thursday
Pvt. John K. Chrispell was killed on Okinawa April 9, 1945
Sherburne - The body of Private John K. Chrispell who was killed in action on Okinawa, April 9, 1945, will arrive in Sherburne at 11:20 Thursday morning via the Delaware Lackawanna and Western Railway. Full military honors will be accorded the returned

---

395 "Pennsylvania, County Marriages, 1885-1950", database with images, FamilySearch (https://familysearch.org/ark:/61903/1:1:KHXT-CRV : 23 September 2017), Peter H Chrispell and Grace A Miller, 1943.
396 "Pennsylvania, County Marriages, 1885-1950", database with images, FamilySearch (https://familysearch.org/ark:/61903/1:1:KHXT-CRV : 23 September 2017), Peter H Chrispell and Grace A Miller, 1943.
397 Findagrave at ancestry.com.
398 Obituary found on page 249.
399 U.S., Find A Grave Index, 1700s-Current.
400 Obituary found on page 249.
401 U.S., Find A Grave Index, 1700s-Current for Lulu Bernice Chrispell Harrington.
402 U.S., Find A Grave Index, 1700s-Current for Lulu Bernice Chrispell Harrington.
403 U.S., Social Security Applications and Claims Index, 1936-2007 for Richard Eugene Harrington.
404 U.S., Social Security Applications and Claims Index, 1936-2007 for Richard Eugene Harrington.

soldier by the Sherburne Legion post 574, with Commander Edwin Awards in charge. The body will be taken from the train directly to Sherburne West Hill Cemetery for burial. Rev. Charles Adams, pastor of the Methodist Church will officiate. Private Chrispell is the son of Peter H. Chrispell of Sherburne. On December 7 the silver and bronze stars were awarded post unamously to Private Chrispell. The star was awarded for gallant action on Okinawa 9 April 1945. After his unit had secured its objective he observed that the company on the left flank was halted by intensive enemy machine gun fire emanating from several pillboxes.

35. Pearl Marguerite Palmer[4] (Ina Elizabeth Webb[3], Thomas H. Webb[2], Henry B. Webb[1]) was born on 21 Sep 1890 in South Dakota [405] and died on 15 Apr 1952 in Los Angeles, California[406]. She married Wallace Holly[407]. He was born on 31 Aug 1890 in Minnesota[408] and died on 27 Jan 1975 in Riverside, California[409].

Wallace W. Holly and Pearle Marguerite Palmer had the following child:
    i.   Wilford W. Holly was born in 1924 in California[410].

---

[405] Ancestry.com, South Dakota, Birth Index, 1856-1917 (Provo, UT, USA, Ancestry.com Operations Inc, 2003), Ancestry.com, http://www.Ancestry.com, South Dakota Department of Health; Pierre, South Dakota; South Dakota, Birth Index, 1856-1917.

[406] Ancestry.com, California Death Index, 1940-1997 (Provo, UT, USA, The Generations Network, Inc., 2000), www.ancestry.com, Date: 1952-04-15. Record for Pearl Palmer Holley.

[407] Ancestry.com, California Death Index, 1940-1997 (Provo, UT, USA, The Generations Network, Inc., 2000), www.ancestry.com, Date: 1952-04-15. Record for Pearl Palmer Holley.

[408] Ancestry.com, Social Security Death Index (Provo, UT, USA, The Generations Network, Inc., 2008), www.ancestry.com, Number: 566-66-1707; Issue State: California; Issue Date: 1962. Record for Wallace Holley.

[409] Ancestry.com, California Death Index, 1940-1997 (Provo, UT, USA, The Generations Network, Inc., 2000), www.ancestry.com, Date: 1975-01-27. Record for Wallace W Holley.

[410] Ancestry.com, 1930 United States Federal Census (Online publication - Provo, UT, USA: Ancestry.com Operations Inc, 2002.Original data - United States of America, Bureau of the Census. Fifteenth Census of the United States, 1930. Washington, D.C.: National Archives and Records Administration, 1930. T626,), Ancestry.com, http://www.Ancestry.com, Year: 1930; Census Place: Inglewood, Los Angeles, California; Roll: 128; Page: 6A; Enumeration District: 1021; Image: 497.0; FHL microfilm: 2339863. Record for Pearl M Holly.

Generation Five

36. Larue Mastin Poole[5] (William Ellsworth Poole[4], Mary H. Webb[3], John H. Webb[2], Henry B. Webb[1]) was born on 14 Mar 1904 in Friendship, New York[411] and died in 1962[412]. He married Opal M. Harsh[413]. She was born on 25 Feb 1906[414] and died on 26 Apr 1991[415]. Larue Mastin Poole and Opal M. Harsh had one child who may still be living.

37. William Alonzo Poole[5] (William Ellsworth Poole[4], Mary H. Webb[3], John H. Webb[2], Henry B. Webb[1]) was born on 15 Nov 1909 in Friendship, New York[416] and died on 12 May 1990 in Eldorado, Kansas[417]. He married Margaret Melva Delong, the daughter of Frank M. Delong and Hazel C. McQuerter[418]. She was born on 23 Apr 1914 in Raton Calfax, New Mexico[419] and died on 01 Jan 2003 in El Dorado, Kansas[420]. William Alonzo Poole and Margaret Melva Delong had three children who may still be living.

The Wichita Eagle, El Dorado - Obituary
Margaret M. Poole, 88, died Sunday, Jan. 12, 2003. Graveside service 10 a.m. Friday, Sunset Lawns Cemetery. Memorial service 11 a.m., First United Methodist Church. Survivors: daughters, Pamela Cogswell of Arvada, Colo., Vicki Hallmark, Peggy Christy, both of El Dorado; sister, Mildred Hower of Winfield; nine grandchildren; 15 great-grandchildren; one great-great-grandchild. Memorial established with First United Methodist Church. Kirby-Morris Funeral Home.

---

[411] Ancestry.com, U.S., Find A Grave Index, 1700s-Current (Provo, UT, USA, Ancestry.com Operations, Inc., 2012), Ancestry.com, http://www.Ancestry.com, Record for Larue M. Poole.

[412] Ancestry.com, U.S., Find A Grave Index, 1700s-Current (Provo, UT, USA, Ancestry.com Operations, Inc., 2012), Ancestry.com, http://www.Ancestry.com, Record for Larue M. Poole.

[413] Ancestr.com Year: 1940; Census Place: Kansas City, Jackson, Missouri; Roll: T627_2180; Page: 19B; Enumeration District: 116-344.

[414] Ancestry.com, Social Security Death Index (Provo, UT, USA, The Generations Network, Inc., 2008), www.ancestry.com, Number: 497-36-6436; Issue State: Missouri; Issue Date: 1951-1952. Record for Opal M. Poole.

[415] Ancestry.com, Social Security Death Index (Provo, UT, USA, The Generations Network, Inc., 2008), www.ancestry.com, Number: 497-36-6436; Issue State: Missouri; Issue Date: 1951-1952. Record for Opal M. Poole.

[416] Ancestry.com, Social Security Death Index (Provo, UT, USA, The Generations Network, Inc., 2008), www.ancestry.com, Number: 442-07-4779; Issue State: Oklahoma; Issue Date: Before 1951. Record for W. A. Poole.

[417] Ancestry.com, Social Security Death Index (Provo, UT, USA, The Generations Network, Inc., 2008), www.ancestry.com, Number: 442-07-4779; Issue State: Oklahoma; Issue Date: Before 1951. Record for W. A. Poole.

[418] Ancestry.com, 1940 United States Federal Census (Provo, UT, USA, Ancestry.com Operations, Inc., 2012), Ancestry.com, http://www.Ancestry.com, Year: 1940; Census Place: El Dorado, Butler, Kansas; Roll: T627_1222; Page: 10B; Enumeration District: 8-22. Record for William A Poole.

[419] Ancestry.com, U.S., Social Security Applications and Claims Index, 1936-2007 (Provo, UT, USA, Ancestry.com Operations, Inc., 2015), Ancestry.com, http://www.Ancestry.com, Record for Margaret Melva Poole

[420] Ancestry.com, U.S., Social Security Applications and Claims Index, 1936-2007 (Provo, UT, USA, Ancestry.com Operations, Inc., 2015), Ancestry.com, http://www.Ancestry.com, Record for Margaret Melva Poole

38. Vera Louise Perkins[5] (Pansey Maude Poole[4], Mary H. Webb[3], John H. Webb[2], Henry B. Webb[1]) was born 11 Feb 1908[421] in Friendship, New York and died 08 Jan 2001 in Friendship, New York[422]. She married Charles Marion McGough, the son of Thomas McGough and Gertrude Baker, on 01 Jul 1927 in Allegany County, New York[423]. He was born on 18 Jul 1905 in Friendship, New York[424] and died in 22 Feb 1954 in Olean, New York[425].

Charles Marion McGough and Vera Louise Perkins had the following child:
    i.   Laura McGough was born and died in 1932[426].

39. Laura Belle Niver[5] (Charles A. Niver, Sr.[4], Adelia M. Webb[3], John H. Webb[2], Henry B. Webb[1]) was born 17 Jan 1903 in Denver Colorado[427] and died 25 April 1990 in New York State[428].

She married Ward Olmsted Maxson, the son of Homer and Mary Maxson on 06 Apr 1923 in Wyoming, New York[429]. He was born 15 Aug 1900 in Pearl Creek, New York and died on 03 Dec 1991[430] in Warsaw, New York[431].

Photo of Laura Belle Niver Maxson found on Ancestry.com.

Ward Olmsted Maxson and Laura Belle Niver had the following children:
    i.   Ward Junior Maxson was born 06 Oct 1923[432] in Perry, New York and died 05 Feb 2007[433]. He married Rene Willima Young and they had one child.

[421] Ancestry.com, U.S., Find A Grave Index, 1700s-Current (Provo, UT, USA, Ancestry.com Operations, Inc., 2012),

[422] Ancestry.com, U.S., Find A Grave Index, 1700s-Current (Provo, UT, USA, Ancestry.com Operations, Inc., 2012),

[423] Ancestry.com. New York, County Marriage Records, 1847-1849, 1907-1936 [database on-line]. Lehi, UT, USA: Ancestry.com Operations, Inc., 2016.
Original data: Marriage Records. New York Marriages. Various New York County Clerk offices.

[424] Ancestry.com, U.S., Find A Grave Index, 1700s-Current (Provo, UT, USA, Ancestry.com Operations, Inc., 2012).

[425] New York State Death Index at Ancestry.com

[426] Ancestry.com, U.S., Find A Grave Index, 1700s-Current (Provo, UT, USA, Ancestry.com Operations, Inc., 2012).

[427] Ancestry.com, U.S., Find A Grave Index, 1700s-Current (Provo, UT, USA, Ancestry.com Operations, Inc., 2012).

[428] Ancestry.com, U.S., Find A Grave Index, 1700s-Current (Provo, UT, USA, Ancestry.com Operations, Inc., 2012).

[429] Ancestry.com. New York, County Marriage Records, 1847-1849, 1907-1936 [database on-line]. Lehi, UT, USA: Ancestry.com Operations, Inc., 2016

[430] Ancestry.com, U.S., Find A Grave Index, 1700s-Current (Provo, UT, USA, Ancestry.com Operations, Inc., 2012).

[431] Ancestry.com, U.S., Find A Grave Index, 1700s-Current (Provo, UT, USA, Ancestry.com Operations, Inc., 2012).

[432] Ancestry.com. *U.S., Social Security Death Index, 1935-2014* [database on-line]. Provo, UT, USA: Ancestry.com Operations Inc, 2014.

[433] Ancestry.com. *U.S., Social Security Death Index, 1935-2014* [database on-line]. Provo, UT, USA: Ancestry.com Operations Inc, 2014.

Photo of Ward Junior Maxson found on Ancestry.com.←

ii. Reginald W. Maxson was born 29 Aug 1925[434] in Perry, New York and died 25 Jan 2001 in Lakewood, California[435]. He married Jaqueline Rose Blackwood and they had one child.

Photo of Reginald W. Maxson found on Ancestry.com.→

iii. Martin Maxson was born in 1927[436] in Perry, New York and died 20 Oct 1928 in Perry, New York[437].

iv. Betsy Niver Maxson was born 11 Aug 1929[438] in Perry, New York and died 07 May 2013 in Warsaw, New York[439]. She married Clayton Eugene Shirley[440]. He was born 27 Sep 1928[441] and died 06 Oct 1997[442].

Photo of Betsy Niver Maxson found on Ancestry.com.

---

[434] Ancestry.com. *U.S., Social Security Death Index, 1935-2014* [database on-line]. Provo, UT, USA: Ancestry.com Operations Inc, 2014.

[435] Ancestry.com. *U.S., Social Security Death Index, 1935-2014* [database on-line]. Provo, UT, USA: Ancestry.com Operations Inc, 2014.

[436] Ancestry.com, U.S., Find A Grave Index, 1700s-Current (Provo, UT, USA, Ancestry.com Operations, Inc., 2012).

[437] Ancestry.com, U.S., Find A Grave Index, 1700s-Current (Provo, UT, USA, Ancestry.com Operations, Inc., 2012).

[438] Ancestry.com, U.S., Find A Grave Index, 1700s-Current (Provo, UT, USA, Ancestry.com Operations, Inc., 2012).

[439] Ancestry.com, U.S., Find A Grave Index, 1700s-Current (Provo, UT, USA, Ancestry.com Operations, Inc., 2012).

[440] Ancestry.com, U.S., Find A Grave Index, 1700s-Current (Provo, UT, USA, Ancestry.com Operations, Inc., 2012).

[441] Ancestry.com, U.S., Find A Grave Index, 1700s-Current (Provo, UT, USA, Ancestry.com Operations, Inc., 2012).

[442] Ancestry.com, U.S., Find A Grave Index, 1700s-Current (Provo, UT, USA, Ancestry.com Operations, Inc., 2012).

Batavia, New York - Betsy M. Shirley, 83 of Perry, died May 7, 2013 at the Wyoming County Nursing Facility in Warsaw. She was born in Perry on August 11, 1929 to the late Ward (Laura Niver) Maxson. Betsy was a 1947 graduate of Perry Central School. She worked in the cafeteria of the Perry Central School for years before she retired. She was a member of the First United Methodist Church in Perry. She enjoyed crocheting, reading and going to visit friends. Along with her parents she is preceded in death by her husband Clayton E. Shirley; daughter Patricia Ann Whitton; siblings Laura Schwab, Mary Dumbleton, Nellie Towneslanckton, Martin, Ward and Reginald Maxson. She is survived by her grandson Jesse R. Whitton of Perry; sister Eva Mae (Devoughn) Speicher of Grants Pass Oregon; son-in-law Brian Whitton of Warsaw; sister-in-law Teresa Shirley, brother-in-law Ronald Shirley along with several nieces, nephews, great nieces and great nephews. Friends are invited to call on Friday May 10, 2013 from 5-8pm at the Eaton-Watson Funeral Home, LLC. 98 N. Main St. in Perry where a Funeral Service will follow 8pm at the Funeral Home. Interment will take place in Glenwood

Cemetery, Perry. Memorials may be made to the First United Methodist Church 35 Covington St. Perry, NY 14530 or to the Office for the Aging 8 Perry Ave. Warsaw, NY 14569.

  v. Mary Ann Maxson was born 21 Oct 1934[443] in Perry, New York and died 04 Mar 1961 in Pinellas, Florida[444]. She married Richard F. Dumbleton on 28 Aug 1954 in Perry, New York[445].

  vi. Nellie M. Maxson was born 12 Jan 1936 in Perry, New York and died 26 Aug 2013 in Batavia, New York. She married Philip Lanckton in 2008[446].

Photo of Nellie M. Maxson found on Ancestry.com.

Batavia. New York - Nellie was born in Perry NY on January 12, 1936 a daughter of the late Ward O. Laura Belle Niver Maxson. Nellie was a 1954 graduate of Perry Central School. She had worked for the former Ben Franklin, Champion Products, Robeson Cutlery, and Perry Knitting Mill, the Perry Central School, Perry Public Library and retired from M&T Bank in 2004. She was a member of the First United Methodist Church in Perry, the Moose Club in Warsaw and the Tuesday Night bowling league. She enjoyed bowling, sewing, cooking, and especially enjoyed the company of her children and grandchildren. She is survived by her husband Philip Lanckton whom she married in

---

[443] Ancestry.com, U.S., Find A Grave Index, 1700s-Current (Provo, UT, USA, Ancestry.com Operations, Inc., 2012).

[444] Ancestry.com. *Florida Death Index, 1877-1998* [database on-line]. Provo, UT, USA: Ancestry.com Operations Inc, 2004.

[445] Ancestry.com, New York State Marriage index.

[446] Obituary included in this book on page 254.

2008, a daughter Susan Butler of Chipley, Fla., 3 sons: Steven (Patricia) Townes , Stuart (Lisa) Townes and Skyler (Carly) Townes all of Perry, 2 sisters: Betsy Shirley of Perry and Eva Mae (Devoughn) Speicher of Grants Pass, Or. Brothers and Sister in-laws: Mary (Jerome) Lemley of Pavilion, Frank Crawford of Fairbanks, Al.,12 grandchildren: Katie Barajas, Susan Martinez, Jenny, David and Patty Ziolkowski, Steven Jr., Amber, Joel, Matthew, Key, Briar and Alexander Townes and 12 great grandchildren, along with many nieces and nephews. PRECEDED IN DEATH BY: along with her parents are her 1st husband Albert Townes who died in 2002, siblings: Laura Schwab, Mary Dumbleton, Martin, Ward and Reginald Maxson, and a brother-in-law: Clayton Shirley. no prior visitation. Graveside service will be held on Wednesday August 29th at 3:00pm at Grace Cemetery in Castile. On Tuesday evening August 28th there with be a gathering at the Perry Vets Club for a Celebration of Life.

       vii.   Laura Belle Maxson was born 01 Jul 1938[447] in Perry, New York and died 31 Jul 2005[448] in Victorville, California. Her last name at the time of her death was Schwab.

40. Harold Cosper Niver[5] (Charles A. Niver, Sr.[4], Adelia M. Webb[3], John H. Webb[2], Henry B. Webb[1]) was born on 02 Mar 1907 in Friendship, New York[449] and died in Oct 1985 in Commack, New York[450]. He married Marian Elaine Chesbro, the daughter of Charles D. Chesbro and Lena Alice Case, on 14 Jun 1933 in Oswego, New York[451]. She was born on 12 Jun 1915 in Fulton, New York[452] and died 17 May 1997[453]. At the time of her death, she had married again to Howard Granzow.

Harold Cosper Niver and Marian Elaine Chesbro had the following children:
       i.   Nancy Jean Niver was born on 04 Nov 1935 in Fulton, New York[454] and died on 15 Nov 1992 in Westerlo, New York[455]. She married Mr. Aylor.
       ii.   Living Niver.

[447] U.S., Social Security Applications and Claims Index, 1936-2007.

[448] U.S., Social Security Applications and Claims Index, 1936-2007.

[449] Ancestry.com, Social Security Death Index (Provo, UT, USA, The Generations Network, Inc., 2008), www.ancestry.com, Number: 111-20-1858; Issue State: New York; Issue Date: Before 1951. Record for Harold Niver.

[450] Ancestry.com, Social Security Death Index (Provo, UT, USA, The Generations Network, Inc., 2008), www.ancestry.com, Number: 111-20-1858; Issue State: New York; Issue Date: Before 1951. Record for Harold Niver.

[451] Ancestry.com, New York, County Marriages, 1847-1849; 1907-1936 (Lehi, UT, USA, Ancestry.com Operations, Inc., 2016), Ancestry.com, http://www.Ancestry.com, Record for Harold Cosper Niver.

[452] Ancestry.com, New York, County Marriages, 1847-1849; 1907-1936 (Lehi, UT, USA, Ancestry.com Operations, Inc., 2016), Ancestry.com, http://www.Ancestry.com, Record for Harold Cosper Niver.

[453] Ancestry.com, U.S., Find A Grave Index, 1700s-Current (Provo, UT, USA, Ancestry.com Operations, Inc., 2012), Ancestry.com, http://www.Ancestry.com.

[454] Ancestry.com, U.S., Social Security Applications and Claims Index, 1936-2007 (Provo, UT, USA, Ancestry.com Operations, Inc., 2015), Ancestry.com, http://www.Ancestry.com, Record for Nancy Jean Niver.

[455] Ancestry.com, U.S., Social Security Applications and Claims Index, 1936-2007 (Provo, UT, USA, Ancestry.com Operations, Inc., 2015), Ancestry.com, http://www.Ancestry.com, Record for Nancy Jean Niver.

41. PFC Glenn W. Niver[5] (Charles A. Niver, Sr.[4], Adelia M. Webb[3], John H. Webb[2], Henry B. Webb[1]) was born on 17 Nov 1910[456] and died on 03 Mar 1994 in Olean, New York[457]. He married Marguerite Ivy Dillon, the daughter of Francis Dillon and Lily Caroline Moore, on 16 May 1945 in England[458]. She was born on 27 Jan 1919 in Weymouth, Dorset, England[459] and died on 26 Oct 2009 in Olean, New York[460]. Pfc Glenn W Niver and Marguerite Ivy Dillon had two children who may still be living.

Photo of Glenn W. Niver and Marguerite Ivy Dillon found on Ancestry.com.

42. Dorothy M. Baker[5] (Robert Oney Baker[4], Ellen M. Webb[3], John H. Webb[2], Henry B. Webb[1]) was born in 1906 in United States[461]. She married John A. Logan on 25 Aug 1923 in Rochester, New York[462]. He was born in 1902[463] and died 03 Jul 1945 in Rochester, New York[464].

---

[456] Ancestry.com, Social Security Death Index (Provo, UT, USA, The Generations Network, Inc., 2008), www.ancestry.com, Number: 079-07-2132; Issue State: New York; Issue Date: Before 1951. Record for Glenn W. Niver.

[457] Ancestry.com, Social Security Death Index (Provo, UT, USA, The Generations Network, Inc., 2008), www.ancestry.com, Number: 079-07-2132; Issue State: New York; Issue Date: Before 1951. Record for Glenn W. Niver.

[458] Ancestry.com, U.S., Find A Grave Index, 1700s-Current (Provo, UT, USA, Ancestry.com Operations, Inc., Ancestry.com, U.S., Find A Grave Index, 1700s-Current (Provo, UT, USA, Ancestry.com Operations, Inc., 2012), Ancestry.com,

[459] Ancestry.com, U.S., Find A Grave Index, 1700s-Current (Provo, UT, USA, Ancestry.com Operations, Inc., Ancestry.com, U.S., Find A Grave Index, 1700s-Current (Provo, UT, USA, Ancestry.com Operations, Inc., 2012), Ancestry.com,

[460] Ancestry.com, U.S., Find A Grave Index, 1700s-Current (Provo, UT, USA, Ancestry.com Operations, Inc., 2012), Ancestry.com, http://www.Ancestry.com.

[461] Ancestry.com, New York, County Marriages, 1847-1849; 1907-1936 (Lehi, UT, USA, Ancestry.com Operations, Inc., 2016), Ancestry.com, http://www.Ancestry.com, Record for Dorothy M Baker

[462] Ancestry.com, New York, County Marriages, 1847-1849; 1907-1936 (Lehi, UT, USA, Ancestry.com Operations, Inc., 2016), Ancestry.com, http://www.Ancestry.com, Record for Dorothy M Baker

[463] Ancestry.com, U.S., Find A Grave Index, 1700s-Current (Provo, UT, USA, Ancestry.com Operations, Inc., 2012), Ancestry.com, http://www.Ancestry.com.

[464] Ancestry.com, U.S., Find A Grave Index, 1700s-Current (Provo, UT, USA, Ancestry.com Operations, Inc., 2012), Ancestry.com, http://www.Ancestry.com.

John A. Logan and Dorothy M. Baker had the following children:

48.   i.   Eleanor June Logan was born on 22 Jul 1924 in New York State[465] and died on 13 Jun 2000[466].

       ii.   Living Logan.

49.   iii.   Walter C. Logan was born on 01 Jul 1927[467] and died on 05 Jul 2014 in Ft. Lauderdale, Florida[468].

       iv.   Living Logan.

43. Helene L. O'Connell[5], (Mildred E. Foote[4], William H. Foote[3], Abigail Webb[2], Henry B. Webb[1]) was born on 04 Apr 1902 in Cortland, New York [469] and died on 08 May 1986 in Rome Hospital, Rome, New York[470]. She married James M. O'Hara, the son of Michael and Margaret O'Hara on 14 Aug 1930 in Cortland, New York[471]. He was born in 1901 in Turin, New York[472] and died on 28 Dec 1955 in Syracuse, New York[473]. James M. O'Hara and Helene L. O'Connell had one child who may still be living.

Helene O'Hara had lived in Rome since 1924. She was a member of St. Peter's Church, the Syracuse University Alumni Association, Theta Phi Alpha Sorority and Phi Beta Kappa National Honor Society. She had three grandchildren at the time of her death.

James O'Hara attended Turin High School and graduated from Utica Free Academy. He was a graduate of Syracuse University and Fordham Law School, New York City. He was an associated for a time at White Plains in practice with the former Judge Humphrey J. Lynch. He opened his Utica law office in 1929 and five years later established a Rome office. From 1932 through 1934 he was sheriff's attorney under the late Albert E. Ellinger and began his term as corporation counsel in 1935. He was a member of the Knights of Columbus, the Elks and belonged to St. Peter's Church.

44. Robert Danicl O'Connell[5], (Mildred E. Foote[4], William H. Foote[3], Abigail Webb[2], Henry B. Webb[1]) was born on 01 Sep 1910 in Cortland, New York[474] and died on 22 Jun 1998 in Bloomfield, Connecticut[475]. He married Maree Basttista on 05 Jun 1937 in[476].

[465] Ancestry.com, U.S., Find A Grave Index, 1700s-Current (Provo, UT, USA, Ancestry.com Operations, Inc., 2012), Ancestry.com, http://www.Ancestry.com, Record for Donald George Stifter.

[466] Obituary of Eleanor June Logan, Rochester Democrat and Chronicle, Rochester, New York - June 14, 2000. Included in this book on page 261.

[467] Ancestry.com, U.S. Public Records Index, Volume 2, Record for Walter C Logan.

[468] Obituary of Walter J. Logan included in this book on page 261.

[469] Obituary, Rome Sentinel, Rome, New York, May 9, 1986.

[470] Obituary, Rome Sentinel, Rome, New York, May 9, 1986.

[471] Obituary, Rome Sentinel, Rome, New York, May 9, 1986.

[472] Obituary, Rome Sentinel, Rome, New York, December 28, 1953.

[473] Obituary, Rome Sentinel, Rome, New York, December 28, 1953.

[474] Obituary, The Hartford Courant, Hartford, Connecticut, June 24, 1998 on line.

[475] Obituary, The Hartford Courant, Hartford, Connecticut, June 24, 1998 on line.

[476] Obituary, The Hartford Courant, Hartford, Connecticut, June 24, 1998 on line.

 The Hartford Courant, June 24, 1998 - *Robert D. O'Connell was a four letter man in High School. He played football under Knute Rockne at Notre Dame. After transferring to Yale in his sophomore year, e played varsity football and basketball, including one season with Albie Booth as captain. He also captained a championship basketball team at Yale in 1032/33, After graduating Yale, he entered Yale Law School and graduated in 1936. His career was in insurance, having worked at the Traveler's Co. and the Aetna Insurance Co. Following his retirement in 1975, he worked as a consultant in Stamford and then New York City until 1984. Mr. O'Connell served for four and a half years in the U.S. Army during World War II, including one and a half years in India with the rank of Captain, working in a Branch of Intelligence.*

Robert Daniel O'Connell and Maree Basttista had four children who may still be living.

45. Laura Abigail Rudd[5] (Lydia Anna Mather[4], Mary Abigal Foote[3], Abigail Webb[2], Henry B. Webb[1]) was born on 18 Feb 1898 in New York State[477] and died on 15 Dec 1993 in Rome, New York[478]. She married Charles Frederick Dolan, the son of Daniel F. Dolan and Mary E. Dillon, on 31 Aug 1916[479] in Utica, New York. He was born on 03 Dec 1891 in Cortland, New York[480] and died in 21 Jan 1937[481]. She later married John J. Dillon, the son of James P. Dillon and Agnes Agen in 1937 in Scranton, Pennsylvania[482]. He was born on 20 Aug 1891 in Utica, New York[483] and died on 12 Aug 1952 in St. Elizabeth Hospital, Utica, New York[484]. Laura was employed for 35 years by the Boston Store. She was a member of St. Paul's Church, Whitesboro, New York. She lived in the Colonial Apartments in Rome in her later years and then at the Stonehedge Nursing Home in Rome, New York. Laura had three great granddaughters at the time of her death John Dillon was educated in Utica Schools. For many years he was a salesman for the Adrean Lee Packing company. He later operated The Barn in North Utica and at the time of his death he was a salesman for the Cudahy Packing Company in Utica, New York. He was a member of St. Peter's Church in North Utica.

---

[477] Ancestry.com, Social Security Death Index (Provo, UT, USA, The Generations Network, Inc., 2008), www.ancestry.com, Database online. Number: 081-14-6242; Issue State: New York; Issue Date: Before 1951. Record for Laura Dillon.

[478] Ancestry.com, Social Security Death Index (Provo, UT, USA, The Generations Network, Inc., 2008), www.ancestry.com, Database online. Number: 081-14-6242; Issue State: New York; Issue Date: Before 1951. Record for Laura Dillon.

[479] Ancestry.com. *New York, County Marriage Records, 1847-1849, 1907-1936* [database on-line]. Lehi, UT, USA: Ancestry.com Operations, Inc., 2016.

[480] Ancestry.com, World War I Draft Registration Cards, 1917-1918 (Provo, UT, USA, The Generations Network, Inc., 2005),

[481] Ancestry.com. *New York, Death Index, 1880-1956* [database on-line]. Lehi, UT, USA: Ancestry.com Operations, Inc., 2017.

[482] Obituary, Utica Daily Press, Utica, New York, August 13, 1952.

[483] Obituary, Utica Daily Press, Utica, New York, August 13, 1952.

[484] Obituary, Utica Daily Press, Utica, New York, August 13, 1952.

Charles Frederick Dolan's World War I draft registration said he worked as a clerk for Hart and Crouse of Utica.

Charles Frederick Dolan and Laura Abigail Rudd had the following child:70.
50.   i.   William Francis Dolan was born on 13 Aug 1917 in Whitesboro, New York[485] and died on 19 Apr 1997 in Rome Memorial Hospital, Rome, New York[486].

46. Lee J. Mallette[5] (Gertrude M. Mather[4], Mary Abigal Foote[3], Abigail Webb[2], Henry B. Webb[1]) was born on 02 Mar 1916 in New York State[487] and died on 23 Nov 1999 in Hemet, California[488]. He married a lady by the name of Alida. Lee J. Mallette lived at 447 E. Madison Ave., El Cajon, California in 1963. Lee J. Mallette and Alida Mallette had three children who may still be living.

47. Helen K. Porter[5] (Julia Catherine Webb[4], Myron D Webb[3], LaFayette Webb[2], Henry B. Webb[1]) was born on 05 Jul 1916 in Lewiston, Idaho[489] and died on 13 Mar 1996 in Conrad, Montana[490]. She married Wayne M. Berland, the son of Bert Berland and Frances Shumaker, on 11 Nov 1946 in Conrad, Montana[491]. He was born on 03 Nov 1919 in Brady, Montana[492] and died on 31 Jan 2000[493].   Wayne M. Berland and Helen K Porter had one child who may still be living.

Helen K. (Porter) Berland, age 79, passed away March 13 at her residence following a long illness. A Vigil Service will be held March 17, at 7:00 p.m. at St. Michael's Catholic Church in Conrad. Mass of Christian Burial will be held March 18, at 11 a.m. at St. Michael's Catholic Church. Interment will be in Mount Olivet Cemetery in Conrad. The Pondera Funeral Home is in charge of arrangements. She was born July 5, 1916 in Lewiston, Idaho. She came to the Conrad area as a child. She graduated from Conrad

[485] Ancestry.com. *U.S., Social Security Death Index, 1935-2014* [database on-line]. Provo, UT, USA: Ancestry.com Operations Inc, 2014.

[486] Ancestry.com. *U.S., Social Security Death Index, 1935-2014* [database on-line]. Provo, UT, USA: Ancestry.com Operations Inc, 2014.

[487] Ancestry.com. *U.S., Social Security Death Index, 1935-2014* [database on-line]. Provo, UT, USA: Ancestry.com Operations Inc, 2014.

[488] Ancestry.com. *U.S., Social Security Death Index, 1935-2014* [database on-line]. Provo, UT, USA: Ancestry.com Operations Inc, 2014.

[489] Ancestry.com, U.S., Social Security Applications and Claims Index, 1936-2007 (Provo, UT, USA, Ancestry.com Operations, Inc., 2015), Ancestry.com, http://www.Ancestry.com, Record for Helen Kathryn Berland.

[490] Ancestry.com, U.S., Social Security Applications and Claims Index, 1936-2007 (Provo, UT, USA, Ancestry.com Operations, Inc., 2015), Ancestry.com, http://www.Ancestry.com, Record for Helen Kathryn Berland.

[491] Ancestry.com, Montana, Marriage Records, 1943-1986 Ancestry.com, http://www.Ancestry.com, Montana Department of Public Health and Human Services; Helena, Montana; Montana State Marriage Records, 1943-1986; Roll Number: 19; Certificate Number Range: Pon 1 - Pon 500. Record for Helen K. Porter.

[492] Ancestry.com, U.S., Find A Grave Index, 1700s-Current (Provo, UT, USA, Ancestry.com Operations, Inc., 2012), Ancestry.com, http://www.Ancestry.com, Record for Wayne M Berland.

[493] Ancestry.com, U.S., Find A Grave Index, 1700s-Current (Provo, UT, USA, Ancestry.com Operations, Inc., 2012), Ancestry.com, http://www.Ancestry.com, Record for Wayne M Berland.

High School and was employed in the office of the County Clerk and Recorder for a number of years. Helen and Wayne Berland were married in Conrad on November 11, 1946. They made their home in Conrad ever since. She was a member of St. Michael's Church. She liked to camp, travel and fish. Survivors include her husband Wayne of Conrad and one son Bill Berland of Albuquerque, NM. Memorials may be sent to the Pondera Peach Hospice or the charity of one's choice.

Generation Six

48. Eleanor June Logan[6] (Dorothy M. Baker[5], Robert Oney Baker[4], Ellen M. Webb[3], John H. Webb[2], Henry B. Webb[1]) was born on 22 Jul 1924 in New York State[494] and died on 13 Jan 2000[495]. She married Donald George Stifter on 12 Mar 1945 in Rochester, New York[496]. He was born on 31 Aug 1924 in Rochester, New York[497] and died on 12 Jun 1988[498].

Rochester Democrat and Chronicle - June 14, 2000
Stifter, Eleanor J. (Logan) January 13, 2000 Predeceased by her loving husband, Donald. Survived by her children, Dan (Char), Cathleen, Gene Paul (Judi) Sandra Blasi, Jerry Lieberman Stifter, grandchildren, Lisa (John) Ahem, Mark, Timm (Carolina) and Ryan Stifter, Daniel and Jeffery Blasi and Kristy Lieberman. Brothers, Vin Logan, Walt (Jean) Logan, Sister Dorothy Lavery, best friend (cousin), Mary Sweeney. Several nieces, nephews and cousins. No prior calling. Friends are invited to her Funeral Mass Sat. June 15th, 12:30 p.m. at Spiritus Christi, Salem UCC, 60 Bittner St.. In Lieu of flowers kindly consider Union Hill Volunteer Ambulance, PO Box 112, Union Hill. Arrangements - Nulton Funeral Home.

Donald George Stifter and Eleanor June Logan had five children who may still be living.

49. Walter C. Logan[6] (Dorothy M. Baker[5], Robert Oney Baker[4], Ellen M. Webb[3], John H. Webb[2], Henry B. Webb[1]) was born on 01 Jul 1927[499] and died on 05 Jul 2014 in Ft. Lauderdale, Florida[500]. He married Jean in 1948[501].

Walter C. Logan, 87 of Ft. Lauderdale, FL, formerly of Rochester, NY, passed away Saturday, July 5, 2014. He is survived by his loving wife, Jean, married 66 years; sons Jack and Steven (Vivian) Logan; granddaughter, Helen Logan and brother, Vincent Logan and many other family members. He is predeceased by his sisters, Eleanor and

---

[494] Ancestry.com, U.S., Find A Grave Index, 1700s-Current (Provo, UT, USA, Ancestry.com Operations, Inc., 2012), Ancestry.com, http://www.Ancestry.com, Record for Donald George Stifter.

[495] Obituary, Rochester Democrat and Chronicle, Rochester, New York - June 14, 2000.

[496] Ancestry.com, New York State Marriage Index 1881-1957.

[497] Ancestry.com, U.S., Find A Grave Index, 1700s-Current (Provo, UT, USA, Ancestry.com Operations, Inc., 2012), Ancestry.com, http://www.Ancestry.com, Record for Donald George Stifter.

[498] Ancestry.com, U.S., Find A Grave Index, 1700s-Current (Provo, UT, USA, Ancestry.com Operations, Inc., 2012), Ancestry.com, http://www.Ancestry.com, Record for Donald George Stifter.

[499] Ancestry.com, U.S. Public Records Index, Volume 2 (Provo, UT, USA, Ancestry.com Operations, Inc., 2010), www.ancestry.com, Record for Walter C Logan.

[500] Obituary of Walter C. Logan included in this book on page 261.

[501] Obituary of Walter C. Logan included in this book on page 261.

Dorothy. The family will receive friends on Wed., July 9th, from 4 to 7 pm at the Kalis-McIntee Funeral Home, 2505 N. Dixie Hwy, Wilton Manors. Mass of Christian Burial will be celebrated on Thursday, July 10th, 11 am in St. Pius, X Catholic Church, 2511 N. Ocean Blvd. Ft. Lauderdale. In Lieu of flowers, memorial donations may be made in Walter's memory to the Abandoned Pet Rescue 1220 NE 26 St. Ft. Lauderdale, FL 33305. Online condolences at KalisMcIntee.com.

Walter C. and Jean Logan had two children who may still be living.

50. William Francis Dolan[6] (Laura Abigail Rudd[5], Lydia Anna Mather[4], Mary Abigail Foote[3], Abigail Webb[2], Henry B. Webb[1]) was born on 13 Aug 1917 in Whitesboro, New York[502] and died on 19 Apr 1997 in Rome Memorial Hospital, Rome, New York[503]. He married Eleanor King, the daughter of Lester King and Leila Jones on 15 Jun 1940 in St. Francis Church, Utica, New York[504]. She was born on 09 Jun 1916 in Utica, New York[505]. and died on 04 Nov 2001 in Rome, New York[506].

Photo of William Francis Dolan and Eleanor King on their wedding day. Photo was in the authors collection.

William was educated in Utica Free Academy and St. Francis DeSales Schools and was a veteran of the U.S. Army Air Corps. He had been employed at Griffiss Air Force Base for 30 years in Civil Engineering retiring in 1969 and he also drove a school bus for Birnie Bus Co. for 28 years, retiring in 1996. He was a communicant of St. Paul's Church, a life member of Knights of Columbus #391 Rome council, a member of Friendly Sons of St. Patrick and was an avid basketball player in the former Rome Industrial League. William was stationed at Fort Slocum in 1936.

Eleanor was a former member of the Tabernacle Baptist Church, Utica, and a member of the Order of Eastern Star, Neowahga Chapter #419, Cazenovia, NY, since 1939. She

---

[502] Ancestry.com. *U.S., Social Security Death Index, 1935-2014* [database on-line]. Provo, UT, USA: Ancestry.com Operations Inc, 2014.

[503] Ancestry.com. *U.S., Social Security Death Index, 1935-2014* [database on-line]. Provo, UT, USA: Ancestry.com Operations Inc, 2014.

[504] Ancestry.com. *U.S., Social Security Death Index, 1935-2014* [database on-line]. Provo, UT, USA: Ancestry.com Operations Inc, 2014.

[505] Ancestry.com. *U.S., Social Security Death Index, 1935-2014* [database on-line]. Provo, UT, USA: Ancestry.com Operations Inc, 2014.

[506] Ancestry.com. *U.S., Social Security Death Index, 1935-2014* [database on-line]. Provo, UT, USA: Ancestry.com Operations Inc, 2014.

worked in several area stores over the years and since 1973 she had been associated with the Rome Family Y where she had taught hundreds of babies and preschool children to swim, plus many adults. Eleanor coached the women's synchronized swim team for 10 years. she taught exercise classes in the water and had the arthritis class for several years. She retired after 20 years at the Y in 1992.

William Francis Dolan and Eleanor King had the following children:

     i.   Patrick C. Dolan was born on 29 Sep 1942 in Utica , New York[507] and died on 28 Feb 2011 in Bonita Springs, Florida[508]. He was married at the time of his death. Patrick graduated from Rome Free Academy and served in the Rome fire Department for 27 years, retiring in January 1998. He was a member of St. Peter's Church in Rome, New York and St. Leo's Church in Bonita Springs, Florida. Pat was a true sportsman. He loved playing golf, hockey and coaching hockey to his grandchildren. He enjoyed hunting, fishing and trapping, and was having the time of his life on his fishing trips on his new boat in the Gulf of Mexico. Patrick C. Dolan and his wife had three children who may still be living.

     ii.   Living Dolan

---

[507] Obituary, Utica Observer Dispatch, Utica, New York, March 3, 2011 online.
[508] Obituary, Utica Observer Dispatch, Utica, New York, March 3, 2011 online.

Chapter Three

Descendants

of

HUMPHREY TURNER

Generation One

1. Humphrey Turner was born on 22 Oct 1593 in Kent, England[1] and died on 05 Jun 1673 in Scituate, Massachusetts[2]. He married Lydia Gamer, the daughter of Richard Gaymer and Margaret Mason, on 24 Oct 1618 in Sandon, Essex, England[3]. She was born on 18 May 1602 in Terling, Essex, England[4] and died in 1669 in Scituate, New England[5].

The Turner name is of Norman-French origin. They were in England as early as 1067, date of the Norman Conquest, when "Le Sire de-Tourneur" accompanies King William in his expedition.

Humphrey Turner, born in England, probably Devonshire, and sailed perhaps from Holland with his family, arriving in Plymouth, New England in 1628. He was a tanner. A house lot was assigned to him in 1629 in Scituate, and built a house in which he probably lived in 1633. His wife, Lydia Gamer, was born in England and died before 1673, in Scituate, New England. Humphrey Turner was among the earliest and most efficient in the settlement of Scituate. He represented the town two years as a deputy to the General Court. He was a commissioner, constable, etc. He was possessed of that judgment, discretion, energy and perseverance of character, which eminently fitted him to be one of the pioneers in the beginning and carrying forward a new settlement. He died in Scituate in 1673.

Humphrey Turner was a tanner by trade.

Church Membership: He was a founding member of Scituate church, 8 January 1634/5. "Goody Turner," presumably his wife, joined the same church Jan 10, 1635/6. Education: He signed his deeds until 1 November 1672, when he made his mark.Offices: Deputy for Scituate to Plymouth General Court, 2 June 1640 through 4 June 1653. Constable for Duxbury, 5 January 1635/6 through 4 June 1639. Grand Jury, 1642 and 1643. Plymouth jury, 4 September 1638. Committee to divide lands in Scituate, 30 Nov 1640. Supervisor of highways, Scituate, June 1647 and 1648. Coroner's Jury 5 June

[1] Ancestry.com, U.S., Find A Grave Index, 1700s-Current (Provo, UT, USA, Ancestry.com Operations, Inc., 2012), Ancestry.com, http://www.Ancestry.com, Record for Humphrey Turner.

[2] Ancestry.com, U.S., Find A Grave Index, 1700s-Current (Provo, UT, USA, Ancestry.com Operations, Inc., 2012), Ancestry.com, http://www.Ancestry.com, Record for Humphrey Turner.

[3] Ancestry.com, U.S., Find A Grave Index, 1700s-Current (Provo, UT, USA, Ancestry.com Operations, Inc., 2012), Ancestry.com, http://www.Ancestry.com, Record for Humphrey Turner.

[4] Ancestry.com, U.S., Find A Grave Index, 1700s-Current (Provo, UT, USA, Ancestry.com Operations, Inc., 2012), Ancestry.com, http://www.Ancestry.com, Record for Humphrey Turner.

[5] Ancestry.com, U.S., Find A Grave Index, 1700s-Current (Provo, UT, USA, Ancestry.com Operations, Inc., 2012), Ancestry.com, http://www.Ancestry.com, Record for Humphrey Turner.

1666 on the body of Mary, wife of Thomas Totman.   In Scituate section of 1643 Plymouth list of men able to bear arms.

Estate: Assessed 9s. in the Plymouth tax lists of 25 March 1633 and 47 March 1634. On 18 May 1633 Humphrey Turner, having obtained leave to make use of a piece of ground by the pond on the western side of the fort, near the town and having enclosed the same with a firm palisado, hath sold his right and title to the same, as also the palisado itself, together with a small randevow, to Josias Winslow, the elder, for and in consideration of eight pounds sterling.

 Birth: Abut 1595 based on estimate date of marriage.

Death: After 1 November 1672 and before 29 May 1673. (A tombstone gives his age in 1673 as 78, and says he was born in 1594, but the stone was erected in 1869.

Marriage: Lydia was living as of 23 July 1669 when she consented to her husband's deed of 1 October 1668, but died by 28 February 1669/70 when she was not named in her husband's will.

Comments: On 17 February 1639, Lydia Turner, daughter of Humphrey Turner, was baptized at Little Baddow, Essex. This one record is not sufficient to make a positive identification of the origin of the immigrant, but it should be noted that William Vassall, who also came to Scituate to reside, had two children baptized at Little Baddow about the same time. At 4 December 1638 court Humphrey Turner was fined twice 3s. each time for non-appearance. On June 7, 1649 Humphrey Turner and others deposed that William Gilson had requested land on behalf of two of his sister's children, when he had brought them from England.

Humphrey Turner had built a house at Scituate by September 1634 and by1636 he had built a second house "on hi lot," and at some point his first house had passed to Goodman Jackson. On 1 January 1637/8 Humphrey Turner was one of a number of freemen of Scituate who complained that their proportions of land were so small that they could not subsist upon them, and the court of assistants granted them a portion of upland and neck between the North and South Rivers and all the meadow between the rivers from North River to Beaver Pond "always provided and upon condition that they make a township there and inhabit upon the said lands"

On 7 March 1639/40 Thomas Roberts of Plymouth sold to Humphrey Turner of Scituate one acre and three-quarters of swamp in Scituate lately purchased of George Lewis of Scituate.

On 27 May 1648 Humphrey Turner of Scituate, tanner, sold to Henry Ewell of Scituate, joiner, all that my ten acres of upland lying and being by the water mill in Scituate.

On 1 October 1668 Humphrey Turner of Scituate, tanner, deeded to my sons, Joseph and Nathaniel Turner, all that my lot of upland lying and being on the easterly side of Taunton River on 23 July 1669 wife consented. On 21 February 1669 Humphrey Turner of Scituate, tanner, deeded to my son Nathaniel Turner of Scituate twenty seven acres of upland at the Third Cliff, with housing, and thirty acres of marsh meadow adjoining. On 24 February 1669 Humphrey Turner, tanner, of Scituate, deeded to my son Thomas Turner of Scituate twenty acres of upland at the Third Cliff, which sometimes was John Whetcomb's, along with nine acres of marsh meadow adjoining. On 1 November 1672 Humphrey Turner of Scituate deeded to my loving son Joseph Turner of Scituate all the right to undivided land in Scituate or any way appertaining to the right of a purchasing freeman of the patent of Plymouth; acknowledged 29 May 1673 by the witnesses, the grantor being deceased.

In his will, dated 28 February 1669/70 and proved 5 June 1673, Humphrey Turner of Scituate, tanner, being weak in body bequeathed to my eldest son John Turner, his farm; to my son Joseph Turner 40 pounds also 12 pounds; to my son John Turner 5 pounds; to my son Daniel Turner 12 pounds; to my son Nathaniel Turner 50 pounds; to my daughter Mary 10 pounds/ and to my daughter Lydia Doughtey 12 pounds; unto my grandchild Humphrey Turner 5 pounds; to my grandchild Mary Doughtey 10 pounds; to my grandchildren Jonathan Turner, Josiah Turner and Elizabeth Turner, being the fruits of my eldest son, 10s. a year; to Son Nathaniel Turner all my livestock both cattle, horses, sheep, etc.; to my son Thomas Turner all my wearing clothes, one wood bed and blankets.

All secondary sources agree in giving Humphrey Turner one wife, Lydia Gamer, but nowhere is there any evidence for this surname. The earliest appearance of the name in print seems to be in Deane (Samuel Deane, *History of Scituate, Massachusetts, from its First Settlement to 1831*).
The two eldest surviving children of Humphrey Turner were both names John. In England at the time of birth of these sons, they could be by the same mother, but the chances are good that they were half siblings and that Humphrey Turner married twice in England. Based on the two paragraphs above we concur with Selim Walker McArthur in his statement that Lydia was "not necessarily his first wife or mother of his eldest son John".
Deane says that Turner "arrived with his family, in Plymouth 1628". He had a house lot assigned him in 1629. This is not supported by any contemporary records, and lots were apparently not assigned in Scituate until 1633.

Lydia's possible maiden name variants were: Gamer, Gaymer, Garner.

Lydia Gaymer was baptized in Terling, Essex, 18 May 1602, the daughter of Richard Gaymer and Margaret Mason. She married Humphrey Turner 24 Oct 1618 in Sandon, Essex, England. She was living in Scituate Massachusetts on 23 July 1669 when she consented to her husband's deed of 1 October 1668, but had died by 28 February 1669[/70] when she was not named in her husband's will.   Their 8 children: John the elder (who married Mary Brewster), John the younger (who married Ann James), Thomas, Lydia Doughty, Mary Parker, Joseph, Nathaniel & Daniel.

Humphrey Turner and Lydia Gamer had the following children:
      i.   John Turner was born on 24 Mar 1622 in Terling, Essex, England[6]. He married Mary Brewster, the daughter of Jonathan Brewster, on 12 Nov 1645[7].
2.   ii.   John Turner was born in 1625[8] and died in 1687 in Scituate, New England[9]. He married Ann James on 25 Apr 1649 in Scituate, Plymouth, Massachusetts, United States[10].
3.   iii.   Thomas Turner was born in 1625 in Essex, England[11] and died in Nov 1688[12].   He married Sarah Hiland on 06 Jan 1651[13].   She was born in 1629 in Tenterden, Ashford Borough, Kent, England[14] and died in Nov 1688 in Scituate, Plymouth County, Massachusetts[15].
4.   iv.   Lydia Turner was born on 17 Feb 1629 in Little Baddoe, Co. Essex, England[16]. She died in 1673 in Scituate, Plymouth County, Massachusetts[17]. She married

---

[6] Familysearch.org, "England Births and Christenings, 1538-1975." Database. FamilySearch. http://FamilySearch.org : 3 March 2017. Index based upon data collected by the Genealogical Society of Utah, Salt Lake City.

[7] Ancestry.com, North America, Family Histories, 1500-2000 (Provo, UT, USA, Ancestry.com Operations, Inc., 2016), Ancestry.com, http://www.Ancestry.com, Book Title: The Tilson genealogy : from Edmond Tilson at Plymouth, N E , 1638 to 1911 : with brief sketches of. Record for John Turner.

[8] Ancestry.com, North America, Family Histories, 1500-2000 (Provo, UT, USA, Ancestry.com Operations, Inc., 2016), Ancestry.com, http://www.Ancestry.com, Book Title: The Tilson genealogy : from Edmond Tilson at Plymouth, N E , 1638 to 1911 : with brief sketches of. Record for John Turner.

[9] Ancestry.com, North America, Family Histories, 1500-2000 (Provo, UT, USA, Ancestry.com Operations, Inc., 2016), Ancestry.com, http://www.Ancestry.com, Book Title: The Tilson genealogy : from Edmond Tilson at Plymouth, N E , 1638 to 1911 : with brief sketches of. Record for John Turner.

[10] Ancestry.com, North America, Family Histories, 1500-2000 (Provo, UT, USA, Ancestry.com Operations, Inc., 2016), Ancestry.com, http://www.Ancestry.com, Book Title: The Tilson genealogy : from Edmond Tilson at Plymouth, N E , 1638 to 1911 : with brief sketches of. Record for John Turner.

[11] Ancestry.com, North America, Family Histories, 1500-2000.

[12] Ancestry.com, Global, Find A Grave Index for Burials at Sea and other Select Burial Locations, 1300s-Current (Provo, UT, USA, Ancestry.com Operations, Inc., 2012), Record for Thomas Turner.

[13] The Great Migration book.

[14] Ancestry.com, Global, Find A Grave Index for Burials at Sea and other Select Burial Locations, 1300s-Current (Provo, UT, USA, Ancestry.com Operations, Inc., 2012), Record for Thomas Turner.

[15] Ancestry.com, Global, Find A Grave Index for Burials at Sea and other Select Burial Locations, 1300s-Current (Provo, UT, USA, Ancestry.com Operations, Inc., 2012), Record for Thomas Turner.

[16] Familysearch.org, "England, Essex Parish Registers, 1538-1997," database, FamilySearch Humphrey Turner in entry for Lydia Turner, 17 Feb 1629, Christening; citing , Little Baddow, Essex, England, Essex Record Office, England; FHL microfilm 560,908.

James Doughty on 15 Aug 1649[18]. He was born in 1624 in Little Baddow, Chelmsford Borough, Essex, England[19].

5.   v.   Mary Turner was born on 25 Jan 1634 in Scituate, New England[20] and died in 1703 in Scituate, Plymouth County, Massachusetts[21]. She married William Parker on 13 Nov 1651 in Scituate, Massachusetts[22]. He was born in 1615 in Kent, England[23] and died on 03 Oct 1684 in Scituate, Massachusetts[24].

       vi.   Joseph Turner was born on 01 Jan 1636 in Scituate, New England[25] and died after 1681. He did not marry[26].

       vii.   Nathaniel Turner was born on 10 Mar 1638 in Scituate, New England[27]. He married Mehitable Rigby, the daughter of John Rigby, on 29 Mar 1664. He later married Abigail Stockbridge on 1691[28].

       viii.   Daniel Turner was born on 23 Nov 1641 in Scituate, Massachusetts[29] and died in 1699 in Scituate, Massachusetts[30]. He married Hannah Randall, the daughter of William Randall, on 20 Jun 1665[31]. She was born on 23 Nov 1644 in Scituate, Massachusetts[32]. She died on 23 Aug 1714 in Scituate, Massachusetts[33].

---

[17] Ancestry.com, U.S., Find A Grave Index, 1700s-Current (Provo, UT, USA, Ancestry.com Operations, Inc., 2012), Ancestry.com, http://www.Ancestry.com, Record for Lydia Doughty.

[18] The Great Migration Begins, Immigrants to New England, 1620-1633.

[19] Ancestry.com, U.S., Find A Grave Index, 1700s-Current (Provo, UT, USA, Ancestry.com Operations, Inc., 2012), Ancestry.com, http://www.Ancestry.com, Record for Lydia Doughty.

[20] Ancestry.com, North America, Family Histories, 1500-2000 (Provo, UT, USA, Ancestry.com Operations, Inc.

[21] Ancestry.com, U.S., Find A Grave Index, 1700s-Current (Provo, UT, USA, Ancestry.com Operations, Inc., 2012), Ancestry.com, http://www.Ancestry.com, Record for Mary Parker.

[22] Ancestry.com, U.S., New England Marriages Prior to 1700 (Provo, UT, USA, Ancestry.com Operations Inc, 2012), www.ancestry.com, Genealogical Publishing Co.; Baltimore, MD, USA; Volume Title: Third Supplement to Torrey's New England Marriages Prior to 1700. Record for Mary Parker

[23] Ancestry.com, U.S., Find A Grave Index, 1700s-Current (Provo, UT, USA, Ancestry.com Operations, Inc., 2012), Ancestry.com, http://www.Ancestry.com, Record for Mary Parker.

[24] Ancestry.com, U.S., Find A Grave Index, 1700s-Current (Provo, UT, USA, Ancestry.com Operations, Inc., 2012), Ancestry.com, http://www.Ancestry.com, Record for Mary Parker.

[25] Ancestry.com, North America, Family Histories, 1500-2000 (Provo, UT, USA, Ancestry.com Operations, Inc.

[26] The Great Migration Begins, Immigrants to New England, 1620-1633.

[27] Ancestry.com, North America, Family Histories, 1500-2000 (Provo, UT, USA, Ancestry.com Operations, Inc.

[28] The Great Migration Begins, Immigrants to New England, 1620-1633.

[29] Ancestry.com, U.S., Find A Grave Index, 1700s-Current (Provo, UT, USA, Ancestry.com Operations, Inc., 2012), Ancestry.com, http://www.Ancestry.com, Record for Daniel Turner.

[30] Ancestry.com, U.S., Find A Grave Index, 1700s-Current (Provo, UT, USA, Ancestry.com Operations, Inc., 2012), Ancestry.com, http://www.Ancestry.com, Record for Daniel Turner.

[31] The Great Migration Begins, Immigrants to New England, 1620-1633.

[32] Ancestry.com, U.S., Find A Grave Index, 1700s-Current (Provo, UT, USA, Ancestry.com Operations, Inc., 2012), Ancestry.com, http://www.Ancestry.com, Record for Daniel Turner.

[33] Ancestry.com, U.S., Find A Grave Index, 1700s-Current (Provo, UT, USA, Ancestry.com Operations, Inc., 2012), Ancestry.com, http://www.Ancestry.com, Record for Daniel Turner.

Generation Two

2. John Turner[2] (Humphrey Turner[1]) was born in 1625[34] and died in 1687 in Scituate, New England[35]. He married Ann James on 25 Apr 1649 in Scituate, Massachusetts[36]. John and his family lived northeast of Hick's swamp, south of the harbor.

John Turner and Ann James had the following children:

     i.   Japheth Turner was born on 09 Feb 1650 in Scituate, New England and died in 1690[37]. He married Hannah Hudson.

     ii.   Ann Turner was born on 23 Feb 1652 in Scituate, New England[38]. She married Joseph Greene.

     iii.   Israel Turner was born on 14 Feb 1654 in Scituate, New England[39]. He married Sarah Stockbridge.

6.   iv.   John Turner was born on 30 Oct 1654 in Scituate, New England[40] and died in Nov 1696 in Guilford, Connecticut Colony[41]. He married Johanna Benton on 16

---

[34] Ancestry.com, North America, Family Histories, 1500-2000 (Provo, UT, USA, Ancestry.com Operations, Inc., 2016), Ancestry.com, http://www.Ancestry.com, Book Title: The Tilson genealogy : from Edmond Tilson at Plymouth, N E , 1638 to 1911 : with brief sketches of. Record for John Turner.

[35] Ancestry.com, North America, Family Histories, 1500-2000 (Provo, UT, USA, Ancestry.com Operations, Inc., 2016), Ancestry.com, http://www.Ancestry.com, Book Title: The Tilson genealogy : from Edmond Tilson at Plymouth, N E , 1638 to 1911 : with brief sketches of. Record for John Turner.

[36] Ancestry.com, North America, Family Histories, 1500-2000 (Provo, UT, USA, Ancestry.com Operations, Inc., 2016), Ancestry.com, http://www.Ancestry.com, Book Title: The Tilson genealogy : from Edmond Tilson at Plymouth, N E , 1638 to 1911 : with brief sketches of. Record for John Turner.

[37] Ancestry.com, North America, Family Histories, 1500-2000 (Provo, UT, USA, Ancestry.com Operations, Inc., 2016), Ancestry.com, http://www.Ancestry.com, Book Title: The Tilson genealogy : from Edmond Tilson at Plymouth, N E , 1638 to 1911 : with brief sketches of. Record for John Turner.

[38] Ancestry.com, North America, Family Histories, 1500-2000 (Provo, UT, USA, Ancestry.com Operations, Inc., 2016), Ancestry.com, http://www.Ancestry.com, Book Title: The Tilson genealogy : from Edmond Tilson at Plymouth, N E , 1638 to 1911 : with brief sketches of. Record for John Turner.

[39] Ancestry.com, North America, Family Histories, 1500-2000 (Provo, UT, USA, Ancestry.com Operations, Inc., 2016), Ancestry.com, http://www.Ancestry.com, Book Title: The Tilson genealogy : from Edmond Tilson at Plymouth, N E , 1638 to 1911 : with brief sketches of. Record for John Turner.

[40] Ancestry.com, Massachusetts, Town and Vital Records, 1620-1988 (Provo, UT, USA, Ancestry.com Operations, Inc., 2011), Ancestry.com, http://www.Ancestry.com, Record for John Turner.

[41] Ancestry.com, U.S., Sons of the American Revolution Membership Applications, 1889-1970 (Provo, UT, USA, Ancestry.com Operations, Inc., 2011), www.ancestry.com, Record for Benjamin Turner.

Dec 1686 in New England[42]. She was born on 08 Oct 1660 in Guilford[43] and died in 1692[44].

      v.   Miriam Turner was born on 08 Apr 1658 in New England[45]. She married Nathan Pickles.

      vi.   Sarah Turner was born on 25 Jul 1665 in Scituate, New England[46]. She married Ichabod Holbrook.

      vii.   Jacob Turner was born on 10 May 1667 in Scituate, New England[47]. He married Jane Vining.

      viii.   David Turner was born on 05 Nov 1670 in Scituate, New England[48]. He married Elizabeth Stockbridge.

      ix.   Phillip Turner was born on 18 Aug 1673 in Scituate, New England[49]. He married Elizabeth Nash.

      x.   Ichabod Turner was born on 09 Apr 1676 in Scituate, New England[50].

3. Thomas Turner[2] (Humphrey Turner[1]) was born in 1625 in Essex, England[51] and died in Nov 1688[52]. He married Sarah Hiland on 06 Jan 1651[53]. She was born in 1629 in

---

[42] Ancestry.com, U.S., New England Marriages Prior to 1700 (Provo, UT, USA, Ancestry.com Operations Inc, 2012), www.ancestry.com, Genealogical Publishing Co.; Baltimore, MD, USA; Volume Title: New England Marriages Prior to 1700. Record for Joanna Turner.

[43] Ancestry.com, U.S., New England Marriages Prior to 1700 (Provo, UT, USA, Ancestry.com Operations Inc, 2012), www.ancestry.com, Genealogical Publishing Co.; Baltimore, MD, USA; Volume Title: New England Marriages Prior to 1700. Record for Joanna Turner.

[44] Ancestry.com, U.S., New England Marriages Prior to 1700 (Provo, UT, USA, Ancestry.com Operations Inc, 2012), www.ancestry.com, Genealogical Publishing Co.; Baltimore, MD, USA; Volume Title: New England Marriages Prior to 1700. Record for Joanna Turner.

[45] Ancestry.com, North America, Family Histories, 1500-2000 (Provo, UT, USA, Ancestry.com Operations, Inc., 2016), Ancestry.com, http://www.Ancestry.com, Book Title: The Tilson genealogy : from Edmond Tilson at Plymouth, N E , 1638 to 1911 : with brief sketches of. Record for John Turner.

[46] Ancestry.com, North America, Family Histories, 1500-2000 (Provo, UT, USA, Ancestry.com Operations, Inc., 2016), Ancestry.com, http://www.Ancestry.com, Book Title: The Tilson genealogy : from Edmond Tilson at Plymouth, N E , 1638 to 1911 : with brief sketches of. Record for John Turner.

[47] Ancestry.com, North America, Family Histories, 1500-2000 (Provo, UT, USA, Ancestry.com Operations, Inc., 2016), Ancestry.com, http://www.Ancestry.com, Book Title: The Tilson genealogy : from Edmond Tilson at Plymouth, N E , 1638 to 1911 : with brief sketches of. Record for John Turner.

[48] Ancestry.com, North America, Family Histories, 1500-2000 (Provo, UT, USA, Ancestry.com Operations, Inc., 2016), Ancestry.com, http://www.Ancestry.com, Book Title: The Tilson genealogy : from Edmond Tilson at Plymouth, N E , 1638 to 1911 : with brief sketches of. Record for John Turner.

[49] Ancestry.com, North America, Family Histories, 1500-2000 (Provo, UT, USA, Ancestry.com Operations, Inc., 2016), Ancestry.com, http://www.Ancestry.com, Book Title: The Tilson genealogy : from Edmond Tilson at Plymouth, N E , 1638 to 1911 : with brief sketches of. Record for John Turner.

[50] Ancestry.com, North America, Family Histories, 1500-2000 (Provo, UT, USA, Ancestry.com Operations, Inc., 2016), Ancestry.com, http://www.Ancestry.com, Book Title: The Tilson genealogy : from Edmond Tilson at Plymouth, N E , 1638 to 1911 : with brief sketches of. Record for John Turner.

[51] Ancestry.com, Global, Find A Grave Index for Burials at Sea and other Select Burial Locations, 1300s-Current (Provo, UT, USA, Ancestry.com Operations, Inc., 2012), Record for Thomas Turner.

[52] Ancestry.com, Global, Find A Grave Index for Burials at Sea and other Select Burial Locations, 1300s-Current (Provo, UT, USA, Ancestry.com Operations, Inc., 2012), Record for Thomas Turner.

[53] The Great Migration Begins, Immigrants to New England, 1620-1633.

Tenterden, Ashford Borough, Kent, England[54] and died in Nov 1688 in Scituate, Massachusetts[55].

Thomas Turner was born in England, either in Kent or Essex, about 1625. His parents were Humphrey Turner and Lydia Gaymer. Between 1630 and 1634, Humphrey brought his family to new England. They settled in Scituate, Plymouth, Massachusetts. Thomas married Sarah Hyland in Scituate on January 6, 1652. Thomas and Sarah both died in November of 1688 in Scituate. Their places of burial are not known.

Thomas Turner and Sarah Hiland had the following child:
      i.   Mary Turner was born on 15 Sep 1658[56] in Scituate, Massachusetts and died in 1704 in Scituate, Massachusetts[57].
      ii.   Nathan Turner was born 08 Dec 1670[58] in Scituate, Massachusetts and died in 1721 in Scituate, Massachusetts[59].

4. Lydia Turner[2] (Humphrey Turner[1]) was born on 17 Feb 1629 in Little Baddoe, Co. Essex, England[60] and died in 1673 in Scituate, Massachusetts[61]. She married James Doughty on 15 Aug 1649[62]. He was born in 1624 in Little Baddow, Chelmsford Borough, Essex, England[63].

James Doughty and Lydia Turner had the following children:
      i.   Mary Doughty was born in 1650[64] and died in 1681[65].
      ii.   James Doughty was born in 1651[66].
      iii.   Elizabeth Doughty was born in 1654[67] and died in 1742[68].

---

[54] Ancestry.com, Global, Find A Grave Index for Burials at Sea and other Select Burial Locations, 1300s-Current (Provo, UT, USA, Ancestry.com Operations, Inc., 2012), Record for Thomas Turner.

[55] Ancestry.com, Global, Find A Grave Index for Burials at Sea and other Select Burial Locations, 1300s-Current (Provo, UT, USA, Ancestry.com Operations, Inc., 2012), Record for Thomas Turner.

[56] Findagrave.com

[57] Findagrave.com

[58] Family trees on Ancestry.com

[59] Family trees on Ancestry.com.

[60] Familysearch.org, "England, Essex Parish Registers, 1538-1997," database, FamilySearch Humphrey Turner in entry for Lydia Turner, 17 Feb 1629, Christening; citing , Little Baddow, Essex, England, Essex Record Office, England; FHL microfilm 560,908.

[61] Ancestry.com, U.S., Find A Grave Index, 1700s-Current (Provo, UT, USA, Ancestry.com Operations, Inc., 2012), Ancestry.com, http://www.Ancestry.com, Record for Lydia Doughty.

[62] The Great Migration Begins, Immigrants to New England, 1620-1633.

[63] Ancestry.com, U.S., Find A Grave Index, 1700s-Current, Record for Lydia Doughty.

[64] Ancestry.com, U.S., Find A Grave Index, 1700s-Current, Record for Lydia Doughty.

[65] Ancestry.com, U.S., Find A Grave Index, 1700s-Current, Record for Lydia Doughty.

[66] Ancestry.com, U.S., Find A Grave Index, 1700s-Current, Record for Lydia Doughty.

[67] Ancestry.com, U.S., Find A Grave Index, 1700s-Current, Record for Lydia Doughty.

[68] Ancestry.com, U.S., Find A Grave Index, 1700s-Current, Record for Lydia Doughty.

iv.   Martha Doughty was born in 1657[69].
v.   Lydia Doughty was born in 1658[70].
vi.   Sarah Doughty was born in 1662[71].
vii.   Samuel Doughty was born in 1664[72].
viii.   Robert Doughty was born in 1667[73].
ix.   Susanna Doughty was born in 1670[74].

5. Mary Turner[2] (Humphrey Turner[1]) was born on 25 Jan 1634 in Scituate, New England[75] and died in 1703 in Scituate, Massachusetts[76]. She married William Parker on 13 Nov 1651 in Scituate[77]. He was born in 1615 in Kent, England[78] and died on 03 Oct 1684 in Scituate, Massachusetts[79].

William Parker and Mary Turner had the following child:
       i.   Lidia Turner was born on 09 May 1653 in Scituate, Massachusetts[80] and died on 07 Sep 1719 in Freetown, Massachusetts[81]. She married Theophilus Wetherell.

---

[69] Ancestry.com, U.S., Find A Grave Index, 1700s-Current (Provo, UT, USA, Ancestry.com Operations, Inc., 2012), Ancestry.com, http://www.Ancestry.com, Record for Lydia Doughty.

[70] Ancestry.com, U.S., Find A Grave Index, 1700s Current (Provo, UT, USA, Ancestry.com Operations, Inc., 2012), Ancestry.com, http://www.Ancestry.com, Record for Lydia Doughty.

[71] Ancestry.com, U.S., Find A Grave Index, 1700s-Current (Provo, UT, USA, Ancestry.com Operations, Inc., 2012), Ancestry.com, http://www.Ancestry.com, Record for Lydia Doughty.

[72] Ancestry.com, U.S., Find A Grave Index, 1700s-Current (Provo, UT, USA, Ancestry.com Operations, Inc., 2012), Ancestry.com, http://www.Ancestry.com, Record for Lydia Doughty.

[73] Ancestry.com, U.S., Find A Grave Index, 1700s-Current (Provo, UT, USA, Ancestry.com Operations, Inc., 2012), Ancestry.com, http://www.Ancestry.com, Record for Lydia Doughty.

[74] Ancestry.com, U.S., Find A Grave Index, 1700s-Current (Provo, UT, USA, Ancestry.com Operations, Inc., 2012), Ancestry.com, http://www.Ancestry.com, Record for Lydia Doughty.

[75] Ancestry.com, North America, Family Histories, 1500-2000

[76] Ancestry.com, U.S., Find A Grave Index, 1700s-Current (Provo, UT, USA, Ancestry.com Operations, Inc., 2012), Ancestry.com, http://www.Ancestry.com, Record for Mary Parker

[77] Ancestry.com, U.S., New England Marriages Prior to 1700 (Provo, UT, USA, Ancestry.com Operations Inc, 2012), www.ancestry.com, Genealogical Publishing Co.; Baltimore, MD, USA; Volume Title: Third Supplement to Torrey's New England Marriages Prior to 1700. Record for Mary Parker.

[78] Ancestry.com, U.S., Find A Grave Index, 1700s-Current (Provo, UT, USA, Ancestry.com Operations, Inc., 2012), Ancestry.com, http://www.Ancestry.com, Record for Mary Parker.

[79] Ancestry.com, U.S., Find A Grave Index, 1700s-Current (Provo, UT, USA, Ancestry.com Operations, Inc., 2012), Ancestry.com, http://www.Ancestry.com, Record for Mary Parker.

[80] Ancestry.com, U.S., Find A Grave Index, 1700s-Current (Provo, UT, USA, Ancestry.com Operations, Inc., 2012), Ancestry.com, http://www.Ancestry.com, Record for Mary Parker.

[81] Ancestry.com, U.S., Find A Grave Index, 1700s-Current (Provo, UT, USA, Ancestry.com Operations, Inc., 2012), Ancestry.com, http://www.Ancestry.com, Record for Mary Parker.

Generation Three

6. John Turner[3] (John Turner[2] , Humphrey Turner[1]) was born on 30 Oct 1654 in Scituate, Massachusetts[82] and died in Nov 1696 in Guilford, Connecticut Colony[83]. He married Johanna Benton on 16 Dec 1686 in New England[84]. She was born on 08 Oct 1660 in Guilford[85] and died in 1692[86].

John Turner and Johanna Benton had the following child:

7.　　i.　　Benjamin Turner Sr. was born in 1689 in Connecticut[87] and died on 25 Nov 1776 in Killingworth, Connecticut[88].

---

[82] Ancestry.com, Massachusetts, Town and Vital Records, 1620-1988 (Provo, UT, USA, Ancestry.com Operations, Inc., 2011), Ancestry.com, http://www.Ancestry.com, Record for John Turner.

[83] Ancestry.com, U.S., Sons of the American Revolution Membership Applications, 1889-1970 (Provo, UT, USA, Ancestry.com Operations, Inc., 2011), www.ancestry.com, Record for Benjamin Turner.

[84] Ancestry.com, U.S., New England Marriages Prior to 1700 (Provo, UT, USA, Ancestry.com Operations Inc, 2012), www.ancestry.com, Genealogical Publishing Co.; Baltimore, MD, USA; Volume Title: New England Marriages Prior to 1700. Record for Joanna Turner.

[85] Ancestry.com, U.S., New England Marriages Prior to 1700 (Provo, UT, USA, Ancestry.com Operations Inc, 2012), www.ancestry.com, Genealogical Publishing Co.; Baltimore, MD, USA; Volume Title: New England Marriages Prior to 1700. Record for Joanna Turner.

[86] Ancestry.com, U.S., New England Marriages Prior to 1700 (Provo, UT, USA, Ancestry.com Operations Inc, 2012), www.ancestry.com, Genealogical Publishing Co.; Baltimore, MD, USA; Volume Title: New England Marriages Prior to 1700. Record for Joanna Turner.

[87] Ancestry.com, Connecticut, Deaths and Burials Index, 1650-1934 (Provo, UT, USA, Ancestry.com Operations, Inc., 2011), www.ancestry.com, Record for Benjamin Turner

[88] Ancestry.com, Connecticut, Deaths and Burials Index, 1650-1934 (Provo, UT, USA, Ancestry.com Operations, Inc., 2011), www.ancestry.com, Record for Benjamin Turner

Generation Four

7. Benjamin Turner Sr.[4] (John Turner[3], John Turner[2] , Humphrey Turner[1]) was born in 1689 in Connecticut[89] and died on 25 Nov 1776 in Killingworth, Connecticut[90]. He married Martha Chapman on 31 Mar 1720 in Killingworth, Connecticut[91]. She was born on 02 Apr 1700 in Middlesex County, Connecticut[92] and died on 30 Aug 1752 in Killingworth, Connecticut[93].

Benjamin Turner Sr. and Martha Chapman had the following children:
8.   i.   Benjamin Turner Jr. was born on 27 May 1722 in Killingworth, Connecticut [94] and died on 11 Mar 1786 in Connecticut[95].
      ii.   Jacob Turner was born on 03 May 1731 in Killingworth, Connecticut[96] and died in 1762[97].
      iii.   Jemina Turner was born on 23 Feb 1733 in Killingworth, Connecticut[98].
      iv.   Reuben Turner was born on 24 Aug 1736 in Killingworth, Connecticut[99].
      v.   Lucey Turner was born on 16 Jul 1739 in Killingworth, Connecticut[100].
      vi.   Peter Turner was born on 03 Oct 1745 in Killingworth, Connecticut[101].
      vii.   Lidea Turner was born on 31 Jan 1746 in Killingworth, Connecticut[102].
      viii.   Paul Turner was born on 25 May 1748 in Killingworth, Connecticut[103].
      ix.   Solaman Turner was born on 08 Dec 1749 in Killingworth, Connecticut[104].

---

[89] Ancestry.com, U.S., Sons of the American Revolution Membership Applications, 1889-1970 (Provo, UT, USA, Ancestry.com Operations, Inc., 2011), www.ancestry.com, Record for Benjamin Turner.

[90] Ancestry.com, U.S., Find A Grave Index, 1700s-Current (Provo, UT, USA, Ancestry.com Operations, Inc., 2012), Ancestry.com, http://www.Ancestry.com, Record for Benjamin Turner.

[91] Ancestry.com, U.S., Find A Grave Index, 1700s-Current (Provo, UT, USA, Ancestry.com Operations, Inc., 2012), Ancestry.com, http://www.Ancestry.com, Record for Benjamin Turner.

[92] Ancestry.com, U.S., Find A Grave Index, 1700s-Current (Provo, UT, USA, Ancestry.com Operations, Inc., 2012), Ancestry.com, http://www.Ancestry.com, Record for Benjamin Turner.

[93] Ancestry.com, U.S., Find A Grave Index, 1700s-Current (Provo, UT, USA, Ancestry.com Operations, Inc., 2012), Ancestry.com, http://www.Ancestry.com, Record for Benjamin Turner.

[94] Ancestry.com, Connecticut Town Birth Records, pre-1870 (Barbour Collection) (Provo, UT, USA, The Generations Network, Inc., 2006), www.ancestry.com, Record for Benjamin Turner.

[95] Ancestry.com, Connecticut, Church Record Abstracts, 1630-1920 (Provo, UT, USA, , 2013), Ancestry.com, http://www.Ancestry.com, Record for Benjamin Turner.

[96] Ancestry.com, U.S., Sons of the American Revolution Membership Applications, 1889-1970 (Provo, UT, USA, Ancestry.com Operations, Inc., 2011), www.ancestry.com, Record for Benjamin Turner.

[97] Ancestry.com, U.S., Sons of the American Revolution Membership Applications, 1889-1970 (Provo, UT, USA, Ancestry.com Operations, Inc., 2011), www.ancestry.com, Record for Benjamin Turner.

[98] Familysearch.org, "Connecticut Births and Christenings, 1649-1906.

[99] Familysearch.org, "Connecticut Births and Christenings, 1649-1906.

[100] Familysearch.org, "Connecticut Births and Christenings, 1649-1906.

[101] Familysearch.org, "Connecticut Births and Christenings, 1649-1906.

[102] Familysearch.org, "Connecticut Births and Christenings, 1649-1906.

[103] Familysearch.org, "Connecticut Births and Christenings, 1649-1906.

Generation Five

8. Benjamin Turner Jr.[5] (Benjamin Turner Sr.[4], John Turner[3], John Turner[2], Humphrey Turner[1]) was born on 27 May 1722 in Killingworth, Connecticut[105] and died on 11 Mar 1786 in Connecticut[106]. He married Martha Davis on 28 Dec 1744 in Killingworth, Connecticut[107]. She was born in 1724[108] and died on 01 Jun 1752 in Connecticut[109]. He later married Elizabeth Griffin on 06 Dec 1753 in Connecticut.[110]

Benjamin Turner Jr. and Martha Davis had the following child:
9.   i.   Paul Turner was born on 16 Feb 1752 in Killingworth, Connecticut[111] and died on 14 Sep 1830[112].

Benjamin Turner Jr. and Elizabeth Griffin had the following children:
        ii.   Elizabeth Turner was born on 04 Nov 1764 in Killingworth, Connecticut[113].
        iii.   John Turner was born on 04 Nov 1764 in Killingworth, Connecticut[114].

---

[104] Familysearch.org, "Connecticut Births and Christenings, 1649-1906.

[105] Ancestry.com, U.S., Sons of the American Revolution Membership Applications, 1889-1970 (Provo, UT, USA, Ancestry.com Operations, Inc., 2011), www.ancestry.com, Record for Benjamin Turner.

[106] Ancestry.com, U.S., Find A Grave Index, 1700s-Current (Provo, UT, USA, Ancestry.com Operations, Inc., 2012), Ancestry.com, http://www.Ancestry.com, Record for Benjamin Turner.

[107] Ancestry.com, Early Connecticut Marriages (Provo, UT, USA, Ancestry.com Operations, Inc., 2012), Ancestry.com, http://www.Ancestry.com, Record for Benjamin Turner.

[108] Ancestery.com, Connecticut, Hale Collection of Cemetery Inscriptions and Newspaper Notices, 1629-1934.

[109] Ancestery.com, Connecticut, Hale Collection of Cemetery Inscriptions and Newspaper Notices, 1629-1934.

[110] Connecticut, Town Marriage Records, pre-1870 (Barbour Collection)

[111] Familysearch.org, "Connecticut Births and Christenings, 1649-1906," database, FamilySearch (https://familysearch.org/ark:/61903/1:1:F74C-B2G : 11 February 2018), Paul Turner, 16 Feb 1752.

[112] Ancestry.com. New York, Wills and Probate Records, 1659-1999 [database on-line]. Provo, UT, USA: Ancestry.com Operations, Inc., 2015.,

[113] Familysearch.org, "Connecticut Births and Christenings, 1649-1906," database, FamilySearch Benjamin Turner in entry for Martha Turner, 04 Nov 1764.

[114] Familysearch.org, "Connecticut Births and Christenings, 1649-1906," database, FamilySearch Benjamin Turner in entry for Martha Turner, 04 Nov 1764.

Generation Six

9.   Paul Turner[6] (Benjamin Turner Sr.[5], Benjamin Turner Sr.[4], John Turner[3], John Turner[2], Humphrey Turner[1]) was born on 16 Feb 1752 in Killingworth, Connecticut[115] and died on 14 Sep 1830[116]. He married Patience Bradley on 03 Aug 1768.

Paul Turner and Patience Bradley had the following children:
10.   i.   John Turner was born on 15 Sep 1775 in Massachusetts[117] and died about 1852[118].
11.   ii.   Sally or Sarah Turner was born on 16 Sep 1777 in West Stockbridge, Massachusetts[119] and died on 03 Aug 1859 in Kortright Center, New York[120].
      iii.   Benjamin Turner was born on 16 Dec 1779 in Massachusetts[121].
12.   iv.   Catherine Turner was born on 06 Dec 1781 in Stockbridge, Massachusetts[122] and died on 10 Mar 1856[123].
      v.   Patience Bradley Turner was born on 06 Nov 1784 in West Stockbridge, Massachusetts[124]. She married John Bunner.
13.   vi.   Mary R. Turner was born on 23 Dec 1789 in Massachusetts[125] and died on 06 May 1869 in Madison, New York[126].
      vii.   Betsey Turner was born in 1792[127]. She married John Gun[128].
14.   viii.   Paul Turner was born in 1794[129]

---

[115] Familysearch.org, "Connecticut Births and Christenings, 1649-1906," database, Paul Turner, 16 Feb 1752.

[116] Ancestry.com. New York, Wills and Probate Records, 1659-1999 [database on-line]. Provo, UT, USA: Ancestry.com Operations, Inc., 2015.

[117] Massachusetts Births and Christenings, "Massachusetts Births and Christenings, 1639-1915," database, FamilySearch (https://familysearch.org/ark:/61903/1:1:VQDH-LZH : 4 December 2014), John Turner, 15 Sep 1775

[118] Findagrave.com in the Hambletville Cemetery, Delaware County, New York.

[119] Ancestry.com, U.S., Find A Grave Index, 1700s-Current (Provo, UT, USA, Ancestry.com Operations, Inc., 2012), Ancestry.com, http://www.Ancestry.com, Record for Silas Henry Goodrich.

[120] Ancestry.com, U.S., Find A Grave Index, 1700s-Current (Provo, UT, USA, Ancestry.com Operations, Inc., 2012), Ancestry.com, http://www.Ancestry.com, Record for Silas Henry Goodrich.

[121] Ancestry.com, Massachusetts, Town and Vital Records, 1620-1988.

[122] Ancestry.com, Massachusetts, Town and Vital Records, 1620-1988.

[123] Ancestry.com, U.S., Find A Grave Index, 1700s-Current (Provo, UT, USA, Ancestry.com Operations, Inc., 2012), Ancestry.com, http://www.Ancestry.com, Record for Catherine Hartwell.

[124] Massachusetts, Town and Vital Records, 1620-1988

[125] Ancestry.com, U.S., Find A Grave Index, 1700s-Current (Provo, UT, USA, Ancestry.com Operations, Inc., 2012), Ancestry.com, http://www.Ancestry.com, Record for Mary R. Webb.

[126] Ancestry.com, U.S., Find A Grave Index, 1700s-Current (Provo, UT, USA, Ancestry.com Operations, Inc., 2012), Ancestry.com, http://www.Ancestry.com, Record for Mary R. Webb.

[127] Familysearch.org trees.

[128] Familysearch.org trees.

[129] Familysearch.org trees.

Generation Seven

10. John Turner[7] (Paul Turner[6], Benjamin Turner Sr.[5], Benjamin Turner Sr.[4], John Turner[3], John Turner[2], Humphrey Turner[1]) was born on 15 Sep 1775 in Massachusetts[130] and died in 1852[131]. He married Polly Esther Burnell[132]. She was born in 08 Sep 1772[133] and died in 26 Nov1846[134].

John Turner and Polly Esther Burnell had the following children:

    i.   Diadamia Turner born in 1801. She died in 1884[135].

15.   ii.   Hopestell C. Turner was born on 28 Jan 1822 in Delaware County, New York[136] and died in after 1905.

    iii.   Amelia Turner was born in 1827 in Delaware County, New York[137].

11. Sally or Sarah Turner[7] (Paul Turner[6], Benjamin Turner Sr.[5], Benjamin Turner Sr.[4], John Turner[3], John Turner[2], Humphrey Turner[1]) was born on 16 Sep 1777 in West Stockbridge, Massachusetts[138] and died on 03 Aug 1859 in Kortright Center, New York[139]. She married Silas Henry Goodrich[140]. He was born on 02 Oct 1773 in Sharon, Connecticut[141] and died on 01 Mar 1849 in Kortright Center, New York[142].

---

[130] Massachusetts Births and Christenings, "Massachusetts Births and Christenings, 1639-1915," database, FamilySearch (https://familysearch.org/ark:/61903/1:1:VQDH-LZH : 4 December 2014), John Turner, 15 Sep 1775

[131] Findagrave.com in the Hambletville Cemetery, Delaware County, New York.

[132] Findagrave.com in Doonans Corners Cemetery, Kortwright, New York.

[133] Findagrave.com in Doonans Corners Cemetery, Kortwright, New York.

[134] Findagrave.com in Doonans Corners Cemetery, Kortwright, New York.

[135] Ancestry.com, American Marriages Before 1699 (Provo, UT, USA, Ancestry.com Operations Inc, 1997), Ancestry.com, http://www.Ancestry.com, Record for Thomas Turner.

[136] Ancestry.com, 1870 United States Federal Census (Provo, UT, USA, The Generations Network, Inc., 2003), www.ancestry.com, Year: 1870; Census Place: Kortright, Delaware, New York; Roll: M593_924; Page: 276A; Family History Library Film: 552423. Record for Hopestell Turner.

[137] Ancestry.com, New York, State Census, 1855 for Delaware County, New York.

[138] Ancestry.com, U.S., Find A Grave Index, 1700s-Current (Provo, UT, USA, Ancestry.com Operations, Inc., 2012), Ancestry.com, http://www.Ancestry.com, Record for Silas Henry Goodrich.

[139] Ancestry.com, U.S., Find A Grave Index, 1700s-Current (Provo, UT, USA, Ancestry.com Operations, Inc., 2012), Ancestry.com, http://www.Ancestry.com, Record for Silas Henry Goodrich.

[140] Ancestry.com, U.S., Find A Grave Index, 1700s-Current (Provo, UT, USA, Ancestry.com Operations, Inc., 2012), Ancestry.com, http://www.Ancestry.com, Record for Silas Henry Goodrich.

[141] Ancestry.com, U.S., Find A Grave Index, 1700s-Current (Provo, UT, USA, Ancestry.com Operations, Inc., 2012), Ancestry.com, http://www.Ancestry.com, Record for Silas Henry Goodrich.

[142] Ancestry.com, U.S., Find A Grave Index, 1700s-Current (Provo, UT, USA, Ancestry.com Operations, Inc., 2012), Ancestry.com, http://wrww.Ancestry.com, Record for Silas Henry Goodrich.

Silas Henry Goodrich and Sally or Sarah Turner had the following children:

    i.   Ira Goodrich was born on 19 Jun 1797[143]. He married Hannah Janes.

    ii.   Erastus Goodrich was born in 1799[144].

    iii.   Amanda Goodrich was born on 04 Jun 1799 in Delaware County, New York[145] and died on 17 Feb 1881 in Delaware County, New York[146].

    iv.   John T. Goodrich was born on 01 Aug 1801[147] and died on 02 Jul 1903 in Matteson, Michigan[148]. He married Patty M. Brownell.

    v.   Hiram M. Goodrich was born on 22 Jul 1803[149].

    vi.   Orrin Goodrich was born on 07 Sep 1805[150] and died on 24 Jul 1869[151]. He married Amelia Wheeler.

    vii.   James Goodrich was born on 02 Feb 1808[152]. He married Mary Copely.

    viii.   Clarissa Goodrich was born on 13 Feb 1810[153] and died on 18 Jan 1887[154]. She married James F. Cleveland on 29 Nov 1829[155]. He was born on 19 Jan 1805[156] and died on 01 Apr 1897[157].

---

[143] Ancestry.com, North America, Family Histories, 1500-2000 Book Title: The Goodrich family in America : a genealogy of the descendants of John and William Goodrich of Wet. Record for Silas Henry Goodrich.

[144] Ancestry.com, North America, Family Histories, 1500-2000 Book Title: The Goodrich family in America : a genealogy of the descendants of John and William Goodrich of Wet. Record for Silas Henry Goodrich.

[145] Ancestry.com, U.S., Find A Grave Index, 1700s-Current (Provo, UT, USA, Ancestry.com Operations, Inc., 2012), Ancestry.com, http://www.Ancestry.com, Record for Silas Henry Goodrich.

[146] Ancestry.com, U.S., Find A Grave Index, 1700s-Current (Provo, UT, USA, Ancestry.com Operations, Inc., 2012), Ancestry.com, http://www.Ancestry.com, Record for Silas Henry Goodrich.

[147] Ancestry.com, North America, Family Histories, 1500-2000 (Provo, UT, USA, Ancestry.com Operations, Inc., 2016), Ancestry.com, http://www.Ancestry.com, Book Title: The Goodrich family in America : a genealogy of the descendants of John and William Goodrich of Wet. Record for Silas Henry Goodrich.

[148] Ancestry.com, U.S., Find A Grave Index, 1700s-Current (Provo, UT, USA, Ancestry.com Operations, Inc., 2012), Ancestry.com, http://www.Ancestry.com, Record for Silas Henry Goodrich.

[149] Ancestry.com, North America, Family Histories, 1500-2000 (Provo, UT, USA, Ancestry.com Operations, Inc., 2016), Ancestry.com, http://www.Ancestry.com, Book Title: The Goodrich family in America : a genealogy of the descendants of John and William Goodrich of Wet. Record for Silas Henry Goodrich.

[150] Ancestry.com, North America, Family Histories, 1500-2000 (Provo, UT, USA, Ancestry.com Operations, Inc., 2016), Ancestry.com, http://www.Ancestry.com, Book Title: The Goodrich family in America : a genealogy of the descendants of John and William Goodrich of Wet. Record for Silas Henry Goodrich.

[151] Ancestry.com, U.S., Find A Grave Index, 1700s-Current (Provo, UT, USA, Ancestry.com Operations, Inc., 2012), Ancestry.com, http://www.Ancestry.com, Record for Silas Henry Goodrich.

[152] Ancestry.com, North America, Family Histories, 1500-2000 (Provo, UT, USA, Ancestry.com Operations, Inc., 2016), Ancestry.com, http://www.Ancestry.com, Book Title: The Goodrich family in America : a genealogy of the descendants of John and William Goodrich of Wet. Record for Silas Henry Goodrich.

[153] Ancestry.com, North America, Family Histories, 1500-2000 (Provo, UT, USA, Ancestry.com Operations, Inc., 2016), Ancestry.com, http://www.Ancestry.com, Book Title: The Goodrich family in America : a genealogy of the descendants of John and William Goodrich of Wet. Record for Silas Henry Goodrich.

[154] Ancestry.com, U.S., Find A Grave Index, 1700s-Current (Provo, UT, USA, Ancestry.com Operations, Inc., 2012), Ancestry.com, http://www.Ancestry.com, Record for Clarrissa Cleveland.

[155] Ancestry.com, U.S., Find A Grave Index, 1700s-Current (Provo, UT, USA, Ancestry.com Operations, Inc., 2012), Ancestry.com, http://www.Ancestry.com, Record for Clarrissa Cleveland.

[156] Ancestry.com, U.S., Find A Grave Index, 1700s-Current (Provo, UT, USA, Ancestry.com Operations, Inc., 2012), Ancestry.com, http://www.Ancestry.com, Record for Clarrissa Cleveland.

[157] Ancestry.com, U.S., Find A Grave Index, 1700s-Current (Provo, UT, USA, Ancestry.com Operations, Inc., 2012), Ancestry.com, http://www.Ancestry.com, Record for Clarrissa Cleveland.

ix.   Amasa J. Goodrich was born on 05 Mar 1810[158] and died on 22 Oct 1870 in East Saint Louis, Illinois[159].

x.   Sally Ann Goodrich was born on 13 Jun 1812[160].

12. Catharine Turner[7] (Paul Turner[6], Benjamin Turner Sr.[5], Benjamin Turner Sr.[4], John Turner[3], John Turner[2], Humphrey Turner[1]) was born on 06 Dec 1781 in Stockbridge, Massachusetts[161] and died on 10 Mar 1856[162]. She married Solomon Hartwell[163]. He was born on 09 Jun 1777 in Fitchburg, Massachusetts[164] and died on 16 Oct 1861[165].

Solomon Hartwell and Catharine Turner had the following child:

i.   Samantha Hartwell was born on 28 May 1814 in Jefferson, New York[166] and died on 23 Feb 1904 in Cazenovia, New York[167]. She married Rev. Lewis Brumley Stone, on 18 Jan 1842[168]. He was born on 01 Sep 1806[169] and died on 17 Aug 1866 in Cazenovia, New York[170].

Samantha (Hartwell) Stone was the daughter of Solomon and Catherine (Turner) Hartwell. She was the 2nd wife of Rev. Lewis Brumley Stone. They were married January 18, 1842. He was a Local Preacher in the New York Conference of the Methodist Episcopal Church.

---

[158] Ancestry.com, North America, Family Histories, 1500-2000 (Provo, UT, USA, Ancestry.com Operations, Inc., 2016), Ancestry.com, http://www.Ancestry.com, Book Title: The Goodrich family in America : a genealogy of the descendants of John and William Goodrich of Wet. Record for Silas Henry Goodrich.

[159] Ancestry.com, U.S., Find A Grave Index, 1700s-Current (Provo, UT, USA, Ancestry.com Operations, Inc., 2012), Ancestry.com, http://www.Ancestry.com, Record for Silas Henry Goodrich.

[160] Ancestry.com, North America, Family Histories, 1500-2000 (Provo, UT, USA, Ancestry.com Operations, Inc., 2016), Ancestry.com, http://www.Ancestry.com, Book Title: The Goodrich family in America : a genealogy of the descendants of John and William Goodrich of Wet. Record for Silas Henry Goodrich.

[161] Ancestry.com, Massachusetts, Town and Vital Records, 1620-1988.

[162] Ancestry.com, U.S., Find A Grave Index, 1700s-Current (Provo, UT, USA, Ancestry.com Operations, Inc., 2012), Ancestry.com, http://www.Ancestry.com, Record for Catherine Hartwell.

[163] Ancestry.com, U.S., Find A Grave Index, 1700s-Current (Provo, UT, USA, Ancestry.com Operations, Inc., 2012), Ancestry.com, http://www.Ancestry.com, Record for Solomon Hartwell.

[164] Ancestry.com, U.S., Find A Grave Index, 1700s-Current (Provo, UT, USA, Ancestry.com Operations, Inc., 2012), Ancestry.com, http://www.Ancestry.com, Record for Solomon Hartwell.

[165] Ancestry.com, U.S., Find A Grave Index, 1700s-Current (Provo, UT, USA, Ancestry.com Operations, Inc., 2012), Ancestry.com, http://www.Ancestry.com, Record for Solomon Hartwell.

[166] Ancestry.com, U.S., Find A Grave Index, 1700s-Current (Provo, UT, USA, Ancestry.com Operations, Inc., 2012), Ancestry.com, http://www.Ancestry.com, Record for Solomon Hartwell.

[167] Ancestry.com, U.S., Find A Grave Index, 1700s-Current (Provo, UT, USA, Ancestry.com Operations, Inc., 2012), Ancestry.com, http://www.Ancestry.com, Record for Solomon Hartwell.

[168] Ancestry.com, U.S., Find A Grave Index, 1700s-Current (Provo, UT, USA, Ancestry.com Operations, Inc., 2012), Ancestry.com, http://www.Ancestry.com, Record for Solomon Hartwell.

[169] Ancestry.com, U.S., Find A Grave Index, 1700s-Current (Provo, UT, USA, Ancestry.com Operations, Inc., 2012), Ancestry.com, http://www.Ancestry.com, Record for Solomon Hartwell.

[170] Ancestry.com, U.S., Find A Grave Index, 1700s-Current (Provo, UT, USA, Ancestry.com Operations, Inc., 2012), Ancestry.com, http://www.Ancestry.com, Record for Solomon Hartwell.

13. Mary R. Turner[7] (Paul Turner[6], Benjamin Turner Sr.[5], Benjamin Turner Sr.[4], John Turner[3], John Turner[2], Humphrey Turner[1]) was born on 23 Dec 1789 in Massachusetts[171] and died on 06 May 1869 in Madison, New York[172]. She married Henry B. Webb[173]. He was born in 1784 in Connecticut[174] and died in 1864 in Madison, New York[175].

FOR MORE ON MARY R. TURNER AND HER DESCENDANTS, PLEASE SEE CHAPTER TWO.

14. Paul Turner[7] (Paul Turner[6], Benjamin Turner Sr.[5], Benjamin Turner Sr.[4], John Turner[3], John Turner[2], Humphrey Turner[1]) was born in 1794 in Davenport, New York and died about 1830 in New York State[176]. He married Ester Cotton. She was born in about 1790 in Middletown, Connecticut.

Paul Turner and Ester Cotton had the following children:
16.   i.   Paul Turner was born on 25 Feb 1814[177] and died on 15 Mar 1893 in Binghamton, New York[178].
17.   ii.   Sarah Turner was born on 30 May 1815 in Onondaga County, New York[179] and died on 18 Mar 1856 in Elbridge, New York[180].

[171] Ancestry.com, U.S., Find A Grave Index, 1700s-Current (Provo, UT, USA, Ancestry.com Operations, Inc., 2012), Ancestry.com, http://www.Ancestry.com, Record for Mary R. Webb.

[172] Ancestry.com, U.S., Find A Grave Index, 1700s-Current (Provo, UT, USA, Ancestry.com Operations, Inc., 2012), Ancestry.com, http://www.Ancestry.com, Record for Mary R. Webb.

[173] Ancestry.com, New York, State Census, 1855 (Provo, UT, USA, Ancestry.com Operations, Inc., 2013), Ancestry.com, http://www.Ancestry.com, Record for Mary Webb.

[174] Ancestry.com, U.S., Find A Grave Index, 1700s-Current (Provo, UT, USA, Ancestry.com Operations, Inc., 2012), Ancestry.com, http://www.Ancestry.com, Record for Henry B. Webb

[175] Ancestry.com, U.S., Find A Grave Index, 1700s-Current (Provo, UT, USA, Ancestry.com Operations, Inc., 2012), Ancestry.com, http://www.Ancestry.com, Record for Henry B. Webb

[176] Ancestry. com - in the New York, Wills and Probate Records, 1659-1999

[177] Ancestry.com, U.S., Find A Grave Index, 1700s-Current (Provo, UT, USA, Ancestry.com Operations, Inc., 2012), Ancestry.com, http://www.Ancestry.com, Record for Paul Turner.

[178] Ancestry.com, U.S., Find A Grave Index, 1700s-Current (Provo, UT, USA, Ancestry.com Operations, Inc., 2012), Ancestry.com, http://www.Ancestry.com, Record for Paul Turner.

[179] Ancestry.com, U.S., Find A Grave Index, 1700s-Current (Provo, UT, USA, Ancestry.com Operations, Inc., 2012), Ancestry.com, http://www.Ancestry.com, Record for Silas C Goodrich.

[180] Ancestry.com, U.S., Find A Grave Index, 1700s-Current (Provo, UT, USA, Ancestry.com Operations, Inc., 2012), Ancestry.com, http://www.Ancestry.com, Record for Silas C Goodrich.

18.   iii.   Erastus G. Turner was born in Nov 1818 in New York State and died on 30 Mar 1881 in Bradford, Pennsylvania[181].

iv.   George W. Turner was born in 1825 in Royalton, New York[182].

19   v.   Nancy S. Turner was born on 20 Aug 1827 in Marshburg, Pennsylvania[183] and died on 03 Feb 1882[184].

vi.   Anna E. Turner was born on 23 Aug 1831 in Ithaca, New York[185] and died on 02 Mar 1916 in Kane, Pennsylvania[186]. She married Mr. Haak.

Photo of Erastus G. Turner found on Ancestry.com.

[181] Ancestry.com, U.S., Find A Grave Index, 1700s-Current

[182] Ancestry.com, U.S., Civil War Draft Registrations Records, 1863-1865 (Provo, UT, USA, Ancestry.com Operations, Inc., 2010), Ancestry.com, http://www.Ancestry.com, National Archives and Records Administration (NARA); Washington, D.C.; Consolidated Lists of Civil War Draft Registration Records (Provost Marshal General's Bureau; Consolidated Enrollment Lists, 1863-1865); Record Group: 110, Records of the Provost Marshal General's Bureau (Civil War); Collection Name: Consolidated Enrollment Lists, 1863-1865 (Civil War Union Draft Records); NAI: 4213514; Archive Volume Number: 3 of 7. Record for George W Turner.

[183] Ancestry.com, Pennsylvania, Death Certificates, 1906-1963, Ancestry.com, http://www.Ancestry.com, Pennsylvania Historic and Museum Commission; Pennsylvania, USA; Pennsylvania (State). Death certificates, 1906-1966; Certificate Number Range: 105601-108300. Record for Nancy Turner.

[184] Ancestry.com, Pennsylvania, Death Certificates, 1906-1963, Ancestry.com, http://www.Ancestry.com, Pennsylvania Historic and Museum Commission; Pennsylvania, USA; Pennsylvania (State). Death certificates, 1906-1966; Certificate Number Range: 105601-108300. Record for Nancy Turner.

[185] Ancestry.com, Pennsylvania, Death Certificates, 1906-1963.

[186] Ancestry.com, Pennsylvania, Death Certificates, 1906-1963.

Generation Eight

15. Hopestell C. Turner[8] (John Turner[7], Paul Turner[6], Benjamin Turner Sr.[5], Benjamin Turner Sr.[4], John Turner[3], John Turner[2], Humphrey Turner[1]) was born on 28 Jan 1822 in Delaware County, New York[187] and died in after 1905. He married Eliza Ann Hunt in 1843. She was born in 1826 in Ulster County, New York[188] and died 29 Mar 1898 in Kortright, New York[189].

Hopestell C. Turner and Eliza Ann Hunt had the following children:
     i.   Polly Evaline Turner was born in Mar 1844 in Delaware County, New York[190] and died on 05 Jun 1916 in Kortright, New York[191].
20.   ii.   William L. Turner was born in Aug 1845 in Delaware County, New York[192] and died on 1903 in Kortright, New York[193].
     iii.   John Turner was born in 1847 in Delaware County, New York[194] and died on 05 Oct 1872[195].
     iv.   Crosby H. Turner was born in Jan 1849 in Delaware County, New York[196]. He married a woman by the name of Mary L. in 1886[197]. She was born in Sep 1862 in New York[198].

[187] Ancestry.com, 1870 United States Federal Census (Provo, UT, USA, The Generations Network, Inc., 2003), www.ancestry.com, Year: 1870; Census Place: Kortright, Delaware, New York; Roll: M593_924; Page: 276A; Family History Library Film: 552423. Record for Hopestell Turner.

[188] Ancestry.com, U.S., Selected Federal Census Non Population Schedules, 1850-1880 (Provo, UT, USA, Ancestry.com Operations, Inc., 2010), Ancestry.com, http://www.Ancestry.com, Census Year: 1850; Census Place: Kortright, Delaware, New York; Archive Collection Number: A2; Roll: 2; Page: 211; Line: 18; Schedule Type: Agriculture. Record for Hopestill Turner.

[189] Ancestry.com, New York, Death Index, 1880-1956.

[190] Ancestry.com, 1900 United States Federal Census (Provo, UT, USA, Ancestry.com Operations Inc, 2004), Ancestry.com, http://www.Ancestry.com, Year: 1900; Census Place: Kortright, Delaware, New York; Roll: 1021; Page: 6B; Enumeration District: 0019; FHL microfilm: 1241021. Record for Hopestill Turner.

[191] Ancestry.com, New York, Death Index, 1880-1956 (Lehi, UT, USA, Ancestry.com Operations, Inc., 2017), Ancestry.com, http://www.Ancestry.com, New York Department of Health; Albany, NY; NY State Death Index; Certificate Number: 35718. Record for Evaline Turner.

[192] U.S., Find A Grave Index, 1600s-Current. Montoza Cemetery, Barryville, New York.

[193] U.S., Find A Grave Index, 1600s-Current. Montoza Cemetery, Barryville, New York.

[194] Ancestry.com, New York, State Census, 1855 (Provo, UT, USA, Ancestry.com Operations, Inc., 2013), Ancestry.com, http://www.Ancestry.com, Record for Hopestill Turner.

[195] U.S., Find A Grave Index, 1600s-Current.

[196] Ancestry.com, New York, State Census, 1855 (Provo, UT, USA, Ancestry.com Operations, Inc., 2013), Ancestry.com, http://www.Ancestry.com, Record for Hopestill Turner.

[197] Ancestry.com, 1900 United States Federal Census (Provo, UT, USA, Ancestry.com Operations Inc, 2004), Ancestry.com, http://www.Ancestry.com, Year: 1900; Census Place: Davenport, Delaware, New York; Roll: 1021; Page: 8B; Enumeration District: 0006; FHL microfilm: 1241021. Record for Crosby H Turner.

[198] Ancestry.com, 1900 United States Federal Census (Provo, UT, USA, Ancestry.com Operations Inc, 2004), Ancestry.com, http://www.Ancestry.com, Year: 1900; Census Place: Davenport, Delaware, New York; Roll: 1021; Page: 8B; Enumeration District: 0006; FHL microfilm: 1241021. Record for Crosby H Turner.

v.   Julia Turner was born in 1851 in Delaware County, New York[199] and died on 21 Jun 1871[200].

vi.   Melissa A. Turner was born in1854 Delaware County, New York[201] and died in 1894[202].

21.   vii.   Addison W. Turner was born on 25 Jun 1854[203] and died on 30 May 1938[204].

viii.   Charles E. Turner was born in Nov 1857 in New York[205] and died in 01 Dec 1935[206].

ix.   Harriet Turner was born in 1863 in New York[207] and died on 24 Jun 1934 in Kortright, New York [208].

16. Paul Turner[8] (PaulTurner[7], Paul Turner[6], Benjamin Turner Sr.[5], Benjamin Turner Sr.[4], John Turner[3], John Turner[2], Humphrey Turner[1]) was born on 25 Feb 1814[209] and died on 15 Mar 1893 in Binghamton, New York[210]. He married Hannah M. Lewis. She was born on 12 Jun 1807[211] in New York State and died on 07 Aug 1899[212].

---

[199] Ancestry.com, New York, State Census, 1865 (Provo, UT, USA, Ancestry.com Operations, Inc., 2014), Ancestry.com, http://www.Ancestry.com, Record for Hopestell Turner.

[200] Ancestry.com, U.S., Find A Grave Index, 1700s-Current (Provo, UT, USA, Ancestry.com Operations, Inc., 2012), Ancestry.com, http://www.Ancestry.com, Record for Julia Turner.

[201] Ancestry.com, New York, State Census, 1865 (Provo, UT, USA, Ancestry.com Operations, Inc., 2014), Ancestry.com, http://www.Ancestry.com, Record for Hopestell Turner.

[202] Ancestry.com, Public Member Trees (Provo, UT, USA, Ancestry.com Operations Inc, 2006), www.ancestry.com, Record for Benjamin Turner.

[203] Ancestry.com, U.S., Find A Grave Index, 1700s-Current (Provo, UT, USA, Ancestry.com Operations, Inc., 2012), Ancestry.com, http://www.Ancestry.com, Record for Addison Turner

[204] Ancestry.com, U.S., Find A Grave Index, 1700s-Current (Provo, UT, USA, Ancestry.com Operations, Inc., 2012), Ancestry.com, http://www.Ancestry.com, Record for Addison Turner

[205] Ancestry.com, 1900 United States Federal Census (Provo, UT, USA, Ancestry.com Operations Inc, 2004), Ancestry.com, http://www.Ancestry.com, Year: 1900; Census Place: Kortright, Delaware, New York; Roll: 1021; Page: 6B; Enumeration District: 0019; FHL microfilm: 1241021. Record for Hopestill Turner.

[206] Ancestry.com, New York, Death Index, 1880-1956.

[207] Ancestry.com, New York, State Census, 1865 (Provo, UT, USA, Ancestry.com Operations, Inc., 2014), Ancestry.com, http://www.Ancestry.com, Record for Hopestell Turner.

[208] Ancestry.com, New York, Death Index, 1880-1956 (Lehi, UT, USA, Ancestry.com Operations, Inc., 2017), Ancestry.com, http://www.Ancestry.com, New York Department of Health; Albany, NY; NY State Death Index; Certificate Number: 38228. Record for Harriet Turner.

[209] Ancestry.com, U.S., Find A Grave Index, 1700s-Current (Provo, UT, USA, Ancestry.com Operations, Inc., 2012), Ancestry.com, http://www.Ancestry.com, Record for Paul Turner.

[210] Ancestry.com, U.S., Find A Grave Index, 1700s-Current (Provo, UT, USA, Ancestry.com Operations, Inc., 2012), Ancestry.com, http://www.Ancestry.com, Record for Paul Turner.

[211] Ancestry.com, U.S., Find A Grave Index, 1700s-Current (Provo, UT, USA, Ancestry.com Operations, Inc., 2012), Ancestry.com, http://www.Ancestry.com, Record for Paul Turner.

[212] Ancestry.com, U.S., Find A Grave Index, 1700s-Current (Provo, UT, USA, Ancestry.com Operations, Inc., 2012), Ancestry.com, http://www.Ancestry.com, Record for Paul Turner.

Paul Turner and Hannah M. Lewis had the following children:
     i.   Esther Turner was born on 22 Apr 1837[213] and died on 04 May 1915[214]. In 1905, Esther was living with her brother, Theodore. She was 70.
     ii.   Albert Turner was born in 1838[215] and died in 1876.
22.   iii.   Theodore A. Turner was born in 1842[216] in New York State and died on 13 Mar 1916.
     iv.   Paul Turner Jr. was born in 1844[217] in New York State and died on 05 Sep 1891 in Binghamton, New York[218].
     v.   Mason Turner was born in Feb 1845[219] in New York State and died on 09 Dec 1857[220].

17. Sarah Turner[8] (PaulTurner[7], Paul Turner[6], Benjamin Turner Sr.[5], Benjamin Turner Sr.[4], John Turner[3], John Turner[2], Humphrey Turner[1]) was born on 30 May 1815 in Onondaga County, New York[221] and died on 18 Mar 1856 in Elbridge, New York[222]. She married Silas C. Goodrich[223]. He was born on 21 Aug 1813 in Onondaga County, New York[224] and died on 04 Apr 1858 in Elbridge, New York[225].

Silas C Goodrich and Sarah Turner had the following child:
     i.   William Jerome Goodrich was born on 18 Jun 1837 in New York[226] and died on 03 Apr 1931 in Orange County, California[227].

18. Erastus G. Turner[8] (PaulTurner[7], Paul Turner[6], Benjamin Turner Sr.[5], Benjamin Turner Sr.[4], John Turner[3], John Turner[2], Humphrey Turner[1]) was born in Nov 1818 in New York[228] and died on 30 Mar 1881 in Bradford, Pennsylvania[229]. He married Parmella Blue Marsh[230] She was born in 1825 in Pennsylvania[231] and died in 1870[232].

---

[213] Ancestry.com, U.S., Find A Grave Index, 1700s, Record for Esther Turner.
[214] Ancestry.com, U.S., Find A Grave Index, 1700s, Record for Esther Turner.
[215] Ancestry.com, U.S., Find A Grave Index, 1700s, Record for A. L. W. Turner.
[216] Ancestry.com, U.S., Find A Grave Index, 1700s, Record for Theodore Turner.
[217] Ancestry.com, U.S., Find A Grave Index, 1700s, Record for Paul Jr Turner.
[218] Ancestry.com, U.S., Find A Grave Index, 1700s, Record for Paul Jr Turner.
[219] Ancestry.com, U.S., Find A Grave Index, 1700s, Record for Mason Turner.
[220] Ancestry.com, U.S., Find A Grave Index, 1700s, Record for Mason Turner.
[221] Ancestry.com, U.S., Find A Grave Index, 1700s, Record for Silas C Goodrich.
[222] Ancestry.com, U.S., Find A Grave Index, 1700s, Record for Silas C Goodrich.
[223] The Will of Sarah's father, Paul Turner found on Ancestry.com in New York Wills
[224] Ancestry.com, U.S., Find A Grave Index, 1700s, Record for Silas C Goodrich.
[225] Ancestry.com, U.S., Find A Grave Index, 1700s, Record for Silas C Goodrich.
[226] Ancestry.com, U.S., Find A Grave Index, 1700s, Record for Silas C Goodrich.
[227] Ancestry.com, U.S., Find A Grave Index, 1700s, Record for Silas C Goodrich.
[228] Ancestry.com, U.S., Find A Grave Index, 1700s, Record for Sylvanus M Turner.
[229] Ancestry.com, U.S., Find A Grave Index, 1700s, Record for Sylvanus M Turner.
[230] Ancestry.com, U.S., Find A Grave Index, 1700s, Record for Sylvanus M Turner.
[231] Ancestry.com, U.S., Find A Grave Index, 1700s, Record for Sylvanus M Turner.
[232] Ancestry.com, U.S., Find A Grave Index, 1700s, Record for Sylvanus M Turner.

Erastus G. Turner and Parmella Blue Marsh had the following children:

23.   i.   Ruth Turner was born in Sep 1843 in Pennsylvania[233] and died in 1903[234].

ii.   Sophrania Turner was born in May 1850 in Pennsylvania[235].

24.   iii.   Sylvanus M. Turner was born on 02 Aug 1852 in Eldred, Pennsylvania[236]and died on 30 Jun 1924 in Eldred, Pennsylvania[237].

Photo of Sylvanus M. Turner found on Ancestry.com.

iv.   Shoubel Cotton Turner was born on 27 Nov 1854 in Bradford County, Pennsylvania[238] and died on 25 Sep 1930 in Noble County, Ohio[239]. He married a woman by the name of Carrie. She was born in 1888[240] and died on 06 Apr 1969[241].

v.   Archibald Turner was born on 02 Jul 1856 in Pennsylvania[242] and died on 10 Dec 1919 in Bradford, Pennsylvania[243].

Photo of Archibald Turner found on Ancestry.com.

[233] Ancestry.com, U.S., Find A Grave Index, 1700s-Current (Provo, UT, USA, Ancestry.com Operations, Inc., 2012), Ancestry.com, http://www.Ancestry.com, Record for Ruth Harris.

[234] Ancestry.com, U.S., Find A Grave Index, 1700s-Current (Provo, UT, USA, Ancestry.com Operations, Inc., 2012), Ancestry.com, http://www.Ancestry.com, Record for Ruth Harris.

[235] Ancestry.com, 1850 United States Federal Census (Provo, UT, USA, The Generations Network, Inc., 2005), www.ancestry.com, Year: 1850; Census Place: Kinzua, Warren, Pennsylvania; Roll: M432_832; Page: 379A; Image: 750. Record for Sophronia Turner.

[236] Ancestry.com, U.S., Find A Grave Index, 1700s, Record for Sylvanus M. Turner.

[237] Ancestry.com, U.S., Find A Grave Index, 1700s, Record for Sylvanus M. Turner.

[238] Ancestry.com, U.S., Find A Grave Index, 1700s-Current (Provo, UT, USA, Ancestry.com Operations, Inc., 2012), Ancestry.com, http://www.Ancestry.com, Record for Shouble Cotton Turner

[239] Ancestry.com, U.S., Find A Grave Index, 1700s-Current (Provo, UT, USA, Ancestry.com Operations, Inc., 2012), Ancestry.com, http://www.Ancestry.com, Record for Shouble Cotton Turner

[240] Ancestry.com, U.S., Find A Grave Index, 1700s-Current (Provo, UT, USA, Ancestry.com Operations, Inc., 2012), Ancestry.com, http://www.Ancestry.com, Record for Shouble Cotton Turner

[241] Ancestry.com, U.S., Find A Grave Index, 1700s-Current (Provo, UT, USA, Ancestry.com Operations, Inc., 2012), Ancestry.com, http://www.Ancestry.com, Record for Shouble Cotton Turner

[242] Pennsylvania Death Certificate on Archibald Turner found on Ancestry.com.

[243] Pennsylvania Death Certificate on Archibald Turner found on Ancestry.com.

    vi.   Henry J. Turner was born in 1858 and was not in the 1870 census with the family.

25.   vii.   Ida May Turner was born in 1860 in Of Corydon Twp, Pennsylvania[244].

    viii.   Ellinora J. Turner was born in 1863 in Pennsylvania[245].

    ix.   Hulda Turner was born in 1864 in Pennsylvania[246].

19. Nancy S. Turner[8] (Paul Turner[7], Paul Turner[6], Benjamin Turner Sr.[5], Benjamin Turner Sr.[4], John Turner[3], John Turner[2], Humphrey Turner[1]) was born on 20 Aug 1827 in Marshburg, Pennsylvania[247] and died on 03 Feb 1882[248]. She first married a man with the last name of Wickman and later married James W. Palmer. He was born on 30 Jan 1807 in Geneva, New York[249] and died on 01 Nov 1883[250].

Mr. Wickman and Nancy S. Turner had the following child:

    i.   Madora Wickman was born in 1851 in New York[251].

James W. Palmer and Nancy S. Turner had the following children:

26.   ii.   Emily Jane Palmer was born on 09 Apr 1862 in Marshburg, Pennsylvania[252] and died on 28 Mar 1940 in Hamlin, Pennsylvania[253].

27.   iii.   Fannie Louis Palmer was born on 04 Jul 1863 in Marshburg, Pennsylvania[254] and died on 30 Dec 1945 in Kane, Pennsylvania[255].

---

[244] Ancestry.com, 1870 United States Federal Census (Provo, UT, USA, Ancestry.com Operations, Inc., 2009), Ancestry.com, http://www.Ancestry.com, Year: 1870; Census Place: Corydon, McKean, Pennsylvania; Roll: M593_1372; Page: 674A; Family History Library Film: 552871. Record for Ida Mary Turner.

[245] Ancestry.com, 1870 United States Federal Census (Provo, UT, USA, Ancestry.com Operations, Inc., 2009), Ancestry.com, http://www.Ancestry.com, Year: 1870; Census Place: Corydon, McKean, Pennsylvania; Roll: M593_1372; Page: 674A; Family History Library Film: 552871. Record for Ellinora J Turner.

[246] Ancestry.com, 1870 United States Federal Census (Provo, UT, USA, The Generations Network, Inc., 2003), www.ancestry.com, Year: 1870; Census Place: Corydon, McKean, Pennsylvania; Roll: M593_1372; Page: 674A; Family History Library Film: 552871. Record for Hulda Turner.

[247] Ancestry.com, Pennsylvania, Death Certificates, 1906-1963 (Provo, UT, USA, Ancestry.com Operations, Inc., 2014), Ancestry.com, http://www.Ancestry.com, Pennsylvania Historic and Museum Commission; Pennsylvania, USA; Pennsylvania (State). Death certificates, 1906-1966; Certificate Number Range: 105601-108300. Record for Nancy Turner.

[248] Ancestry.com, Pennsylvania, Death Certificates, 1906-1963 (Provo, UT, USA, Ancestry.com Operations, Inc., 2014), Pennsylvania Historic and Museum Commission; Pennsylvania, USA; Pennsylvania (State). Death certificates, 1906-1966; Certificate Number Range: 105601-108300. Record for Nancy Turner.

[249] Ancestry.com, Pennsylvania, Death Certificates, 1906-1963 (Provo, UT, USA, Ancestry.com Operations, Inc., 2014), Pennsylvania Historic and Museum Commission; Pennsylvania, USA; Pennsylvania (State). Death certificates, 1906-1966; Certificate Number Range: 105601-108300. Record for Nancy Turner.

[250] Ancestry.com scanned photo of gravestone.

[251] Ancestry.com and The Church of Jesus Christ of Latter-day Saints, 1880 United States Federal Census (Provo, UT, USA, Ancestry.com Operations Inc, 2010), Ancestry.com, http://www.Ancestry.com, Year: 1880; Census Place: La Fayette, McKean, Pennsylvania; Roll: 1154; Page: 378C; Enumeration District: 092. Record for Madora Wickham.

[252] Ancestry.com, U.S., Find A Grave Index, 1700s-Current (Provo, UT, USA, Ancestry.com Operations, Inc., 2012), Ancestry.com, http://www.Ancestry.com, Record for Emily J. Nogar.

[253] Ancestry.com, U.S., Find A Grave Index, 1700s-Current (Provo, UT, USA, Ancestry.com Operations, Inc., 2012), Ancestry.com, http://www.Ancestry.com, Record for Emily J. Nogar.

[254] Ancestry.com, Pennsylvania Death Certificate for Fannie Louis Morrison.

[255] Ancestry.com, Pennsylvania Death Certificate for Fannie Louis Morrison.

iv.   Louisa M. Palmer was born on 12 Jun 1865 in Marshburg, Pennsylvania[256] and died on 10 Feb 1943 in Bradford, Pennsylvania[257].

v.   Ella Palmer was born in 1874 in Pennsylvania[258].

---

[256] Ancestry.com, Pennsylvania Death Certificate for Louisa M. Palmer.

[257] Ancestry.com, Pennsylvania Death Certificate for Louisa M. Palmer.

[258] Ancestry.com and The Church of Jesus Christ of Latter-day Saints, 1880 United States Federal Census (Provo, UT, USA, Ancestry.com Operations Inc, 2010), Ancestry.com, http://www.Ancestry.com, Year: 1880; Census Place: La Fayette, McKean, Pennsylvania; Roll: 1154; Page: 378C; Enumeration District: 092. Record for Ella Palmer.

Generation Nine

20. William L. Turner[9] (Hopestell C. Turner[8], John Turner[7], Paul Turner[6], Benjamin Turner Sr.[5], Benjamin Turner Sr.[4], John Turner[3], John Turner[2], Humphrey Turner[1]) was born in Aug 1845 in Delaware County, New York[259] and died in 1903 in Barryville, New York[260]. He married a woman by the name of Delia M[261]. She was born in 1845 in New York[262] and died in 1918[263].   William L. Turner and his wife, Delia M., were buried in the Montoza Cemetery, Barryville, New York.

William L Turner and Delia M Turner had the following children:
>   i.   M. Lee Turner was born in 1871[264].
>   ii.   Ralph Turner was born in 1875[265].

21. Addison W. Turner[9] (Hopestell C. Turner[8], John Turner[7], Paul Turner[6], Benjamin Turner Sr.[5], Benjamin Turner Sr.[4], John Turner[3], John Turner[2], Humphrey Turner[1]) was born on 25 Jun 1854[266] and died on 30 May 1938[267]. He married Elizabeth Elwyn in 1882[268]. She was born in 1864[269] and died on 21 Feb 1931[270].

Addison W. Turner and Elizabeth Elwyn had the following child:
>   i.   Nora Turner was born in Jun 1883 in New York[271].

[259] U.S., Find A Grave Index, 1600s-Current. Montoza Cemetery, Barryville, New York.

[260] U.S., Find A Grave Index, 1600s-Current. Montoza Cemetery, Barryville, New York.

[261] U.S., Find A Grave Index, 1600s-Current. Montoza Cemetery, Barryville, New York.

[262] U.S., Find A Grave Index, 1600s-Current. Montoza Cemetery, Barryville, New York.

[263] U.S., Find A Grave Index, 1600s-Current. Montoza Cemetery, Barryville, New York.

[264] Ancestry.com, New York, State Census, 1875 (Provo, UT, USA, Ancestry.com Operations, Inc., 2013), Ancestry.com, http://www.Ancestry.com, Record for William L Turner.

[265] Ancestry.com, New York, State Census, 1875 (Provo, UT, USA, Ancestry.com Operations, Inc., 2013), Ancestry.com, http://www.Ancestry.com, Record for William L Turner.

[266] Ancestry.com, U.S., Find A Grave Index, 1700s-Current (Provo, UT, USA, Ancestry.com Operations, Inc., 2012), Ancestry.com, http://www.Ancestry.com, Record for Addison Turner

[267] Ancestry.com, U.S., Find A Grave Index, 1700s-Current (Provo, UT, USA, Ancestry.com Operations, Inc., 2012), Ancestry.com, http://www.Ancestry.com, Record for Addison Turner

[268] Ancestry.com, U.S., Find A Grave Index, 1700s-Current (Provo, UT, USA, Ancestry.com Operations, Inc., 2012), Ancestry.com, http://www.Ancestry.com, Record for Elizabeth Turner.

[269] Ancestry.com, U.S., Find A Grave Index, 1700s-Current (Provo, UT, USA, Ancestry.com Operations, Inc., 2012), Ancestry.com, http://www.Ancestry.com, Record for Elizabeth Turner.

[270] Ancestry.com, U.S., Find A Grave Index, 1700s-Current (Provo, UT, USA, Ancestry.com Operations, Inc., 2012), Ancestry.com, http://www.Ancestry.com, Record for Elizabeth Turner.

[271] Ancestry.com, 1900 United States Federal Census (Provo, UT, USA, Ancestry.com Operations Inc, 2004), Ancestry.com, http://www.Ancestry.com, Year: 1900; Census Place: Meredith, Delaware, New York; Roll: 1021; Page: 5A; Enumeration District: 0021; FHL microfilm: 1241021. Record for Addison Turner.

22. Theodore A. Turner[9] (Paul Turner[8], Paul Turner[7], Paul Turner[6], Benjamin Turner Sr.[5], Benjamin Turner Sr.[4], John Turner[3], John Turner[2], Humphrey Turner[1]) was born in 1842[272] in New York State and died on 13 Mar 1916[273]. He married Elvira Andrews, the daughter of Ransom and Orphia Andrews, in 1862[274]. She was born in Jun 1845 in New York[275] and died in 1901[276].

Theodore A Turner and Elvira Andrews had the following children:
28.   i.   Albert Lewis Turner was born in 1864[277] and died in 1936[278].
      ii.   Ida May Turner was born in 1867 in New York[279].
     iii.   George H. Turner was born in Apr 1870 in New York[280] and died on 19 Jul 1918 in Binghamton, New York[281]. He married Mary C. Hotaling[282]. She was born in 1869 in United States[283] and died on 17 Sep 1925 in Binghamton, New York[284].

---

[272] Ancestry.com, U.S., Find A Grave Index, 1700s-Current, Record for Theodore Turner.

[273] Ancestry.com, U.S., Find A Grave Index, 1700s-Current, Record for Theodore Turner.

[274] Ancestry.com, 1900 United States Federal Census (Provo, UT, USA, The Generations Network, Inc., 2004), www.ancestry.com, Year: 1900; Census Place: Binghamton Ward 12, Broome, New York; Page: 5; Enumeration District: 0027. Record for Elvira L Turner.

[275] Ancestry.com, 1900 United States Federal Census (Provo, UT, USA, The Generations Network, Inc., 2004), www.ancestry.com, Year: 1900; Census Place: Binghamton Ward 12, Broome, New York; Page: 5; Enumeration District: 0027. Record for Elvira L Turner.

[276] Ancestry.com, U.S., Find A Grave Index, 1700s-Current (Provo, UT, USA, Ancestry.com Operations, Inc., 2012), Ancestry.com, http://www.Ancestry.com, Record for Theodore Turner.

[277] Ancestry.com, U.S., Find A Grave Index, 1700s-Current (Provo, UT, USA, Ancestry.com Operations, Inc., 2012), Ancestry.com, http://www.Ancestry.com, Record for Albert Lewis Turner.

[278] Ancestry.com, U.S., Find A Grave Index, 1700s-Current (Provo, UT, USA, Ancestry.com Operations, Inc., 2012), Ancestry.com, http://www.Ancestry.com, Record for Albert Lewis Turner.

[279] Ancestry.com and The Church of Jesus Christ of Latter-day Saints, 1880 United States Federal Census (Provo, UT, USA, Ancestry.com Operations Inc, 2010), Ancestry.com, http://www.Ancestry.com, Year: 1880; Census Place: Binghamton, Broome, New York; Roll: 810; Page: 104D; Enumeration District: 035. Record for Theodore Turner.

[280] Ancestry.com, U.S., Find A Grave Index, 1700s-Current (Provo, UT, USA, Ancestry.com Operations, Inc., 2012), Ancestry.com, http://www.Ancestry.com, Record for George H. Turner.

[281] Ancestry.com, U.S., Find A Grave Index, 1700s-Current (Provo, UT, USA, Ancestry.com Operations, Inc., 2012), Ancestry.com, http://www.Ancestry.com, Record for George H. Turner.

[282] Ancestry.com, U.S., Find A Grave Index, 1700s-Current (Provo, UT, USA, Ancestry.com Operations, Inc., 2012), Ancestry.com, http://www.Ancestry.com, Record for George H. Turner.

[283] Ancestry.com, U.S., Find A Grave Index, 1700s-Current (Provo, UT, USA, Ancestry.com Operations, Inc., 2012), Ancestry.com, http://www.Ancestry.com, Record for George H. Turner.

[284] Ancestry.com, U.S., Find A Grave Index, 1700s-Current (Provo, UT, USA, Ancestry.com Operations, Inc., 2012), Ancestry.com, http://www.Ancestry.com, Record for George H. Turner.

23. Ruth Turner[9] (Erastus G. Turner[8], Paul Turner[7], Paul Turner[6], Benjamin Turner Sr.[5], Benjamin Turner Sr.[4], John Turner[3], John Turner[2], Humphrey Turner[1]) was born in Sep 1843 in Pennsylvania[285] and died in 1903[286]. She married William H. Harris[287]. He was born on 12 Sep 1838 in Jersey Shore, Pennsylvania[288] and died on 27 Sep 1922 in Warren County, Pennsylvania[289].

William H. Harris and Ruth Turner had the following children:

29.   i.   Ella Harris was born on 23 Dec 1853 in Pennsylvania[290] and died on 21 in Kinzua, Pennsylvania[291].

30.   ii.   Carrie Muir Harris was born on 03 Sep 1872 in Kinzua, Pennsylvania[292] and died on 10 Jan 1953 in North Warren, Pennsylvania[293].

Photo of Ruth Turner Harris with her two daughters, Ella and Carrie Harris found on Ancestry.com.

[285] Ancestry.com, U.S., Find A Grave Index, 1700s-Current (Provo, UT, USA, Ancestry.com Operations, Inc., 2012), Ancestry.com, http://www.Ancestry.com, Record for Ruth Harris.

[286] Ancestry.com, U.S., Find A Grave Index, 1700s-Current (Provo, UT, USA, Ancestry.com Operations, Inc., 2012), Ancestry.com, http://www.Ancestry.com, Record for Ruth Harris.

[287] Ancestry.com, U.S., Find A Grave Index, 1700s-Current (Provo, UT, USA, Ancestry.com Operations, Inc., 2012), Ancestry.com, http://www.Ancestry.com, Record for Ruth Harris.

[288] Ancestry.com, U.S., Find A Grave Index, 1700s-Current, Record for Ruth Harris.

[289] Ancestry.com, U.S., Find A Grave Index, 1700s-Current, Record for Ruth Harris.

[290] Ancestry.com, Pennsylvania, Death Certificates, 1906-1963 (Provo, UT, USA, Ancestry.com Operations, Inc., 2014), Pennsylvania Historic and Museum Commission; Pennsylvania, USA; Pennsylvania (State). Death certificates, 1906-1966; Certificate Number Range: 053001-056000. Record for Ella J Merrison.

[291] Ancestry.com, Pennsylvania, Death Certificates, 1906-1963, Pennsylvania Historic and Museum Commission; Pennsylvania, USA; Pennsylvania (State). Death certificates, 1906-1966; Certificate Number Range: 053001-056000. Record for Ella J Merrison.

[292] Ancestry.com, U.S., Find A Grave Index, 1700s-Current, Record for Ruth Harris.

[293] Ancestry.com, U.S., Find A Grave Index, 1700s-Current, Record for Ruth Harris.

24.   Sylvanus M. Turner[9] (Erastus G. Turner[8], Paul Turner[7], Paul Turner[6], Benjamin Turner Sr.[5], Benjamin Turner Sr.[4], John Turner[3], John Turner[2], Humphrey Turner[1]) was born on 02 Aug 1852 in Eldred, Pennsylvania[294] and died on 30 Jun 1924 in Eldred, Pennsylvania[295]. He married Evelyn Bennett in 1874[296]. She was born on 24 Jan 1859 in Bradford, Pennsylvania[297] and died on 30 May 1943 in Warren, Pennsylvania[298].

Photo of Sylvanus M. Turner and his wife Evelyn Viola Bennett found on Ancestry.com.

Sylvanus M. Turner and Evelyn Bennett had the following children:

31.   i.   Grace K. Turner was born on 11 Sep 1876[299] and died on 17 Sep 1943[300].

32.   ii.   Lucy Eveline Turner was born on 19 Aug 1878 in Eldred, Pennsylvania[301]. She died on 06 Sep 1974 in Hornell, New York[302].

iii.   Clara Gertrude Turner was born in 1879 in Eldred, Pennsylvania[303] and died on 02 Oct 1885 in Eldred, Pennsylvania[304].

33.   iv.   Wellman Ellery Turner was born on 20 Sep 1881 in Eldred, Pennsylvania and died on 07 Mar 1953 in Ceres, New York[305].

34.   v.   Truman Herbert Turner was born on 14 Oct 1882[306] and died in 1933[307].

vi.   Ernest Sylvanus Turner was born on 16 Aug 1884 in Bullis Mills, Pennsylvania[308] and died on 09 Jun 1906 in Conestoga, Pennsylvania[309].

---

[294] Ancestry.com, U.S., Find A Grave Index, 1700s-Current, Record for Sylvanus M Turner.

[295] Ancestry.com, U.S., Find A Grave Index, 1700s-Current, Record for Sylvanus M Turner.

[296] Ancestry.com, 1900 United States Federal Census, Year: 1900; Census Place: Ceres, McKean, Pennsylvania; Page: 5; Enumeration District: 0103. Record for Sylvanus M Turner.

[297] Ancestry.com, U.S., Find A Grave Index, 1700s-Current, Record for Sylvanus M Turner.

[298] Ancestry.com, U.S., Find A Grave Index, 1700s-Current, Record for Sylvanus M Turner.

[299] Ancestry.com, U.S., Find A Grave Index, 1700s-Current, Record for Erwin Maxson.

[300] Ancestry.com, U.S., Find A Grave Index, 1700s-Current, Record for Erwin Maxson

[301] Ancestry.com, U.S., Find A Grave Index, 1700s-Current, Record for Sylvanus M Turner.

[302] Ancestry.com, U.S., Find A Grave Index, 1700s-Current, Record for Sylvanus M Turner.

[303] Ancestry.com, U.S., Find A Grave Index, 1700s-Current, Record for Sylvanus M Turner.

[304] Ancestry.com, U.S., Find A Grave Index, 1700s-Current, Record for Sylvanus M Turner.

[305] Ancestry.com, Pennsylvania, Death Certificates, 1906-1963 (Provo, UT, USA, Ancestry.com Operations, Inc., 2014, Pennsylvania Historic and Museum Commission; Pennsylvania, USA; Pennsylvania (State). Death certificates, 1906-1966; Certificate Number Range: 023851-026550. Record for Wellman Turner.

[306] Ancestry.com, U.S., Find A Grave Index, 1700s-Current (Provo, UT, USA, Ancestry.com Operations, Inc., 2012), Ancestry.com, http://www.Ancestry.com, Record for Truman Herbert Turner.

[307] Ancestry.com, U.S., Find A Grave Index, 1700s-Current, Record for Truman Herbert Turner.

[308] Ancestry.com, U.S., Find A Grave Index, 1700s, Record for Ernest Sylvanus Turner.

[309] Ancestry.com, U.S., Find A Grave Index, 1700s-Current (Provo, UT, USA, Ancestry.com Operations, Inc., 2012), Ancestry.com, http://www.Ancestry.com, Record for Ernest Sylvanus Turner.

vii.   Edith M. Turner was born on 05 Oct 1884 in Eldred, Pennsylvania[310] and died on 07 Oct 1885 in Eldred, Pennsylvania[311].

35.   viii.   Permilla A. Turner was born in Sep 1886 in Bullis Mills, Pennsylvania[312] and died on 12 Dec 1932 in Olean, New York[313].

Photo of Sylvanus M. Turner with his wife, Evelyn Bennett, with seven of their ten children found on Ancestry.com.

36.   ix.   Rexford Archibald Turner was born on 30 Oct 1887 in Ceres, New York[314] and died on 06 Dec 1966[315].

---

[310] Ancestry.com, U.S., Find A Grave Index, 1700s-Current Record for Sylvanus M Turner.

[311] Ancestry.com, U.S., Find A Grave Index, 1700s-Current Record for Sylvanus M Turner.

[312] Ancestry.com, U.S., Find A Grave Index, 1700s-Current Record for Philip Arthur Hodges.

[313] Ancestry.com, U.S., Find A Grave Index, 1700s-Current Record for Philip Arthur Hodges.

[314] Ancestry.com, Pennsylvania, Death Certificates, 1906-1963 (Provo, UT, USA, Ancestry.com Operations, Inc., 2014), Ancestry.com, http://www. Museum Commission; Pennsylvania, USA; Pennsylvania (State). Death certificates, 1906-1966; Box Number: 2503; Certificate Number Range: 119701-122550. Record for Rexford A Turner.

[314] Ancestry.com, Pennsylvania, Death Certificates, 1906-1963 (Provo, UT, USA, Ancestry.com Operations, Inc., 2014), Ancestry.com, http://www. Museum Commission; Pennsylvania, USA; Pennsylvania (State). Death certificates, 1906-1966; Box Number: 2503; Certificate Number Range: 119701-122550. Record for Rexford A Turner.

[314] Ancestry.com, U.S., Find A Grave Index, 1700s-Current Record for Sylvanus M Turner..

[314] Ancestry.com, U.S., Find A Grave Index, 1700s-Current Record for Sylvanus M Turner.

[314] Ancestry.com, Pennsylvania Death Certificate for Fannie Louis Morrison.

[314] Ancestry.com, Pennsylvania Death Certificate for Fannie Louis Morrison.Ancestry.com, Pennsylvania Historic and Museum Commission; Pennsylvania, USA; Pennsylvania (State). Death certificates, 1906-1966; Box Number: 2503; Certificate Number Range: 119701-122550. Record for Rexford A Turner.

[315] Ancestry.com, U.S., Find A Grave Index, 1700s-Current (Provo, UT, USA, Ancestry.com Operations, Inc., 2012), Ancestry.com, http://www.Ancestry.com, Record for Sylvanus M Turner.

x.   Infant Turner was born on 04 Dec 1889[316] and died on 04 Dec 1889[317].

25. Ida May Turner[9] (Erastus G. Turner[8], Paul Turner[7], Paul Turner[6], Benjamin Turner Sr.[5], Benjamin Turner Sr.[4], John Turner[3], John Turner[2], Humphrey Turner[1]) was born in 1860 in Of Corydon Twp, Pennsylvania[318]. She married Martin Luther Haven[319]. He was born on 24 Sep 1845 in Bradford, Pennsylvania[320] and died on 21 Jan 1933 in Bradford, Pennsylvania[321].

Martin Luther Haven and Ida May Turner had the following children:
37.   i.   Goodrich Erastus Haven was born on 21 Aug 1885 in Custer City, Pennsylvania[322] and died on 03 Nov 1962 in Bradford, Pennsylvania[323].
       ii.   Benjamin C. Haven was born on 22 Dec 1888[324] and died on 24 Jan 1922 in Bradford, Pennsylvania[325].

26. Emily Jane Palmer[9] (Nancy S. Turner[8], Paul Turner[7], Paul Turner[6], Benjamin Turner Sr.[5], Benjamin Turner Sr.[4], John Turner[3], John Turner[2], Humphrey Turner[1]) was born on 09 Apr 1862 in Marshburg, Pennsylvania[326] and died on 28 Mar 1940 in Hamlin, Pennsylvania[327]. She married Russell Harvey Nogar on 30 Dec 1895 in Smethport, Pennsylvania[328]. He was born on 03 May 1863 in New York[329] and died on 08 Feb 1947 in Kane, Pennsylvania[330].

Russell Harvey Nogar and Emily Jane Palmer had the following children:
38.   i.   Marion Elizabeth Nogar was born on 07 Feb 1899 in Hazel Hurst, Pennsylvania[331] and died on 28 Mar 1940 in Kasson, Pennsylvania[332].
       ii.   Marguerite Christian Nogar was born in 1902.

---

[316] Ancestry.com, U.S., Find A Grave Index, 1700s-Current Record for Sylvanus M Turner.

[317] Ancestry.com, U.S., Find A Grave Index, 1700s-Current Record for Sylvanus M Turner.

[318] Ancestry.com, 1870 United States Federal Census (Provo, UT, USA, Ancestry.com Operations, Inc., 2009), Ancestry.com, http://www.Ancestry.com, Year: 1870; Census Place: Corydon, McKean, Pennsylvania; Roll: M593_1372; Page: 674A; Family History Library Film: 552871. Record for Ida Mary Turner.

[319] Ancestry.com, Pennsylvania Death Certificate for Ida May Haven.

[320] Ancestry.com, Pennsylvania Death Certificate for Ida May Haven.

[321] Ancestry.com, Pennsylvania Death Certificate for Ida May Haven.

[322] Ancestry.com, Pennsylvania Death Certificate for Goodrich Erastus Haven.

[323] Ancestry.com, Pennsylvania Death Certificate for Goodrich Erastus Haven.

[324] Ancestry.com, Pennsylvania Death Certificate for Benjamin C. Haven.

[325] Ancestry.com, Pennsylvania Death Certificate for Benjamin C. Haven.

[326] Ancestry.com, Pennsylvania Death Certificate for Emily Jane Nogar.

[327] Ancestry.com, Pennsylvania Death Certificate for Emily Jane Nogar.

[328] Ancestry.com, Pennsylvania, Marriages, 1852-1968 (Lehi, UT, USA, Ancestry.com Operations, Inc., 2016), Ancestry.com, http://www.Ancestry.com, Record for Emma Palmer.

[329] Ancestry.com, Pennsylvania, Marriages, 1852-1968 (Lehi, UT, USA, Ancestry.com Operations, Inc., 2016), Ancestry.com, http://www.Ancestry.com, Record for Emma Palmer.

[330] Ancestry.com, Pennsylvania, Marriages, 1852-1968, Record for Emma Palmer.

[331] Ancestry.com, U.S., Find A Grave Index, 1700s-Current, Record for Russell Shirley Swanson.

[332] Ancestry.com, U.S., Find A Grave Index, 1700s-Current, Record for Russell Shirley Swanson

27.   Fannie Louis Palmer[9] (Nancy S. Turner[8], Paul Turner[7], Paul Turner[6], Benjamin Turner Sr.[5], Benjamin Turner Sr.[4], John Turner[3], John Turner[2], Humphrey Turner[1]) was born on 04 Jul 1863 in Marshburg, Pennsylvania[333] and died on 30 Dec 1945 in Kane, Pennsylvania[334]. She married Thomas Delbert Morrison, the son of Abraham and Amararitha Morrison, in 1885[335].   He was born on 25 Dec 1859 in Franklin, Pennsylvania[336] and died on 01 Apr 1941 in Kane, Pennsylvania[337].

Thomas Delbert Morrison and Fannie Louis Palmer had the following children:
       i.   Maude Ethel Morrison was born on 12 Oct 1886 in Marshburg, Pennsylvania[338] and was still alive in the 1940 census.
       ii.   Leon Leroy Morrison was born on 27 Dec 1887[339] and died on 09 May 1956 in Cisco, Texas[340]. He married Roxie J. Teafateller, the daughter of C. C. and Etta N. Teafateller, on 25 Aug 1949 in Texas[341]. She was born in 1930[342].
       iii.   Thomas Adrian Morrison was born on 20 Jun 1890 in Kane, Pennsylvania[343] and died in Jan 1972 in Kane, Pennsylvania[344].
       iv.   Lloyd James Morrison was born on 28 Oct 1892 in Kane, Pennsylvania[345] and died in Jan 1980[346]. He married a girl by the name of Eliza.
       v.   Edith Eva Morrison was born on 19 Jan 1896[347] and died in Apr 1977 in Kane, Pennsylvania[348].
       vi.   Helen Louie Morrison was born on 07 Mar 1907 in Kane, Pennsylvania[349].

---

[333] Ancestry.com, Pennsylvania Death Certificate for Fannie Louis Morrison.

[334] Ancestry.com, Pennsylvania Death Certificate for Fannie Louis Morrison.

[335] Ancestry.com, 1900 United States Federal Census; Census Place: Wetmore, McKean, Pennsylvania; Page: 15; Enumeration District: 0125. Record for Fannie S Morrison.

[336] Ancestry.com, Pennsylvania Death Certificate for Thomas Delbert Morrison.

[337] Ancestry.com, Pennsylvania Death Certificate for Thomas Delbert Morrison.

[338] Ancestry.com. *U.S., Social Security Applications and Claims Index, 1936-2007*. Provo, UT, USA: Ancestry.com Operations, Inc., 2015.

[339] Ancestry.com, Texas, Death Certificates, 1903-1982 (Provo, UT, USA, Ancestry.com Operations, Inc., 2013), , Texas Department of State Health Services; Austin Texas, USA. Record for Leon Leroy Morrison.

[340] Ancestry.com, Texas, Death Certificates, 1903-1982 (Provo, UT, USA, Ancestry.com Operations, Inc., 2013), , Texas Department of State Health Services; Austin Texas, USA. Record for Leon Leroy Morrison.

[341] Ancestry.com, Texas, Select County Marriage Records, 1837, Grayson County Clerk's Office; Sherman, Texas; Grayson County Marriage Records. Record for L E E Morrison.

[342] Ancestry.com, Texas, Death Certificates, 1903-1982 (Provo, UT, USA, Ancestry.com Operations, Inc., 2013), , Texas Department of State Health Services; Austin Texas, USA. Record for Leon Leroy Morrison.

[343] Ancestry.com, U.S. World War II Draft Registration Cards, Record for Thomas Adrian Morrison.

[344] Ancestry.com, Social Security Death Index Issue State: Pennsylvania; Issue Date: Before 1951. Record for Thomas Morrison.

[345] Ancestry.com, U.S. World War II Draft Registration Cards, 1942 for the State of Pennsylvania; Record Group Title: Records of the Selective Service System, 1926-1975; Record Group Number: 147; Series Number: M1951.

[346] Ancestry.com, U.S., Find A Grave Index, 1700s-Current, Record for Lloyd Morrison.

[347] Ancestry.com, U.S., Find A Grave Index, 1700s-Current, Record for Eva Morrison.

[348] Ancestry.com, U.S., Find A Grave Index, 1700s-Current, Record for Eva Morrison.

[349] Ancestry.com, Pennsylvania, Birth Certificates, 1906-1910 (Lehi, UT, USA, Ancestry.com Operations, Inc., 2015), Ancestry.com, http://www.Ancestry.com, Pennsylvania Historical and Museum Commission; Harrisburg, Pennsylvania; Box Number: 74; Certificate Number: 26663. Record for Helen Louie Morrison.

Generation Ten

28.   Albert Lewis Turner[10] (Theodore A. Turner[9], Paul Turner[8], Paul Turner[7], Paul Turner[6], Benjamin Turner Sr.[5], Benjamin Turner Sr.[4], John Turner[3], John Turner[2], Humphrey Turner[1]) was born in 1864[350] and died in 1936[351]. He married Nellie Paige[352]. She was born in 1864[353] and died in 1938[354].

Albert Lewis Turner and Nellie E Paige had the following children:
39.   i.   Henry W. Turner was born on 23 May 1901 in Binghamton, New York[355], and died on 03 Oct 1974 in Pinellas, Florida[356]
40.   ii.   Ellen May Turner was born on 12 Dec 1905 in Johnson City, New York[357] and died on 15 Sep 1991 in Binghamton, New York[358].

29.   Ella Harris[10] (Ruth Turner[9], Erastus G. Turner[8], Paul Turner[7], Paul Turner[6], Benjamin Turner Sr.[5], Benjamin Turner Sr.[4], John Turner[3], John Turner[2], Humphrey Turner[1]) was born on 23 Dec 1853 in Pennsylvania[359] and died on 21 May 1937 in Kurzua, Pennsylvania[360]. She married William Oscar Jennings Morrison, the son of Ezra

---

[350] Ancestry.com, U.S., Find A Grave Index, 1700s-Current (Provo, UT, USA, Ancestry.com Operations, Inc., 2012), Ancestry.com, http://www.Ancestry.com, Record for Albert Lewis Turner.

[351] Ancestry.com, U.S., Find A Grave Index, 1700s-Current (Provo, UT, USA, Ancestry.com Operations, Inc., 2012), Ancestry.com, http://www.Ancestry.com, Record for Albert Lewis Turner.

[352] Ancestry.com, U.S., Find A Grave Index, 1700s-Current (Provo, UT, USA, Ancestry.com Operations, Inc., 2012), Ancestry.com, http://www.Ancestry.com, Record for Albert Lewis Turner.

[353] Ancestry.com, U.S., Find A Grave Index, 1700s-Current (Provo, UT, USA, Ancestry.com Operations, Inc., 2012), Ancestry.com, http://www.Ancestry.com, Record for Albert Lewis Turner.

[354] Ancestry.com, U.S., Find A Grave Index, 1700s-Current (Provo, UT, USA, Ancestry.com Operations, Inc., 2012), Ancestry.com, http://www.Ancestry.com, Record for Albert Lewis Turner.

[355] Ancestry.com, Social Security Death Index (Provo, UT, USA, The Generations Network, Inc., 2008), www.ancestry.com, Number: 077-10-8037; Issue State: New York; Issue Date: Before 1951. Record for Henry Turner.

[356] Ancestry.com, Florida Death Index, 1877-1998 (Provo, UT, USA, The Generations Network, Inc., 2004), www.ancestry.com, Record for Henry W Turner.

[357] Ancestry.com, U.S., Find A Grave Index, 1700s-Current (Provo, UT, USA, Ancestry.com Operations, Inc., 2012), Ancestry.com, http://www.Ancestry.com, Record for Albert Lewis Turner

[358] Ancestry.com, U.S., Find A Grave Index, 1700s-Current (Provo, UT, USA, Ancestry.com Operations, Inc., 2012), Ancestry.com, http://www.Ancestry.com, Record for Albert Lewis Turner

[359] Ancestry.com, Pennsylvania, Death Certificates, 1906-1963 (Provo, UT, USA, Ancestry.com Operations, Inc., 2014), Ancestry.com, http://www.Ancestry.com, Pennsylvania Historic and Museum Commission; Pennsylvania, USA; Pennsylvania (State). Death certificates, 1906-1966; Certificate Number Range: 053001-056000. Record for Ella J Merrison.

[360] Ancestry.com, Pennsylvania, Death Certificates, 1906-1963 (Provo, UT, USA, Ancestry.com Operations, Inc., 2014), Ancestry.com, http://www.Ancestry.com, Pennsylvania Historic and Museum Commission; Pennsylvania, USA; Pennsylvania (State). Death certificates, 1906-1966; Certificate Number Range: 053001-056000. Record for Ella J Merrison.

and Janet Morrison, in 1884[361]. He was born in Oct 1854 in Pennsylvania[362] and died on 27 May 1904[363]. She later married G. Elmer Croft, the son of John R. Croft and Sarah A. Sykes, on 31 Oct 1908 in Chautauqua, New York[364]. He was born on 25 Dec 1870 in Fulton County, Pennsylvania[365]and died on 02 Nov 1943 in Huntingdon, Pennsylvania[366].

William Oscar Jennings Morrison and Ella Harris had the following children:
<ul>
<li>i.   Carrie Morrison</li>
<li>ii.   Ella Morrison</li>
</ul>

Photo of William Oscar Jennings Morrison found on Ancestry.com.

30. Carrie Muir Harris[10] (Ruth Turner[9], Erastus G. Turner[8], Paul Turner[7], Paul Turner[6], Benjamin Turner Sr.[5], Benjamin Turner Sr.[4], John Turner[3], John Turner[2], Humphrey Turner[1]) was born on 03 Sep 1872 in Kinzua, Pennsylvania[367] and died on 10 Jan 1953 in North Warren, Pennsylvania[368]. She married John A. Clicquennoi in 1891[369]. He was born on

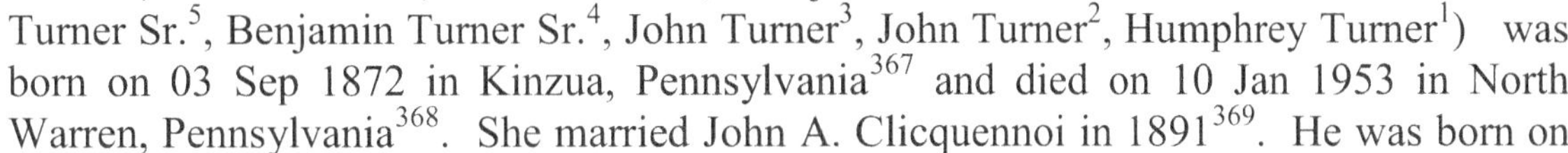

[361] Ancestry.com, 1900 United States Federal Census (Provo, UT, USA, Ancestry.com Operations Inc, 2004), Ancestry.com, http://www.Ancestry.com, Year: 1900; Census Place: Kinzua, Warren, Pennsylvania; Page: 4; Enumeration District: 0140. Record for Ella J Morrison.

[362] Ancestry.com, U.S., Find A Grave Index, 1700s-Current (Provo, UT, USA, Ancestry.com Operations, Inc., 2012), Ancestry.com, http://www.Ancestry.com, Record for Oscar Jennings Morrison.

[363] Ancestry.com, U.S., Find A Grave Index, 1700s-Current (Provo, UT, USA, Ancestry.com Operations, Inc., 2012), Ancestry.com, http://www.Ancestry.com, Record for Oscar Jennings Morrison.

[364] Ancestry.com, New York, County Marriages, 1847-1849; 1907-1936 (Lehi, UT, USA, Ancestry.com Operations, Inc., 2016), Ancestry.com, http://www.Ancestry.com, Record for G Elmer Croft.

[365] Ancestry.com, Pennsylvania, Death Certificates, 1906-1963 (Provo, UT, USA, Ancestry.com Operations, Inc., 2014), Ancestry.com, http://www.Ancestry.com, Pennsylvania Historic and Museum Commission; Pennsylvania, USA; Pennsylvania (State). Death certificates, 1906-1966; Certificate Number Range: 096651-099350. Record for George E Croft.

[366] Ancestry.com, Pennsylvania, Death Certificates, 1906-1963 (Provo, UT, USA, Ancestry.com Operations, Inc., 2014), Ancestry.com, http://www.Ancestry.com, Pennsylvania Historic and Museum Commission; Pennsylvania, USA; Pennsylvania (State). Death certificates, 1906-1966; Certificate Number Range: 096651-099350. Record for George E Croft.

[367] Ancestry.com, U.S., Find A Grave Index, 1700s-Current (Provo, UT, USA, Ancestry.com Operations, Inc., 2012), Ancestry.com, http://www.Ancestry.com, Record for Ruth Harris.

[368] Ancestry.com, U.S., Find A Grave Index, 1700s-Current (Provo, UT, USA, Ancestry.com Operations, Inc., 2012), Ancestry.com, http://www.Ancestry.com, Record for Ruth Harris.

[369] Ancestry.com. *U.S., Find A Grave Index, 1600s-Current* [database on-line]. Provo, UT, USA: Ancestry.com Operations, Inc., 2012. Record for John A. Clicquennoi.

02 Sep 1862 in the United States of America[370] and died on 16 Jan 1939 in Warren County, Pennsylvania[371].

John A. Clicquennoi and Carrie Muir Harris had the following children:
     i.   Floyd H. Clicquennoi was born on 22 Jun 1894[372] and died 30 Apr 1950[373]. Floyd married Janette Wiley on 16 Apr 1927 in Chautauqua, New York[374]. She was born in New York in 1902[375].
     ii.   Ruth Clicquennoi was born in Feb 1898 in Pennsylvania[376] and died in 1983[377].

31. Grace K. Turner[10] (Sylvanus M. Turner[9], Erastus G. Turner[8], Paul Turner[7], Paul Turner[6], Benjamin Turner Sr.[5], Benjamin Turner Sr.[4], John Turner[3], John Turner[2], Humphrey Turner[1]) was born on 11 Sep 1876[378] and died on 17 Sep 1943[379]. She married Erwin E. Maxson. He was born on 05 Dec 1869 in McKean County, Pennsylvania[380] and died on 05 May 1930[381].

Erwin E Maxson and Grace K Turner had the following children:
41.   i.   Winona Maxson was born on 02 Mar 1895 in Bullis Mills, Pennsylvania[382] and died on 09 Jan 1915 in Bullis Mills, Pennsylvania[383].
42.   ii.   Hazel E. Maxson was born on 03 Aug 1896[384] and died on 19 Mar 1956[385].

---

[370] Ancestry.com. *U.S., Find A Grave Index, 1600s-Current* [database on-line]. Provo, UT, USA: Ancestry.com Operations, Inc., 2012. Record for John A. Clicquennoi.

[371] Ancestry.com. *U.S., Find A Grave Index, 1600s-Current* [database on-line]. Provo, UT, USA: Ancestry.com Operations, Inc., 2012. Record for John A. Clicquennoi.

[372] U.S., Headstone Applications for Military Veterans, 1925-1963.

[373] U.S., Headstone Applications for Military Veterans, 1925-1963.

[374] Ancestry.com, New York County Marriages.

[375] Ancestry.com, New York County Marriages.

[376] US. Findagrave at Ancestry.com.

[377] US. Findagrave at Ancestry.com.

[378] Ancestry.com, U.S., Find A Grave Index, 1700s-Current, Record for Erwin Maxson.

[379] Ancestry.com, U.S., Find A Grave Index, 1700s-Current, Record for Erwin Maxson.

[380] Ancestry.com, U.S., Find A Grave Index, 1700s-Current, Record for Erwin Maxson.

[381] Ancestry.com, U.S., Find A Grave Index, 1700s-Current, Record for Erwin Maxson.

[382] Ancestry.com, Pennsylvania, Death Certificates, 1906-1963 (Provo, UT, USA, Ancestry.com Operations, Inc., 2014), Ancestry.com, http://www.Ancestry.com, Pennsylvania Historic and Museum Commission; Pennsylvania, USA; Pennsylvania (State). Death certificates, 1906-1966; Certificate Number Range: 111661-114850. Record for Winona Mildred Stillman.

[383] Ancestry.com, Pennsylvania, Death Certificates, 1906-1963 (Provo, UT, USA, Ancestry.com Operations, Inc., 2014), Ancestry.com, http://www.Ancestry.com, Pennsylvania Historic and Museum Commission; Pennsylvania, USA; Pennsylvania (State). Death certificates, 1906-1966; Certificate Number Range: 111661-114850. Record for Winona Mildred Stillman.

[384] Ancestry.com, U.S., Find A Grave Index, 1700s-Current (Provo, UT, USA, Ancestry.com Operations, Inc., 2012), Ancestry.com, http://www.Ancestry.com, Record for Albert G. Olson.

[385] Ancestry.com, U.S., Find A Grave Index, 1700s-Current (Provo, UT, USA, Ancestry.com Operations, Inc., 2012), Ancestry.com, http://www.Ancestry.com, Record for Albert G. Olson.

iii.   Eva G. Maxson was born in Jun 1898 in Cattaraugus County, New York[386] and died on 13 Dec 1905 in Bullis Mills, Pennsylvania[387].

43.   iv.   Irene Gladys Maxson was born on 26 Jun 1901[388] and died on 15 Sep 1954 in Ithaca, New York[389].

v.   Elmer S. Maxson was born on 13 Jun 1904[390] and died on 14 Apr 1926 in Bolivar, New York[391].

vi.   Ernestine Ruby Maxson was born on 24 Aug 1909 in Pennsylvania[392] and died on 24 Jan 1923[393].

44.   vii.   Ernest Woodrow Maxson was born on 19 Nov 1912 in Shinglehouse, Pennsylvania[394] and died on 20 Oct 1991[395].

45.   viii.   Welcome Rexford Maxson was born on 30 Oct 1916 in Eldred McKea, Pennsylvania[396] and died on 27 May 1990[397].

32. Lucy Eveline Turner[10] (Sylvanus M. Turner[9], Erastus G. Turner[8], Paul Turner[7], Paul Turner[6], Benjamin Turner Sr.[5], Benjamin Turner Sr.[4], John Turner[3], John Turner[2], Humphrey Turner[1]) was born on 19 Aug 1878 in Eldred, Pennsylvania[398] and died on 06

[386] Ancestry.com, U.S., Find A Grave Index, 1700s-Current (Provo, UT, USA, Ancestry.com Operations, Inc., 2012), Ancestry.com, http://www.Ancestry.com, Record for Eva G. Maxson.

[387] Ancestry.com, U.S., Find A Grave Index, 1700s-Current (Provo, UT, USA, Ancestry.com Operations, Inc., 2012), Ancestry.com, http://www.Ancestry.com, Record for Eva G. Maxson.

[388] Ancestry.com, U.S., Find A Grave Index, 1700s-Current (Provo, UT, USA, Ancestry.com Operations, Inc., 2012), Ancestry.com, http://www.Ancestry.com, Record for Irene Appleby.

[389] Ancestry.com, U.S., Find A Grave Index, 1700s-Current (Provo, UT, USA, Ancestry.com Operations, Inc., 2012), Ancestry.com, http://www.Ancestry.com, Record for Irene Appleby.

[390] Ancestry.com, U.S., Find A Grave Index, 1700s-Current (Provo, UT, USA, Ancestry.com Operations, Inc., 2012), Ancestry.com, http://www.Ancestry.com, Record for Elmer S. Maxson.

[391] Ancestry.com, U.S., Find A Grave Index, 1700s-Current (Provo, UT, USA, Ancestry.com Operations, Inc., 2012), Ancestry.com, http://www.Ancestry.com, Record for Elmer S. Maxson.

[392] Ancestry.com, U.S., Find A Grave Index, 1700s-Current (Provo, UT, USA, Ancestry.com Operations, Inc., 2012), Ancestry.com, http://www.Ancestry.com, Record for Ernestine Ruby Maxson.

[393] Ancestry.com, U.S., Find A Grave Index, 1700s-Current (Provo, UT, USA, Ancestry.com Operations, Inc., 2012), Ancestry.com, http://www.Ancestry.com, Record for Ernestine Ruby Maxson.

[394] Ancestry.com, U.S., Find A Grave Index, 1700s-Current (Provo, UT, USA, Ancestry.com Operations, Inc., 2012), Ancestry.com, http://www.Ancestry.com, Record for Ernest Woodrow Maxson.

[395] Ancestry.com, U.S., Find A Grave Index, 1700s-Current (Provo, UT, USA, Ancestry.com Operations, Inc., 2012), Ancestry.com, http://www.Ancestry.com, Record for Ernest Woodrow Maxson.

[396] Ancestry.com, U.S., Find A Grave Index, 1700s-Current (Provo, UT, USA, Ancestry.com Operations, Inc., 2012), Ancestry.com, http://www.Ancestry.com, Record for Welcome Rexford Maxson.

[397] Ancestry.com, U.S., Find A Grave Index, 1700s-Current (Provo, UT, USA, Ancestry.com Operations, Inc., 2012), Ancestry.com, http://www.Ancestry.com, Record for Welcome Rexford Maxson.

[398] Ancestry.com, U.S., Find A Grave Index, 1700s-Current (Provo, UT, USA, Ancestry.com Operations, Inc., 2012), Ancestry.com, http://www.Ancestry.com, Record for Sylvanus M Turner.

Sep 1974 in Hornell, New York[399]. She married Harley B. McDowell[400]. He was born on 08 Feb 1878[401] and died on 29 Aug 1959[402].

Harley B. McDowell and Lucy Eveline Turner had the following children:

46.   i.   Azelda Iona McDowell was born in 1905 in Pennsylvania[403] and died in 1969[404].

       ii.   Orla McDowell was born in 1911 in Pennsylvania[405].

47.   iii.   Henriette McDowell was born on 14 Aug 1912 in Shinglehouse, Pennsylvania[406] and died on 03 Nov 1975 in Hornell, New York[407].

33.   Wellman Ellery Turner[10] (Sylvanus M. Turner[9], Erastus G. Turner[8], Paul Turner[7], Paul Turner[6], Benjamin Turner Sr.[5], Benjamin Turner Sr.[4], John Turner[3], John Turner[2], Humphrey Turner[1]) was born on 20 Sep 1881 in Eldred, Pennsylvania[408] and died on 07 Mar 1953 in Ceres, New York[409]. He married Clara Sutton[410].   She was born on 19 Oct 1883[411] and died on 09 Mar 1948[412].

---

[399] Ancestry.com, U.S., Find A Grave Index, 1700s-Current (Provo, UT, USA, Ancestry.com Operations, Inc., 2012), Ancestry.com, http://www.Ancestry.com, Record for Sylvanus M Turner.

[400] Ancestry.com, U.S., Find A Grave Index, 1700s-Current (Provo, UT, USA, Ancestry.com Operations, Inc., 2012), Ancestry.com, http://www.Ancestry.com, Record for Harley B. McDowell.

[401] Ancestry.com, U.S., Find A Grave Index, 1700s-Current (Provo, UT, USA, Ancestry.com Operations, Inc., 2012), Ancestry.com, http://www.Ancestry.com, Record for Harley B. McDowell.

[402] Ancestry.com, U.S., Find A Grave Index, 1700s-Current (Provo, UT, USA, Ancestry.com Operations, Inc., 2012), Ancestry.com, http://www.Ancestry.com, Record for Harley B. McDowell.

[403] Ancestry.com, U.S., Find A Grave Index, 1700s-Current (Provo, UT, USA, Ancestry.com Operations, Inc., 2012), Ancestry.com, http://www.Ancestry.com, Record for Azelta Baldwin.

[404] Ancestry.com, U.S., Find A Grave Index, 1700s-Current (Provo, UT, USA, Ancestry.com Operations, Inc., 2012), Ancestry.com, http://www.Ancestry.com, Record for Azelta Baldwin.

[405] Ancestry.com, 1920 United States Federal Census (Provo, UT, USA, The Generations Network, Inc., 2005), www.ancestry.com, Year: 1920; Census Place: Shinglehouse, Potter, Pennsylvania; Roll: T625_1648; Page: 3A; Enumeration District: 130. Record for Orla Mcdowell.

[406] Ancestry.com, U.S., Find A Grave Index, 1700s-Current (Provo, UT, USA, Ancestry.com Operations, Inc., 2012), Ancestry.com, http://www.Ancestry.com, Record for Henrietta Lee.

[407] Ancestry.com, U.S., Find A Grave Index, 1700s-Current (Provo, UT, USA, Ancestry.com Operations, Inc., 2012), Ancestry.com, http://www.Ancestry.com, Record for Henrietta Lee.

[408] Ancestry.com, Pennsylvania, Death Certificates, 1906-1963 (Provo, UT, USA, Ancestry.com Operations, Inc., 2014), Ancestry.com, http://www.Ancestry.com, Pennsylvania Historic and Museum Commission; Pennsylvania, USA; Pennsylvania (State). Death certificates, 1906-1966; Certificate Number Range: 023851-026550. Record for Wellman Turner.

[409] Ancestry.com, Pennsylvania, Death Certificates, 1906-1963 (Provo, UT, USA, Ancestry.com Operations, Inc., 2014), Ancestry.com, http://www.Ancestry.com, Pennsylvania Historic and Museum Commission; Pennsylvania, USA; Pennsylvania (State). Death certificates, 1906-1966; Certificate Number Range: 023851-026550. Record for Wellman Turner.

[410] Ancestry.com, U.S., Find A Grave Index, 1700s-Current (Provo, UT, USA, Ancestry.com Operations, Inc., 2012), Ancestry.com, http://www.Ancestry.com, Record for Wellman Elroy or Ellery Turner.

[411] Ancestry.com, U.S., Find A Grave Index, 1700s-Current (Provo, UT, USA, Ancestry.com Operations, Inc., 2012), Ancestry.com, http://www.Ancestry.com, Record for Wellman Elroy or Ellery Turner.

[412] Ancestry.com, U.S., Find A Grave Index, 1700s-Current (Provo, UT, USA, Ancestry.com Operations, Inc., 2012), Ancestry.com, http://www.Ancestry.com, Record for Wellman Elroy or Ellery Turner.

Wellman Passed away at the home of his niece and nephew, Mr. and Mrs. Robert Howard in Ceres, NY., where he had lived for four months. He was the son of S.N. and Evelyn (Bennett) Turner. In 1899 he married Miss Clara Sutton who preceded him in death in 1948. Most of his adult life he had lived in West Valley, NY. At the time of his death he was survived by three sons, Herbert Turner of Cuba, NY., Dudley Turner of West Valley, NY and Raymond Turner of Collins, NY; two daughters, Mrs. Albert Ayers of Lower Bank NJ., and Mrs. Julia Reynolds of Perrysburg, NY: One brother, Rexford Turner of Ceres, NY; One sister, Mrs. Lucy McDowell of Wellsville, NY along with 12 grandchildren, 7 great-grandchildren and several nieces and nephews. The funeral was held at the Howard Funeral Home in Shinglehouse, PA on March 10, 1953.

Wellman Ellery Turner and Clara Sutton had the following children:

       i.   Herbert Turner was born on 29 Jun 1901[413] and died on 18 Mar 1988[414].

       ii.   Evelyn E. Turner was born in 1904[415] and died on 25 Sep 1908 in East Olean, New York[416].

48.   iii.   Dudly Otis Turner was born on 10 Sep 1905[417] and died in Jan 1984 in Little Valley, New York[418].

49.   iv.   Mary Christina Turner was born on 01 Jul 1907 in New York[419] and died on 24 Apr 1994[420].

50.   v.   Raymond Elwood Turner was born on 02 Aug 1915 in New York[421] and died on 05 Oct 2012[422].

       vi.   Julia Millicent Turner was born on 08 Mar 1918 in West Valley, New York[423] and died on 23 Dec 2001 in Dade City, Florida[424]. She married John E. Reynolds on 24 Dec 1940 in Olean, New York.

---

[413] Ancestry.com, U.S., Find A Grave Index, 1700s-Current -Record for Evelyn E. Turner.

[414] Ancestry.com, U.S., Find A Grave Index, 1700s-Current -Record for Herbert Turner.

[415] Ancestry.com, U.S., Find A Grave Index, 1700s-Current -Record for Herbert Turner.

[416] Ancestry.com, U.S., Find A Grave Index, 1700s-Current -Record for Evelyn E. Turner.

[417] Ancestry.com, Social Security Death Index (Provo, UT, USA, The Generations Network, Inc., 2008), www.ancestry.com, Number: 122-18-6958; Issue State: New York; Issue Date: Before 1951. Record for Dudley Turner.

[418] Ancestry.com, Social Security Death Index (Provo, UT, USA, The Generations Network, Inc., 2008), www.ancestry.com, Number: 122-18-6958; Issue State: New York; Issue Date: Before 1951. Record for Dudley Turner.

[419] Ancestry.com. *U.S., Social Security Applications and Claims Index, 1936-2007* [database on-line]. Provo, UT, USA: Ancestry.com Operations, Inc., 2015.

[420] Ancestry.com. *U.S., Social Security Applications and Claims Index, 1936-2007* [database on-line]. Provo, UT, USA: Ancestry.com Operations, Inc., 2015.

[421] Ancestry.com, U.S., Find A Grave Index, 1700s-Current (Provo, UT, USA, Ancestry.com Operations, Inc., 2012), Ancestry.com, http://www.Ancestry.com, Record for Raymond Elwood Turner.

[422] Ancestry.com, U.S., Find A Grave Index, 1700s-Current (Provo, UT, USA, Ancestry.com Operations, Inc., 2012), Ancestry.com, http://www.Ancestry.com, Record for Raymond Elwood Turner.

[423] Ancestry.com, Social Security Death Index, Record for Julia M. Reynolds.

[424] Ancestry.com, Social Security Death Index, Record for Julia M. Reynolds.

34. Truman Herbert Turner[10] (Sylvanus M. Turner[9], Erastus G. Turner[8], Paul Turner[7], Paul Turner[6], Benjamin Turner Sr.[5], Benjamin Turner Sr.[4], John Turner[3], John Turner[2], Humphrey Turner[1]) was born on 14 Oct 1882[425] and died in 1933[426]. He married Flora Alberta Terrette, the daughter of Frank Terrette and Hannah Sponceler, on 14 Oct 1914 in Allegany, New York[427]. She was born in 1895 in Myrtle, Pennsylvania[428] and died in 1986[429].

Truman Herbert Turner and Flora Alberta Terrette had the following children:

   i.   Carl V. Turner was born on 31 Aug 1915[430] and died on 09 Feb 2001[431].
   ii.   Ruth A. Turner was born on 05 May 1917[432] and died on 29 Dec 2010[433].

35.   Permilla A. Turner[10] (Sylvanus M. Turner[9], Erastus G. Turner[8], Paul Turner[7], Paul Turner[6], Benjamin Turner Sr.[5], Benjamin Turner Sr.[4], John Turner[3], John Turner[2], Humphrey Turner[1]) was born in Sep 1886 in Bullis Mills, Pennsylvania[434] and died on 12 Dec 1932 in Olean, New York[435]. She married Philip Arthur Hodges[436].   He was born in 1885 in Pennsylvania[437] and died on 03 Jun 1951 in Wellsville, New York[438].

Photo of Permilla A. Turner found on Ancestry.com.

[425] Ancestry.com, U.S., Find A Grave Index, 1700s-Current (Provo, UT, USA, Ancestry.com Operations, Inc., 2012), Ancestry.com, http://www.Ancestry.com, Record for Truman Herbert Turner.

[426] Ancestry.com, U.S., Find A Grave Index, 1700s-Current (Provo, UT, USA, Ancestry.com Operations, Inc., 2012), Ancestry.com, http://www.Ancestry.com, Record for Truman Herbert Turner.

[427] Ancestry.com, New York, County Marriages, 1847-1849; 1907-1936 (Lehi, UT, USA, Record for Truman Herbert Turner

[428] Ancestry.com, U.S., Find A Grave Index, 1700s-, Record for Truman Herbert Turner.

[429] Ancestry.com, U.S., Find A Grave Index, 1700s-, Record for Truman Herbert Turner..

[430] Ancestry.com, U.S., Find A Grave Index, 1700s-Current, Record for Carl V. Turner.

[431] Ancestry.com, U.S., Find A Grave Index, 1700s-Current, Record for Carl V. Turner.

[432] Ancestry.com, U.S., Find A Grave Index, 1700s-Current, Record for Ruth A. Turner.

[433] Ancestry.com, U.S., Find A Grave Index, 1700s-Current, Record for Ruth A. Turner..

[434] Ancestry.com, U.S., Find A Grave Index, 1700s-Current, Record for Philip Arthur Hodges.

[435] Ancestry.com, U.S., Find A Grave Index, 1700s-Current, Record for Philip Arthur Hodges.

[436] Ancestry.com, U.S., Find A Grave Index, 1700s-Current, Record for Philip Arthur Hodges.

[437] Ancestry.com, U.S., Find A Grave Index, 1700s-Current, Record for Philip Arthur Hodges.

[438] Ancestry.com, U.S., Find A Grave Index, 1700s-Current, Record for Philip Arthur Hodges.

Philip Arthur Hodges and Permilla A Turner had the following children:
51.   i.   Leah E. Hodges was born on 12 Aug 1905[439] and died on 06 Sep 1999 in Albany, New York[440].
       ii.   Harold Philip Hodges was born on 11 Jul 1910[441] and died on 09 Mar 1939[442].
       iii.   Winifred Hodges was born in Pennsylvania[443] and may still be living.
       iv.   Antoinette Hodges was born in Pennsylvania[444] and may still be living.

36.   Rexford Archibald Turner[10] (Sylvanus M. Turner[9], Erastus G. Turner[8], Paul Turner[7], Paul Turner[6], Benjamin Turner Sr.[5], Benjamin Turner Sr.[4], John Turner[3], John Turner[2], Humphrey Turner[1]) was born on 30 Oct 1887 in Ceres, New York[445] and died on 06 Dec 1966[446]. He married Margaret Christine O'Toole on 05 May 1906 in Portville, Cattaraugus, New York[447]. She was born on 27 Sep 1884 in Pennsylvania[448] and died in 1971[449].

Photo of Rexford Archibald Turner found on Ancestry.com.

Rexford Archibald Turner and Margaret Christine O'Toole had the following children:
       i.   Infant Turner was born on 07 Mar 1907[450] and died on 23 Mar 1907[451].
52.   ii.   Margaret Alice Turner was born on 17 Mar 1908 in Eldred, Pennsylvania[452] and died on 08 Nov 1995 in Coudersport, Pennsylvania[453].

[439] Ancestry.com, U.S., Find A Grave Index, 1700s-Current, Record for Leah E. Gleason.

[440] Ancestry.com, U.S., Find A Grave Index, 1700s-Current, Record for Leah E. Gleason.

[441] Ancestry.com, U.S., Find A Grave Index, 1700s-Current, Record for Philip Arthur Hodges.

[442] Ancestry.com, U.S., Find A Grave Index, 1700s-Current, Record for Philip Arthur Hodges.

[443] Ancestry.com, 1930 United States Federal Census (Provo, UT, USA, The Generations Network, Inc., 2002), www.ancestry.com, Year: 1930; Census Place: Olean, Cattaraugus, New York; Page: 8B; Enumeration District: 0039. Record for Philip A Hodges.

[444] Ancestry.com, 1930 United States Federal Census (Provo, UT, USA, The Generations Network, Inc., 2002), www.ancestry.com, Year: 1930; Census Place: Olean, Cattaraugus, New York; Page: 8B; Enumeration District: 0039. Record for Philip A Hodges.

[445] Ancestry.com, U.S., Find A Grave Index, 1700s-Current (Provo, UT, USA, Ancestry.com Operations, Inc., 2012), Ancestry.com, http://www.Ancestry.com, Record for Rexford Archibald Turner.

[446] Ancestry.com, U.S., Find A Grave Index, 1700s-Current (Provo, UT, USA, Ancestry.com Operations, Inc., 2012), Ancestry.com, http://www.Ancestry.com, Record for Rexford Archibald Turner.

[447] Ancestry.com, New York Marriage Index.

[448] Ancestry.com, U.S., Find A Grave Index, 1700s-Current, Record for Rexford Archibald Turner.

[449] Ancestry.com, U.S., Find A Grave Index, 1700s-Current, Record for Rexford Archibald Turner..

[450] Ancestry.com, U.S., Find A Grave Index, 1700s-Current, Record for Rexford Archibald Turner.

[451] Ancestry.com, U.S., Find A Grave Index, 1700s-Current, Record for Rexford Archibald Turner.

[452] Ancestry.com, U.S., Find A Grave Index, 1700s-Current (Provo, UT, USA, Ancestry.com Operations, Inc., 2012), Ancestry.com, http://www.Ancestry.com, Record for Margaret A Howard.

[453] Ancestry.com, U.S., Find A Grave Index, 1700s-Current (Provo, UT, USA, Ancestry.com Operations, Inc., 2012), Ancestry.com, http://www.Ancestry.com, Record for Margaret A Howard.

53.   iii.   Lucy Elizabeth Turner was born on 20 Mar 1910 in Ceres, Pennsylvania[454] and died on 06 Jun 1986 in Pennsylvania[455].
54.   iv.   Erwin P. Turner was born on 23 Sep 1912[456] and died on 27 Dec 1997[457].
55.   v.   Lena Agnes Turner was born on 19 Sep 1914[458] and died in Aug 1981 in Ceres, New York[459].
56.   vi.   John Archibald Turner was born on 31 Aug 1916 in Ceres, New York[460] and died on 25 Jan 2000[461].

37. Goodrich Erastus Haven[10] (Ida May Turner[9], Erastus G. Turner[8], Paul Turner[7], Paul Turner[6], Benjamin Turner Sr.[5], Benjamin Turner Sr.[4], John Turner[3], John Turner[2], Humphrey Turner[1]) was born on 21 Aug 1885 in Custer City, Pennsylvania[462] and died on 03 Nov 1962 in Bradford, Pennsylvania[463]. He married Iza Bell Kessler, the daughter of Jerome Kessler and Lola Thornton[464]. She was born on 28 Dec 1887[465] and died on 08 Apr 1949[466].

Goodrich Erastus Haven and Iza Bell Kessler had the following children:
57.   i.   Jennie M. Haven was born on 20 Dec 1906[467] and died on 02 Apr 1969[468].
58.   ii.   Martin Goodrich Haven was born on 06 Mar 1908 in Custer City, Pennsylvania[469] and died on 14 Jun 1974 in Bradford, Pennsylvania[470].

---

[454] Ancestry.com, Pennsylvania, Birth Certificates, 1906-1910 (Lehi, UT, USA, Ancestry.com Operations, Inc., 2015), Ancestry.com, http://www.Ancestry.com, Pennsylvania Historical and Museum Commission; Harrisburg, Pennsylvania; Box Number: 312; Certificate Number: 50460. Record for Lucy Elizabeth Turner.

[455] Ancestry.com, Social Security Death Index (Provo, UT, USA, The Generations Network, Inc., 2008), www.ancestry.com, Number: 116-20-6890; Issue State: New York; Issue Date: Before 1951. Record for Lucy Howard

[456] Ancestry.com. *U.S., Find A Grave Index, 1600s-Current* [database on-line]. Provo, UT, USA: Ancestry.com Operations, Inc., 2012. Record for Erwin P. Turner.

[457] Ancestry.com. *U.S., Find A Grave Index, 1600s-Current* [database on-line]. Provo, UT, USA: Ancestry.com Operations, Inc., 2012. Record for Erwin P. Turner.

[458] Ancestry.com, Social Security Death Index (Provo, UT, USA, The Generations Network, Inc., 2008), www.ancestry.com, Number: 128-30-9807; Issue State: New York; Issue Date: 1955-1957. Record for Lena Spees.

[459] Ancestry.com, Social Security Death Index (Provo, UT, USA, The Generations Network, Inc., 2008), www.ancestry.com, Number: 128-30-9807; Issue State: New York; Issue Date: 1955-1957. Record for Lena Spees.

[460] Ancestry.com, U.S., Social Security Applications and Claims Index, 1936-2007 (Provo, UT, USA, Ancestry.com Operations, Inc., 2015), Ancestry.com, http://www.Ancestry.com, Record for John Archibald Turner.

[461] Ancestry.com, U.S., Social Security Applications and Claims Index, 1936-2007 (Provo, UT, USA, Ancestry.com Operations, Inc., 2015), Ancestry.com, http://www.Ancestry.com, Record for John Archibald Turner.

[462] Ancestry.com, Pennsylvania Death Certificate for Goodrich Erastus Haven.

[463] Ancestry.com, Pennsylvania Death Certificate for Goodrich Erastus Haven.

[464] Ancestry.com, Pennsylvania Death Certificate for Goodrich Erastus Haven.

[465] Pennsylvania Historic and Museum Commission; Pennsylvania, USA; Pennsylvania (State). Death certificates, 1906–1966; Certificate Number Range: 031801-034350. Record for Iza Keesler Buckley.

[466] Pennsylvania Historic and Museum Commission; Pennsylvania, USA; Pennsylvania (State). Death certificates, 1906–1966; Certificate Number Range: 031801-034350. Record for Iza Keesler Buckley.

[467] Ancestry.com. *U.S., Find A Grave Index, 1600s-Current,* Record for Jennie M. Kelly.

[468] Ancestry.com. *U.S., Find A Grave Index, 1600s-Current,* Record for Jennie M. Kelly.

[469] Ancestry.com, U.S. WWII Draft Cards Young Men, 1940-1947. Record for Martin Goodrich Haven.

[470] Ancestry.com. *U.S., Find A Grave Index, 1600s-Current* [database on-line]. Provo, UT, USA: Ancestry.com Operations, Inc., 2012. Record for Martin Goodrich Haven.

iii.   Jerome W. Haven was born on 10 Nov 1910 in Custer City, Pennsylvania[471] and died on 25 Apr 1920 in Bradford, Pennsylvania[472]. Jerome died from a fractured skull. He attempted to cross the track of the B.R. and P.R.R. in front of a moving freight train was struck by the pilot of the engine and was fatally hurt accidently.

iv.   Lillian Ida Haven was born on 07 Jul 1912 in Pennsylvania[473]. She married Franklin Julius Peterson[474]. He was born on 19 Feb 1911 in MT Jewett, Pennsylvania[475].

v.   Gretchen Haven was born on 15 Mar 1916[476] and died on 30 Mar 1916 in Bradford, Pennsylvania[477].

38. Marion Elizabeth Nogar[10] (Emily Jane Palmer[9], Nancy S. Turner[8], Paul Turner[7], Paul Turner[6], Benjamin Turner Sr.[5], Benjamin Turner Sr.[4], John Turner[3], John Turner[2], Humphrey Turner[1]) was born on 07 Feb 1899 in Hazel Hurst, Pennsylvania[478] and died on 28 Mar 1940 in Kasson, Pennsylvania[479]. She married Elmer Wilhelm Swanson, the son of John Swanson and Josephine Hokenton, on 19 Jan

Photo of Marion Elizabeth Nogar Swanson found on Ancestry.com.

[471] Ancestry.com, Pennsylvania, Death Certificates, 1906-1963 (Provo, UT, USA, Ancestry.com Operations, Inc., 2014).

[472] Ancestry.com, Pennsylvania, Death Certificates, 1906-1963 (Provo, UT, USA, Ancestry.com Operations, Inc., 2014).

[473] Ancestry.com, Public Member Trees (Provo, UT, USA, Ancestry.com Operations Inc, 2006), www.ancestry.com, Record for Goodrich Erastus Haven.

[474] Ancestry.com, 1930 United States Federal Census (Provo, UT, USA, Ancestry.com Operations Inc, 2002), Ancestry.com, http://www.Ancestry.com, Year: 1930; Census Place: Bradford, McKean, Pennsylvania; Page: 18B; Enumeration District: 0009. Record for Lillian Peterson.

[475] Ancestry.com, U.S., Evangelical Lutheran Church in America, Swedish American Church Records, 1800-1946 (Lehi, UT, USA, Ancestry.com Operations, Inc., 2017), Ancestry.com, http://www.Ancestry.com, Archives of the Evangelical Lutheran Church in America; Elk Grove Village, IL, USA; Parish: Zion Lutheran Church; ELCA Film Number: S679-681; SSIRC Film Number: S-680. Record for Franklin Julius Peterson.

[476] Ancestry.com, Pennsylvania Death Certificate for Gretchen Haven.

[477] Ancestry.com, Pennsylvania Death Certificate for Gretchen Haven.

[478] Ancestry.com, U.S., Find A Grave Index, 1700s-Current (Provo, UT, USA, Ancestry.com Operations, Inc., 2012), Ancestry.com, http://www.Ancestry.com, Record for Russell Shirley Swanson.

[479] Ancestry.com, U.S., Find A Grave Index, 1700s-Current (Provo, UT, USA, Ancestry.com Operations, Inc., 2012), Ancestry.com, http://www.Ancestry.com, Record for Russell Shirley Swanson.

1918 in Cattaraugus, New York[480]. He was born on 05 Mar 1895 in McKean County, Pennsylvania[481] and died on 13 Nov 1973 in Kane, McKean County, Pennsylvania[482]. Elmer Wilhelm Swanson and Marion Elizabeth Nogar had the following children:

i.   Russell Shirley Swanson was born in Feb 1921[483] and died on 11 May 2008 in McKean County, Pennsylvania[484]. He married a woman by the name of Marian C.[485] She was born on 09 Sep 1922[486] and died on 20 Nov 2013[487].

ii.   Ralph Elmer Swanson was born on 11 Nov 1927 in Hazel Hurst, Pennsylvania[488] and died on 12 Jan 1999 in Overgaard, Arizona[489].

iii. Dale Swanson was born in Pennsylvania and could still be alive.

[480] Ancestry.com, New York, County Marriages, 1847-1849; 1907-1936 (Lehi, UT, USA, Ancestry.com Operations, Inc., 2016), Ancestry.com, http://www.Ancestry.com, Record for Marion Nogar

[481] Ancestry.com, U.S., Find A Grave Index, 1700s-Current (Provo, UT, USA, Ancestry.com Operations, Inc., 2012), Ancestry.com, http://www.Ancestry.com, Record for Russell Shirley Swanson.

[482] Ancestry.com, U.S., Find A Grave Index, 1700s-Current (Provo, UT, USA, Ancestry.com Operations, Inc., 2012), Ancestry.com, http://www.Ancestry.com, Record for Russell Shirley Swanson.

[483] Ancestry.com, U.S., Find A Grave Index, 1700s-Current (Provo, UT, USA, Ancestry.com Operations, Inc., 2012), Ancestry.com, http://www.Ancestry.com, Record for Russell Shirley Swanson.

[484] Ancestry.com, U.S., Find A Grave Index, 1700s-Current (Provo, UT, USA, Ancestry.com Operations, Inc., 2012), Ancestry.com, http://www.Ancestry.com, Record for Russell Shirley Swanson.

[485] Ancestry.com, U.S., Find A Grave Index, 1700s-Current (Provo, UT, USA, Ancestry.com Operations, Inc., 2012), Ancestry.com, http://www.Ancestry.com, Record for Russell Shirley Swanson.

[486] Ancestry.com, U.S., Find A Grave Index, 1700s-Current (Provo, UT, USA, Ancestry.com Operations, Inc., 2012), Ancestry.com, http://www.Ancestry.com, Record for Russell Shirley Swanson.

[487] Ancestry.com, U.S., Find A Grave Index, 1700s-Current (Provo, UT, USA, Ancestry.com Operations, Inc., 2012), Ancestry.com, http://www.Ancestry.com, Record for Russell Shirley Swanson.

[488] Ancestry.com, U.S., Find A Grave Index, 1700s-Current (Provo, UT, USA, Ancestry.com Operations, Inc., 2012), Ancestry.com, http://www.Ancestry.com, Record for Elmer Wilhelm Swanson.

[489] Ancestry.com, U.S., Find A Grave Index, 1700s-Current (Provo, UT, USA, Ancestry.com Operations, Inc., 2012), Ancestry.com, http://www.Ancestry.com, Record for Elmer Wilhelm Swanson.

Generation Eleven

39. Henry W. Turner[11] (Albert Lewis Turner[10], Theodore A. Turner[9] ,Paul Turner[8], Paul Turner[7], Paul Turner[6], Benjamin Turner Sr.[5], Benjamin Turner Sr.[4], John Turner[3], John Turner[2], Humphrey Turner[1]) was born on 23 May 1901 in Binghamton, New York[490] and died on 03 Oct 1974 in Pinellas, Florida[491]. He married Mary Ethel Kreidler on 31 May 1902 in Moscow, Pennsylvania[492] and died on 25 Jul 1981 in Saint Petersburg, Florida[493].

Henry W Turner and Mary Ethel Kreidler had the following children:
i.   Henry A. Turner was born in New York State and may still be alive.
ii.   Richard Wallace Turner was born on 14 Mar 1924 in Johnson City, New York[494] and died on 04 Aug 2004[495]. He married Caroline Elizabeth Davis, the daughter of Norman Edward Davis and Myrtle Ella Sanders, on 08 Oct 1944 in New Hanover, North Carolina[496]. She was born on 07 Jul 1923 in Wilmington, North Carolina[497] and died on 07 Dec 2000[498].
iii.   Roger L. Turner was born in New York[499] and may still be living.

40. Ellen May Turner[11] (Albert Lewis Turner[10], Theodore A. Turner[9] ,Paul Turner[8], Paul Turner[7], Paul Turner[6], Benjamin Turner Sr.[5], Benjamin Turner Sr.[4], John Turner[3], John Turner[2], Humphrey Turner[1]) was born on 12 Dec 1905 in Johnson City, New York[500]

---

[490] Ancestry.com, Social Security Death Index (Provo, UT, USA, The Generations Network, Inc., 2008), www.ancestry.com, Number: 077-10-8037; Issue State: New York; Issue Date: Before 1951. Record for Henry Turner.

[491] Ancestry.com, Florida Death Index, 1877-1998 (Provo, UT, USA, The Generations Network, Inc., 2004), www.ancestry.com, Record for Henry W Turner.

[492] Ancestry.com, U.S., Find A Grave Index, 1700s-Current (Provo, UT, USA, Ancestry.com Operations, Inc., 2012), Ancestry.com, http://www.Ancestry.com, Record for Henry W. Turner.

[493] Ancestry.com, U.S., Find A Grave Index, 1700s-Current (Provo, UT, USA, Ancestry.com Operations, Inc., 2012), Ancestry.com, http://www.Ancestry.com, Record for Henry W. Turner.

[494] Ancestry.com, U.S., Social Security Applications and Claims Index, 1936-2007 (Provo, UT, USA, Ancestry.com Operations, Inc., 2015), Ancestry.com, http://www.Ancestry.com, Record for Richard Wallace Turner.

[495] Ancestry.com, U.S., Social Security Applications and Claims Index, 1936-2007 (Provo, UT, USA, Ancestry.com Operations, Inc., 2015), Ancestry.com, http://www.Ancestry.com, Record for Richard Wallace Turner.

[496] Ancestry.com, North Carolina, Marriage Records, 1741-2011 (Provo, UT, USA, Ancestry.com Operations, Inc., 2015), Ancestry.com, http://www.Ancestry.com, Record for Richard W Turner.

[497] Ancestry.com, North Carolina, Birth Indexes, 1800-2000 (Provo, UT, USA, Ancestry.com Operations Inc, 2005), Ancestry.com, http://www.Ancestry.com, Record for Caroline Elizabeth Davis.

[498] Ancestry.com, U.S., Social Security Applications and Claims Index, 1936-2007 (Provo, UT, USA, Ancestry.com Operations, Inc., 2015), Ancestry.com, http://www.Ancestry.com, Record for Caroline Elizabeth Davis.

[499] National Archives and Records Administration, U.S. World War II Army Enlistment Records, 1938-1946 (Provo, UT, USA, The Generations Network, Inc., 2005), www.ancestry.com, Record for Roger L Turner.

[500] Ancestry.com, U.S., Find A Grave Index, 1700s-Current (Provo, UT, USA, Ancestry.com Operations, Inc., 2012), Ancestry.com, http://www.Ancestry.com, Record for Albert Lewis Turner.

and died on 15 Sep 1991 in Binghamton, New York[501]. She married Carl Charles Senedaker, the son of Alinzer and Mertie Larena Snedaker, on 03 Jul 1930 in Broome, New York[502]. He was born on 04 Jun 1902 in Binghamton, New York[503] and died on 11 Mar 1971 in Johnson City, New York[504]. Carl Charles Senedaker and Ellen May Turner had two children who may still be living.

41. Winona Maxson[11] (Albert Lewis Turner[10], Theodore A. Turner[9], Paul Turner[8], Paul Turner[7], Paul Turner[6], Benjamin Turner Sr.[5], Benjamin Turner Sr.[4], John Turner[3], John Turner[2], Humphrey Turner[1]) was born on 02 Mar 1895 in Bullis Mills, Pennsylvania[505] and died on 09 Jan 1915 in Bullis Mills, Pennsylvania[506]. She married Donald E Stillman, the son of Oramel B Stillman and Pearl Wilson, on 28 Feb 1914 in Allegany, New York[507]. He was born on 31 Jul 1893[508].

from Findagrave member, Cherie Officer and the Portville (NY) Review, Thursday, January 14, 1915 Page One. Winona and her husband, Don Stillman lived in Shinglehouse, PA. She passed away at the home of her parents, Mr. and Mrs. E.E. Maxson three days after giving birth to a baby. She was born on McCrae Book, later the family moved to Main Settlement in the Town of Portville, NY then moved to Shinglehouse, PA and moved back to McCrae Brook in 1916 where they owned a farm. Winona married Donald Stillman on 28 February 1914 and they had resided in Shinglehouse, PA. Besides her Husband, Parents and baby she was survived by three sisters, two brothers (names not stated) and her grandparents, Mr. and Mrs. E.V. Turner and Mr. and Mrs. Maxson. The funeral was held at the M.E. Church in Portville on 11 January 1915 with burial at Chestnut Hill Cemetery.

---

[501] Ancestry.com, U.S., Find A Grave Index, 1700s-Current (Provo, UT, USA, Ancestry.com Operations, Inc., 2012), Ancestry.com, http://www.Ancestry.com, Record for Albert Lewis Turner

[502] Ancestry.com, New York, County Marriages, 1847-1849; 1907-1936 (Lehi, UT, USA, Ancestry.com Operations, Inc., 2016), Ancestry.com, http://www.Ancestry.com, Record for Ellen M Turner.

[503] Ancestry.com, U.S., Find A Grave Index, 1700s-Current (Provo, UT, USA, Ancestry.com Operations, Inc., 2012), Ancestry.com, http://www.Ancestry.com, Record for Carl Charles Snedaker.

[504] Ancestry.com, U.S., Find A Grave Index, 1700s-Current (Provo, UT, USA, Ancestry.com Operations, Inc., 2012), Ancestry.com, http://www.Ancestry.com, Record for Carl Charles Snedaker.

[505] Ancestry.com, Pennsylvania, Death Certificates, 1906-1963 (Provo, UT, USA, Ancestry.com Operations, Inc., 2014), Ancestry.com, http://www.Ancestry.com, Pennsylvania Historic and Museum Commission; Pennsylvania, USA; Pennsylvania (State). Death certificates, 1906-1966; Certificate Number Range: 111661-114850. Record for Winona Mildred Stillman.

[506]Ancestry.com, Pennsylvania, Death Certificates, 1906-1963 (Provo, UT, USA, Ancestry.com Operations, Inc., 2014), Ancestry.com, http://www.Ancestry.com, Pennsylvania Historic and Museum Commission; Pennsylvania, USA; Pennsylvania (State). Death certificates, 1906-1966; Certificate Number Range: 111661-114850. Record for Winona Mildred Stillman.

[507] Ancestry.com, New York, County Marriages, 1847-1849; 1907-1936 (Lehi, UT, USA, Ancestry.com Operations, Inc., 2016), Ancestry.com, http://www.Ancestry.com, Record for Winona B Maxson.

[508] Ancestry.com, Pennsylvania, Death Certificates, 1906-1963 (Provo, UT, USA, Ancestry.com Operations, Inc., 2014), Ancestry.com, http://www.Ancestry.com, Pennsylvania Historic and Museum Commission; Pennsylvania, USA; Pennsylvania (State). Death certificates, 1906-1966; Certificate Number Range: 111661-114850. Record for Winona Mildred Stillman.

Donald E Stillman and Winona Maxson had the following child:
i.   Winonia Mildred Stillman was born on 06 Jan 1915 in Pennsylvania[509] and died on 01 Dec 1915 in Eldred, Pennsylvania[510].

42. Hazel E. Maxson[11] (Grace K. Turner[10], Sylvanus M. Turner[9], Erastus G. Turner[8], Paul Turner[7], Paul Turner[6], Benjamin Turner Sr.[5], Benjamin Turner Sr.[4], John Turner[3], John Turner[2], Humphrey Turner[1]) was born on 03 Aug 1896[511] and died on 19 Mar 1956[512]. She married Albert G. Olson[513]. He was born on 25 Apr 1899[514] and died on 07 Aug 1966[515].

Albert G. Olson and Hazel E. Maxson had the following children:
i.   PFC Harold A. Olson was born on 12 Aug 1921 in Shinglehouse, Pennsylvania[516] and died on 07 May 2013 in Coudersport, Pennsylvania[517].
ii.   Hazen Carl Olson was born on 07 Sep 1924 in Titusville, Pennsylvania[518] and died on 01 Mar 1939 in Conewango, Pennsylvania[519].
iii.   Living Olson.

43. Irene Gladys Maxson[11] (Grace K. Turner[10], Sylvanus M. Turner[9], Erastus G. Turner[8], Paul Turner[7], Paul Turner[6], Benjamin Turner Sr.[5], Benjamin Turner Sr.[4], John Turner[3],

[509] Ancestry.com, Pennsylvania, Death Certificates, 1906-1963 (Provo, UT, USA, Ancestry.com Operations, Inc., 2014), Ancestry.com, http://www.Ancestry.com, Pennsylvania Historic and Museum Commission; Pennsylvania, USA; Pennsylvania (State) Death certificates, 1906-1966; Certificate Number Range: 111661-114850. Record for Winona Mildred Stillman.

[510] Ancestry.com, Pennsylvania, Death Certificates, 1906-1963 (Provo, UT, USA, Ancestry.com Operations, Inc., 2014), Ancestry.com, http://www.Ancestry.com, Pennsylvania Historic and Museum Commission; Pennsylvania, USA; Pennsylvania (State). Death certificates, 1906-1966; Certificate Number Range: 111661-114850. Record for Winona Mildred Stillman.

[511] Ancestry.com, U.S., Find A Grave Index, 1700s-Current (Provo, UT, USA, Ancestry.com Operations, Inc., 2012), Ancestry.com, http://www.Ancestry.com, Record for Albert G. Olson.

[512] Ancestry.com, U.S., Find A Grave Index, 1700s-Current (Provo, UT, USA, Ancestry.com Operations, Inc., 2012), Ancestry.com, http://www.Ancestry.com, Record for Albert G. Olson.

[513] Ancestry.com, U.S., Find A Grave Index, 1700s-Current (Provo, UT, USA, Ancestry.com Operations, Inc., 2012), Ancestry.com, http://www.Ancestry.com, Record for Albert G. Olson.

[514] Ancestry.com, U.S., Find A Grave Index, 1700s-Current (Provo, UT, USA, Ancestry.com Operations, Inc., 2012), Ancestry.com, http://www.Ancestry.com, Record for Albert G. Olson.

[515] Ancestry.com, U.S., Find A Grave Index, 1700s-Current (Provo, UT, USA, Ancestry.com Operations, Inc., 2012), Ancestry.com, http://www.Ancestry.com, Record for Albert G. Olson.

[516] Ancestry.com, U.S., Find A Grave Index, 1700s-Current (Provo, UT, USA, Ancestry.com Operations, Inc., 2012), Ancestry.com, http://www.Ancestry.com, Record for Harold A.. Olson.

[517] Ancestry.com, U.S., Find A Grave Index, 1700s-Current (Provo, UT, USA, Ancestry.com Operations, Inc., 2012), Ancestry.com, http://www.Ancestry.com, Record for Albert G. Olson.

[518] Ancestry.com, U.S., Find A Grave Index, 1700s-Current (Provo, UT, USA, Ancestry.com Operations, Inc., 2012), Ancestry.com, http://www.Ancestry.com, Record for Hazen Carl Olson.

[519] Ancestry.com, U.S., Find A Grave Index, 1700s-Current (Provo, UT, USA, Ancestry.com Operations, Inc., 2012), Ancestry.com, http://www.Ancestry.com, Record for Hazen Carl Olson.

John Turner[2], Humphrey Turner[1]) was born on 26 Jun 1901[520] and died on 15 Sep 1954 in Ithaca, New York[521]. She married Phill Terrence Appleby, the son of L. D. Appleby and Alice Mae Wolcott, on 02 Jul 1920 in Allegany, New York[522]. He was born on 10 Feb 1899[523] and died in Mar 1978 in Mount Morris, New York [524].

Phill Terrence Appleby and Irene Gladys Maxson had the following children:
59.   i.   Loraine E. Appleby was born on 15 Apr 1921 in Bolivar, New York[525] and died on 11 Jan 2005 in Olean, New York[526].

        ii.   Arthur L. Appleby was born on 31 Aug 1922[527] and died on 14 Oct 1968[528].

        iii.   Phylis G. Appleby was born on 15 Mar 1927 in Olean, New York[529] and died on 01 Mar 2001[530].   She married William H. Ford[531].   He was born on 20 Apr 1924[532] and died on 03 Dec 1988[533].

        iv.   Alice M. Appleby was born on 08 Dec 1933 in Pennsylvania[534] and died on 29 Sep 2006[535]. She married Kenneth Abrams on 11 Sep 1954 in Ithaca, New York[536].

44. Ernest Woodrow Maxson[11] (Grace K. Turner[10], Sylvanus M. Turner[9], Erastus G. Turner[8], Paul Turner[7], Paul Turner[6], Benjamin Turner Sr.[5], Benjamin Turner Sr.[4], John Turner[3], John Turner[2], Humphrey Turner[1]) was born on 19 Nov 1912 in Shinglehouse,

[520] Ancestry.com, U.S., Find A Grave Index, 1700s-Current (Provo, UT, USA, Ancestry.com Operations, Inc., 2012), Ancestry.com, http://www.Ancestry.com, Record for Irene Appleby.

[521] Ancestry.com, U.S., Find A Grave Index, 1700s-Current (Provo, UT, USA, Ancestry.com Operations, Inc., 2012), Ancestry.com, http://www.Ancestry.com, Record for Irene Appleby.

[522] Ancestry.com, New York, County Marriages, 1847-1849; 1907-1936 (Lehi, UT, USA, Ancestry.com Operations, Inc., 2016), Ancestry.com, http://www.Ancestry.com, Record for Phill T Appleby.

[523] Ancestry.com, U.S., Find A Grave Index, 1700s-Current (Provo, UT, USA, Ancestry.com Operations, Inc., 2012), Ancestry.com, http://www.Ancestry.com, Record for Phill Terrence Appleby.

[524] Ancestry.com, U.S., Find A Grave Index, 1700s-Current (Provo, UT, USA, Ancestry.com Operations, Inc., 2012), Ancestry.com, http://www.Ancestry.com, Record for Phill Terrence Appleby.

[525] Ancestry.com, U.S., Find A Grave Index, 1700s-Current (Provo, UT, USA, Ancestry.com Operations, Inc., 2012), Ancestry.com, http://www.Ancestry.com, Record for Loraine E. Straight.

[526] Ancestry.com, U.S., Find A Grave Index, 1700s-Current (Provo, UT, USA, Ancestry.com Operations, Inc., 2012), Ancestry.com, http://www.Ancestry.com, Record for Loraine E. Straight.

[527] Ancestry.com, U.S., Find A Grave Index, 1700s-Current (Provo, UT, USA, Ancestry.com Operations, Inc., 2012), Ancestry.com, http://www.Ancestry.com, Record for Arthur L. Appleby.

[528] Ancestry.com, U.S., Find A Grave Index, 1700s-Current (Provo, UT, USA, Ancestry.com Operations, Inc., 2012), Ancestry.com, http://www.Ancestry.com, Record for Arthur L. Appleby.

[529] Ancestry.com, U.S., Find A Grave Index, 1700s-Current (Provo, UT, USA, Ancestry.com Operations, Inc., 2012), Ancestry.com, http://www.Ancestry.com, Record for Phyllis G. Ford.

[530] Ancestry.com, U.S., Find A Grave Index, 1700s-Current (Provo, UT, USA, Ancestry.com Operations, Inc., 2012), Ancestry.com, http://www.Ancestry.com, Record for Phyllis G. Ford.

[531] Ancestry.com, U.S., Find A Grave Index, 1700s-Current, Record for William H. Ford.

[532] Ancestry.com, U.S., Find A Grave Index, 1700s-Current, Record for William H. Ford.

[533] Ancestry.com, U.S., Find A Grave Index, 1700s-Current, Record for William H. Ford.

[534] Ancestry.com, U.S., Find A Grave Index, 1700s-Current, Record for Alice Abrams..

[535] Ancestry.com, U.S., Find A Grave Index, 1700s-Current, Record for Alice Abrams.

[536] Ancestry.com, U.S., Find A Grave Index, 1700s-Current (Provo, UT, USA, Ancestry.com Operations, Inc., 2012), Ancestry.com, http://www.Ancestry.com, Record for Alice Abrams.

Pennsylvania[537] and died on 20 Oct 1991[538]. He married a girl by the name of Fern G.[539]. She was born on 22 Sep 1915 in Alma, New York[540] and died on 26 Mar 1998[541].

Ernest Woodrow Maxson and Fern G. Maxson had the following child:
    i.   Erwin D. Maxson was born on 26 Dec 1937[542] and died on 08 Jul 2009[543].

45. Welcome Rexford Maxson[11] (Grace K. Turner[10], Sylvanus M. Turner[9], Erastus G. Turner[8], Paul Turner[7], Paul Turner[6], Benjamin Turner Sr.[5], Benjamin Turner Sr.[4], John Turner[3], John Turner[2], Humphrey Turner[1]) was born on 30 Oct 1916 in Eldred McKea, Pennsylvania[544] and died on 27 May 1990[545]. He married Lucille Kemp[546]. She was born on 30 Aug 1919 in Shinglehouse, Pennsylvania[547] and died on 17 Aug 2017 in Coudersport, Pennsylvania[548].

Welcome Rexford Maxson and Lucille Kemp had the following child:
    i.   Ronald W. Maxson was born on 31 Aug 1940[549] and died on 27 Mar 1985[550].

46. Azelda Iona McDowell[11] (Lucy Eveline Turner[10], Sylvanus M. Turner[9], Erastus G. Turner[8], Paul Turner[7], Paul Turner[6], Benjamin Turner Sr.[5], Benjamin Turner Sr.[4], John

---

[537] Ancestry.com, U.S., Find A Grave Index, 1700s-Current (Provo, UT, USA, Ancestry.com Operations, Inc., 2012), Ancestry.com, http://www.Ancestry.com, Record for Ernest Woodrow Maxson.

[538] Ancestry.com, U.S., Find A Grave Index, 1700s-Current (Provo, UT, USA, Ancestry.com Operations, Inc., 2012), Ancestry.com, http://www.Ancestry.com, Record for Ernest Woodrow Maxson.

[539] Ancestry.com, U.S., Find A Grave Index, 1700s-Current (Provo, UT, USA, Ancestry.com Operations, Inc., 2012), Ancestry.com, http://www.Ancestry.com, Record for Ernest W. Maxson.

[540] Ancestry.com, U.S., Find A Grave Index, 1700s-Current (Provo, UT, USA, Ancestry.com Operations, Inc., 2012), Ancestry.com, http://www.Ancestry.com, Record for Fern G. Maxson.

[541] Ancestry.com, U.S., Find A Grave Index, 1700s-Current (Provo, UT, USA, Ancestry.com Operations, Inc., 2012), Ancestry.com, http://www.Ancestry.com, Record for Fern G. Maxson.

[542] Ancestry.com, U.S., Find A Grave Index, 1700s-Current (Provo, UT, USA, Ancestry.com Operations, Inc., 2012), Ancestry.com, http://www.Ancestry.com, Record for Ernest W. Maxson.

[543] Ancestry.com, U.S., Find A Grave Index, 1700s-Current (Provo, UT, USA, Ancestry.com Operations, Inc., 2012), Ancestry.com, http://www.Ancestry.com, Record for Ernest W. Maxson.

[544] Ancestry.com, U.S., Find A Grave Index, 1700s-Current (Provo, UT, USA, Ancestry.com Operations, Inc., 2012), Ancestry.com, http://www.Ancestry.com, Record for Welcome Rexford Maxson.

[545] Ancestry.com, U.S., Find A Grave Index, 1700s-Current (Provo, UT, USA, Ancestry.com Operations, Inc., 2012), Ancestry.com, http://www.Ancestry.com, Record for Welcome Rexford Maxson.

[546] Ancestry.com, U.S., Find A Grave Index, 1700s-Current (Provo, UT, USA, Ancestry.com Operations, Inc., 2012), Ancestry.com, http://www.Ancestry.com, Record for Welcome Rexford Maxson.

[547] Ancestry.com, U.S., Find A Grave Index, 1700s-Current (Provo, UT, USA, Ancestry.com Operations, Inc., 2012), Ancestry.com, http://www.Ancestry.com, Record for Welcome Maxson.

[548] Ancestry.com, U.S., Find A Grave Index, 1700s-Current (Provo, UT, USA, Ancestry.com Operations, Inc., 2012), Ancestry.com, http://www.Ancestry.com, Record for Welcome Maxson.

[549] Ancestry.com, U.S., Find A Grave Index, 1700s-Current (Provo, UT, USA, Ancestry.com Operations, Inc., 2012), Ancestry.com, http://www.Ancestry.com, Record for Welcome Maxson

[550] Ancestry.com, U.S., Find A Grave Index, 1700s-Current (Provo, UT, USA, Ancestry.com Operations, Inc., 2012), Ancestry.com, http://www.Ancestry.com, Record for Welcome Maxson

Turner[3], John Turner[2], Humphrey Turner[1]) was born in 1905 in Pennsylvania and died in 1969[551]. She married Arthur Herbert Baldwin, the son of Allan Baldwin and Agnes Haye, on 27 May 1926 in Cattaraugus, New York[552]. He was born on 02 Jul 1900[553] and died in Jan 1973 in Emporium, Pennsylvania[554].

Arthur Herbert Baldwin and Azelda Iona McDowell had the following children:

    i.   Robert A. Baldwin was born on 04 Jul 1927[555] and died on 13 Sep 2007[556].

    ii.   John Baldwin was born in Pennsylvania and my still be living·

47. Henriette E. McDowell[11] (Lucy Eveline Turner[10], Sylvanus M. Turner[9], Erastus G. Turner[8], Paul Turner[7], Paul Turner[6], Benjamin Turner Sr.[5], Benjamin Turner Sr.[4], John Turner[3], John Turner[2], Humphrey Turner[1]) was born on 14 Aug 1912 in Shinglehouse, Pennsylvania[557] and died on 03 Nov 1975 in Hornell, New York[558]. She married David Gerald Lee on 07 Aug 1933 in Allegany, New York[559]. He was born in 1912 in New York[560] and died on 23 Feb 2010 in Texas[561].

Photo of Henriette E. McDowell Lee found on Ancestry.com.

David Gerald Lee and Henriette E. Mcdowell had four children who may still be living.

---

[551] Ancestry.com, U.S., Find A Grave Index, 1700s-Current (Provo, UT, USA, Ancestry.com Operations, Inc., 2012), Ancestry.com, http://www.Ancestry.com, Record for Azelta Baldwin

[552] Ancestry.com, New York, County Marriages, 1847-1849; 1907-1936 (Lehi, UT, USA, Ancestry.com Operations, Inc., 2016), Ancestry.com, http://www.Ancestry.com, Record for Azelda Iona McDowell.

[553] Ancestry.com, Social Security Death Index (Provo, UT, USA, The Generations Network, Inc., 2008), www.ancestry.com, Number: 209-09-7206; Issue State: Pennsylvania; Issue Date: Before 1951. Record for Arthur Baldwin.

[554] Ancestry.com, Social Security Death Index (Provo, UT, USA, The Generations Network, Inc., 2008), www.ancestry.com, Number: 209-09-7206; Issue State: Pennsylvania; Issue Date: Before 1951. Record for Arthur Baldwin.

[555] Ancestry.com, U.S., Find A Grave Index, 1700s-Current (Provo, UT, USA, Ancestry.com Operations, Inc., 2012), Ancestry.com, http://www.Ancestry.com, Record for Azelta Baldwin.

[556] Ancestry.com, U.S., Find A Grave Index, 1700s-Current (Provo, UT, USA, Ancestry.com Operations, Inc., 2012), Ancestry.com, http://www.Ancestry.com, Record for Azelta Baldwin.

[557] Ancestry.com, U.S., Find A Grave Index, 1700s-Current (Provo, UT, USA, Ancestry.com Operations, Inc., 2012), Ancestry.com, http://www.Ancestry.com, Record for Henrietta Lee.

[558] Ancestry.com, U.S., Find A Grave Index, 1700s-Current (Provo, UT, USA, Ancestry.com Operations, Inc., 2012), Ancestry.com, http://www.Ancestry.com, Record for Henrietta Lee.

[559] Ancestry.com, U.S., Find A Grave Index, 1700s-Current (Provo, UT, USA, Ancestry.com Operations, Inc., 2012), Ancestry.com, http://www.Ancestry.com, Record for Henrietta Lee.

[560] Ancestry.com, U.S., Find A Grave Index, 1700s-Current (Provo, UT, USA, Ancestry.com Operations, Inc., 2012), Ancestry.com, http://www.Ancestry.com, Record for David G. Lee.

[561] Ancestry.com, U.S., Find A Grave Index, 1700s-Current (Provo, UT, USA, Ancestry.com Operations, Inc., 2012), Ancestry.com, http://www.Ancestry.com, Record for David G. Lee.

48.   Dudly Otis Turner[11] (Wellman Ellery Turner[10], Sylvanus M. Turner[9], Erastus G. Turner[8], Paul Turner[7], Paul Turner[6], Benjamin Turner Sr.[5], Benjamin Turner Sr.[4], John Turner[3], John Turner[2], Humphrey Turner[1]) was born on 10 Sep 1905[562] and died in Jan 1984 in Little Valley, New York[563]. He married Fannie Bell, the daughter of William Bell and Maud Reynolds, on 19 Oct 1926 in Cattaraugus, New York[564]. She was born on 12 Oct 1908[565] and died in Apr 1979 in West Valley, New York[566].

Dudly Otis Turner and Fannie Bell had the following children:

     i.   Marie B. Turner was born on 07 Jun 1928 in Olean, New York[567] and died on 21 Sep 2013 in Salamanca, New York[568]. She married Bernard Westfall on 04 Jul 1950 in Ashford, New York[569]. He was born on 20 Apr 1919[570] and died on 03 Nov 2005[571].

LITTLE VALLEY - *Marie B. Westfall, 85, of Little Valley passed away Saturday (Sept. 21, 2013) at Absolut of Salamanca. She was born June 7, 1928, in Olean, a daughter of the late Dudley and Fannie Bell Turner. On July 4, 1950, she married Bernard Westfall, who predeceased her. Mrs. Westfall had worked in the Wollen Mills in Salamanca, Setter Stix, Brooks Market, Bush Industries and the in the cafeteria at Little Valley Central School. She and her husband also had a dairy farm on Kyler Hill Road for many years. She was a member of St. Michael's Lutheran Church and the Little Valley American Legion Auxiliary. She is survived by a son, Dale Westfall of Little Valley; a daughter, Angela (Rick) Dowd of Little Valley; seven grandchildren and 11 great-grandchildren; and also a brother, Richard (Joyce) Turner of Springville. Besides her husband, she was predeceased by a sister, Lahoma "Tiny"*

[562] Ancestry.com, Social Security Death Index (Provo, UT, USA, The Generations Network, Inc., 2008), www.ancestry.com, Number: 122-18-6958; Issue State: New York; Issue Date: Before 1951. Record for Dudley Turner.

[563] Ancestry.com, Social Security Death Index (Provo, UT, USA, The Generations Network, Inc., 2008), www.ancestry.com, Number: 122-18-6958; Issue State: New York; Issue Date: Before 1951. Record for Dudley Turner.

[564] Ancestry.com, New York, County Marriages, 1847-1849; 1907-1936 (Lehi, UT, USA, Ancestry.com Operations, Inc., 2016), Ancestry.com, http://www.Ancestry.com, Record for Dudley Otis Turner

[565] Ancestry.com. *U.S., Social Security Death Index, 1935-2014* [database on-line]. Provo, UT, USA: Ancestry.com Operations Inc, 2014.

[566] Ancestry.com. *U.S., Social Security Death Index, 1935-2014* [database on-line]. Provo, UT, USA: Ancestry.com Operations Inc, 2014.

[567] Ancestry.com, U.S., Find A Grave Index, 1700s-Current (Provo, UT, USA, Ancestry.com Operations, Inc., 2012), Ancestry.com, http://www.Ancestry.com, Record for Marie B. Westfal.l

[568] Ancestry.com, U.S., Find A Grave Index, 1700s-Current (Provo, UT, USA, Ancestry.com Operations, Inc., 2012), Ancestry.com, http://www.Ancestry.com, Record for Marie B. Westfall.

[569] Ancestry.com, New York State, Marriage Index, 1881-1967 (Lehi, UT, USA, Ancestry.com Operations, Inc., 2017), Ancestry.com, http://www.Ancestry.com, New York State Department of Health; Albany, NY, USA; New York State Marriage Index. Record for Marie B Turner.

[570] Ancestry.com, U.S., Find A Grave Index, 1700s-Current (Provo, UT, USA, Ancestry.com Operations, Inc., 2012), Ancestry.com, http://www.Ancestry.com, Record for Marie B. Westfall.

[571] Ancestry.com, U.S., Find A Grave Index, 1700s-Current (Provo, UT, USA, Ancestry.com Operations, Inc., 2012), Ancestry.com, http://www.Ancestry.com, Record for Marie B. Westfall.

Westfall. Friends may call at the Mentley Funeral Home Inc., 411 Rock City St. in Little Valley, on Monday (Sept. 23, 2013) from noon to 2 p.m., at which time and place funeral services will be held. Burial will be in Little Valley Rural Cemetery.

      ii.   LaHoma A. Turner was born in 1930 in New York[572] and died in 1968[573]. She married Emil C. Westfall, the son of Martin J. and Freda C. Westfall, on 19 Mar 1948 in E. Otto, New York[574]. He was born in 1928[575] and died in 1985[576].

49. Mary Christina Turner[11] (Wellman Ellery Turner[10], Sylvanus M. Turner[9], Erastus G. Turner[8], Paul Turner[7], Paul Turner[6], Benjamin Turner Sr.[5], Benjamin Turner Sr.[4], John Turner[3], John Turner[2], Humphrey Turner[1]) was born on 01 Jul 1907 in New York[577] and died on 24 Apr 1994[578]. She married James William Albert Ayers[579]. He was born on 25 Jul 1901[580].   James William Albert Ayers and Mary Christina Turner had three children who may still be living.

50. Raymond Elwood Turner[11] (Wellman Ellery Turner[10], Sylvanus M. Turner[9], Erastus G. Turner[8], Paul Turner[7], Paul Turner[6], Benjamin Turner Sr.[5], Benjamin Turner Sr.[4], John Turner[3], John Turner[2], Humphrey Turner[1]) was born on 02 Aug 1915 in New York[581] and died on 05 Oct 2012[582]. He married Dolores Mae Jordan[583].   She was born on 03 May 1921[584] and died on 10 Jul 2012[585].

---

[572] Ancestry.com. *U.S., Find A Grave Index, 1600s-Current* [database on-line]. Provo, UT, USA: Ancestry.com Operations, Inc., 2012. Record for Lahoma A. Westfall.

[573] Ancestry.com. *U.S., Find A Grave Index, 1600s-Current* [database on-line]. Provo, UT, USA: Ancestry.com Operations, Inc., 2012. Record for Lahoma A. Westfall.

[574] New York State Department of Health; Albany, NY, USA; *New York State Marriage Index*

[575] Ancestry.com. *U.S., Find A Grave Index, 1600s-Current* [database on-line]. Provo, UT, USA: Ancestry.com Operations, Inc., 2012. Record for Emil C. Westfall.

[576] Ancestry.com. *U.S., Find A Grave Index, 1600s-Current* [database on-line]. Provo, UT, USA: Ancestry.com Operations, Inc., 2012. Record for Emil C. Westfall.

[577] Ancestry.com. *U.S., Social Security Applications and Claims Index, 1936-2007* [database on-line]. Provo, UT, USA: Ancestry.com Operations, Inc., 2015.

[578] Ancestry.com. *U.S., Social Security Applications and Claims Index, 1936-2007* [database on-line]. Provo, UT, USA: Ancestry.com Operations, Inc., 2015.

[579] Ancestry.com, 1930 United States Federal Census (Provo, UT, USA, The Generations Network, Inc., 2002), www.ancestry.com, Year: 1930; Census Place: Washington, Burlington, New Jersey; Page: 1B; Enumeration District: 0074. Record for Mary C Ayres.

[580] Ancestry.com, 1930 United States Federal Census (Provo, UT, USA, The Generations Network, Inc., 2002), www.ancestry.com, Year: 1930; Census Place: Washington, Burlington, New Jersey; Page: 1B; Enumeration District: 0074. Record for Mary C Ayres.

[581] Ancestry.com, U.S., Find A Grave Index, 1700s-Current (Provo, UT, USA, Ancestry.com Operations, Inc., 2012), Ancestry.com, http://www.Ancestry.com, Record for Raymond Elwood Turner.

[582] Ancestry.com, U.S., Find A Grave Index, 1700s-Current (Provo, UT, USA, Ancestry.com Operations, Inc., 2012), Ancestry.com, http://www.Ancestry.com, Record for Raymond Elwood Turner.

[583] Ancestry.com, U.S., Find A Grave Index, 1700s-Current (Provo, UT, USA, Ancestry.com Operations, Inc., 2012), Ancestry.com, http://www.Ancestry.com, Record for Dolores May Turner.

[584] Ancestry.com, U.S., Find A Grave Index, 1700s-Current (Provo, UT, USA, Ancestry.com Operations, Inc., 2012), Ancestry.com, http://www.Ancestry.com, Record for Dolores May Turner.

Raymond Elwood Turner and Dolores Mae Jordan had the following children:

  i. Larry Dean Turner was born on 25 Feb 1939 in Olean, New York[586] and died on 17 Nov 2006 in Florida[587].

  ii. Donna Rae Turner was born on 23 Jan 1946[588] and died on 21 May 1963[589].

51. Leah E. Hodges[11] (Permilla A. Turner[10], Sylvanus M. Turner[9], Erastus G. Turner[8], Paul Turner[7], Paul Turner[6], Benjamin Turner Sr.[5], Benjamin Turner Sr.[4], John Turner[3], John Turner[2], Humphrey Turner[1]) was born on 12 Aug 1905[590] and died on 06 Sep 1999 in Albany, New York[591]. She married Ralph Earl Gleason, the son of E. B. Gleason and Matilda Clair, on 13 Feb 1935 in Allegany, New York[592]. He was born on 10 Mar 1902[593] and died in Apr 1984 in Albany, New York[594].   Ralph Earl Gleason and Leah E Hodges had one child who may still be living.

52. Margaret Alice Turner[11] (Archibald Turner[10], Sylvanus M. Turner[9], Erastus G. Turner[8], Paul Turner[7], Paul Turner[6], Benjamin Turner Sr.[5], Benjamin Turner Sr.[4], John Turner[3], John Turner[2], Humphrey Turner[1]) was born on 17 Mar 1908 in Eldred, Pennsylvania[595] and died on 08 Nov 1995 in Coudersport, Pennsylvania[596]. She married Harold Dexter Howard, the son of Edwin Howard and May Cornelius on 26 Nov 1925 in 1925 in Cattaraugus, New York[597]. He was born on 08 Jul 1905[598] and died on 15 Oct

[585] Ancestry.com, U.S., Find A Grave Index, 1700s-Current (Provo, UT, USA, Ancestry.com Operations, Inc., 2012), Ancestry.com, http://www.Ancestry.com, Record for Dolores May Turner.

[586] Ancestry.com, U.S., Find A Grave Index, 1700s-Current (Provo, UT, USA, Ancestry.com Operations, Inc., 2012), Ancestry.com, http://www.Ancestry.com, Record for Dolores May Turner.

[587] Ancestry.com, U.S., Find A Grave Index, 1700s-Current (Provo, UT, USA, Ancestry.com Operations, Inc., 2012), Ancestry.com, http://www.Ancestry.com, Record for Dolores May Turner.

[588] Ancestry.com, U.S., Find A Grave Index, 1700s-Current (Provo, UT, USA, Ancestry.com Operations, Inc., 2012), Ancestry.com, http://www.Ancestry.com, Record for Dolores May Turner.

[589] Ancestry.com, U.S., Find A Grave Index, 1700s-Current (Provo, UT, USA, Ancestry.com Operations, Inc., 2012), Ancestry.com, http://www.Ancestry.com, Record for Dolores May Turner.

[590] Ancestry.com, U.S., Find A Grave Index, 1700s-Current (Provo, UT, USA, Ancestry.com Operations, Inc., 2012), Ancestry.com, http://www.Ancestry.com, Record for Leah E. Gleason.

[591] Ancestry.com, U.S., Find A Grave Index, 1700s-Current (Provo, UT, USA, Ancestry.com Operations, Inc., 2012), Ancestry.com, http://www.Ancestry.com, Record for Leah E. Gleason.

[592] Ancestry.com, New York, County Marriages, 1847-1849; 1907-1936 (Lehi, UT, USA, Ancestry.com Operations, Inc., 2016), Ancestry.com, http://www.Ancestry.com, Record for Ralph E Gleason.

[593] Ancestry.com, Social Security Death Index (Provo, UT, USA, The Generations Network, Inc., 2008), Record for Ralph Gleason.

[594] Ancestry.com, Social Security Death Index (Provo, UT, USA, The Generations Network, Inc., 2008), Record for Ralph Gleason.

[595] Ancestry.com, U.S., Find A Grave Index, 1700s-Current (Provo, UT, USA, Ancestry.com Operations, Inc., 2012), Ancestry.com, http://www.Ancestry.com, Record for Margaret A Howard.

[596] Ancestry.com, U.S., Find A Grave Index, 1700s-Current (Provo, UT, USA, Ancestry.com Operations, Inc., 2012), Ancestry.com, http://www.Ancestry.com, Record for Margaret A Howard.

[597] Ancestry.com, New York, County Marriages, 1847-1849; 1907-1936 (Lehi, UT, USA, Ancestry.com Operations, Inc., 2016), Ancestry.com, http://www.Ancestry.com, Record for Margaret Alice Turner.

1991[599]. Harold Dexter Howard and Margaret Alice Turner had one child who may still be living.

53.   Lucy Elizabeth Turner[11] (Archibald Turner[10], Sylvanus M. Turner[9], Erastus G. Turner[8], Paul Turner[7], Paul Turner[6], Benjamin Turner Sr.[5], Benjamin Turner Sr.[4], John Turner[3], John Turner[2], Humphrey Turner[1]) was born on 20 Mar 1910 in Ceres, Pennsylvania[600] and died on 06 Jun 1986 in Pennsylvania[601]. She married Robert Bernard Howard, the son of Henry F. Howard and Ella Meyers[602]. He was born on 10 Nov 1905 in Ceres, New York[603] and died on 07 Sep 1991[604].

Robert Bernard Howard and Lucy Elizabeth Turner had the following children:
     i.   Robert Henry Howard was born on 19 Apr 1929[605] and died on 27 Nov 1962[606].

     ii.   Donald R. Howard was born on 31 Jan 1931[607] and died on 03 Mar 2008 in Bradford, Pennsylvania[608]. He married a woman by the name of Donna E.[609]. She was born in 1931 in Houlton, Maine[610] and died on 22 Mar 1990[611].

[598] Ancestry.com, U.S., Find A Grave Index, 1700s-Current (Provo, UT, USA, Ancestry.com Operations, Inc., 2012), Ancestry.com, http://www.Ancestry.com, Record for Harold D. Howard

[599] Ancestry.com, U.S., Find A Grave Index, 1700s-Current (Provo, UT, USA, Ancestry.com Operations, Inc., 2012), Ancestry.com, http://www.Ancestry.com, Record for Harold D. Howard.

[600] Ancestry.com, Pennsylvania, Birth Certificates, 1906-1910 (Lehi, UT, USA, Ancestry.com Operations, Inc., 2015), Ancestry.com, http://www.Ancestry.com, Pennsylvania Historical and Museum Commission; Harrisburg, Pennsylvania; Box Number: 312; Certificate Number: 50460. Record for Lucy Elizabeth Turner.

[601] Ancestry.com, Social Security Death Index (Provo, UT, USA, The Generations Network, Inc., 2008), www.ancestry.com, Number: 116-20-6890; Issue State: New York; Issue Date: Before 1951. Record for Lucy Howard

[602] Ancestry.com. *Web: Pennsylvania, Find A Grave Index, 1682-2012* [database on-line]. Provo, UT, USA: Ancestry.com Operations, Inc., 2012. Record for Robert B. Howard.

[603] Ancestry.com, U.S. WWII Draft Cards Young Men, 1940-1947 (Lehi, UT, USA, Ancestry.com Operations, Inc., 2011), Ancestry.com, http://www.Ancestry.com, The National Archives in St. Louis, Missouri; St. Louis, Missouri; Record Group: Records of the Selective Service System, 147; Box: 1155. Record for Robert Bernard Howard.

[604] Ancestry.com. *U.S., Social Security Applications and Claims Index, 1936-2007* [database on-line]. Provo, UT, USA: Ancestry.com Operations, Inc., 2015. Record for Robert Bernard Howard.

[605] Ancestry.com, U.S., Headstone Applications for Military Veterans, 1925-1963 (Provo, UT, USA, Ancestry.com Operations, Inc., 2012), www.ancestry.com, Record for Robert Henry Howard.

[606] Ancestry.com, U.S., Find A Grave Index, 1700s-Current (Provo, UT, USA, Ancestry.com Operations, Inc., 2012), Ancestry.com, http://www.Ancestry.com, Record for Robert Henry Howard.

[607] Ancestry.com, U.S., Find A Grave Index, 1700s-Current (Provo, UT, USA, Ancestry.com Operations, Inc., 2012), Ancestry.com, http://www.Ancestry.com, Record for Donald R. Howard.

[608] Ancestry.com, U.S., Find A Grave Index, 1700s-Current (Provo, UT, USA, Ancestry.com Operations, Inc., 2012), Ancestry.com, http://www.Ancestry.com, Record for Donald R. Howard.

[609] Ancestry.com, U.S., Find A Grave Index, 1700s-Current (Provo, UT, USA, Ancestry.com Operations, Inc., 2012), Ancestry.com, http://www.Ancestry.com, Record for Donald R. Howard.

[610] Ancestry.com, U.S., Find A Grave Index, 1700s-Current (Provo, UT, USA, Ancestry.com Operations, Inc., 2012), Ancestry.com, http://www.Ancestry.com, Record for Donald R. Howard.

[611] Ancestry.com, U.S., Find A Grave Index, 1700s-Current (Provo, UT, USA, Ancestry.com Operations, Inc., 2012), Ancestry.com, http://www.Ancestry.com, Record for Donald R. Howard.

Donald R. Howard, 77 ,0f Shinglehouse, died Monday (March 3, 2008) in Charles Cole Memorial. Hospital, Coudersport, after a short illness. Born January 16,1931 in Bradford, he was a son of Robert and Lucy Turner Howard. On March 26, 1949 in Hornell, NY, he married Donna E. George, who died on March 22,1990. He attended Shinglehouse High School. Mr. Howard served with the Olean National Guard. He was a salesman for Chapman-Burrows Furniture Store in Genesee for many years and later owned Howard 's Hardware in Shinglehouse from 1967 until he retired in 1986. Earlier he had a Christmas tree farm in Genesee. He was a member of Sharon Lodge #598 F &AM in Shinglehouse where he was a past master and had held the office of Tyler for many years. He was a member of the Coudersport Consistory and a member of the Shinglehouse American legion Post 530. Surviving are a daughter, Tracy L. (Will) Worthington of Eldred; three sons Kenneth J. Howard of Lakeland, Florida, Jeffrey W.(Darlene) Howard and Mick (Lisa) Howard, both of Shinglehouse; eight grandchildren: Jessica (John) Marshall ,Dustin Howard, Dylan Howard, Andy (Danielle)Howard, Tonya (Israel) Alonzo, Craig (Amy) Worthington, Ryan Worthington, and Derek (Ashley) Worthington; nine great-grandchildren; a Sister, Jean Gross of Ceres; four brothers, Richard (Jean) Howard of Richburg, NY, Jack (Nickki) Howard of Shinglehouse, James (Liz) Howard of Florida, and William (Mindy) Howard of Shinglehouse; and several nieces and nephews. In addition to his parents and wife, Mr. Howard was predeceased by two brothers, Robert Howard and Paul Howard. Funeral services were held at the Virgil L. Howard Funeral Home, Shinglehouse, on Thursday (March 6, 2008) . The Rev. Russell J. Horning, pastor of the First Baptist Church, Shinglehouse, and Pastor Robert Howard, Mr. Howard's nephew, of Whitesville, NY, officiated. Burial was in the Maple Grove Cemetery, Shinglehouse.

   iii. Richard Earl Howard was born on 30 Jun 1933 [612] and died on 23 Mar 2010 in Richburg, New York[613].

   iv. Paul Franklin Howard was born on 23 Nov 1934 in Olean, New York[614] and died on 13 Sep 2001[615].

   v. Linda Diane Howard was born in 1953[616] and died in 1953[617].

---

[612] Ancestry.com, Social Security Death Index (Provo, UT, USA, The Generations Network, Inc., 2008), www.ancestry.com, Issue State: New York; Issue Date: 1951. Record for Richard E. Howard.

[613] Ancestry.com, Social Security Death Index (Provo, UT, USA, The Generations Network, Inc., 2008), www.ancestry.com, Issue State: New York; Issue Date: 1951. Record for Richard E. Howard.

[614] Ancestry.com, U.S., Social Security Applications and Claims Index, 1936-2007 (Provo, UT, USA, Ancestry.com Operations, Inc., 2015), Ancestry.com, http://www.Ancestry.com, Record for Paul Franklin Howard.

[615] Ancestry.com, U.S., Social Security Applications and Claims Index, 1936-2007 (Provo, UT, USA, Ancestry.com Operations, Inc., 2015), Ancestry.com, http://www.Ancestry.com, Record for Paul Franklin Howard.

[616] Ancestry.com, U.S., Find A Grave Index, 1700s-Current (Provo, UT, USA, Ancestry.com Operations, Inc., 2012), Ancestry.com, http://www.Ancestry.com, Record for Linda Diane Howard.

[617] Ancestry.com, U.S., Find A Grave Index, 1700s-Current (Provo, UT, USA, Ancestry.com Operations, Inc., 2012), Ancestry.com, http://www.Ancestry.com, Record for Linda Diane Howard.

54.   Erwin P. Turner[11] (Archibald Turner[10], Sylvanus M. Turner[9], Erastus G. Turner[8], Paul Turner[7], Paul Turner[6], Benjamin Turner Sr.[5], Benjamin Turner Sr.[4], John Turner[3], John Turner[2], Humphrey Turner[1]) was born on 23 Sep 1912[618] and died on 27 Dec 1997[619]. He married Florence May Kemp[620]. She was born on 31 Mar 1918 in Pennsylvania[621] and died on 16 May 2006 in Shinglehouse, Pennsylvania[622]. He later married Nellie Beatrice Young on 30 Oct 1954 in Hinsdale, New York [623].

Photo of Erwin P. Turner found on Ancestry.com.

Erwin P. Turner and Florence Mae Kemp had the following children:

    i.   Helen Turner was born on 24 Nov 1933 in Pennsylvania[624] and died on 20 Jun 2008 in Shinglehouse, Pennsylvania[625]. She married Frederick Erwin App[626]. He was born on 18 May 1920 in Olean, New York[627] and died on 15 Apr 1996 in Coudersport, Pennsylvania[628].

Photo of Helen Turner App found on Ancestry.com.

ii.   John Turner may still be alive.

iii.   Charles Jay Turner was born on 28 Nov 1938 in Olean, New York[629] and died on 23 Jun 2003[630].

---

[618] Ancestry.com. *U.S., Find A Grave Index, 1600s-Current* [database on-line]. Provo, UT, USA: Ancestry.com Operations, Inc., 2012. Record for Erwin P. Turner.

[619] Ancestry.com. *U.S., Find A Grave Index, 1600s-Current* [database on-line]. Provo, UT, USA: Ancestry.com Operations, Inc., 2012. Record for Erwin P. Turner.

[620] Ancestry.com, 1940 United States Federal Census (Provo, UT, USA, Ancestry.com Operations, Inc., 2012), www.ancestry.com, Year: 1940; Census Place: Ceres, McKean, Pennsylvania; Roll: m-t0627-03568; Page: 3B; Enumeration District: 42-19. Record for Erwin Turner.

[621] Ancestry.com. *U.S., Social Security Applications and Claims Index, 1936-2007* [database on-line]. Provo, UT, USA: Ancestry.com Operations, Inc., 2015.

[622] Ancestry.com. *U.S., Social Security Applications and Claims Index, 1936-2007* [database on-line]. Provo, UT, USA: Ancestry.com Operations, Inc., 2015.

[623] Ancestry.com, New York state Marriage index for Erwin P. Turner.

[624] Ancestry.com, U.S., Find A Grave Index, 1700s-Current, Record for Helen M App.

[625] Ancestry.com, U.S., Find A Grave Index, 1700s-Current, Record for Helen M App.

[626] Ancestry.com, U.S., Find A Grave Index, 1700s-Current, Record for Helen M App.

[627] Ancestry.com, U.S., Find A Grave Index, 1700s-Current, Record for Helen M App.

[628] Ancestry.com, U.S., Find A Grave Index, 1700s-Current, Record for Helen M App.

iv.   Leonard Turner
v.   Gordon Eugene Turner was born on 23 Dec 1943 in Olean, New York[631] and died on 31 Jul 2001[632].

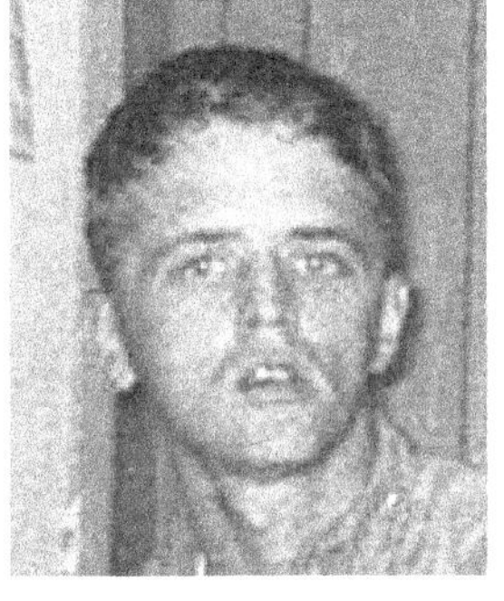

Photo of Gordon Eugene Turner found on Ancestry.com.

55.   Lena Agnes Turner[11] (Archibald Turner[10], Sylvanus M. Turner[9], Erastus G. Turner[8], Paul Turner[7], Paul Turner[6], Benjamin Turner Sr.[5], Benjamin Turner Sr.[4], John Turner[3], John Turner[2], Humphrey Turner[1]) was born on 19 Sep 1914[633] and died in Aug 1981 in Ceres, New York[634]. She married Kenneth Roland Spees on 01 Sep 1933 in Allegany, New York[635]. He was born on 13 Apr 1911 in New York[636] and died in Sep 1979[637].

Kenneth Roland Spees and Lena Agnes Turner had the following child:
i.   Genette A. Spees was born in 1947[638] and died in 1968[639]. She married on 01 Sep 1933 in Allegany, New York[640].

56.   John Archibald Turner[11] (Archibald Turner[10], Sylvanus M. Turner[9], Erastus G. Turner[8], Paul Turner[7], Paul Turner[6], Benjamin Turner Sr.[5], Benjamin Turner Sr.[4], John Turner[3], John Turner[2], Humphrey Turner[1]) was born on 31 Aug 1916 in Ceres, New York[641] and died on 25 Jan 2000[642]. He married Olive Elizabeth Payne[643]. She was born

[629] Ancestry.com, U.S., Social Security Applications and Claims Index, 1936-2007 (Provo, UT, USA, Ancestry.com Operations, Inc., 2015), Ancestry.com, http://www.Ancestry.com, Record for Charles Jay Turner.
[630] Ancestry.com, U.S., Social Security Applications and Claims Index, 1936-2007 (Provo, UT, USA, Ancestry.com Operations, Inc., 2015), Ancestry.com, http://www.Ancestry.com, Record for Charles Jay Turner.
[631] Ancestry.com, U.S., Social Security Applications and Claims Index, 1936-2007 for Gordon Eugene Turner.
[632] Ancestry.com, U.S., Social Security Applications and Claims Index, 1936-2007 for Gordon Eugene Turner.
[633] Ancestry.com, Social Security Death Index (Provo, UT, USA, The Generations Network, Inc., 2008), www.ancestry.com, Number: 128-30-9807; Issue State: New York; Issue Date: 1955-1957. Record for Lena Spees.
[634] Ancestry.com, Social Security Death Index (Provo, UT, USA, The Generations Network, Inc., 2008), www.ancestry.com, Number: 128-30-9807; Issue State: New York; Issue Date: 1955-1957. Record for Lena Spees.
[635] Ancestry.com, New York, County Marriages, 1847-1849; 1907-1936 (Lehi, UT, USA, Ancestry.com Operations, Inc., 2016), Ancestry.com, http://www.Ancestry.com, Record for Lena Turner.
[636] Ancestry.com, U.S., Find A Grave Index, 1700s-Current (Provo, UT, USA, Ancestry.com Operations, Inc., 2012), Ancestry.com, http://www.Ancestry.com, Record for Kenneth Roland Spees.
[637] Ancestry.com, U.S., Find A Grave Index, 1700s-Current (Provo, UT, USA, Ancestry.com Operations, Inc., 2012), Ancestry.com, http://www.Ancestry.com, Record for Kenneth Roland Spees.
[638] Ancestry.com, New York, County Marriages, 1847-1849; 1907-1936 (Lehi, UT, USA, Ancestry.com Operations, Inc., 2016), Ancestry.com, http://www.Ancestry.com, Record for Ganette A. Spees.
[639] Ancestry.com, U.S., Find A Grave Index, 1700s-Current (Provo, UT, USA, Ancestry.com Operations, Inc., 2012), Ancestry.com, http://www.Ancestry.com, Record for Kenneth Roland Spees.
[640] Ancestry.com, U.S., Find A Grave Index, 1700s-Current (Provo, UT, USA, Ancestry.com Operations, Inc., 2012), Ancestry.com, http://www.Ancestry.com, Record for Kenneth Roland Spees.
[641] Ancestry.com, U.S., Social Security Applications and Claims Index, 1936-2007 (Provo, UT, USA, Ancestry.com Operations, Inc., 2015), Ancestry.com, http://www.Ancestry.com, Record for John Archibald Turner.
[642] Ancestry.com, U.S., Social Security Applications and Claims Index, 1936-2007 (Provo, UT, USA, Ancestry.com Operations, Inc., 2015), Ancestry.com, http://www.Ancestry.com, Record for John Archibald Turner.

on 09 Feb 1919[644] and died on 15 Aug 2004 in Tucson, Arizona[645].   John Archibald Turner and Olive Elizabeth Payne had four daughters.

57.   Jennie M. Haven[11] (Goodrich Erasutus Haven [10], Ida May Turner[9], Erastus G. Turner[8], Paul Turner[7], Paul Turner[6], Benjamin Turner Sr.[5], Benjamin Turner Sr.[4], John Turner[3], John Turner[2], Humphrey Turner[1]) was born on 20 Dec 1906[646] and died on 02 Apr 1969[647].   She married Harry Thomas Kelly[648]. He was born on 27 Oct 1902 in Pennsylvania[649] and died on 07 Dec 1979 in Garfield Heights, Ohio[650].

Harry Thomas Kelly and Jennie M. Haven had the following children:
        i.   Lois Marion Kelly may was born 15 Aug 1925[651] and died on 12 Feb 2001 in East McKeesport, Pennsylvania[652].
60.   ii.   Harry Thomas Kelly, Jr. was born in 05 Oct 1926[653] and died on 29 Apr 1974.
        iii.   Living Kelly.
        iv.   Living Kelly.

58. Martin Goodrich Haven[11] (Goodrich Erasutus Haven [10], Ida May Turner[9], Erastus G. Turner[8], Paul Turner[7], Paul Turner[6], Benjamin Turner Sr.[5], Benjamin Turner Sr.[4], John Turner[3], John Turner[2], Humphrey Turner[1]) was born on 06 Mar 1908 in Custer City,

[643] Ancestry.com, U.S., Find A Grave Index, 1700s-Current (Provo, UT, USA, Ancestry.com Operations, Inc., 2012), Ancestry.com, http://www.Ancestry.com, Record for Olive Elizabeth Turner.

[644] Ancestry.com, U.S., Find A Grave Index, 1700s-Current (Provo, UT, USA, Ancestry.com Operations, Inc., 2012), Ancestry.com, http://www.Ancestry.com, Record for Olive Elizabeth Turner.

[645] Ancestry.com, U.S., Find A Grave Index, 1700s-Current (Provo, UT, USA, Ancestry.com Operations, Inc., 2012), Ancestry.com, http://www.Ancestry.com, Record for Olive Elizabeth Turner.

[646] Ancestry.com. *U.S., Find A Grave Index, 1600s-Current* [database on-line]. Provo, UT, USA: Ancestry.com Operations, Inc., 2012. Record for Jennie M. Kelly.

[647] Ancestry.com. *U.S., Find A Grave Index, 1600s-Current* [database on-line]. Provo, UT, USA: Ancestry.com Operations, Inc., 2012. Record for Jennie M. Kelly.

[648] Ancestry.com. *U.S., Find A Grave Index, 1600s-Current* [database on-line]. Provo, UT, USA: Ancestry.com Operations, Inc., 2012. Record for Jennie M. Kelly.

[649] Ancestry.com and Ohio Department of Health, Ohio, Deaths, 1908-1932, 1938-2007 (Provo, UT, USA, Ancestry.com Operations Inc, 2010), Ancestry.com, http://www.Ancestry.com, Certificate: 094123; Volume: 23902. Record for Harry T Kelly.

[650] Ancestry.com and Ohio Department of Health, Ohio, Deaths, 1908-1932, 1938-2007 (Provo, UT, USA, Ancestry.com Operations Inc, 2010), Ancestry.com, http://www.Ancestry.com, Certificate: 094123; Volume: 23902. Record for Harry T Kelly.

[651] Ancestry.com. *U.S., Social Security Death Index, 1935-2014* [database on-line]. Provo, UT, USA: Ancestry.com Operations Inc, 2014. Record for Lois M. Kelly.

[652] Ancestry.com. *U.S., Social Security Death Index, 1935-2014* [database on-line]. Provo, UT, USA: Ancestry.com Operations Inc, 2014. Record for Lois M. Kelly.

[653] Ancestry.com. *U.S., Department of Veterans Affairs BIRLS Death File, 1850-2010* [database on-line]. Provo, UT, USA: Ancestry.com Operations, Inc., 2011. Record for Harry Thomas Kelly, Jr.

Pennsylvania[654] and died on 14 Jun 1974 in Bradford, Pennsylvania[655]. He married Hazel Marion Bly on 20 Jul 1927 in Cattaraugus, New York[656]. She was born in 1913[657].

Martin Goodrich Haven and Hazel Marion Bly had the following child:
      i.   William Martin Haven was born on 11 Aug 1929 in Bradford, Pennsylvania[658] and died on 15 Jul 2000[659].

---

[654] Ancestry.com, U.S. WWII Draft Cards Young Men, 1940-1947 (Lehi, UT, USA, Ancestry.com Operations, Inc., 2011), Ancestry.com, http://www.Ancestry.com, The National Archives in St. Louis, Missouri; St. Louis, Missouri; Record Group: Records of the Selective Service System, 147; Box: 1045. Record for Martin Goodrich Haven.

[655] Ancestry.com. *U.S., Find A Grave Index, 1600s-Current* [database on-line]. Provo, UT, USA: Ancestry.com Operations, Inc., 2012. Record for Martin Goodrich Haven.

[656] Ancestry.com, New York, County Marriages, 1847-1849; 1907-1936 (Lehi, UT, USA, Ancestry.com Operations, Inc., 2016), Ancestry.com, http://www.Ancestry.com, Record for Martin G Haven.

[657] Ancestry.com, New York, County Marriages, 1847-1849; 1907-1936 (Lehi, UT, USA, Ancestry.com Operations, Inc., 2016), Ancestry.com, http://www.Ancestry.com, Record for Martin G Haven.

[658] Ancestry.com. *U.S., Social Security Applications and Claims Index, 1936-2007* [database on-line]. Provo, UT, USA: Ancestry.com Operations, Inc., 2015. Record for William Martin Haven.

[659] Ancestry.com. *U.S., Social Security Applications and Claims Index, 1936-2007* [database on-line]. Provo, UT, USA: Ancestry.com Operations, Inc., 2015. Record for William Martin Haven.

Generation Twelve

59.   Lorraine E. Appleby[12] (Irene Gladys Maxson[11] , Grace K. Turner[10], Sylvanus M. Turner[9], Erastus G. Turner[8], Paul Turner[7], Paul Turner[6], Benjamin Turner Sr.[5], Benjamin Turner Sr.[4], John Turner[3], John Turner[2], Humphrey Turner[1]) was born on 15 Apr 1921 in Bolivar, New York [660] and died on 11 Jan 2005 in Olean, New York[661]. She married Merle Kenneth Straight[662]. He was born on 25 Nov 1917 in Andover, New York[663] and died on 10 Jan 1947 in Annin, Pennsylvania[664].   Merle Kenneth Straight and Loraine E. Appleby four children who may still be living.

Olean, NY - Loraine A. Straight of 350 Front St. died Tuesday (January 11, 2005) in the Olean General Hospital.   Born April 15, 1921 in Bolivar, NY she was the daughter of Phill and Irma Maxson Appleby. On July 16, 1940 in Eldred, PA she married Kenneth Merle Straight who predeceased her January 10, 1947.   Mrs. Straight was a graduate of Otto-Eldred High School and worked for McGraw Edison Co., now Cooper Power Systems, in Olean for over 30 years, retiring in 1983.   She attended Christ United Methodist Church in Olean and had been very active as a volunteer for the former St. Francis Hospital as well as a day captain for Meals on Wheels through the RSVP program. She was a former Lady Elk in Olean and was a former member of the Olean Senior League. She also served as an ombudsman for the former Cattaraugus County Nursing Home (now The Pines) in Olean.   Surviving are two sons Steven "Jim" (Anne) Straight of Olean and Clayton John Straight; 2 daughters Katherine (James) Martel of Rochester and Merleyn Kay Straight of Rogue River, OR; 4 grandchildren; 2 great grandchildren; 1 sister Alice Abrams of Tucson, AZ and several nieces and nephews.   In addition to her husband and parents she was predeceased by a stepmother Minerva Fagan; a son Arthur Straight in April 1986; a granddaughter Stephanie Martel; 2 brothers Arthur A. Appleby and Lawrence P. Appleby and 1 sister Phyllis Ford.   Burial

---

[660] Ancestry.com, U.S., Find A Grave Index, 1700s-Current (Provo, UT, USA, Ancestry.com Operations, Inc., 2012), Ancestry.com, http://www.Ancestry.com, Record for Loraine E. Straight.

[661] Ancestry.com, U.S., Find A Grave Index, 1700s-Current (Provo, UT, USA, Ancestry.com Operations, Inc., 2012), Ancestry.com, http://www.Ancestry.com, Record for Loraine E. Straight.

[662] Ancestry.com, U.S., Find A Grave Index, 1700s-Current (Provo, UT, USA, Ancestry.com Operations, Inc., 2012), Ancestry.com, http://www.Ancestry.com, Record for Loraine E. Straight.

[663] Ancestry.com, Pennsylvania, Death Certificates, 1906-1963 (Provo, UT, USA, Ancestry.com Operations, Inc., 2014), Ancestry.com, http://www.Ancestry.com, Pennsylvania Historic and Museum Commission; Pennsylvania, USA; Pennsylvania (State). Death certificates, 1906-1966; Certificate Number Range: 003601-006150. Record for Merle Kenneth Straight.

[664] Ancestry.com, Pennsylvania, Death Certificates, 1906-1963 (Provo, UT, USA, Ancestry.com Operations, Inc., 2014), Ancestry.com, http://www.Ancestry.com, Pennsylvania Historic and Museum Commission; Pennsylvania, USA; Pennsylvania (State). Death certificates, 1906-1966; Certificate Number Range: 003601-006150. Record for Merle Kenneth Straight.

will be in Maple Lawn Cemetery, Bolivar, NY.   Memorials may be made to The Rehabilitation Center 1439 Buffalo St. Olean, NY or to a charity of the donor's choice.

60. Harry Thomas Kelly Jr.[12] (Jennie M. Haven[11], Goodrich Erastus Haven[10] , Ida May Turner[9], Erastus G. Turner[8], Paul Turner[7], Paul Turner[6], Benjamin Turner Sr.[5], Benjamin Turner Sr.[4], John Turner[3], John Turner[2], Humphrey Turner[1]) was born in 05 Oct 1926[665] and died in on 29 Apr 1974[666]. He married Maxine Sarah Keck[667].   She was born on 13 Aug 1918[668] and died on 10 Jan 1971 in Pennsylvania[669].

Harry Thomas Kelly Jr. and Maxine Sarah Keck had the following child:
   i.   Ralph Eugene Kelly was born in 1939[670] and died on 10 Jul 1967[671].

---

[665] U.S., Social Security Applications and Claims Index, 1936-2007. Record for Harry Thomas Kelly, Jr.

[666] U.S., Social Security Applications and Claims Index, 1936-2007. Record for Harry Thomas Kelly, Jr.

[667] Ancestry.com. *U.S., Find A Grave Index, 1600s-Current* [database on-line]. Provo, UT, USA: Ancestry.com Operations, Inc., 2012. Record for Maxine S. Kelly.

[668] Ancestry.com. *U.S., Find A Grave Index, 1600s-Current* [database on-line]. Provo, UT, USA: Ancestry.com Operations, Inc., 2012. Record for Maxine S. Kelly.

[669] Ancestry.com. *U.S., Find A Grave Index, 1600s-Current* [database on-line]. Provo, UT, USA: Ancestry.com Operations, Inc., 2012. Record for Maxine S. Kelly.

[670] Ancestry.com. *U.S., Find A Grave Index, 1600s-Current* [database on-line]. Provo, UT, USA: Ancestry.com Operations, Inc., 2012. Record for Maxine S. Kelly.

[671] Ancestry.com. *U.S., Find A Grave Index, 1600s-Current* [database on-line]. Provo, UT, USA: Ancestry.com Operations, Inc., 2012. Record for Maxine S. Kelly.

INDEX

In some cases the spelling of surnames are different between the parents and the children. For instance: Reed and Read and Kowalewski and Kowlewski.

Women are listed under their maiden names and married names. Women's maiden names are in ( ); their married names are in [ ].

Individuals with unknown surnames are listed at the beginning of the index.

John Baptist, 146
Karen Susanne [Dwyer], 200, 209
Living, 199
Marie (Longtin), 199
Mary Agnes (Foote), 74, 75, 146, 147
Susan [Ellenwood], 199, 209
Esmond, Elam Marie [Palermo], 192
Ewell, Henry, 266
Ewen, Marjorie [Chrispell]., 249
Eyler, Mary Elizabeth [Henrick], 126

-F-

Fagin/Fagan
Adelia M. (Webb), 215, 221, 222
Alice F. (?), 234
Ann H. (?), 234
Anna, 222
Anna Maude [Williams], 233
Charles Read, 222, 233, 234
Clifford, 234
Cora (Aylesworth), 233
Francis J., 234
George H., 222, 233
Hazel A. [Howe], 234
John, 221, 222
Kenneth P., 234
Sally Foliett [Chrispell], 222, 232, 233
Ferguson, Nancy [Priest], 10
Fillman, Emma Palestine [Merrick], 192
Fisher, Esther [Murphy], 132
Fitch, Albert, 24
Fjelsta
Nils, 114
Rachel (Ellertson), 114
Rose Melvina [Priest], 114
Fletcher, Amelia F. [Longtin], 199
Foote
Abigail (Webb), 5, 24, 214, 217, 218
Abigail (Hosley), 23, 217
Agnes E., 25
Alice (Henry), 229
Anna Mariah (Weaver), 228, 229
Carl L., 77
Catherine (Price), 24
Ceila G. (Walker), 77

Charles Lewis, 24, 26, 76, 77
Clara E., 229
Clarence E., 229
Claudia C. (Baker), 78
Edna Cecelia [Hickey], 75
Earl E., 77, 149, 150
Earl James, 24, 26, 78
George Henry, 229
George Lynn Jr., 25, 74, 75
George L. Sr., 5, 23, 24, 217, 218
Harold, 77
Hazel J. (Dailey), 149, 150
Hazel E., [Rousseau], 78, 150, 151
Isabel Lydia [Hart] [Light] [Earley], 75, 148, 149
Jay Dean, 24, 25
Jessie Selkrigg, 23, 217
Lizzie (Dolaway), 25
Lydia Marie (Leigh). 5, 6, 23, 24
Mary Abigail [Mather], 218, 229, 230
Mary Agnes [Emery], 74, 75, 146, 147
Mary Etta (Clancy) , 74, 75
Mary (O'Dell), 228
Mildred E. [O'Connell], 229, 241, 242
Sarah E. [Hansen], 150
Stewart J., 77
William H., 218, 228, 229
Zoola (Read), 76, 77
Ford
Phylis G. (Appleby), 310
Wililam H., 310
Forgy, Martha Susannah [Miller], 128
Fowler
Amanda Melcina [Priest], 43
James 11
Frank, Rev. Irving,
Frece, Lottie M. [Puffer], 85
Freeman, Evelyn Catherine [Todd], 109
Fretwell
Fannie Sparks (Ramsey), 136
Leona Leota, 136, 137
William L., 136
Fritzlan
Jean Alma [Thomas], 102, 103
Myrtle Rebecca, 102
Winslow Homer, 102
Fusenig
Beulah E. (Todd), 112, 113

Nicholas Dudley, 113
Nicholas Joseph Jr., 112, 113

-G-

Gage, Mary [Moore], 244
Gagnier, Celina [Emery], 146
Gallagher
Charlotte [Kowalewski], 161
Mary Frances [Corey], 163
Gamer/Gaymer
Lydia [Turner], 265, 267, 268, 272
Margaret (Mason), 265, 268
Richard, 265, 268
Gausted
Annie (Jordshaugen), 153
Clara B. [Ledebuhr], 153, 154
Oscar, 153
George, Edith [Clark], 67
Gifford
Alma [Wood], 35
Burton, 24
Gilson, William, 266
Gleason
E. B., 315
Leah E. (Hodges), 303, 315
Matilda (Clair), 315
Ralph Earl, 315
Goodrich
Amanda, 279
Amasa J., 280
Amelia (Wheeler), 279
Clarissa [Cleveland], 279
Erastus, 279
F.N., 12
Hiram M., 279
Ira, 279
James, 279
John T., 279
Mary (Copely), 279
Orrin, 279
Patty M. (Brownell), 279
Sally or Sarah (Turner), 277, 278, 279
Sally Ann, 280
Sarah (Turner), 281, 285
Silas C., 285
Silas Henry, 278, 279
William Jerome, 285
Gordon, Rosa Ann [Berry], 34
Grant
Alexander, 187
Isabel (Simpson), 187
Granzow, Howard 255
Green, Matthew, 50

Obituaries & Newspaper Articles

-R-